VENTURE CAPITAL AND PRIVATE EQUITY
A Casebook

Third Edition

Josh Lerner
Harvard Business School
and
National Bureau of Economic Research

Felda Hardymon
Harvard Business School

Ann Leamon
Harvard Business School

John Wiley & Sons, Inc.

Dedication

To Mugsy, Boxy, Morgan, and Money
To Bluesy
To JB

Publisher	Susan Elbe
Production Manager	Pam Kennedy
Acquisitions Editor	Judith R. Joseph
Project Editor	Cindy Rhoads
Production Editors	Kelly Tavares, Sarah Wolfman-Robichaud
Managing Editor	Kevin Dodds
Illustration Editor	Benjamin Reece
Cover Design	Benjamin Reece
Cover Photo	© Digital Vision/Getty Images

This book was set in New Caledonia by Leyh Publishing, LLC and printed and bound by Hamilton Printing. The cover was printed by Lehigh Press.

This book is printed on acid-free paper. ♾

ISBN 0-471-23069-3

Printed in the United States of America

10 9 8 7 6 5 4 3 2 1

Acknowledgements

The writing of a case study is an activity that involves many people. From the initial conception of a case to its publication and revision involves practitioners, students, and colleagues at one's own and other schools. Thus, the problem with the acknowledgements section of a casebook is not deciding who to include, but rather worrying about those one has left out!

First, it is important to note that a number of case studies were jointly written with colleagues, students, and practitioners. Beyond these co-authors, many others provided assistance. The partners and managers of the many private equity groups, institutions, and companies featured in these cases not only agreed to be the subject of the analyses, but generously set aside time to answer many questions, review numerous drafts, and make many helpful suggestions. Chris Allen responded to numerous requests for data, often under severe time constraints. Colleagues at Harvard Business School and many other business schools offered numerous suggestions after reading or teaching these cases. We also thank the many reviewers for the constructive comments and suggestions, which have helped us raise the quality of the book. Marianne D'Amico and Suzanne Plummer managed the many logistical details regarding the casewriting process and provided unflagging administrative support. Lillian Coltin, Patricia Hathaway, Sandy Frey, and Soebagio Notosoehardjo in the Case Records department handled the permissions and submission process of (too often) last-minute cases with grace, humor, and speed. The Harvard Business School's Division of Research generously funded the considerable cost of developing these case studies. Cindy Rhoads and Heather King at John Wiley & Sons and Kevin Dodds and Jennifer Wasson of Leyh Publishing provided key assistance in the production of the volume. The assistance and encouragement of Judith Joseph and Leslie Kraham at Wiley was critical in the development of the volume.

Finally, Josh thanks Wendy for putting up with his travels on casewriting trips, Felda thanks Dena for her unstinting help and long-suffering support in managing two careers and his colleagues at Bessemer Venture Partners for their support, and Ann thanks John for waving her off and welcoming her back.

About the Authors

Josh Lerner is the Jacob H. Schiff Professor of Investment Banking at Harvard Business School, with a joint appointment in the Finance and Entrepreneurial Management Units. He graduated from Yale College with a special divisional major that combined physics with the history of technology, and he worked for several years on issues concerning technological innovation and public policy at the Brookings Institution, for a public-private task force in Chicago, and on Capitol Hill. He then earned a Ph.D. in Harvard's Economics Department.

Much of his research, which is collected in *The Venture Capital Cycle* (1999), *The Money of Invention* (2001), and *Innovation and Its Discontents* (2004), focuses on the structure and role of venture capital organizations. He organizes the Entrepreneurship and Innovation Policy and the Economy Groups at the National Bureau of Economic Research and serves as coeditor of their publication, *Innovation Policy and the Economy*. In addition, he is a research associate in the NBER's Corporate Finance and Productivity Programs.

In the 1993–94 academic year, he introduced an elective course for second-year MBAs on private equity finance. In recent years, "Venture Capital and Private Equity" has consistently been one of the top electives at Harvard Business School. In addition, he chairs and teaches private equity executive education courses, teaches several doctoral classes, and plays a variety of administrative roles at the university.

Felda Hardymon is a professor of Management Practice at the Harvard Business School and a career venture capitalist. He joined Bessemer Venture Partners (BVP) in 1981 and continues as a general partner. BVP is among the oldest venture firms (1911) and is a long-standing specialist in early stage investing.

He has led BVP's investments in more than sixty companies in the software, communications, and retail sectors, including Cascade Communications, Parametric Technology, Staples, and MSI. Previously he was a vice president of BDSI, the original venture subsidiary of General Electric Company, where he led investments in Ungermann-Bass, Stratus Computer, and Western Digital. He has served on the board of the National Venture Capital Association, where he was chairman of the Tax Committee. He received a B.S. from Rose Polytechnic Institute, a Ph.D. (mathematics) from Duke University, and an MBA (Baker scholar) from Harvard Business School.

Ann Leamon is a senior research associate at the Harvard Business School. She came to Harvard after six years as a senior business analyst at L. L. Bean and three years at Central Maine Power Company as a senior economic and load forecaster. Her work in local area load forecasting won an Industry Innovators award from the Electric Power Research Institute, and she published several papers and addressed conferences on the project.

At Harvard, she cofounded the Center for Case Development and has written more than forty cases. She left that position to collaborate with Professors Lerner and Hardymon in the further development of the "Venture Capital and Private Equity" course. She also handles corporate communications for Bessemer Venture Partners. She earned a B.A. (honors) in German from University of King's College/Dalhousie and an M.A. in economics from University of Montana, where she studied urban redevelopment.

Table of Contents

1

Private Equity Today and Tomorrow

The 1980s and 1990s saw a tremendous boom in the private equity industry. The pool of U.S. private equity funds—partnerships specializing in venture capital, leveraged buyouts, mezzanine investments, build-ups, distressed debt, and related investments—has grown from $5 billion in 1980 to just under $300 billion at the beginning of 2004. Private equity's growth over that period has outstripped that of almost every class of financial product.

Despite this growth, many questions about private equity remain unanswered, and many of its features continue to be mysterious. How do venture capital and buyout funds create value? What explains this tremendous growth in these funds? What explains the process of boom and bust: the rapid increases in fund-raising in the late 1960s, mid-1980s and late 1990s, and the precipitous declines in the 1970s, early 1990s, and early 2000s? To what extent is the model developed and refined over the past several decades likely to likely to be translated into other countries and types of investments? This volume explores these exciting and important questions.

WHAT IS PRIVATE EQUITY?

A natural first question is "What constitutes a private equity fund?" Many start-up firms require substantial capital. A firm's founder may not have sufficient funds to finance these projects alone and therefore must seek outside financing. Entrepreneurial firms that are characterized by significant intangible assets, that expect years of negative earnings, and that have uncertain prospects, are unlikely to receive bank loans or other debt financing. Similarly, troubled firms that need to undergo restructurings may find external financing difficult to raise. Private equity organizations finance these high-risk, potentially high-reward projects. They protect the value of their equity stakes by undertaking careful due diligence before making the investments and retaining powerful oversight rights afterwards.

Typically, these investors do not primarily invest their own capital, but rather raise the bulk of their funds from institutions and individuals. Large institutional investors, such as pension funds and university endowments, are likely to want illiquid long-run investments such as private equity in their portfolio. Often, these groups have neither the staff nor the expertise to make such investments themselves.

The private equity industry was, in its initial decades, a predominantly American phenomenon. It had its origins in the family offices that managed the wealth of high-net-worth individuals in the last decades of the nineteenth century and the first decades of the twentieth century. Wealthy families such as the Phippes, Rockefellers, Vanderbilts, and Whitneys invested in and advised a variety of business enterprises, including the predecessor entities to AT&T, Eastern Airlines, and McDonnell Douglas. Gradually, these families began involving outsiders to select and oversee these investments.

The first formal private equity firm was established shortly after World War II. American Research and Development (ARD) was formed in 1946 by MIT President Karl Compton, Harvard Business School Professor Georges F. Doriot, and Boston business leaders. A small group of venture capitalists made high-risk investments into emerging companies that were based on technology developed for World War II. The success of the investments ranged widely: almost half of ARD's profits during its twenty-six-year existence as an independent entity came from its $70,000 investment in Digital Equipment Company in 1957, which grew in value to $355 million. Because institutional investors were reluctant to invest, ARD was structured as a publicly traded closed-end fund and marketed mostly to individuals. The few other venture organizations begun in the decade after ARD's formation were also structured as closed-end funds.

The first venture capital limited partnership, Draper, Gaither, and Anderson, was formed in 1958. Imitators soon followed, but limited partnerships accounted for a minority of the venture pool during the 1960s and 1970s. Most venture organizations raised money either through closed-end funds or Small Business Investment Companies (SBICs), federally guaranteed risk-capital pools that proliferated during the 1960s. While the market for SBICs in the late 1960s and early 1970s was strong, incentive problems ultimately led to the collapse of the sector. The annual flow of money into private equity during its first three decades never exceeded a few hundred million dollars and usually was substantially less. During these years, while a few funds made a considerable number of investments in buyouts and other transactions involving mature firms, private equity organizations were universally referred to as venture capital funds.

The activity in the private equity industry increased dramatically in late 1970s and early 1980s. Industry observers attributed much of the shift to the U.S. Department of Labor's clarification of the Employee Retirement Income Security Act's "prudent man" rule in 1979. Prior to this year, the legislation limited pension funds from investing substantial amounts of money into venture capital or other high-risk asset classes. The Department of Labor's clarification of the rule explicitly allowed pension managers to invest in high-risk assets, including private equity. Numerous specialized funds—concentrating in areas such as leveraged buyouts, mezzanine transactions, and such hybrids as venture leasing—sprang up during these years. Another important change in the private equity industry during this period was the rise of the limited partnership as the dominant organizational form.

The subsequent years saw both very good and trying times for private equity investors. On the one hand, during the 1980s, venture capitalists backed many of the most successful high-technology companies, including Cisco Systems, Genentech, Microsoft, and Sun Microsystems. Numerous successful buyouts—such as Avis, Beatrice, Dr Pepper, Gibson Greetings, and McCall Pattern—garnered considerable public attention in the 1980s. At the same time, commitments to the private equity industry during this decade were uneven. The annual flow of money into venture capital funds increased by a factor of ten during the first half of the 1980s, but it steadily declined from 1987 through 1991. Buyouts underwent an even more dramatic rise through the 1980s, followed by a precipitous fall at the end of the decade.

Much of this pattern was driven by the changing fortunes of private equity investments. Returns on venture capital funds had declined sharply in the mid-1980s after being exceedingly attractive in the 1970s. This fall was apparently triggered by overinvestment in a few industries, such as computer hardware, and the entry of many inexperienced venture capitalists. Buyout returns underwent a similar decline in the late 1980s, due largely to the increased competition between groups for transactions. As investors became disappointed with returns, they committed less capital to the industry.

The 1990s saw these patterns repeated on an unprecedented scale. Much of the decade saw dramatic growth and excellent returns in almost every part of the private equity industry. This recovery was triggered by several factors. The exit of many inexperienced investors at the beginning of the decade ensured that the remaining groups faced less competition for transactions. The healthy market for initial public offerings during much of the decade meant that it was easier for all investors to exit private equity transactions. Meanwhile, the extent of technological innovation—particularly in information technology-related industries—created extraordinary opportunities for venture capitalists. New capital commitments to both venture and buyout funds rose in response to these changing circumstances, increasing to record levels by the late 1990s and 2000.

But as is often the case, the growth of private equity increased at a pace that was too great to be sustainable. Institutional and individual investors—attracted especially by the tremendously high returns being enjoyed by venture funds—flooded money into the industry at unprecedented rates. In many cases, groups staggered under the weight of capital. In other cases, groups that should have not raised capital succeeded in garnering considerable funds. Too rapid growth led to overstretched partners, inadequate due diligence, and in many cases, poor investment decisions. The industry will need to address the legacy of this growth in the first years of the twenty-first century.

But the most revolutionary changes in the private equity in recent years have not been in the patterns of investment, but rather in the structure of the private equity groups themselves. Private equity organizations, while in the business of funding innovation, had been remarkably steadfast in retaining the limited partnership structure since the mid-1960s. In recent years, however, a flurry of experimentation has taken hold in the industry. Among the changes seen are the establishment of affiliate funds in different regions and nations and the expansion of the funds offered by buyout funds to include real estate, mezzanine, and bond funds.

What explains these sudden changes on the part of the major private equity groups in recent years? We believe that this reflects a more fundamental shift in the industry, as private equity groups struggle to address the increasing efficiency of their investing. Facing increased competition, they are seeking to find new ways to differentiate themselves.

Evidence of the increased efficiency of the private equity industry can be seen in many places. While venture capital for much its first decades had the flavor of a cottage industry, with a considerable number of relatively small groups working alongside one another, today it is much more competitive.

Given this changed competitive environment, the leading groups are increasingly seeking to differentiate themselves from the mass of other investors. They are employing a variety of tools to build up and distinguish their "brands," which will help distinguish themselves from other investors. These steps include the strategic partnerships, provision of additional services, and aggressive fund-raising described above, as well as many other initiatives to extend build their visibility in the United States and abroad.

To be sure, private equity is not unique in this transformation. For instance, the investment banking industry underwent a similar transformation in the 1950s and 1960s, as the leading "bulge bracket" firms solidified their leadership positions. The gap between the leading banks and the following ones greatly increased during this years, as the leading groups greatly enhanced their range of activities and boosted their hiring of personnel. Similarly, the management of the major banks was transformed during these years, as procedures were systematized and management structures formalized.

WHY IS PRIVATE EQUITY NEEDED?

Private equity plays a critical role in the American economy and increasingly around the globe as well. The types of firms that private equity organizations finance—whether young start-ups hungry for capital or ailing giants that need to restructure—pose numerous risks and uncertainties that discourage other investors.

In this section, we will first review the risks that these firms pose. We will then consider briefly how private equity organizations address these problems. Finally, we will discuss why other financiers, such as banks, often cannot address these problems as effectively as private equity groups.

The financing of young and restructuring firms is a risky business. Uncertainty and informational gaps often characterize these firms, particularly in high-technology industries. These information problems both make it difficult to assess these firms and permit opportunistic behavior by entrepreneurs after the financing is received.

To briefly review the types of conflicts that can emerge in these settings, conflicts between managers and investors ("agency problems") can affect the willingness of both debt and equity holders to provide capital. If the firm raises equity from outside investors, the manager has an incentive to engage in wasteful expenditures (e.g., lavish offices) because he may benefit disproportionately from these but does not bear their entire cost. Similarly, if the firm raises debt, the manager may increase risk to undesirable levels. Because providers of capital recognize these problems, outside investors demand a higher rate of return than would be the case if the funds were internally generated.[1]

Additional agency problems may appear in the types of entrepreneurial firms in which private equity groups invest. For instance, entrepreneurs might invest in strategies, research, or projects that have high personal returns but low expected monetary payoffs to shareholders: consider the founder of a biotechnology company who chooses to invest in a certain type of research that brings him great recognition in the scientific community but provides little return for the venture capitalist. Similarly, entrepreneurs may receive initial results from market trials indicating little demand for a new product, but they may want to keep the company going because they receive significant private benefits from managing their own firm.

Even if the manager is motivated to maximize shareholder value, information gaps may make raising external capital more expensive or even preclude it entirely. Equity offerings of firms may be associated with a "lemons" problem: if the manager is better informed about the investment opportunities of the firm and acts in the interest of current shareholders, then he will issue new shares only when the company's stock is overvalued. Indeed, numerous studies have documented that stock prices decline upon the announcement of equity issues, largely because of the negative signal sent to the market. This "lemons" problem leads investors to be less willing to invest in young or restructuring firms, or to be unwilling to invest at all. Similar information problems have also been shown to exist in debt markets.[2]

---

1. The classic treatment of these problems is in Michael C. Jensen, and William H. Meckling, "Theory of the Firm: Managerial Behavior, Agency Costs, and Ownership Structure," *Journal of Financial Economics* 3 (1976): 305–360.

2. The "lemons" problem was introduced in George A. Akerlof, "The Market for 'Lemons': Qualitative Uncertainty and the Market Mechanism," *Quarterly Journal of Economics* 84 (1970): 488–500. Discussions of the implications of this problem for financing decisions are in Bruce C. Greenwald, Joseph E. Stiglitz, and Andrew Weiss, "Information Imperfections in the Capital Market and Macroeconomic Fluctuations," *American Economic Review Papers and Proceedings* 74 (1984): 194–199, and in Stewart C. Myers and Nicholas S. Majluf, "Corporate Financing and Investment Decisions When Firms Have Information That Investors Do Not Have," *Journal of Financial Economics* 13 (1984): 187–221.

More generally, the inability to verify outcomes makes it difficult to write contracts that are contingent upon particular events. This inability makes external financing costly. Many economic models[3] argue that when investors find it difficult to verify that certain actions have been taken or certain outcomes have occurred—even if they strongly suspect the entrepreneur has followed a certain action that was counter to their original agreement, they cannot prove it in court—external financing may become costly or difficult to obtain.

If the information problems could be eliminated, these barriers to financing would disappear. Financial economists argue that specialized intermediaries, such as private equity organizations, can address these problems. By intensively scrutinizing firms before providing capital and then monitoring them afterward, they can alleviate some of the information gaps and reduce capital constraints. Thus, it is important to understand the tools employed by private equity investors as responses to this difficult environment, which enable firms to ultimately receive the financing that they cannot raise from other sources. It is the nonmonetary aspects of private equity that are critical to its success. It is these tools—the screening of investments, the use of convertible securities, the syndication and staging of investments, and the provision of oversight and informal coaching—that we shall highlight in the second module of the course.

Why cannot other financial intermediaries (e.g., banks) undertake the same sort of monitoring? While it is easy to see why individual investors may not have the expertise to address these types of agency problems, it might be thought that bank credit officers could undertake this type of oversight. Yet even in countries with exceedingly well-developed banking systems, such as Germany and Japan, policymakers seek to encourage the development of a private equity industry to ensure more adequate financing for risky entrepreneurial firms.

The limitations of banks stem from several of their key institutional features. First, because regulations in the United States limit banks' ability to hold shares, they cannot freely use equity to fund projects. Taking an equity position in the firm allows the private equity group to proportionately share in the upside, guaranteeing that the investor benefits if the firm does well. Second, banks may not have the necessary skills to evaluate projects with few tangible assets and significant uncertainty. In addition, banks in competitive markets may not be able to finance high-risk projects because they are unable to charge borrowers rates high enough to compensate for the firm's riskiness. Finally, private equity funds' high-powered compensation schemes give these investors incentives to monitor firms more closely, because their individual compensation is closely linked to the funds' returns. Banks, corporations, and other institutions that have sponsored venture funds without such high-powered incentives have found it difficult to retain personnel, once the investors have developed a performance record that enables them to raise a fund of their own.[4]

3. Important examples include Sanford Grossman and Oliver D. Hart, "The Costs and Benefits of Ownership: A Theory of Vertical and Lateral Integration," *Journal of Political Economy* 94 (1986): 691–719, and in Oliver D. Hart and John Moore, "Property Rights and the Nature of the Firm," *Journal of Political Economy* 98 (1990): 1119–1158.

4. The limitations of bank financing are explored in such theoretical and empirical academic studies as Joseph E. Stiglitz and Andrew Weiss, "Credit Rationing in Markets with Incomplete Information," *American Economic Review* 71 (1981): 393–409, and in Mitchell A. Petersen and Raghuram G. Rajan, "The Effect of Credit Market Competition on Lending Relationships," *Quarterly Journal of Economics* 110 (1995): 407–444.

ABOUT THIS VOLUME

This volume is based on a course introduced at Harvard Business School in the 1993–94 academic year. "Venture Capital and Private Equity" has attracted students interested in careers as private equity investors, as managers of entrepreneurial firms, or as investment bankers or other intermediaries who work with private equity groups and the companies that they fund. These cases have also been used in a variety of other settings, such as executive education courses at Harvard and graduate and undergraduate entrepreneurship courses at many other business schools. This third edition has been extensively revised to reflect the many changes in the industry in recent years.

A natural question for a reader to ask is what he or she will learn from this volume. This casebook has three goals:

- First, the private equity industry is complex. Participants in the private equity industry make it even more complicated by using a highly specialized terminology. These factors lead to the world of venture capital and buyout investing often appearing impenetrable to the uninitiated. Understanding the ways in which private equity groups work—as well as the key distinctions between these organizations—is an important goal.

- Second, private equity investors face the same problems that other financial investors do, but in extreme form. An understanding of the problems faced in private equity—and the ways that these investors solve them—should provide more general insights into the financing process. Thus, a second goal is to review and apply the key ideas of corporate finance in this exciting setting.

- Finally, the process of valuation is critical in private equity. Disputes over valuation—whether between an entrepreneur and a venture capitalist or between a private equity group raising a new fund and a potential investor—are commonplace in this industry. These disputes stem from the fact that valuing early stage and restructuring firms can be very challenging and highly subjective. This casebook explores a wide variety of valuation approaches, from techniques widely used in practice to methods less frequently seen in practice today but likely to be increasingly important in future years.

The volume is divided into four modules. Its organization of the first three sections mirrors that of the private equity process, which can be viewed as a cycle. The cycle starts with the raising of a private equity fund; proceeds through the investment in, monitoring of, and adding value to firms; continues as the private equity group exits successful deals and returns capital to the investors; and renews itself with the seeking of additional funds. Each module will begin with an overview that depicts the themes and approaches of the section. Different classes, however, may choose to use this volume in different ways.[5] Thus, it may be helpful to briefly summarize the organization of the volume at the outset.

The first module of *Venture Capital and Private Equity* examines how private equity funds are raised and structured. These funds often have complex features, and the legal issues involved are frequently arcane. But the structure of private equity funds has a profound effect on the behavior of venture and buyout investors. Consequently, it is as important for the entrepreneur raising private equity to understand these issues as

---

5. While some courses may follow closely the order of cases in the volume, others may deviate substantially. For instance, a course concentrating on entrepreneurial finance may focus on cases in the second and third modules in the volume.

it is for a partner in a fund. The module will seek not only to understand the features of private equity funds and the actors in the fundraising process, but also to analyze them. We will map out which institutions serve to increase the profits from private equity investments as a whole and which institutions seem designed mostly to shift profits between the parties.

The second module of the course considers the interactions between private equity investors and the entrepreneurs they finance. These interactions are at the core of what private equity investors do. We will seek to understand these interactions through two perspectives.

We first consider how the activities undertaken by private equity organizations are a response to the challenges that the firms in their portfolio pose. We highlight how firms in a private equity portfolio typically pose three critical problems, which make it difficult for them to meet their financing needs through traditional mechanisms, such as bank loans. This module will illustrate these approaches with examples from a wide variety of industries and private equity transactions.

The second approach emphasizes the influence of the circumstances of the private equity organization itself. There is typically no one "right" investment decision. Rather, the proper response to any given situation will reflect the circumstances of the private equity organization, such as the extent to which successful fund-raising in the future can be assured and the experience of the individual investment professionals.

The third module of *Venture Capital and Private Equity* examines the process through which private equity investors exit their investments. Successful exits are critical to ensuring attractive returns for investors and, in turn, to raising additional capital. But private equity investors' concerns about exiting investments—and their behavior during the exiting process itself—can sometimes lead to severe problems for entrepreneurs. We will employ an analytic framework very similar to that used in the first module of the course. We will seek to understand which institutional features associated with exiting private equity investments increase the overall amount of profits from private equity investments, and which actions seem to be intended to shift more of the profits to particular parties.

The final module considers the future of the private equity industry. We highlight a number of examples where groups are grappling with the changing competitive environment, whether by creating affiliates or reorganizing their structure. We also consider efforts to transplant the venture model into other settings. These cases will allow us not only to explore the future of the private equity industry, but also to review the key themes developed during the course.

A number of cases running through this volume emphasize one more theme: the challenge of managing a career in private equity. We consider the implications of a choice between different private equity organizations and investment opportunities from the perspective of a recent MBA graduate. In numerous other cases, we will consider not just the overall situations, but also the career implications for the individuals involved in the decisions

At the same time, it is important to emphasize that there are many opportunities for learning about venture capital and private equity outside of this volume. The four module notes—and many of the topical notes interspersed in the body of the text—suggest further readings. These range from trade journals such as the *Private Equity Analyst* and the *Venture Capital Journal* to handbooks on the legal nuances of the private equity process to academic studies. In addition, a note at the end of this volume provides a systematic overview of many information sources for readers who wish to explore a particular aspect of the private equity industry in more detail.

THE FUTURE OF PRIVATE EQUITY

The cases and notes in this volume are designed to provide an understanding of the history of the private equity industry's development and the workings of the industry today. Because the case studies must of necessity look at events in the past, they may provide less guidance about the future of the private equity industry. The question of how the venture and buyout industries will evolve over the next decade is a particularly critical one because the growth during the 1980s and 1990s was so spectacular. It is natural to ask whether the gains made in these years can be sustained. Put another way, how severe will be the retrenchment that the industry is undergoing?

These are fair questions. As will be highlighted throughout this volume, short-run shifts in the supply of or demand for private equity investments can have dramatic effects. For instance, periods with a rapid increase in capital commitments have historically led to fewer restrictions on private equity investors, larger investments in portfolio firms, higher valuations for those investments, and lower returns for investors.

These patterns have led many practitioners to conclude that the industry is inherently cyclical. In short, this view implies that periods of rapid growth generate so many problems that periods of retrenchment are sure to follow. These cycles may lead us to be pessimistic about the prospects for the industry in the years to come.

It is important, however, to also consider the *long-run* determinants of the level of private equity, not just the short-run effects. In the short run, intense competition between private equity groups may lead to a willingness to pay a premium for certain types of firms. This is unlikely to be a sustainable strategy in the long run: firms that persist in such a strategy will earn low returns and eventually be unable to raise follow-on funds.

The types of factors that determine the long-run steady-state supply of private equity in the economy are more fundamental. These are likely to include the pace of technological innovation in the economy, the degree of dynamism in the economy, the presence of liquid and competitive markets for investors to sell their investments (whether markets for stock offerings or acquisitions), and the willingness of highly skilled managers and engineers to work in entrepreneurial environments. However painful the short-run adjustments, these more fundamental factors are likely to be critical in establishing the long-run level.

When one examines these more fundamental factors, there appears to have been quite substantial changes for the better over the past several decades.[6] We will highlight two of the determinants of the long-run supply of private equity in the United States, where these changes have been particularly dramatic: the acceleration of the rate of technological innovation and the decreasing "transaction costs" associated with private equity investments.

---

6. It is also worth emphasizing that despite its growth, the private equity pool remains relatively small. For every $1 of private equity in the portfolio of U.S. institutional investors, there is about $25 of publicly traded equities. The ratios are even more uneven for overseas institutions. At the same time, the size of foreign private equity pool remains far below the United States. The disparity can be illustrated by comparing the ratio of the private equity investment to the size of the economy (gross domestic product). In 2002, this ratio was about five times higher in the United States than in East and South Asia, and two times higher in the United States than in Western Europe. (These statistics are taken from the European Venture Capital Association, *EVCA Yearbook*, Zaventum, Belgium, European Venture Capital Association, 2003; Asian Venture Capital Journal, *Venture Capital in Asia: 2004 Edition*, Hong Kong, Asian Venture Capital Journal, 2003; and World Bank, *World Development Indicators*, Washington, World Bank, 2003.) At least to the casual observer, these ratios seem modest when compared to the economic role of new firms, products, and processes in the developed economies.

While the increase in innovation can be seen though several measures, probably the clearest indication is in the extent of patenting. Patent applications by U.S. inventors, after hovering between 40,000 and 80,000 annually over the first eighty-five years of this century, have surged over the past decade to 150,000 per year. This does not appear to reflect the impact of changes in domestic patent policy, shifts in the success rate of applications, or a variety of alternative explanations. Rather, it appears to reflect a fundamental shift in the rate of innovation.[7] The breadth of technology appears wider today than it has been ever before. The greater rate of intellectual innovation provides fertile ground for future investments, especially by venture capitalists.

A second change has been decreasing cost of making new private equity investments. The efficiency of the private equity process has been greatly augmented by the emergence of other intermediaries familiar with its workings. The presence of such expertise on the part of lawyers, accountants, managers, and others—even real estate brokers—has substantially lowered the transaction costs associated with forming and financing new firms or restructuring existing ones. The increasing number of professionals and managers familiar with and accustomed to the employment arrangements offered by private equity-backed firms (such as heavy reliance on stock options) has also been a major shift. In short, the increasing familiarity with the private equity process has made the long-term prospects for such investments more attractive than they have ever been before.

As the various cases in this volume highlight, much is still not yet known about the private equity industry. The extent to which the U.S. model will spread overseas and the degree to which the American model will—or can—be adapted during this process are particularly interesting questions. It seems clear, however, that this financial intermediary will be an enduring feature on the global economic landscape in the years to come.

---

7. These changes are discussed in Samuel Kortum and Josh Lerner, "Stronger Protection or Technological Revolution: What Is Behind the Recent Surge in Patenting?", *Carnegie-Rochester Conference Series on Public Policy* 48 (1998): 247–304.

2

Martin Smith: January 2002

Martin Smith faced an enviable dilemma, but a dilemma nonetheless. A second-year student in the MBA program at Harvard Business School, Smith's private equity job hunt had been successful: so much so that he had three opportunities. One of these offers, from Knowledge Capital Partners, had just arrived, but with the proviso that he accept or reject the offer by the next morning. As he walked in the deepening winter twilight to the campus gymnasium, Shad Hall, he wondered what he should do.

During the course of his job search, Smith had come to appreciate the very substantial differences between funds. The first firm he had an offer from, Newport Partners, was one of the oldest buyout firms in the country. It had acquired an enviable track record until the past three years, when two new initiatives—a technology investment program and an internationalization effort—had gone badly astray. As a result of this failure, its most recent fundraising effort had fallen well below its initial target. The reconstituted senior management team had promised dramatic changes, but Smith was unsure how to assess this offer. The second offer was from a private equity fund associated with a consulting group. The partners of Knowledge Capital had experienced remarkable success investing in transactions brought to it by (or identified in concert with) its clients. But here, too, Smith found reason for worry. The group's most recent fund, Knowledge Capital III, was almost five times the size of the previous effort. Moreover, Smith wondered whether the fund's success might be straining the relationship with its consulting firm parent. Finally, Smith had the opportunity to join one of his former roommates in running a "search fund." His colleague had identified some wealthy individuals who were not only willing to support their search for an undervalued company over the next year and a half, but also to provide much of the capital that they would ultimately need to close the transaction.

Another important consideration for Smith was the compensation packages that the different groups offered. Knowledge Capital offered relatively modest base pay (at least by the standards of the private equity industry) and made no provision for a share of the carried interest. On the other hand, if he joined Newport Partners, Smith would receive a higher base level of compensation and was assured of receiving a share of the

Professor Josh Lerner prepared this case. HBS cases are developed solely as the basis for class discussion. Cases are not intended to serve as endorsements, sources of primary data, or illustrations of effective or ineffective management.

fund's profits by the end of the next year. The rewards from the search fund were potentially the greatest, but also the most uncertain. While he realized that joining a private equity group as an associate was a long-run investment, Smith was also keenly aware of the impending need to pay off the substantial debt that he had accumulated while attending Harvard Business School.

OPPORTUNITIES IN THE PRIVATE EQUITY INDUSTRY IN 2002

The U.S. private equity industry had been little more than a cottage industry until the late 1970s. While the first funds were established in the 1940s, the industry had largely relied on individual investors for its first three decades. Very little of the substantial pools of capital associated with pension funds had gone into private equity, due both to the funds' unfamiliarity with the asset class and their fears that such investments violated federal standards.

The U.S. Department of Labor addressed these concerns in 1979 by clarifying the "prudent man rule," unleashing a wave of capital into private equity funds that continued for two decades. Virtually without exception, each year had seen more money invested in private equity, typically into limited partnerships with a contractually specified ten-year life. (The investors served as limited partners—so named because their liability was typically limited to the amount they invested—while the private equity group served as the general partners.) Exhibit 2.1 illustrates the growth of commitments to private equity funds over this period.

The exhibit also illustrates the changing mixture between funds devoted to making leveraged buyout and venture capital investments.[1] The growing share of venture investments could be attributed in large part to the success of these investments in the

---

EXHIBIT 2.1

PATTERN OF PRIVATE EQUITY FUND-RAISING, 1980–2001

Billions of 1999 $s

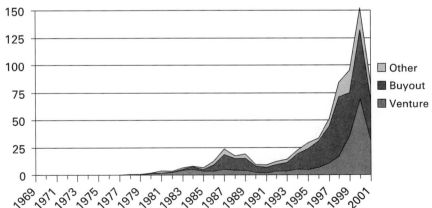

Source: Compiled from the *Private Equity Analyst* and unpublished records of Asset Alternatives.

Note: 2001 through November only.

---

1. For an overview of the private equity industry, see Paul Gompers and Josh Lerner, *The Money of Invention* (Boston: Harvard Business School, 2001).

mid- to late 1990s. Exhibit 2.2 summarizes the annual returns from venture and buy-out investments.

Private equity groups were traditionally very lean organizations, operating without substantial staffs of analysts or associates. This reluctance to add staff was seen as imparting at least two advantages. First, the organizations' small size led to a great deal of flexibility. Private equity, particularly in recent years, was a highly competitive business, where investment opportunities often needed to be acted upon quickly. Small groups could react rapidly with firsthand knowledge. Second, the performance of each partner and associate could be carefully observed and attributed, and compensation and promotion decisions made accordingly. The ability to carefully measure performance limited the internal political activities so common in corporate life.

In recent years, though, the number of employees in private equity organizations had climbed. This partially reflected the success of partnerships in raising additional capital and their need to invest these funds rapidly. Exhibit 2.3 illustrates the recent growth of the private equity industry. While many private equity funds shunned recent graduates of MBA programs, preferring to hire people with experience in operating firms, recruitment of MBA graduates had also increased. Exhibit 2.3 also indicates the increase in recruitment of Harvard Business School graduates into private equity investing.

The use of compensation in private equity organizations had also undergone a substantial evolution with the recent growth of the private equity industry. Initially, there had been distinct schemes employed within traditional independent partnerships and groups affiliated with investment or commercial banks. (These affiliated groups have made up about 25 percent of the private equity groups active over the past twenty-five years, though a smaller share of the dollars invested.)[2] Private equity funds would

EXHIBIT 2.2

PRIVATE EQUITY RETURNS, BY YEAR

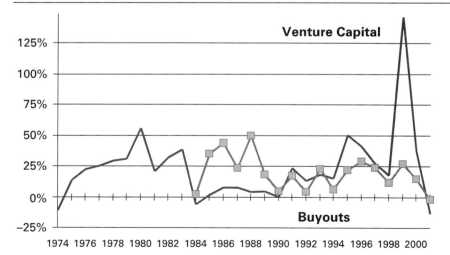

Source: Compiled from various databases of *Venture Economics.*

Note: 2001 based on first six months only.

2. The prevalence and performance of institutionally affiliated private equity groups are summarized in Paul A. Gompers and Josh Lerner, "Conflict of Interest and Reputation in the Issuance of Public Securities: Evidence from Venture Capital," *Journal of Law and Economics* 42 (April 1999) 53–80.

EXHIBIT 2.3

GROWTH OF PRIVATE EQUITY INDUSTRY, 1982–2001

	National Venture Capital Association Member Organizations (includes many buyout investors)	Harvard Business School Students Accepting Venture Capital or Buyout Positions	Total Venture Capital Principals (includes some but not all buyout and corporate investors)
1982	114	NA	963
1983	130	NA	1,134
1984	144	NA	1,380
1985	180	9	1,495
1986	191	18	1,664
1987	207	20	1,874
1988	225	11	1,954
1989	229	20	2,053
1990	223	12	2,081
1991	220	11	2,136
1992	201	8	2,250
1993	193	19	2,301
1994	187	16	2,347
1995	179	22	2,481
1996	194	44	2,679
1997	240	70	2,883
1998	310	103	3,021
1999	370	117	NA
2000	425	138	NA
2001	437°	114	NA

Sources: Compiled from unpublished National Venture Capital Association, Harvard Business School, and Venture Economics records.

Notes: °As of October 2001.

   NA = Not available.

typically pay an annual salary plus a share of the capital gains (or "carried interest") harvested in that year (the latter would be received only by the partners). Affiliated groups, which typically did not employ a partnership structure (they usually simply invested the parent institution's capital, rather than that of outside investors) generally provided employees with a salary and bonus. Even with the bonus, however, the compensation level in the affiliated funds was rarely equal to that of independent funds, and many of the leading private equity groups had been established by individuals who had left captive private equity groups such as those of the Bank of Boston, Citibank, the First National Bank of Chicago, and Security Pacific (now Bank of America).

During the 1990s, the patterns of compensation began subtly changing. In particular, the sharp demarcation between affiliated and independent groups blurred. A number of affiliated groups, eager to limit the defection of personnel, took two new approaches. Many such organizations adopted "shadow" compensation schemes that more directly tied their employees' rewards to their performance. Other institutions allowed their private equity groups to raise part of their funds from outside investors, rather than just from the sponsoring institution. For the funds raised from outsiders, there would be a provision for carried interest, at least some of which would be payable to the group's partners.

Meanwhile, intense competition for talented partners and associates had led independent groups to begin awarding bonuses in addition to salaries and carried interest. While precise data were difficult to obtain, survey estimates of compensation levels by the consulting firm William M. Mercer are summarized in Exhibits 2.4 and 2.5.

One factor that these surveys did not fully capture was the presence of co-investment rights. Many private equity groups allowed both partners and associates to invest in their transactions. In some cases there were few restrictions; in other groups, the investors were required to invest an equal amount in each transaction to address the limited partners' concerns about potential incentive and conflict-of-interest problems. In particular, institutional investors were often concerned that large investments by the general partners would reduce their own stakes in the most attractive opportunities, and that general partners would spend a disproportionate amount of time with the companies in which they had personally invested. In many organizations, associates were extended loans with which to make investments. In many cases, these loans were at a reduced interest level or were required to be repaid only to the extent that the investments yielded any proceeds.

MARTIN SMITH

Martin Smith had a background that made him attractive to many buyout organizations. After earning an undergraduate degree in economics at the University of Pennsylvania's

---

EXHIBIT 2.4

COMPENSATION OF PRIVATE EQUITY INVESTORS ($000s)

	Salary and Bonus		Total Compensation°		Carried Interest (%)†	
	Median	75th	Median	75th	Median	% Eligible
Managing general partner	$703	$1,403	$1,051	$4,778	4.0%	88%
Senior partner	630	1,110	841	1,727	2.4	88
Midlevel partner	359	622	465	990	1.6	82
Junior partner	249	348	253	395	0.5	72
Senior associate	155	202	163	219	0.2	45
Associate	121	150	125	151	0.1	34
Analyst	74	90	75	90	NA	5

Notes:

° Total compensation includes carried interest distributions as well as salary and bonus.

† Carried interest percentage is for most recent fund. The median is calculated only for those with a positive carried interest. Not all firms have a carried interest plan.

Source: 2001 Private Equity Firms Compensation Survey, conducted by William M. Mercer, Inc., New York, 2001. I thank Steve Brown and Randall Fast for their assistance.

EXHIBIT 2.5

COMPENSATION OF SENIOR PARTNERS AND SENIOR ASSOCIATES IN PRIVATE EQUITY FUNDS OF DIFFERENT TYPES ($000s)

	Senior Partners		Senior Associates	
	Median Salary and Bonus	Median Total Compensation	Median Salary and Bonus	Median Total Compensation
All Funds:	$630	$841	$155	$163
Lowest third in size	275	296	116	116
Middle third in size	784	833	147	194
Highest third in size	865	1,121	161	163
Private Firms:	600	636	160	160
Lower half in size	350	471	113	113
Upper half in size	874	1,105	168	170
Institutional Funds:	838	1,228	147	180
Lower half in size	625	833	140	140
Upper half in size	850	1,900	147	180

Source: 2001 Private Equity Firms Compensation Survey, Conducted by William M. Mercer, Inc., New York, 2001. I thank Steve Brown and Randall Fast for their assistance.

Wharton School, he had joined the investment bank Goldman, Sachs as an analyst in its corporate finance group. While his work there had sharpened his financial analysis skills, after two years he had tired of the endless parade of spreadsheets. Shortly thereafter, he joined a "B2B" (business-to-business) company geared toward helping midsized firms manage their financial planning and strategy. Although the firm ultimately proved to be a victim of the 2000–01 Internet downdraft, the experience offered Smith the chance to work closely with a number of chief financial officers of midsized firms, as well as with investment bankers and private equity groups. While in business school, his coursework had only reinforced Smith's desire to join the private equity industry after graduation.

At the same time, he had pursued an effective strategy in identifying private equity opportunities. First, he had focused on the private equity groups that were most likely to be interested in him. Smith had realized that without a significant technical background, it was unlikely that the many groups specializing in venture capital investments would see him as attractive. Consequently, he had targeted groups undertaking buyout and build-up investments.

Another important element had been avoiding more marginal private equity organizations. Smith had been contacted by a number of groups that were in the process of raising a first fund and had seen his resume in the Venture Capital and Principal Investment Club's Web site. Rather than seriously pursuing these positions, he had focused on more established groups.

Finally, he had extensively researched the private equity industry in order to target organizations that fit his skill set and to understand their situations. His steps included identifying what groups had just raised funds or were likely to be raising funds in the upcoming year (and hence likely to be thinking about adding personnel), researching the key deals that the partnerships had invested in, and seeking to ascertain the different groups' investment philosophies. As he narrowed his job search, he sought firsthand information about the groups from portfolio companies and an institutional investor. While this was time consuming and occasionally raised eyebrows at the private equity groups with whom he was interviewing, he believed it was only prudent. After all, accepting a position with a private equity group could be seen as a decision that required the same degree of due diligence as any other investment. The only difference was that here the investment was not of money—just a substantial amount of Smith's "human capital"!

THE DILEMMA

By mid-January, Smith's research yielded the offers from the established firms of Newport and Knowledge, plus the entrepreneurial search fund. Exhibit 2.6 summarizes the track records of the two established organizations.

If the organizations were being evaluated on the basis of "marquee value," no doubt Smith would give the nod to Newport Partners. This fund was one of the first

---

EXHIBIT 2.6

HISTORICAL PERFORMANCES OF PRIOR FUNDS

Newport Partners

Fund	Date	Size (millions)	Fund Return (%)[1]	Venture Economics Median (%)	Venture Economics Top ¼ (%)	General Partner (GP) Performance
				—as of 6/30/01—		
Fund IV	1990	$500	28% (2.5 times $)	13%	21%	A winner across the board
Fund V	1995	$1,000	19% (1.8 times $)	8%	18%	Powered by two key successful deals
Fund VI	1998	$1,510	–6% (0.8 times $)	2%	10%	Numerous disappointments
Fund VII	2001	$1,200	(just raised)			

Knowledge Capital Partners

Fund	Date	Size (millions)	Fund Return (%)*	Venture Economics Median (%)	Venture Economics Top ¼ (%)	General Partner (GP) Performance
				—as of 6/30/01—		
Fund I[†]	1993–96	$100	27% (2.4 times $)	16%	23%	Three deals were particular winners
Fund II	1997	$210	43% (2.0 times $)	4%	23%	Uniformly successful
Fund III	2001	$1,000	(just raised)			Dramatic step-up in size

Notes: Comparison data is for all buyout funds, but does not include all other private equity organizations.

* Return is net to the limited partners after fees and carried interest. The ratio of total fund value (distributions plus the reported value of fund assets) to paid-in capital is also reported.

† This was not a formal fund, but rather a collection of individual deals. The terms of these deals varied, and frequently did not entail a formal carried interest for the limited partners.

Source: Compiled from Venture Economics, VentureXpert Database, http://www.ventureeconomics.com.

to undertake leveraged buyout investments. While the organization did not raise its formal fund until 1978, it had its origins in the "family office" of a wealthy New England clan, which had begun investing in restructurings and recapitalizations as early as the 1950s. The fund had undertaken a number of high profile—and very successful—buyout transactions in each of the decades that followed.

By the end of 1990s, however, the group's fortunes had taken a turn for the worse. After researching press accounts and conversations with industry observers, Smith concluded that at least two fateful decisions had led to these disappointments. First, like many buyout firms, Newport had decided that it could not ignore the technology boom of the late 1990s. Nearly 20 percent of the sixth fund had been devoted to a buyout of a telecommunications test and measurement equipment firm, whose prospects had declined precipitously with those of the industry itself. If the share price of the small fraction of the company that remained publicly traded was to be believed, the firm had lost more than three-quarters of its value since the time of the original investment. Another investment—three rounds of financing for a consulting firm that was focused on helping old-line manufacturers conduct e-commerce—was smaller in size (about 6 percent of the total capital), but had been liquidated for a total loss.

The second decision had been to undertake an international expansion effort. The firm had opened costly offices in Frankfurt, Prague, and Warsaw, seeking to capitalize on the coming integration of the leading Eastern European nations into the European Community. The offices had not, however, been able to identify much in terms of attractive deal flow that met Newport's criteria. In particular, the only investment, the buyout of a Czech auto parts plant, had been plagued by shoddy products and labor unrest since its completion.

As a result of these disappointments, raising Newport's seventh fund had been arduous. The partners had originally set a target of $2 billion, and Smith suspected that—as is often the case—the fund's partners had actually hoped to raise a larger amount. Instead, the final closing in February 2001 had been for $1.2 billion, less than the $1.5 billion sixth fund.

On the other hand, Newport had begun what it labeled a "back to basics" effort to address these problems. In particular, Newport's legendary senior partner, Townsend "Sandy" Beech, had returned to assume the role of managing general partner on a full-time basis. (Beech, who had overseen many of Newport's most successful deals since the late 1960s, had since 1997 been largely focused an effort to build the world's fastest catamaran, in the hopes of being able to bring the America's Cup race back to the East Coast of the United States.) As part of this initiative, the two partners and three associates who had aggressively championed Newport's technology deals had left the firm, as had the twelve investment professionals stationed in Europe. After these changes, the firm was left with eleven seasoned partners with a diverse array of backgrounds (included a fairly even mix of those with financial, consulting, and operating experience), who were distributed among offices in New York, Dallas, and Chicago.

Knowledge Capital Partners presented a very different scenario from that of Newport. The organization had begun as a natural outgrowth of the midsized Washington, D.C.-based consulting firm Knowledge Partners. The consultants, in conjunction with close business associates, had initially invested their own funds in special situations emerging from consulting projects. For instance, one of their initial triumphs had been the spin-off of a small luggage manufacturing operation from a diversified conglomerate. After completing a consulting project for the large firm in which they had recommended that the unit be spun out, the partners had approached the senior management team and offered to purchase the unit for $50 million. During the next two years, the partners had sharply trimmed the product line and started a new marketing campaign that repositioned the product as an upscale product. They had sold the product shortly thereafter to an Italian firm for $100 million, yielding attractive returns on their equity investment of $10 million.

Knowledge Capital had raised its first formal fund in 1997 (labeled Knowledge Capital Partners II, LP, to reflect the fact that the group had been active in the market earlier). Shortly before the $210 million fund closed, the two consulting partners who had been most closely involved in the management of the investments joined the fund full-time, as did two seasoned professionals from East Coast buyout firms who had extensive experience managing turnarounds and rapidly growing firms. This fund employed a strategy similar to that of the first fund and had enjoyed considerable success. It had purchased a number of middle-market firms and smaller corporate divisions that needed substantial restructuring and strategic repositioning and then implemented these changes. In the summer of 2001, the firm had raised its third fund. Reflecting its remarkable success, the fund had raised $1 billion.

Smith was very attracted to the firm's clear strategy, the quality of the partners, and its proven record of success. Indeed, among his peers in business school, this was one of the groups with the greatest "buzz" or interest level. At the same time, there were a number of causes for worry. First, the rapid growth of the fund was worrisome. Not only had the capital under management grown dramatically in the past year, but also the total number of investment professionals had climbed from fourteen to thirty-seven. This growth was particularly an issue since the fund had traditionally specialized in small to midsized investments that required intensive involvement by the operating partners. To what extent could the model "scale" as the private equity organization grew?

As Smith talked with his classmates and friends, he highlighted a second concern as well: the relationship between the consulting firm and the private equity fund. One of his classmates told of his experiences at another consulting group that had a private equity fund. Not only did the consultants resent the high levels of compensation that the private equity professionals enjoyed, but they also found the fund put them at a disadvantage when competing for new clients: competing consulting firms would assert to potential clients that the consultant favored solutions that would create opportunities for its private equity fund. Smith also learned about investment bank–affiliated funds where the partners had to pass on promising transactions because they competed with long-standing clients of the bank's corporate finance division. When he had raised this concern with the partners at the fund, they had been quite dismissive. Rather, they emphasized the historical synergies between the consulting and private equity activities. They also noted that the presence of the private equity activity had made it easier for the firm to recruit new consultants. Smith wondered, however, whether such tensions would appear, now that the third fund, with so much more money, had been raised.

The third option was quite different. Steve Avery, one of Smith's roommates in his first year at Harvard Business School, was seeking to persuade Smith to join a search fund that he had organized. Avery, who had graduated with the class of 2001, had spent the past year (while working as a consultant at McKinsey & Co.) negotiating a complex contract with a number of entrepreneurs he had met when they attended the Harvard Business School's Owner-President-Manager program in the spring of 2001. The executives had agreed to finance Avery and a partner for eighteen months while they looked for a prospective company to buy out. When they found a potential candidate, the six executives agreed to contribute up to $6 million in financing for the transaction, conditional on its meeting with their approval. They also agreed to provide informal advice and counsel as the business evolved.

In exchange, the investors would receive their principal back, in addition to a share of the capital gains. In particular, the investors would receive 90 percent of the capital gains until they had obtained a 10 percent rate of return, then 80 percent of the gains until they received a return of 25 percent, and then 70 percent of the gains thereafter. Avery and Avery, assuming that Smith decided to take up this offer, would divide the remainder of the gains equally.

To be sure, there were real risks associated with this offer. Steve and Smith might not be able to identify an attractive takeover target in the allotted time, or at least one that would meet the investors' approval. Even if they identified such a business, the managers might be unwilling to be acquired by a relatively inexperienced investor group. Raising the additional financing needed to complete the deal might be difficult, particularly if the current recession proved to be long-lived.

But on the other hand, there were real potential benefits. The recent economic downturn meant that many promising small business were locked out from the equity and credit markets. Moreover, Smith had found at least a dozen examples of Harvard MBAs who had employed a similar strategy upon graduating from business school and had purchased firms.

Smith wondered how to interpret these offers, and how much importance to place on compensation in his choice between the three funds. Newport's offer had been an attractive one, with total compensation of about $170,000. While he would not receive any share of the fund's profits initially, the partners had indicated that if things worked out well, Smith would receive such a share at the end of 2003. At the same time, he was aware that Newport did not have a tradition of "promoting from within": instead, associates tend to work for four or five years at the firm and then go on to other private equity organizations. While Beech had assured Smith that this policy was likely to shift in the future, it was unclear how substantial such a shift would be.

Knowledge Capital's offer was about 30 percent lower in terms of compensation. Nor was it clear when Smith would begin sharing in the capital gains; when he had raised that issue, the partners had rather abruptly indicated that it was premature to discuss this question. Finally, in the search fund, there were no guarantees beyond the $90,000 salary that the search fund investors would pay Smith during his first year. If they identified a successful deal, however, the returns could be very dramatic.

The Private Equity Cycle: Fundraising

The first module of *Venture Capital and Private Equity* examines how private equity funds are raised and structured. These funds often have complex features, and the legal issues involved are frequently arcane. But the structure of private equity funds profoundly affects the behavior of venture and buyout investors. Consequently, it is important to understand these issues, whether one intends to work for, receive money from, or invest in or alongside private equity funds.

The module will seek not only to understand the features of private equity funds and the actors in the fundraising process, but also to analyze them. We will map out which institutions serve primarily to increase the profits from private equity investments as a whole, and which seem designed mostly to shift profits *between* the parties. We will seek to understand the functions of and reasons for each aspect of private equity fundraising.

WHY THIS MODULE?

The structuring of venture and buyout funds may initially appear to be a complex and technical topic, one better left to legal specialists than general managers. Private equity partnership agreements are complex documents, often extending for hundreds of pages. Practitioner discussions of the structure of these firms are rife with obscure terms such as "reverse clawbacks."

But the subject is an important one, for the features of private equity funds—whether management fees, profit sharing rules, or contractual terms—have a profound effect on the behavior of these investors. It is clearly important to understand these influences if one is seeking to work for a private equity fund. But an understanding of these dynamics will also be valuable for the entrepreneur financing his company through these investors, the investment banker underwriting a firm backed by private equity funds, the corporate development officer investing alongside venture capitalists in a young company, and the pension fund manager placing her institution's capital into a fund.

This note was prepared by Professor Joshua Lerner for the sole purpose of aiding classroom instructors in the Venture Capital and Private Equity course.

An example may help to illustrate this point. Almost all venture and buyout funds are designed to be "self-liquidating": that is, to dissolve after ten or twelve years. The need to terminate each fund imposes a healthy discipline, forcing private equity investors to take the necessary but painful step of terminating underperforming firms in their portfolios. (These firms are sometimes referred to as the "living dead" or "zombies.") But the pressure to raise an additional fund can sometimes have less pleasant consequences. Young private equity organizations frequently rush young firms to the public marketplace in order to demonstrate a successful track record, even if the companies are not ready to go public. This behavior, known as "grandstanding," can harm the long-run prospects of the firms dragged prematurely into the public markets.

A second rationale for an examination of the concerns and perspectives of institutional investors and intermediaries is that they provide an often-neglected avenue into the private equity industry. Many students diligently pursue positions at the traditional private equity organizations, but neglect other routes to careers as private equity investors. A position evaluating private equity funds and putting capital to work in these organizations is likely to lead to a network of relationships with private equity investors that may eventually pay handsome dividends.

THE FRAMEWORK

Many actors participate in the private equity fundraising drama. Investors—whether pension funds, individuals, or endowments—each have their own motivations and concerns. These investors frequently hire intermediaries. Sometimes these "gatekeepers" play a consultative role, recommending attractive funds to their clients. In other cases, they organize funds-of-funds of their own. Specialized intermediaries concentrate on particular niches of the private equity industry, such as buying and selling interests in limited partnerships from institutional investors. In addition, venture and buyout organizations are increasingly hiring placement agents who facilitate the fundraising process.

This module will examine each of these players. Rather than just describing their roles, however, we will highlight the rationales for and impacts of their behavior. Some institutions and features have evolved to improve the efficiency of the private equity investment process, while others appear to be designed primarily to shift more of the economic benefits to particular parties.

Investing in a private equity fund is in some respects a leap of faith for institutional investors. Most pension funds and endowments typically have very small staffs. At the largest organizations, a dozen professionals may be responsible for investing several billion dollars each year. Meanwhile, private equity funds undertake investments that are either in risky new firms pursuing complex new technologies or in troubled mature companies with numerous organizational pathologies and potential legal liabilities.

Many of the features of private equity funds can be understood as responses to this uncertain environment, rife with many information gaps. For instance, the "carried interest"—the substantial share of profits allocated to the private equity investors—helps address these information asymmetries by ensuring that all parties gain if the investment does well. Similarly, pension funds hire gatekeepers to ensure that only sophisticated private equity funds with well-defined objectives get funded with their capital.

At the same time, other features of private equity funds can be seen as attempts to *transfer* wealth between parties, rather than efforts to increase the size of the overall amount of profits generated by private equity investments. An example was the drive by many venture capital funds in the mid-1980s—a period when the demand for their services was very strong—to change the timing of their compensation. Prior to this point, venture capital funds had typically disbursed all the proceeds from their first few successful investments to their investors, until the investors had received their original invested capital back. The venture capitalists would then begin receiving a share of the subsequent investments that they exited. Consider a fund that had raised capital of $50 million, whose first three successful investments yielded $25 million each. Under the traditional arrangement, the proceeds from the first two offerings would have gone entirely to the institutional investors in their fund. The venture capitalists would have only begun receiving a share of the proceeds at the time that they exited the third investment.

In the mid-1980s, venture capitalists began demanding—and receiving—the right to start sharing in even the first successfully exited investments. The primary effect of this change was that the venture capitalists began receiving more compensation early in their funds' lives. Put another way, the net present value of their compensation package increased considerably. It is not surprising, then, that as the inflow into venture capital weakened in the late 1980s, institutional investors began demanding that venture capitalists return to the previous approach of deferring compensation.

This twin tension—between behavior that increases the size of the "pie" and actions that simply change the relative sizes of the slices—runs through this module. We will attempt to both understand the workings of and the reasons for the key features of these funds using this framework.

THE STRUCTURE OF THE MODULE

The first half of the module introduces the key elements of the private equity fund-raising process. Among the actors whose structure and concerns we will examine are institutions, private equity investors, funds-of-funds, and gatekeepers. We will put particular emphasis on the agreements that bring these parties together into limited partnerships. Because they play such an important role in shaping behavior, compensation terms will be a special focus.

The second half of the module looks at the raising of two funds by private equity organizations. We look at private equity organizations with very different histories and investment targets. The funds that emerged from these circumstances reflected not only the differences between the investments that each fund promised to make, but also each group's ability to persuade—or demand—a better deal from its investors. We will consider a variety of issues, from the role of the key institutions in the fundraising process to how the performance of these funds should be assessed.

FURTHER READING ON PRIVATE EQUITY FUND-RAISING AND PARTNERSHIPS

Legal Works

JOSEPH W. BARTLETT, *Equity Finance: Venture Capital, Buyouts, Restructurings, and Reorganization* (New York: Wiley, 1995), chapters 24 and 29.

CRAIG E. DAUCHY AND MARK T. HARMON, "Structuring Venture Capital Limited Partnerships," *The Computer Lawyer* 3 (November 1986): 1–7.

MICHAEL J. HALLORAN, LEE F. BENTON, ROBERT V. GUNDERSON, JR., KEITH L. KEARNEY, AND JORGE DEL CALVO, *Venture Capital and Public Offering Negotiation* (Englewood Cliffs, NJ: Aspen Law and Business, 1997 and updates), volume 1, chapters 1 and 2.

Practitioner and Journalistic Accounts

Asset Alternatives, *Directory of Alternative Investment Programs* (Wellesley, MA: Asset Alternatives, 2003).

Asset Alternatives, *Private Equity Analyst-Holt Compensation Survey* (Wellesley, MA: Asset Alternatives, 2003).

Asset Alternatives, *Private Equity Fund of Funds: State of the Market* (Wellesley, MA: Asset Alternatives, 2003).

Asset Alternatives, *Terms and Conditions of Private Equity Partnerships* (Wellesley, MA: Asset Alternatives, 2003).

PAUL A. GOMPERS AND JOSH LERNER, *The Money of Invention* (Boston: Harvard Business School Press, 2001), chapters 5–6.

William M. Mercer, Inc., *Key Terms and Conditions for Private Equity Investing*, 1997.

Venture Economics, *Directory of Limited Partners* (Newark: Venture Economics, 2003).

Numerous articles in *Buyouts, Private Equity Analyst,* and *Venture Capital Journal.*

Academic Studies

JOHN H. COCHRANE, "The Risk and Return of Venture Capital," National Bureau of Economic Research Working Paper no. 8066, 2001.

GEORGE W. FENN, NELLIE LIANG, AND STEPHEN PROWSE, "The Private Equity Market: An Overview," *Financial Markets, Institutions and Instruments* 6 (no. 4, 1997): 70–100.

PAUL A. GOMPERS AND JOSH LERNER, "Risk and Reward in Private Equity Investments: The Challenge of Performance Assessment," *Journal of Private Equity* 1 (Winter 1997): 5–12.

PAUL A. GOMPERS AND JOSH LERNER, *The Venture Capital Cycle* (Cambridge, MIT Press, 2004), chapters 2–6.

PAUL A. GOMPERS AND JOSH LERNER, "What Drives Venture Fundraising?" *Brookings Papers on Economic Activity—Microeconomics* (1998): 149–192.

THOMAS HELLMANN, "Venture Capital: A Challenge for Commercial Banks," *Journal of Private Equity* 1 (Fall 1997): 49–55.

BLAINE HUNTSMAN AND JAMES P. HOBAN JR., "Investment in New Enterprise: Some Empirical Observations on Risk, Return and Market Structure," *Financial Management* 9 (Summer 1980): 44–51.

LESLIE A. JENG AND PHILIPPE C. WELLS, "The Determinants of Venture Capital Funding: Evidence Across Countries," *Journal of Corporate Finance* 6 (September 2000): 241–284.

STEVEN N. KAPLAN AND ANTOINETTE SCHOAR, "Private Equity Performance: Returns, Persistence, and Capital." National Bureau of Economic Research Working Paper no. 9807, 2003.

JOSH LERNER AND ANTOINETTE SCHOAR, "The Illiquidity Puzzle: Theory and Evidence from Private Equity," *Journal of Financial Economics,* forthcoming.

PATRICK R. LILES, *Sustaining the Venture Capital Firm* (Cambridge: Management Analysis Center, 1977).

3

Yale University Investments Office: June 2003

Burly men lugged boxes full of computer equipment and office furniture. Throughout the office, files were being boxed up and carted off. The Yale University Investments Office was in the process of moving from a converted Victorian-era mansion on the Yale campus, its home for the past dozen years, to an office building a few blocks away.

Yale's chief investment officer, David Swensen, looked over the hectic scene. Whatever the short-run pain of the move, he mused, the benefits of having the Investments Office staff on a single floor were sure to be substantial.

His thoughts turned to the larger challenges associated with the management of the university's Endowment, which totaled $11.0 billion in June 2003. Under Swensen's leadership, and with the guidance and approval of the Investment Committee, Yale had developed a rather different approach to Endowment management, including substantial investments in less efficient equity markets such as private equity (venture capital and buyouts), real assets (real estate, timber, oil, and gas), and "absolute return" investing. This approach had generated successful, indeed enviable, returns. Swensen and his staff were proud of their record and believed that Yale should probably focus even more of its efforts and assets in these less efficient markets. At the same time, the very success of their strategy had generated new questions. How far did they think Yale should or could go in this direction? How should they respond to the growing popularity of the approach they had chosen? Given the difficult times that private equity funds were facing, should this asset class continue to play an integral role in Yale's portfolio?

Professor Josh Lerner prepared this case. HBS cases are developed solely as the basis for class discussion. Cases are not intended to serve as endorsements, sources of primary data, or illustrations of effective or ineffective management.

BACKGROUND[1]

Ten Connecticut clergymen established Yale in 1701. Over its first century, the college relied on the generosity of the Connecticut General Assembly, which provided more than half of its funding. The creation of a formal endowment for Yale was triggered by the 1818 disestablishment of Congregationalism as Connecticut's state religion. Students and alumni alike demanded that the school respond by establishing a divinity school to offer theological instruction. To fund this effort, numerous alumni made large gifts, the first in a series of successful fund drives. While Yale used many of these donations to buy land and construct buildings, other funds were invested in corporate and railroad bonds, as well as equities. By the century's end, the Endowment had reached $5 million.

The growth of the Endowment rapidly accelerated during the first three decades of the twentieth century. This was due both to several enormous bequests and to aggressive investments in equities, which comprised well over half the Endowment's portfolio during the "roaring" 1920s. In 1930, equities represented 42 percent of the Yale Endowment; the average university had only 11 percent.[2] Yale avoided severe erosion of its Endowment during the Great Depression in the 1930s, however, because many quite recent bequests were kept in cash or Treasuries, rather than being invested in equities.

In the late 1930s, Treasurer Laurence Tighe decided that the share of equities in Yale's portfolio should be dramatically reduced. Tighe argued that higher taxes were likely to expropriate any corporate profits that equity holders would otherwise receive even if a recovery were to occur. He argued that bonds would consequently perform better than stocks. His decision, which stipulated that at least two dollars would be held in fixed income instruments for every dollar of equity, set the template for Yale's asset allocation over the next three decades. The treasurer and trustees continued to manage the Endowment themselves during this period, selecting individual bonds and high-yield or income-oriented stocks for the portfolio. These policies seemed very prudent in the late 1930s and 1940s. But unfortunately, they were less well suited for the bull market of the 1950s and 1960s. In the mid- and late 1960s, in response, the Endowment's trustees decided upon two substantial policy shifts.

First, the trustees decided to increase substantially the university's exposure to equity investments. In this decision, they were influenced by a task force sponsored by McGeorge Bundy, president of the Ford Foundation. This committee—which included Kingman Brewster, president of Yale—argued that most university endowments had taken too conservative an approach: "It is our conclusion that past thinking by many endowment managers has been overly influenced by fear of another major crash. Although nobody can ever be certain what the future may bring, we do not think that a long-term policy founded on such fear can survive dispassionate analysis."[3]

Second, Yale decided to contract out much of the portfolio management function to an external advisor. The school helped found a new Boston-based money manager, Endowment Management and Research Corporation (EM&R), whose principals were well-known successful growth stock investors recruited from other Boston money

1. This section is based on Brooks Mather Kelley, *Yale: A History* (New Haven: Yale University Press, 1974); David F. Swensen, *Pioneering Portfolio Management: An Unconventional Approach to Investment Management* (New York: Free Press, 2000); and Yale University Investments Office, *The Yale Endowment* (New Haven: Yale University, 2002).

2. General university information is from Institutional Department, Scudder, Stevens & Clark, *Survey of University and College Endowment Funds* (New York: Scudder, Stevens & Clark, 1947).

3. Advisory Committee on Endowment Management, *Managing Educational Endowments: Report to the Ford Foundation* (New York: Ford Foundation, 1969).

management firms. The plan was that EM&R would function as a quasi-independent external firm and would be free to recruit additional clients. Yale would be its largest client and would have priority over other clients.

The high expectations for EM&R were never realized. Like other universities, Yale saw its Endowment's value plummet in the ensuing years because of a "bear" market, accelerating inflation, and operating deficits. Between 1969 and 1979, the inflation-adjusted value of Yale's Endowment declined by 46 percent. While the investment performance was not unusual relative to other endowments, it nonetheless severely strained the financial fabric of the university. Yale terminated its relationship with EM&R in 1979 and embarked upon a program to use a variety of external advisors in its evolving asset management framework.

DAVID SWENSEN AND THE INVESTMENTS OFFICE IN 2003

In 1985, David Swensen was hired to head the Investments Office. William Brainard, Yale's provost at the time, and world-renowned economist James Tobin persuaded their former student—Swensen had earned his Ph.D. in Economics at Yale in 1980—to leave his post at Lehman Brothers. The position offered not only the opportunity to help Yale, but also the possibility of some teaching in Yale College as well.

In the succeeding eighteen years, Swensen built the capabilities of the Yale Investments Office. Most importantly, he recruited and developed a quite small but very high-quality internal staff. Dean Takahashi, whom Swensen had known as a Yale student, was recruited into the Investments Office and became Swensen's primary lieutenant. The two worked extremely closely. In fact, in the preface to Swensen's book, *Pioneering Portfolio Management,* he described the contents as his and his colleague's "joint intellectual property." A number of other staff members had also been recruited over the years, often recent graduates of Yale College. There were a total of twenty employees (sixteen professionals) in the office in June 2003. Swensen encouraged his staff to be active members of the larger Yale community, and he had chosen his office's near-campus location to signal that the Investments Office was an integral part of the university and its financial management function.

Swensen defined the role of the Investments Office broadly. Reporting to the president and to an Investment Committee (described below), the Investments Office had overall responsibility for Endowment matters. While most of its day-to-day activities involved evaluating, selecting, monitoring, and overseeing external investment advisors, it also played a critical role in the entire policy-making process. For example, it was responsible for recommendations on both the investment policy and the spending policy for the Endowment—that is, in broad terms, how the money should be invested and how much of it could be spent in any given year.

The Investment Committee, to which the Investments Office reported, was composed of influential and knowledgeable Yale alumni, a number of whom were quite active in different segments of the asset management business. The committee as a whole functioned as an active, involved board, meeting quarterly and providing advice, counsel, and ultimately approval of the various investment managers. In addition, David Swensen often consulted individual members of the Investment Committee on issues within their areas of specific expertise. This helped guide the thinking and recommendations of the Investments Office on key issues, and it fostered an atmosphere of advice and support within which the Investments Office could take quite different and sometimes unconventional stances if it believed in them and could convince the Investment Committee of their merit.

Investment Philosophy

Perhaps the most fundamental difference between Yale and other universities was its investment philosophy. Swensen was fond of quoting John Maynard Keynes' maxim that "worldly wisdom teaches us that it is better for reputation to fail conventionally than to succeed unconventionally."[4] Nonetheless, Swensen was willing to take "the risk of being different" when it seemed appropriate and potentially rewarding. By not following the crowd, Yale could develop its investment philosophy from first principles, which are summarized below.

First, Swensen strongly believed in equities, whether publicly traded or private. He pointed out that equities are a claim on a real stream of income, as opposed to a contractual sequence of nominal cash flows (such as bonds). Since the bulk of a university's outlays are devoted to salaries, inflation can place tremendous pressure on its finances. Not only do bonds have low expected returns relative to more equity-like assets, but they also often perform poorly during periods of rising or highly uncertain inflation. To demonstrate convincingly why he believed in the long-run advantages of equity investing, Swensen would often refer to the actual cumulative long-run returns over past decades. An original one-dollar investment in December 1925 in large-company U.S. stocks would be worth $1,775 by the end of 2002 and small-company stocks, $6,816; a comparable investment in U.S. Treasury bonds would be worth $60 and Treasury bills, $17.[5]

A second principle was to hold a diversified portfolio. In general, Yale believed that risk could be more effectively reduced by limiting aggregate exposure to any single asset class, rather than by attempting to time markets. While Swensen and his staff usually had their own informed views of the economy and markets, they believed that most of the time those views were already reflected in market prices. They thus tended to avoid trying to time short-run market fluctuations and would overweight or underweight an asset class only if a persuasive case could be made that market prices were measurably misvalued for understandable reasons.[6]

A third principle was to seek opportunities in less efficient markets. Swensen noted that over the previous decade, the difference in performance between U.S. fixed income managers in the twenty-fifth and seventy-fifth percentiles (of their performance universe) was minimal, and the difference in performance between U.S. common stock portfolio managers in the twenty-fifth and seventy-fifth percentiles was approximately 3 percent per annum. In private equity, in contrast, this same performance difference exceeded 20 percent per annum. This suggested that there could be far greater incremental returns to selecting superior managers in nonpublic markets characterized by incomplete information and illiquidity, and that was exactly what Swensen and his staff endeavored to do.

Fourth, Swensen believed strongly in using outside managers for all but the most routine or indexed of investments. He thought these external investment advisors should be given considerable autonomy to implement their strategies as they saw fit, with relatively little interference from Yale. These managers were chosen very carefully, however, after a lengthy and probing analysis of their abilities, their comparative advantages,

---

4. John M. Keynes, *The General Theory of Employment Interest and Money* (New York: Harcourt Brace, 1936), chapter 12.

5. R. G. Ibbotson Associates, *Stocks, Bonds, Bills and Inflation* (Chicago: R. G. Ibbotson Associates, 2003).

6. Yale actively rebalanced its portfolio to maintain its target asset allocations, however, and this led to frequent short-term adjustments in its holdings. For instance, as equity values rose in the summer of 1987, Yale sold stocks in order to return to its target allocation level. After the stock market crash later that year, the Endowment repurchased many of the same securities as it sought to raise its asset allocation back to the target level.

their performance records, and their reputations. The Investments Office staff was responsible for developing close and mutually beneficial relationships with each of these external managers. The staff members prided themselves on knowing their managers very well, on listening carefully to their ongoing advice, and on helping to guide them, if and when appropriate, on policy matters. From time to time, the Investments Office effectively "put a team in business" by becoming a new manager's first client. And it was not uncommon for managers to consider Yale one of their most important clients.

Finally, the Yale philosophy focused critically on the explicit and implicit incentives facing outside managers. In Swensen's view, most of the asset management business had poorly aligned incentives built into typical client-manager relationships. For instance, managers typically prospered if their assets under management grew very large, not necessarily if they just performed well for their clients. The Investments Office tried to structure innovative relationships and fee structures with various external managers so as to better align the managers' interests with those of Yale, insofar as that was possible.

Recent Asset Allocation and Performance Results

Yale's Investment Committee annually reviewed its Endowment portfolio to decide on target allocations to the various asset classes. The actual allocations in recent years are shown in Exhibit 3.1, which illustrates the recent upward trend in the allocation to the private equity, real assets, and absolute return classes, as well as the current (2003) target allocations. The comparable asset allocations for several groups of university endowments are shown in Exhibits 3.2 and 3.3. Private equity allocations for large institutions (including both pension funds and endowments) are shown in Exhibit 3.4.

As a part of the planning process, the Investments Office compared its "mean-variance analysis" of the expected returns and risks from its current allocation to those of past Yale allocations and the current mean allocation of other universities. These computations, which relied on specific assumptions about the expected returns, volatilities, and correlations among asset classes, posed several issues. First, because these relationships can change dramatically over time, the Investments Office did not just rely mechanically on historical data, but instead modified the historical numbers based on its own experience. Second, the Investment Office imposed limits on the amount that could be invested in each asset class. If it did not, the optimization program would instruct Yale to hold no domestic equities (or even to short-sell this asset class), and to instead invest in the more illiquid alternatives. This result followed naturally from the assumptions of the model: for instance, private equity was projected to have nearly twice the real return of U.S. equities (11.4 percent versus 6.0 percent), albeit with a higher standard deviation (29.1 percent versus 20.0 percent). (Over the previous decade, actual returns had been considerably higher for both asset classes, and standard deviations—measured quarterly—had been lower.) The imposition of these constraints reflected the need of the university to diversify its holdings as well as the substantially greater imprecision with which Yale could assess the risk and return of its alternative assets. The results of this comparative mean variance analysis are shown in Exhibit 3.5.

In addition, the Investments Office examined the long-run implications of its allocation for the "downside risk" to the Endowment. In keeping with a quantitative format for analyzing long-run downside risk that had been used previously, the office examined the probability that the income stream from the Endowment would fall by more than 10 percent (adjusted for inflation) over a five-year period; the office also examined the probability that the inflation-adjusted value of the Endowment would fall by more than one-half over the next fifty years. To undertake this

EXHIBIT 3.1

ASSET ALLOCATIONS OF YALE ENDOWMENT, 1985–2002

	1985	1986	1987	1988	1989	1990	1991	1992	1993	1994	1995	1996	1997	1998	1999	2000	2001	2002	Current (2000) Target Allocation
Domestic equity	61.6%	63.5%	61.7%	56.8%	53.2%	48.0%	30.7%	27.5%	23.9%	21.2%	21.8%	22.6%	21.5%	19.2%	15.1%	14.2%	15.5%	15.4%	15.0%
Foreign equity	6.3	8.6	10.8	14.0	15.4	15.2	14.8	15.3	16.5	14.6	12.5	12.4	12.8	12.1	11.1	9.0	10.6	12.8	15.0
Bonds	10.3	12.7	14.6	15.0	16.3	21.2	21.2	22.7	22.5	16.5	12.2	12.3	12.5	10.1	9.6	9.4	9.8	10.0	7.5
Cash	10.1	5.0	2.1	2.1	0.3	0.9	0.9	0.5	0.1	0.6	1.8	0.9	-0.2	-2.5	1.5	8.1	6.2	0.3	0.0
Real assets	8.5	7.5	7.2	7.7	8.7	8.0	7.9	7.1	6.0	8.6	13.5	11.2	11.5	13.0	17.9	14.9	16.8	20.5	20.0
Private equity	3.2	2.7	3.6	4.4	6.1	6.7	8.3	10.4	14.4	18.1	17.2	20.2	18.6	21.0	23.0	25.0	18.2	14.4	17.5
Absolute return	0.0	0.0	0.0	0.0	0.0	0.0	15.9	16.5	16.6	20.1	21.0	20.7	23.3	27.1	21.8	19.5	22.9	26.5	25.0

Notes: Asset allocations are on June 30 of each year.

Private equity includes venture capital and buyouts (and oil and gas and forestland through 1998).

Absolute return includes hedge funds, high-yield bonds, distressed securities, and event arbitrage.

Real assets includes real estate and (since 1999) oil and gas and forestland.

Source: Yale University documents.

EXHIBIT 3.2

ASSET ALLOCATIONS OF LARGE UNIVERSITY ENDOWMENTS, 1985–2002

	1985	1986	1987	1988	1989	1990	1991	1992	1993	1994	1995	1996	1997	1998	1999	2000	2001	2002
Domestic equity	51.5%	52.1%	53.8%	50.2%	46.1%	45.3%	43.5%	44.4%	43.0%	41.6%	42.8%	41.1%	42.3%	39.9%	36.3%	36.5%	30.1%	29.3%
Foreign equity	2.0	2.6	3.0	5.2	6.6	6.6	7.8	8.1	10.2	14.3	15.2	14.0	15.9	14.7	14.5	15.0	13.9	14.3
Bonds	26.4	28.3	26.0	26.2	27.5	29.2	30.2	30.7	26.9	22.4	17.5	20.1	18.0	15.9	15.0	17.4	17.8	23.1
Cash	10.8	8.8	8.9	7.7	6.9	6.9	6.1	5.2	4.6	3.2	4.1	3.2	3.1	2.5	3.0	2.8	2.5	-0.2
Real estate	4.8	4.9	5.2	4.3	5.1	4.4	4.2	3.7	3.7	4.2	5.1	5.2	5.2	6.9	6.6	4.7	6.3	5.9
Private equity	2.7	1.9	2.0	5.8	6.6	6.2	6.2	5.9	6.6	7.7	8.0	8.1	7.2	8.2	11.1	13.9	12.1	9.9
Absolute return	0.0	0.0	0.0	0.0	0.0	0.1	0.6	0.8	3.3	5.2	6.2	6.7	6.9	10.1	11.3	8.3	13.2	14.7
Other	1.8	1.4	1.1	0.6	1.2	1.3	1.4	1.2	1.7	1.5	1.1	1.6	1.5	2.0	2.1	1.2	4.1	3.1

Notes: Asset allocations are on June 30 of each year.

Large funds are defined as those with more than $1 billion in assets in 1998 through 2002, as those with more than $400 million in assets in 1988 through 1997, and as those with more than $200 million in assets in 1985 through 1987.

Private equity includes venture capital, buyouts, and oil and gas.

Funds are weighted equally in calculating average allocations in 1985 through 1987.

Absolute return includes hedge funds, high-yield bonds, distressed securities, and event arbitrage.

Funds are weighted by size in calculating average allocations in 1988 through 1994.

The 1985–1987 classifications may not be completely analogous to those in other years.

Source: Compiled from National Association of College and University Business Officers, *2002 NACUBO Endowment Study,* Washington, DC, National Association of College and University Business Officers, 2003 (and earlier years).

EXHIBIT 3.3

ASSET ALLOCATIONS OF ALL UNIVERSITY ENDOWMENTS, 1985–2002

	1985	1986	1987	1988	1989	1990	1991	1992	1993	1994	1995	1996	1997	1998	1999	2000	2001	2002
Domestic equity	46.1%	48.7%	51.4%	46.4%	48.5%	48.1%	47.1%	47.1%	48.5%	47.2%	49.2%	51.6%	52.6%	52.4%	53.7%	41.4%	49.5%	47.3%
Foreign equity	0.8	1.1	1.6	1.5	1.8	2.4	2.4	3.2	4.2	7.5	9.5	9.5	11.2	11.0	10.6	14.1	9.9	10.1
Bonds	30.6	30.6	30.8	33.8	32.2	33.9	35.3	35.3	34.4	32.2	28.3	27.3	25.2	24.9	23.1	21.1	24.9	26.9
Cash	14.5	13.1	12.6	14.2	13.0	10.9	10.1	9.9	7.6	7.1	6.5	5.4	4.8	4.1	4.0	3.5	4.1	3.9
Real estate	4.2	3.9	2.2	2.5	2.7	2.9	2.9	2.3	2.1	2.1	2.3	2.0	2.0	2.2	2.1	3.0	2.4	2.7
Private equity	0.7	0.6	0.7	0.9	1.1	1.0	1.1	0.9	1.1	1.2	1.3	1.4	1.4	1.4	2.2	8.7	2.6	2.4
Absolute return	0.0	0.0	0.0	0.0	0.0	0.0	0.2	0.3	1.1	1.8	2.0	2.2	2.4	3.6	3.8	7.0	4.2	5.1
Other	3.1	2.0	0.7	0.6	0.7	0.7	0.9	1.0	0.9	0.9	0.9	0.5	0.4	0.4	0.5	1.1	2.3	1.6

Notes: Asset allocations are on June 30 of each year.

Private equity includes venture capital, buyouts, and oil and gas.

Absolute return includes hedge funds, high-yield bonds, distressed securities, and event arbitrage.

All funds are weighted equally in calculating average allocations.

The 1985 and 1986 classifications may not be completely analogous to those in other years.

Source: Compiled from National Association of College and University Business Officers, *2002 NACUBO Endowment Study,* Washington, DC, National Association of College and University Business Officers, 2003 (and earlier years).

EXHIBIT 3.4

ASSET ALLOCATIONS OF MAJOR PENSION FUNDS
AND ENDOWMENTS TO PRIVATE EQUITY, 1992–2001

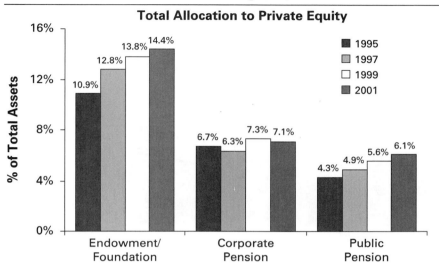

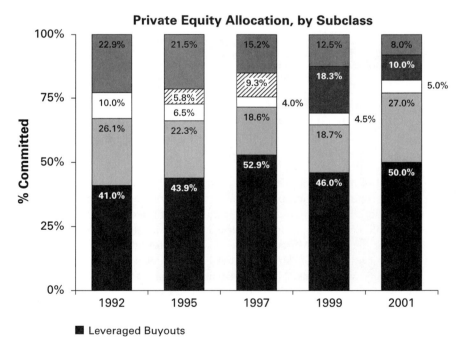

Note: 2001 computation is only for North American-based institutions. In the allocation by subclass, international private equity is reported as a distinct class only between 1992 and 1997.

Source: Goldman, Sachs & Co. and Frank Russell Capital Inc., *2001 Report on Alternative Investments by Tax-Exempt Organizations*, November 2001.

EXHIBIT 3.5

YALE'S HISTORICAL RISK AND RETURN PROFILE

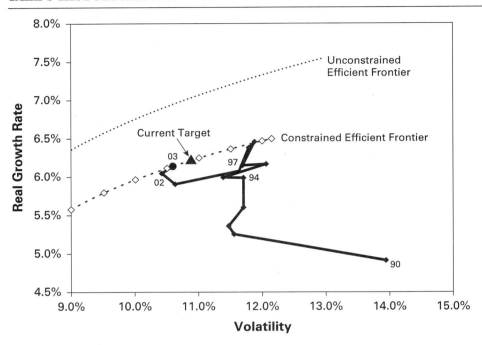

Source: University documents.

analysis, the Investments Office employed a probabilistic Monte Carlo analysis, which simulated and compiled thousands of possible random outcomes drawn from an assumed distribution of returns and correlations used in the simpler "mean-variance analysis." This "downside risk analysis" suggested that the probability of a 10 percent spending fall in purchasing power within any five-year period was 23 percent and of a 50 percent fall over a fifty-year horizon was 11 percent.

Yale's allocation philosophy and distinctive approach to investing had paid off handsomely. In fiscal year 2002, the fund had returned 0.7 percent. The positive return, while small, compared favorably to the 18.0 percent decline in the S&P 500 and the 9.2 percent decline in Morgan Stanley Capital International (MSCI) Europe, Australasia, and Far East (EAFE). Moreover, the Endowment managed to overcome substantial private equity writedowns. This performance was above Yale's large peers (Columbia, Harvard, MIT, Princeton, and Stanford) who averaged –2.6 percent, as well as all universities as measured by National Association of College and University Business Officers (a mean of –6.0 percent). Even more impressive had been the fund's long-run performance since Swensen and Takahashi arrived at Yale. Over the fifteen years ending in June 2002, Yale's annualized return was 14.2 percent, exceeding the return of all other colleges and universities. This result was more than 2.7 percent per annum better than Yale's "peers" (other nontaxable endowments with over $1 billion in assets) and about 4.3 percent per annum better than the average of all such endowments.[7] (The Endowment's performance

7. Had the Yale Endowment generated investment performance over the previous fifteen years at the equal-weighted average of all university endowments, the Endowment in June 2002 would have been $5.1 billion smaller.

during recent years is compared to that of other universities in Exhibit 3.6; a more detailed breakdown of Yale's returns by asset class is reported in Exhibit 3.7.) Yale's record placed it in the top 1 percent in SEI Investments' rankings of large institutional investors.[8] Not only had the average return been high, but the Endowment also had avoided losing funds: the university had not had a negative return since 1988.

The primary reason for Yale's superior long-term performance record had been the returns generated by the portfolio's active managers. Manager selection accounted for more than half of the superior performance by Yale relative to the average endowment over the last five years. As expected, the Endowment's excess returns had been greatest in the least efficient markets. Over the ten years ending in June 2002, the annualized differences between Yale's asset class returns and related benchmarks were 0.9 percent in the most efficiently priced asset class, bonds, and 23.1 percent in what is probably the least efficient market, private equity.

The Investments Office and the Investment Committee had been pleased with these results. As their experience with the distinctive approach grew and they became more confident of their ability to produce sustained above-average results, they adjusted their spending policy upward. In 1992, in response to an Investments Office recommendation, the Yale Corporation adjusted the university's long-term target spending rate upward from 4.50 percent to 4.75 percent of Endowment assets; and in 1995, it adjusted the rate upward again to 5 percent.[9] The university was thus benefiting from the strength of its investment program in two ways, both from a larger Endowment and from the justified increase in the target spending rate. The substantial Endowment also played a role in Yale's receiving the highest rating to finance capital projects (AAA/Aaa) from the two leading bond rating agencies and in the university's ability to borrow money at extremely favorable interest rates.

The Management of Marketable Securities

The investment philosophy outlined above guided Yale's management decisions in all of its asset classes. For example, Swensen and Takahashi approached bonds with skepticism. They viewed the Endowment's current target allocation of 7.5 percent in bonds primarily as a disaster reserve, guarding against a severe drop in asset values and/or deflation (such as in the Great Depression). Yale held U.S. government issues almost exclusively; Swensen was skeptical about whether returns from U.S. corporate bonds adequately compensated investors for the added default risk and the callability of corporate issues. He was quite skeptical of foreign fixed income securities as well.

Unlike most of the rest of its portfolio, the Investments Office managed its bond portfolio internally. Swensen believed that the government bond market was so efficient, and the spread between the performance of government bond fund managers so small, that it did not make sense to hire an outside manager. The portfolio was managed with no attempt to add value through trading on interest rate movements. The Endowment staff attempted to generate incremental returns only through modest security selection bets—for example, by using private placements issued by the Private Export Funding Corporation (PEFCO), which were backed by the full faith and credit of the U.S. government.

Yale also owned a substantial number of U.S. common stocks, though the current target allocation, 15 percent of assets, was surprisingly small relative to almost all other

8. Corporate defined benefit plans with in excess of $100 million in assets.

9. The amount of the Endowment spent each year was based on a simple formula, namely, the spending rate (currently 5 percent) times the current value of the Endowment, with a 30 percent weight, and the value of last year's spending increased by inflation, with a 70 percent weight.

EXHIBIT 3.6

RETURNS OF ALL UNIVERSITY ENDOWMENTS, YALE ENDOWMENT, AND BENCHMARK INDICES, FISCAL YEARS 1980–2002 (%)

	1980	1981	1982	1983	1984	1985	1986	1987	1988	1989	1990	1991	1992	1993	1994	1995	1996	1997	1998	1999	2000	2001	2002	Annualized 1980–2002 Return
Equal-weighted mean	12.6	14.7	-0.2	40.9	-2.5	25.4	26.3	13.9	1.4	13.9	10.0	7.3	13.3	13.4	2.9	15.7	17.3	20.5	18.0	11.0	13.0	-3.6	-6.0	12.0
Dollar-weighted mean	NA	NA	NA	46.0	-2.9	26.1	30.3	16.6	1.1	14.9	10.9	6.2	14.1	14.5	4.4	16.9	20.6	21.7	18.6	11.9	23.8	-2.7	-4.2	NA
Yale	18.7	22.7	-4.5	50.1	-0.2	25.8	36.0	22.8	-0.2	17.3	13.1	2.1	13.2	17.3	12.0	15.7	25.7	21.8	18.0	12.2	41.0	9.2	0.7	16.2
S&P 500	17.0	20.4	-11.5	60.9	-4.8	30.7	35.6	25.1	-7.0	20.5	16.5	7.4	13.5	13.6	1.4	26.0	26.0	34.7	30.2	22.8	7.2	-14.8	-18.0	13.9
Wilshire 5000	19.2	25.2	-15.0	66.5	-8.7	31.2	35.3	20.1	-5.9	19.5	12.8	7.0	13.9	16.6	1.2	24.7	26.2	29.3	28.9	19.6	9.5	-15.3	-16.6	13.4
Long-term bond index	7.3	-1.6	14.0	24.9	2.9	26.8	20.4	4.1	7.2	12.1	7.1	10.1	15.5	15.8	-1.3	12.1	4.5	7.4	11.3	3.0	5.0	10.3	8.8	9.7
Consumer price index	14.4	9.6	7.1	2.6	4.2	3.8	1.8	3.7	4.0	5.2	4.7	4.7	3.1	3.0	2.5	3.0	2.8	2.3	1.7	2.0	3.7	3.2	1.1	4.0

Notes: Fiscal years end on June 30 of each year.

The first two averages include endowments that report returns net and gross of fees.

No data on dollar-weighted mean or net-of-fee equal-weighted mean returns are available for 1980 through 1982 and 2000 through 2002 (for net-of-fee returns only). Annualized returns are computed for shorter periods.

Yale's returns are reported net of fees.

Source: Compiled from National Association of College and University Business Officers, *2002 NACUBO Endowment Study*, Washington, DC, National Association of College and University Business Officers, 2003 (and earlier years).

EXHIBIT 3.7

RETURNS OF YALE ENDOWMENT, BY ASSET CLASS

Asset Class	Yale 2002 Return	Target Benchmark	Benchmark 2002 Return	Yale versus Benchmark	Yale Three-Year Annualized	versus Benchmark	Yale Ten-Year Annualized	versus Benchmark
Domestic equity	−6.4	Wilshire 5000	−16.6	10.2	11.5	19.7	16.9	5.9
Foreign equity	11.9	Foreign composite	−3.8	15.7	5.1	10.9	9.4	4.7
Fixed income	8.5	LB	8.8	−0.3	8.5	0.5	8.2	0.9
Real assets[a]	9.5	HEPI + 6%	10.1	−0.5	14.1	3.8	15.3	6.7
Private equity	−23.3	HEPI + 10%	14.1	−37.5	49.3	35.1	36.9	23.1
Absolute return	7.3	HEPI + 8%	12.1	−4.8	14.7	2.2	12.1	0.3
Total Endowment	0.7	Composite benchmark	6.4	−5.7	15.7	8.2	16.9	5.7

[a] This includes only real estate prior to June 30, 1999.

Notes: All returns are net of management fees.

Returns are for periods ending June 30, 2002.

LB = Lehman Brothers U.S. Treasury Index.

HEPI = Higher Education Price Index.

The total benchmark return is calculated using Yale's target allocations. In June 2003, Yale's Investment Committee agreed to alter its benchmarks. For instance, private equity would be compared to a composite of Cambridge Associates private equity indices and a 10 percent real return.

Source: University documents.

large institutional investors. Although Yale had been an early adopter of indexing, as the Investments Office staff had become increasingly confident in its ability to find superior managers it eliminated the passive portfolio in favor of a small number of active equity managers. These managers shared several characteristics. First, the majority of Yale's active equity managers tended to emphasize disciplined approaches to investing that could be clearly articulated and differentiated from others. Swensen and Takahashi were convinced that disciplined fundamental-based approaches, when intelligently applied, could generate reliable and superior long-run performance. There were, in addition, several small stock-picking firms among Yale's managers, firms that specialized in a particular industry or type of investing—for example, a technology specialist fund, one specializing in North American oil-and-gas firms, and another that held only biotechnology stocks. Not surprisingly, none of Yale's managers tended to emphasize market timing, nor did they emphasize fuzzy or intuitive investment approaches that were difficult to articulate. The university's managers tended to be smaller independent organizations that were owned by their investment professionals. Other things being equal, Yale preferred managers willing to "co-invest" and to be compensated commensurate with their investment performance. Swensen and Takahashi worried that money managers working at many organizations tended to emphasize growth in assets at the expense of performance and that ownership by a large institution reduced organizational stability and dampened incentive to perform.

Foreign equities, another 15 percent of Endowment assets, were a valuable source of diversification, since their returns tended to be only partially correlated with those of the U.S. equity market. But Yale had encountered some real frustrations in transferring its model for successful domestic equity investing to foreign markets. First, the selection of appropriate active money managers had proven particularly challenging. The relatively slower development of institutional investing in many foreign countries meant that there were fewer sophisticated "U.S. style" money managers abroad, managers with credible audited investment performance records and specialized disciplined investment processes. Perhaps more critically, many leading foreign fund managers appeared to work for larger organizations that were in turn owned by large financial institutions, which raised concerns between Swensen and Takahashi about misaligned incentives. Unlike in the United States, there were very few independent investment advisors owned solely by their professionals. In spite of these problems, Yale had recently been successful in identifying and hiring investment managers based in London, Singapore, and Hong Kong and saw this as one of the near-term "bright spots" in its portfolio.

Senior Director Takahashi found the emerging equity markets of Asia, Latin America, and Eastern Europe particularly intriguing because of the widespread opportunities to find undervalued securities in these less efficient markets. By June 2003, roughly 6,500 companies were listed on emerging stock market exchanges, amounting to 21 percent of all listed companies in the world. While the market capitalization of these stocks represented 10 percent of the non-U.S. market capitalization, the economies of emerging markets amounted to more than 28 percent of non-U.S. GDP in dollar terms and roughly twice that amount when adjusted for purchasing power. In addition to attractive investment opportunities, emerging markets also provided portfolio diversification since their returns generally had low correlation with those of the United States. Furthermore, emerging markets were growing rapidly, at nearly twice the rate of developed countries. There were concerns, of course, including whether these growth prospects would translate into strong investment returns. Although the link between growth and profitability for the corporations of these countries was widely assumed, Takahashi was concerned that the link was weak at best. Nonetheless, he believed that the rapid rate of change in emerging markets provided opportunities for active managers to earn superior returns.

Takahashi believed that Yale's foreign equity portfolio should be heavily weighted toward emerging markets, but he was concerned with the limited universe of acceptable managers conducting research-intensive, fundamentally based analysis. Many of the top global emerging markets funds had grown to have many billions of dollars of assets under management, making it difficult to deploy assets in smaller, less well-followed corporations. On the other hand, small funds often lacked the resources to research and cover the tremendous breadth of global emerging markets. Yale had seven emerging markets managers in its portfolio. One was a large U.S.-based value manager who used a blend of judgmental and quantitative analysis to allocate between countries and choose stocks. Another was a large London-based global emerging markets manager who used bottom-up fundamental research to invest in a concentrated portfolio. Five were small regionally focused managers—one investing in Africa, one in Eastern Europe, one in Russia, and two in Southeast Asia—concentrating on intensively researched value plays.

Yale's emerging market portfolio had generated an annualized 7.4 percent return over the previous decade, 5.8 percent annually in excess of its benchmark.[10] Although Takahashi believed that such excess returns were not sustainable in the long run, he thought that emerging markets generally would continue to be less efficient and provide more opportunities for excess returns than developed markets. While the Investment Committee did not set a distinct target for emerging market equity holdings, it did so indirectly through the definition of a foreign equity benchmark. Currently, foreign equity returns were compared to a benchmark index that was composed one-half by the MSCI EAFE Index and one-half by the MSCI Emerging Markets Free Index. One issue for Yale was that positions in emerging market securities were held by managers other than those in the publicly traded foreign equity portfolio. For instance, some of Yale's absolute return managers held substantial positions in companies based in developing nations.

A final, more diffuse category of publicly traded investments was called "absolute return" strategies, to which Yale currently allocated 25 percent of its assets. These included a variety of funds specializing in eclectic mixtures of strategies designed to exploit market inefficiencies. Yale divided these investments into two broad categories: event-driven and value-driven. Event-driven strategies generally involved creating hedged positions in mispriced securities and were dependent on a specific corporate event, such as a merger or bankruptcy settlement, to achieve targeted returns. Value-driven strategies also entailed hedged investments in mispriced securities, but they relied on changing company fundamentals or increasing market awareness to drive prices toward fair value. The common denominator of these strategies was that their returns were expected to be equitylike, yet not highly correlated with any particular financial market. It consequently made sense to evaluate their investment performance in terms of the absolute returns achieved, rather than relative to any indices of market performance.

Yale's commitment to this asset class was tested in 1998, when many hedge funds suffered in the "flight to liquidity" that followed Russia's August 1998 default on its debt obligations. During this period, many expensive (but liquid) assets rose in price, and many cheap (illiquid) assets became cheaper. Even though some of these pricing anomalies were likely to be short-lived—for example, Treasury bonds maturing in twenty-nine

---

10. The benchmark used until 1999 was the International Finance Corporation (IFC) Global Emerging Index, and MSCI Emerging Markets Free Index thereafter.

years traded at a substantial discount to those maturing in thirty years—a number of investors panicked after the collapse of the Long-Term Capital Management fund and demanded the return of their capital. As a result, some funds were forced to liquidate positions at exceedingly unfavorable prices. While in most cases the university was insulated from the effects of other investors' sales because the fund managers had established separate accounts for Yale's investment, in other cases, Yale's funds were commingled with other investors. In these instances, Yale's returns suffered: the ill-timed selling decisions depressed the returns of all investors. As a result of this experience, Yale redoubled its efforts to use separate accounts that insulated Yale's investments from poorly timed acts of other investors. The university's use of its market power recalled steps that had been taken in the difficult fund-raising environment that real estate funds faced after the early 1990s savings and loan crisis, when Yale obtained more attractive terms on its funds— for instance, insisting that its fund managers share in the capital gains only above a given rate of return (a "hurdle rate").

While the influx of money into hedge funds in the previous few years had certainly posed challenges, Yale was convinced that it would still succeed in this area. While the returns of certain sectors of the industry might suffer from such changes, these problems were far from universal. In particular, the fund influx might pose special challenges for funds concentrating on merger arbitrage and distress, since the pool of opportunities was relatively finite. For funds specializing in relative value plays, though, the influx of capital should not matter nearly as much, since the opportunities for investment were quite broad.

THE MANAGEMENT OF PRIVATE EQUITY

Domestic Venture Capital and Buyout Funds

While Yale had been among the first universities to invest in private equity, entering into its first buyout partnership in 1973 and its first venture capital partnership in 1976, the pace of investing had dramatically increased over time. Exhibit 3.8 summarizes the size of and returns from Yale's private equity portfolio.

Yale's private equity investment strategy was consistent with its overall investment philosophy. First, the Investments Office placed a premium on building long-term relationships with a limited number of premier organizations. More than 90 percent of Yale's portfolio was invested in multiple funds sponsored by the university's group of general partners. Yale's prestige, name, and long experience in private equity investing made it a desirable client and allowed it to invest in some well-regarded funds that might otherwise have been closed.

Second, Yale emphasized private equity organizations that took a "value-added" approach to investing (the hallmark of the venture capital industry). Yale shied away from any funds that sought to generate the bulk of their returns from simply buying assets at attractive prices, refinancing them, and "flipping" them. Its philosophy was explained in a discussion of buyout organizations: "While financial skill is a vital component of LBO investing, we seek firms that build fundamentally better businesses. Financial engineering skill is a commodity, readily available and cheaply priced. Value-added operational experience, however, is rare."[11]

11. David F. Swensen, Dean J. Takahashi, and Timothy R. Sullivan, "Private Equity—Portfolio Review," memorandum to Investment Committee (September 29, 1994), p. 5.

EXHIBIT 3.8

RETURNS AND SIZE OF PRIVATE EQUITY INVESTMENTS OF THE YALE ENDOWMENT, 1978–2002

Fiscal Year	Venture	LBO	Int'l	Total	Portfolio Value	Endowment Value
1978	27.2%	35.3%	NA	33.9%	3.2	545
1979	−2.2	−3.0	NA	−2.8	3.4	578
1980	208.1	231.9	NA	225.5	8.4	669
1981	33.3	−16.6	NA	−0.5	15.6	793
1982	25.6	−47.5	NA	−2.2	19.3	741
1983	123.4	−10.1	NA	91.4	38.6	1,089
1984	3.7	41.6	NA	9.2	37.3	1,061
1985	−10.1	5.6	NA	−5.0	42.0	1,083
1986	2.6	34.0	NA	15.8	46.9	1,739
1987	25.4	23.9	NA	24.3	75.7	2,098
1988	−0.7	7.3	−1.9%	3.3	91.0	2,044
1989	−0.3	38.7	13.4	23.4	120.7	2,336
1990	15.6	7.8	−4.4	11.8	173.7	2,571
1991	11.6	14.7	−10.0	6.1	226.8	2,567
1992	28.3	7.2	4.1	14.6	294.2	2,833
1993	13.6	57.3	−0.2	32.3	464.9	3,219
1994	20.2	18.7	24.0	24.6	640.6	3,529
1995	37.8	26.3	13.1	27.0	682.4	3,390
1996	124.8	30.9	33.7	60.2	896.6	4,860
1997	37.6	22.3	90.2	36.2	1,125.6	5,790
1998	38.5	46.4	1.9	29.0	1,382.8	6,624
1999	133.9	24.8	−15.4	37.8	1,993.6	7,199
2000	701.0	35.1	38.3	168.5	2,513.7	10,085
2001	9.0	−14.7	−3.9	−5.4	1,943.0	10,725
2002	−39.9	−11.2	−0.7	−23.3	1,492.0	10,524
Three-year	256.0	0.5	12.6	49.3		
Five-year	107.4	8.4	2.9	39.4		
Ten-year	53.5	18.9	18.0	36.9		
Since inception	35.3	21.6	15.7	31.4		
Venture Economics Benchmark Return	17.6	13.9	11.9			
2002 share in Yale Portfolio	35.1	54.9	9.9			

Notes: Returns are for year ending June 30 of each year. Value of private equity portfolio and Endowment are as of June 30 and are expressed in millions of dollars.

NA indicates that Yale had no investments in the asset class during that year, or that the investments were not classified as private equity.

The Yale fiscal year returns are internal rates of return calculated on a daily basis. Multiyear returns are based on internal rates of return using quarterly data.

"Venture Economics Benchmark Return" is the pooled internal rate of return from inception until June 30, 2002, for all funds of each type in the Venture Economics database. The international compilation includes only European funds.

The row entitled "2002 Share in Yale Portfolio" refers to the share of Yale private equity portfolio devoted to this subclass on June 30, 2002.

Source: Compiled from Venture Economics, *VentureXpert Database*, http://www.ventureeconomics.com, and university documents.

Yale believed that value-added investors could generate incremental returns independent of how the broader markets were performing. In addition, such investors might also find better deals at cheaper prices, deals away from the auction process that others did not see. For instance, Clayton & Dubilier (where Yale served as limited partner) had purchased Lexmark International from IBM and Allison Engine from General Motors after establishing close relationships with those corporations. As a general rule, though, Yale was willing to give considerable latitude to its firms to define sensibly the types of private equity deals that they wanted to do.

Another key principle was to select organizations in which the incentives were properly aligned. For instance, Yale was reluctant to invest in private equity organizations affiliated with larger financial institutions. Such situations, the Investments Office believed, were fertile breeding grounds for conflicts of interest, or lack of incentives for the people actually doing the deals, or both. In addition, Yale preferred an overall structure for each of its funds such that the private equity firm could just cover its ongoing costs from the annual fees, earning essentially all of its economic returns from the "carry" tied directly to investment performance. This policy could at times be problematic: for instance, several of the most successful venture funds had dramatically increased their annual management fee income during the 1990s. While Yale would have liked to insist that the bulk of the compensation be linked to investment performance, in many cases it had been unable to persuade the venture partners to change the proposed compensation scheme. Some of these venture organizations were sufficiently attractive that the Investments Office decided to participate in their funds anyway. In other cases, because of fundamental changes in the private equity firm's investment strategy or organizational structure, Yale declined to participate.

When Yale's private equity portfolio was compared to those of other universities, three patterns stood out. First, Yale had traditionally had a considerably greater exposure to this area: in the latter half of the 1990s, Yale had a target allocation to private equity in excess of 20 percent, considerably more than other schools (see Exhibits 3.2 and 3.3). Second, Yale had a larger fraction of its holdings concentrated in the funds of top-flight firms. A third difference related to the composition of the private equity investments. In general, many funds could be categorized as either buyout or venture capital funds, though in the late 1990s the distinction between the two had become increasingly blurred as buyout funds purchased technology firms and even invested in start-up firms. The mixture of most major universities' endowments was heavily weighted toward venture capital funds, with the average large endowment (dollar-weighted) holding nearly three-fifths of its private equity investments in this asset class. In contrast, Yale had shifted over time: the proportion of the private equity portfolio in traditional venture capital had declined from 46 percent in June 1990 to 27 percent in June 1997 and then risen again (to 35 percent in June 2002). These shifts reflected not a changing policy objective, but rather were the result of both factors within Yale's control—such as "bottom up" assessments of which individual funds offered the highest returns—and factors outside Yale's control—such as drawdown schedules of private equity managers.

Yale had recently lowered its target allocation to private equity to 17.5 percent. This decision reflected several considerations. First, beginning in 2000, its actual holdings in private equity had fallen rapidly. The shrinkage initially reflected many funds distributing shares in successful IPOs in 2000, and then firms rapidly writing down unsuccessful investments. Moreover, fund-raising by the premier groups that Yale typically invested in fell rapidly after 2000; many groups reduced the size of existing funds and sharply slowed their investment rates as they grappled with the troubled firms in their portfolio. (Exhibit 3.9 summarizes the inflow into private equity over the past two decades.) Many of the groups

EXHIBIT 3.9

PRIVATE EQUITY FUNDRAISING, BY FUND TYPE, 1980–2002

	1980	1981	1982	1983	1984	1985	1986	1987	1988	1989	1990	1991	1992	1993	1994	1995	1996	1997	1998	1999	2000	2001	2002
Venture capital	0.6	0.9	1.3	2.6	3.4	2.1	2.1	3.7	3.1	3.3	1.9	1.4	2.6	2.9	4.2	4.7	6.6	6.1	19.0	35.6	73.9	37.3	7.7
Buyouts/Corporate finance	0.1	0.1	0.4	0.6	1.5	1.1	4.3	9.6	7.9	8.8	4.6	4.3	6.7	8.2	13.2	19.0	22.8	19.1	57.2	39.0	74.5	56.7	36.2
Mezzanine	0.0	0.1	0.0	0.8	0.2	0.8	2.4	4.1	1.7	2.6	1.2	1.7	0.8	0.5	1.2	2.4	1.4	2.7	2.8	4.3	5.4	4.7	2.1
Other	0.0	0.0	0.1	0.2	0.0	0.3	0.2	0.1	0.4	0.2	0.2	0.3	0.6	1.2	0.8	2.2	1.3	3.3	13.1	16.6	2.3	16.1	8.9
Total	0.7	1.1	1.8	2.4	5.1	4.3	9.0	17.5	13.1	14.9	6.9	7.7	10.7	12.8	19.4	28.4	32.1	31.3	92.2	95.5	174.1	114.7	54.9

Notes: All figures are in billions of dollars.

Other investments include funds-of-funds, secondary purchase funds, and venture leasing funds.

Source: Compiled from *The Private Equity Analyst* and the records of Asset Alternatives. I thank Steven Galante for his help.

that had returned to the market raised far smaller funds than those they had raised in 1999 and 2000. While some members of the Investment Committee felt that the 25 percent target should be retained, by mid-2002 the Investment Committee reached a consensus that a lower target better reflected the current environment.

At the same time, Swensen and Takahashi believed that Yale should stay committed to private equity for two reasons. First, from its inception in 1973 to June 2002, Yale's private equity portfolio had delivered an annual rate of return of over 31 percent (with a standard deviation of returns over the past twenty-five years of 55 percent). Second, over its nearly thirty years of investing, Yale had developed a deep understanding of the process and strong relationships with key managers, which served as an important competitive advantage. An important aspect of this advantage was the continuity of the team managing the private equity program. Swensen, Takahashi, and Director Timothy Sullivan had worked together on the portfolio for more than a decade and a half.

Another substantial question was whether the same groups would succeed in future years. Private equity had been subject to a boom-and-bust cycle since at least the 1960s, with high returns attracting new investors, who flooded money into the sector until returns deteriorated, whereupon they withdrew. But the unprecedented growth of the private equity industry appeared to have changed the industry in some permanent ways. First was the scale at which private equity groups operated. These concerns were particularly acute on the buyout side, where multibillion-dollar funds had become the norm. The Investments Office was concerned that these groups would pursue low-risk, low-return transactions, in order to ensure their ability to raise a follow-on fund (with the substantial associated fees), rather than following innovative strategies that had the potential of generating higher returns. As Tim Sullivan noted, "Many LBO firms appear to have explicitly lowered their return hurdles in order to compete for transactions, particularly at the larger end of the market, pricing deals to yield returns in the mid-to-high teens."[12] As a consequence, some of these large funds had experienced defections of key personnel who sought to begin new funds of their own. When investing in middle-market buyout groups, Yale often found itself becoming progressively more uncomfortable as the groups raised larger and larger sums. More generally, Yale noted with concern that a number of leading buyout groups were positioning themselves as "asset managers"—for instance, raising absolute return, venture capital, mezzanine, and real estate funds in addition to their core buyout funds. Sullivan worried that such moves would profoundly affect the incentives of the private equity organizations, as they lowered their return expectations and made excessively safe investments. In the most extreme manifestation of this phenomenon, private equity groups such as Thomas H. Lee Co. and Warburg, Pincus had sold stakes in themselves to other asset managers. Yale feared that such transactions, while financially attractive to the private equity groups' founders, would lead to conflicts of interest between the private equity investment activity and the other asset management businesses.[13] The second major change involved the new classes of investors active in the industry (see Exhibit 3.10). Despite the downturn in the returns,

12. David F. Swensen, Dean J. Takahashi, Timothy R. Sullivan, Alan S. Forman, and Seth D. Alexander, "Private Equity—Portfolio Review," October 7, 1999, p. 15.

13. On the venture capital side, the Investments Office was concerned about the plethora of venture organizations that were planning to raise very large funds, even if smaller than the billion-dollar funds of few years back. While the Investments Office was aware that many venture investors were convinced that the "minimum efficient scale" of a venture capital organization had increased, they were again concerned about the incentive effects of the increase in fee income.

EXHIBIT 3.10

PRIVATE EQUITY FUND-RAISING, BY INVESTOR TYPE, 1980–2002 (%)

	1980	1981	1982	1983	1984	1985	1986	1987	1988	1989	1990	1991	1992	1993	1994	1995	1996	1997	1998	1999	2000	2001	2002
Pension funds	29.8	23.1	33.3	31.4	34.1	33.0	50.1	39.0	45.9	36.4	52.5	42.2	47.8	46.8	49.1	49.7	45.4	NA	NA	48.6	40.1	41.7	45.4
Banking/insurance	13.3	15.2	14.0	12.0	13.2	10.9	10.4	15.0	9.4	12.6	9.2	5.4	16.4	15.9	17.0	17.8	19.5	NA	NA	13.5	23.3	24.5	16.1
Endowments/foundations	13.9	11.8	6.8	7.8	5.7	7.7	6.3	10.0	11.6	12.3	12.6	24.1	11.4	13.0	11.7	12.4	12.6	NA	NA	13.0	21.1	21.8	10.7
Individuals/families	15.4	23.1	20.3	20.9	14.7	13.0	11.8	12.0	8.4	6.1	11.4	12.3	10.4	7.1	10.3	8.4	7.5	NA	NA	4.9	11.8	9.4	12.0
Others	27.6	26.8	25.6	27.9	33.4	35.4	21.4	24.0	24.7	32.6	14.3	16.0	14.0	17.3	11.8	11.7	15.1	NA	NA	20.0	3.7	2.6	15.9

Notes: Prior to 1992, the tabulations include only investments in venture capital funds; thereafter, all private equity funds.

Others include corporations, foreign investors (except for 2000 and 2001), and government bodies (excluding pension funds).

Commitments by funds-of-funds are not included in the tabulations.

NA = not available.

Source: Compiled from *The Private Equity Analyst* and the records of Venture Economics. I thank Jesse Reyes and Anthony Romanello for their help.

numerous overseas institutions and state pension funds seemed to have a voracious appetite for private equity. Many of these investments seemed to be made in a very undisciplined manner, as inexperienced investors backed virtually every group that would accept a substantial check. The presence of these newcomers suggested that intense price competition would continue to affect the private equity industry in the years to come.

Nonetheless, Yale hoped that it could continue to realize attractive returns from this asset class, just as it had during the 1980s and 1990s. First, the Investments Office noted, the deterioration of performance in the 1990s had been far from uniform across firms. While very poor returns characterized some new "spin-off" organizations as well as some established organizations that had grown in an undisciplined manner, many of the funds managed by top-tier private equity organizations had continued to generate superior returns. Because Yale had concentrated its portfolio in several of these funds, such as those organized by Bain Capital, Berkshire Partners, Greylock, and Kleiner Perkins, the university believed its private equity managers would produce superior performance, even in a difficult environment for private equity.

Second, Yale had a considerable understanding of the private equity process, which allowed it to manage investments in sophisticated ways. One example of Yale's innovative management was the hedging of its positions. Yale carefully tracked the holdings of the private equity firms in which it invested.[14] When Yale believed that it had too large an exposure to any particular publicly traded firm, it sought to hedge that exposure through short sales and derivatives. Short sales and put options would generate offsetting profits if the share price declined. This effectively helped reduce the danger of a severe drop in the public market wiping out the gains of a private equity investment. This hedging strategy had allowed Yale to receive a higher return from its early 1990s investment in Snapple, which declined substantially between its peak fourteen months after it was taken public and the liquidation of Thomas H. Lee Equity Partners' position. Moreover, this hedging allowed Yale to continue to invest in promising private equity funds during the boom period of the late 1990s: had the university not reduced its overall exposure through hedging, the exposure would have been so far above target that the Investments Office could not in good conscience have continued to make new commitments.

Finally, there were important benefits to being in the private equity market at all times. If Yale were to decide not to invest with a top-tier firm merely because the market was overheated, it might not be able to persuade the organization to accept its money when later market conditions were more favorable. As Tim Sullivan concluded, if Yale were to alter its steady commitment to private equity and seek to time the market, top-tier firms "would not want Yale's unreliable money."[15]

This confidence was borne out by an analysis of Yale's venture capital returns. The Investments Office found that it had enjoyed its highest returns from the groups where it was strictly rationed in terms of how much it could invest; put another way, the clubs where it was hardest to get in truly were the best! This pattern held whether the Endowment looked at large funds or small funds. While Yale had made numerous investments into less well-known funds in hopes of backing the "leaders of tomorrow," these had generated more mixed results. A few funds had generated superior returns, but the

14. Private equity organizations typically do not sell the shares of firms in their portfolios at the time they go public. They generally promise the underwriter to continue to hold them for a period of months (often termed the "lock-up" period). Many will continue to hold shares after the lock-up period expires, if they believe the shares will appreciate further.

15. David F. Swensen, Dean J. Takahashi, and Timothy R. Sullivan, "Private Equity—Venture Capital Strategy," memorandum to the Investment Committee (March 4, 1992), p. 7.

overall level of performance trailed the established funds in Yale's portfolio and "few of these firms have become consistent members of Yale's roster of active managers."[16]

International Private Equity Funds

An area of continuing interest was international private equity. While Yale's initial strategy had been concentrated on the United Kingdom and France (at the end of 1995 nearly half its foreign investments had been based there), it had also explored developing markets. One noteworthy characteristic was Yale's avoidance of the developing countries of Asia, which represented the largest single share of many large institutions' international private equity portfolios during much of the 1990s.[17]

The Investments Office's move into international private equity had been the consequence of a cautious planning process. As the U.S. market became increasingly competitive, Yale paid more attention to overseas markets where far fewer funds were competing for deals, suggesting the possibility of more attractive valuations. While many other institutional investors saw international private equity as particularly promising, Yale eschewed the typical strategy of investing in large funds devoted to buyouts in Europe and Asia. This reflected several considerations. First, many of the leading foreign private equity investors were subsidiaries or affiliates of large financial institutions. As discussed above, Endowment Director Timothy Sullivan was concerned that such situations were rife with compensation and conflict-of-interest problems. Second, the Investments Office often found it quite difficult to evaluate foreign private equity organizations. In most countries, Yale lacked the strong network of relationships that it could rely upon in the United States to assess the quality of potential new partners. A possible alternative was to invest in a number of the new very large "global private equity" funds that were being sponsored by established and well-regarded U.S. firms. Sullivan liked some of these firms and approved of their incentive structures, but he was a little troubled by the U.S. firms' obvious lack of experience and track records in these very different foreign markets. The managers of these global funds suggested that they should become the solution for Yale's problems, but Sullivan was unconvinced.

At the same time, international private equity investing carried real risks, as Yale's experience in Eastern Europe illustrated. Yale had made a small initial investment in a Russian "quasi-private equity" fund, which took stakes in both thinly traded public corporations and smaller private firms. As the fund family enjoyed spectacular successes in the mid-1990s, Yale took a significant amount of money off the table, but reinvested a considerable share of its gains. This fund family experienced sharply negative returns after the Russian debt crisis of 1998. Overall, the Eastern Bloc investment yielded Yale an annualized return in the mid-20 percent range—but in a strikingly uneven manner that was not for the faint of heart!

There were also private equity funds being raised to invest in Latin America and in Southeast and Southern Asia. Yale had been able to identify a number of these emerging market funds that were managed by general partners that seemed attractive by normal standards: small entrepreneurial firms, with operational experience on the ground

16. David F. Swensen, Dean J. Takahashi, Timothy R. Sullivan, Seth D. Alexander, and Robert F. Wallace, "Private Equity—Venture Capital Decision Making Assessment," memorandum to the Investment Committee, May 22, 2003, p. 17.

17. For instance, Asia represented 35 percent of all non-U.S. private equity commitments by major institutional investors in 1995. In light of disappointing returns, this share had fallen to 16 percent by 2001. Goldman, Sachs & Co. and Frank Russell Capital, Inc., *2001 Report on Alternative Investing by Tax-Exempt Organizations* (November 2001).

in these emerging markets, some co-investment and/or incentive fees, and an apparently keen sense of where upside opportunities might lie. And it was tempting to participate in some of these funds, as a very long-term contrarian bet if nothing else. But the problems of evaluating and selecting managers were challenging here, perhaps more severe than in almost any other asset class.

THE MANAGEMENT OF REAL ASSETS

Another important class was real assets, which included real estate, oil-and-gas, and timberland investments. The Investments Office believed that properly managed real estate provided an interesting set of investment opportunities. The returns from real property tended to be uncorrelated with those from marketable common stock and, in the long run, real property might produce returns protected from inflation. Most importantly, real estate was a quite inefficient, cyclical market where Yale might well be able to generate very attractive returns if it could find the right managers with the right strategies and the right incentive structures. As in other asset classes, Yale concentrated on pure equity investments, avoiding mortgages and other debt. The Investments Office shunned managers who were just financial advisors who might buy existing buildings with stable rent rolls and apply a little financial engineering. Instead, the office sought to establish relationships with real estate operators who had a competitive advantage, either by property type or market, and preferably with a focus on an out-of-favor sector.

Historically, Yale's real estate portfolio had consisted primarily of a single Manhattan office building at 717 Fifth Avenue, a direct investment that had been singled out and recommended by a group of alumni in the 1970s. The property, which was located at the intersection of 56th Street and for many years had featured the Steuben Glass showroom, performed very well. Yale paid $14 million for a 50 percent interest in 1978 and $47 million for the remaining 50 percent in 1994.

In spite of the strong performance, the challenges in managing 717 Fifth Avenue came to reinforce Yale's strong preference for external management of Endowment assets. When Steuben Glass announced its intention to vacate its Fifth Avenue retail space to move to a Madison Avenue location, Yale Real Estate Director Alan Forman quickly discovered firsthand the near impossibility of engaging an agent with an owner's mentality. He subsequently devoted a significant amount of his time to finding suitable replacement tenants—Hugo Boss and Escada—and supervising a major construction project to accommodate their needs.

Ultimately, Yale's October 2002 sale of 717 Fifth Avenue generated spectacular results. The sales price of $611 per square foot represented one of the highest prices ever paid for an arm's-length sale of a Manhattan office property. Over the twenty-four-year holding period, Yale realized a 19.3 percent per annum return on its investment.

During the late 1980s, Yale had been substantially underweighted in real estate because it could not identify enough attractive investment opportunities during that period. But beginning around 1990, Yale came to believe that the decline in asset values associated with the savings and loan crisis had created a compelling opportunity. Accordingly, the Investments Office began increasing its real estate investments.

Many institutional investors, having been severely burned, were still wary if not totally dismissive of this asset class. Yale's strategy was to focus on deliberately contrarian segments of the real estate market where most other investors feared to tread. They sought out partners who targeted distressed sellers and who possessed the operating expertise to implement value-added strategies that could realize substantial returns over the medium term. For example, Yale engaged managers to buy (1) downtown and suburban office buildings from insurance companies facing financial pressures or banks that had foreclosed; (2) close-in developable land, a highly illiquid property type, especially in a capital-constrained environment; or (3) strip shopping centers that needed a reconfiguration or a redirected marketing effort.

Perhaps predictably, Yale had encountered some interesting challenges in implementing this real estate strategy. First, Yale felt that the institutional real estate industry was dominated by firms that were compensated through transaction fees or fees based upon assets under management, rather than by sharing in the profits generated for their investors. These firms thus had every incentive to keep their investors' capital tied up over long periods of time, leading to asset accumulation and retention, rather than generation of superior investment returns. (During the early 1980s, the Endowment had invested a small amount of money in a number of pools managed by well-known real estate advisors, many of which had performed rather poorly.) Because of these factors, Yale had decided not to deal with the established group of institutional real estate advisors. Luckily, the collapse of the real estate market had provided the Investments Office with an opportunity to find some new firms that might be hungry for funds and that might consequently be willing to accept new kinds of incentive structures. From Yale's perspective, the Investments Office wanted to borrow ideas from, and improve upon, the incentive structures typical in private equity funds. In particular, they wanted all the real estate principals' activities to be focused on one pool at a time, they wanted the principals to make a significant cash investment in the pool (sometimes called co-investment), they preferred an intermediate term strategy for the pool (after which they might or might not invest in a later pool), and they wanted most of the principals' compensation to come at the end of the fund and to be linked to investors' returns.

Over time, working their networks, the Investments Office staff had been able to find a number of independent firms with excellent real estate operating skills that were eager to forge this kind of relationship. But most of these firms were not well known, even by knowledgeable real estate investors. Unlike in private equity, where Yale participated in funds considered to be the premier institutional funds, few people knew or even recognized the names of most of their real estate funds. Yale was often the lead investor in these funds, with a sizable percentage of the limited partnership interest. Although it had proven difficult to expand the size of the total real estate portfolio very quickly this way, Yale had gradually built a portfolio. While it would have been much easier, of course, to use some of the larger better-known institutional real estate advisors to expand the real estate portfolio quickly, this would surely have meant compromising on Yale's desired strategy and incentive structures—compromises with which the Investments Office was not comfortable.

The other side of the real assets portfolio was the oil-and-gas and timberland partnerships. In some ways, this market remained an attractive one. A substantial supply of energy properties had come to market in recent years, as major oil companies downsized and smaller firms consolidated. While some independent firms had been able to raise capital from the public marketplace, the supply of institutional money for such properties remained relatively limited. Timberland was in an even earlier stage of development, having been added to the portfolios of relatively few institutional investors. Large forest products companies were under considerable pressure to sell forestland to enhance shareholder value.

It was difficult, however, to find well-designed oil-and-gas partnerships led by attractive managers. Much of the partnership-raising business appeared to be in the hands of agents, who were compensated primarily on the basis of arranging deals. In addition, there were quite a few operators who seemed to get rich, even if their clients did not.

Furthermore, assessing the skills of the general partners in these funds was often difficult. In many cases, individuals raised funds on the basis of their participation in earlier successful partnerships. But it was generally very difficult for the Investments Office to determine which partner had been responsible for a key discovery or production success.[18] Yale's general impression was that investment opportunities and partnerships with sterling track records, unblemished reputations, and proper deal structures were quite uncommon in the oil-and-gas industry.

As a result, Yale's investments in oil-and-gas tended to emphasize two investment models. The first focused on partnerships in the business of acquiring existing oil fields and enhancing their operations. In contrast to the high-risk world of exploration, it was somewhat easier to assess performance and responsibility here. Furthermore, the long-term assets provided relatively predictable income and protection from energy-related inflation. The other approach applied a private equity investment model whereby Yale invested in partnerships pursuing equity investments in oil-and-gas and energy service companies.

Forestland was another attractive area for future exploration. Yale had invested in two partnerships focused on sustainable harvesting of softwood and hardwood forestland in the United States. Yale Investments Director Seth Alexander believed that the conventional assessment of natural resource funds did not fully capture the fact that they offered a steady stream of inflation-sensitive payments in addition to the potential to add value through active management, making such investments far more attractive than commodity indexes. Recent timberland investments were acquired at substantial discounts to the standing value of the timber that offered projected low double-digit returns assuming that prices remained stable. This seeming anomaly was due to two factors. First, overleveraged timber companies were being forced by fiscal pressures to sell assets at attractive prices. Second, forestland had not traditionally been managed to maximize the rate of return, which created good opportunities for sophisticated operators. This appeared to be a ripe area for further expansion in the years to come; however, the opportunity to acquire attractively priced timberland might be fleeting.

By mid-2003, the Endowment had more than 20 percent of its assets invested in real assets, just above the target allocation of 20 percent. On the one hand, Investment Office staff members were pleased because real estate performance had been strong, outpacing substantially the National Council of Real Estate Investment Fiduciaries (NCREIF) Property Index (NPI). The incentive structures put in place with their real estate managers a few years earlier were providing a powerful motivation to maximize returns through property sales. Moreover, ten-year performance of 15.3 percent indicated that Yale's allocation to real estate had served the Endowment well over a long period of time. The 26.2 percent ten-year return of Yale's oil-and-gas portfolio validated the University's strategy of partnering with operations-focused, value-added firms. While the early returns on Yale's timber portfolio were promising, the true success of the program would become apparent only with the passage of time.

Even with an actual allocation for real assets near the target level, the Investments Office worried about the future allocation to the asset class. Because the University's managers found only occasional attractive investment opportunities, large commitments to real estate, oil-and-gas, and timber funds remained undrawn. The staff worried that the real assets portfolio might not be large enough to serve the needs of the Endowment as a whole. Swensen had gained comfort in the past from

18. This was in contrast to venture or buyout investing, where individual partners' successes and failures could be more or less assessed by examining who represented the partnership as a director on various firms' boards.

Yale's substantial real assets allocation, which might provide protection in the event of a significant further downturn in the U.S. stock market, and worried about the adequacy of the portfolio's projected size.

FUTURE DIRECTIONS

In July 2003, Swensen and Takahashi believed that they probably wanted to continue with a heavy weighting in what they viewed as less efficient markets. On the other hand, were private investments, which had been so important in contributing to Yale's superior returns over the years, still attractive in a market flooded with capital? How should Yale allocate its new commitments in this overheated environment? In particular, how should the new investments be allocated across venture, buyout, international, real estate, and natural resource funds? What should be the mix between new groups and established organizations? Should Yale expand its international program to include a greater emphasis on Asia and continental Europe?

Looking beyond the short run, Swensen and Takahashi wondered about the risks and challenges that the coming years would pose to the Yale Endowment. Over the past few years, the fraction of traditional publicly traded securities in the Endowment fell below 40 percent for the first time. This seemed like an important transition. Just how far could such securities—and fixed income in particular—be reduced? At some point, should they begin to worry seriously about issues of decreasing portfolio liquidity, and the increasing difficulty in determining precise valuations for the Endowment?[19] Similarly, should they worry about the implications of this evolution for staffing? Should they worry about the fact that an increasing fraction of the portfolio did not really have meaningful benchmarks against which they could reliably measure their managers, themselves, and the success of their strategies? The feedback in these asset classes came only in the very long term, perhaps too long for most individuals' decision horizons. In the long run, how should they think about the issues of risk? Would it really be true that private markets offered greater returns? In the long run, would it be viable for Yale to adopt an asset allocation that was considerably different from that of its closest peers, such as Harvard, Princeton, and Stanford? More generally, could these few Endowments as a group persist with asset allocations that were very different from those of almost every other institutional investor?

---

19. For example, valuation issues arise in terms of the estimates used in the spending rule, which had originally assumed that market prices would be available to value the assets.

4

Acme Investment Trust: January 2001

The three members of the private equity group at Acme Investment Trust—an $8 billion pension fund of a major manufacturing concern—gathered for their weekly meeting in the conference room in their suburban Ohio offices. Despite the seemingly routine nature of the meeting, today they faced an intriguing dilemma.

On the face of it, their decision today—whether or not to invest $40 million into Hicks, Muse, Tate & Furst's fifth fund—was little different from many others they had considered in previous meetings. But there was also quite a unique aspect to the decision: the investment came with a personal guarantee from the funds' general partners. In particular, the partners guaranteed a 20 percent return over a five-year period to the limited partners on $200 million already invested by the fund in thirteen Internet-related transactions.

This offer posed numerous questions in the minds of the Acme private equity team. To what extent was this offer a signal of the partners' confidence in their investment ability, or was it a sign of anxiety about the ability to raise their next fund? How would such a guarantee affect the behavior of the investment team? What would be the impact on the economics of the partnership itself?

HICKS, MUSE, TATE & FURST

Thomas Hicks was one of the legendary entrepreneurs of the private equity industry. Not only was he the cofounder and lead partner at one of the top buyout groups in the nation, but he also had an influence and visibility that many of his peers lacked: owner of numerous Dallas professional sports franchises, confidant to George W. Bush, and major benefactor of the University of Texas and many other causes.

Professor Josh Lerner prepared this case from published sources. HBS cases are developed solely as the basis for class discussion. Cases are not intended to serve as endorsements, sources of primary data, or illustrations of effective or ineffective management.

HISTORY[1]

Tom Hicks spent much of his youth in Port Arthur, a rough-and-tumble southeast Texas town where his father had moved his family after taking part in a purchase of a local radio station. After earning a marketing degree from the University of Texas in 1968, he took a banking position in Chicago. A project researching small business investment companies (federally sponsored venture capital funds that proliferated in the 1960s) kindled his interest in private equity. After receiving an MBA from the University of Southern California, he joined J. P. Morgan and won a coveted spot in its private equity unit. This position was followed by private equity work at the First Dallas Capital Corp. and the Dallas office of Summit Partners.

Hicks had gone into private equity investing on his own in 1977. He had raised $4 million to finance a buyout of a company that made aluminum windows. When it was successful, he and a partner invested in thirty-four companies, most in the oil-and-gas industry. These firms, however, suffered dramatically after the drop in oil prices in the early 1980s, and Hicks was forced to start afresh.

In 1984, Hicks raised his first fund, with Robert Haas, a Cleveland lawyer. The $90 million fund, Hicks & Haas, enjoyed a number of successes. Most spectacular was the purchase of Dr Pepper's Texas bottling operations for an enterprise value of $100 million in 1985. When combined with subsequent acquisitions, this enterprise (then known as Dr Pepper/Seven Up) was sold to Cadbury Schweppes in 1995 for $2.5 billion. The fund's other investments also had enjoyed considerable success.

Not only was the fund financially successful, but it also set the template for investments by Hicks and his partners in the years to come. The fund employed the then-uncommon "buy-and-build" strategy. The fund would acquire a well-run "platform" company and then add smaller acquisitions. During this period, Hicks also established several crucial relations with outside investors and managers. Finally, the fund sought to differentiate itself by specializing in transactions far from the New York City hub of most buyout funds.

In 1989, Hicks teamed up with John E. Muse—a Tyler, Texas, native who had graduated from the Air Force Academy and had a successful career in corporate finance with Prudential Securities—to raise Hicks, Muse & Co. In 1991, the group was renamed Hicks, Muse, Tate & Furst (HMTF), to reflect the contributions of partners Charles Tate and Jack Furst. The group closed on its first fund later that year.

The rapid growth and success of the group—summarized in Exhibit 4.1—could be attributed to a number of factors. In large part, the group continued the strategy first developed at Hicks & Haas. For instance, the funds focused on a handful of industries such as television, radio, outdoor advertising, manufacturing, food, and consumer branded products. A single company would become the foundation for a series of investments, and then the enterprise would be taken public or sold. The group had close ties to a number of key operating executives who were familiar with its approach. In

---

1. This section is based on a variety of press accounts, especially Gary Jacobson, "Hicks, Haas Seek Buyouts on Their Own," *Dallas Morning News* (December 17, 1989), p. 1H; Stephanie A. Forest, "Where LBO Means 'Let's Be Offbeat,'" *Business Week* (July 1, 1996), p. 86; James F. Peltz, "A 'Buy and Build' Strategy Takes LBO Firm Hicks Muse to the Top of its Field," *Los Angeles Times* (March 15, 1998), p. D1ff; "When Deal-Maker Hicks Shoots, He Usually Scores: Opportunity, Determination Built Business-Sports Empire," *Dallas Morning News* (July 11, 1999), p. A1ff.

EXHIBIT 4.1

HICKS, MUSE, TATE & FURST U.S. FUND PERFORMANCE[°]

Fund	Year of First Closing	Amount Raised ($ Million)	Gross Internal Rate of Return[†]
Hicks & Haas	1985	90	321.7%
HMTF I	1989	270	34.1
HMTF II	1993	700	29.6
HMTF III	1996	2,540	17.5
HMTF IV	1998	4,100	NM[‡]
HMTF V	2000	—[§]	NM[‡]

Note: Table does not include European and Latin American funds.

[°] As of December 31, 2000.

[†] Total IRR calculated assuming each investment is made concurrently (the "time zero" method).

[‡] Internal rates of return are not meaningful due to the early stage of the fund and the large number of the investments held at cost.

[§] Fund had not yet had its final closing.

Source: Hicks, Muse, Tate & Furst.

---

many cases, these outsiders would serve as management affiliates to the fund, providing day-to-day management of companies in the portfolio. The group also focused for many years on transactions in mid-America. As Muse observed, "For many people in the heartland—the Midwest and South—they click better with us than with some guy with a yellow tie and slicked-back hair from New York City."[2]

The buyout of DuPont's electronics supplier business (subsequently renamed Berg Electronics), illustrated the group's approach. At the time of its purchase for $330 million, the firm was generating revenues of $380 million and $18 million of earnings before interest, taxes, depreciation, and amortization (EBITDA). The buyout group, working in conjunction with management affiliate James Mills of St. Louis (a long-time Hicks collaborator), determined that the group had the potential to generate an EBITDA of $65 million. Five years later, after eight add-on acquisitions totaling $155 million, Mills and Hicks, Muse had succeeded in increasing the firm's EBITDA to $185 million. During the period, the firm's equity value increased more than thirteenfold.

The group successfully addressed other challenges as well. Hicks, Muse had been characterized by a degree of cohesion that was often rare among private equity groups; for instance, all named partners remained with the firm over the years. Also remarkable was the willingness of the partners to invest in building support staff. By the end of 2000, the firm's eight partners were supported by thirty investment professionals and seventy-five staff members.

INTERNATIONAL EXPANSION[3]

Hicks, Muse had increasingly embarked on an international strategy. The private equity group had raised a Latin American fund with committed capital of $960 million in 1998 and a €1.5 billion European fund in 1999.

---

2. Allen Myerson, "Texans Like Home-Cooked Deals: Big Bucks in Backslapping Style," *Denver Post* (August 1, 1994), p. E1.

3. The section is based on a wide assortment of press accounts.

These funds had been deployed in the same aggressive manner that had been a hallmark of Hicks, Muse's North American operations. For instance, in 1999, the fund had acquired Hillsdown Holdings (which encompassed Buxted chickens and Typhoo tea, among other brands) for 870 million pounds, the largest buyout to date in the United Kingdom. Some of these foreign investments had done quite well. For instance, in December 2000, the fund had sold Mumm and Perrier Jouet, which it had purchased eighteen months before for €290 million (over half of which was debt), to Allied Domecq for about €580 million.

But in other cases, the fund had been forced to scale back its international ambitions. For instance, in September 2000, the firm had abandoned its plans to raise an international early stage partnership with two publicly traded Internet firms that also had done extensive venture investments, CMGI of the United States and Pacific Century CyberWorks of Hong Kong. Its second Latin American fund, originally targeted at $750 million, had undertaken a first closing of $125 million in December 2000. At the time of the closing, the partners acknowledged that they now expected to ultimately raise only between one-third to one-half of the original target in light of the difficult fund-raising environment.

THE CHALLENGES OF HMTF IV[4]

In contrast to the earlier funds, Hicks, Muse, Tate & Furst Fund IV had encountered mixed results. In January 1998, the fund had invested $250 million of equity in a joint acquisition with Kohlberg, Kravis, Roberts & Co. of Regal Cinemas, the largest movie chain in the nation. By November 2000, Regal had acknowledged that it had violated the covenants on its bank debt and was exploring restructuring alternatives.[5] On the other hand, oil exploration company Triton Energy, in which the fund invested $350 million in 1998 and 1999, promised to generate a substantial return for the fund.

But the bulk of Hicks, Muse's troubles had stemmed from half a dozen investments made in 1999 and 2000 that were somewhat different from those it had made previously. In particular, the firm had invested $1.2 billion in broadband communications and technology service firms. Not only were these industries dissimilar from those in which Hicks, Muse had traditionally invested, but so was the investment type. These had been PIPE (Private Investments in Public Equities) transactions, which involved the purchase of minority stakes in already public entities.

PIPEs represented an alternative financing source for public equity firms that either chose not to or could not access the public equity markets.[6] These investments were made either in the form of common stock or convertible securities (preferred stock or debt) that could be exchanged into common stock. Because these securities were not registered with the U.S. Securities and Exchange Commission (SEC), they could not be sold until registered with the SEC (often, but not always, a routine step). Activity in the PIPEs market is summarized in Exhibit 4.2.

---

4. This section is based on a variety of press accounts, especially Kara Scannell, "Hicks Muse Suffers a Bet on Stocks in Telecom Sector," *Wall Street Journal* (August 23, 2000); Mitchell Schnurman, "The Seduction of Tom Hicks," *Fort Worth Star-Telegram* (August 15, 2001), p. 1ff; and "Texan Bull," *Economist* 357 (December 16, 2000).

5. Bruce Orwall and Gregory Zuckerman, "Regal Considers Filing for Bankruptcy," *Wall Street Journal* (November 15, 2001), p. B11.

6. The next three paragraphs are based in large part on Steve Louden, Sanjay Morey, William Russell, and Brian Suvigne, "Hicks, Muse, Tate, and Furst: A Foray into Unfamiliar PIPE Investments," unpublished paper, 2001.

EXHIBIT 4.2

PIPE ACTIVITY

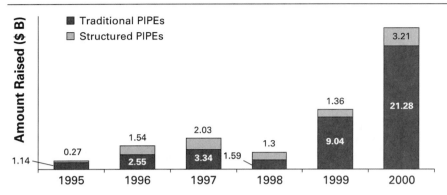

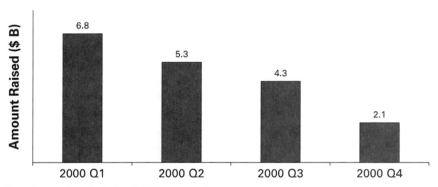

Note: Lower chart includes all PIPE transactions.

Source: Compiled from http://www.placementtracker.com.

These securities were typically sold to the investors at a discount, often 10 percent to 12 percent. This was considerably greater than that which the purchasers of a follow-on offering of common stock (which can be immediately sold) enjoy, namely 0.5 percent to 3 percent.[7] If the convertible structure was used, typically the exercise price for the conversion of the preferred shares into common stock was set at a premium to the current stock price, to ensure that the investor did not "flip" the shares. In exchange for the purchase of a PIPE, private equity investors frequently received control rights, including representation on the firm's board.[8]

7. This discount has varied over time, with higher discounts seen in the 1990s than in earlier decades. For a discussion, see Kenneth Kim and Hyun-Han Shin, "The Underpricing of Seasoned Equity Offerings: 1983–1998," Unpublished working paper, University of Wisconsin at Milwaukee and State University of New York at Buffalo, 2001.

8. Hedge funds, mutual funds, and others also purchase PIPEs. These investors may or may not receive similar control provisions. The size of a PIPE transaction is often around 10 percent of the firm's equity, since the large U.S. exchanges require that when a company issues equity equal to 20 percent or more of the firm's common stock at a discounted price, it must first seek shareholder approval.

PIPEs took on two different forms. Traditional PIPEs would convert into a fixed number of shares, regardless of the company's fortunes. During the late 1990s, however, structured PIPEs, more colorfully know as "death spiral" or "toxic" PIPEs, became popular, especially with hedge funds. Through a variety of mechanisms, these ensure that the investors receive a set rate of return. To accomplish this, these securities adjusted the conversion ratio when the firm's stock price fared poorly, allowing the preferred holders to receive a larger share of the firm's common stock. The onset of bad news for a firm with such a security outstanding was thus doubly bad news for the common stock holders: first, the firm would be less profitable, and second their equity stake might be substantially diluted. As a result, bad news in these cases could trigger a rapid decline in the share price.

Between April 1999 and April 2000, Hicks, Muse had invested about $1.2 billion in six PIPE transactions. (The transactions are summarized in Exhibit 4.3. As is typical for PIPE investments by buyout groups, these were structured as traditional preferred investments, with a fixed conversion rate.) The investments attracted considerable discussion at the time. Some observers saw them as an opportunity to transfer the buyout group's model to an important new sector of the economy, but others had reservations about whether the firm would be able to succeed in these quite different sectors.

By June 2000, it was determined that the highly visible PIPEs investments would be assigned to the fourth fund, rather than split equally between the fourth and fifth fund as originally intended. (The fund had made these investments—as well as the start-up investments discussed below—using the proceeds from a nearly $2 billion bridge loan that it had negotiated in 1999 from a number of banks. Hicks, Muse had frequently employed this strategy in order to take advantage of attractive investment opportunities that were identified before the fund-raising process was complete.) Meanwhile, the $300 million investment in the Pan American Sports Network, which appeared to be progressing extremely well, would be assigned to the fifth fund.

In any case, these six investments had all encountered severe performance problems in the months that followed the NASDAQ correction of April 2000. Not only did their sectors perform poorly, but in many cases, the firms' stock price performed

---

EXHIBIT 4.3

HICKS, MUSE'S PIPE INVESTMENTS

Company Name	Announcement Date	Stock Price°	Amount Invested ($ million)	Conversion Price	Premium°	Dividend Rate	Maturity	Ownership on Conversion
Globix	11/08/99	$33.25	80	$40.00	20%	7.50%	2014	19%
ICG	2/28/00	22.22	240	28.00	26	8.00	2015	19
RCN Corp.	3/18/99	35.50	250	39.00	10	7.00	2014	14
Rhythms NetConnections	2/07/00	34.00	260	37.50	10	8.25	2015	8
Teligent, Inc.	11/05/99	42.69	210	57.50	35	7.75	2014	14
Viatel Inc.	2/01/00	35.50	170	46.25	30	7.50	2015	14

° Based on stock price three days before transaction.

Source: Compiled from press accounts.

significantly worse than industry benchmarks.[9] Press accounts suggested that investors in at least some of these firms had a limited ability to monitor management activities.[10] The stock price performance of these funds is summarized in Exhibit 4.4.

EXHIBIT 4.4

STOCK PRICE PERFORMANCE OF HICKS, MUSE PIPE INVESTMENTS

Globix

ICG

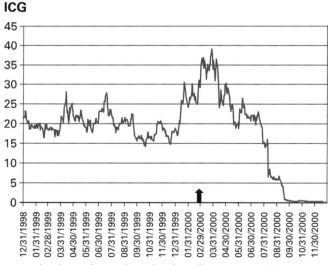

Notes: The chart indicates the (split-adjusted) movement of the common stock of each firm.

The arrow indicates the date of the announcement of the Hicks, Muse investment.

Source: Datastream and U.S. Securities and Exchange Commission findings.

(Continues)

9. Between March 15, 2001, and December 31, 2001, the six companies lost 96 percent of their value. During the same interval, the Ibbotson small-capitalization equity index fell by 26 percent and the NASDAQ telecommunications index by 60 percent.

10. Paul M. Sherer and Gary McWilliams, "Out of Line: How a Brash Provider of Internet Services Became Unplugged," *Wall Street Journal,* November 13, 2000, pp. A1ff.

EXHIBIT 4.4 *(CONTINUED)*

STOCK PRICE PERFORMANCE OF HICKS, MUSE PIPE INVESTMENTS

RCN

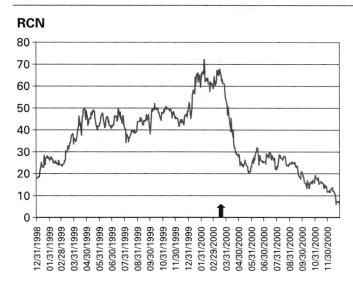

Rhythms NetConnections

(Continues)

COMPENSATION IN THE PRIVATE EQUITY INDUSTRY[11]

At the start of the twenty-first century, private equity investors were typically compensated in two ways: a share of the profits and an annual fee. These two elements, however, displayed many variations. For instance, the way in which the fee was calculated and the timing of the profit sharing varied tremendously from firm to firm.

11. For a more detailed treatment of this topic, as well as data on recent trends, see Josh Lerner, "A Note on Private Equity Partnership Agreements," Harvard Business School note No. 294-084 (Boston: Harvard Business School Publishing, 2000).

EXHIBIT 4.4 *(CONTINUED)*

STOCK PRICE PERFORMANCE OF HICKS, MUSE PIPE INVESTMENTS

Teligent

Viatel

The percentage of profits retained by private equity investors was known as the carried interest. This share had historically been about 20 percent, although more established venture funds frequently commanded higher carried interests. In recent years, it had become more common to make the carried interest contingent on the performance of the fund. For instance, the carried interest might be 20 percent until the limited partners received a 30 percent rate of return on their investment, whereupon the carried interest increased to 25 percent.

The second element of compensation was management fees. These fees, which were typically paid quarterly, financed day-to-day operations. In many funds, the fees changed over time. For instance, the fees would often be reduced in later years, reflecting the expectation that the partnership's costs would be lower during the "harvesting period." The fees might also contain provisions for inflation adjustments. The base used to calculate the fee varied. While most agreements computed the annual fee as a percentage of invested capital, in some cases the value of the partnership's assets was used.

There were also many differences in the timing of compensation. Over 90 percent of the funds contained some provision that ensured that the private equity investors did not unconditionally receive distributions.

Most restrictions are of two types. The standard partnership agreement of the 1960s and 1970s called for the private equity investors to receive distributions only after their limited partners had received their invested capital back. Any subsequent distributions were then split according to the carried interest. This arrangement, however, was perceived to have a negative effect on the choice of securities distributed.[12] This was because private equity investors frequently distributed securities of firms that they had taken public, rather than selling the shares and distributing cash.[13] Before the committed capital had been returned, some private equity investors were perceived to distribute overvalued securities. Undervalued securities were retained until after committed capital was returned and the investor was eligible to receive distributions.

During the 1980s, a new contractual form allowed private equity investors to receive capital gains as long as the value of the portfolio exceeded 100 percent, 125 percent, or some other multiple of the invested capital. (The multiple was referred to as hurdle rate.) Under these arrangements, the cost basis of each investment was first returned to the limited partners. The remainder—the capital gain on this particular investment—was then divided between the limited and general partners according to the agreed-upon formula. Consider the distribution of 1,000 shares of a company that the private equity investors had purchased for \$2/share and currently trading at \$12/share, under a contract where the proceeds were divided 80% – 20%. The limited partners would receive shares with a value of \$10,000 [$1,000 \times (\$2 + 0.8 \times (\$12 - \$2))$] and the general partners shares worth \$2,000 [$1,000 \times (0.2 \times (\$12 - \$2))$].[14]

Private equity organizations that had persuaded their investors to allow them to receive accelerated profit-sharing were significantly older and larger. Industry observers argued that the ability of larger partnerships to accelerate their compensation through a hurdle rate reflected their market power. For instance, a Venture Economics report noted, "Although there are some limited partners which believe they should receive their original capital back before the general [partners] begin to share in the profits, most of the limited [partners] . . . were aware that it was difficult to demand, particularly with more experienced groups."[15]

---

12. Venture Economics, *Venture Capital Performance–1989*, Needham, Venture Economics, 1989.

13. Private equity investors have at least two reasons for distributing securities rather than cash. First, the limited partners usually include both tax-paying and tax-exempt investors, who may have different preferences concerning the timing of security sales. Second, distributions of securities are valued (both in the partnerships' internal accounting and in the records of gatekeepers and other monitors) using the share price prior to the distribution. The actual price that a private equity investor might realize if he sold a large block of a thinly traded security might be considerably lower. See Venture Economics, "A Perspective on Venture Capital Management Fees," *Venture Capital Journal* 27 (December 1987), 10–14.

14. Some recent funds have gone to the other extreme: they do not allow the private equity investors to receive capital gains until *more* than 100 percent of invested capital has been returned to investors. These tend to have been raised by smaller and younger organizations.

15. Venture Economics, "Stock Distributions–Fact, Opinion and Comment," *Venture Capital Journal* 27 (August 1987), 8–14.

THE OFFER[16]

In its November 2000 letter to Acme and other potential limited partners, Hicks, Muse outlined several changes from its initial plans.

- First, the group would only seek to raise between $3 billion and $4 billion, rather than the $4.5 billion target that had been set originally. (The firm had previously abandoned its plans to seek a separate $1.5 billion "new economy" fund.)

- Second, the group would discontinue investing in "new economy" firms and would instead invest in "consumer branded, manufacturing and media sectors, which had been part of [Hicks, Muse's] traditional and very successful strategy."[17]

- Finally, the group's portfolio of thirteen high-technology investments, known as HMTF Holdings, would be guaranteed a rate of return of at least 20 percent. In the worst-case scenario, where all investments were liquidated, the fund's eight partners would provide limited partners with their original capital back plus an amount equal to a return of 20 percent over the investment holding period. (The partners indicated, however, that they anticipated that this scenario would not occur, since some investments, such as Vectrix Corp. and The Realm.com, had solid management teams and attractive prospects.)

Some potential limited partners attributed the offer to the difficulties of the private equity fund-raising environment. They pointed out that buyout industry had grown considerably in size, while the investment environment had become considerably more difficult. For instance, purchase prices had risen, bank debt for transactions was harder to access, and the success of Hicks, Muse and other groups (e.g., Golder, Thoma, Cressy & Rauner) in consolidation investments had attracted many imitators. These trends are summarized in Exhibit 4.5.

Others saw the potential risk that the members of the buyout group were taking on as a positive signal. For instance, Brad Pacheco, spokesman for the $177 billion California Public Employee's Retirement Fund, commented, "They're looking out for investors and will take the hit themselves if the investments sour."[18] Richard Holbein, an investment consultant for the Arkansas and Louisiana teachers' pension funds, noted that the offer "goes a long way to showing the character of the general partners."[19]

16. This section is based on assorted press accounts, especially Katherine Campbell, "Hicks Partners are Ready to Reach into Their Own Pockets," *Financial Times* (November 14, 2000), p. 35; Leslie Green, "Hicks Muse Lowers Fund Target, Closes on $1.2 Billion," *Buyouts* 14 (January 8, 2000) pp. 1, 62; and Steven Lipin, "New Hicks Muse Fund Offers Guarantee," *Wall Street Journal* (November 8, 2000), p. A4.

17. Ricki Fulman, "Unusual Offer: Pension Funds Consider Hicks Muse's Guaranteed 20 percent Return for Portfolio," *Pensions and Investments* 28 (November 13, 2000), p. 2.

18. *Ibid.*

19. "Hicks Muse Giving Investors Guarantee on Returns: The Offer is Reportedly Drawing Interest and Erasing Doubts about the Leveraged Buyout Firm," *Los Angeles Times* (November 9, 2000), p. C4.

EXHIBIT 4.5

LEVERAGED BUYOUT MARKET TRENDS

	1992	1993	1994	1995	1996	1997	1998	1999	2000
Total fund-raising ($B)	6.7	8.2	13.2	19.0	22.8	19.1	57.2	39.0	63.5
Transaction volume ($B)	9.6	11.0	13.0	20.9	29.0	29.7	41.0	63.4	39.0
Number of transactions	270	255	228	272	277	275	306	386	283
Purchase price as a multiple of EBITDA	NA	5.4×	6.5×	7.0×	7.1×	8.6×	8.3×	7.4×	6.7×
Average equity contribution in buyouts	22%	25%	26%	24%	23%	30%	32%	36%	38%

Notes: Transaction volume and number only includes traditional buyout investments, not other investments by buyout funds.

      EBITDA = Earnings before interest, taxes, depreciation, and amortization.

      NA = Not available.

Source: Compiled from *Buyouts, Private Equity Analyst,* and other publications. I thank S&P Portfolio Management Data for the information on average equity contribution.

5

A Note on Private Equity Partnership Agreements

Venture capital and leveraged buyouts are by necessity long-run investments. Consequently, the vast majority of U.S. private equity today is raised through private partnerships with a life span of ten years or longer. To govern these investments, complex contracts have sprung up. These contracts provide an insight into the complex challenge of raising and managing a private equity fund.

There are three critical aspects to these contracts: the structure of the funds, the restrictions placed on their activities, and the incentives offered to the private equity investors. This note considers each of these aspects in turn.[1]

HOW THE FUND IS STRUCTURED

Private equity funds typically have limited and general partners. The limited partners are institutional and individual investors who provide capital. These are limited in the sense that their liability extends only to the capital that they contribute. If, for instance, the fund invests in a company that produces a drug that kills some patients, the victims' relatives cannot sue the partnership's investors for damages. The general partners—typically the private equity investors who manage the fund—may be directly liable, however.[2]

---

1. This section is based on Asset Alternatives, *Private Equity Partnership Terms and Conditions*, Wellesley, MA: Asset Alternatives, 1999; Joseph W. Bartlett, *Equity Finance: Venture Capital, Buyouts, Restructurings, and Reorganization*, New York: Wiley, 1995; Paul A. Gompers and Josh Lerner, "The Use of Covenants: An Empirical Analysis of Venture Partnership Agreements," *Journal of Law and Economics* 39 (October 1996), 566–599; Jack S. Levin, *Structuring Venture Capital, Private Equity and Entrepreneurial Transactions*, Chicago: Commerce Clearing House, 1994; Venture Economics, *Terms and Conditions of Venture Capital Partnerships*, Needham, MA: Venture Economics, 1989; and Venture Economics, *Terms and Conditions of Venture Capital Partnerships—1992*, Needham, MA: Venture Economics, 1992.

2. Private equity investors protect themselves, at least partially, by not serving directly as the general partners. Rather, they create a corporation that serves as the general partner, of which they in turn are shareholders.

A private equity fund is typically raised in several stages. Initial investors in a private equity fund are often eager to avoid opportunistic behavior by the general partners as they raise additional funds. As a result, a series of contractual provisions govern the fund-raising process.

The first of these provisions is a minimum size of investment. General partners will typically set a minimum size for institutional investors and a smaller minimum for individual investors. Limited partners have at least two reasons for being concerned about the number of partners. Under the Investment Company Act of 1940, funds with more than a few hundred partners (originally one hundred) must register as investment advisors. This imposes complex regulatory and disclosure requirements. More generally, the costs of administering a private equity fund increase with the number of limited partners.

Most contracts stipulate an explicit minimum and maximum size for the fund. In many cases, limited partners have distinct preferences about fund sizes. If the general partners are unable to attract additional capital from other investors, the initial investors may prefer that the fund be disbanded. The general partners' inability to raise additional funds may imply that other potential limited investors have adverse information that the initial investors do not have.[3] They will in many cases also be concerned that the fund not become too large, lest the management skills of the general partners be strained. In many cases, the private equity investors are allowed to exceed the maximum size stated in the contract by 10 percent or 20 percent, as long as they explicitly obtain permission from the existing limited partners. The limited partners who enter late almost always are required to pay the same up-front and organization fees as the original limited partners, and they may be restricted from a share of the interest earned on the original limited partner's initial capital commitments.

Prior to the 1986 Tax Reform Act, the contribution of the general partners to the funds was invariably 1 percent. This was because 1 percent was the minimum contribution by a general partner required by law. Since this act, general partners are free to contribute as much or as little as they desire. In most cases, however, 1 percent is still the general partners' contribution. Deviations are confined to small funds, particularly first funds raised by private equity partnerships. In these cases, a substantial minority of firms contribute either a smaller or larger percentage. A few funds allow firms not to make the contributions in cash, but rather in non–interest bearing notes.

Contracts uniformly have a "takedown" schedule, which specifies how the funds committed by the limited partners will be paid into the fund. Neither the limited nor general partners are usually eager for the funds to be paid in immediately. Since the private equity partnership will invest the funds gradually, if the funds are simply sitting in the fund's bank account, they will depress the partnership's rate of return. Typically partnership agreements will call for a set amount to be disbursed at closing (most often between 10 percent and 33 percent). The dates of subsequent payments may be set in the agreement or else left to the general partner's discretion. Larger funds are more likely to leave the schedule to the discretion of the general partners. Even if they are left to the private equity investors' discretion, minimum and maximum periods usually are set. Typically all the funds are drawn down by between the second and fourth anniversaries of the fund's formation.

Private equity partnerships almost always have a life of about ten years. They usually can be extended for at least two more years. In some cases, permission of the limited

---

3. This is similar to provisions in the riskiest of initial public offerings, the "best efforts" offering. If the underwriter cannot sell a minimum number of shares in a best efforts offering, the offering will be canceled, and the initial investors will be refunded.

partners is required; in other cases, only extensions beyond this point need permission. In general, the decision to extend the life of the partnership is not controversial.

Almost all partnerships allow the limited partners to terminate their investments in the partnership under certain extreme conditions. These include the death or withdrawal of the general partners or the bankruptcy of the fund. Most agreements also allow the limited partners to dissolve the partnership or replace the general partners if between 51 percent and 100 percent of the limited partners believe that the general partner is damaging the fund. Often, however, the parties in these cases end up in court.[4]

Most contracts will also have provisions for defaulting limited partners who fail to meet their capital commitments. In many cases, the general partners reserve the right to charge interest for late payments, to seize the limited partner's stake in whole or part, or even to sue the limited partner. In other cases, the terms are less onerous. The general partners may agree to help to market the limited partner's interest or to pay the limited partner an amount that reflects the current fair market value of the partnership interest (or a fraction of this value). In many cases, if a pension fund must withdraw from a private equity fund due to the complex regulations promulgated by the U.S. Department of Labor, these penalties are waived. In addition, limited partners can frequently transfer their shares to other parties, conditional on the approval of the general partners.

WHAT THE PRIVATE EQUITY INVESTORS CAN AND CANNOT DO

An area of protracted negotiation is the discretion with which the general partner can run the private equity fund. In the 1960s and 1970s, partnership agreements contained few such restrictions. These early venture capital organizations were free to invest as they saw fit. As the 1980s progressed, however, institutional investors began viewing themselves as holding a portfolio of private equity funds, each with a distinct focus. They demanded contractual provisions that would limit general partners' ability to deviate from their area of expertise. A few of the very oldest organizations, however, have managed to maintain simple contracts with few restrictions.[5] These covenants can be divided into three broad classes: the overall management of the fund, the activities of the general partners, and the permissible types of investments.

Management of the Fund

The first of these restrictions relates to the size of investment in any one firm. These provisions are intended to ensure that the general partners do not attempt to salvage an investment in a poorly performing firm by investing significant resources in follow-on funding. The private equity investors typically do not receive a share of profits until the limited partners have received their original investment back. Consequently, the general partners' share of profits can be thought of as a call option. The general partner may gain disproportionately from increasing risk of the portfolio at the expense of

---

4. Articles about such disputes include E. S. Ely, "Dr. Silver's Tarnished Prescription," *Venture* 9 (July 1987), 54–58; "Iowa Suits Test LPs' Authority to Abolish Fund," *Private Equity Analyst* 4 (May 1994), 1 and 9; and "Madison L.P.s Oust G.P., Legal Skirmish Ensues," *Buyouts* (October 23, 1995), 4.

5. It might be wondered why these issues need to be specified within the original partnership agreement. Could not, for instance, the limited partners serve as directors, overseeing the investment decisions of the private equity investors? In actuality, limited partners can retain their limited liability only if they are not involved in the day-to-day operations of the fund. Thus, once the fund is formed, they are limited to a purely consultative role, such as service on the firm's advisory board. This makes the careful delineation of rights in the original partnership agreement critical.

diversification. This limitation is frequently expressed as a percentage of capital invested in the fund (typically called committed capital). Alternatively, it may be expressed as a percent of the current value of the fund's assets. In a few cases, a limit may be placed on the aggregate size of the partnership's two or three largest investments.

The second class of restriction limits the use of debt. As option holders, the general partners may be tempted to increase the variance of their portfolio's returns by leveraging the fund. Partnership agreements often limit the ability of private equity investors to borrow funds themselves or to guarantee the debt of their portfolio companies (which might be seen as equivalent to direct borrowing). Partnership agreements may restrict debt to a set percentage of committed capital or assets, and in some instances also restrict the maturity of the debt, to ensure that all borrowing is short-term.[6]

The third restriction relates to co-investments with the private equity organization's earlier and/or later funds. Many private equity organizations manage multiple funds, formed several years apart, which can lead to opportunistic behavior. Consider, for instance, a venture organization whose first fund has made an investment in a troubled firm. The general partners may find it optimal for their second fund to invest in this firm, in the hopes of salvaging the investment.[7] Consequently, partnership agreements for second or later funds frequently contain provisions that the fund's advisory board must review such investments or that a majority (or supermajority) of the limited partners approve these transactions. Another way in which these problems are limited is by the requirement that the earlier fund invest simultaneously at the same valuation. Alternatively, the investment may be allowed only if one or more unaffiliated private equity organizations simultaneously invest at the same price.

A fourth class of covenant relates to reinvestment of profits. Private equity investors may have several reasons to reinvest funds, rather than distribute profits to the limited partners. First, many partnerships receive fees on the basis of either the value of assets under management or adjusted committed capital (capital less any distributions). Distributing profits will reduce these fees. Second, reinvested capital gains may yield further profits for the general (as well as the limited) partners.[8] The reinvestment of profits may require approval of the advisory board or the limited partners. Alternatively, such reinvestment may be prohibited after a certain date, or after a certain percent of the committed capital is invested.

Activities of the Private Equity Investors

Five frequently encountered classes of restrictions limit the activities of the general partners. The first of these restricts the ability of the general partners to invest personal funds

---

6. A related provision—found in virtually all partnership agreements—is that the limited partners will avoid unrelated business taxable income. Tax-exempt institutions must pay taxes on UBTI, which is defined as the gross income from any unrelated business that the institution regularly carries out. If the venture partnership is generating significant income from debt-financed property, the limited partners may have tax liabilities.

7. Distortions may also be introduced by the need for the private equity investors to report an attractive return for their first fund as they seek capital for a third fund. Many venture funds will write up the valuation of firms in their portfolios to the price paid in the last venture round. By having the second fund invest in one of the first fund's firms at an inflated valuation, they can (temporarily) inflate the reported performance of their first fund.

8. Another reason why private equity investors may wish to reinvest profits is that such investments are unlikely to be mature at the end of the fund's stated life. The presence of investments that are too immature to liquidate is a frequently invoked reason for extending the partnership's life beyond the typical contractual limit of ten years. In these cases, the private equity investors will continue to generate fees from the limited partners (though often on a reduced basis).

in firms. If general partners invest in selected firms, they may devote excessive time to these firms and may not terminate funding if the firms encounter difficulties. To address this problem, general partners are often limited in the size of the investment that they can make in any of their fund's portfolio firms. This limit may be expressed as a percentage of the total investment by the fund, or (less frequently) of the net worth of the private equity investor. In addition, the private equity investors may be required to seek permission from the advisory board or limited partners. An alternative approach employed in some partnership agreements is to require the private equity investors to invest a set dollar amount or percentage in every investment made by the fund.[9]

A second restriction addresses the reverse problem: the sale of partnership interests by general partners. Rather than seeking to increase their personal exposure to selected investments, general partners may sell their share of the fund's profits to other investors. While the general partnership interests are not totally comparable with the limited partners' stakes (for instance, the general partners will typically only receive a share of the capital gains after the return of the limited partners' capital), these may still be attractive investments. The limited partners are likely to be concerned that such a sale would reduce the general partners' incentives to monitor their investments. Partnership agreements may prohibit the sale of general partnership interests outright, or else require that these sales be approved by a majority (or supermajority) of the limited partners.

A third area for restrictions on the general partners is future fund-raising. The raising of an additional fund will raise the management fees that the general partners receive, and it may reduce the attention that they pay to existing funds. Partnership agreements may prohibit fund-raising by the general partners until a set percentage of the portfolio has been invested or until a given date. Alternatively, fund-raising may be restricted to a fund of a certain size or focus (e.g., a venture organization may be allowed to raise a buyout fund, whose management would presumably be by other general partners).

In a similar vein, some partnership agreements restrict other actions by general partners. Because outside activities are likely to reduce the attention paid to investments, private equity investors may be restricted to spending "substantially all" (or some other fraction) of their time managing the investments of the partnership. Alternatively, the general partners' ability to be involved in businesses other than the companies in which the private equity fund has invested may be restricted. These limitations are often confined to the first years of the partnership, or until a set percent of the fund's capital is invested, when the need for attention by the general partners is presumed to be the largest.

A fifth class of covenant relates to the addition of new general partners. By hiring less experienced general partners, private equity investors may reduce the burden on themselves. The quality of the oversight provided, however, is likely to be lower. As a result, many funds require that the addition of new general partners be approved by either the advisory board or a set percentage of the limited partners.

It should be noted that while many issues involving the behavior of the general partners are addressed through partnership agreements, several others typically are not. One subject that is almost never discussed is the vesting schedule of general partnership interests. If a general partner leaves a private equity organization early in the life

---

9. Another issue relating to co-investment is the timing of the investments by the general partners. In some cases, venture capitalists involved in the establishment of a firm will purchase shares at the same time as the other founders at a very low valuation, then immediately invest their partnership's funds at a much higher valuation. Some partnership agreements address this problem by requiring venture capitalists to invest at the same time and price as their funds.

of the fund, he may forfeit all or some of his share of the profits. If the private equity investors do not receive their entire partnership interest immediately, they are less likely to leave the fund soon after it is formed. A second issue is the division of the profits between the general partners. In the case of some funds, most of the profits accrue to the older general partners, even if the younger private equity investors are providing the bulk of the day-to-day management. While these issues are addressed in agreements between the general partners, they are rarely discussed in the contracts between the general and limited partners.

Types of Investments

The third family of covenants limits the types of assets in which the fund will invest. These restrictions are typically structured in similar ways: the private equity fund is allowed to invest no more than a set percentage of capital or asset value in a given investment class. An exception may be made if the advisory board or a set percentage of the limited partners approve. Occasionally, more complex restrictions will be encountered, such as the requirement that the sum of two asset classes not exceed a certain percent of capital.

Two fears appear to motivate these restrictions on investments. First, the general partners may be receiving compensation that is inappropriately large. For instance, the average money manager who specializes in investing in public securities receives an annual fee of about 0.5 percent of assets, while private equity investors receive 20 percent of profits in addition to an annual fee of about 2.5 percent of capital. Consequently, limited partners seek to limit the ability of private equity investors to invest in public securities. Similarly, the typical investment manager receives a one-time fee of 1 percent of capital for investing an institution's money in a private equity fund. Partnership agreements often also include covenants that restrict the ability of the general partners to invest capital in other private equity funds.

A second concern is that the general partners will invest in classes of investments in which they have little expertise, in the hope of gaining experience. For instance, during the 1980s, many venture capital funds began investing in leveraged buyouts. Those that developed a successful track record proceeded to raise funds specializing in buyouts; many more, however, lost considerable sums on these investments.[10] Similarly, many firms explored investing in foreign countries during the 1980s. Only a relative handful proved sufficiently successful to raise funds specializing in these investments.

HOW ARE PRIVATE EQUITY INVESTORS COMPENSATED?[11]

Even with these covenants, the key limited partners in private equity funds—for instance, pension fund trustees and university overseers—find it challenging to monitor the funds in their portfolio or to select the funds most likely to do well. This reflects the difficult environment in which general partners operate. The typical firms backed by general partners have severe information problems, very important strategic and operational decisions to make, and substantial capital needs.

10. The poor performance of venture-backed LBOs such as Prime Computer has been much discussed in the popular press; quantitative support of these claims is found in analyses of the returns of funds with different investment objectives by Venture Economics.

11. This section is based on Paul A. Gompers and Josh Lerner, "An Analysis of Compensation in the U.S. Venture Capital Partnership," *Journal of Financial Economics* 51 (January 1999), 3–44, and subsequent updates by the authors.

In order to ensure the success of their investments, general partners must carefully work with and oversee entrepreneurs and portfolio companies. These activities help the general partners assess the activities of their portfolio companies. But given the difficulty of observing the interactions between general partners and company managers, and the long gestation period from the time that investments are made until they are exited, it is difficult for limited partners to ensure optimal behavior after they commit to the fund.

The structure of private equity partnerships, in which a large share of the compensation depends on the fund's performance, helps solve the limited partners' difficulties in evaluating potential investment opportunities. The design of an appropriate incentive scheme for the general partners can play a critical role in alleviating these problems.

In particular, the carried interest may be important for two reasons. First, it provides an incentive for the private equity manager to work hard, even if his effort cannot be observed. It may be that in the initial funds, a private equity manager will work diligently even without explicit pay-for-performance incentives because if he can establish a good investment track record, he will gain additional compensation in later funds because of the increased ease of fund-raising. Once a reputation has been established, explicit incentive compensation is needed to induce the proper effort levels. A second possibility is the signal that accepting a large portion of compensation in the form of carried interest may provide. If the institutional investors see that a new private equity manager is willing to take a cut in his base fee in the hopes of making a substantial amount of carried interest, they may be more willing to invest in that fund: the move signals that the venture capitalist is confident of his ability to create value.

The management fee also plays an important role. Traditionally, private equity groups were exceedingly "lean" organizations: aside from some spending on support staff, travel, and office space, there was little overhead. Thus, most of the management fees flowed to investment professionals.

But over the past few years, a flurry of experimentation has characterized the private equity industry. Among the changes seen are partnerships between venture capital and buyout organizations, sometimes in conjunction with corporations; the establishment of affiliate funds in different regions and nations; and the launching of physical and "virtual" incubators by private equity groups. Each of these efforts requires a greater investment in people and infrastructure, which places far great demands on management fees than traditional efforts.

Our research has examined the evolution of compensation in private equity partnerships over the past two decades. This information has been gathered from a broad cross-section of institutional investors and intermediaries. As suggested above, the results provide important insights into the evolution of compensation. Because investors often focus on the level of carried interest, we first consider the level that the carry has taken across various private equity types, e.g., U.S. venture capital, U.S. buyout, and non-U.S. funds.

One particularly interesting pattern is the role of private equity firm reputation on the level of carried interest charged by the fund. Reputation is, of course, a difficult thing to measure. Instead, one has to examine characteristics of private equity groups that we suspect are related to reputation. In this analysis, we focus on the size of the private equity fund being raised. Fund size is a useful measure of investment track record: investors will provide larger sums to investors with proven success, even if they have not raised any earlier funds. Fund size, however, may also capture differences in industry or geographic focus.[12] The patterns of carried interest for various

---

12. Ideally, we would have a measure of the cumulative experience of the general partners associated with the fund. While we try to address this problem by considering buyout, non-U.S., and venture funds separately, we realize that this measure is inexact.

types and sizes of private equity funds are presented in Exhibit 5.1. We tabulate the carried interest for the more than 650 funds in our sample raised between 1995 and 2000. We show the average carried interest for U.S. venture capital funds, other U.S. private equity funds, and non-U.S. private equity funds across various size categories from under $50 million in committed capital to more than $1 billion. For both U.S. nonventure private equity funds and non-U.S. funds, the carried interest deviates little from 20 percent.

The pattern within U.S. venture capital funds, however, is strikingly different. Carried interest in all groups (except those funds between $50 million and $100 million in committed capital) are significantly higher than 20 percent. The carried interest rises steadily for funds above $100 million, reaching an average of nearly 24 percent for the largest venture capital funds.

These depictions of the average level of carried interest are somewhat misleading, as they disguise the fact that these measures are very concentrated. This point is illustrated in Exhibit 5.2, which shows the distribution of the carried interest for U.S. venture capital and buyout and other private equity firms. The vast majority of funds have carried interest of 20, 25, or 30 percent.

Because the organized venture capital funds have a longer history in the United States, we next explore the changes in the mean level of carried interest for venture capital funds raised between 1978 and 2000. These results are shown in Exhibit 5.3. Surprisingly, despite the widespread belief that carried interest on venture capital funds

EXHIBIT 5.1

CARRIED INTEREST, BY FUND TYPE AND SIZE, 1995–2000

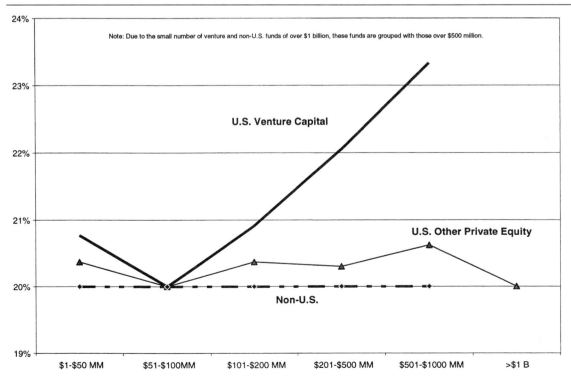

EXHIBIT 5.2

DISTRIBUTION OF CARRIED INTEREST, BY FUND TYPE

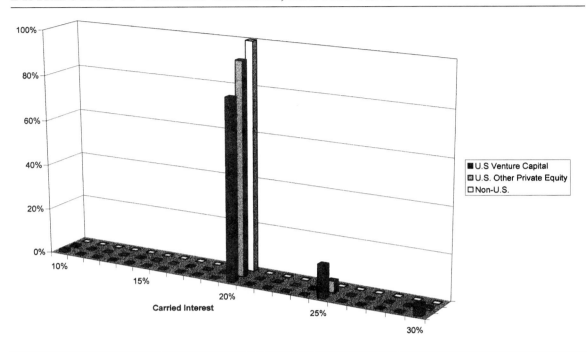

EXHIBIT 5.3

AVERAGE CARRIED INTEREST OF VENTURE CAPITAL FUNDS, BY YEAR

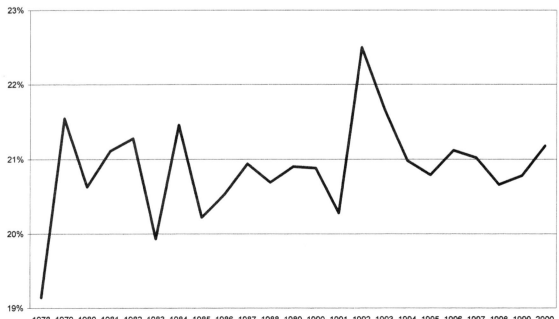

has been steadily rising in recent years, the trend is highly volatile. There appears to be little upward trend in carried interest when all funds are considered.[13]

How do we reconcile the results of Exhibits 5.1 and 5.3? The increased visibility of the large, successful venture capital groups has generated substantial press. In the accounts of these successful venture capital funds, journalists often focus on the rising carried interest they have received. As an industry, however, carried interest has not risen appreciably.

We next examine management fees. It is surprising that relatively little attention has been paid to the pattern that these fees have taken. These fees are a significant fraction of venture capitalist's compensation. They are, however, calculated in myriad ways. Fixed fees may be specified as a percent of the committed capital (the amount of money investors have committed to provide over the life of the fund), the value of fund's assets, or some combination or modification of these two measures. Both the base used to compute the fees and the percentage paid as fees may vary over the life of the fund. These differences make it difficult to do a straightforward comparison among the various funds.

Thus, we use two measures of fixed fees to gauge their importance for general partners. The first measure of fees that we examine is the level of fees in the third year of the fund. The choice of the third year reflects several important features of fees in private equity partnerships. First, fees in the early years are often lower than they are in later years. For most of the funds in our sample, fees reach their maximum percentage by the third anniversary of the fund. A second pattern also makes the third anniversary appropriate. Many funds reduce their fees after a certain number of years or when a new fund is raised (typically after the third anniversary of the fund's closing).

The level of fees in year three for U.S. venture capital, U.S. nonventure private equity, and non-U.S. private equity are presented in Exhibit 5.4.[14] The funds are once again those that were raised between 1995 and 2000. For non-U.S. funds and U.S. nonventure private equity funds, fees decline with fund size. Fees for the smallest funds average nearly 2.4 percent. For non-U.S. private equity funds, fees decline to 1.9 percent while for U.S. nonventure private equity, fees decline even further, to 1.6 percent. Once again, U.S. venture capital funds have a very different fee pattern. Fees increase across all fund size groups with the highest fees, as a percentage of committed capital, being paid to the largest funds.

This measure, however, actually understates the changes. In particular, many of the changes in fees have been in the rates charged during the initial and final years of the funds. An alternative to simply looking at the level of management fees is to examine the net present value implications of various compensation terms.

A net present value analysis requires assumptions about the drawdowns of capital, the rate of return on investments, and the timing of the distribution of returns to general and limited partners. In our analysis of compensation, we project out the returns to limited and general partners under various return scenarios. We discount relatively certain compensation (e.g., fees based on committed capital) at 10 percent, while applying a 20 percent discount rate to more uncertain compensation (such as carried interest paid, returns to the limited partners, or fees based on net asset value). These calculations take into account the entire stream of fees that limited partners agree to pay out over the lifetime of the private equity fund. In other words, calculating the net present value of fees

13. Both 1978 and 1992 are extreme cases. Both were poor markets, where relatively few funds were raised. Thus, these measures are considerably "noisier" that the others.

14. In this calculation, as well as the one below, we make a series of assumptions about fund drawdowns, investment rate, and performance, which are spelled out in detail in the article cited in footnote 11.

EXHIBIT 5.4

MANAGEMENT FEE IN YEAR 3, BY FUND TYPE AND SIZE, 1995–2000

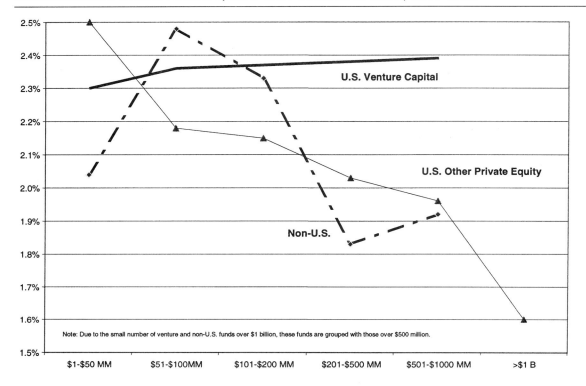

Note: Due to the small number of venture and non-U.S. funds over $1 billion, these funds are grouped with those over $500 million.

and the net present value of carried interest is a better measure of the burden that they place on the fund's potential return to the limited partners.

We compute the net present value of *all* management fees that are specified in the partnership agreement. We express the value as a percent of the committed capital. We discount relatively certain compensation (e.g., fees based on committed capital) at 10 percent, while applying a 20 percent discount rate to more uncertain compensation (such as fees based on net asset value). This calculation takes into account the entire stream of fees that limited partners agree to pay out over the lifetime of the private equity fund. In other words, calculating the net present value of fees is a better measure of the burden that they place on the fund.

Exhibit 5.5 reports the mean net present value of the base compensation as a percentage of committed capital for the industry segment that has seen the most dramatic changes, venture capital. The basic pattern has been one of declining fees, that is, the average level of fees for all funds is lower for funds raised after 1993 than those raised earlier. The changing pattern across groups with different experience levels, however, is quite striking. For funds raised prior to 1992, the level of fees declined with prior fund-raising experience, that is, experienced venture capitalists actually charged lower fees. (Because these groups raised larger funds, the actual fees received were actually larger for these groups.) After 1993, however, the pattern reversed. The most experienced venture capital organizations now charge substantially higher fees than inexperienced firms. The fees of these experienced groups have increased substantially from the level of fees that these funds charged prior to the recent fund-raising boom.

EXHIBIT 5.5

VENTURE CAPITAL FEES OVER FUND LIFE (AS % OF COMMITTED CAPITAL)

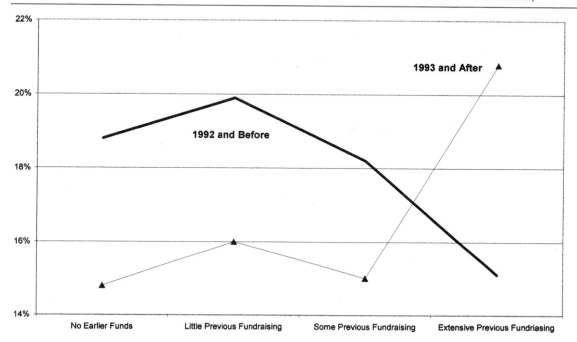

6

Grove Street Advisors

> When you commit to a venture capital fund as a limited partner, you're tying up your money for ten years based on someone's past performance.
> —Peter Dolan, Harvard Management Company

> …And now the past is irrelevant.
> —Clint Harris

One summer day in 2003, Clint Harris, managing partner and cofounder of Grove Street Advisors, studied the pictures of submarines that decorated his office wall and remembered taking the Graduate Management Admission Test while under the polar ice cap. His record on that examination had sent him to Harvard Business School and thence to a career in private equity. He knew that his most recent venture was now facing a test of its own as he and his partners sought to strengthen their business in the new world of private equity as an asset class to which public entities had a permanent allocation (see Exhibit 6.1 for bios and organizational chart).

Grove Street Advisors (GSA) was an intermediary that managed individually tailored private equity investment programs for large institutions, primarily public pension funds. Six months after its incorporation in May 1998, GSA had achieved national notice when the California Public Employees' Retirement System (CalPERS) chose the four-person firm to develop a program for its $350 million commitment to venture capital. Since then, the firm had grown to twenty-four people with over $3 billion under management from CalPERS, the Oregon Public Employees' Retirement Fund, and NIB Capital, a Dutch pension fund manager. It had 60 percent of its investments in venture firms, 35 percent in buyouts, and the balance in special situations, including two hedge funds.

GSA provided a range of services. First and foremost, it created and managed dedicated funds-of-funds for its clients. CalPERS, for instance, had wanted to invest in venture capital, primarily in Silicon Valley, to diversify its private equity portfolio and invest in enterprises in its own home state, and to share in the asset's lucrative returns.

Professors Felda Hardymon and Josh Lerner, Senior Research Associate Ann Leamon, and Frank Angella (HBS MBA '01) prepared this case with help from Christopher Allen in providing Exhibit 6.4. HBS cases are developed solely as the basis for class discussion. Cases are not intended to serve as endorsements, sources of primary data, or illustrations of effective or ineffective management.

EXHIBIT 6.1a

BIOGRAPHIES OF GSA'S MANAGEMENT TEAM

Clint P. Harris: Founder and Managing Partner

Experience: Prior to founding Grove Street in 1998, Harris was a founder and managing director of Advent International. During his fourteen years with the firm, Advent grew to become one of the world's largest and most successful private equity firms operating both in the United States and internationally. He served on Advent's investment committee responsible for more than 250 transactions. He also designed and raised more than $800 million in capital for a broad range of dedicated investment programs for both corporate and institutional investors. Prior to Advent, Harris spent seven years as a management consultant and Partner with Bain & Company, where he helped establish Bain's Japanese practice and opened Bain's first office in Germany, and five years as a naval officer serving on nuclear submarines.

Education: Undergraduate AB and engineering degrees from Dartmouth College and an MBA from Harvard University, where he was a Baker scholar.

David B. Mazza: Founder and Managing Partner

Experience: Prior to founding Grove Street in 1998, Mazza was the founder and managing partner of Mazza & Riley, which under his leadership became the largest and best-known executive search practice serving the venture capital industry. During his twenty-year career in executive search, he recruited more than forty general partners for leading venture capital firms, and more than forty CEO/COOs in venture capital backed portfolio companies. Through that process, he developed a very broad range of contacts and relationships. These contacts have also resulted in a small but highly successful deal origination practice where Mazza was able to package an attractive investment opportunity with a top-quality management team and capital raised from the venture industry.

Education: Undergraduate degree in sociology from Brown University and an MBA from Harvard University.

Catherine A. Crockett: Founder and General Partner

Experience: Prior to founding GSA in 1998, Crockett built a successful fourteen-year career in the design and implementation of private equity investment programs where there was both a financial and business development objective. In total, she has led the formation of venture capital funds as well as private equity investment programs with nearly $400 million under management for major corporate and state pension fund investors. Her clients/programs included the states of Michigan, Florida, Kansas, and Kentucky as well as the Federal Communications Commission, Puerto Rico and a number of foreign governments and agencies.

Education: Undergraduate degree in government and business administration from the University of Notre Dame and an MPA from Harvard's Kennedy School.

Barry J. Gonder: General Partner

Experience: Gonder joined GSA in 2001 after five years as senior investment officer of the CalPERS Alternative Investment Management Program, where he was responsible for managing the Alternative Investment and Private Equity portfolios. During his tenure at CalPERS, he built the program from $1.4 billion invested to $9 billion invested and $19 billion of commitments. Previously, he spent a decade with The Travelers Companies, where he managed private equity investments, served as director of research for Travelers Common Stock Group, and was responsible for the foreign investment portfolio. At Connecticut Mutual, Gonder served as senior investment officer responsible for alternative investments and private equity placements, initiated a private equity program and completed the organization's first direct venture capital, mezzanine debt, and partnership transactions.

Education: Undergraduate degree in economics from Vassar College and an MBA from the University of North Carolina.

(Continues)

EXHIBIT 6.1a (CONTINUED)

BIOGRAPHIES OF GSA'S MANAGEMENT TEAM

Ann St. Germain: General Partner and CFO

Experience: St. Germain joined Grove Street in 1999 after more than seventeen years experience in public accounting including thirteen years in Ernst & Young's private equity practice, where she was promoted to the partnership in 1997. At E&Y, she was one of three partners working with Advent International with primary responsibility for planning, organizing, administering, and successfully completing over forty financial audits. In addition, she has over a decade of experience in fund accounting and reporting, as well as portfolio company due diligence.

Education: BS in accounting from Syracuse University and a CPA.

Source: Company information.

EXHIBIT 6.1b

GSA ORGANIZATIONAL CHART

GROVE STREET ADVISORS

Grove Street Advisors
22 Employees Dedicated to Private Equity

Partners

Catherine Crockett	Dave Mazza	Clint Harris	Barry Gonder	Ann St. Germain
General Partner	Managing Partner	Managing Partner	General Partner	General Partner/CFO

Investment Team · Finance & Accounting Team

Ajay Saini — VP Finance

Principals

Frank Angella — Principal	Chris Yang — Principal

Mark Davidson — Controller · Roberto Ramirez — Dir. Client Reporting

Associates

Gamell Robles — Funds Coordinator	Jessica Feldt — Associate	TBH — Associate	TBH — Associate

Carol Lodge — Accountant · Amy Phaneuf — Accountant · Lisa Smith — Accountant · Jennifer Lefebvre — Finance Manager

Support Staff

Diane Facendola — Assistant	Nancy Fitzgerald — Assistant	Patricia Lewis — Assistant	Debbie Lindsay — Assistant	Cindy Sullivan — Assistant	Nate Lao — IT Manager

TBH = To Be Hired, replacement of Associates who departed for business school

Total Staff: 22 → 24

Confidential – Proprietary to GSA

Source: Company information.

Largely through the relationships established by cofounder David Mazza, GSA also identified and sometimes provided the initial funding for new and emerging private equity firms, laying the groundwork for CalPERS, NIB, and Oregon to establish long-term relationships with firms that, it was hoped, would become top-quartile performers. GSA had also done some direct co-investing beside the venture capital (VC) firms in its portfolio, although this effort was largely suspended in 2000.

By mid-2003, though, the landscape in which GSA operated had changed. As Catherine Crockett, GSA's third cofounder, had said, "In 1998, no one was offering customized funds-of-funds. We saw that hole in the market and we drove a semi into it. The market has evolved since then and the question is what do we do next."

The market had indeed evolved and was continuing to respond to a multitude of forces. The limited partners (LPs) were becoming more sophisticated. Pension funds that earlier would not have considered private equity now looked to allocate a proportion of their holdings to alternative assets—and this was not just big state organizations but even the pension fund of Trenton, New Jersey. With the increased money looking to move into the sector, there were more intermediaries, and they offered more products. The number of fund-of-funds managers worldwide had grown from seven in 1990 to 104 in 2001, and other intermediaries had entered the sector.[1] In addition to traditional products such as funds-of-funds and their variations, gatekeepers screened groups before pension funds even considered them. Consultants and rating agencies could tell LPs where and how much they should invest. Secondary markets had evolved, allowing an organization to buy a position in a fund from an LP that wanted to sell. A few groups would securitize an LP's future income stream from a private equity portfolio, and others traded the positions like derivatives. Information providers such as Thomson Financial (parent of Venture Economics) made the industry, known for its secrecy, more transparent and made it easier for LPs to approach general partners (GPs) directly.

GSA was considering several options. It could continue as it was, offering customized funds-of-funds to large clients, or to a greater number of smaller groups. Several small groups, including a family office, had recently approached the firm. GSA could offer more general, yet still specialized, funds-of-funds, devoted to emerging managers, for instance, or to biotech. Lastly, it could renew its dormant co-investing effort. Each strategy posed its own set of challenges for the firm in terms of skill sets, staffing levels, and structure. Complicating the issue was the broader question of disclosure, because public pension funds had been pressured to reveal the performance of their private equity investments. CalPERS had published GSA's fund-level results (see Exhibit 6.2); venture firms feared that sensitive portfolio company valuations would be the next target of curious journalists. Would that reduce venture firms' willingness to accept pension fund money? If so, what did that mean for GSA?

INTERMEDIARIES

By 2003, there were a number of ways for investors to participate in private equity. The simplest was to invest directly in private firms. This, however, required specialized knowledge, support staff, deal flow, and a significant amount of money. Some families formed their own organizations to manage private equity investments—the Rockefellers had Venrock, the Phippses created Bessemer Venture Partners, and J. H. Whitney founded his eponymous firm. Some companies, such as General Electric and Intel, and insurance companies like Travelers and Allstate, had similar efforts. For most entities, whether institutions or individuals, the costs of such an operation were prohibitive.

The next simplest approach was to pool funds with other investors and invest in a general partnership (e.g. a VC or buyout fund) that had its own deal flow, support staff, and domain knowledge. In exchange for a commitment of several million dollars, a management fee of 2–3 percent, and carried interest (a share of the profits) between 20 percent

---

1. *Private Equity Funds-of-Funds State of the Market* (Asset Alternatives Research Report, 2nd edition, May 2003), p. 20.

EXHIBIT 6.2

CALIFORNIA EMERGING VENTURES PERFORMANCE AS OF JUNE 2003

Capital Committed by CalPERS to CEV Programs	
At GSA discretion	$1,330 million
CalPERS co-investments	$1,500 million
Total	$2,830 million

Status of CEV Program as of 6/30/03	
Capital committed to funds	$2,404 million
Capital drawn by funds	$1,082 million
—of which GP fees & expenses	*~$133 million*
Portfolio value	$856 million

Performance Metrics	
CEV Funds' IRR	−14.0%
Top Quartile Benchmark for Venture	−15.6%
Median benchmark for Venture	−23.9%

Note: Benchmark data from Cambridge Associates for vintage years 1999 through 2002, weighted for CEV capital commitments.

Source: Company information.

and 30 percent, the limited partners could leave the details of finding, making, managing, and exiting the investments to the GPs. Major endowments, high-net-worth individuals, and some (mostly private) institutions followed this approach. The earliest limited partners were individuals. Some institutions had participated in private equity since the 1960s, with more entering the asset class in the late 1970s and early 1980s. These LPs had invested in nascent top-tier firms just as they were established.

By the mid-1980s, returns to private equity had started to generate attention beyond the institutions, endowments, and individuals that had historically participated. In part this stemmed from the Department of Labor's 1979 clarification of the "prudent person" rule, which not only allowed pension funds to invest in private equity, but also held that a prudent portfolio would include a range of risk and return in its investments (see Exhibit 6.3 for text of the rule). Until then, public pension funds had rarely invested in anything riskier than bonds and very large capitalization public equities.[2] In the early 1980s, both public and governmental pension funds started investing in buyout funds, and in the middle of the decade, these funds, with their billions of dollars, were starting to sniff around the edges of venture capital. What they found created the need for a new investment vehicle.

Private equity, but especially VC, exhibited a curious phenomenon—top-performing firms tended to remain as such over time. One study found that excellent performance persisted not just to the successor fund of an outperformer, but even to the fund after that. One explanation was that good performance put talented GPs in touch with talented entrepreneurs, generating proprietary deal flow or allowing top-tier funds into promising

2. While government pension funds, such as CalPERS, were exempt from the Department of Labor rules, they tended to refer to them for guidance.

EXHIBIT 6.3

THE "PRUDENT MAN" RULE CLARIFICATION OF 1979

The Department is of the opinion that (a) generally, the relative riskiness of a specific investment or investment course of action does not render such investment or investment course of action either per se prudent or per se imprudent, and (b) the prudence of an investment decision should not be judged without regard to the role that the proposed investment or investment course of action plays within the overall plan portfolio. Thus, although securities issued by a small or new company may be a riskier investment than securities issued by a "blue chip" company, the investment in the former company may be entirely proper under the Act's [Employee Retirement Income Securities Act of 1974] "prudence" rule.

Source: 44 Fed. Reg. 37,221, at 37,222 (June 26, 1979), found in Sutkowski & Rhoads Law Offices Ltd., http://www.erisalawfirm.com, accessed August 26, 2003.

---

deals at more favorable terms, due to perceived benefits from the association with the group.[3] Being attached to a good fund, it appeared, generated enough returns for everyone involved that they had little incentive to move.

Top-tier private equity organizations, then, could raise as much money as they wanted from a few select LPs, often those that had previously backed the firm, sometimes even from its inception. These top firms had little need to take money from new LPs, especially those that were not familiar with the asset class. This situation was different in buyouts, where the firms were much less particular in their choice of LPs. As Clint Harris noted, "Buyout firms always need money because their deals tend to be so big." Essentially shut out of the top-tier of VC, new entrants could always resort to the lower tiers—with vastly inferior results. In fact, LPs that could not get into a "top-quartile" VC fund, with a return above 16.1 percent, were better off in public equities, where returns hovered around 15 percent, as compared to a VC median IRR of 4 percent.[4] Furthermore, public equities had the added benefit of liquidity (see Exhibit 6.4).

In addition, there were structural barriers. A small investor, whether an individual or a small pension fund, would be hard pressed to meet the typical investment limit in a VC fund, a $2 million minimum and a $5 million maximum for a $100 million fund (higher for a billion-dollar fund) and still maintain any sort of portfolio diversification. A large investor, on the other hand, had too much money to conform to a $5 million maximum. A good example in the mid-1990s was CalPERS, which had a two-person Alternative Investments staff charged with committing $15 billion to private equity. A $5 million investment required time and attention that the rest of the portfolio could scarcely afford.

Thus, an investor looking to get into the private equity asset class had to find a top-tier firm to attain rewards worth the risk and illiquidity. But in a Catch-22 of sorts, in order to get into a top-tier fund, an LP had to be in a top-tier fund already—or offer some unique benefit—because otherwise it had too much or too little money and lacked the necessary expertise and connections. Another challenge lay in timing. Traditionally, firms raised funds only every three years or so. An LP looking to put a lot of money into private equity (PE) not only had to have access to the right funds, but also needed

---

3. Steven Kaplan and Antoinette Schoar, "Private Equity Performance: Returns Persistence and Capital," *National Bureau of Economic Research*, Working Paper 9807, June 2003, passim.

4. Data from Venture Economics, http://www.venturexpert.com, accessed September 30, 2003.

EXHIBIT 6.4

RETURN ON INVESTMENT TO VARIOUS ASSET CLASSES, 1980–2002

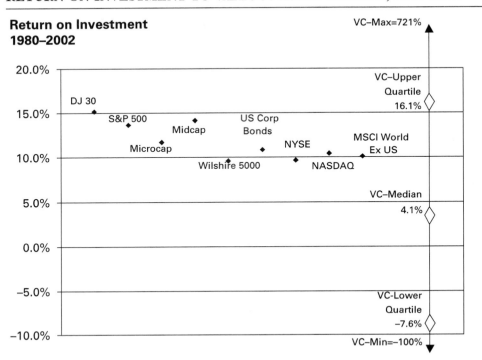

Note: Non-VC options are returns to various stock and bond index funds. All indicators include failed firms.

Source: Adapted from Venture Economics (Cumulative IRR for All Venture Capital) and Thomson Financial Datastream.

---

to be prepared to invest when those firms were raising money (see Exhibit 6.5 for fund-raising activity among a sample of firms).

Funds-of-funds evolved as a way to answer this need. A classic fund-of-funds acted much like a mutual fund for stocks. By aggregating many small investments, a fund-of-funds solved the diversification problem because investors could contribute smaller amounts. A fund-of-funds used its expertise to conduct due diligence on the multiple private equity funds available, and it had the contacts to access high-quality PE organizations. It also mediated between the GPs and new LPs, explaining the arcane ways of venture investing and shielding the GP from the questions and concerns of inexperienced investors. For this service, the fund-of-fund managers charged a combination of fees and carry (a share of the profits) that varied, depending on the cachet of the firm and the preferences of the client. Some charged a flat fee regardless of the amount of money under management; others had a fee that ranged between 0.5 percent and 1.2 percent of funds either under management or committed. Starting in the late 1990s, some fund-of-funds managers had begun charging carry above a hurdle; other groups did not (see Exhibits 6.6a–6.6c for the distribution of fees and carry among

EXHIBIT 6.5a

TOP VC FIRMS AS DEFINED BY HAMILTON LANE ADVISORS

Firm Name	Year Founded	Firm Name	Year Founded
Accel Partners	1983	Mohr Davidow Ventures	1983
Austin Ventures, L.P.	1979	Morgenthaler Ventures	1968
Benchmark Capital	1995	New Enterprise Associates	1978
Bessemer Venture Partners	1911	Norwest Venture Partners	1961
Charles River Ventures	1970	Oak Investment Partners	1978
Draper Fisher Jurvetson	1985	Polaris Venture Partners	1996
Greylock	1965	Redpoint Ventures	1996
Highland Capital Partners	1988	Sequoia Capital	1972
Kleiner Perkins Caufield & Byers	1972	Sevin Rosen Funds	1981
Lightspeed Venture Partners	1971	Sierra Ventures	1981
Matrix Partners	1977	Sigma Partners	1984
Mayfield Fund	1969	U.S. Venture Partners	1981
Menlo Ventures	1976	Venrock Associates	1969

Note: The list is based on both qualitative and quantitative factors, including market position, strength of team, and historical returns, and it is updated regularly. Firms are ranked alphabetically.

The founding year is from Venture Expert, http://www.ventureexpert.com, accessed December 5, 2003, and company Web sites.

Source: Hamilton Lane Advisors.

EXHIBIT 6.5b

FUNDS RAISED BY VC FIRMS LISTED ABOVE, 1998–2002

Year	No. of Funds	Total Target ($ mil)	Gross Period Amount Raised ($ mil)	Net Period Amount Raised ($ mil)
1998	26	3,296.1	4,396.4	4,396.4
1999	32	7,195.0	11,170.8	11,170.8
2000	38	13,410.6	20,064.7	20,064.7
2001	18	7,155.0	10,793.0	10,793.0
2002	14	6,631.1	77.1	–3,485.7*
5-year Total	**124**	**37,687.8**	**46,502.0**	**42,939.2**

* In 2002, firms returned money from funds that they decided they could not reasonably deploy in the changed venture environment. Thus, although $77 million was raised that year, the firms in this sample returned or reduced funds by a total of $3,485.7 million.

Source: http://www.ventureexpert.com, accessed November 13, 2003.

EXHIBIT 6.6a

MANAGEMENT FEES AMONG FUND-OF-FUNDS MANAGERS

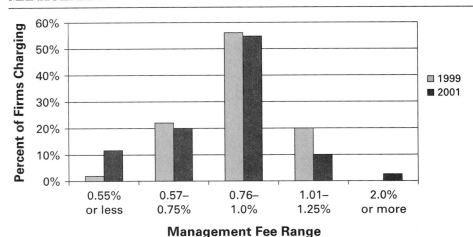

Source: Adapted from *Private Equity Funds-of-Funds State of the Market* (Asset Alternatives Research Report, 2nd edition, 2002), p. 56.

EXHIBIT 6.6b

CARRIED INTEREST RATES AMONG FUND-OF-FUNDS MANAGERS

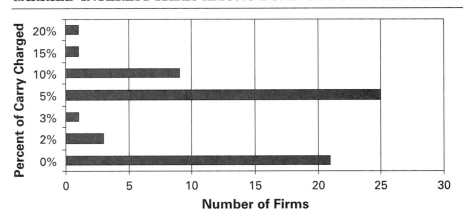

Source: Adapted from *Private Equity Funds-of-Funds State of the Market* (Asset Alternatives Research Report, 2nd edition, 2002), p. 59.

managers). For large investors, a fund-of-funds could manage a significant amount of money, parceling it out into various firms and handling the day-to-day details (see Exhibit 6.7 for the fund-of-funds' role). Despite the concern of many pension funds in keeping fees low, top funds-of-funds such as HarbourVest and Horsley-Bridge could charge an annual fee of 1 percent over a fund's twelve-year life.

Along with increasing money in the alternative asset markets came demands for more refined products. In the **classic blind pool,** the LP put money into a fund based

EXHIBIT 6.6c

HURDLE RATES AMONG FUND-OF-FUNDS MANAGERS

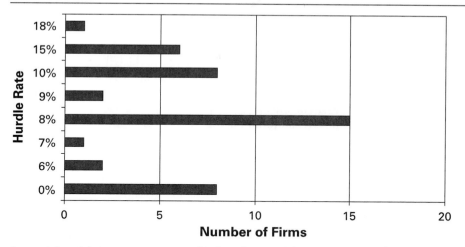

Source: Adapted from *Private Equity Funds-of-Funds State of the Market* (Asset Alternatives Research Report, 2nd edition, May 2003), pp. 61–62.

EXHIBIT 6.7

ROLE OF FUNDS-OF-FUNDS IN SCALING LP CONTRIBUTIONS

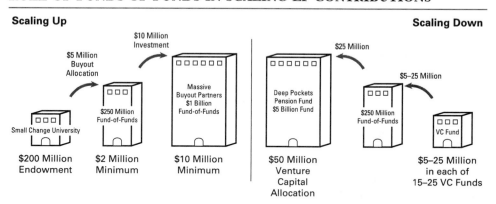

Source: Private Equity Funds-of-Funds State of the Market (Asset Alternatives Research Report, 2nd edition, May 2003.

on its prospectus (high tech, buyouts, or a balance of the two, for instance) and the fund manager allocated the monies to funds that met those qualifications. A **targeted fund-of-funds** allowed the LP more control of its investments, focusing on specific sectors (biotech, for instance) or geographies (a western pension fund might prefer to support western businesses). A **customized fund-of-funds** gave even more control to the LP. The fund manager would work with the LP to design a program that directly met the LP's needs. Sometimes, the LP even retained final authority over which funds would receive its investments. The line between the managers of funds like these (termed nondiscretionary funds) and **consulting services** provided by firms like Cambridge Associates and Wilshire was blurry, as the consultants would help determine optimal portfolio allocations for their clients and even suggest funds in which the client should invest. It was usually left up to the client to access the fund or fund-of-funds and manage its investment.

Pension fund advisors (generically known as **gatekeepers**) provided a similar service. For a set fee, these firms would help pension funds both allocate their funds across asset classes and evaluate the funds in which they could invest. Gatekeepers might also provide "outside opinion" on potential investments, fulfilling the requirement that state pension funds have such a review of investments. These were known for the extensive questionnaires that prospective fund managers, whether LBO or VC funds or funds-of-funds, had to fill out.

Along with the consultants and gatekeepers, a host of other alternative asset groups had evolved. Information providers, both rating agencies/consultants like Cambridge Associates and news sources like Thomson Financial, became more widely used. The rating agencies assessed the performance of the various VC firms, providing a report card of sorts for the LPs. These firms were compensated on a fee-for-service or a subscription basis. Based on these recommendations, the LP would invest in a firm or a fund-of-funds. Often, the candidate funds had to be screened by a gatekeeper.

Once an organization had invested in an alternative asset vehicle, it could call upon a number of groups to help manage that investment. In addition to standard reporting organizations such as Venture Economics, asset managers such as Franklin Park Advisors could help manage the risk of an LP's portfolio. An LP investing in a top-quartile fund-of-funds might find that it was overexposed to the telecommunications sector, as a majority of the top funds had invested in that area. Franklin Park could help it sell off some of these positions. Thus, an LP holding shares in telecommunications through a fund-of-funds that included Sequoia, Oak Investment Partners, and Mayfield would have to sell its position in one of those funds, rather than getting out of individual companies. These advisors also could assist in distribution management and, as happened in 2001 and 2002, in shedding entire positions on the secondary market when LPs were either overallocated in private equity or could not meet calls for capital pledged in more affluent days.

Other firms specialized in achieving liquidity for this notoriously illiquid asset class. Several groups would securitize the income stream from a private equity portfolio; others would strip off the income stream and sell that separately, as a derivative. These options were used, for the most part, by larger LPs that had a long history in private equity. In a number of cases, these strategies had been unsuccessful, due to insufficient demand and the difficulty of pricing them appropriately.

By 2003, as the public equity markets endured a second year of slumping performance, alternative assets markets exhibited a curious dynamic. Some of the more significant historical players, such as Yale University and JP Morgan Chase, were reducing their allocations. This was due in part to "denominator degradation"—in a sinking market, private equity holdings, which were re-valued only periodically, tended to lag the immediate price adjustments of publicly held stock, inadvertently inflating the value of the private equity portfolios. When an endowment targeted a certain percent for investment in alternative assets and the public markets fell, the portfolio might end up overweighted in private assets without increasing its investment activity. Thus, 2003 saw Yale scaling back its allocation from 22 percent to 17.5 percent to adjust. JP Morgan Chase halved its private equity commitment from 20 percent of capital to 10 percent in response to the tremendous losses it had suffered in the NASDAQ crash.[5]

Simultaneously, smaller organizations, especially state and even city pension funds, were pressured to increase their allocations. This was a response to the lackluster performance of public equities, to the organizations' historical underexposure to alternative assets, and to demographic trends. State and city pension funds faced an imminent burden with the aging of the Baby Boom generation. While over half of all pensions then offered were defined contribution plans (that is, the worker invested through an employer-sponsored scheme, often with an employer match, but without a guaranteed payout at retirement), the bulk of past plans were defined benefit, in which the employer guaranteed a certain income per month to the retiree. With more people retiring and fewer paying into such plans and the public markets slumping, the fund sponsors needed venture-level returns to keep the plans solvent. While the Internet bubble had left many suspicious of VC, the experience had amply demonstrated the asset's capacity for generating above-market returns. For a defined benefit plan sponsor, even modestly positive returns would outperform the markets of the early 2000s; thus, an increasing number of smaller pension funds were looking to put money in alternative assets even as the bigger players pulled back (see Exhibit 6.8 for capital committed to funds-of-funds).

PENSION FUNDS AND PRIVATE EQUITY

Perhaps more than any other type of LP, public pension funds had a difficult time with private equity. Unlike other players, these funds knew that their performance

EXHIBIT 6.8

COMMITMENTS TO FUNDS-OF-FUNDS, 1995–2001

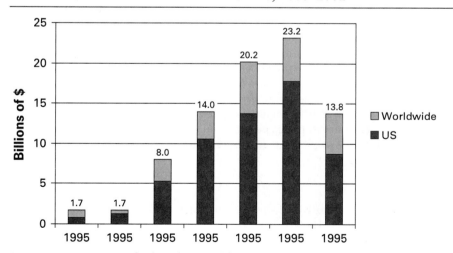

Source: *Private Equity Funds-of-Funds State of the Market* (Asset Alternatives Research Report, 2nd edition, May 2003), p. 24.

5. Robert Clow and Lina Saigol, "Big Banks Nurse Private Equity Wounds," FT.com (December 12, 2002), p. 1.

and decisions could become political fodder. Their governance boards tended to be large, and often lacked a background in finance and investing. The staff, all state employees, was compensated on a state salary scale. Particularly talented individuals were often recruited away by the groups in which they invested. Relatively few had direct private equity experience, and even fewer had VC expertise and contacts. Worse yet, their reputations would likely suffer far more from a bad decision than they would be burnished by a good one.

Nonetheless, although the ERISA rule clarification in 1979 applied only to private pension funds, public pension funds began investing in private equity, initially in buyouts. Not only did buyouts provide better returns in the 1980s, but they also were easier for multibillion-dollar funds to invest in. For a small staff managing a $100 billion fund, even a 2 percent allocation to private equity was $2 billion. The buyout industry, with average funds above $120 million in most of the 1980s, could handle this volume far better than could VC, where average funds in that decade never exceeded $50 million.[6] In addition, a buyout fund had a shorter life, tying up the investment for between seven and ten years, rather than the ten to twelve of a VC fund.

Eventually, however, the public pension funds ran against two phenomena. Returns to buyouts sagged in the early 1990s, as those to VC began rising. In addition, as the target allocations rose from 0 to 2 to 5 to 7 percent for CalPERS in 1996, the sheer amount of money entering the buyout market meant that an organization of CalPERS's size would be competing against itself for deals, as it had money in all the good buyout funds. The pension funds had to get into VC.

Here, however, they encountered a number of structural barriers. Not only did they have too much money to allocate and not enough contacts within the industry to get into the best firms, but each limited partnership would tie up the money for at least ten years. With pension fund boards changing every few years, this meant that the chairman who approved a given investment would rarely be in place to enjoy its rewards. VC also required a back office to respond to capital calls, and an investment staff prepared to weather the rigors of the J-curve, that early period of a fund's life before investments were harvested. Last, to guard against uninformed decisions, pension funds were often required to have a gatekeeper approve their decisions. To gather the necessary information, the gatekeepers routinely required potential funds to fill out 100-page questionnaires. As Barry Gonder, former senior investment officer for CalPERS and now a general partner at GSA, explained, "If you want to get in to Kleiner Perkins, you don't go to them with a 100-page questionnaire. You go to them, get down on your knees, and beg." As additional disincentives for VC funds, most public pension funds also had a time-consuming approval process for each fund-level investment, and needed elaborate and detailed quarterly reports from the GPs.

CALPERS

In 1998, CalPERS faced an additional challenge. Despite a private equity investment effort since 1990, it had only succeeded in allocating $1 billion of its target allocation of $15 billion to that sector. In 1996, it had hired Gonder, who had an extensive background in private equity and venture capital investing for Connecticut Mutual Insurance and Travelers Insurance, to create a world-class private equity program and ramp its private equity allocation up to 5 to 10 percent of its assets. CalPERS's board had found itself unable to invest in the booming Silicon Valley venture scene ninety miles away, not only because of the scale of its allocation but also because GPs viewed the

---

6. Data from Venture Expert at www.ventureexpert.com, accessed August 27, 2003.

organization as having a difficult process and as being tough (or difficult, depending on one's perspective) negotiators, particularly with regard to fee structures.[7] For example, CalPERS's chief investment officer in the mid-1990s had attempted to lead a revolt against the fee structure of the big buyout house Kohlberg, Kravis & Roberts. Instead of changing the structure of a 1.6 percent fee and 20 percent carry, KKR excluded CalPERS and raised its fund on the original terms.[8]

Gonder said:

> When I came to CalPERS, I found that 89 percent of private equity was in big leveraged buyout funds. There was little venture, and even less in the top-tier. It wasn't surprising—I found that it took us nine months and one week to approve a transaction. The staff had no discretion; everything had to go to the investment committee.[9] The investment committee was the entire board and met ten times a year. These people are hard-working and dedicated; it's just that the process did not meet the needs of the top-tier venture capitalists. We had to create a mechanism for CalPERS to access the top-tier venture firms in a way that met both of their needs.

Early in his tenure with CalPERS, Gonder encountered the need for this mechanism directly. As he explained, "I called partners at several of the top-tier firms with whom I'd invested when I was at Connecticut Mutual and Travelers. I said, 'I'd like to invest with you.' They said, 'Sure, Barry, let's talk. Who are you with now?' I'd say, 'CalPERS,' and there would be a moment of silence, and they would say, 'Well, good luck to you.'"

GROVE STREET ADVISORS

At the end of 1997, Clint Harris and Catherine Crockett, with advisory help from David Mazza, decided to fill that need. Harris, who had joined Bain Consulting when it was at forty employees and left when it had 1,000 to help Peter Brooke start Advent International, described the genesis of the idea:

> The idea for Grove Street came from my experience in raising money for Advent. Here was a firm founded on Peter Brooke's reputation from TA Associates and the concept of an international network of private equity firms. Yale and Harvard backed us; it was a classic first-time fund with proven people, but regardless of Peter's record, we had no chance of raising money from the gatekeepers. In 1997, we raised our fourth fund of $1.3 billion in about six months, and by this time we were talking with some gatekeepers. We spent a huge proportion of our time and energy with these organizations, and at the end of the period, the fund was oversubscribed and we called the gatekeepers to let them know we were closing it. Two could not have cared less. Two said they could not invest in an international fund—so why were they talking with a fund named Advent International? And two said they were very interested but needed two more months to complete their analysis. The way the gatekeepers ran their businesses made no sense to me, and I could not understand why large institutional investors would

7. Vishesh Kumar, "No More Mr. Mean Guy," *Industry Standard* (April 27, 2001).

8. Barry Rehfeld, "No Alternative," *Institutional Investor* (April 1997), p. 75.

9. This has since changed and the staff has discretion for investments up to $100 million as long as there is an outside opinion.

want to have such representation. Yet they controlled a large amount of the money available to private equity.

So I began thinking about how I would design a firm in that space. There seemed to be a much better business model than that which was being used, and if you could pull it off, there were some really attractive things about the market. For one, public pension fund managers have to use an outside advisor, so the business is not going to go away. Also, if your group could gain the respect of the private equity fund managers, they'd serve as your sales force, because fund managers are always asking one another about the good LPs. It's a circular question; you can find the good funds by finding the good LPs. And if you structured the relationship correctly, you could measure your performance and develop a defensible position.

Crockett came from a different but complementary background. With a degree from Harvard's Kennedy School of Government, she had been involved in economically targeted investment (ETI), the use of private equity—broadly defined to include research and development, buyouts, tech commercialization, and venture capital—for economic development. She said, "After fifteen years, I needed a change. I had evaluated markets; identified, evaluated, and built management teams; structured LP agreements; created partnership teams—and all in the toughest markets. With GSA, I could do it in any market I wanted!"

Harris and Crockett had worked together on some of her projects, first with another partner and later with her own firm, the Gazelle Group. Crockett's experience gave the new firm some important advantages in its plan to create customized private equity investment programs for small public pension funds. She noted, "I knew the concerns of the pension funds and I knew the very unique culture of government entities. Just the fact that I'd done ETI turned out to be valuable."

Mazza, a sectionmate of Harris at Harvard Business School, initially served as an advisor to Harris and Crockett. Having sold his second company, a recruiting firm, to Korn Ferry International in 1996, he was not quite ready to throw himself into building yet another business from scratch. Harris and Crockett very much wanted him to join them due to his fifteen years of experience in recruiting GPs to venture firms and senior executives to portfolio companies. Said Harris, "Dave's sense of people flow meant that we wouldn't just identify teams, we'd be able to complete them." While he formally recruited fifty or more general partners, he also informally introduced numerous CEOs and general partners to his venture capital clients, who ended up working with those firms. Mazza explained:

> For about a decade, from 1985 to 1995, the venture capital recruiting market was small but growing fast. One other search professional, Steve Potter, who founded the Highland Search Group, and I handled the vast majority of it. Between Steve and myself, we recruited over 100 general partners and probably an equal number of associates, vice presidents, and principals. To accomplish that, we interviewed over 1,000 private equity professionals, meaning that collectively, we knew just about everyone in the market. Once I sold my firm, that dynamic changed, but I still retained my long-term relationships that included someone in almost every firm in the industry. So, when I call for references on someone, I'm usually talking to people who trust me and will give me an accurate read on a situation.

THE CALPERS CONNECTION

GSA's founders met Barry Gonder and Rick Hayes in the summer of 1998. Gonder and Hayes felt that CalPERS should have a customized portfolio with access to top-quartile venture capital, especially the Silicon Valley firms. With Gonder's industry background, he also brought an unusual requirement—he wanted an alignment of interests between CalPERS and the group managing its VC effort. This meshed with Harris's belief that GSA should operate and be compensated like a VC fund—with a fee, carry above a hurdle, and the GSA partners' commitment to co-invest alongside CalPERS. This had been highly unusual in the early funds-of-funds but was becoming more common in the late 1990s (refer to Exhibits 6.6a–6.6c for typical fund-of-funds compensation rates).

CalPERS distributed a request for proposals for its $350 million (over three to four years) private equity investment effort. Thirty firms responded, one of them GSA. The process involved filling out the requisite questionnaire, proposing a structure, and providing references. From the thirty applicants, CalPERS chose four finalists, which made two-hour presentations to the board. On October 22, five months after GSA had opened its doors, it learned that it had won the assignment. With that news and the knowledge that there would be enough work to keep everyone busy, Mazza agreed to join as general partner.

GSA's program had three components. First was California Emerging Ventures I (CEV I), a $350 million dedicated fund-of-funds that GSA would invest at its discretion.[10] No more than $25 million would go to any one fund, and no more than 10 percent would go to international vehicles. Of the $350 million, between $250 million and $300 million would go into fund partnerships, while up to $100 million could be co-invested directly in portfolio companies. The second aspect focused on identifying and funding new teams. Termed the "turnkey" program, this tapped into Mazza's extensive network of private equity personnel. In addition to forming new teams, GSA would also fund these new groups. The last component of the CalPERS program involved a nondiscretionary fund for investment opportunities that GSA discovered and brought to CalPERS's attention.

One of GSA's most effective selling points was its willingness to transfer the relationship with the VC firm eventually to the client. The process would work as follows:

1. GSA would invest $10 million from its CalPERS fund (CEV I) in a good fund. As Crockett described it, "We'd say, 'We're GSA, you know us. We want you to get to know CalPERS through us.'"

2. When the VC firm raised another fund, GSA would again invest $10 million from its CalPERS fund (CEV I or a successor) and provide CalPERS the ability and discretion to co-invest up to an additional $40 million of CalPERS's own money alongside GSA. This gave the VC firm a chance to know CalPERS more directly, and gave CalPERS a very cost-effective way to invest. In this phase of the process, GSA was compensated with a reduced fee structure.

3. In the third fund, all the money came from CalPERS and the investment went into the CalPERS core portfolio. GSA would receive no compensation at this stage of the relationship.

---

10. In a "discretionary" fund, once the manager and LP agree to an investment charter, the fund can be invested as the manager sees fit without approval of the LP. A "nondiscretionary" fund requires approval of the LP for each investment decision.

GSA's attention to new and emerging funds was another point of differentiation. Of the $250 million to $300 million that would go to fund investments, one-third was earmarked for emerging funds because, as Harris described:

> I have seen that many partners get to the middle of their careers and they're ready for a change, whether to get their name on the door or because they're worried about the succession plan. The reason that Harvard and Yale have such large allocations in so many great firms is that they backed them at the beginning. We're committed to getting CalPERS into the exciting new and emerging funds that will end up in the top-tier. And with CalPERS's money, there's a better chance that they can succeed, because they won't have to spend the same amount of time fund-raising; they can get to the business of investing.

The compensation structure had two aspects and was designed to reward GSA for exemplary performance. GSA charged a fee slightly lower than the typical pooled fund-of-funds and reduced it by increments over time (see Exhibit 6.6a). Over the life of the program, the fee was less than half that of a typical fund-of-funds and matched the actual workload. Carry generally conformed to industry norms (see Exhibit 6.6b) and was paid only above a performance hurdle higher than the industry average (see Exhibit 6.6c). "At returns of 18 percent or so, the compensation structure is equivalent to the level of a typical large institutional fund-of-funds provider," said Harris. "Below that, we're a better deal, and above that we earn more but only on the strength of performance."

NEW AND EMERGING FUNDS

GSA invested in new funds in two ways. The first was a conventional investment in a fund being raised by a new group. The second approach was more proactive. Mazza's network often brought word of new groups that were forming. CalPERS, with $6 billion to get into VC, had lots of money to put to work. GSA would take a lead investor role and would make a significant investment, getting in on the ground floor with a promising new group. It would usually negotiate a lower level of fees and carry in the first fund, and any discounts on fees would be shared with CalPERS. It was hoped that this early support would assure CalPERS of a seat at future funds (see Exhibit 6.9a for the lifecycles of private equity fund managers).

Mazza's network conveyed side benefits as well. In one example, when CalPERS was considering investing in an LBO fund, Mazza's friends in the LBO search industry warned that half the partners in that fund were actively interviewing for other positions. CalPERS passed on the opportunity.

Mazza had been involved in starting new firms in the past, explaining:

> I'd made some introductions that had gotten firms off the ground—Highland Capital, for instance, and North Bridge. With North Bridge, I'd been helping two friends with some career advice and finally decided to introduce them. I told them I didn't know if they'd make it through breakfast because they had such different styles but both had good track records investing in information technology companies. They have proceeded to build one of the top venture capital funds of the '90s.
>
> What you find is that people know each other in this industry, but they rarely know if a colleague is unhappy in a certain situation. As a trusted third

EXHIBIT 6.9a

LIFE CYCLES OF PRIVATE EQUITY FUND MANAGERS

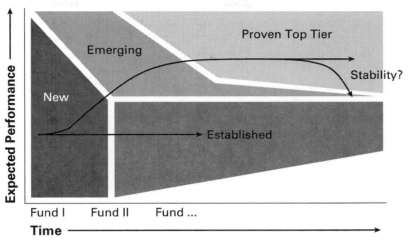

Source: Company information.

party, though, I become privy to that information, and can make matches. The new team will almost always figure out a way to work together for the first few funds. After all, it's their name on the door and their independent reputation to make, and they'll work really hard. In the fourth or fifth fund, if the personal chemistry has been poor, it is possible that the partners will opt to part ways. At that point they have made their names, money for their LPs and themselves, and they have a reduced incentive to make it work. This is obviously a worst case scenario, but by then, they have developed a track record, a larger team and the fund itself has been established, so there is less reliance on any single individual.

He described the difference with GSA as, "Now, though, we're not just introducing people; we can write a check to get them off the ground." (See Exhibit 6.9b for new funds GSA had backed.)

On Beyond CEV I

Before the documents on CEV I were signed in early 1999, GSA had obtained places in both Technology Crossover Ventures and idealab!, investments that produced immediate successes and allowed GSA to report a 322 percent IRR in its first quarter's report to CalPERS. During 1999, GSA also assisted in the creation of two firms: Audax, a private equity holding company founded by two ex-Bain Capital partners, and Solera Capital.

The entire VC industry was on fast-forward. Crockett said:

In 1999, a lot of good firms came onto the market. We had expected to invest CEV I over a normal fund cycle of two or three years, but the normal cycle

---

EXHIBIT 6.9b

FUNDS ESTABLISHED THROUGH GSA'S EMERGING FUNDS PROGRAM

Audax Group—The first spinout from Bain Capital, the Audax Group is a broad-based alternative asset investment management group with buyout and mezzanine investing teams.

Solera Capital—Strong NYC-based team focused on later-stage venture capital and growth equity.

New Mountain Capital—A buyout firm founded by a former senior partner from Forstmann Little.

MPM BioEquities—The industry's first premier healthcare "crossover" vehicle investing in small public companies and late-stage private deals, MPM BioEquities was launched in cooperation with MPM Capital, the largest biotechnology-focused healthcare venture capital group in the world.

Falconhead Capital—A joint venture with IMG, the world's leading sports, entertainment and lifestyle management and marketing company, Falconhead Capital is a $215 million fund that focuses on private equity investments where Falconhead's exclusive, contractual relationship with IMG can deliver proprietary investment opportunities, access to key employees for due diligence, and significant value to portfolio companies.

Source: Company information.

> became one year. We had to decide how to respond. We could invest in, say, eight of the top funds that we wanted this year. Then next year, assuming they were out raising money again, to be a good partner we would either have to invest again, which would be unusual out of the same CEV pool, or be seen as uncertain money and pass in order to invest with another good fund. We'd planned to get into twenty-five funds or so—but over three years. Now we could either invest in eight, three times in three years, or all twenty-five in one. Together with CalPERS, we decided to create a follow-on pool of capital and accelerate the process lest we miss the chance at some really good funds.

CalPERS committed $400 million to CEV II in June 2000 and $500 million to CEV III in March 2001, both on the same terms as CEV I. In addition, CalPERS created a supplemental pool to invest in funds alongside CEV II and III when GSA could obtain a larger allocation and CalPERS wanted more than $25 million of the fund. GSA received reduced compensation on these extra investments, but this strategy facilitated the transfer process. Mazza commented, "We had demonstrated that we could get into good funds." By the end of 2002, GSA managed a total of $2.75 billion for CalPERS, including about $1.25 billion in the dedicated funds-of-funds and $1.5 billion in nondiscretionary supplemental investments. The direct investment program had been halted in mid-2000.

GSA had stopped the direct investment program for several reasons. The first was staff. GSA had been staffed to invest CEV I over three years. With fund-raising velocity almost tripling, the firm simply did not have sufficient resources to manage the fund investment activity and the direct investment activity equally well. Harris explained:

> We want to add value to the funds in which we participate. Money is cheap, but if we can provide a recruitment lead or a lead on a deal, we've distinguished ourselves. It's also great due diligence; the best way to learn about

people is to do a deal with them. But there were conflicts of interest—a firm might offer us a good deal and one they had trouble financing, and there'd be an implicit quid pro quo—and the sheer amount of time that it took distracted us from the core fund-of-funds program.

In addition, Harris noted, "We felt that the pricing was going crazy. It was difficult to get into the first round of a good deal, and the follow-ons were wildly expensive." GSA only invested approximately $25 million of the $100 million intended for the direct investment program. The rest was reallocated to special situations (including secondary opportunities)[11] and funds.

Thus far, the relationships and the concept of getting in on the ground floor had been working for both GSA and CalPERS, despite some challenges. In 2002, a newspaper had sued CalPERS to disclose the results from its venture capital investments, usually highly secret and guarded information (see Exhibits 6.10a and 6.10b for the results CalPERS published). CalPERS had established a policy to disclose only fund-level results, not any information at the portfolio company level, but other public institutions (most notably The University of Texas) disclosed fund-level performance as well as selected terms from LP agreements. Some other LPs, looking for larger positions in funds, had tried to make this a reason to shut CalPERS out of firms that it had backed initially. Crockett commented, "The disclosure issue can be handled with careful reporting. But it did strain the trust of some nervous GPs. Most of them, 90 percent, are fine but a few are skittish."

Mazza elaborated:

> Before we were involved with CalPERS, some VCs were scared of their onerous process. Disclosure has brought back that uneasiness. It's a little counterintuitive; the best venture firms are frequently the ones most sensitive to disclosure. But you can see it—they are smaller, perform better, and can pick and choose their investors. So why deal with any LP issue if they don't have to?

Running CEV

GSA aimed to make decisions in six weeks. Harris said, "Venture capitalists have to say 'No' a hundred times. It's how you say that 'No' that makes all the difference. I see no reason that we cannot run this process in the same way that a venture capitalist runs

---

EXHIBIT 6.10a

GSA'S RESULTS FOR CALPERS AS OF JUNE 2003

Fund Description	Vintage Year	Capital Committed	Cash In	Cash Out	Cash Out & Remaining Value	Net IRR	Investment Multiple
California Emerging Ventures I, LLC	1999	954,252,442	567,122,081	56,673,037	448,161,418	(11.42)	0.79×
California Emerging Ventures II, LLC	2000	1,360,275,465	515,583,437	45,657,730	388,849,334	(17.83)	0.75×
California Emerging Ventures III, LLC	2001	552,602,084	31,806,895	245,558	18,716,043	(49.54)	0.59×

Source: http://www.calpers.ca.gov/invest/aim/aim.asp, accessed November 13, 2003.

---

11. A secondary opportunity occurred when an LP already in a private equity fund wanted to sell that position.

EXHIBIT 6.10b

CEV CONSTITUENT FUNDS' PERFORMANCE AS OF JUNE 30, 2003

The following exhibit is an excerpt from the CalPERS Web site and reflects only the GSA-managed programs (CEV, CEV II, and CEV III) as of June 30, 2003, updated quarterly and posted on the CalPERS Web site at http://www.calpers.ca.gov/invest/aim/aim-detail. The introductory section below must be viewed by every user who accesses performance data on any of CalPERS's fund commitments, not just those managed by GSA.

How to Read the Performance Review Table

The table, which is updated quarterly, provides information on the status of the CalPERS private equity commitments. The left-hand column lists all funds to which CalPERS has committed capital. The column "Capital Committed" identifies the original amount CalPERS agreed to invest in each fund. "Cash In" represents capital contributed for investments and management fees. "Cash Out" represents distributions CalPERS has received from the fund.

Reported performance may reflect a variety of factors. One fund may be in the formative stage when management fees have a larger negative impact on results in the initial years (see our Private Equity Performance Review section that discusses the J-Curve Effect). Another fund may be realizing investments in some companies and distributing the proceeds to investors. Performance may also be influenced by the performance cycle within industries or the strategies in which funds invest, such as technology versus manufacturing, or venture capital versus buyout. There are no generally accepted standards, practices, or policies for reporting private equity valuations. Generally, private equity partnerships take ten to twelve years to realize full value. Most general partners tend to have a conservative valuation approach, and as a result interim reported values could differ materially from the values realized when portfolio companies are sold. For these reasons it is not always meaningful to compare the interim returns or multiples for funds, particularly for funds of different vintage years or investment strategies.

In evaluating private equity performance, CalPERS emphasizes using both the realized IRR along with "Cash Out & Remaining Value" divided by the Cash In. Interim IRRs by themselves are not the best indicators of how a fund is performing or how it will perform over its full life.

Note: The reported value figures shown are reported by the general partners. For funds formed during or after a vintage year of 1998, the investment multiple was noted as "N/M," which means Not Meaningful. Industry practice dictates that these funds are in the early stages of their investment life cycle and any performance analysis done on these funds would not generate meaningful results as private equity funds are understood to be long-term investments. It is strongly advised that you review our information on the J-Curve Effect: Earning Acceptable Returns under the Private Equity Performance Review area for detailed explanation. The term "N/A" means Not Available.

Fund Description	Vintage Year°	Capital Committed	Cash In	Cash Out	Cash Out & Remaining Value	Net IRR†	Investment Multiple‡
Aberdare Ventures II, L.P.	2002	$20,000,000	$3,265,005	$0	$2,441,509	(27.60)%	0.75×
Aberdare Ventures, L.P.	1999	2,500,000	2,011,000	0	1,083,009	(20.30)	0.54×
Acacia Venture Partners II, L.P.	1999	10,000,000	8,249,076	507,479	1,728,968	(48.20)	0.21×
Alloy Ventures 2000, L.P	2000	10,000,000	8,000,000	1,037,310	6,922,117	(9.00)	0.87×
Alloy Ventures 2002, L.P.	2002	10,000,000	1,500,000	220,974	1,717,846	26.80	1.15×
Apax Israel II L.P.	1999	5,000,000	3,850,000	762,404	1,699,950	(33.40)	0.44×

Notes: IRRs and multiples are irrelevant at the early stage of these funds' lives.

° Vintage Years are determined based on the later of i) the date CEV first contributed capital to the fund or ii) the date the fund made its first investment.

† IRR is calculated based upon actual dates of cash flows and quarter-end valuations. The IRR calculation includes interest paid, if applicable.

‡ Multiple is calculated as "Cash Out + Remaining Value" divided by "Cash In."

§ Berkshire values its portfolio annually; therefore interim IRRs are not necessarily representative of intrayear changes in value.

|| "Cash In" was drawn for organization costs and management fees only, no investments made to date.

Commitment is denominated in foreign currency, therefore U.S. dollar commitment will fluctuate quarter-to-quarter.

Source: http://www.calpers.ca.gov/invest/aim/aim-detail.asp?FundOfFunds=2, accessed November 13, 2003.

(Continues)

EXHIBIT 6.10b (CONTINUED)

CEV CONSTITUENT FUNDS' PERFORMANCE AS OF JUNE 30, 2003

Fund Description	Vintage Year°	Capital Committed	Cash In	Cash Out	Cash Out & Remaining Value	Net IRR[†]	Investment Multiple[‡]
Applied Genomic Technology Capital Fund, L.P.	2001	5,000,000	2,375,000	0	1,582,748	(26.20)	0.67×
ARCH Venture Fund V, L.P.	2001	12,500,000	5,812,500	18,949	4,819,201	(12.00)	0.83×
ArrowPath Fund II, L.P.	2001	5,000,000	1,075,000	175,348	865,908	(18.80)	0.81×
Atlas Venture Fund VI, L.P.	2001	6,200,000	1,230,226	0	872,967	(28.60)	0.71×
Audax Mezzanine Fund, L.P.	2002	100,000,000	23,901,597	585,034	22,496,779	(7.30)	0.94×
Audax Private Equity Fund, L.P.	2000	100,000,000	61,600,549	2,600,613	51,988,446	(11.50)	0.84×
Audax Venture Fund, L.P.	2000	11,250,000	11,250,000	1,169,453	4,632,513	(30.20)	0.41×
Austin Ventures VII, L.P.	1999	15,000,000	10,363,634	618,728	6,209,988	(23.60)	0.60×
Austin Ventures VIII, L.P.	2001	41,500,000	10,250,000	1,149,429	6,944,395	(31.20)	0.68×
Battery Ventures VI, L.P.	2000	7,500,000	3,862,500	780,574	2,351,601	(30.50)	0.61×
Bay Partners X, L.P.	2001	20,000,000	4,000,000	0	2,637,520	(27.00)	0.66×
Berkshire Fund VI, Limited Partnership§	2002	25,000,000	3,368,411	787	3,668,950	21.20	1.09×
BlueStream Ventures, L.P.	2000	7,500,000	4,125,000	440,879	1,840,759	(33.20)	0.45×
Carmel Software Fund (Delaware) L.P.	2000	2,500,000	1,187,500	0	678,094	(29.60)	0.57×
Clearstone Venture Partners I-B, L.P.	1999	2,500,000	2,500,000	5,986,137	6,834,037	156.90	2.73×
Clearstone Venture Partners II-A, L.P.	1999	20,000,000	12,600,000	2,977,316	7,800,916	(18.90)	0.62×
Commonwealth Capital Ventures III, L.P. (A)	2000	5,000,000	2,075,000	0	1,161,929	(35.10)	0.56×
Convergence Ventures II, L.P.	1999	5,000,000	4,218,500	0	792,526	(49.40)	0.19×
DCM III, L.P.	2000	25,000,000	10,625,000	551,750	7,727,468	(21.00)	0.73×
Draper Fisher Jurvetson Fund VII, L.P.	2000	25,000,000	8,437,500	0	4,666,229	(34.00)	0.55×
F.V.E., L.P.	2002	7,610,624	4,718,587	0	3,439,216	(31.30)	0.73×
FBR Technology Venture Partners II (QP), L.P.	2000	2,500,000	2,035,000	90,694	371,463	(48.90)	0.18×
FFC Partners II, L.P.	2000	6,000,000	2,930,603	12,472	2,650,515	(6.50)	0.90×
Fletcher Spaght Ventures, L.P.	2001	5,000,000	725,000	0	466,567	(39.90)	0.64×
Focus Ventures II, L.P.	2000	5,000,000	3,150,000	172,242	923,971	(43.60)	0.29×
Frontenac VIII Limited Partnership	2000	10,000,000	4,700,000	25,026	1,605,814	(50.80)	0.34×
Gemini Israel III Limited Partnership	2000	2,500,000	1,375,000	0	936,660	(17.80)	0.68×
General Catalyst Group II, L.P.	2001	25,000,000	7,500,000	0	6,304,214	(14.60)	0.84×
General Catalyst Group, LLC	2000	3,975,000	3,378,750	0	1,804,232	(22.30)	0.53×
Global Catalyst Partners II, L.P.	2002	5,000,000	1,500,000	0	1,048,090	(43.10)	0.70×
Granite Global Ventures (Q.P.) L.P.	2001	7,500,000	3,187,500	0	2,008,267	(32.90)	0.63×
GRP II, L.P.	2000	5,000,000	1,850,132	18,950	1,380,999	(15.60)	0.75×
HealthCap IV, L.P.#	2002	6,119,216	761,415	0	574,526	(27.90)	0.75×
Healthcare Focus Fund, L.P.	2001	30,000,000	17,250,000	0	15,354,341	(10.10)	0.89×
Highland Capital Partners V Limited Partnership	2000	5,000,000	3,358,546	739,693	2,164,110	(17.70)	0.64×
Highland Capital Partners VI Limited Partnership	2001	35,000,000	5,162,500	0	3,770,831	(30.40)	0.73×

(Continues)

EXHIBIT 6.10b *(CONTINUED)*

CEV CONSTITUENT FUNDS' PERFORMANCE AS OF JUNE 30, 2003

Fund Description	Vintage Year*	Capital Committed	Cash In	Cash Out	Cash Out & Remaining Value	Net IRR†	Investment Multiple‡
ICPE, L.P.	2000	2,389,376	2,110,279	0	156,195	(48.50)	0.07×
I-Hatch Ventures, L.P.	2000	3,625,000	2,554,684	0	1,120,666	(28.30)	0.44×
Index Ventures II (Delaware), L.P.	2001	5,000,000	847,339	0	597,134	(26.40)	0.70×
Insight Capital Partners III, L.P.	1999	7,500,000	7,381,407	1,744,216	4,711,025	(16.20)	0.64×
Insight Venture Partners IV, L.P.	2000	40,000,000	15,200,000	383,160	10,186,908	(26.00)	0.67×
Institutional Venture Partners X, L.P.	2001	10,000,000	5,000,000	0	3,840,206	(15.90)	0.77×
International Life Sciences Fund III (LP1), L.P.	2002	10,000,000	1,250,000	0	831,652	(33.40)	0.67×
Israel Seed IV, L.P.	2000	2,500,000	1,187,500	0	559,454	(32.50)	0.47×
Jerusalem Venture Partners IV, L.P.	2001	7,500,000	2,925,000	0	1,961,006	(24.90)	0.67×
JMI Equity Fund IV, L.P.	1999	2,500,000	1,319,093	118,874	887,097	(15.40)	0.67×
Kettle Partners Limited Partnership II	2000	2,500,000	1,491,250	0	423,657	(51.60)	0.28×
KPS Special Situations Fund II, L.P.	2003	10,000,000	882,477	0	812,294	(94.40)	0.92×
Lake Capital Partners L.P.	2002	10,000,000	402,180	0	0	(90.70)	0.00×
Lighthouse Capital Partners III, L.P.	1999	10,000,000	8,500,000	7,021,866	9,333,078	4.50	1.10×
Lighthouse Capital Partners IV, L.P.	2000	50,000,000	30,000,000	2,500,000	23,773,919	(11.60)	0.79×
Lightspeed Venture Partners VI, L.P.	2000	40,000,000	14,474,995	431,402	8,334,366	(29.90)	0.58×
Lime Rock Partners II, L.P.	2003	10,000,000	2,077,903	0	1,920,530	(19.40)	0.92×
Menlo Ventures IX, L.P.	2001	15,000,000	4,500,000	0	3,477,670	(18.90)	0.77×
Morgan Stanley Dean Witter Venture Partners IV, L.P.	1999	5,000,000	4,058,432	0	1,346,391	(32.20)	0.33×
Morgenthaler Partners VII, L.P.	2001	10,000,000	2,500,000	0	1,972,953	(19.70)	0.79×
MPM BioVentures III-QP, L.P.	2002	50,000,000	8,500,000	0	7,688,313	(15.20)	0.90×
MPM BioVentures II-QP, L.P.	2000	5,000,000	4,075,000	0	2,989,734	(13.60)	0.73×
Nautic Partners V, L.P.	2000	10,000,000	3,586,890	1,449	2,803,826	(27.60)	0.78×
New Enterprise Associates 10, Limited Partnership	2000	75,000,000	35,625,000	2,526,546	28,998,356	(13.10)	0.81×
New Enterprise Associates 9, Limited Partnership	1999	5,000,000	4,900,000	158,463	1,978,687	(29.10)	0.40×
New Mountain Partners, L.P.	2000	100,025,000	33,253,179	10,425,607	44,422,149	17.90	1.34×
North Bridge Venture Partners IV-B, L.P.	1999	10,000,000	6,400,000	1,687,252	4,649,055	(16.80)	0.73×
North Bridge Venture Partners V-A, L.P.	2001	40,000,000	8,000,000	1,453,634	5,742,040	(27.80)	0.72×
Oak Investment Partners IX, Limited Partnership	1999	10,000,000	8,125,000	541,235	2,803,275	(40.90)	0.35×
Oak Investment Partners X, Limited Partnership	2001	25,000,000	8,829,690	0	5,568,071	(31.00)	0.63×
OVP Venture Partners VI, L.P.	2001	5,000,000	637,500	0	400,248	(47.80)	0.63×
Oxford Bioscience Partners III L.P.	1999	2,500,000	2,312,500	0	1,446,607	(18.80)	0.63×
Oxford Bioscience Partners IV L.P.	2001	30,000,000	11,250,000	0	10,886,547	(3.30)	0.97×
Palomar Ventures II, L.P.	2000	7,500,000	2,257,500	0	1,609,945	(26.00)	0.71×

(Continues)

EXHIBIT 6.10b (CONTINUED)

CEV CONSTITUENT FUNDS' PERFORMANCE AS OF JUNE 30, 2003

Fund Description	Vintage Year°	Capital Committed	Cash In	Cash Out	Cash Out & Remaining Value	Net IRR[†]	Investment Multiple[‡]
Partech International Ventures IV	2000	5,000,000	2,162,571	0	812,601	(35.80)	0.38×
Pinnacle Ventures I-B, L.P.	2002	30,040,859	6,008,625	0	5,204,762	(34.07)	0.87×
Pitango Capital Fund III (USA) L.P.	2000	5,000,000	2,800,000	0	1,798,326	(21.60)	0.64×
Polaris Venture Partners IV, L.P.	2002	10,000,000	300,000	0	142,172	(64.40)	0.47×
Prism Venture Partners III, L.P.	2000	5,000,000	4,175,000	0	2,275,078	(26.30)	0.54×
Prism Venture Partners IV, L.P.	2001	25,000,000	8,000,000	0	6,021,854	(22.00)	0.75×
Quadrangle Capital Partners L.P.	2000	50,000,000	27,114,204	0	29,495,149	7.50	1.09×
Redpoint Ventures II, L.P.	2000	9,000,000	3,240,000	0	1,996,382	(25.20)	0.62×
Reliant Equity Partners, L.P.‖	N/A‖	25,000,000	1,162,189	0	14,808	N/A	0.01×
Rosewood Capital IV, L.P.	2000	50,000,000	20,422,765	467,050	12,079,054	(30.90)	0.59×
Schroder Ventures International Life Sciences Fund II, L.P. 1	1999	10,000,000	9,500,000	732,106	7,654,366	(8.90)	0.81×
Sequel Limited Partnership II	1999	7,500,000	6,825,000	300,604	2,744,685	(28.30)	0.40×
Sequel Limited Partnership III	2000	25,000,000	8,000,000	229,093	5,157,302	(28.60)	0.64×
Sevin Rosen Fund VIII L.P.	2000	10,290,000	4,596,750	0	2,780,198	(32.80)	0.60×
Sierra Ventures VIII-A, L.P.	2000	20,000,000	6,000,000	0	3,977,890	(23.90)	0.66×
Skyline Venture Partners Qualified Purchaser Fund III, L.P.	2001	5,000,000	1,550,000	0	1,348,804	(13.90)	0.87×
Solera Partners, L.P.	2000	75,000,000	20,717,009	29,445	14,576,024	(14.80)	0.70×
Spectrum Equity Investors IV, L.P.	2000	75,000,000	30,375,000	9,927,195	24,310,677	(16.80)	0.80×
Sports Capital Partners CEV, LLC	2001	122,000,000	65,284,910	0	43,674,542	(30.56)	0.67×
Summit Accelerator Fund, L.P.	1999	1,500,000	945,000	131,689	569,482	(19.90)	0.60×
Summit Ventures VI-A, L.P.	2001	25,000,000	4,250,000	298,443	3,512,982	(17.30)	0.83×
TA IX, L.P.	2000	61,500,000	19,680,000	0	19,075,245	(2.00)	0.97×
TA Subordinated Debt Fund, L.P.	2000	38,500,000	10,587,500	2,464,000	11,911,773	8.20	1.13×
Tallwood II, L.P.	2002	5,000,000	500,000	0	367,420	(48.70)	0.73×
TCV III (Q), L.P.	1999	7,775,000	7,775,000	7,332,639	10,108,530	17.10	1.30×
TCV IV, L.P.	1999	25,000,000	17,465,000	2,694,553	17,698,199	.60	1.01×
Telecom Partners III, L.P.	1999	1,700,000	1,560,000	30,000	123,499	(62.00)	0.08×
Three Arch Capital, L.P.	2001	40,000,000	16,300,000	213,552	13,808,950	(10.80)	0.85×
Three Arch Partners III, L.P.	2000	2,500,000	937,500	9,383	667,309	(19.20)	0.71×
Trident Capital Fund - V, L.P.	2000	5,293,999	1,808,800	0	1,312,678	(21.30)	0.73×
Trinity Ventures VIII, L.P.	2000	6,000,000	1,590,000	197,377	980,680	(27.30)	0.62×
U.S. Venture Partners VIII, L.P.	2001	25,000,000	7,500,000	0	4,914,095	(28.50)	0.66×
Updata Venture Partners II, L.P.	2001	5,000,000	2,125,000	1,272,329	2,289,132	9.60	1.08×
VantagePoint Venture Partners III (Q), L.P.	1999	15,000,000	11,100,000	1,835,473	5,562,673	(30.20)	0.50×
VantagePoint Venture Partners IV (Q), L.P.	2000	50,000,000	12,000,000	0	5,072,579	(41.90)	0.42×
Vector Capital II, L.P.	1999	5,000,000	3,750,000	0	3,820,275	.60	1.02×
Ventures West 7 U.S. Limited Partnership	2000	5,000,000	3,315,112	312,357	2,592,357	(14.60)	0.78×
Weiss, Peck & Greer Venture Associates V, L.L.C.	1999	5,000,000	4,589,670	1,841,663	4,135,094	(4.80)	0.90×
WIIG Communications Partners, L.P.	2000	2,500,000	1,936,537	61,759	614,625	(47.10)	0.32×
Worldview Technology Partners IV, L.P.	2001	9,065,012	3,594,079	256,681	2,078,490	(26.10)	0.58×

its own. We need to minimize the time we spend on deals we don't do, focus on the deals we do, and respect the time of the people we work with."

Ann St. Germain, general partner and chief financial officer, joined GSA from Ernst & Young just after the CEV I contract was signed. She managed the reporting functions, which were complex despite the small number of clients. The group received data on each of its funds as well as every portfolio company, and it prided itself on providing customized reports to its clients.

OREGON AND NIB

In 2001, GSA had won a $250 million contract to manage a dedicated fund-of-funds for the Oregon Public Employees Retirement Fund (OPERF), an $80 billion institutional investor and an original investor in KKR's first fund in 1981. Its challenge was scale, as its $35 billion asset pool made it difficult to make investments of less than $50 million. It also lacked the time to find and evaluate emerging fund managers. For OPERF, GSA would target small venture and buyout funds.

GSA followed a policy of charging essentially the same total fee to each major client, although in a combination of fees and carry that responded to each client's particular concerns. OPERF was willing to pay a fee that was roughly 35 percent higher than CalPERS's over the life of the program, in exchange for a higher hurdle rate before GSA received carry.

NIB, the Dutch pension fund manager and a private equity fund manager in its own right, had sought out GSA in early 2002. NIB Private Equity managed €14 billion for the two major Dutch pension funds, which had a total of €205.5 billion in assets. Henry Robin, the head of U.S. investments for the firm, which had given GSA $100 million to invest in new and emerging partnerships, explained:

> We wanted to commit $300 million per year to the U.S. venture market. Historically, we had accomplished our allocation historically primarily through funds-of-funds, but we wanted now to invest directly in top-quartile firms. GSA will help us to accomplish our long-term objectives—we want to have money with roughly twenty-five top-tier managers over the next three years or one complete fund-raising cycle. And that is very hard to do when you have very few existing relationships and want to disburse large amounts of money, especially with the GPs raising smaller sums these days. GSA had a unique model in that it will hand the relationships off to us. We're patient. We expect to invest in about ten unproven, but high-potential funds through the GSA mandate. Let's say that after a few years one-third shows strong promise or definitive success, one-third is average, and one-third is poor. We would take the top one-third and invest with them directly when they raise their next fund. If we continue to do this with emerging managers, after a few years, we will have a number of managers in the new, top-tier firms where we were original investors with a guaranteed allocation each time they raise a subsequent fund.

NIB's strategy focused on developing a pool of emerging funds with which it had established relationships in the event that they emerged as high performers. Crockett said, "We will invest their money the first time and introduce them. Then, if performance is good, they would likely bring the relationship inside in the second fund."

By summer 2003, GSA had invested in Tallwood Venture Capital, a first-time venture firm, on NIB's behalf. Robin said, "We've met them, they know our faces and our staff. We were involved during the due diligence. We're very pleased thus far."

As with OPERF, GSA customized the compensation structure to meet specific NIB requests. However, the compensation structure was essentially equivalent to GSA's first two programs when viewed as a total package.

The Future

With over $3 billion under management barely five years after opening its doors, GSA had exceeded its founders' wildest dreams. Crockett said, "We had thought we'd get three small clients and prove the model, get three larger ones and prove it more, and then get three really big ones. Instead, we got CalPERS right off the bat." With the added competition in the market, though, GSA had to consider its options (see Exhibit 6.11 for competitive strategies).

Harris and his partners were building a sustainable business. He pointed to the distribution of ages and experience within the firm as part of its strength, noting, "Dave and I are in our fifties and have been in this business for a long time. Catherine and Barry are in their forties; they have deep experience and are in the prime of their careers. Then we have a full complement of principals and associates who want to make a name for themselves. Public pension funds need to have this kind of continuity in their intermediaries, and we have a solid platform from which to grow the business."

Dedicated Funds-of-funds

One option was continuing with the dedicated fund-of-funds model and expanding it to more clients. While GSA had succeeded at this to date, it faced challenges in scaling.

EXHIBIT 6.11

IMPORTANCE GIVEN TO VARIOUS COMPETITIVE STRATEGIES BY FUNDS-OF-FUNDS' MANAGERS

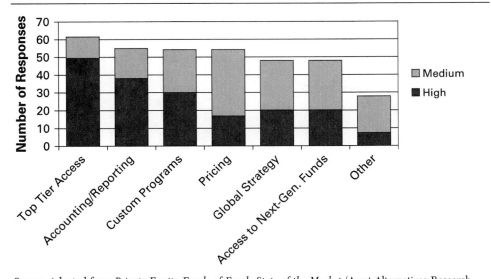

Source: Adapted from *Private Equity Funds-of-Funds State of the Market* (Asset Alternatives Research Report, 2nd edition, 2002), p. 45.

"There are only about four really big funds out there," said Gonder. "CalPERS, the Canada Pension Planning Board, NIB, and TIAA-CREF. CalPERS was a unique situation at a unique time. The others might need us for a targeted program, like NIB's, but not on the scale of the CalPERS program."

Crockett elaborated:

> We could go for more and smaller groups—the size of Oregon, for instance. Six or so at $250 million over three years would be efficient for us. We'd still be able to give the type of customized client service that we've done. At ten, this model gets wobbly and we have to look at the time spent on client services as opposed to investment decisions. I'm not sure how we'd do with even smaller groups yet—around $50 million. How small can we go?

Going Small

GSA had recently encountered three attractive opportunities with organizations looking to allocate smaller amounts, in the range of $100 million each, to private equity. One was a state pension fund that had sent a request for proposals to manage its $300 million VC account over three years. GSA had won the account, only to learn it would be split into thirds. Yet the award was renewable and seemed likely to grow over time.

The second opportunity involved a high-net-worth family office seeking a firm to take over management of its existing VC and buyout portfolio, as well as to make new investments. This would introduce GSA to the family office market. It was a source of stable money and was not subject to disclosure, which made it an attractive funding source for top-tier VC firms.

The last opportunity was with the pension fund of a European country targeting U.S. venture funds. This promised to be a stable, solid relationship over time and it would be easy for GSA to service. Harris felt that funds liked overseas money because they wanted to diversify their funding sources and there were no disclosure issues.

Working with smaller amounts of committed capital, however, challenged the scalability of GSA's model. Harris said, "There are tremendous economies of scale in the investment business. We put a huge amount of work into doing the due diligence on funds, and once we've invested, we monitor performance and report to our client. It's far more efficient for us to invest $20 million than $5 million."

Reviving Direct Investment

Another option was reviving the direct investment operation. Harris said, "It offers a natural complement to the business because we have a natural deal flow through our relationships. But we'd have to build a separate organization to do it; we can't wear both hats." Current clients seemed unconcerned about whether GSA did direct investing. It did, however, help GSA gain in-depth knowledge of firms in which it might invest.

Gonder commented, "It's more efficient if we put our money into a top-tier fund. To make one $5 million or $10 million direct investment, you have to put a huge amount of resources behind it. We leverage our time better on the fund side. Besides, the fund relationship is potentially continuous, while direct investing is a one-off."

Harris said, "But the fundamental synergy between a direct investment program and the way we work with the funds is still there." Direct investing did, however, pose some significant challenges. Buyout funds were far easier to invest with, as they preferred to control a syndicate and having an LP as part of the syndicate assured a fairly passive partner. As Harris observed, "If you trust them, you don't have to do a lot of additional work and they're glad to see you. And since you've already given them a bunch of your money, you'd better trust them." In 2003, GSA had a buyout portfolio, which it had lacked in 2000.

Venture deals were more difficult. Harris explained:

> There's a different dynamic in VC deals. In the early round of a good deal, the VC firms first want to get as much as they can for themselves. Their second priority is to syndicate with other VC firms that can help out with this or future deals. To give a chunk of a good early deal to an LP is a nuisance. For an LP to get into an early deal burns a lot of goodwill. You can get into the follow-ons far more easily. In 2000, follow-ons were ridiculously overpriced. Now, though, there are some really good ones out there. The problem then is that you have to do all your own due diligence because your interests and those of the current investors are not perfectly aligned. You need more staff.

Mainstream Fund-of-funds

Harris considered offering a mainstream fund-of-funds. "We really don't have a cash-on-cash track record yet," he said. "CEV I beats Cambridge Associates' top-tier benchmark—over the comparable period they're at negative 15.6 percent, we're negative 14 percent. That's not enough to raise a fund on. We'd have to differentiate ourselves, possibly on emerging fund managers. But even that will take some time. If we've chosen the right new funds, we'll have seats at the best funds in ten years." The challenge of the emerging managers' funds, though, was the amount of effort involved. "For every emerging manager fund," said Harris, "there's a huge amount of due diligence and organizational help. And in the end, we can only invest at most $10 million from one client."

Mazza agreed that the team first needed a track record. Once that was established, he felt that a hybrid fund-of-funds might offer an answer, as he explained:

> If we had five clients with the same objectives, we could write five $10 million checks and really put a new fund on the map. We'd become fund-makers. But we rarely find that—usually someone wants emerging venture teams and someone wants proven buyout funds. We may offer some degree of customization, more than the typical fund-of-funds but less than the total customization we provide to each of our clients now.

However, Crockett wondered about the firm's positioning, saying, "Does the market really need yet another commingled fund-of-funds?"

Strong Currents Ahead

GSA had just received an RFP from a large state pension fund looking for someone to help build a $1.5 billion diversified private equity program from scratch over seven or eight years. The group wanted to pay only a fee, no carry. Harris wondered if GSA should reply and convince the state to place a smaller amount, perhaps $200 million, with it. "Our business is to do the hard part and get the economics of a fund-of-funds," he mused.

If GSA could maintain its historic performance relative to the industry, it would acquire a respectable track record as the industry recovered. In a few years, it could raise a traditional fund-of-funds. "We wouldn't be differentiated then," Harris thought. "We'd have better terms and conditions, but we'd essentially be competing with the big brand-name funds-of-funds. And if you get too big, you become an index fund because you're in everything."

The co-investing effort could provide a new avenue for growth. Given the downturn in the industry, Harris could staff it without trouble. But would the old issues of distraction and quid pro quos endure? Harris said:

> When we started the firm, our approach made the most sense to the most experienced investors. We were lucky that CalPERS, a large, experienced investor, gave us the chance to prove our model, at just the right time. Now that we've proved the approach, where do we want to take it? Do we continue doing big dedicated accounts, or do we become a fund-of-funds, or move into smaller dedicated accounts? How big can we get relative to the market without becoming an index?

7

A Note on the Private Equity Fund-Raising Process

The process by which private equity groups raise funds is often shrouded in obscurity. While established groups can often raise their new funds in a matter of weeks, if not days, the process is very different for less established private equity organizations. For these groups, the fund-raising process can prove to be painfully slow.

This note seeks to remove some of the mystery from the fund-raising process. It highlights three aspects. First, the key actors in the fund-raising drama are considered. We then consider the special case of first-time funds, and the challenges that these organizations face. Finally, we consider the broader question of what determines the overall level of private equity fund-raising.

THE ACTORS

The general partners are the venture capitalists or private equity investors who are responsible for the day-to-day management of the fund. While they receive a substantial share of the capital gains from the fund, the general partners typically only contribute a modest amount of its capital. U.S. tax law formerly stipulated that the general partners needed to invest at least one percent of the capital in a limited partnership. While this requirement has been relaxed, 1 percent remains the typical share to invest. Particularly in first-time funds and in very large buyout funds, much of this investment may be in the form of notes, rather than cash. This reflects the fact that the general partners may not have the liquid resources to place this much capital into the fund upfront.

In two circumstances, however, it is common to see general partners making larger investments. The first is first-time funds, when establishing the credibility with potential limited partners may be very difficult. The general partners may consequentially supply a larger share of the capital. Not only does this contribution allow the fund to achieve a "critical mass" in some cases, but it also signals the commitment of the general partners to the success of the fund. (Some limited partners, however, find such

Professor Josh Lerner prepared this note as the basis for class discussion rather than to illustrate either effective or ineffective handling of an administrative situation.

large commitments worrisome, believing that the venture capitalists may become unwilling to make risky but attractive investments.) The other circumstance is becoming increasingly common: established funds whose partners have amassed significant amounts of wealth. In these instances, the partners may desire to put more and more of the capital into the fund, even if it "crowds out" other investors.

The limited partners include a wide array of individual and institutional investors, from families to pension funds to corporations. They often vary widely in their experience and sophistication. While established university endowments and old-line families may have long-standing relationships with well-established venture and buyout funds, many investors find themselves "on the outside looking in." Without established relationships, they are likely to find it hard to invest in top-tier organizations. In many cases, these investors also lack the experience (or the confidence) to identify which first-time private equity groups are attractive, and consequentially they refuse to invest in funds organized by less-established organizations as a rule.

There are also several distinct kinds of limited partners. One of these, the special limited partner, will be discussed in detail in the next section. Another is the "friend" of the fund. These friends include successful entrepreneurs who had been backed by the venture fund and former general partners who have retired from the fund. These friends typically invest in a special companion fund, which often has more favorable terms than the main fund.

Also on the stage are a variety of intermediaries. Some of these are hired by the limited partners, others by the general partners.

Investment advisors, or "gatekeepers," have been a fixture in the private equity world since the early 1970s.[1] The first such organization was established in 1972, when the First National Bank of Chicago established an advisory group as part of its trust department. (This operation was ultimately purchased in a management buyout in 1989 and took on the name Brinson Partners. Among the other pioneers of the advisory business were Bigler Investment Management and Horsley Bridge Partners, formerly known as Horsley Keough.) These organizations typically provide advisory services to some clients (who still make the ultimate decision where to invest) while exercising discretionary control over other clients' assets. Typically, these advisors will set up separate accounts for the larger investors, but comingle the assets of smaller investors into one or more "funds-of-funds."

The 1990s saw a dramatic growth in and increasing specialization of funds-of-funds. Many new entrants organized these funds, most notably the major investment banks, which raised multibillion funds from their high net worth clients. The new funds included some geared towards certain classes of investors, such as the Common Fund (university and other educational endowments) and FLAG Venture Partners (high net worth families). Others targeted certain investment niches: for instance, international private equity funds, minority-managed funds, and those based in a particular state. In the late 1990s, some funds-of-funds were even established to invest in a single fund.[2] The fund organizers typically charge an annual fee based on capital under management, typically around one percent. Some funds-of-funds, however, also receive a share of the carried interest in addition to management fees.

---

1. For a more detailed discussion of the role of investment advisors, see "University Technology Ventures," Harvard Business School case no. 201-043.

2. Many buyout groups welcomed investments by new investors, but had high minimum investment amounts due to federal securities regulations. By investing through a fund, a number of individuals who could not otherwise reach the minimum investment size could obtain access to the private equity fund.

A related set of intermediaries are the consulting firms. These groups, such as Venture Economics and Cambridge Associates, help limited partners make investment decisions but do not actually manage funds themselves. Rather, they monitor the performance of the private equity groups and the industry as a whole. These organizations provide institutional and individual investors with a view of the relative performance of the groups already in their portfolio and investments that they are considering. In some cases, they may even make recommendations to limited partners as to whether to invest in particular funds or not.

Placement agents play a similar role for the general partners. While the typical private equity group raises a fund only every two or three years, these organizations continually represent groups that are raising funds. Thus, they maintain close ties to the leading investors and have a keen sense of the market. Placement agents range from the major investment banks (e.g., Merrill Lynch) to specialist boutiques (for instance, the Monument Group) to myriad one-person shops. Traditionally, established placement agents worked only for buyout groups. In recent years, however, as venture organizations have begun raising considerably larger funds from a more diverse base of investors, more of these groups have retained placement agents as well.

The fees charged by these groups for their services are highly variable. For the very largest buyout funds, the fee may be as low as one-half of a percent of the capital actually raised by the placement agent. For a first-time fund, on the other hand, the fee may be as high as three percent of the fund's total capital. In these instances, some of the fee may be demanded upfront (on a nonrefundable basis, even if the fund-raising is unsuccessful), and the placement agent may even ask for some of the general partners' carried interest as well.

THE SPECIAL CHALLENGE OF FIRST-TIME FUNDS

Nowhere is the inefficiency of the private equity fund-raising process more apparent than in the raising of first-time funds. Many investors are reluctant to invest in an unproven team. Even if the partners have successful individual track records, their failure to have worked together before as a team may deter investors. Horror stories abound of groups who spent more than two years on the road fund-raising, in some cases visiting a single investment advisor a dozen times before being told that investor did not invest in first-time funds as a matter of principle.

How does one raise a fund without a track record, when to obtain a track record one needs a fund? New private equity organizations have addressed this conundrum in several ways.

The first is to identify investors who are not purely motivated by financial returns, but instead seek some strategic benefit from the fund. For instance, a state pension fund may reserve a certain portion of its venture capital allocation for funds based the state, in the hopes of stimulating local economic development. Similarly, a corporation with extensive activity in an industry not well served by existing venture funds (e.g., advanced ceramics) may find it attractive to invest in a new fund specializing in this area. In these cases, the investors are willing to accept a lower expected financial return in return for the indirect benefits that the investment will provide.[3]

---

3. Along similar lines, many first-time funds have found individual investors (particularly those with a background in hedge funds or investment banking) to have a greater appetite for risk than institutional investors, and willing to accept the higher variance of returns that come with first-time funds.

A second strategy is to establish an alliance with an existing institution. In some cases, first-time funds have established ties with investment banks or existing private equity groups. These arrangements typically entail the joint ownership of the management company that runs the private equity group. In many instances, the strategic partner has an important role in the governance of the fund, even to the point of having the right to review and approve all investment decisions.

While such an alliance may impart credibility to a fledgling private equity group, it also comes with some real costs. Other investors may fear that the institutional partner will distort the investment decisions (e.g., blocking otherwise promising investments that potentially compete with its longstanding clients). Alternatively, they may fear that having much of the profits flow to the institution will weaken the incentives of the private equity investors. Even if the fund can be raised and invested, problems may ensue. Many private equity groups with such ties have gone on to establish stellar track records and realized that the institutional ties were no longer needed to raise funds. In a number of cases, the investors have found their partnership ties time-consuming and costly to unwind.

The final strategy is to recruit what is termed a lead investor (often termed a special limited partner). Such an investor typically contributes a significant percentage of the capital of the fund. It may also provide some "seed funding" to the general partners before the fund closes, in order to cover the often-substantial costs associated with marketing a new fund.

In exchange, the special limited partner typically benefits in at least two ways. For instance, if a special limited partner contributes $25 million to a first-time fund with a total of $100 million in capital commitments, it will receive 25 percent of the payouts to the limited partners. Since the limited partners typically receive 80 percent of the capital gains of a first-time fund, this translates into 20 percent of the overall profits from the fund. In addition, the special limited partner is likely to receive a share of the fund's carried interest. In this example, the special limited partner may receive in addition one-quarter of the carried interest, or 5 percent of the overall profits of the fund. (This is frequently referred to as five "points.") Finally, the special limited partner may pay lower management fees than other limited partners.

Involving a special limited partner, however, may prove costly to the general partners. First, these payments directly reduce the returns of the private equity investors. Second, the investors may need to make important concessions regarding the governance of the fund, such as allowing the special limited partner to control a powerful advisory board that monitors the fund's activities. Finally, these concessions can alienate other potential investors in the fund. These investors may demand similar concessions for themselves, even if they are not making the "leap of faith" of investing first in the fund that the special limited partner did.

THE DETERMINANTS OF FUND-RAISING ACTIVITY

In the last section of this note, we consider a broader question: what determines the overall level of private equity fund-raising? This is a question that can be best answered from a vantage point of 30,000 feet, rather than the 300-foot altitude that has characterized most of the discussion in the note.

At the same time, however, this is a very practical question. As the cases in this module have repeatedly emphasized, the ebb and flow of private equity fund-raising can have a profound effect on private equity groups. An understanding of fund-raising dynamics can thus provide an important competitive advantage to private equity investors.

Various factors may affect the level of commitments to private equity organizations. These may be divided into those that affect either the supply of or the demand for private equity.[4] By the *supply* of private equity, we mean the relative desire of institutional investors to commit capital to the sector.

The number of entrepreneurs with good ideas who want financing determines the *demand* for private equity. It is very likely that decreases in capital gains tax rates might increase commitments to the funds, even though the bulk of the funds come from tax-exempt investors. Even a modest a drop in the capital gains tax rate may have a substantial effect on the willingness of corporate employees to become entrepreneurs, thereby increasing the need for private equity. This increase in demand due to greater entrepreneurial activity may lead to more fund-raising.

Both the supply of and demand for private equity may be stimulated by a robust public equity markets. A vibrant public market permits new firms to issue shares, allowing entrepreneurs and investors to ultimately achieve liquidity and unlock the value in their firms. Furthermore, it has been suggested that only when such a public market exists can private equity investors make a credible commitment to entrepreneurs that they will ultimately relinquish control of the firms in which they invest.[5]

The paragraphs above have emphasized rational explanations for the variability in private equity fund-raising. But some critics attributed the apparent cyclicality in the amount of venture funds raised to irrational forces.[6] They have argued that institutional investors are prone to either over- or underinvest in speculative markets such as venture capital and private equity. They suggest that this apparently irrational pattern of investing can explain the extreme swings in fund-raising. Furthermore, these works argue that such dramatic swings may hinder entrepreneurship and innovation in the American economy.

Empirical research has explored these various claims in the context of U.S. venture capital funds.[7] (Buyout fund-raising remains to be explored.) Strong evidence supports the claims regarding capital gains tax rates: lower capital gains taxes seem to have a particularly strong effect on the amount of venture capital supplied by tax-exempt investors. This suggests that the primary mechanism by which capital gains tax cuts affect venture fund-raising is by increasing the demand of entrepreneurs for capital. If the effect were on the supply of funds, changes in tax rates should have affected the contribution by taxable entities more dramatically.

A number of other factors influence venture capital fund-raising. Not surprisingly, regulatory changes such as the Department of Labor's shift in 1979 shift in the "prudent man" rule had an important impact on commitments to private equity funds. In addition, performance influences fund-raising. Higher returns—which are typically associated with periods with large number of initial public offerings—lead to greater capital commitments to new funds.

4. The ideas in this paragraph are from James M. Poterba, "How Burdensome Are Capital Gains Taxes? Evidence from the United States," *Journal of Public Economics* 33 (1987): 157–172; and James M. Poterba, "Venture Capital and Capital Gains Taxation," in Lawrence Summers, editor, *Tax Policy and the Economy,* Cambridge: MIT Press, 1989.

5. See the discussion, for instance, in Bernard S. Black and Ronald J. Gilson, "Venture Capital and the Structure of Capital Markets: Banks versus Stock Markets," *Journal of Financial Economics* 47 (1998): 243–277; and Philippe Aghion, Patrick Bolton, and Jean Tirole, "Exit Options in Corporate Finance: Liquidity versus Incentives," unpublished working paper, Harvard University, 2000.

6. Examples include Michael C. Jensen, "Corporate Control and the Politics of Finance," *Journal of Applied Corporate Finance* 4 (Summer 1991): 13–33; and William A. Sahlman and Howard Stevenson, "Capital Market Myopia," *Journal of Business Venturing* 1 (1986): 7–30.

7. Paul A. Gompers and Josh Lerner, "What Drives Venture Capital Fundraising?", Brookings Papers on Economic Activity: *Microeconomics* (1998) 149–192.

A related study examines the factors that influence venture capital fund-raising in twenty-one countries.[8] It finds that the strength of the IPO market is an important factor in the determinant of venture capital commitments, echoing the conclusions of Black and Gilson. The strength of the IPO market does not, however, seem to influence commitments to early stage funds as much as later-stage ones. While this work represents an important initial step, much more remains to be explored.

One provocative finding from this analysis is that government policy can have a dramatic impact on the current and long-term viability of the venture capital sector. In many countries, policymakers face a dilemma. The relatively few entrepreneurs active in these markets face numerous daunting regulatory restrictions, a paucity of venture funds focusing on investing in high-growth firms, and illiquid markets where investors do not welcome IPOs by young firms without long histories of positive earnings. It is often unclear where to begin the process of duplicating the success of the United States. In these settings, it may well be that well-targeted government efforts can play an important and positive role.

8. Leslie A. Jeng and Philippe C. Wells, "The Determinants of Venture Capital Funding: Evidence Across Countries," *Journal of Corporate Finance*, 6 (2000), 241–289.

8

Gold Hill Venture Lending

"I would hate to give birth to a child that bites me."
—Ken Wilcox, CEO, Silicon Valley Bank

"Without the SVB partnership, we're not worse than any other venture debt fund. But with it, we're much better."
—David Fischer, partner, Gold Hill

It was hard to get inspired about February in the Northeast, mused David Fischer, a partner and cofounder of Gold Hill Venture Lending (Gold Hill), as he stared out at the frozen landscape beyond the window of the jet landing at the Harrisburg, Pennsylvania airport for yet another fund-raising meeting. He was trying to raise $200 million for a first-time venture debt fund associated with Silicon Valley Bank (SVB), a major technology lender, but after nine months of grueling effort and rejection—polite rejection but rejection nonetheless—Fischer felt almost as lifeless as the ice-covered grasses beyond the runway. He was starting to fear that the difficult market of 2003 might not be ready for this project, but he hoped that the changes in the fund's structure would make it more appealing to potential investors.

The idea of an affiliated fund seemed to offer significant synergies to all parties. SVB owned a share of Gold Hill's management company and also was a limited partner in the fund. Its $20 million commitment was the largest thus far. Gold Hill would share SVB's deal flow, back office, sales force, database, and its twenty-year history with entrepreneurs, venture firms, and individual venture investors. It would have the option to do any appropriate deal that came to SVB—a substantial deal stream given that SVB banked over 60 percent of the venture-backed start-ups in North America. Even in the recent downturn among venture-backed companies, venture debt had performed well. SVB's internal rate of return (IRR) between 1996 and 2002, from positions in 437 companies, was 19.48

Professors Felda Hardymon and Josh Lerner and Senior Research Associate Ann Leamon prepared this case. HBS cases are developed solely as the basis for class discussion. Cases are not intended to serve as endorsements, sources of primary data, or illustrations of effective or ineffective management.

percent overall, with 9.42 percent from loans, and a net loss ratio of 3.5 percent.[1] During their careers with SVB, Gold Hill's team of Fischer, Sean Lynden, Frank Tower, and Tim Waterson had been associated with deals that produced half of the bank's warrant income, which had come from 30 percent of the companies that took venture debt.[2]

Gold Hill's partners planned to syndicate with SVB but also to make their own loans, in which they would introduce the bank. Because returns from venture debt came through both interest and warrants, Gold Hill would receive a steady stream of income from interest payments, with an equitylike upside from the warrants. As with any venture-type investment, receiving income from the warrants required funding the right companies. The relationship with SVB, which had strong ties to the venture community, would help as SVB knew the deals that were in process and the venture capitalists that were creating them. Fischer and his partners also had long-standing relationships with the venture community.

It had, Fischer thought as he went through the jetway, seemed like such an obviously good idea. He knew that fund-raising for a first-time fund would be tough and that the competition would be stiff. As he was struggling to raise his $200 million, Lighthouse Capital had closed its fifth fund at $366 million. Pinnacle had closed on $100 million in July 2002 and was aiming to raise a second $100 million before it closed its fund. Maybe, Fischer mused, there was no more room for another venture debt fund, especially one with a bank sponsor. It seemed that those potential investors intrigued by venture debt were wary of the fund's connection with SVB, and those intrigued by the institutional sponsorship found venture debt distasteful.

A lot was riding on this meeting, he admitted to himself in the taxi. He and his partners had recently discussed raising a smaller fund—in addition to SVB's $20 million, which might go to $25 million, they had another $10 million in solid commitments and could easily reach $50 million. Perhaps in this wary environment, they should go with the $50 million and prove the model. Then, with a track record of solid returns, they could raise more money, countering objections with experience. Yet Fischer thought that venture debt really had a place in this market, for companies, venture capitalists, and investors alike. He wanted to close the $200 million. He just had to allay the investors' concerns.

VENTURE LENDING[3]

The process of funding a new venture forced the entrepreneur to trade ownership for cash. An entrepreneur had a good idea and no money. The riskier the idea, the more equity the owner would have to give up to receive funding. Over time, a number of methods and sources had arisen to fund businesses, including individual (angel) investors, angel groups, private and corporate venture capital, venture leasing, and a few banks, of which SVB was one. Each had a role to play in a start-up's lifecycle (see Exhibit 8.1). Each also had its own benefits and disadvantages to an entrepreneur. Each was looking for the company to grow and create value and eventually yield a return on its investment in a liquidity event.

---

1. The net loss ratio is defined as loans that had been written off as uncollectible as a percentage of the total value of venture loans made, and it applies only to the venture debt portfolio. SVB's nonperforming loans overall (those more than ninety days overdue, and those for which there was no reasonable expectation that principal and interest would be paid) for the year ending December 31, 2002, amounted to 1 percent of total gross loans and 0.5 percent of total assets.
2. A warrant is the right to purchase stock in the future at a preapproved price.
3. This section based on Felda Hardymon and Ann Leamon, "Silicon Valley Bank," Harvard Business School (Boston, MA, 2000), Note no.800-332.

EXHIBIT 8.1

FUNDING CONTINUUM

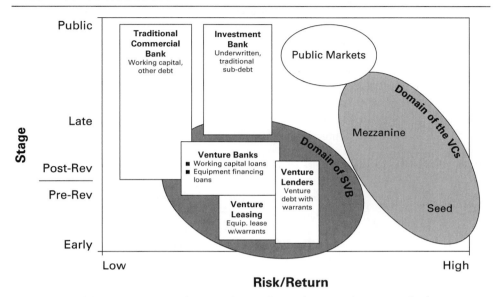

Source: Adapted from Leamon & Hardymon, "Silicon Valley Bank," Harvard Business School No. 800–133, p. 19.

Venture lending was a blanket term that covered a number of situations in which a start-up that did not have revenues (pre-revenue or pre-rev) received a loan in exchange for paying interest and granting warrants. Venture lending, which first appeared in the early 1970s, included venture leasing (also called asset based lending), venture debt, and subordinated debt. When nonbank entities offered these facilities, they usually were organized like venture capital (VC) partnerships. The distinctions were as follows:

- Venture leasing: Developed particularly to respond to the needs of the semiconductor industry, where required equipment could run into the hundreds of millions of dollars, a venture lessor would buy a piece of equipment and lease it to the company with payments over a number of years, typically three. The company would make payments of principal and interest and grant warrants based on the value of the equipment. The company never owned the equipment, so it never had to deal with issues of salvage. In additional, the accounting rules favored leasing.[4] At the end of the period, the company could purchase the equipment for its residual value. Because the lessor could always repossess the asset if the company failed to make payments, the interest rate was lower than typically charged on an unsecured debt vehicle. If the company went public or was purchased, the leasing firm could exercise its warrants.[5] Many firms established guidelines for this combination based upon the risk inherent in the deal: the least risky project could have an implicit return (assuming the

---

4. Josh Lerner, "A Note on the Venture Leasing Industry," Harvard Business School Note no. 9-294-069, p. 4.

5. *Ibid.*

payment of all lease and purchase payments but excluding any return from warrants) of 9 percent to 10 percent with no warrants, while the most risky might run as high as 17 percent with warrant coverage of 25 percent to 40 percent.[6]

- Venture debt: This was a secured loan that could be used to finance either equipment or growth capital. An equipment loan differed from venture leasing only in that the company owned the equipment and was repaying the lender for the money used to purchase it. Usually the interest on these facilities was 7 percent to 9 percent, with 3 percent or 4 percent warrant coverage. A growth capital loan was an open loan that was not based on equipment. The interest rate was higher, usually around 10–12 percent, with 10 percent warrants. Usually, both of these loans had three-year terms and were secured by a blanket lien[7] on the company's assets or its enterprise value (intellectual property in addition to hard assets), giving the lender a senior position in the capital structure. If the company went bankrupt, this lender would receive its cash back before the holders of equity or subordinated debt did. In the case of equipment financing, the lender could repossess the machinery; in the case of growth capital, the lender could exercise its lien on the company's assets. In some situations, a company might have venture debt and later, once it had generated revenue, an accounts receivable loan. The two lenders would become co-lenders; both would have secured loans but the venture lender would "carve out" a portion of the assets that secured its loan to secure the accounts receivable facility. Thus, the venture debt blanket lien would cover everything except the accounts receivable securing that loan. If the company went bankrupt, the two lenders would be repaid first, from the proceeds of their collateral.

- Subordinated debt: A subordinated debt position meant that there was a more senior layer of debt in the capital structure. In a liquidation, the holders of senior debt would be repaid first, and only then would the subordinated debt holders receive anything, with equity holders being paid last. The line between venture debt and sub debt could become blurred if the company, having taken venture debt, then took a loan that would be senior in the capital structure, such as an accounts receivable loan. Generally, venture debt term sheets required that the venture lender approve any loans senior to that position; rarely was that approval withheld. Thus, a venture debt position supported by a blanket lien on the company's assets could become subordinated to later financings unless the venture debt lender stipulated that it would maintain a senior position and was willing to carve out some portion of its collateral.

Warrants conveyed the right to purchase shares of stock at a stated price within a given time period.[8] In the case of private firms, the price was usually the per-share price from the most recent venture round, and the time period five or ten years. A warrant was often expressed as a percentage of the value of the cash advanced. Warrant coverage of 10 percent on a loan or a piece of equipment worth $1 million conveyed the lender the right to buy shares worth 10 percent of $1 million, or $100,000, if exercised within the allowed timeframe. If the most recent round had established a price of $5 per share, the lender would receive a warrant for the purchase of 20,000 shares of stock ($100,000 ÷ $5).[9]

---

6. Josh Lerner, *Venture Capital & Private Equity: A Casebook* (New York: John Wiley & Sons, 2000), p. 294.

7. Defined as "a catchall term that refers to every imaginable type of collateral owned by the borrower," per Thomas P. Fitch, *Dictionary of Banking Terms*, 4th edition (Hauppauge, NY: Barrons, 2000).

8. Robert N. Anthony and James S. Reece, *Accounting Principles* (Homewood IL: Irwin, 1989), p. 226.

9. Lerner, *Venture Capital & Private Equity*, p. 293. While this rule of thumb was often used in practice, the amount of warrant coverage provided very little guidance to its economic value.

Venture lending could benefit all the parties involved. For the lender, the arrangement offered a regular stream of monthly payments at a healthy interest rate along with the chance of equity-type upside should the warrants be worthwhile. The venture capitalists backing the company could avoid dilution and preserve the company's equity. The company could save its equity for future financings. These would occur later, thanks to the debt's cash infusion, and hopefully at a higher valuation that would offset the debt's drawback of regular repayments.[10] Equity, it was thought, should be used for expenses that drove the company forward, such as hiring and research and development, rather than office chairs or computers. Lenders relied both on the investors' ability to choose good firms and on their presumed willingness to support the investment with future funding, and thus tried to maintain good relationships with the best venture capitalists. Further reducing risk, the loan usually closed just after a major equity infusion, increasing the possibility that the debt would be paid off before the company's money ran out.

VENTURE DEBT

Venture lending methods began evolving in the early 1970s but took different forms on the East and West Coasts. Venture leasing was common on the West Coast, while venture debt took hold on the East Coast, largely due to the activity of the Bank of New England (BoNE).

Traditional banks avoided loans to fledging firms because they failed the traditional banking standard known as "belt and suspenders"; the ability to repay a loan either from operating cash flow or from the value of underlying assets. The period of a company's life before it started generating revenue was the domain of equity financing. Banks became involved only when the firm had revenues, operating cash flow, and accounts receivable, despite the quality or amount of venture backing, because a future equity infusion was not viewed as an acceptable form of collateral.

In the early 1970s, Allyn Woodward and Art Snyder at BoNE began questioning these assumptions. They examined the cash flows of start-up companies and decided that pre-revenue, pre-product companies with venture backing had the *highest* likelihood of repaying a loan because the venture capitalists could be relied upon to provide an additional equity infusion to protect their interest. Secondly, venture capitalists tended to fund only companies that already had or could create significant intellectual property. This implied two possible means of repayment: the equity infusion or, as backup, the sale of intellectual property, such as technology patents or copyrights.

Venture-backed start-ups also represented a relatively liquid business model, especially attractive to a bank. Essentially, a pre-revenue company going through rounds of venture financing would receive a large infusion of cash, deposit it in a low-interest account, and gradually draw it down before a new round injected more cash, providing low-cost stable capital to the bank that held those deposits. Because the energy, creativity, and commitment of the entrepreneur and the VC backer would be greater early in the company-building process, Woodward felt that the earlier stages of a company's life, counterintuitively, were the safest for the banking relationship. If the company thrived, it could then use the bank's more traditional products.

This complete inversion of conventional banking wisdom created a huge emotional barrier to competitors. Until 1990, BoNE dominated the East Coast venture lending market. Its willingness to provide equipment loans precluded the development of venture leasing companies, which remained a West Coast phenomenon. In 1986, it entered into an agreement with a West Coast institution, SVB, in which SVB syndicated loans

10. Vyvyan Tenorio, "Venture Lenders Fill Comdisco Void," *The Daily Deal* (October 4, 2002).

too large for its asset base with the larger eastern bank. This move would have a significant impact on the future of venture lending.

Years later, Gold Hill's Fischer described the venture lending model this way:

> We are concerned with financing risk, the possibility that the company will receive a future round of financing. What matters there is the company's ability to bring in rounds of follow-on financing. One major consideration is the quality of the venture capitalists involved. There is a big difference between the ability of top-tier and non–top-tier venture capitalists in attracting investors to subsequent rounds. Admittedly, that's not the only determinant—there's the market space, the business model, the margins, and various company-specific aspects. Even the best top-tier firm would have trouble getting follow-on interest in an online pet food retailer. But basically, if we have identified the top VC firms and the top practitioners within them—which we have—we can get our arms around financing risk. Operating risk, which venture lenders don't need to assess as carefully, is a different story. If you back a later-stage company that is already up and running, as a mezzanine fund would, you are trying to predict operating risk. There can be all sorts of exogenous shocks—foreign devaluations, natural disasters, changes in input pricing— that are far less predictable than the behavior of a small number of people with a track record of building nascent businesses.

SILICON VALLEY BANK[11]

Four card-playing California businessmen had founded SVB in 1983 to answer the need they saw for a bank to fund West Coast start-ups. The successes of Tandem Computer, Apple, and Intel had illustrated the possibility of high-flying performance from very humble origins in markets and with products that many people had never imagined.

In 1986, SVB had formed a syndicate with the larger BoNE to handle West Coast deals that exceeded its resources, rather than share them with its regional competitors. The arrangement worked well until January 1990, when BoNE announced a $1 billion loss. Although this occurred in areas unrelated to the bank's technology loans, the leaders of the technology practice, Fischer, Woodward, and Ken Wilcox, left BoNE and merged with SVB, forming Silicon Valley East.

In 1992, Woodward moved west to become the chief banking officer at SVB, and Wilcox became the head of Silicon Valley East. In the wake of losses due to its exposure to the overheated California real estate market, the bank restricted its focus to technology, life sciences, and the California premium wine industry.

By the later 1990s, the venture debt market had defined itself. Banks or debt funds would make a loan to a start-up, usually for working capital or equipment, at interest rates between 7 percent and 12 percent, and receive warrants and, sometimes, co-investment rights in the next round. Collateral was usually a first lien on all assets (see Exhibit 8.2 for typical venture debt term sheet). Although SVB dominated the market with a 60 percent share among venture-backed companies, it faced fierce competition primarily from nonbank entities. Among them were GATX Ventures, Comdisco Ventures, Lighthouse Capital Partners, Transamerica Technology Finance, and Western Technology Investments (WTI) (see Exhibit 8.3 for venture debt funds raised). Observed one venture capitalist, "The venture debt funds would trail around after the top-tier venture

---

11. This section is abstracted from Felda Hardymon and Ann Leamon, "Silicon Valley Bank," *HBS* 800-332.

EXHIBIT 8.2

TYPICAL VENTURE DEBT AGREEMENT FOR A COMPANY RAISING ITS FIRST ROUND

Borrower: HiFi WiFi

Loan Amount: Total = $2 million in two disbursements: $1 million on signing, with a second payment of $1 million upon close of $16 million in equity.

Term: Thirty-six months

Collateral: First lien on all assets°

Funding Syndicate: Two top-tier VC firms

Yield: 10 percent from interest and 22–25 percent from interest and warrants.

Warrants: 100,000 shares to be redeemed at the price of the Series A round (still under negotiation at the time of this agreement)

Right to invest: $500,000 in next round.

Source: Gold Hill.

°A lien is the right to take and sell or hold the property of a debtor. A lien on all assets meant that the lender could take anything from furniture to intellectual property to satisfy the company's debt.

---

capitalists. As soon as a company received a round, the debt guys would be there offering loans. Some of the debt firms barely cared about the interest rate; all they wanted was the warrants." This was very much an Internet bubble–related phenomenon, Fischer recalled: "There was little due diligence, no concern about an interest rate. These groups papered the market with term sheets."

Of all the venture debt funds in the bubble, Comdisco was the most notoriously aggressive. Founded in 1969, Comdisco (formerly Computer Discount Corporation) leased mainframe computers and provided disaster recovery services, and its revenues had reached $4 billion by the late 1990s. Its venture operation, Comdisco Ventures, had been established in 1987 to lease equipment to pre-revenue start-ups in exchange for equity stakes.[12] By 2000, the venture group had invested $3 billion in venture-backed start-ups, mostly in subordinated debt positions with Internet and telecommunications companies. Its most extreme product, dubbed "Godzilla," had provided loans over $5 million (one was $15 million) to pre-revenue companies largely in exchange for warrants. When the NASDAQ fell, Comdisco's stock price plummeted from its peak of $53 per share in March 2000 to $1 per share a year later. In July 2001, the entire company declared bankruptcy; it emerged in 2002 to wind up operations and sell assets to satisfy creditors. GATX, which specialized in leasing aircraft and rail cars, had shuttered its venture debt operation in December 2002 after taking a $97.8 million provision for possible losses. It listed assets of $280 million at the time.[13]

SVB, constrained by banking regulations from lending large amounts to a single company during the boom, had tried to compete by offering a complete suite of banking services to start-ups and by a focus on "granularity," or taking a large number of smaller venture debt positions rather than making a small number of large bets. It too had suffered from the NASDAQ crash, but while the venture firms had savaged Comdisco in

---

12. Sandra Jones, "The Crash of Comdisco," *Crain's Chicago Business* (November 5, 2001).

13. Vyvyan Tenorio, "GATX Exits VC Debt Business, Returns to Roots," *The Daily Deal* (December 19, 2002).

EXHIBIT 8.3

VENTURE DEBT PROVIDERS

Name of Fund	Money Raised ($ Millions)	Date Closed	Comments
Pinnacle Ventures°	$100 (1st close)	July 2002	Founded by an ex-Comdisco exec, Redpoint was a major LP. Aimed to close on an additional $100 million by April 2003; appears to have fallen short and to have raised about $125 million.
Costella Kirsch[†]	$100	Dec. 2002	
Western Technology Investments[‡]	$720	May 2003	In three funds, has raised more than $1 billion since 1994.
Lighthouse Capital V[§]	$366	May 2003	Oversubscribed; initial target was $300 million.
Venture Credit[ǁ]		Late 2002	Failed to raise fund.
Montage Capital Fund of Terra Nova Capital Partners[ǁ]	$100	June 2002	
Transamerica Technology Finance[#]	NA	NA	U.S. division of a major Dutch financial organization with over $280 billion in assets.
Comerica°°	NA	NA	Total assets of $45 billion. Obtained greater California presence through 2001 purchase of Imperial Bancorp ($7 billion in assets).
Silicon Valley Bank	NA	NA	$4 billion in assets, California-based.

Sources:

° Vyvyan Tenorio, "Venture Lending Fills Void," *The Daily Deal* (October 4, 2002).

† Venture One data.

‡ http://www.westerntech.com, accessed December 19, 2003.

§ Matthew Sheahan, "Venture Lender Lighthouse Attracts $366 Million," *Venture Capital Journal* (July 1, 2003).

ǁ "Borrowing Binge," *Red Herring* (January 6, 2003), in http://www.redherring.com, accessed December 19, 2003.

http://www.transamericafinance.com, accessed December 19, 2003.

°° Bill Stoneman, "Comerica Plugs Along," *American Banker* (June 23, 2002), p. 17.

restructuring their companies, SVB had not suffered a similar fate. "SVB is there for the long run," said one observer. "They have deep connections in the community and they're a bank. Each loan was not big enough that it was worth risking the relationship."

By 2003, even in the face of the economic slump, SVB's business model had held. While its warrant-related revenue had fallen, this was a minor share of the total income generated by the bank's other services and loans. The slow economy reduced its loan activity and the levels of fees on mergers and acquisitions, and portfolio write-downs by the venture firms in which it was invested had reduced the value of those holdings. Nonetheless, loan balances had risen for the last three quarters of 2002, reaching the highest quarterly average loan balance in the company's history, while deposit balances had remained constant for over a year. Non-performing loans[14] had held steady since

---

14. Nonperforming loans were those that were more than 90 days behind the repayment schedule and/or had no reasonable hope that principal and interest would be paid.

the end of 2001 at approximately 1 percent of total gross loans (see Exhibit 8.4a–8.4c for financials).[15] A member of the SVB board commented, "Their performance reflects that fact that this is a real bank, not a bunch of venture-capital wannabees. Because they're a bank, they must focus on downside protection, not upside potential."

With the expansion of bank operations allowed by the Gramm-Leach-Bliley Act of 1999, SVB's parent, Silicon Valley Bancshares, had incorporated itself as a bank holding company, and the organization had expanded its business to include not only commercial banking services such as deposit and collections and traditional lending services but also international services and investment and advisory services through SVB Securities, a licensed broker-dealer. A subsidiary, Alliant Partners, provided investment-banking services, and Woodside Asset Management, another subsidiary, acted as an investment advisor to the high-net-worth individuals served by the private banking department. The

---

EXHIBIT 8.4a

SVB'S INCOME STATEMENT

Year ending Dec. 31, in $ millions	2002	2001	2000	1999	1998
Interest and Fees on Loans	156.2	184.9	189.1	163.0	139.1
Interest and Dividends on Investment Securities	53.5	90.0	114.2	87.7	64.8
Fed Funds Sold/Securities Sold under Resale Agreement	2.9	25.4	83.5	31.2	21.3
Interest Income, Bank	**212.6**	**300.3**	**386.8**	**281.9**	**225.2**
Total Interest Expense	**17.9**	**37.3**	**56.9**	**76.4**	**78.6**
Net Interest Income	**194.7**	**263.0**	**329.8**	**205.4**	**146.6**
Loan Loss Provision	3.9	16.7	54.6	52.4	37.2
Net Interest Income after Loan Loss Provision	**190.8**	**246.3**	**275.2**	**153.0**	**109.5**
Fees & Commissions from Operations	9.1	6.2	3.3	2.8	1.7
Commissions and Fees from Securities Activities	30.7	41.6	35.8	4.5	0.5
Investment Securities Gains	(9.8)	(12.4)	37.1	1.1	5.2
Foreign Currency Gains	15.2	12.7	18.6	14.0	7.4
Other Revenue	30.5	30.3	95.3	36.5	8.3
Noninterest Income, Bank	**75.6**	**78.4**	**190.1**	**58.9**	**23.2**
Labor and Related Expenses	(104.3)	(90.5)	(123.7)	(76.2)	(45.4)
Other Expense	(82.1)	(93.0)	(74.7)	(49.5)	(40.6)
Noninterest Expense, Bank	**(186.4)**	**(183.5)**	**(198.4)**	**(125.7)**	**(83.6)**
Income before Tax	80.1	141.2	267.0	86.2	49.0
Income Tax Total	26.7	53.0	107.9	34.0	20.1
Net Income	**53.4**	**88.2**	**159.1**	**52.2**	**28.9**

Source: Compiled from SVB's filings with the U.S. Securities and Exchange Commission.

(Continues)

15. "Silicon Valley Bancshares Reports Fourth Quarter Earnings," *PR Newswire* (January 16, 2003).

EXHIBIT 8.4b (CONTINUED)

SVB'S BALANCE STATEMENT

Year ending Dec. 31, in $ millions	2002	2001	2000	1999	1998
Cash and Equiv.	239.9	228.3	332.6	278.1	123.0
Fed. Funds Sold	202.7	212.2	1,389.7	898.0	399.2
Securities	1,535.7	1,833.2	2,107.6	1,747.4	1,397.5
Loans	2,086.1	1,767.0	1,716.5	1,623.0	1,611.9
Loan Loss Allowance	(70.5)	(72.4)	(73.8)	(71.8)	(46.0)
Furniture/Equipment	39.9	39.2	30.2	18.7	16.7
Depreciation	(22.0)	(17.4)	(11.7)	(8.0)	(5.3)
Goodwill	100.5	96.4	0.0	NA	NA
Accrued Interest/Other	70.9	85.6	135.6	110.9	48.5
Total Assets	**4,183.2**	**4,172.1**	**5,626.8**	**4,596.4**	**3,545.5**
Noninterest Bearing Deposits	1,892.1	1,737.7	2,448.8	1,928.1	921.8
Interest Bearing Deposits	1544.0	1643.3	2413.6	2181.3	2348.0
Total Deposits	**3,436.1**	**3,381.0**	**4,862.4**	**4,109.4**	**3,269.8**
Total Short-term Borrowings	9.1	41.2	0.0	NA	NA
Total Long-term Debt	56.9	64.3	38.6	38.5	38.5
Total Debt	**66.0**	**105.5**	**38.6**	**38.5**	**38.5**
Minority Interest	43.2	28.3	30.7	0.0	NA
Other Liabilities	47.6	29.8	81.1	79.6	21.3
Total Liabilities	**3,592.8**	**3,544.6**	**5,012.7**	**4,227.5**	**3,329.6**
Paid-in Capital	100.0	196.1	280.0	153.4	94.1
Retained Earnings	476.6	423.3	335.1	176.0	123.9
Other Equity, Total	13.7	8.1	(1.0)	39.3	(2.1)
Total Equity	**590.4**	**627.5**	**614.1**	**368.9**	**215.9**
Total Liabilities and Shareholders' Equity	**4,183.2**	**4,172.1**	**5,626.8**	**4,596.4**	**3,545.5**
Total Common Shares Outstanding	40.6	45.4	49.0	44.8	41.4
Price per share ($)	18.30	26.70	34.60	24.75	8.52
Number of Employees	1,019	981	959	700	590
Number of Common Shareholders	8,573	9,340	770	600	721

Source: Compiled from SVB's filings with the U.S. Securities and Exchange Commission.

---

holding company also participated in merchant banking operations that included two limited partnerships, a venture capital fund, and a fund-of-funds.[16]

SVB AND GOLD HILL

SVB was the "800-pound gorilla" of technology lending. It had had 30,000 clients over its twenty-year history, and its twenty-six offices housed 175 relationship managers (sales

16. Silicon Valley Bancshares, "Silicon Valley Bancshares: Annual Report 2002," (December 31, 2002), pp. 3–6.

EXHIBIT 8.4c

SVB'S HISTORIC LOAN PERFORMANCE (VENTURE DEBT AND STANDARD COMMERCIAL LOANS)

	Avg. Loan Balance (Millions)	Loan Yield	Net Loss Ratio	Warrant Income (000s)
1991	$ 317.7		0.05%	$ 565
1992	446.0		0.28	1,214
1993	484.7		0.41	5,762
1994	542.1	10.80%	1.57	2,840
1995	618.0	11.90	0.18	8,205
1996	689.1	11.50	1.02	5,389
1997	903.5	11.10	0.67	5,480
1998	1,240.6	10.60	2.36	6,657
1999	1,422.4	10.30	1.34	33,003
2000	1,473.9	12.20	1.20	86,322
2001	1,459.7	11.20	1.44	86,500
2002	1,508.2	8.90°	0.35	1,661

Source: SVB. Average Loan Balance, Loan Yield, and warrant figures are for all commercial loans. Net Loss Ratio excludes nontechnology and life science charge-offs in 1999 and 2000.

°2002 loan yield is an estimate.

representatives) supported by a back office of eighty. It had more than 200 VC funds as clients and had invested in more than 200 funds itself. Among venture-backed companies, it saw over 95 percent of all deals and had a 60 percent market share, which was rising (see Exhibit 8.5 for recent market share trends). As of December 31, 2002, the firm held 1,818 separate warrant issues in 1,355 companies and had invested directly in twenty-five companies. Warrant income for 2002 had dropped to $1.7 million, a sharp decline from the $86 million peak in 2000, but the remaining warrants still held promise for the future. SVB also held private equity investments in another twenty-four

EXHIBIT 8.5

SVB'S MARKET SHARE OF A AND B ROUNDS

	A&B Rounds	SVB Clients	Market Share
Q401	59	36	61%
Q102	131	59	45
Q202	131	85	65
Q302	56	29	52
Q402	38	30	79
Total	**415**	**239**	**58**

Source: SVB and Venture Wire.

companies through its VC fund, Silicon Valley BancVentures, LP, and had positions in twenty VC funds through its fund-of-funds, SVB Strategic Investors Fund, LP.

SVB had experience in raising money for private equity funds. In 2000, the fund-of-funds, SVB Strategic Investors Fund, L.P., had initially raised $135 million (eventually reduced to $122 million) to invest in top-tier venture partnerships, and SVB's VC operation, Silicon Valley BancVentures, had raised $56.1 million to co-invest in emerging technology and life sciences companies. In both cases, the bank had invested enough for a 10 percent ownership. The money raised, though, had largely come from individuals who were bank friends, family, and clients, rather than institutional investors.

With Gold Hill, the bank was setting up a subsidiary to do something that SVB already did—offer venture debt to companies backed by top-tier venture capitalists—but, in a departure from its experience, with funds from institutional investors. SVB had considered a venture debt fund for a long time before setting up Gold Hill. Ken Wilcox, now CEO of SVB, said:

> In 1995, a few people in our merchant bank who had come to us from a venture leasing background wanted to set up a venture debt fund. I was vehemently against it. They saw it as a chance to get the bank to raise the money for them while they were compensated on a fees-and-carry basis. I felt that the skills involved in venture debt were not especially different from those that our account officers employ on a daily basis. We compete with venture debt funds and we do a good job at it. The only reason that venture debt folks should get more money, I felt, was that they had raised their own funds and sourced their own deals—and in this early version, the venture debt folks wanted to use the bank to do both of these.

By 2002, though, Wilcox's thinking had changed:

> The industry has changed in the last six years, and part of it was our fault. In 1996 or so, we went for a market share grab and offered a product called Quick-Start—a $400,000 preapproved loan with a rate of prime or prime plus 1 percent, 3 percent warrant coverage, no financial covenants, and no due diligence or approval process—to companies backed by the top VC firms. But competitors came back with $500,000, then $600,000 and we one-upped each other until it was $1 million. Just as we decided this was a bad idea, Comdisco came into the market with the Godzilla product, loaning $3–10 million. Even though Comdisco has imploded, this experience fundamentally changed the market, and the average size of a venture debt facility today is between $3 million and $4 million, substantially higher than it was before 1996. For us to participate in this market, as a regulated entity using money from depositors, we have to syndicate our deals. Over the last eighteen months, we've had to share 270 deals. We see almost all of them, and we end up winning over half. We spend a lot of time working these deals, creating the networks that access them, doing due diligence, putting them through our credit process, and developing the right financing package for them. By syndicating, we are essentially giving away a lot of work. But we can't supply a $3 million venture debt facility by ourselves. We finally decided that we should set up a fund so that we're syndicating with a friendly firm and sharing in the proceeds.

In 2003, even without Comdisco and GATX, the venture debt market included a number of nonbank entities, such as Pinnacle and Lighthouse, and one bank, Comerica, in addition to SVB. Comerica's technology presence was minor, but it occasionally offered unconventional deals, up to $2 million with interest rates of 1 percent above prime[17], 3 percent warrant coverage and other favorable terms. Said Wilcox, "Monetizing our deal flow is essential for the bank to survive in this highly competitive environment."

Venture capitalists and entrepreneurs had become more comfortable with the entire concept of venture debt. With the recent move to smaller financing rounds and subsequent funding tied to milestones, the availability of venture debt was important both financially and emotionally. Gold Hill's Fischer commented:

> There is a CEO we simply love. Not only has he generated great returns, but even when he didn't succeed, he's done everything he could to ensure that the bank was made whole. He just started a new company with backing from a top-tier firm. Before it can get more funding, the company has to be generating revenue. Under the Gold Hill fund structure, we could supply a $5 million venture debt line, split $4 million from us and $1 million from SVB, with 10 percent warrant coverage, 10 percent interest, and a three-year term. To the CEO, having this facility gives him emotional security that he won't be trying to arrange a bridge line when he really should be focused on closing customers. And the venture investors are delighted that they won't have to be arranging a bridge financing, that the company has a far greater chance of hitting its targets. This also means that the next round will likely occur at a higher valuation, because the company has actually achieved the milestone. This extends the runway without chewing up equity (see Exhibit 8.6).

While early start-up firms had to rely on venture debt for all their bank loans, a company about to start generating revenues would want alternatives, as a pure venture debt vehicle was an expensive financing method. In such situations, Gold Hill would

---

EXHIBIT 8.6

IMPACT OF VENTURE DEBT ON AN ENTREPRENEUR'S CASH BURN

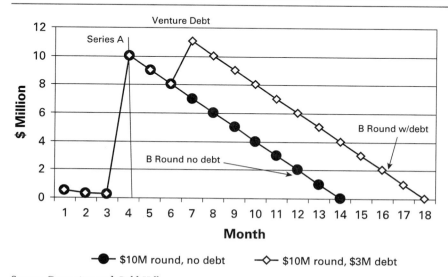

Source: Casewriter and Gold Hill.

---

17. The reference rate banks use in pricing short-term loans to their most creditworthy customers.

provide some venture debt and bring in SVB with a lower-priced alternative such as a working capital line. The fund would "carve out" a portion of its typical blanket lien to allow SVB the collateral necessary for its loan. Fischer explained:

> The recent deal was very competitive because the entrepreneur was so well known. Our key competitive advantage is that we could bundle a straight term loan from Gold Hill with an SVB working capital line. This provides a company with a lower-cost solution than if the CEO had to take venture debt for the entire amount. Lighthouse can't bundle like we can. We like to say that we provide a relationship product.

Gold Hill had greater latitude in the amount it could loan, the interest rate it could charge, and the warrants it could take than did SVB (see Exhibit 8.7 for comparison). The bank had regulators that protected the depositors' money. The fund had no such regulators. Instead, the Securities and Exchange Commission ensured that Gold Hill's investors were accredited (that is, had incomes or assets above a certain amount) and were thus assumed to be sophisticated enough to understand the risk and, in the worst case, wealthy enough to afford to lose their investment. The regulators knew that SVB was invested in Gold Hill, and as long as it was a minor position ($20 million from a $4.2 billion asset base), there was no problem, and Gold Hill was not subject to bank-related regulation.

The relationship was symbiotic. Gold Hill would leverage SVB's access to deals and acquaintance with venture capitalists. SVB would offer the fund any venture debt deals

EXHIBIT 8.7

COMPARISON OF TERMS FROM GOLD HILL, SVB, AND OTHER NONBANK PROVIDER

Term	SVB	Nonbank Provider	Gold Hill
Amount	$2 million	$3 million	$3 million
Terms	30 months amortization° for Hardware 24 months amortization for Software	6 months interest only, 42 months amortization[†]	36 months amortization
Formula[‡]	100% of invoice up to 35% for soft costs	Nonformula No invoices required	Nonformula No invoices required
Yield	8%	7.5%	8.0%
Warrant Coverage	5%	7.5%	7.5%
Collateral	All asset lien	All asset lien	All asset lien
Covenants[§]	2 milestone covenants	None	None

Source: Gold Hill.

Notes:

° Period over which principal and interest are paid.

† Payments cover interest only for the first six months, then principal and interest for forty-two months.

‡ Amount of the loan that can be drawn down for a given expense. "Nonformula" means that any amount, up to the full loan, can be drawn.

§ Language through which a borrow agrees to do certain things; in this case, achieve certain milestones.

that it encountered, allowing the bank to focus on providing its other products to these and other companies. Gold Hill's "sweet spot" was deals above $1.5 million, an area in which SVB had a 78 percent share. Working with Gold Hill would give SVB a better chance of reaching early stage companies backed by the best VC firms. SVB's approach of syndicating with other funds had worried venture capitalists and entrepreneurs who feared managing yet another syndicate. The relationship with Gold Hill allowed SVB to provide a streamlined transparent financing package.

SVB, which constantly monitored the VC firms in the market and the partners within them, had identified a changing group of seventy venture capital firms with exemplary performance. Gold Hill planned to focus on the top 30 percent of these firms, and within them, up to 125 of the best individual partners. Between 1996 and 2002, SVB had found that its loans to the top seventy firms had produced an all-in IRR[18] of 26.16 percent, while the IRR for the top 25 was 40.71 percent. Multiples, respectively, were 1.25× and 1.34× (see Exhibit 8.8 for SVB's performance details).

To invest $200 million in four years, Gold Hill hoped to do thirty-five to forty deals per year. Its target group of venture capitalists could be assumed to do two Series A or B deals each year, with roughly 67 percent taking some venture debt. Gold Hill's pace, roughly 20 percent of the annual deal flow, would allow the firm to lose a few deals to competitors and still meet its targets.

EXHIBIT 8.8

POOLED RESULTS FOR SVB'S VENTURE DEBT 1996–1999, AS OF SEPTEMBER 30, 2002

	All Venture Loans[°]	SVB 70[†]	GH 25[‡]
Number of Loans/Companies	1,024/618	247/119	144/65
Total $ Disbursed (millions)	$346	$81	$49
Total $ Repaid (millions)	$434	$141	$102
Warrant Income($ millions)	$57	$50	$478
Loss Ratio	1.88%	2.02%	1.70%
Loan-only Gross IRR	8.76%	9.71%	9.75%
All-In Gross IRR[§]	24.36%	61.86%	85.76%
Return Multiple	1.26	1.74	2.10

Source: SVB.

Notes: Results reflect all actual cash flows through November 30, 2002. For loans with balances as of November 30, 2002, all future payments were assumed to be made as agreed. No value was given to unrealized warrants.

° Actual returns from all venture debt loans made between 1996 and 1999.

† Results from loans made to companies backed by the seventy venture capital firms that SVB had deemed the top performing.

‡ Results from loans made to companies backed by the best performing twenty-five of the top seventy venture firms.

§ All-in refers to returns based on loans and warrants.

---

18. IRRs that included both interest payments and receipts from warrants.

GOLD HILL'S STRUCTURE

The effort to design Gold Hill had started in 2001, and in early 2002, Fischer joined Sean Lynden on the project. At the time, Gold Hill—then called The Silicon Valley Bank Venture Debt Fund— was envisioned as tightly connected to the bank. The Gold Hill employees would work part-time at the bank and receive typical bank compensation packages. SVB would have seats on Gold Hill's Investment Committee and get a share of the fees. Fischer said, "We didn't really understand the institutional investors. There was an 'if you build it, they will come,' mentality—institutional investors would flock to us because SVB was so dominant."

Between February and May 2002, Fischer and Lynden wrote the initial placement memo. Between May and November, Fischer said, "We were out there presenting to people and getting beaten up. Our placement agent got us in front of qualified top-tier institutional investors, so you could say we were getting beaten up by the best." The key concerns that prospective LPs mentioned were the fund's independence from the bank in terms of decision making and employment, a compensation system that would align the interests of the general partners (GPs) and LPs, and fees and how they were spent. "The LPs were willing to pay fees, but they didn't want those fees to go to anything except building the fund," Fischer noted. In addition, he said, "There was the matter of the first-time fund. Although we'd been doing this for the bank for years, we couldn't say that we'd done it with a fund before."

The final concern that potential LPs expressed was that the team had not yet been identified. Fischer was on the East Coast and Lynden on the West, but this was still an admittedly skeletal organization. Frank Tower, who joined in early 2003, commented, "It was really hard to raise funds without the team together. LPs want to see who will be managing the money." Along with Tower, Tim Waterson completed the Gold Hill GP contingent.

By then, SVB and the Gold Hill team had decided to restructure the fund in response to the wary LPs' feedback. Gold Hill would be a separate entity with SVB as a formal part-owner and investor. Employees of Gold Hill would have to quit SVB, and they would be compensated on a fee-and-carry basis rather than a straight salary (see Exhibit 8.9 for term sheet). "When we went back to the market," said Fischer:

> People were more willing to listen to us. We were more in step with what LPs were looking for from a fund. When we had first been in the market, we were caught as the balance of power shifted from the GPs to the LPs in the wake of the bursting of the Internet bubble. At that point, LPs were mad at the GPs and we were caught in the middle. Since the bursting of the bubble, LPs can be selective and dictate terms to a far greater extent than they could two or three years ago, especially with first-time funds. There's a big difference now between the established funds and the new ones—everyone wants to get into the old, established funds whereas the new funds have a hard time. But Pinnacle, a new venture debt fund, had closed a good sum, and Lighthouse, albeit established, was oversubscribed! So it couldn't have been the product. It had to be the structure. LPs didn't like what they saw in the SVB Debt Fund structure; it was too much a sponsored fund and they felt that interests weren't aligned enough. Once we changed the structure and had a solid team in place, raising a first-time fund with an institutional affiliation was still tough, but not impossible.

EXHIBIT 8.9

SUMMARY TERMS FOR GOLD HILL VENTURE LENDING I (ABRIDGED)

Item	Description
Amount to Be Raised	$200 million, up to $250 million.
Subscription Price	Minimum investment of $500,000 for individual investors, $2 million for institutions.
Closing Date	One year after the date on which the fund has raised more than $40 million.
Revocations/Withdrawals	None unless subject to special regulation.
Drawdowns	Capital commitments to be delivered as needed with at least ten days' notice.
Fund Objectives & Strategy	To generate superior returns by providing debt financing with warrant coverage to portfolio companies and, to a lesser extent, by making direct equity investments in those companies.
Term	Ten years, with up to three one-year extensions.
SVB's Capital Contribution	Commitment of $20 million, split between an LP interest and interest in the GP.
Timing of Distributions	In cash or marketable securities as determined by the GP.
Apportionment of Distributions	First: 100 percent of all investors in proportion to paid-in capital contributions until equal to the contributions made to date and an 8 percent per annum return, calculated like compound interest.
	Second: 100 percent to the GP until the GP has received its carried interest of 20 percent of the sum of the distributed preferred return and total distributions.
	Third: 80 percent to all fund investors and 20 percent to the GP.
Clawback	Yes, net of tax.
Reinvestment	For the first four years, the fund will reinvest the principal payment on loans, net of reserves and expenses, in new loans and equity securities.
Management Fee	The fund will pay a management fee to Gold Hill Capital Management, Inc. of 2 percent per year of the total committed fund capital for the first seven years, then 1.5 percent for the next two years, and 1 percent thereafter.
Financial Reports	Investors will receive quarterly and annual reports, annual audited financial statements and quarterly unaudited financial statements, and information necessary for income tax returns.
Removal of the General Partner	With or without cause by affirmative vote of the majority. The GP's interest would then be converted to that of an LP.

Source: Gold Hill.

The Team

Gold Hill's four-person founding team had over sixty years of experience in venture lending through up and down cycles (see Exhibit 8.10 for biographies). Fischer's interest in the project stemmed from a self-confessed entrepreneurial bent.

> This is like one of the spin-offs of our tech clients. But rather than separating, we'll be partnering closely with SVB, leveraging the bank's strengths and history, and adding value back to it. This is a chance for me to build off my history of managing all the bank offices outside of Northern California. We're not competing with the bank. We're adding to its strengths while building what we hope will be a sustainable business.

EXHIBIT 8.10

BIOGRAPHIES OF GOLD HILL TEAM

David Fischer has been exclusively dedicated to financing early stage technology and life science companies for more than eighteen years. He spent thirteen years at Silicon Valley Bank, where he held a variety of lending, venture capital liaison, and management positions. In his last assignment, he was responsible for all the bank's sales operations outside Northern California, a portfolio of more than $800 million in loans, and more than 100 warrant-based transactions.

Fischer has been a voting member of Silicon Valley Bank's Investment Committee, which has approved investments in more than 100 venture capital funds and into approximately fifty venture-backed technology and life science companies. He was also on the Investment Committee for Silicon Valley BancVentures, a $56 million direct equity fund that invests in early stage companies backed by top-tier venture funds.

Before joining Silicon Valley Bank in 1990, Fischer served for four years as a lender in Bank of New England's Technology group. Fischer is involved with various community and professional organizations, including the Pan Mass Challenge for the Jimmy Fund and the Advisory Board of the New England High Tech Charity Foundation. He earned a BA in economics from Middlebury College in Vermont. He has received his Chartered Financial Analyst (CFA) designation and is a member of the Association for Investment Management Research and the Boston Security Analysts Society.

Sean Lynden has been serving the financial needs of technology and life science companies for over eleven years, in both business development and portfolio management roles. He joined Silicon Valley Bank in 1992 and has sourced, negotiated, structured, monitored, and approved hundreds of loan transactions. In his last role as director of strategic planning, Lynden analyzed the venture capital investment environment affecting technology lending — identifying current and potential target markets, conducting client needs assessments, and helping formulate Silicon Valley Bank's overall business strategy.

Previously, Lynden was a founder and manager of Silicon Valley Bank's Northern California Semiconductor practice, where he had direct responsibility for Silicon Valley Bank's marketing efforts in the fabless semiconductor, EDA, and semiconductor equipment niches. During this time, Lynden maintained strong credit quality in a $125 million loan portfolio during a severe downturn in the semiconductor industry.

Lynden also served as a senior credit officer for Silicon Valley Bank's software, online services, and life sciences practices in Northern California. In this role he had individual loan approval authority of $5 million and served as a member of Silicon Valley Bank's Loan Committee. Lynden helped form the Corporate Finance group, and he also managed a team of analysts responsible for monitoring and tracking $500 million in loan commitments.

Lynden holds a BA from Stanford University and completed a certificate program at the Pacific Coast Banking School at the University of Washington.

Source: Gold Hill.

(Continues)

EXHIBIT 8.10 (CONTINUED)

BIOGRAPHIES OF GOLD HILL TEAM

Frank Tower has more than twelve years' experience working with early stage information technology and life science companies. For the past two years, Tower served as a senior credit officer in Silicon Valley Bank's Boston office—responsible for more than $400 million in loan commitments concentrated in Boston, New York, and Philadelphia.

Tower has worked with Silicon Valley Bank's regional lending teams in sourcing, structuring, negotiating, and managing more than 250 client relationships, while maintaining excellent credit quality in a period of economic turmoil. In this capacity, he had individual approval authority for loans up to $5 million, served on the Loan Committee, Credit Council, Joint Leadership, and Internal Communications committees.

Before his recent focus in Boston, Tower served as senior vice president and manager of Silicon Valley Bank's Mid-Atlantic office in Reston, Va., which he established. From 1995 to 1998, he cultivated relationships with companies, venture capitalists, and key referral sources to grow the portfolio from zero to seventy-two clients with $60 million in credit commitments. He hired, trained, and managed a team of seven professionals in all aspects of sourcing, structuring, negotiating, and underwriting commercial loan transactions.

Tower is very active in the technology community. He served as a board member of the Mid-Atlantic Venture Association and the MindShare CEO Forum. He also served on the selection and coaching committees for the Mid-Atlantic Venture Fair. From 1998 to 2000, Tower was a general partner of Blue Rock Capital, a regional $51 million seed and early stage information technology fund. At Blue Rock, Tower played an active role in the screening, due diligence, and structuring of twelve portfolio investments. He served as a director or observer of four companies during his tenure. Tower joined Silicon Valley Bank in 1992 from Replica Corporation, where he was controller of this venture-backed, interactive game company. He holds a BS in finance and investments from Babson College.

Tim Waterson has been lending and providing banking services to early stage technology companies in the Northern California since 1980. Waterson joined Silicon Valley Bank in 1994 as a team leader in the Northern California Technology Lending division. In 1996, he assumed responsibility for the Northern California Software Industry practice, where he had direct responsibility for the marketing, sales, and lending activity to all Bay Area software companies. In this capacity, Waterson generated substantial warrant income for the bank.

In 1998, Waterson was appointed manager of Silicon Valley Bank's Southwest Lending division, where he also acted as the division credit officer. He has sourced, structured, negotiated, and closed hundreds of venture lending transactions. From January 2000 until he joined Gold Hill, he had been responsible for Silicon Valley Bank's Products and Services group—overseeing Silicon Valley Bank's national leasing, asset-based, and specialty finance lending activities.

Waterson has supervised portfolios of up to $500 million in venture lending activity at Silicon Valley Bank. As head of the Products and Services group he also developed online banking products for early stage venture companies, cash management products, and international services and support.

Before joining Silicon Valley Bank, Waterson started and managed the first Northern California Business Lending group for Citigroup. He also spent four years in Bank of America's High Technology Lending division, where he managed the relationship with Apple Computer at its earliest stages. He is a member of the University of California Haas School of Business Entrepreneurs Forum. He is a graduate of UCLA with a BA in economics, and he earned an MBA in finance from Santa Clara University.

During their careers, the Gold Hill partners had originated, negotiated, and managed over $2 billion of venture loans during both the biggest run-up and the most sustained collapse of venture activity in the sector's history. While underwriting over 1,000 early stage venture loans, they had established close ties throughout the VC community, facilitating due diligence and deal flow. In addition, they could rely upon SVB's 175-person staff of relationship managers.

The four would have equal ownership. The general partners would receive a 20 percent carry after an 8 percent preferred return to the LPs; because SVB owned a share of the general partner and contributed so significantly to the fund, it would split the carry with the partners for this fund. The 2 percent management fee, based on committed capital, would decline after seven years to 1.5 percent for two years and 1 percent thereafter, funding salaries for the partners and support staff and covering management expenses (see Exhibit 8.11 for the fee flow).

The total staff of Gold Hill would number ten. In addition to the general partners, there would be associates and several analysts, who would help with due diligence and monitoring the portfolio. The organization would be split between the East and West Coasts, with offices in Newton, Massachusetts, outside Boston, and Santa Clara, California, colocated with SVB's main office. Fischer was comfortable with the dispersion. "It all comes back to the strong teamwork culture at SVB," he said. "We have grown up in it and it's natural to keep in touch even despite distance."

EXHIBIT 8.11

RELATIONSHIP OF GOLD HILL, SVB, AND LPs

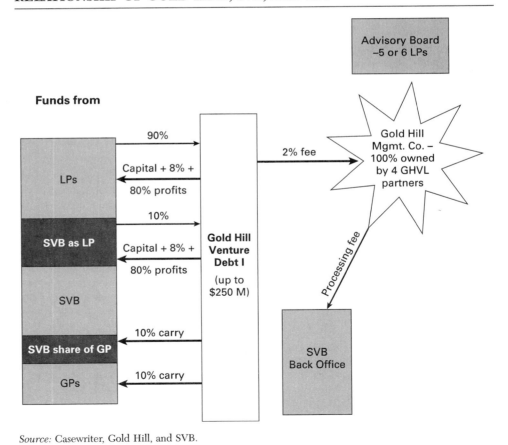

Source: Casewriter, Gold Hill, and SVB.

Gold Hill planned to make term loans of between $1 and $5 million to finance equipment purchases or working capital. The loans would amortize over thirty-six to forty-eight months, carry a 9 percent to 12 percent fixed interest rate, and convey warrants of 5–15 percent of the loan amount. Collateral would range from a specific lien to a blanket lien, and Gold Hill would try to get the right to invest in the next financing round.[19] The ideal loan size, Fischer said, "is $2.5 million or $3 million. We're very careful with $5 million. Venture investors don't like to see big chunks of debt in a company, and putting that much in might complicate future financings."

Deal Sharing

Gold Hill would be the preferred lending partner for SVB. For both entitles, part of the attraction of the arrangement was that it required no change in SVB's business model. Said Fischer, "The relationship managers will be doing the same thing. It's just that if it's a venture debt deal, they'll bring us in instead of a third-party lender. If Gold Hill finds a deal before SVB does, we'll make every effort to bring in the bank. Given the value of that partnership, it's only right that it should work both ways. We'll do everything we can to bring SVB into deals we source on our own."

The SVB relationship managers on whom the model relied were financially motivated to find good lending opportunities for both organizations. On top of a salary, they received annual bonuses based on the overall revenue of their portfolio and on the income stream from warrants. In 2002, with a mere $1.7 million in warrant income, SVB had paid no warrant-related bonuses at all. While this experience showed that warrant income was not reliable, it inspired the staff to find the best possible companies as clients.

The bank also provided information on the overall activity in the market. Fischer said, "SVB knows the best partners at VC firms, from their track record of picking good companies, sticking with them, and taking care of the bank if things don't work out. We won't follow any name-brand firm blindly; we want to understand the partner's expertise." SVB's data helped to answer one of the two key questions that Fischer had with every deal, as he described:

> The first is whether the company is fundable from an equity investor's perspective. Then the information from the bank helps us to determine whether the syndicate is functional. Sometimes we have the information ourselves; sometimes we use data from the bank. SVB has twenty years of history on all the best venture capitalists; how they work together, their track record through good times and bad. This definitely helps us to assess risk.

The information sharing also benefited entrepreneurs and venture capitalists. As Tower explained, "As a client of Gold Hill, there are benefits beyond our ability to just provide financing. Our clients are part of the SVB family. We have national and local events that build connections among the technology community, such as monthly executive lunches, VC panels, and networking events. SVB banks a lot of companies so we're a good source for job leads for CEOs and for venture capitalists looking to staff their portfolio companies."

The Investment Process

The investment process allowed Gold Hill and SVB to share information while making independent decisions. It proceeded through the following steps:

---

19. The use of a specific asset as collateral.

1. Deal flow: This was a function of the relationships of both the Gold Hill team and SVB with the venture community. Neither Fischer nor Wilcox saw any reason that SVB would see less than its historic 95 percent of all venture deals. Gold Hill might access deal flow from different sources, as well.

2. Selection: Fischer said, "In choosing a deal, it's crucial to understand both financing risk and operating risk." Financing risk was a function of the VC syndicate, and the company's market and business plan. Because Gold Hill relied upon a future equity infusion as one of its means of repayment, the VC firm's track record in choosing and then fully backing young companies was critical. Next, the Gold Hill partners would judge the strength of the company's management team and the market it intended to target. Finally, the partners would evaluate whether the financing round would create intellectual property or increase the enterprise value. All of these helped to determine the amount of financing risk Gold Hill would be taking on.

3. Due diligence: While the Gold Hill team would conduct its own due diligence, it would also access the results of SVB's credit checks and the bank's data on the venture firm's record and the existence and strength of competing portfolio companies. This information would reduce the risk of funding duplicate companies in a crowded market. It would also shed light on management's capital plan and potential burn rate. If the management had worked with SVB before, any history of mismanagement would be abundantly clear. A final area of examination was the company's potential return and its fit with the portfolios of the venture firms backing it.

4. Investment decision: Each organization would make a separate and independent credit decision. SVB would decide through its standard credit process. Gold Hill would decide through a unanimous vote of its partners. One entity could lend to a company that the other declined. If SVB needed help with the loan and Gold Hill declined, the bank could then syndicate with another partner.

5. Monitoring: There were two levels of monitoring. One was the day-to-day business of billing for interest and principal and reconciling accounts. The other was the higher-level review of business operations, such as the burn rate and progress toward profitability. SVB's back office, which was ten times larger than that of any other fund, handled the former tasks, in exchange for a service fee that Gold Hill paid. SVB would bill for and collect regular interest payments. Clients would send duplicate reporting packages to SVB and Gold Hill. SVB would analyze the financials and copy Gold Hill on the results; Gold Hill could conduct additional analysis or request more information from the company if it felt necessary. For the higher-level operational monitoring, the Gold Hill partners maintained active, close connections with the companies in which they were invested. To work out problem situations, SVB and Gold Hill had structured an agreement (an "intercreditor agreement"). Either the entity with the greater amount of money at risk or the one suggesting the more stringent approach to recovery would lead the effort.

Gold Hill planned to recycle its principal as a way to boost the fund's returns. For the first four years of the fund's life, Gold Hill would make new loans from the principal payments coming in from old loans. Thus, as a company paid down the principal of its loan, that money was recycled into loans to other companies, essentially leveraging the size of the fund. Interest income, gains from warrants, and equity gains from any co-investment opportunities would be distributed when received. While LPs would supply

$200 million and pay a management fee on that sum, they would receive interest and warrants on approximately $325 million in loans, according to the model.

Compensation

Wilcox had reservations about the compensation structure, as he explained:

> Don't get me wrong; I think the world of the Gold Hill team. But venture capital boutiques just pay too much. We are doing most of the work for the Gold Hill team, and we're lending our good name to the fund-raising. These guys had worked for a salary and a bonus for years doing the same thing they're doing now, and they'd done a great job. Why are they suddenly going to have conflicts of interest if they aren't being overcompensated? But the institutional money managers wouldn't have it any other way.

Fischer replied:

> The institutional investors wanted to ensure that our interests were aligned with theirs. They didn't want us compensated by the bank. Unless the warrants we take are fantastically valuable, I won't become rich off this fund; in fact, I'd do better if I stayed at the bank. If we raise three or four successful funds, then I'll make money, but then I will have proved that this is a good model and everyone—the bank, the bank's shareholders, and the LPs—will be doing well.

Conflicts of Interest

While the Gold Hill team and SVB felt that the fund offered investors a unique way to take advantage of the upside of equity while keeping the floor return of debt by leveraging SVB's unique window into the market, the fund-raising was difficult. Wilcox said, "One of the really challenging aspects has been understanding the viewpoints of the LPs. It's so foreign to us—they seem to have no deadlines and they're very skeptical. Maybe it's because they were burnt in the last cycle, maybe it's typical for a first-time fund, but they were *very* skeptical."

All of the participants expressed concerns about possible conflicts of interest. Wilcox was concerned that Gold Hill's allegiance would gradually drift away from the bank. "It's not that we've ever expected they'd do anything good for us but bad for the LPs. It's more like we're concerned they might do more with our competitors than with us."

Fischer felt this was unlikely, saying:

> I can't envision a better partner than SVB. Because of our history and the value of the partnership, we'd never do anything to compromise the bank. We think we have the opportunity to help SVB have better pricing in its products—we'll take on the riskier stuff, they can do what they do best and offer more mainline bank products. But at the end of the day, we're lenders, not venture capitalists. Working together, we'll be able to provide a more complete package at a better price that benefits all the parties involved.

The Gold Hill partners were aware that some competitors might try to use the connection with the bank to scare potential investee companies. Nonbank funds could claim that Gold Hill might encourage its partner to "sweep funds," or garnish accounts, if the company banked at SVB and fell behind on Gold Hill loans.

LPs expressed a number of concerns. Some feared that SVB, at $4.2 billion, was a prime takeover target, given its niche business and good brand name, a situation that might change the nature of the fund. Wilcox felt that the probability of such an event was very low. "Can I say never? Of course not. But I can say that while our stock has been up and down of late, we're pursuing strategies that will strengthen the rebounds and we're nowhere near being takeover bait."

Nonetheless, some institutions recalled all too clearly investing in funds managed by Hambrecht & Quist only to have the parent taken over by Chase, thus changing the deal. "If I had wanted Chase to manage my money, I would have given my money to Chase in the first place," was the general reaction of those LPs. "Why should I put myself in a similar situation?"

Others were concerned about the potential conflicts of interest between SVB and Gold Hill. These could arise in a number of ways if SVB and Gold Hill were invested in the same company but in securities with different seniority, especially if SVB's position were senior to Gold Hill's. The LPs wondered whether SVB, in a liquidation situation, would forego some recovery of its loan to ensure that Gold Hill would get something back on a more subordinate position. Fischer maintained that this missed the point, as Gold Hill and SVB would be co-lenders with equal seniority.

Another concern was the entire status of an affiliated fund. Some institutions believed that "particularly severe conflicts between investor goals and money manager actions appear in 'financial supermarkets.'"[20] Gold Hill, it was feared, might be pressured to help SVB out of a bad loan or be talked into making a bad loan to support its parent's goals. "I'm paid based on the fund's performance," Fischer said.

> I have no compensation from the bank; the bank can't fire me. Why would I do a thing like that? SVB understands we have to be selective and only do forty deals a year. So those have to be the best deals, because SVB isn't just a bank we work with but our partner, our co-owner, and our LP. If we want to have a successful family of funds, we have to make our decisions in the best interests of our LPs. We truly believe our differentiator is our relationship with SVB. To maximize the potential of the fund, we must maximize the relationship with the bank. The best returns for the LPs will come from having the best relationship with the bank. Deals where the bank is competing with us in some way won't do that. We will need to manage the tension between our fiduciary responsibility to our LPs and our need for a strong relationship with the bank. I strongly believe we can do this to the ultimate success of everyone.

The fact that a portion of the fund's revenues and returns would be shared with SVB, some LPs argued, might create perverse incentives. For one, it could increase the likelihood that the fund's partners would leave for shops where they could receive 100 percent of the reward for their work. Secondly, the partners might be inclined to devote more attention to those deals in which their parent was more interested, through reasons of relationships or sales of additional products, rather than to those where the potential for return to the fund itself was greatest. "Financial conglomerates," wrote one institutional LP, "generally seek income growth regardless of the consequences for investment performance."[21]

Other potential investors had cited wariness with venture debt itself and whether there was sufficient demand in the market. Some companies, although initially enthusiastic about

---

20. David Swenson, *Pioneering Portfolio Management* (New York: The Free Press, 2000), p. 261.
21. Swenson, p. 261.

taking venture debt, had become far less intrigued after they received a term sheet. More-over, some LPs viewed venture debt returns as insufficient, claiming they were taking venture risk yet receiving debt returns. Fischer thought this stood the argument on its head. Yet other LPs, especially those for large endowments, claimed that venture debt was difficult to fit into a portfolio. This school held that their portfolios "swung for the fences," expecting the best returns in good years and simply exceeding a VC benchmark in bad ones. In such a case, they argued, "why do I need a risk mitigator?"

THE PITCH

Fischer felt any conflicts could be resolved. "Without the SVB partnership we're not any different from Lighthouse or Pinnacle. We wouldn't be worse than they are, but with SVB, we're far better. The advantages are so great to both parties that we'll find a way to work through any issues that arise."

He knew that some LPs saw the benefits of venture debt. One had said, "Venture debt is an essential part of every venture-backed company's financial geology." Unfortunately, that LP had invested in both Lighthouse and Pinnacle.

Was there just no more appetite in the market for another venture debt fund? How, short of closing a small fund and proving themselves, could he show the wary LPs that the Gold Hill model would work?

The Private Equity Cycle: Investing

The second module of the course considers the interactions between private equity investors and the entrepreneurs that they finance. These interactions are at the core of what private equity investors do.

We will approach these interactions through a framework that seeks to understand the actions of private equity investors along two dimensions. First, we will explore the particular challenges that young and restructuring firms pose to private equity investors. Second, we will understand how the competitive situation facing the private equity firm itself determines its interactions with the firms in its portfolio.

WHY THIS MODULE?

It is easy to build a case that the financing and guidance of dynamic private businesses lie at the heart of the private equity process. The frequently complex interactions between investors and the firms in their portfolios could fill several courses! In order to help organize this complex material, we will approach the cases in this module through two frameworks.

First, we categorize the reasons why the types of firms backed by private equity investors find it difficult to meet their financing needs through traditional mechanisms, such as bank loans. These difficulties can be sorted into four critical factors: uncertainty, asymmetric information, intangible firm assets, and varying market conditions. At any point in time, these factors determine the choices that a firm faces. As a firm evolves, however, these factors can change in rapid and unanticipated ways.

We also highlight the manner in which the circumstances of the private equity group can affect the investment decision. In some cases, an imminent need to approach limited partners for capital—or an imminent decision as to whether an investment professional is to be promoted to partner—may lead to the rejection of an

This note was prepared by Professor Joshua Lerner for the sole purpose of aiding classroom instructors in the Venture Capital and Private Equity course.

otherwise attractive transaction. In other cases, concerns about competition from within and outside the private equity industry are leading groups to undertake substantial investments in the services they provide entrepreneurs. These company- and private equity organization–level issues will help organize our analyses of the complex interactions between private equity investors and the firms in their portfolios.

THE FRAMEWORK (1): THE FINANCING CHALLENGE

Entrepreneurs rarely have the capital to see their ideas to fruition and must rely on outside financiers. Meanwhile, those who control capital—for instance, pension fund trustees and university overseers—are unlikely to have the time or expertise to invest directly in young or restructuring firms. It might be thought that the entrepreneurs would turn to traditional financing sources, such as bank loans and the issuance of public stock, to meet their needs. A variety of factors, though, deny these financing sources to some of the most potentially profitable and exciting firms.

Private equity investors are almost invariably attracted to firms that find traditional financing difficult to arrange. Why are these firms difficult to finance? Whether managing a $10 million seed investment pool or a $5 billion leveraged buyout fund, private equity investors are looking for companies that have the potential to evolve in ways that create value. This evolution may take several forms. Early stage entrepreneurial ventures are likely to grow rapidly and respond swiftly to the changing competitive environment. Alternatively, the managers of buyout and build-up firms may create value by improving operations and acquiring other rivals. In each case, the firm's ability to change dynamically is a key source of competitive advantage, but also a major problem to those who provide the financing.

As mentioned above, the characteristics of these dynamic firms will be analyzed using a four-factor framework. The first of these, uncertainty, is a measure of the array of potential outcomes for a company or project. The wider the dispersion of potential outcomes, the greater the uncertainty. By their very nature, young and restructuring companies are associated with significant levels of uncertainty. Uncertainty surrounds whether the research program or new product will succeed. The response of a firm's rivals may also be uncertain. High uncertainty means that investors and entrepreneurs cannot confidently predict what the company will look like in the future.

Uncertainty affects the willingness of investors to contribute capital, the desire of suppliers to extend credit, and the decisions of firms' managers. If managers are averse to taking risks, it may be difficult to induce them to make the right decisions. Conversely, if entrepreneurs are overoptimistic, then investors want to curtail various actions. Uncertainty also affects the timing of investment. Should an investor contribute all the capital at the beginning, or should the investment be staged through time? Investors need to know how information-gathering activities can address these concerns and when they should be undertaken.

The second factor, asymmetric information, is distinct from uncertainty. Given daily involvement with the firm, an entrepreneur knows more about the company's prospects than investors, suppliers, or strategic partners. Various problems develop in settings where asymmetric information is prevalent. For instance, the entrepreneur may take detrimental actions that investors cannot observe: perhaps undertaking a riskier strategy than initially suggested or not working as hard as the investor expects. The entrepreneur might also invest in projects that build up personal reputation at the investors' expense.

Asymmetric information can also lead to selection problems. Entrepreneurs may exploit the fact that they know more about the project or their abilities than investors do. Investors may find it difficult to distinguish between competent entrepreneurs and incompetent ones. Without the ability to screen out unacceptable projects and entrepreneurs, investors are unable to make efficient and appropriate decisions.

The third factor affecting a firm's corporate and financial strategy is the intangible nature of many firms' assets. Firms that have tangible assets—e.g., machines, buildings, land, or physical inventory—may find financing easier to obtain or may be able to obtain more favorable terms. It is more difficult to abscond with the firm's source of value when it relies on physical assets. When the most important assets are intangible, such as trade secrets, raising outside financing from traditional sources may be more challenging.

Market conditions also play a key role in determining the difficulty of financing firms. Both the capital and product markets may be subject to substantial variations. The supply of capital from public investors and the price at which this capital is available may vary dramatically. These changes may be a response to regulatory edicts or shifts in investors' perceptions of future profitability. Similarly, the nature of product markets may vary dramatically, whether due to shifts in the intensity of competition with rivals or in the nature of the customers. If there is exceedingly intense competition or a great deal of uncertainty about the size of the potential market, firms may find it very difficult to raise capital from traditional sources.

THE FRAMEWORK (2): THE IMPACT OF THE PRIVATE EQUITY ORGANIZATION'S SITUATION

While the circumstances of the firm are important, so too are those of the private equity group itself. Three classes of circumstances are among the most influential in shaping private equity organizations' strategies.

In some cases, actions taken in previous fund-raising cycles can profoundly shape private equity investments. For instance, a private equity group may commit to investing in certain types of industries or stages at the time that the fund is raised, and consequently be hesitant to deviate from the stated plan. In a similar manner, the allocation of responsibility and compensation at the time that a fund closes may substantially affect the investment decisions made, even if in hindsight the private equity organization would have been far better off with another arrangement.

In other instances, it is the concerns about the raising of subsequent funds that are critical. For instance, the fact that the venture capital organization will soon be in the market with a new fund may drive the partners to refinance a troubled portfolio company, in order to avoid a write-off that might lead potential investors to question their performance. Similarly, groups may worry about a series of large failures endangering a private equity organization's "franchise" with limited partners. As a result, they may seek to balance the portfolio between highly risky investments offering the potential for large returns and a number of more modest but safer investments (for instance, syndicated investments in the latter financing rounds of transactions originated by other private equity groups). These concerns are at work not only at the organizational level, but also among individuals: worries about promotion and relative compensation can also profoundly affect private equity professionals' decisions.

Finally, concerns about the group's success in persuading top-flight entrepreneurs to choose their capital are important as well. During the early days of the industry, established private equity organizations had the upper hand in bargaining with entrepreneurs: there were relatively few alternatives to venture financing. The pool of private equity was also quite small. As a consequence, when groups found themselves interested in the same transaction, they often chose to share (or "syndicate") the transaction rather than to compete with each other. Today, the situation has changed dramatically. Not only has the amount of private equity expanded sharply, but groups are also facing increasing competition from sophisticated angel investors, incubators, and groups of high-net-worth investors organized by investment banks and other intermediaries. As a result, leading private equity groups today are increasingly engaging in what might be termed "branding": seeking to dramatically expand the range of services provided to and their visibility among entrepreneurs. Through such steps, the organizations seek to differentiate themselves from competitors within and outside the private equity industry.

THE STRUCTURE OF THE MODULE

This module will illustrate these two frameworks with examples from a wide variety of private equity funds and industries. We will carefully identify the types of problems that emerge in transactions involving different industries, countries, types of transactions, and private equity fund circumstances. We will then see how private equity groups respond to these changing settings by, for instance, altering deal structures.

A second important aspect of this module will be to explore the institutional and legal aspects of each type of private equity transaction. Among the specific issues raised in private equity transactions that we will consider are:

- The investment criteria, deal terms, and post-transaction tactics of venture capital investors
- The alternative criteria and approaches employed by latter-stage investors, as well as the associated providers of debt financing to these firms
- The nature of transactions that incorporate elements both of venture capital and buyouts, such as technology buyouts
- The extent to which deal structures can be translated into overseas markets, such as developing nations
- The various ways in which valuation issues are addressed, including many of the methodologies specific to the private equity industry and the opportunities for the application of new valuation techniques
- The relationship between financing choices and firm strategy
- The structure and implementation of relationships with strategic co-investors
- The restructuring of entrepreneurial ventures in distress

FURTHER READING ON PRIVATE EQUITY INVESTING

Legal Works

Joseph W. Bartlett, *Equity Finance: Venture Capital, Buyouts, Restructurings, and Reorganization* (New York: Wiley, 1995), chapters 5–10 and 16–27.

Michael J. Halloran, Lee F. Benton, Robert V. Gunderson, Jr., Keith L. Kearney, and Jorge del Calvo, *Venture Capital and Public Offering Negotiation* (Englewood Cliffs, NJ: Aspen Law and Business, 1997 and updates), volume 1, chapters 5 through 9.

Jack S. Levin, *Structuring Venture Capital, Private Equity, and Entrepreneurial Transactions* (Boston: Little, Brown, 2000), chapters 2–8.

Practicing Law Institute, *Venture Capital* (Commercial Law and Practice Course Handbook Series), New York, Practicing Law Institute, various years, various chapters.

Practitioner and Journalistic Accounts

Jeff Anapolsky, "How to Structure and Manage Leveraged Build-Ups," *Journal of Private Equity* 1 (Summer 1998): 33–50.

Asset Alternatives, *The Venture Capital Analyst: Health Care* [periodical and annual overview] (Wellesley, MA: Asset Alternatives, 2004 and earlier years).

Asset Alternatives, *The Venture Capital Analyst: Technology* [periodical] (Wellesley, MA: Asset Alternatives, 2004 and earlier years).

Asset Alternatives, *VentureOne Deal Terms Report* (Wellesley, MA: Asset Alternatives, 2003).

Leonard A. Batterson, *Raising Venture Capital and the Entrepreneur* (Englewood Cliffs, NJ: Prentice-Hall, 1986).

Coopers & Lybrand, *Three Keys to Obtaining Venture Capital* (New York: Coopers & Lybrand, 1993).

Paul A. Gompers and Josh Lerner, *The Money of Invention* (Boston, Harvard Business School Press, 2001), chapters 2–3.

Udayan Gupta, editor, *Done Deals: Venture Capitalists Tell Their* Stories (Boston: Harvard Business School Press, 2000).

Steve Harmon, *Zero Gravity: Riding Venture Capital from High-Tech Start-Up to Breakout IPO* (Princeton: Bloomberg Press, 1999).

Harold M. Hoffman and James Blakey, "You *Can* Negotiate with Venture Capitalists," *Harvard Business Review* 65 (March–April 1987): 16–24.

James L. Plummer, *QED Report on Venture Capital Financial Analysis* (Palo Alto: QED Research, 1987).

PriceWaterhouseCoopers, *Money Tree Report* (New York: PriceWaterhouseCoopers, 2004 and earlier).

Ruthann Quindlen, *Confessions of a Venture Capitalist: Inside the High-Stakes World of Start-Up Financing* (New York: Warner Books, 2000).

Randell Stross, *eBoys* (New York: Crown, 2000).

Many accounts in *Buyouts, Private Equity Analyst,* and *Venture Capital Journal.*

Academic Studies

George P. Baker and Karen H. Wruck, "Organizational Changes and Value Creation in Leveraged Buyouts: The Case of O. M. Scott & Sons Company," *Journal of Financial Economics* 25 (December 1989): 163–190.

George W. Fenn, Nellie Liang, and Stephen Prowse, "The Private Equity Market: An Overview," *Financial Markets, Institutions, and Instruments* 6 (#4, 1997): 27–69.

Paul A. Gompers and Josh Lerner, *The Venture Capital Cycle* (Cambridge: MIT Press, 2004), chapters 7–12.

Paul Halpern, Robert Kieschnick, and Wendy Rotenberg, "On the Heterogeneity of Leveraged Going Private Transactions," *Review of Financial Studies* 12 (Summer 1999): 281–309.

Thomas F. Hellmann and Manju Puri, "The Interaction between Product Market and Financing Strategy: The Role of Venture Capital," *Review of Financial Studies* 13 (#4, 2000): 959–984.

STEVEN N. KAPLAN AND PER STRÖMBERG, "Characteristics, Contracts, and Actions: Evidence from Venture Capital Analyses," National Bureau of Economic Research Working Paper no. 8764, 2003.

STEVEN N. KAPLAN AND PER STROMBERG, "Financial Contracting Theory Meets the Real World: An Empirical Analysis of Venture Capital Contracts," *Review of Economic Studies* 70: April 2003, 281–315.

STEVEN N. KAPLAN AND RICHARD S. RUBACK, "The Valuation of Cash Flow Forecasts: An Empirical Analysis," *Journal of Finance* 50 (September 1995): 1059–1093.

STEVEN N. KAPLAN AND JEREMY STEIN, "The Evolution of Buyout Pricing and Financial Structure in the 1980s," *Quarterly Journal of Economics* 108 (May 1993): 313–358.

SAMUEL KORTUM AND JOSH LERNER, "Assessing the Impact of Venture Capital on Innovation," *Rand Journal of Economics* 31 (Winter 2000): 674–692.

KRISHNA G. PALEPU, "Consequences of Leveraged Buyouts," *Journal of Financial Economics* 27 (September 1990): 247–262.

CHRISTINE C. PENCE, *How Venture Capitalists Make Investment Decisions* (Ann Arbor: UMI Research Press, 1982).

WILLIAM A. SAHLMAN, "The Structure and Governance of Venture Capital Organizations," *Journal of Financial Economics* 27 (October 1990): 473–521.

TYZOON T. TYEBJEE AND ALBERT V. BRUNO, "A Model of Venture Capitalist Investment Activity," *Management Science* 30 (September 1984): 1051–1066.

9

Adams Capital Management: March 2002

One morning in March 2002, the five general partners (see Exhibit 9.1) of Adams Capital Management, Inc. (ACM), a $700 million early stage venture capital firm, argued amiably over the last jelly doughnut before the start of their meeting. They had convened in ACM's Pittsburgh office, as they did every six weeks, for an intensive two-day meeting to review their twenty-seven portfolio companies and to evaluate new investment opportunities in their target industries—information technology (IT) and telecommunications/semiconductors. This meeting, though, had an unusual agenda item: "ACM's 'markets first' strategy—is it still appropriate for today's investment environment?"

ACM's investment strategy, in which the partners focused on particular markets to identify attractive opportunities and then managed the resulting portfolio companies in a defined and structured way, had served the firm well through the good times, with performances in or close to the top quartile for its first and second funds (see Exhibit 9.2 for performance data). Much had changed, however, in the five years since ACM's first fund had closed. The investment environment had gone from robust to hysterical to what now appeared to be a full-fledged collapse in 2001, extending into 2002. By early 2002, the market collapse had been exacerbated by a general sense of economic uncertainty, fueled by threats of war, accounting improprieties, the Wall Street analyst scandal, and declining private equity prices.

ACM had adopted its strategy in part to differentiate itself for potential limited partners. But the partners also believed that the loose structure of most venture firms—where each investor was often given wide leeway in determining which, and how many, markets and business models to invest in—could cause a firm to lose sight of the portfolio as a whole. Without a "markets first" strategy, through which the entire firm agreed upon the markets of interest *before* considering individual companies, the partners felt that firms would invest more on the basis of the fashion of the moment than on business fundamentals or market analysis.

Professors Felda Hardymon and Josh Lerner and Senior Research Associate Ann Leamon prepared this case. This is a rewritten version of "Adams Capital Management," by Felda Hardymon and Bill Wasik, HBS No. 899-256 (Boston: Harvard Business School Publishing, 1999). HBS cases are developed solely as the basis for class discussion. Cases are not intended to serve as endorsements, sources of primary data, or illustrations of effective or ineffective management.

EXHIBIT 9.1

BIOGRAPHIES OF ACM'S GENERAL PARTNERS

Joel P. Adams

Joel P. Adams founded Adams Capital Management in 1994 and has led its growth to $700 million capital under management. Before establishing ACM, Adams served for eight years as vice president and general partner of Fostin Capital Corp., a Pittsburgh-based, family-owned investment firm. Prior to working for Fostin, Adams served for seven years as a nuclear test engineer for General Dynamics, where he managed chemical, electrical and mechanical engineering teams and directed nuclear power plant sea trials. Adams is a director of several private and public companies, a member of several charitable organizations, a frequently requested speaker on the topic of venture capital, and a board member of Carnegie Mellon University.

Education

- M.S. in industrial administration, Carnegie Mellon University
- B.S. in nuclear engineering, State University of New York at Buffalo

Martin Neath

Martin Neath, who helped build Tivoli Systems, Inc., now an IBM company, into a multibillion-dollar software and service operation, joined Adams Capital Management in August 2001 as a general partner. Neath was the seventh employee and first application engineer at Tivoli when he began his career there in 1990, after working at Texas Instruments for five years. While at Tivoli, Neath was responsible for product strategy and development, marketing, customer support, product services and information technology, and he was extensively involved in sales and customer service. Tivoli went public in 1995 and was acquired by IBM a year later. Neath served as executive vice president of Tivoli, overseeing much of the company's day-to-day operations, including five business units, engineering, corporate marketing, customer service, training and education, office of the chief technology officer, and North American sales. In 1998, he was named a member of the IBM Senior Management Group (SMG), a team of the top 300 executives from around the world charged with the overall responsibility for IBM's strategy and business execution. After retiring from IBM in 1999, Martin helped build several emerging growth technology companies in the Austin area, including two years as president and COO of Works, Inc., a provider of procurement applications to midsize companies.

Education

- B.S. in computer science, Tufts University

N. George Ugras

N. George Ugras joined Adams Capital Management in 1999 as a general partner after spending a year as an investment professional at APAX Partners, a private equity firm in New York. Prior to joining APAX Partners, Ugras spent four years as a management consultant at McKinsey & Co. in New York, working closely with clients in the telecommunications and media industries on strategic and operational issues.

Education

- Research Fellow, physics, California Institute of Technology
- Ph.D. with honors, applied physics, Yale University
- B.S. in engineering physics, Fairleigh Dickinson University

(Continues)

EXHIBIT 9.1 (CONTINUED)

BIOGRAPHIES OF ACM'S GENERAL PARTNERS

William A. Frezza

Bill Frezza joined Adams Capital Management in 1997 as a general partner. Prior to his work at Adams Capital, Frezza was founder and president of Wireless Computing Associates, providing technology strategy and consulting services to major vendors in the telecommunications industry. Frezza served as the director of marketing and business development for Ericsson, Inc.'s wireless data division and has extensive engineering and product management experience from General Instrument Corp. and Bell Laboratories. He has also been involved in several start-up ventures, holds seven patents, and was a columnist for *Internet Week*.

Education

- M.S. in electrical engineering, Massachusetts Institute of Technology
- B.S. in biology, Massachusetts Institute of Technology
- B.S. in electrical engineering, Massachusetts Institute of Technology

Jerry S. Sullivan

Jerry Sullivan joined Adams Capital Management in 1997 as a general partner. Prior to joining the team, Sullivan was president of Design Technologies, Inc., focusing on evaluating and assessing the design and manufacturing processes used in electronic product creation. He came to Design Technologies from Microelectronics and Computer Technology Corporation (MCC), where he served as vice president. Prior to joining MCC, Sullivan spent several years at Tektronix and ten years with N.V. Philips. In addition, Jerry honed his international management skills through five years on location with Philips in Europe.

Education

- Advanced Management Program, Harvard Business School
- Ph.D. in physics, University of Colorado
- B.S. in engineering, University of Colorado

Source: Adams Capital Management.

EXHIBIT 9.2

INVESTMENT RETURNS FOR ACM FUNDS AS OF DECEMBER 31, 2001

	ACM I (starting 9/30/97)	ACM II (starting 12/31/99)	ACM III (starting 12/31/00)
Russell 2000 Index	14.2%	–0.3%	2.7%
NASDAQ	17.2%	–51.8%	–20.8%
Upper Quartile Private Equity IRR	60.9%	–2.1%	–16.0%
ACM Net IRR to LPs	**63.5%**	**–1.3%**	**–25.9%**

Source: Adams Capital Management.

But the previous eighteen months had turned recent experience on its head. The partners wondered whether now was the time to change their strategy significantly, and if so, in what way.

VENTURE INVESTING IN 2002

The final years of the 1990s had seen an unprecedented run-up in venture activity. Everything had increased—the amounts of capital raised, the management fees paid, the amounts invested, the prices that companies could command, the exit valuations received, and the speed with which investments became liquid (see Exhibit 9.3).

In 2001, the party had come to a grinding halt. After a decade marked by continually rising amounts of capital flowing into venture funds, the first half of 2001 had seen roughly the same amount raised as the first *quarter* of 2000. Nor had this trend reversed in the latter half of the year; fund-raising for the entire year had trailed 2000 by half. Moreover, the run-up of the preceding years had generated a significant overhang of funds raised but not yet disbursed. This was reflected in the growth of the median fund size, which had risen from $250 million in 1990 to well over $500 million a decade later.[1]

The numbers of deals, their price levels, and the size of the rounds in 2001 had all fallen considerably from the levels of the previous year (see Exhibit 9.4). This reflected the fact that almost three years of record-breaking venture activity had funded too many companies chasing too few customers in almost all technology sectors. In addition, the larger companies that portfolio firms targeted as customers had cut their capital expense budgets and were suffering from the backlog of earlier technology investments that had not yet been fully implemented. Spending on technology fell off sharply. As a result, portfolio companies performed significantly below expectations, often forcing their investors to resort to inside rounds for continued financing. The number of inside rounds for 2001 had doubled compared with the year before.[2]

EXHIBIT 9.3

VENTURE FUNDS RAISED

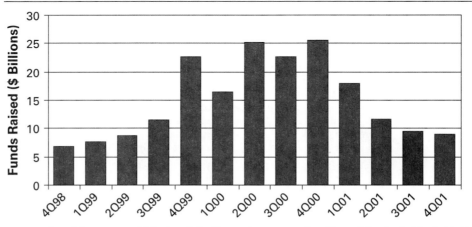

Source: Adapted from an unpublished study by VentureOne presented to Silicon Valley Bank, March 30, 2002.

---

1. Unpublished study by VentureOne presented to Silicon Valley Bank, March 30, 2002.
2. *Ibid.*

EXHIBIT 9.4

VENTURE INVESTMENT BY QUARTER

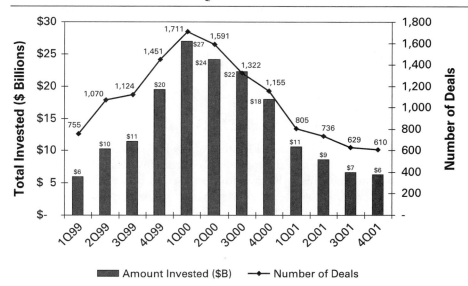

Source: Adapted from an unpublished study by VentureOne presented to Silicon Valley Bank, March 30, 2002.

A further complication for the venture capital (VC) industry was the longer path to liquidity. The initial public offering (IPO) market had dried up—the first half of 2001 had seen nine venture-backed IPOs, compared with 111 in the same period in 2000. Mergers and acquisitions had become the primary path to liquidity, although 2001 saw far fewer of these transactions as well, and at far lower prices.[3]

ADAMS CAPITAL MANAGEMENT

Joel Adams, founder of ACM, grew up in Phelps, New York, a small town between Rochester and Syracuse. "My dad owned a dairy farm," he recalled, "and on his program, as soon as you turned six, you started getting up at 4:45 in the morning and doing chores." Adams was fifteen when his mother passed away, leaving his father with no choice but to delegate most of his wife's responsibilities to the three kids. Looking back on those days, Adams said, "At the time the confluence of events was a hell of a wake-up call for a teenager, but I learned invaluable lessons about money and time management."

After graduating from the University of Buffalo in 1979, Adams joined nuclear submarine manufacturer General Dynamics, where he became a test engineer, the lead engineer responsible for starting and testing a sub's nuclear reactor and representing General Dynamics during the Navy's sea trials of the new boats. In 1984, he moved to Pittsburgh to attend the business school at Carnegie Mellon University (CMU), lured by its strong program in entrepreneurship.

During Adams' second year at CMU, he worked part-time for Fostin Capital, a small VC firm that invested on behalf of the Fosters, a wealthy Pittsburgh family. Adams

3. *Ibid.*

joined Fostin after graduation as a junior partner, just as the firm closed a new $14 million fund. Shortly thereafter, the firm and Adams became involved with APA/Fostin I, a joint venture formed with Patricof & Co. to manage the $40 million fund that the state of Pennsylvania wanted to invest in VC.

In 1992, APA/Fostin II closed at $60 million. The following year, after seven years with the firm, Adams, CFO Andrea Joseph, longtime secretary Lynn Patterson, and former partner Bill Hulley formed Adams Capital Management, Inc., to handle the Fostin portion of the new fund. ACM raised its first fund, the $55 million ACM I, in 1996, and it had a strategy.

DISCONTINUITY-BASED INVESTING

Ever since he had joined Fostin, Adams had been dissatisfied with what he considered a lack of focus and discipline in the firm's investing style. "Here's a nuclear engineer, walking into this industry, with a very small fund in Pittsburgh whose strategy was to be diversified by stage, by industry, *and* by geography," Adams recalled. "After about a year, I said, 'This isn't a strategy at all.' You could do anything." He was especially dismayed by the method of developing deal flow. Rather than learning about markets and then targeting specific deals within them, he said, "The approach at Fostin was to open the mail in the morning" to see what business plans had arrived.

Two of Adams' experiences at Fostin acquainted him with the power of targeted investing. The first was his involvement with Sherpa Corporation, a developer of software applications for engineering product data management. "I understood the issues of engineering data management from my days at General Dynamics," Adams said. "I was a much smarter investor looking at an industry that I knew." Not only was he a better investment manager and board member, he realized, but he was also a better negotiator. "Entrepreneurs are passionate and biased about their businesses," he said. "If the first time I hear about a market is from the entrepreneur, I'm at a big disadvantage."

His second revelation was even more powerful. Seeking a computer in 1987, Adams happened to learn about a mail-order operation in Texas called PCs Limited that custom-built personal computers and undercut retail prices. After speaking with the company's CEO, Michael Dell, Adams invested $750,000 in the future Dell Computer's first outside venture round. At the end of 2000, this holding was worth $470 million.

Adams realized that Dell had created such an explosion of value by exploiting a *discontinuity*—a dramatic and sudden change in a large and established market. In this instance, the discontinuity involved distribution. The rise of direct distribution snuck up on the large personal computer manufacturers, which had highly entrenched networks of retail dealers. These networks, Adams noted, "couldn't be unwound overnight." Dell could build a multibillion-dollar business from scratch because his large and sleepy competitors could not respond to this distribution discontinuity in time.

As ACM expanded, Adams resolved that any new partners would be engineers and bring their technical training to bear in thorough examinations of a few promising markets. By 2002, ACM's strategy had evolved to focus on investments in markets that the partners already knew well and had already identified as attractive.

A few initial prerequisites had developed over time. The first was that the companies in which ACM invested would sell to businesses, not consumers, and their value propositions would be driven by return on investment (ROI). "That's ROI for the customers, not us," said Adams. "Our first question is, 'If somebody is going to buy this company's product, what does the CFO recommendation look like?'" The second criterion was that the business was "first-generation applied technology," or one of the first companies to use a given technology for a specific application.

In keeping with the partners' engineering backgrounds, the firm focused on the IT and telecommunications/semiconductor industries, areas that were, in their view, experiencing significant discontinuities, shifts in existing markets that would create opportunities for start-up companies to become leaders. Within these industries, ACM's partners focused on identifying four primary causes of discontinuities (see Exhibit 9.5):

1. *Standards*. Despite the emergence of a technology standard in some fields, existing manufacturers would often cling to their proprietary technologies in an attempt to preserve their captive customer base. Even as customers demanded the standard, the existing manufacturers perceived it as a threat to their oligopolistic market positions and were reluctant to adopt it. One such example was FORE Systems, which built communications devices that conformed to the asynchronous transfer mode (ATM) standard for communications in wide-area networks. The

---

EXHIBIT 9.5

ACM'S VIEW OF DISCONTINUITIES

Discontinuity: The Mother of Opportunity

Our strategic focus is built upon the concept of a discontinuity—a circumstance or event that disrupts the equilibrium in a particular industry and creates new entry opportunities. Discontinuities are rapid and permanent structural changes in established markets that incumbents, hindered by economics or aging infrastructure, are not able to respond to in a timely fashion.

Examples of specific discontinuities that create new entry points into large established markets include:

- The development of software technology allowing protection of content without proprietary hardware;
- The introduction of competition to the utility industry to permit customer choice among power producers, leaving incumbent utilities burdened with uneconomical infrastructures;
- The changes in the FDA approval processes affecting the introduction of advanced, technology-driven diagnostic devices supporting the convergence of new technologies into tightly integrated, software-based lifesaving systems;
- The emergence of communications protocols that support efficient transaction clearing over public networks, allowing digital content owners to greatly lower distribution costs and improve customer service;
- The move to a property-based spectrum management regime via FCC spectrum auctions, vastly increasing the amount of spectrum available for the introduction of innovative narrowband and broadband wireless technologies.

Compelling market opportunities that can be exploited by breakthrough innovation are created by discontinuities such as **industry standards, regulations, technology convergence,** and **distribution.** And because even the best product or service will not stimulate great returns in a small or mediocre market, we focus on established markets approaching a billion dollars in size. We constantly watch these markets for discontinuities and the emerging companies that are positioned to take advantage of them. This is where we concentrate our investments.

Source: Adams Capital Management.

big players at the time, AT&T/Lucent and Northern Telecom, each had proprietary protocols for those communications. These manufacturers clearly had the technical prowess and market muscle to exploit ATM as well, but they were slow to do so for fear of cannibalizing their own market shares. In April 1999, FORE was acquired by GEC plc for $4.5 billion.

2. *Regulation.* Unexpected regulatory changes could force market players to adapt quickly to a new market reality. An example of such a dislocation had occurred in the U.S. cellular market, where a host of new opportunities and networks had emerged after the government's creation of the PCS spectrum. From a technology point of view, the new spectrum provided a chance for GSM, the cheaper and more easily deployed base station technology popular in the rest of the world, to gain ground on the unwieldy proprietary technology dominant in the United States. GSM equipment manufacturers and the upstart carriers that provided the service used their agility in the new regulatory environment to challenge the giants.

3. *Technology.* A technology-based discontinuity could take two forms. In one, it could appear as a whiz-bang package that took big competitors months or years to duplicate, such as Apple's Macintosh operating system. Alternatively, it could involve the convergence of technologies that had hitherto been separate, requiring innovation to allow these once-disparate systems to interact. An example here was the rise of corporate remote access, which forced companies to buy technology that would connect the public carrier telephone networks to the corporations' internal local area networks.

4. *Distribution.* Dell Computer provided the ultimate example of a distribution-based discontinuity—the rise of mail order completely surprised existing personal computer manufacturers, to the great enrichment of Dell and its shareholders. ACM watched for other such disruptions in established distribution channels.

This top-down approach to identifying markets was crucial in helping ACM achieve consensus about and control over where its partners would invest. Adams had a firm belief: "Market due diligence is the only due diligence you can do independent of a transaction. If you present the partners with the industry and market dynamics ahead of time, then we can all talk about each other's prospective deals and leverage each other's knowledge base and contacts before we make an investment."

ACM's approach to identifying discontinuities included its Discontinuities Roundtable, a group of advisors who met periodically with the ACM partners to identify and discuss market discontinuities that could lead to fruitful investment theses. The twenty-person roundtable comprised industry experts and observers who attended meetings depending on the topic at hand. Among their number had been Clayton Christensen of the Harvard Business School, known for his research on how innovation affected markets; George Kozmetsky, founder and backer of more than 200 companies; Atiq Raza, former CEO of AMD, the chip maker that competed against Intel; and Mike Maples, former chief technology officer of Microsoft. The process required partners to write discontinuity white papers that advanced the investment thesis and to present them to a roundtable of appropriate experts drawn from the pool. The group would discuss the merits of the thesis under consideration, usually agreeing to pursue two or three of the eight to ten papers presented in a meeting. The meetings would also identify other avenues for future exploration.

Once an investment thesis was thoroughly vetted by the Discontinuities Roundtable, the ACM partners would systematically search for deals in that domain. Sometimes this meant identifying pockets of excellence in the appropriate technology and supporting entrepreneurs as they formed a company. In other cases, partners would find an opportunity by sorting through several existing potential investments. This intensive process gave the partners deep knowledge of the companies' opportunities and therefore made ACM more attractive as an investment partner.

Structured Navigation

Along with a systematic approach to identifying markets, ACM also developed a system for managing its investments, called "structured navigation." The system was born out of the observation that early stage technology companies shared many of the same benchmarks and needed many of the same elements to succeed. Jerry Sullivan, a general partner who had joined the firm from MCC, Tektronix, and Phillips, explained: "Our investments typically have high development costs coupled with the direct sales force characteristic of early stage companies. The majority of our investments—90 percent—are software-based, so resource planning and allocations are well understood by all of our general partners. We feel that our structured navigation strategy applies to all companies within the model."

Aspects of the structured navigation included:

1. *Round out the management team.* Like most other VC firms, ACM was deeply involved in helping its entrepreneurs complete their management teams. "Almost 80 percent of the time, we're the first money in, so the entrepreneur has been trying to build a management team without capital," said Martin Neath, a former vice president with IBM and now an ACM general partner. "People are going to join a company that has some capital behind it, so we fundamentally believe that if you've got a great opportunity that's well funded, you're going to attract a lot of talent." ACM had devoted significant resources to the creation of its Services Group to help its portfolio companies in this area.

2. *Obtain a corporate partner or endorsement.* The notion that an early stage company, hoping to exploit a sea change in a large existing market, could forge a partnership (an endorsement, a distribution deal, or an equity investment) with one of the very players from which it hoped to steal market share seemed entirely contradictory. But the ACM partners believed that this should almost always be possible. From ACM's perspective, forging these relationships early would often create other exit opportunities while on a path to a public offering.

3. *Gain early exposure to industry and investment banking analysts.* Industry analysts such as Gartner, Giga, and Forrester often created the first wave of market interest in a new technology. This group's validation could speed the acceptance or application of a new technology. While industry analysts could help create a market for the technology, analysts at investment banking firms could create an exit for the company, and ACM tried to make sure they met the portfolio companies early. "First of all, the good analysts really do understand the businesses of these little companies," explained George Ugras, a general partner in ACM's Silicon Valley office. "But the second thing is, [bankers are] in the fee business, and they need to put marriages together. ... [Introducing the two parties early] is a tactic that will set you up for deals later on."

4. *Expand the product line.* A first-generation applied technology company would be confronted by high initial costs of development and sales. Bill Frezza, the general

partner in ACM's Boston office, observed, "The marginal cost of the development for subsequent products or the next sale is much lower." Once the first product using the new technology had been developed and a base of customers secured, the costs of leveraging that technology into another, similar product and selling it into a base of existing accounts was comparatively small. But "sometimes the entrepreneur hasn't thought that out yet," he noted. "Our approach ensures that the companies are adequately focused on this value creation opportunity."

5. *Implement best practices.* ACM's partners felt that their entrepreneurs should focus on developing products and selling them to customers, not on structuring stock option packages or compensation plans. After working with dozens of companies with similar structures, the partners felt that they could provide boilerplate versions of effective plans.

ACM used these five "steps" (in no particular order) to manage its investments, keeping track of which steps each company had finished and which it still needed to complete. The process, the partners felt, not only made their investments more successful but also provided the partners in four offices across the United States with a commonly understood internal barometer of a company's progress (see Exhibit 9.6 for offices). "If ten months into a deal you can't attract talented people, corporations don't care, and you can't get the bankers interested—you're learning something," Sullivan said. "And maybe you ought to get out."

EXHIBIT 9.6

ACM'S OFFICES

Geographic Presence

Source: Adams Capital Management.

DEFENDING THE STRATEGY

Was it really necessary to formulate such a rigorous strategy for investing in early stage businesses? Adams admitted that, to a certain extent, the strategy was motivated by the practical necessities faced by a small firm based in Pittsburgh raising a $55 million fund in 1996. "We had to get ourselves above the muck, and the way you do that is with a well-defined, market-centric strategy that you execute in a disciplined manner," he said.

But Adams also balked at the conventional wisdom about VC and venture capitalists—namely, that VC was a personality-driven business and that successful venture capitalists were all genius deal makers whose vision turned everything they touched into gold. "I just don't buy the 'rock star' model that many venture firms promote," Adams said.

Instead, he wanted to build a venture firm in the same way that most businesses were built—with a structure in which any of its employees were, in principle, replaceable. "We wanted to develop a system where you could throw anybody out of here and the thing will still cook along," he said. "We wanted to build a system for executing this business. All of us are engineers, we think that way. We're not rock stars. We have a system for finding areas that are of interest, getting deals, and making them valuable. That's what we do."

Over the previous five years, the partners felt that the strict adherence to strategy, combined with the systematic portfolio management that navigation provided, had served the firm well. During that period, ACM I had invested in fifteen companies for a total cost basis of $53 million. That fund, primarily invested by four partners operating out of offices in Pittsburgh, Philadelphia (later Boston), and Austin, Texas, had distributed stock valued at $122.7 million. Based on the early success of that fund, ACM had raised the $150 million ACM II in 1999, followed quickly by the $420 million ACM III in 2000 (see Exhibit 9.7 for fund statistics).

ACM in 2002

The discussions at the March general partner meeting centered on the investment pace of ACM III, the new $420 million fund. Since closing in November 2000, the partners had made ten investments (see Exhibit 9.8 for companies). In the fund's prospectus, ACM had committed to its limited partners that it would make twenty to twenty-five investments in the IT and telecommunications/semiconductor industries, with no more than 10 percent of the fund's total value in any one company. Each company had conformed to ACM's strategy, despite the market decline. Frezza explained:

> We're on target with investing Fund III, and we've been able to find compelling opportunities with extremely low—and therefore attractive—valuations. These will enable us to generate returns in any market conditions. When valuations are unrealistic in the investment phase, only unrealistic valuations in the exit phase will give you the returns you need. It's true that the industry, at times, appears to be caught in an investment decision "paralysis" with this $100 billion of uninvested cash that you hear about, but we continue to execute our strategy diligently, and we have found some extremely attractive deals in our domains.

Sullivan pointed to recent data on capital spending by the *Fortune* 1,000, an important source of partners, customers, and acquirers for many of ACM's portfolio companies:

> Software spending was flat to down in 2001 and expected to be the same for 2002. Telecom equipment spending was down approximately 30 percent in 2001 and is expected to be lower in 2002. Overall, the economy appears to

EXHIBIT 9.7a

ACM'S THREE FUNDS, PERFORMANCE AS OF DECEMBER 31, 2001

	ACM I	ACM II	ACM III
Inception	December 8, 1997	October 8, 1999	November 17, 2000
Contributed capital	$ 55,000,000	$ 105,000,000	$ 69,300,000
Capital due from partners	—	45,000,000	350,700,000
Committed capital	55,000,000	150,000,000	420,000,000
Realized gains or (losses)	110,203,081	—	—
Unrealized gains or (losses)	(10,912,252)	4,631,220	(2,996,000)
Income from investments	—	91,181	—
Net operating loss from inception	(4,261,745)	(6,717,322)	(10,446,432)
Gross value of partnership	150,029,084	148,005,079	406,557,568
Less distributions	(122,699,588)	—	—
Net Partnership Capital (includes capital due from partners)	$ 27,329,496	$ 148,005,079	$ 406,557,568
Percentage increase from inception	**172.78%**	**–1.33%**	**–3.2%**
Represented by:			
Value of current portfolio investments $	27,254,967	$ 96,598,696	$ 55,148,155
Cash and temporary investments	103,069	6,415,192	751,103
Capital due from partners	—	45,000,000	350,700,000
Other net current assets	(28,540)	(8,809)	(41,690)
Partnership Capital	**27,329,496**	**148,005,079**	**406,557,568**
Less capital due from partners	—	(45,000,000)	(350,700,000)
Current Net Partnership Capital	27,329,496	103,005,079	55,857,568

Source: Adams Capital Management.

EXHIBIT 9.7b

ACM I'S PORTFOLIO COMPANY IRRs FOR EXITED INVESTMENTS AS OF DECEMBER 31, 2001

Date	Company	Cost	Proceeds	Gain/Loss	IRR
1/1/1999 & 9/99	Coretek (acq. by Nortel)	$ 3,227,718	$ 122,699,588	$ 119,471,870	495%
11/97 & 12/99	AirNet Communications	5,271,045	553,346	(4,717,699)	–69%
11/97—10/99	Triton Network	2,315,443	1,040,491	(1,274,952)	–32%
9/97	Physicians Data Corp.	1,300,000	43,611	(1,256,389)	–68%
3/98 & 8/98	Reciprocal	2,019,749	—	(2,019,749)	NA

Source: Adams Capital Management.

EXHIBIT 9.8

ACM III'S COMPANIES AS OF MARCH 1, 2002

Initial Investment	Company Name	Sector
11/00	Intrinsity, Inc.	Telecommunications/Semiconductor
2/01	Revenue Technologies Corp.	IT
3/01	Optellios, Inc.	Telecommunications/Semiconductor
6/01	InfoLibria, Inc.	IT
6/01	SmartOps Corp.	IT
7/01	Lovoltech, Inc.	Telecommunications/Semiconductor
7/01	Works, Inc.	IT
7/01	TimeSys Corp.	IT
8/01	AmberWave Systems Corp.	Telecommunications/Semiconductor
2/02	Flashline, Inc.	IT

Source: Adams Capital Management.

be in a macro-recession, and the telecom equipment industry is in a depression. We still expect some consolidation among the biggest players in telecom. It will be a slow and painful process that could last well beyond 2002, but the data are not showing a permanent shift away from technology investments. Technology investments that create efficiencies, generate cost savings, and improve performance or productivity are the main catalysts driving economic growth. Every one of our portfolio companies provides real solutions that create these improvements—otherwise, we wouldn't have invested.

Although a protracted downturn could prove troublesome, Neath felt that venture-backed companies would still have a place in any eventual recovery:

The *Fortune* 500 will use venture-backed firms to stay viable in the global economy. Start-up companies—and most of them will be venture-backed—take the risk out of new technologies. When the checkbooks reopen, the pent-up demand should bode well for our portfolio companies. Whether they'll be successful depends on how well we know our markets and how well we navigate them.

Adams agreed. "I still think that this is an excellent time to be investing in early stage applied technology companies. We're going to look back in a few years and say that some of the best VC-backed technology investments of this decade were made in the 2001–2002 time frame."

At the same time, though, the near-term outlook was uncertain. "You have to admit that the discontinuity well has gone pretty dry in telecom and IT," Ugras said.

The partners determined they had three options if they wanted to revise the firm's strategy. They could go deep, they could go broad, or they could, as they put it, "go all out."

GOING DEEP

The partners had watched the trends in engineering with interest. Increasingly, design work was done in the United States, and, once the product was standardized, the routine engineering work was outsourced to India, where talented engineers were available for far less than their U.S. counterparts. "Now," Adams observed, "Chinese universities are graduating 125,000 engineers a year. Engineering is being commoditized."

As a result, one option for ACM was to focus on the more fundamental building blocks of technology within its current targeted industries—areas such as components, advanced and specialty materials, and special techniques for production processes, which were less likely to be commoditized. Investing in applied materials was, however, a difficult field. The major players in materials and basic components, New Enterprise Associates' CMEA (Chemical and Materials Enterprise Associates) fund and Ampersand Ventures, had tried this strategy, only to expand their focus in the past five years to include IT, life sciences, and software investments.[4] In fact, Ampersand's Specialty Materials and Chemicals II fund, established in 1992, had invested 40 percent of its $40 million in biotechnology companies. By 2001, only eight firms, or 13 percent of Ampersand's 64-company portfolio, were classified as advanced specialty materials. For CMEA, the proportion was even lower, at 6 percent, or five firms.[5] Rather than focusing on advanced specialty materials, the firms were using their knowledge of the field to identify promising technologies in other sectors.[6] Ampersand, for instance, had shifted from advanced materials to specialty materials, moving toward products that were closer to the consumer—vinyl fencing, composites for medical products, and germicidal soaps.

The shift in emphasis had several drivers. The advanced materials sector was characterized by long lead times and high capital intensity. 3M and Du Pont, which had the patience and the strategic interest to back extensive efforts as a type of outsourced research and development, provided fierce competition to traditional VC firms. Said Charlie Yie, general partner at Ampersand:

> We backed a nanotechnology company that was developing superior industrial drill bits. It was an eight-year effort, and we lost everything in the end. It wasn't losing the money that was the biggest problem; it was the eight years invested. Advanced materials share many of the risks of biotechnology—long lead times and capital intensity—but none of its appeal to investors. At the same time, though, if you back the firm that develops the next nylon or Corian, you have incredible returns.

GOING BROAD

Another option that the partners considered was increasing the size of the firm. Until now, ACM had only hired partners, looking for the expertise and experience provided by people of that level. In a market with fewer deals, though, perhaps the firm should leverage its position as a top-quartile fund and hire a number of associates to search for promising concepts. Frezza observed, "There is a lot of good talent on the street now—maybe we should take advantage of this."

Additional personnel would increase the number of potential deals that could be discovered, whether at trade shows, university laboratories, or through various journals. Staffing up would also relieve some of the burden on the general partners, who now did everything from writing the initial white papers on potential areas of focus through discovering companies, negotiating deals, and sitting on boards, with the many disparate

4. David Rotman, "Venture Capital," *Chemical Week* (May 29, 1996), p. 22.

5. Data from VentureSource, http://www.venturesource.com, accessed January 2, 2003.

6. http://www.ampersandventures.com, accessed January 2, 2003.

duties involved. A few good associates might be able to do the research to find the next exciting sector or support the partners in due diligence. Investing ACM III's $420 million at $20 million per company would add another eleven companies to the ten already in the fund's portfolio, increasing the work load for each partner. "At some point, the time we'd invest in training an associate might be worthwhile," Ugras mused.

Yet that time investment worried the partners, who feared turning ACM into an academy for venture capitalists. They were also concerned about just how many of their tasks could be delegated. "Even without rock stars, there's an element of relationship in VC," Neath said. "Unless you have a really good associate, who is likely to leave for a partner position elsewhere, the CEO wants to talk to the partner."

Additionally, ACM's strategy required deep understanding on the part of the partners. "You get a better understanding of the CEO's grasp of his field and his technology in a direct conversation," Frezza commented. "To what degree will we be willing to rely on an associate for primary knowledge of the company, the technology, and the market?" While the partners knew that staffing up and delegating had worked for some top-tier firms, Adams was concerned that the deep domain expertise on which ACM had built its reputation might be diluted by hiring associates fresh from MBA programs and its performance degraded by devoting partner time and energy to training them.[7]

VC firms had also encountered organizational challenges in expanding their scope and numbers. Adding personnel required venture capitalists to become personnel managers to a certain degree, creating career paths, determining compensation strategies, and managing performance in a way that was not necessary in a four-person partnership.

Expanding ACM's investment focus—into medical equipment, for instance—posed other challenges. Firms that had done so had found that the new experts had to educate the other partners on specialized areas, making the deal approval process tedious, time consuming, and cumbersome. Additionally, if one sector was underperforming, those that were successful often resented the burden of making up the losses. If the underperformance endured, that sector expert might be cut, leaving the remaining portfolio in the hands of the existing nonexperts. This had happened to a number of firms in the late 1990s, as high technology consistently outperformed life sciences. Many firms that had invested in both fields moved out of the life sciences sector, leaving a small group of life science companies adrift in a technology-focused firm.

GOING ALL OUT

The final option was for the firm to be more aggressive in its approach. In ACM I, the company had invested an average of $3.5 million in fifteen companies, leading eleven of these deals and taking board seats on ten of them. By the time the investee company had completed several subsequent rounds, it was difficult for ACM to maintain a significant ownership position. In ACM II, which closed in December 1999, the firm invested larger amounts, $9.5 million (including reserves), in fourteen companies. These deals usually had only a handful of co-investors, and ACM was able to attain greater ownership in the deals it wanted to continue backing. With ACM III, the group had invested an average of $15.3 million (including reserves) in ten early stage companies by early 2002, often as the only institutional investor (see Exhibit 9.9 for portfolio).

The partners contemplated continuing this trend. By being countercyclical and increasing its stake in its portfolio companies, ACM would essentially place a major bet

7. This discussion was informed by Noam Wasserman, "The Upside-Down Venture Capitalist," unpublished Ph.D. dissertation, 2002.

EXHIBIT 9.9

ACM'S PORTFOLIO

Name	Fund	1st Investment Date	Board Seat? (Yes/No)	Amount ($Thous)	Stage	Company Status
AirNet Communications Corporation	1	11/1/1997	Y	4,001	Expansion	Went public
AmberWave Systems Corporation	2, 3	12/1/1999	Y	15,625	Early stage	Privately held
Bluestone Software, Inc. (FKA: Bluestone, Inc.)	Pre-ACM	4/18/1997	Y	2,604	Expansion	Went public
CAVU, Inc. (AKA: E-xpedient)	1, 2	2/11/2000	Y	16,153	Early stage	Bankrupt
CoManage Corporation	1	10/7/1998	Y	5,378	Early stage	Privately held
Context Media, Inc.	1, 2	3/21/2000	Y	6,750	Early stage	Privately held
CoreTek, Inc.	1	1/15/1999	Y	3,500	Early stage	Acquired
Cytyc	Pre-ACM	3/1/1989	Y	3,858	Early stage	Went public
Dell	Pre-ACM	11/30/1987	Y	750	Early stage	Went public
Factory Logic Software, Inc.	2	7/17/2000	Y	4,000	Early stage	Privately held
FFWD, Inc. (FKA: eToll, Inc.)	2	7/28/2000	Y	14,024	Expansion	Privately held
First Avenue Networks, Inc. (FKA: Advanced Radio Telecom)	1	6/8/1999	N	3,000	Expansion	Went public
Flashline	3	2/1/2002	Y	6,000	Expansion	Privately held
Hologix, Inc. (FKA: MBA Technologies, Inc.)	1	6/1/1998	Y	6,218	Expansion	Out of business
InfoLibria, Inc.	1, 3	6/14/2001	Y	10,011	Early stage	Out of business
Integrated Micromachines, Inc. (AKA: IMMI)	2	4/11/2000	Y	10,470	Expansion	Privately held
Intellego (FKA: Physicians Data Corporation)	1	9/12/1997	Y	1,300	Early stage	Bankrupt
Intrinsity, Inc. (FKA: EVSX)	2, 3	11/8/2000	Y	17,507	Early stage	Privately held
Journee Software, Inc.	2	4/14/2000	Y	8,863	Expansion	Privately held
Lovoltech, Inc.	2, 3	4/1/2000	Y	8,600	Early stage	Privately held
MedAcoustics, Inc.	1	9/15/1999	Y	3,813	Expansion	Out of business
MediaDNA, Inc. (AKA: eLuminator)	2	10/1/1999	Y	4,550	Early stage	Acquired
ModeTek, Inc.	2	5/1/2000	Y	8,140	Early stage	Privately held
NetSolve, Inc. (FKA: Southwest Network Services, Inc.)	Pre-ACM	11/30/1989	Y	6,168	Expansion	Went public

(Continues)

EXHIBIT 9.9 (CONTINUED)

ACM'S PORTFOLIO

Name	Fund	1st Investment Date	Board Seat? (Yes/No)	Amount ($Thous)	Stage	Company Status
nLight Photonics Corporation	2	1/17/2001	N	2,980	Expansion	Privately held
NP Photonics, Inc.	2	8/1/2000	Obs	2,500	Early stage	Privately held
Optellios, Inc.	3	3/15/2001	Y	3,510	Early stage	Privately held
Partnerware Technologies, Inc.	1	10/3/1999	Y	4,500	Expansion	Out of business
Reciprocal, Inc. (FKA: Rights Exchange, Inc.)	1	3/16/1998	Obs	2,019	Expansion	Out of business
ReturnCentral.com	2	4/1/2000	Y	6,667	Early stage	Privately held
Revenue Technologies Corporation	3	2/1/2001	Y	4,900	Early stage	Privately held
Sensys Medical, Inc. (FKA: Instrumentation Metrics, Inc.)	1	2/25/1998	Obs	2,112	Later stage	Privately held
SmartOps Corporation	3	6/5/2001	Y	8,000	Early stage	Privately held
TimeSys Corporation	3	7/1/2001	Y	8,994	Early stage	Privately held
Triton Network Systems, Inc.	1	12/1/1997	N	2,315	Early stage	Went public
VBrick Systems, Inc.	1	3/23/1999	Y	5,020	Early stage	Privately held
Works, Inc.	3	7/23/2001	Y	10,000	Expansion	Privately held

Source: Adams Capital Management.

Note: Obs = Observer status.

and then support it. The future might lie in raising a number of $400 million funds and taking stakes of 35–45 percent in twenty to twenty-five companies. Although Coretek, ACM I's major home run, had been sold to Nortel for $1.4 billion, the partners believed that the future lay in $200 million exits. Each $200 million exit represented an $80 million opportunity. "With twenty or twenty-five investments per fund," Sullivan observed, "we would have to do well on a quarter of them to achieve respectable returns for our limited partners." The group felt that such performance was possible.

This strategy presented two major problems, though. In a particularly difficult market, far fewer companies might succeed. If a downturn cost ACM its entire investment in half the portfolio, every single remaining company would have to be a significant success just to return capital. Moreover, execution might be difficult. ACM would have to find companies good enough that the firm would want to own 35 percent to 45 percent. Competitively, ACM would not be able to compromise—it would have to get 35 percent to 45 percent ownership or walk. This might preclude it from syndicating, even with a good co-investor and even if the company might prefer additional venture backers. It might be doubly hard to find companies that were not only superb but also wanted ACM as their sole venture backer.

This strategy would impose its own costs on ACM. Without the complementary networks of other venture firms in the deal and their contacts with potential partners, customers, and executives, ACM would have to supply these contacts itself. The firm might have to hire someone to help with such tasks or add partners with complementary networks.

TO BOLDLY GO . . .

Given the dramatic changes in the economic environment, the partners knew they had to act quickly. Some of the portfolio companies were struggling, as other technology companies funded by the overexuberant venture markets had converged on the same shrinking pool of customers beset by their own financial woes. Venture firms too had sustained heavy losses and were concentrating on rescuing their existing deals rather than searching for new investments.

This latter change could have two opposing effects on ACM. There might be less competition for new deals, perhaps allowing ACM to gain greater visibility within the industry and with top-tier VC firms. Yet ACM's existing co-investors were distracted by internal dynamics, reductions in management fees and fund sizes, and the need to reply to concerns among their limited partners, forcing ACM to devote more time and resources to the portfolio.

Were ACM's systems imprisoning it or protecting it? Was now the time to become more aggressive and more opportunistic? Should ACM enter new markets? Would the discontinuity process help or hinder this change? Would structured navigation be more or less effective in the new environment?

From a broader perspective, the partners had to wonder if the private equity industry itself had encountered a discontinuity. If so, what would be the best way for ACM to exploit it?

10

Martin Smith: May 2002

Martin Smith gazed out the window of his Westport, Connecticut, office overlooking the sun-sparkling waters of Long Island Sound and sighed. Had things gone according to plan, he mused, he would be scuba diving in brilliant blue Caribbean waters. Instead, he was working, or rather delaying work by contemplating the temperature difference between the waters outside his window and those of the Virgin Islands. Apparently, he was not the only one laboring on this Sunday morning: the "bing" of the elevator sounded faintly in the background.

After weighing job offers from three leveraged buyout firms as a second-year student at the Harvard Business School, Smith had decided to accept a position at Newport Partners. Unlike some of his less fortunate colleagues, he had had a number of offers from which to choose, as his background had made him attractive to many buyout organizations. With a degree in economics from the University of Pennsylvania's Wharton School, he had joined the investment bank Goldman, Sachs as an analyst in its corporate finance group. After two years, he had grown tired of the endless parade of spreadsheets and joined a startup that helped midsized firms manage their financial planning and strategy. Before this firm failed during the 2000–2001 Internet collapse, Smith had worked closely with a number of chief financial officers in midsized firms, as well as investment bankers and partners in private equity groups. The firm's demise had given Smith the chance to leave the business world to attend Harvard Business School and round out his skill set.

In assessing job offers, Smith had ultimately put a great deal of weight on the certification—or "stamp of approval"—that working at an "old line" group such as Newport would provide. Newport Partners was a top-tier buyout firm: within the private equity community, it had a strong "brand name" and had historically sponsored very successful partnerships. The group, originally the investment arm of a wealthy New England family, had built up a franchise in restructurings and recapitalizations beginning in the 1950s. By 2002, the group consisted of eleven seasoned partners with a range of backgrounds that encompassed financial, consulting, and operation experience. Smith had not anticipated the tremendous workload facing the organization. Although

Senior Research Associate Ann K. Leamon and Professors G. Felda Hardymon and Josh Lerner prepared this case solely as the basis for class discussion. Cases are not intended to serve as endorsements, sources of primary data, or illustrations of effective or ineffective management.

its seventh fund had fallen short of its $2 billion goal, closing on $1.2 billion in February 2001, it still ranked among the top ten highest-closing funds in that difficult year. Recent trends had seen the volume of LBO deals fall dramatically, along with the amount of money invested—one top-tier fund had invested in only one deal in the previous twenty months. Confronted by fewer opportunities and facing the loss of seventeen investment professionals after Newport abandoned initiatives in technology and in Europe, the remaining staff was evaluating more potential investments than ever.

Smith had received an urgent call three weeks before from Townsend "Sandy" Beech, Newport's legendary senior partner. Beech had indicated in no uncertain terms that Smith should begin work as soon as possible. As a result, Smith's long-awaited (and much deserved!) dive trip to the Caribbean had been canceled. Instead, he had driven to Westport immediately after finishing his last final examination and begun work the next day.

If there was a silver lining to these events, Smith mused, it was that he was getting exposure to challenging investment decisions much earlier than he had anticipated. His current assignment was a case in point. On Friday afternoon, Beech had forwarded him three presentations for possible buyout targets. In the e-mail, he had asked Smith to make a presentation about the merits of the three proposals at the partners' meeting on Monday morning. The potential investments were in many respects similar, but each appeared to have its own strengths and weaknesses. A brief conversation with Beech on Saturday, when he had called from the Worrell 1,000 catamaran race, where he was observing innovative designs, had supplied a number of other considerations.

Smith looked back to his blank computer screen and wondered which investment to recommend.

THE U.S. LBO INDUSTRY

A number of trends had made the buyout business more challenging in the late 1990s and early 2000s than in the previous decade, when it had achieved a certain degree of notoriety. The 1980s had seen the breakup of a number of conglomerates, often underproductive and underleveraged firms that were ripe for efficiency-increasing measures. By the early 1990s, though, companies had learned the lessons of the 1980s and were operating more efficiently, both in terms of finance and operations. The senior managing director at one buyout firm observed, "Corporate America is generally more efficient than in the 1980s. There are not as many [situations] where you can just cut expenses and capital expenditures and . . . realize a great return on investment. You have to be prepared to add value in some way."[1]

Even when a buyout firm found a good target, which had become more difficult as the economy shifted from leverageable manufacturing firms to more ephemeral service companies, obtaining the necessary leverage to complete the deal was a challenge. While the market for high-yield (junk) bonds had grown significantly during the 1990s, leverage multiples were much lower than had been the case in the previous decade. In addition, the senior debt market was seriously constrained, due both to tougher government regulations in the wake of the savings and loan scandal, and to the consolidation of the banking market itself.

This changed the typical financing structure for a buyout deal, along with the possible returns. The average equity contribution to a buyout increased from 18 percent in 1987

---

1. David Ying, quoted in Robert Pease, "Strategies for Successful Buyout Investing," (Wellesley, MA: Asset Alternatives, 2001), p. 27.

to 38 percent in 2000, while senior debt fell from 56 percent to 33 percent. With the increasing sophistication of target company sellers, the field was more challenging than ever.

The year 2001 had been no exception to that trend. Fund-raising had fallen by almost half, from 2000's $63.5 billion to $35 billion. Funds complained that good companies were harder to find than ever, as sellers waited for valuations to recover. Nonetheless, some firms had closed significant funds in 2001. Kohlberg Kravis Roberts, famed for performing the biggest LBO on record when it paid $31 billion for RJR Nabisco in 1989, closed a $6 billion fund; Blackstone Capital Partners closed on $4 billion; and Credit Suisse First Boston's (CSFB's) DLJ Merchant Banking Partners III closed on $2.2 billion, which put the total fund at $5.4 billion. Six other funds had a first close above $1 billion.[2]

Increasingly, buyout funds were moving away from the mega-buyouts that had made the industry its name and pursuing niche strategies. New strategies included investing in the less-efficient small-company segment, establishing a specialty investment focus, developing operating expertise to aid companies after acquisition, and diversifying geographically and into broader areas of private equity, such as venture capital and mezzanine financing.[3]

THE INVESTMENT CHOICES

The three presentations that Smith had before him (see Appendix 10.1) were a study in parallels and contrasts. They shared many elements, yet each had distinct strengths. One seemed to have the best management, the second appeared to be in a fast-growing market, and the third had strong brand identity, which would serve it well as its distribution channels evolved.

Rustica Industries

The first of these, Rustica Industries Corp., was the largest manufacturer of industrial wire and polymer systems (similar to the plastic-coated wire closet inserts available through home-organization services) in the United States. With five divisions, it addressed the foodservices, healthcare, commercial products, consumer, and international markets. The firm had a 65 percent market share, six times larger than its closest competitor, and more than 25 percent of its revenues came from products developed in the past five years. Rustica, headquartered in Wilkes-Barre, Pennsylvania, had manufacturing in four U.S. states and in Canada, and was essentially managed by Peter Volpe, who had been with the company for sixteen years. Volpe, age forty-one, was the heir apparent of the retiring CEO. On average, the management team had more than ten years of experience with the firm.

For the twelve months ending March 31, 2002, the company had $136.2 million in revenue and earnings before interest, taxes, depreciation, and amortization (EBITDA) of $22.1 million. Management projected growth to reach $158.7 million in 2005, with EBITDA of $27.8 million. The purchase price was in the vicinity of $145 million and would be facilitated by $100 million worth of debt and subordinated debt.[4] Because the company had been such a stable performer through the years, Newport's senior partner Sandy Beech thought arranging the debt financing would be relatively straightforward.

2. Leslie Green, "Fund-Raising Hardly Compares to Last Year," *Buyouts* (January 7, 2002), p. 1.

3. Pease, p. 15.

4. Abbreviated as "sub-debt," these unsecured loans stood behind senior debt in repayment preference but carried higher interest and frequently included some warrants as well.

At the same time, Smith was concerned about the firm's low capacity utilization and its relative saturation of the market. While financing would allow it to take advantage of acquisition opportunities, he was not quite sure where these might come from. Moreover, the business had relatively low barriers to entry, whether from domestic firms or international entities.

A report from a management-consulting firm indicated substantial potential for the manufacturing side of the business to increase its efficiency at little cost. However, Smith wondered whether the management, which had been focused on marketing, would be able to implement these changes.

Yellowstone Cattle Bank

Yellowstone Cattle Bank (YCB) was a privately held company headquartered in Milwaukee, Wisconsin. It provided payment processing services to regional (small- and medium-sized) merchants and home businesses that accepted credit, charge, and debit cards and checks. Founded in May 1992, YCB was the forty-fourth largest payment processing company by volume, and the twenty-fourth by number of merchant customers.

In 2000, its operating income was $10.1 million, up from $6.8 million the previous year and from break-even five years before.[5] Once acquired, the growth rate was expected to be above 20 percent for the next four years. Net income was projected to grow similarly. More importantly, YCB's customer base had grown from 12,000 to 40,500 merchants over the previous five years and was expected to grow to 77,000 going forward. YCB's growth stemmed from overall expansion of the industry. Industrywide, credit card dollar volume had increased more than 74 percent in the past five years, with credit card use growing from 15 percent to 20 percent of all transactions. Moreover, the factors stimulating this growth were still in place and likely to persist into the near future. In addition, debit card usage was also increasing and could be expected to provide additional growth.

The enterprise value was expected to be close to $75 million, about half the comparable public market valuation. Comparable public companies had recently sold for 30.1× last twelve months (LTM) net income, while YCB's price represented a multiple of 12.6×.

YCB operated in a fragmented and consolidating industry, to the point where the ten largest bank card processors accounted for roughly 70 percent of total charge volume, up from 45 percent six years before. Ultimately, YCB could prove an attractive target as larger processors tried to move down-market to capture higher margins and companies that had a proven track record of organic growth.

Smith was concerned that YCB presented a fundamentally different sort of transaction. The available stock represented only 40 percent of the total equity and was owned by a passive investor. Newport would not be able to exercise significant influence outside of whatever it could negotiate in a shareholders agreement at the outset. Management and other shareholders had indicated that they would be willing to enter into such an agreement; nevertheless, the details were yet to be determined.

At the same time, this deal was extremely attractively priced. Newport would receive its 40 percent for $30 million. Given the fragmented nature of the market, Smith anticipated that the firm could increase its ownership through participating in various later acquisitions.

Management was more of a question mark. Smith had found a handwritten note in the file mentioning that the CEO was notoriously strongwilled and had a habit of driving off potential seconds-in-command. Yet his record of growth had been impeccable and he was primarily responsible for the sterling results thus far.

5. YCB was essentially a specialty bank and thus revenues were not as meaningful as operating income.

Wildflower Corporation

Wildflower was a leading manufacturer of painting applicator products including brushes, rollers, and related accessories.

It had the reputation for providing the "product of choice" for the professional segment of the paint applicator market and had 21 percent of the $192 million domestic professional painter market, with its nearest competitor holding 15.6 percent. Its brand was regarded as the leader in the professional segment in terms of both product quality and brand reputation. The company was located in Portland, Oregon and Fond du Lac, Wisconsin and employed more than 250 people.

Wildflower was being offered to Newport for $88 million by a large conglomerate that was divesting the firm for strategic reasons. The company had recently reported $44 million in revenues for the year with 27.4 percent gross margins and $11.8 million in EBITDA. The company's CAPEX expenditures over the past several years had been insignificant, less than $1 million. Moreover the company was expected to continue its recent historical growth rate of approximately 13 percent per year to reach $70 million with an EBITDA of $20 million by 2005. Wildflower's increased growth was expected to come from the future growth of Home Depot, Lowe's, and other professional segment "big box" retailers, which continue to grow at 25 percent to 30 percent annually. The momentum was fueled both by same store sales increases and by new store openings. Wildflower's penetration into the mass market channel not only strengthened the company's position in the $192 million professional segment, but also gave Wildflower access to the largely untapped $400 million consumer segment.

The paint applicator industry was relatively fragmented. The memorandum that Smith received had statements by management claiming that a number of possible acquisitions would provide significant potential synergies when combined with the company's existing brand reputation and distribution network. In fact, the company had recently executed a letter of intent to purchase a small paint brush and roller manufacturer with $4 million in sales and reported discussions with numerous potential targets that would likely be accretive to cash flows and credit ratios. Management had been with the company for approximately seven years.

EVALUATING THE CHOICES

As he looked again out the window, Smith wondered which investment to recommend. Ideally, he mused, he would have several weeks to sort through these issues, make customer calls, and consult with market experts. But this was not to be!

He also wondered how Beech would receive his presentation. In the two weeks that he had been at Newport he had already noticed that they had very different approaches to looking at transactions. While Smith began by seeking to understand the underlying business and market dynamics, Beech's approach seemed to be surprisingly unsystematic. Smith wondered how much of this was due to their differing backgrounds. Smith had an economics and financial background, and Beech had majored in poetry at Bennington College. After a brief and unsuccessful career as a writer in New York City, he had joined his father's boutique investment bank of Hornblower, Beech, & Palm. Beech's entry into private equity had been almost accidental: upon graduating from the Amos Tuck School at Dartmouth (which his father had also attended), he had joined the private equity affiliate of a New York commercial bank after failing to obtain a position with any of the leading venture or buyout firms. To Smith, it seemed surprising that a buyout investor could have succeeded while employing such an intuitive, seemingly scattershot, approach.

While Smith was sometimes frustrated by Beech's approach, he still had to admit that at least a few of the points that the senior partner had raised in their conversation yesterday were very valid. In particular, he had highlighted the issue of "getting back to basics." Beech had stressed the need to find a few good, small deals in reliable areas to reinvigorate the firm's reputation with the limited partners and in the industry as a whole. In particular, it was important to reestablish strong relationships with the banks that provided debt to Newport's transactions. He therefore particularly wanted to avoid any deals that seemed "too fluffy."

Moreover, Newport had gained its reputation when it was one of the few LBO partnerships and could buy companies cheaply, leverage them heavily, live with the debt, and flip them to a market hungry for initial public offering and mergers and acquisitions. Now, Beech had emphasized, "It's a new world. We have to develop a clear focus and execute flawlessly around it." Smith knew that firms had developed styles—Golda, Thoma, Cressey, and Rauner had developed the concept of buying a platform firm and consolidating an industry around it; some firms, such as Bain Capital, created efficiencies and added value by changing the acquisition's strategy; yet others, such as Thomas H. Lee & Company, emphasized growth LBOs, buying firms that could add value through organic growth as opposed to financial leverage. Smith anticipated that his recommendations would have to address the style that each deal would represent.

Finally, there was "The Resource Problem." When Smith had first heard this term, which seemed to be dropped into every partner-to-partner conversation, he thought it referred to the shortfall in the last fund. How could such a famous firm be concerned about resources? During his first week, Julia Romana, a 1999 graduate of Harvard Business School and a principal in the firm, clued Smith in:

> Look, I know it seems crazy with all of the people trying to get into private equity, much less a firm like this, but the truth is our biggest problem is scarcity of *partner time*. Especially now that we've lost so many professionals. The sellers want to deal with the senior partners, and they're the only people the banks will talk to! For example, Sandy is working six deals and is essentially maxed out. Principals and associates do what we can to extend the partners' time, but the portfolio CEOs aren't interested in talking to us. In the end, the good deals need a Newport partner actively involved, if they're going to get done. If there is anything influencing decisions around here, it's this problem—we call it The Resource Problem and it's serious. We had to pass on what we knew was an interesting syndicated international deal because Sandy was tied up with the Internet fund and couldn't get overseas. It turned out to be Seat Pagine, the Italian yellow pages [which went public and created a return of 30× for the buyout firms involved, primarily Bain Capital, CVC Europe, and Barings Capital]. We not only missed a big payday, but we allowed Bain to move up a notch in the competitive food chain. Now they are competing with us on every deal.

Romana's description of Newport "passing" on Seat had been particularly poignant. Smith had just heard that Seat had actually turned down a Newport term sheet that had her as the designated Newport lead. Romana was a smart investor who spoke fluent Italian, and Smith was keenly aware of what the Seat situation had cost her in stature within the firm. He thought about that as he turned back to his computer screen to review the presentations one more time.

APPENDIX 10.1

THE THREE INVESTMENTS—RUSTICA INDUSTRIES

Rustica Industries Corp.

Agenda

Introduction
Company Overview
Business Segment Summaries
Transaction Overview
Historical and Projected Financial Results
Senior Credit Facilities

Acquisition Rationale

- Industry leader
- Achieved superior rates of revenue growth
  - Increased share in existing markets
  - Development of new products and markets
- Diverse revenue stream
- Opportunities for profit management
- Strong management team that has successfully managed the business independently from current owners
- Opportunities to penetrate significant new markets and high-growth product areas

---

Company Overview

- Founded in 1929
- Largest manufacturer of industrial wire and polymer storage systems in the U.S.
- 65% share of U.S. industrial sales, six times larger than its closest industry competitor
- Ability to create new products to meet the needs of its targeted customer base and identify new market for its existing products
- 26% of Rustica's revenues are generated from products that were developed in the past five years
- Established reputation for quality and wide product range
- Extensive distribution channels and broad range of business segments served
- Headquartered in Wilkes-Barre, PA, with manufacturing sites in PA (2), CA, GA, OH, and Ontario Canada

---

Company Overview: Net Sales & EBITDA by Division

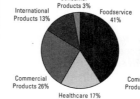

LTM Net Sales by Division
Net Sales $136.2 M

Consumer Products 3%
International Products 13%
Foodservice 41%
Commercial Products 26%
Healthcare 17%

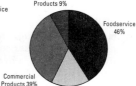

LTM EBITDA by Division
EBITDA: $22.1 M

International Products 9%
Foodservice 46%
Commercial Products 39%
Healthcare 18%

LTM Ended March 31, 2002

Company Overview: Largest Manufacturer in Wire Shelving Industry

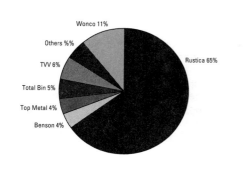

Wonco 11%
Others %%
TVV 6%
Total Bin 5%
Top Metal 4%
Benson 4%
Rustica 65%

Company Overview:
Rustica has increased its share of industry sales over the past five years, despite premium pricing

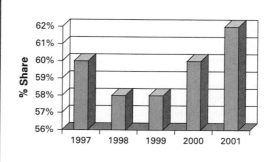

% Share

1997 1998 1999 2000 2001

(Continues)

APPENDIX 10.1 (CONTINUED)

THE THREE INVESTMENTS—RUSTICA INDUSTRIES

Company Overview: Financial Highlights

($MM)	1999	2000	2001	LTM (3/31/02)
Net Sales	$112.4	$122.9	$133.9	$136.2
% Growth	2.6%	9.4%	9.0%	NA
Gross Profit (Excl. Depreciation)	$48.5	$53.3	$61.2	$62.4
EBITDA	$16.8	$16.5	$20.6	$22.1
Share of Industry Sales	**58%**	**60%**	**62%**	**NA**

Company Overview: Opportunities

- Cost reduction opportunities primarily in manufacturing and distribution
- Currently operating at an average capacity utilization of only 65% to 70%
- Incremental sales should yield high variable margins, thereby increasing overall profitability
- Lower production costs should provide the opportunity to increase penetration in price-sensitive markets

Foodservice Division

- The Foodservice division generates 41% to 46% of total sales and EBITDA, respectively.
- The cornerstone of Rustica's business
- Supplies a wide range of high quality wire shelving and storage systems, food preparation cabinets, carts, and "poker-chip" dish dollies
- Network of 95 independent manufacturer's reps sells to foodservice equipment dealers (65%), directly to food service chains (25%), and through OEMs and catalogs (10%)
- End users: 70% commercial, 30% non-commercial (schools)

Company Overview:
2000 Shares of Foodservice Wire Shelving Products

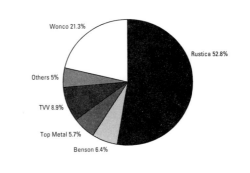

Foodservice Division: Outlook

- Restauraunts are constantly remodeling/refurbishing for aesthetics to improve positioning/sales
  - ❑ Shelving products account for a minimal portion of such refurbishment costs
- New product introductions generate incremental sales of Rustica products at fast food establishments
- Industry requires substantial use of shelving products
  - ❑ Replacement orders
  - ❑ Sanitation requirements

Healthcare Division

- The Healthcare division generates 17% and 18% of total sales and EBITDA, respectively
- Sells Rustica's full line of core products plus a wide range of specialty products
- Customer base of more than 3,000 healthcare institutions
- Focus on developing "specialty" products to meet specific healthcare needs (e.g., emergency carts, surgical case carts)
- Maximizes efficiency of healthcare staff and operations, which is a necessity in the current environment

(Continues)

APPENDIX 10.1 *(CONTINUED)*

THE THREE INVESTMENTS—RUSTICA INDUSTRIES

Healthcare Division: Outlook

- Management believes that this division has an opportunity to capitalize on the recent focus on the healthcare industry.
  - ❏ Help reduce costs
  - ❏ Increased efficiency
- Leverage strong customer base
- Strategic alliances
- New product introduction should increase market penetration

---

Commercial Products Division

- The Commercial Products division generates 26% and 39% of total sales and EBITDA, respectively
- Established to serve all domestic industries outside of the foodservice and healthcare industries, including:
  - ❏ Industrial materials
  - ❏ Laboratories
  - ❏ Electronics
  - ❏ Supermarket
- Sells the same range of "core" Rustica products as well as specialty items such as:
  - ❏ Security storage
  - ❏ Printed circuit board
  - ❏ Specialized workbenches

Commercial Products Division: Outlook

- Fastest growing segment due to new products and focused market development efforts
- Strong growth and new products in the electronics and supermarket sectors should result in increased revenue contribution
- The proportion of this division's sales attributable to core wire products should decline as a result of increased sales of "value added" solutions
- Revenue growth should continue due to perceived productivity enhancement of Company's products for customers

---

Consumer Products Division

- The Consumer Products division generates 3% of toal sales
- The products are adaptations of Rustica's commercial products, with a focus on home entertainment and garage products
- Sold through specialty retail stores, Do-It-Yourself centers, and catalogs
- Negative EBITDA over past 3 years due to high product prices, which caused a major home repair retailer to drop the line

---

Consumer Products Division: Outlook

- The company has refocused its attention on higher end catalog sales and new product development
- Current efforts to reduce manufacturing costs and increase outsourcing should yield increased profitability and penetration in this price-sensitive market

---

International Division

- The International division generates 13% and 9% of total sales and EBITDA, respectively
- Rustica's international export activities cover a wide range of foreign markets, although the Company focuses on Canada, Western Europe, and the Asia/Pacific region
- Lower profitability due to higher sales, marketing, and distribution costs
- Lack of market penetration due to limited strategic focus of local distributors

(Continues)

APPENDIX 10.1 *(CONTINUED)*

THE THREE INVESTMENTS—RUSTICA INDUSTRIES

International Division: Outlook

- Recent efforts to expand the international sales force should result in increased market penetration
- Continuous effort to expand market-specific distributors

Summary Financial Projections

($MM)	LTM (3/31/02)	2002	2003	2004	2005
Net Sales	$136.2	$139.4	$144.9	$151.4	$158.7
% Growth	NA	4.1%	4.0%	4.5%	4.8%
EBITDA	$22.1	$21.8	$24.1	$25.8	$27.8
% of Sales	16.2%	15.6%	16.6%	17.1%	17.5%
Interest Expense	–	$8.0	$7.9	$7.4	$6.9
CAPEX	$3.0	$4.0	$4.0	$4.0	$4.0
EBITDA /Interest	2.8x	2.7x	3.1x	3.5x	4.0x
EBITDA– CAPEX /Interest	2.4x	2.2x	2.6x	2.9x	3.5x
Debt/EBITDA	4.5x	4.4x	3.6x	3.0x	2.4x

Senior Credit Facilities: Company Strengths

- Largest manufacturer in the industry: a 65% share of domestic industrial wire and polymer shelving sales
- Stable Operating Performance: Rustica has increased revenues and share of industry sales throughout the economic cycle
- Diverse Revenue stream: Rustica's success in increasing its share of sales can be attributed to its ability to create new products, to meet the needs of its target market, and to identify new markets for its existing products
- New Product Development: Currently, 26% of Rustica's revenues are from products developed in the past five years

Senior Credit Facilities: Company Strengths

- Improved Profitability Opportunities: significant cost savings that may be achieved through reduction in manufacturing and distribution costs
- Operating Leverage: with the current moderate level of capacity utilization, any incremental sales would yield extremely high variable margins
- Favorable Market Trends: when the economy rebounds, demand for the Company's wire and polymer storage systems should similarly increase
- Strong and Focused Management Team: demonstrated ability to effectively operate through the economic cycle while executing a focused business plan

(Continues)

APPENDIX 10.1 (CONTINUED)

THE THREE INVESTMENTS—YELLOWSTONE CATTLE BANK (YCB)

Yellowstone Cattle Bank

Agenda

Introduction
Company Overview
Business Segment Summaries
Transaction Overview
Historical and Projected Financial Results
Senior Credit Facilities

Investment Opportunity

- Emerging leader in a fast growing market
- Opportunities for profit improvement
- Strong management team since inception still on board
- Attractively priced minority interest available

Company Overview

- Founded in May 1995
- Provides processing payment services to mid-market banks
- Currently 44th largest payment processing company by volume, but 24th by number of merchants serviced
- Proven growth from less than $200K of payment processed in first year to over $1.5 billion in 2001
- Since inception, the merchant base has grown to over 40,500 (over 35%/year compounded).
- Industry wide credit card processing has grown 74% in the past five years and is expected to continue or even accelerate growth.
- $6mm in net income in 2001
- Existing passive investor willing to sell shares at an attractive price

---

Company Overview:
YCB is among the fastest growing operations in the industry

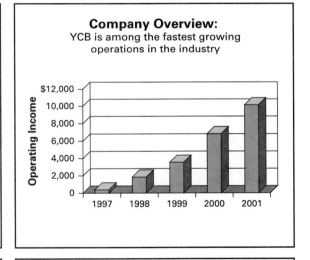

Company Overview:
Financial Highlights

($MM)	1998	1999	2000	2001
Operating Income	$1,919	$3,676	$6,885	$10,052
% Growth	N/M	91.6	87.3	46.0
Net Income	$1,168	$2,233	$4,167	$5,958
Total Merchants	18,875	25,575	34,807	40,500

Company Overview:
Cost Savings Opportunities

- Currently backend services and switch services outsourced
- Plan underway to integrate backend services by late 2002
- Company to build switch services by early 2003
- Savings at current volumes:
  - $50k–$80k/mo backend services
  - $60k/mo switch services

(Continues)

APPENDIX 10.1 (CONTINUED)

THE THREE INVESTMENTS—YELLOWSTONE CATTLE BANK (YCB)

Business Model

Transaction Element	Merchant	YCB	Visa/Mcard Assoc	Issuing Bank
Purchase price Payment	$100.00	–$100.00		
Merchant Discount	–$1.95	$1.95		
Transaction Fee	–$0.20	$0.20		
Interchange Fee		–$1.40		$1.40
Association Fee		–$0.08	$0.08	
Issuing Bank Payment		$100.00		–$100.00
Cardholder Payment				$100.00
Net Proceeds	**$97.85**	**$0.67**	**$0.08**	**$1.40**
Switch (front end)		–$0.07		
Back End		–$0.06		
Proceeds available to cover		**$0.54**		

Merchant Breakdown by Type

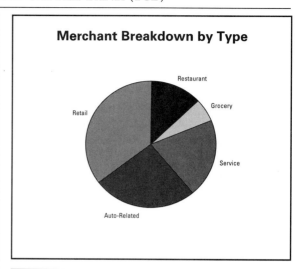

The Market Has and Will Continue to Grow Rapidly

	Dollar Volume ($ mm)				Share of Payment Methods				CAGR
	1990A	1995A	2000A	2005E	1990A	1995A	2000A	2005E	1995–2005
Checks	$1,821	$2,112	$2,265	$2,118	61%	55%	44%	31%	0.0%
Cash	582	704	742	786	20	18	14	11	1.1
Credit	432	754	1,288	7,983	15	20	25	29	10.2
Debit	9	46	364	962	0	1	7	14	35.6
Other	128	215	463	1,028	4	6	9	15	16.9
Total	2,972	3,830	5,121	6,877	100	100	100	100	6.0

Company Overview:
YCB is among the fastest growing operations in the industry

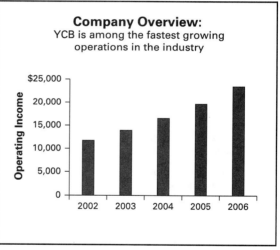

(Continues)

APPENDIX 10.1 (CONTINUED)

THE THREE INVESTMENTS—WILDFLOWER INC.

Wildflower, Inc.

Agenda

Introduction
Product Overview
Industry Overview
Company Overview
Transaction Overview
Historical and Projected Financial Results
Syndications Overview

Acquisition Rationale

- Premier brand name in stable, mature industry
- Solid relationships in both the growing mass merchant and specialty paint store channels
- Strong growth potential in the larger "do-it-yourself" (DIY) consumer segment
- International expansion opportunities
- Acquisition opportunities in fragmented industry
- Strong cash flow with minimal capital requirements
- Experienced management team

Paint Brushes and Rollers

- Brushes:
  - Solid wood handle, stainless steel ferrule, natural hog bristles or synthetic filament, special technology to eliminate shedding and increase efficiency of use while painting
- Rollers:
  - Specialty formulated fabric that enhances paint pick-up and release, solvent resistant core (for multiple uses), special treatments on fabric to resist matting, shedding, and linting

---

Paint Industry Sales are Stable and Growing

- Paint industry has demonstrated consistent 5% growth
- Industry less affected by economic downturns; sales follow steady maintenance cycle of repair and remodel
- Demand expected to increase with number of aging buildings

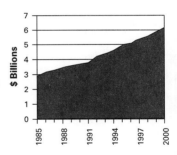

Source: Current Industrial Report M29F and estimates by Impact Marketing Consultants.

U.S. Sales of Paint Applicator Products

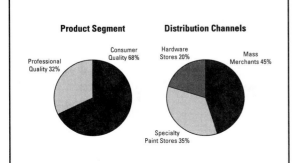

Product Segment

Consumer Quality 68%
Professional Quality 32%

Distribution Channels

Hardware Stores 20%
Mass Merchants 45%
Specialty Paint Stores 35%

Mass Merchants are Expanding Sales

- Sales growing 25% to 30% per year through increased same store sales and new store openings
- Provides access to growing consumer DIY segment
- Stores use strong brands as "pull through" products to attract professionals
- Lowe's and Home Depot lead the trend

Sales within Mass Merchant Channel

Other 21%
Home Depot 44%
Builder's Square 8%
Lowe's 19%

Source: Adapted from *National Home Center News,* April 13, 1998; Excludes major non-home improvement mass merchandisers such as Wal-Mart.

(Continues)

APPENDIX 10.1 (CONTINUED)

THE THREE INVESTMENTS—WILDFLOWER INC.

Strong Price/Value Perception

- Professionals are relatively price insensitive for high quality products
- Paint applicators represent less than 2% of the cost of a professional paint job
- Professionals will pay more for quality applicators due to longer useful life, increased ease of application, reduced job time, and better paint finish

Competitive Overview

- Wildflower has 21.4% of the professional paint applicator market
- Top 4 producers have 65% of professional market, but it fragments below that; "other" has a 21% share
- Total sales $192 million

2000E U.S. Paint Applicator Sales

Manufacturer	% of Professional Market ($192M)	% of Consumer Market ($408M)	% of Total Sales ($600M)
Wildflower	21.4%	0.0%	6.8%
EZ Cover	3.6	31.4	22.5
Panther Paint	3.6	19.1	14.2
Booster Brush	15.6	11.0	12.5
Ribberset/Williams	13.0	3.7	6.7
Other U.S.	20.8	2.5	8.3
Importers	0.0	24.5	16.7

Note that a growing proportion of professional quality product is sold through mass merchants to consumers.

Company Overview

- Wildflower, Inc. was founded in 1925.
- Leading manufacturer of professional quality paint applicators in the U.S.
- Strong customer base in specialty paint stores (68%) and mass merchant (20%) channels
- Established reputation for quality professional products
- Headquarters in Portland, OR and Philadelphia, PA with additional manufacturing in Wisconsin
- Net sales $44.2MM, EBITDA of $11.8MM (LTM February 28, 2002)

Wildflower's Brand Investment

- Over 40 years of grass-roots marketing efforts to build trust with professional painters
- Finest available raw materials
- Product quality reinforced through advertising, packaging, and apprenticeship programs
- **Resulting in:**
  - Most widely recognized brand in paint applicator products
  - Customer survey indicates products represent good value due to increased useful life and high-quality perception
  - Strong customer demand an all channels

Wildflower's Historical Financials

Net Revenues and Growth

Adjusted EBITDA & Margin

APPENDIX 10.1 (CONTINUED)

THE THREE INVESTMENTS—WILDFLOWER INC.

Wildflower Business Strategy

- Continue expansion in mass merchant segment
  - ❑ Same store sales growth of 3% to 5% per year
  - ❑ Increase penetration of new store openings
- Improve brand recognition with consumer customers
  - ❑ Cross-market existing professional products to the DIYers
  - ❑ Product innovations to target retail consumer segment
- Leverage brand to increase roller sales to 50% of sales (currently 27%)
- Selectively pursue international expansion opportunities
- Improve manufacturing productivity

Continued Expansion in Major Merchandiser Segment

- Mass merchants represent significant growth opportunities for Wildflower
  - ❑ 25% to 30% annual growth since the 1980s
  - ❑ Expansion of the DIY consumer segment
- Wildflower will continue its expansion into the segment by:
  - ❑ Leverage its existing relationship to expand into Home Depot's planned new stores in 2002
  - ❑ Increase its presence from 45% of Lowe's stores to 75% (from 200 to 375 stores)
  - ❑ Sell to other mass merchant customers

Improve Brand Recognition with Consumer Customers

- Cross-market existing professional products to DIYers
  - ❑ 70% of current sales are to professional painters
  - ❑ Leverage Home Depot's push into DIY market
- Create innovative products like Aviva brand to target upscale DIY consumer market

Leverage Wildflower Brand to Increase Roller Sales

- Wildflower's product mix historically 28% rollers to brushes
- Rollers command higher margins; in the U.S., rollers have 51% market share
- Wildflower's goal is a 50/50 mix, to be achieved though new marketing efforts and competitively priced roller line for the mass merchant channel

International Expansion Opportunities

- Europe presents a key opportunity as it switches from oil-based to latex paints
- Strategic alliances with Dupont that include annual cash payments and material discounts that total up to $300K to Wildflower
- Expanded European sales force and presence at trade shows
- Acquisitions would jump-start European presence and leverage Wildflower's manufacturing technology
- Apprenticeship program at premier UK painting school develops trust of professional painters in training

Wildflower's Projected Financials

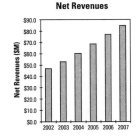

Net Revenues

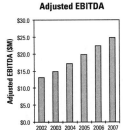

Adjusted EBITDA

(Continues)

APPENDIX 10.1 (CONTINUED)

THE THREE INVESTMENTS—WILDFLOWER INC.

Wildflower Business Strategy

- Wildflower's revenue growth of 13.2% driven mostly by growth in mass merchant channel, remainder of business grows at 3%
- Relatively constant gross margin assumptions with further benefits from fixed cost leverage
- Capital Expenditures projected to remain relatively constant at $1 million per year
  - ❏ Annual maintenance capital expenditures historically averaged $0.5 million

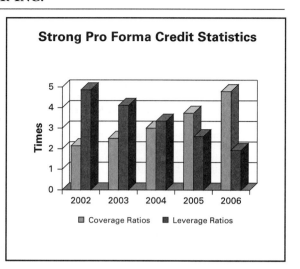

Strong Pro Forma Credit Statistics

Company Strengths

- Market leader in a mature and stable industry
- Strong relationships with mass merchants and specialty stores
- Significant growth opportunities in the consumer and roller markets
- Quality premium products difficult to imitate
- International expansion opportunities
- Consolidation opportunity in fragmented industry
- Limited exposure to import competition in premium segment
- Newport sponsorship

11

AIT Group PLC

On July 18, 2002, Rob Stavis and Jeremy Levine, of Bessemer Venture Partners, stared disbelieving as the words crackled out of the speakerphone. "The investors have said that they won't take a split price," said Guy Peters, the broker doing a share placement for Stavis and Levine's current deal. "They won't take any step-up at all, and we're still £4 million short." The investment in AIT Group Plc, a UK-based software firm that had hit a major liquidity crisis one month before, suddenly looked seriously in doubt.

AIT Group (LSE: AGP) had been put up for sale on June 18, 2002, after it had re-stated its annual earnings for the second time in two weeks and further delayed publication of its annual results. The market, already skittish after the two-year decline in the valuations of technology stocks and worried about AIT's burgeoning debt load, had dumped the stock, driving its price to 38.5 pence, down 63 percent from its previous close[1] and off 98 percent from its high of £18.80.[2] The stock was suspended from trading on the London Stock Exchange and the company's bank would not offer a further line of credit.

Bessemer Venture Partners (BVP), a U.S. venture capital firm with a long history of investing in early stage companies, had become involved in the deal through Nicholas Randall, a CEO whom BVP had backed in the past. Randall had joined forces with Richard Hicks, AIT's founder, former CEO, non-executive chairman, and most recently, non-executive member of the board, who had returned from sailing across the Atlantic to find that his company was in trouble, and was determined to save it.[3] Along with the

---

1. Anonymous, "AIT Loses More Than Half of Value after Delaying Results," *Wall Street Journal Europe* (June 14, 2002).

2. For the time period of this case, the pound was worth, on average, $1.50.

3. UK corporations had two kinds of directors on their main boards—executive directors who were usually full-time employees with full management roles, and nonexecutive directors who usually were not employees and had no operational responsibilities. The role of the latter was to provide independent advice and guidance and to protect the interests of shareholders. The term "director" had also become used for a management level corresponding to vice president in U.S. companies. In this case, "director" will be used as a title, and "member of the board" will refer to nonexecutive directors.

Arbib family, local businesspeople who had just sold a major mutual fund company, Hicks, Randall, and BVP were planning to restart AIT and keep it as a going concern.

Key to refinancing the company was a "step-up," the sale of shares at different prices. The investor group had proposed a two-stage deal: it would lend the company £6 million, which would convert to equity at 5 pence per share. A public offering of £11 million worth of shares at a price of 10.5 pence per share would follow, and the group had committed to take an additional £2.5 million of the shares at that price as well, raising £13.5 million in total. Guy Peters, the broker from Old Mutual Securities (OMS) who was handling the offering, had thought he could sell that amount with little trouble, given AIT's history, up to 2002, as a profitable company and positive initial feedback from potential investors.[4] The pricing, however, had changed a week into the process. The institutional investors that Peters approached had lobbied to reduce the price differential, which was subsequently changed to 3.5 pence (p) for the loan conversion and 6 pence for the shares in the public offering. Now, after the core investor group had already made a £2 million line of credit available to AIT and hired a number of high-priced experts to help with the due diligence, they had just learned that the investors would only take a straight 3.5p/3.5p deal.

When the call was over, Stavis asked, "So, Jeremy, what do you think? Would you walk?"

Levine replied, "I keep thinking over the due diligence findings. I still think it's a good company. But can we get a deal to work?"

Stavis grimaced. "We've already incurred close to £1 million in fees," he said. "But we shouldn't let that cloud our judgment. The real question is whether it's a good investment."

CUSTOMER RELATIONSHIP MANAGEMENT SOFTWARE

In the late 1990s and into 2000, customer relationship management (CRM) software received a lot of attention. By connecting the "back end" of customer account data to the "front end" of customer interactions, these systems allowed providers of anything from financial services to chemicals to tailor their offerings to a customer's needs and to handle all aspects of a customer interaction from one station rather than with multiple transfers across different departments. Thus, when a customer complained to a cell-phone service provider, the representative could access the person's usage patterns, average bill, and recent marketing offers, then craft a resolution based on the degree to which the firm actually wanted to retain the customer's business. Based on a customer's account balances, a bank could place a call either in an automated queue or directly with a customer service representative.

Ideally, such a system would allow perfect price discrimination—the provision of exactly the level of service desired at exactly the price the customer was willing to pay—and allow the provider to maximize profitability. In the real world, implementing CRM generally involved enterprise-level headaches. Customer-facing front-ends, designed for ease of use in retrieving a few key pieces of information, had to be connected to back-end systems that often bordered on the arcane, having been designed for the very specific needs of highly trained individuals in the accounting department. Linking a customer record with name and address to a lifetime order, payment, and profitability history in real time was no trivial task.

---

4. OMS has been spun out of the Old Mutual group since this occurred. Renamed Arbuthnot, it is now part of the Secure Trust Banking Group.

CRM software and service providers reveled in triple-digit growth rates through 1999 and 2000.[5] Only when the economic slump began in earnest did the investment rate slow. By March 2002, only 36 percent of North American executives of Global 3,500 companies were considering the purchase of CRM software, down from 62 percent the previous year.[6] By August 2002, this figure had fallen to 15 percent.[7]

The European CRM market shared the pain. From triple digit rates in the late 1990s, growth had fallen to 21 percent in 2001 and was expected to barely register 8 percent in 2002. The next two years, 2003 and 2004, were expected to see 14 percent growth.[8]

Much of the decline stemmed from the realization that CRM implementations were expensive both in terms of money and company time. One study cited expenditures of $2 to $7 on integration services for every $1 spent on the software itself.[9] Return on investment was elusive—one survey found that half the firms with such systems considered them failures,[10] and 60 percent of companies with the package from Siebel, the market-dominating firm, had yet to see positive results, even two years after implementation.[11] For vendors of CRM software, the economy exacerbated the situation, as 65 percent of CRM revenues had come from those sectors hit hardest by the recession—financial services, telecommunications, and high technology.[12]

AIT, in contrast, could cite several instances where large institutions had benefited from its software. After installing AIT's 3R, the Woolwich Building Society, a financial institution, had seen sales climb from an industry average of 1.2 products per customer to nearly 3. The Woolwich credited this change and a concurrent increase in market capitalization to a combination of 3R and an accompanying corporate change program. Commented Richard Hicks, AIT's founder, "As in so many cases isolated technology change is not sufficient to create these results, but the corporate change would not have been possible without new technology."

CRM software usually was sold directly through the firm that both developed the package and did the extensive customization work necessary to install it. Gradually, however, the installation work was outsourced to third-party integrators, allowing the software provider to concentrate on product development.

Siebel Systems dominated the global market, with twice as large a share as that of SAP, the second-place player.[13] Other firms included Oracle and PeopleSoft. AIT Group, Onyx, and Chordiant were smaller players with niche products. By the start of 2002, most were performing below their previous levels (see Exhibit 11.1 for industry performance).

5. Anonymous, "European CRM Market Slows Down Drastically," *Europemedia* (September 18, 2002), p. 1.

6. Tom Pohlmann, "Benchmark March 2002 Data Overview," *Forrester Research*, http://www.forrester.com/ER/Research/DataOverview/0,2740,14399,00.html, March 2002, accessed November 7, 2002.

7. Tom Pohlmann, "Benchmark August 2002 Data Overview," *Forrester Research*, http://www.forrester.com/ER/Research/DataOverview/0,2740,14595,FF.html, August 2002, accessed November 7, 2002.

8. Anonymous, "European CRM Market Slows Down Drastically—Report," *Europemedia* (September 18, 2002), p. 1.

9. Jennifer Maselli, "Making CRM Fit," *Information Week* (June 24, 2002), p. 32.

10. Study by the Gartner Group, cited in Anonymous, "Survey: Always-on People," *The Economist* (February 2, 2002), p. S9.

11. Brian Albright, "Still a Boom Market for Application Software," *Frontline Solutions* (September 2002, p. 10).

12. Timothy Dolan, "Siebel Systems, Inc. 'Hold,'" *Deutsche Bank Securities* (October 18, 2002).

13. Albright, "Still a Boom Market for Application Software."

EXHIBIT 11.1

COMPETITOR PERFORMANCE, 2000 AND 2001

	Total Sales ($ millions)			Profit bef. Tax ($millions)			Raw Beta	Mkt. Cap. ($ millions)	Debt ($ millions)
	12/31/01	12/31/00	% Change	12/31/01	12/31/00	% Change			
Siebel Systems	2,048.4	1,795.4	14%	404.1	384.4	5%	3.36	12,937.00	300.00
Chordiant	76.0	33.7	126%	−42.1	−35.4	−19%	1.68	419.23	0.08
Onyx	97.0	119.0	−18%	−97.0	−4.5	−2,056%	2.17	168.81	0.42
10-Year UK Government Bond	4.85%								
90-Day UK Gov't T-Bill	4.06%								

Sources: Annual report data from all companies, obtained through OneSource, January 29, 2003; Datastream; and Bloomberg Financial.

Note: Betas over period of June 18, 2000 to June 18, 2002.

AIT GROUP PLC

Richard Hicks founded Applied Interactive Technology (AIT) in Henley-on-Thames, west of London, in 1986. He explained, "I wasn't a typical entrepreneur, but I wanted to do something interesting and make some money." Located in a room above a barber's shop in the picturesque town, the company evolved from a software consultant developing graphical user interfaces for the then-new personal computers into a producer and installer of custom CRM software, primarily for United Kingdom financial institutions. In 1995, AIT introduced 3R, its second-generation product, developed in partnership with Computer Sciences Corporation (CSC), a U.S. firm. 3R provided multichannel customer communications for call centers, and operated on almost any platform.[14] AIT provided the sales, customization, and installation services, which were substantial because the product had to be closely integrated into the customer's existing system. CSC received royalties from every sale.

The company was profitable from the start. As it grew, customers would contract with it on projects ranging from £3 million to £10 million, paying as costs were incurred. Hicks kept the company in Henley, saying, "It was convenient for me; it was a pretty place. Buyers would make a day outing of it when they came for a demonstration."

In 1997, AIT went public on the Official List of the London Stock Exchange (LSE), raising £5 million (see Exhibit 11.2 for a description of the United Kingdom's stock market regulatory regime). Its market capitalization hit a peak of £400 million (see Exhibit 11.3 for AIT's stock price over time). By this time, many of the United Kingdom's financial institutions were running AIT's software as their front end, and paying a steady stream of maintenance fees.

The following year, Hicks began reducing his involvement with the company. Carl Rigby, formerly director (vice president) of sales, became CEO in 1998 and chairman in 2000. The executives decided to accelerate the shift from a services model and focus more on developing and selling their own product, in part to control their destiny

---

14. Kamran Butt and Steve Robertson, "AIT Group: Performing Strongly in Turbulent Times," *Dresdner Kleinwort Wasserstein Research* (May 27, 2002), p. 14.

EXHIBIT 11.2

UK STOCK MARKET REGULATION

The UK securities environment was broadly similar to that in the United States. As in the United States, there were two major stock exchanges: the senior Official List, which was the London Stock Exchange's (LSE) principal market for listed companies, and the junior market known as the Alternative Investment Market (AIM), which had more flexible rules and less stringent listing requirements. The Official List comprised more than 2,000 UK companies and 500 overseas firms, while more than 850 firms had been admitted to AIM. Small emerging UK companies would list on AIM just as emerging companies in the United States listed on NASDAQ. AIM companies could apply to the LSE Official List after trading on AIM for two years. The legal framework had recently been updated through the Financial Services and Markets Act 2000, a massive work that detailed the role of the regulatory body, the Financial Services Authority (FSA), along with the processes for applications and suspensions of listing, prospectus requirements, penalties for the breach of listing rules (market abuse), and general procedures. Although its regulatory role was akin to that of the U.S. Securities and Exchange Commission, the FSA also possessed the power to levy unlimited fines on companies or individuals deemed to have abused the market by giving false or misleading information.

While the FSA managed the listing and the ongoing disclosures for companies on the Official List, the LSE itself regulated these for companies on AIM. To list on AIM, a company had to comply with regulations published in the Public Offers of Securities Regulations of 1995, along with the LSE's AIM Rules; incorrect or misleading information carried civil and/or criminal liability. Once a company had managed to get listed on either the Official List or AIM, it had to obey the LSE's rules for trading. All companies incorporated in the United Kingdom had to file information with the government as specified by the Companies Act 1985. Yet one more entity was involved during takeovers, the Panel on Takeovers and Mergers. This self-regulating body, which was not part of the government, oversaw the operation of The City Code on Takeovers and Mergers, which was designed to ensure fair and equal treatment of all shareholders, and provided an orderly framework within which takeovers could occur.

Sources: Timothy Oldridge, partner at Taylor Wessing; http://www.londonstockexchange.com, accessed January 13, 2003; and http://www.sec.gov, accessed January 13, 2003.

EXHIBIT 11.3

AIT'S MONTHLY AVERAGE CLOSING STOCK PRICE TO DECEMBER 2001 AND FTSE 100 INDEX

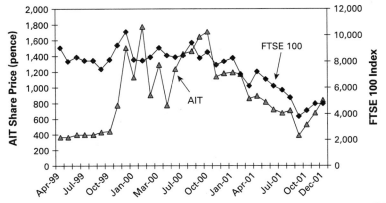

Sources: Adapted from Datastream, January 29, 2003; and OneSource, http://globalbb.onesource.com, accessed January 29, 2003.

but also to exploit the capabilities of the Internet. Nick Randall, a member of the investor group, observed, "They wanted to become a £100 million company, and they knew that they needed their own product to do so."

Portrait, the new product, offered several improvements over 3R. Like 3R, it linked across different databases within an enterprise, but it functioned essentially as a platform on which third-party installers or even business analysts could build their own functionality. 3R's installation had required such specialized expertise that AIT had maintained a substantial installation force and sold directly; Portrait could be sold and installed by third-party system integrators.

2001

AIT seemed to have hit its stride in 2000 and 2001. Under CEO Rigby's leadership, the company won several awards as a top place to work in the United Kingdom, with such amenities as a concierge and shopping delivery service, a subsidized personal trainer, extensive training opportunities, and generous bonuses. AIT also employed a corporate visionary and an artist-in-residence to ensure a creative workplace. In this high growth period, the company enjoyed unusually low staff turnover.

At the same time, the company posted impressive results (see Exhibit 11.4). Revenues for the year ending March 31, 2000 reached £21.7 million, with net income of £2.5 million; the following year saw 56 percent growth to £33.9 million in revenue as net income climbed 40 percent to £3.5 million. The company's market capitalization hit a high of £400 million, despite the general carnage in the surrounding CRM market. Revenue growth of 20 percent was forecast for 2001/2002.

In September 2001, Richard Hicks, the founder, departed on his sailboat for a transatlantic crossing.[15] That same month, AIT purchased IMA, a bankrupt U.S.-based developer of call center software. The merger had several justifications: new management had streamlined operations; the company had a history of developing and selling products through integrators, which would provide some pointers to AIT; IMA complemented AIT with strength in the U.S. and in nonfinancial sectors; and the Portrait product seemed to provide a good transition story from IMA's EDGE package, which was at the end of its life. EDGE was installed at about 350 enterprises and had generated annual revenues of $50 million at its peak. AIT acquired IMA for $16 million, $10 million up front and the balance over the following year. The entire amount was in cash, in part because the bankruptcy court judge would not accept stock. AIT arranged for bank financing, the first debt it had ever required, and planned a possible rights (share) offering for early 2002 to pay off the loan.

Also in 2001, AIT invested £3.4 million in a start-up that provided outsourced call center services. The new firm would also demonstrate a model installation of Portrait.

In addition, the company signed its first reseller agreements, lining up five firms as third-party installers. To support its global expansion, AIT announced plans to establish offices in Australia and Singapore.

AIT's semiannual results to September 30, 2001 (UK companies did not have to release quarterly results) announced revenue of £22.3 million, up 57 percent from the same period the previous year, pretax profit up 34 percent to £2.7 million, and R&D spending up 72 percent to £4.3 million. Nationwide Bank had just announced that it would implement Portrait. In February 2002, though, as the London Stock Exchange slogged through the collapse of its own technology sector amid the Enron-inspired wariness about corporate accounting, analysts began questioning details of the results. In particular, they

---

15. Simon Goodley, "If AIT's Broke, Is Hicks in Time to Fix It?" *The Daily Telegraph* (August 13, 2002), p. 30.

EXHIBIT 11.4a

AIT'S HISTORICAL FINANCIALS, WITH PROJECTED FY '02 AS OF MID-JULY 2002

(in £ millions)	BVP's Estimate for Year Ending 3/31/02	Year Ending 3/31/01	Year Ending 3/31/00	
Total Revenues	**36.2**	**33.9**	**21.7**	
Continuing operations	31.8	33.9	21.7	
Revenues from acquired firm	4.4			
Total Operating Expenses	**44.9**	**28.9**	**18.1**	
Cost of goods sold	23.1	15.0	9.5	
—of which, R&D	9.5	5.7	2.2	
Depreciation	0.1	0.1	0.1	
SG&A expense	16.8	10.7	6.9	
Other operating expense	4.9	3.1	1.6	
Operating Income	**(8.7)**	**5.0**	**3.6**	
Share of associates' operating loss	(0.5)	—	—	
Profit (loss) on ordinary activities before finance charges	(9.2)	5.0	3.6	
Finance Income/(Charge)				
Interest receivable & similar income	0.218	0.115	0.041	
Interest payable	(0.296)	(0.012)	(0.025)	
Net finance income/(charge)	(0.078)	0.103	0.016	
Pretax Income/(Loss)	**(9.3)**	**5.1**	**3.7**	
Tax on profit on ordinary activities	1.0	(1.6)	(1.2)	
Net Income before Extra Items/ Preferred Dividends	**(8.3)**	**3.5**	**2.5**	
Dividends	0.3	0.7	0.6	
Retained Profit	**(8.6)**	**2.8**	**1.9**	
Retained profit brought forward	8.7	5.9	4.0	
Retained profit transferred to reserves	0.1	8.7	5.9	
Earnings Per Share (fully diluted)	(40.64)p	16.2p	11.8p	

Source: Anonymous, "AIT Group PLC," *Multex Global Estimates* (May 16, 2002); Butt & Robertson, "AIT Group: Performing Strongly in Turbulent Times," *Dresdner Kleinwort Wasserstein Research* (May 27, 2002); AIT Annual reports for years ending March 31, 2000–March 31, 2000, OneSource, accessed January 29, 2003; and casewriter.

Note: Interest rates were variable, usually 2 percent above London Interbank Offered Rate (LIBOR). For July 18, 2002, LIBOR on overnight loans was 3.4 percent; http://www.bba.org.uk, accessed April 24, 2003.

seized upon the inconsistency of a £6 million negative cash flow with the operating profit of £2.7 million.[16] Members of the board of directors, among them the CFO, had sold £6.4 million in shares since August 2001.[17] The CFO was appointed COO in December 2001

16. Neil Hume, "Market Forces—AIT's Pluses Add Up to a Minus," *The Guardian* (February 21, 2002), p. 26.
17. *Ibid.*

EXHIBIT 11.4b

AIT'S HISTORICAL BALANCE SHEET

(in £ millions)	BVP's Projected Balance Sheet Postrefinancing	BVP's Estimate for Year Ending 3/31/02	Year Ending 3/31/01	Year Ending 3/31/00
Fixed Assets				
Intangible assets (goodwill from IMA purchase)	2.5	13.1	—	—
Tangible assets	2.0	2.0	1.6	0.5
Investments°	—	2.5	0.5	0.5
Total Fixed Assets	**4.5**	**17.6**	**2.1**	**1.0**
Current Assets				
Accounts receivable due within one year	9.7	9.7	9.1	9.4
Cash at bank and on hand†	17.0	4.2	11.5	5.3
Total Current Assets	**26.7**	**13.9**	**20.6**	**14.7**
Total Assets	**31.2**	**31.5**	**22.7**	**15.7**
Liabilities				
Current Liabilities—Due within One Year				
Bank loans‡	—	8.0	—	—
Balance due on IMA purchase§	—	4.0		
Anticipated severance costs in turnaround	3.0	—		
Accounts payable	2.0	2.0	2.7	0.9
Accruals, deferred income, social security tax‖	6.2	7.2	4.6	3.3
Annual payments on long-term leases —land & buildings	1.6	1.6	1.4	1.3
Annual payments on other leases (cars, equipment)	2.2	2.2	2.2	1.3
Total Current Liabilities	**15.0**	**25.0**	**10.9**	**6.8**

(Continued)

and resigned on February 18, 2002, exercising £1 million worth of options shortly before he did so.[18] By the end of February, the stock had fallen to 590 pence.

Spring 2002

On May 2, 2002, AIT announced the imminent release of full year results that would be "in line with market expectations."[19] On May 31, the company announced a £1.1 million profit shortfall due to contract deferrals.[20] Four members of the board of directors, including Hicks, the founder, and CEO Rigby, lent the company £1 million to meet a payment due on the IMA purchase.

In June, the news became grimmer. The United Kingdom's stock market regulator, the Financial Services Authority (FSA), began an investigation into the circumstances

---

18. Anonymous, "AIT Group PLC Director Shareholding," *Regulatory News Service* (January 8, 2002).

19. Anonymous, "AIT Sees FY Sales, Pretax Pft in Line with Expectations," *Dow Jones International News* (May 2, 2002).

20. Anonymous, "AIT Group Sees GPB 1.1M Rev, Pft Shortfall," *Dow Jones International News* (May 31, 2002).

EXHIBIT 11.4b (CONTINUED)

AIT'S HISTORICAL BALANCE SHEET

(in £ millions)	BVP's Projected Balance Sheet Postrefinancing	BVP's Estimate for Year Ending 3/31/02	Year Ending 3/31/01	Year Ending 3/31/00
Liabilities Due after More Than One Year				
Bank loans#	6.0	—	—	—
Balance due on IMA purchase	2.3	—	—	—
Director loans°°	0.8	—	—	—
Provision for liabilities & charges	—	0.1	—	—
Provision for onerous supply charges	1.9	—	—	—
Provision for onerous lease	1.0	—	—	—
Total Long-term Liabilities	**12.0**	**—**	**—**	**—**
Total Liabilities	**27.0**	**25.1**	**10.9**	**6.8**
Equity shareholders' funds	4.1	3.3	3.1	3.0
Retained profits	0.1	0.1	8.7	5.9
Total Equity & Liability	**31.2**	**31.5**	**22.7**	**15.7**
Number of shares (millions)	31.5	20.6	20.6	20.6
Market Cap. (in £ million as of 12/31/01)		£247.400		
Raw Beta (as of 12/31/01)		1.960		
Volatility		0.055		
Standard Deviation		0.235		

Sources: AIT Annual reports for years ending March 31, 2000, to March 31, 2002; Institutional Shareholder Services, "Global Proxy Analysis: AIT Group," September 9, 2002; OneSource accessed February 4, 2003; and casewriter.

Notes:

° After financing, the goodwill from the IMA purchase would be reduced by £10.6 million, and the firm's investments would be written off.

† This does not match the £16 million net post financing due to cash on hand.

‡ This reflects the bank's revolving credit facility granted when AIT purchased IMA. The credit facility was £8 million with a committed overdraft up to a total of £11 million at an interest rate of LIBOR (in mid-July 2002, 3.4 percent) plus 2 percent.

§ The balance due on IMA ($6.5 million/£4 million) was to be paid in full by September 2002. This would be amended as part of the refinancing to a long-term facility of $3.5 million/£2.3 million due over five years, at an interest rate of 2 percent over LIBOR.

‖ The social security tax liability fell due to the anticipated reduction in head count postfinancing.

At the time of closing, the bank would be repaid £3 million and would convert £2 million into equity, for a net reduction in AIT's debt to the bank of £5 million and a total level of bank debt of £6 million. The bank debt, including overdraft, was £11 million before the payment and the anticipated debt for equity swap. The bank debt level had increased by £3 million between March 31, 2002, and mid-July 2002.

°° In April and May 2002, members of the board of directors lent the company £1.35 million to make payments due on the IMA acquisition. As part of the financing, £600,000 would be repaid and the balance converted into term loans to be repaid by August 2004, thus reclassified from short-term to long-term.

surrounding the profit warning and whether the company deliberately misled the markets.[21] As AIT changed its auditor from Arthur Andersen to Deloitte & Touche, the company failed its audit. On June 13, the company announced that fact and issued another

21. Dearbail Jordan, "AIT Faces Inquiry after Profits Warning," *The Times* (June 1, 2002), p. 54; and Richard Fletcher, "City—FSA Investigates 'Market Abuse' at Software Group," *The Sunday Telegraph* (August 11, 2002), p. 2.

EXHIBIT 11.4c

AIT'S ESTIMATED CASH FLOW STATEMENT AS OF MID-JULY 2002

(in £ million)	Year Ending 3/31/02	Year Ending 3/31/01	Year Ending 3/31/00
Net cash (outflow)/ inflow from operations	–3.6	9.0	2.7
Net interest (paid)/received	–0.1	0.1	—
Taxes paid°	–1.2	–1.1	–1.1
Capital expenditure	–0.4	–1.3	–0.2
Net inflow from assets held for resale	—	—	0.2
Acquisition	–9.7	—	—
Equity dividends paid and planned°	–0.7	–0.7	–0.6
Financing†	8.5	0.1	—
(Decrease)/Increase in Cash	**–7.2**	**6.1**	**1.0**

Sources: AIT Group annual reports for years ending March 2000–2002; and casewriter.

Notes:

° These figures differ from Exhibit 11.4a because they reflect actual payments made during the year. AIT paid taxes on account over the course of the year but the P&L reflects the refund the company eventually received. The equity dividend figure for YE '02 reflects the payment of YE '01's dividend, which occurred in the period.

† Financing includes £466,000 from the issue of new shares, net of expenses, and £8 million in bank debt due in less than one year. The loan note used in acquiring the subsidiary was not included.

profit warning.[22] This time, net income fell by £4.3 million. An estimated £6.7 million profit as of May 30 had dwindled to almost nothing (see Exhibit 11.5 for profit estimates). AIT had debt of £10.5 million against a bank facility of £11.5 million.[23] The shares, which had been steadily losing value throughout the spring, tumbled further, from 66.5p to 38.5p overnight. The board, after being told that it would be impossible to refinance AIT on the stock market, instructed UBS Warburg to sell the company. Warned one rating company, "AIT could go into receivership [an insolvency procedure initiated by the U.K. bankers]. Avoid the shares."[24] On June 19, trading in AIT's shares was suspended (see Exhibit 11.6 for stock price).

THE RESCUERS

On June 20, Nicholas (Nick) Randall was returning home to Henley-on-Thames from Asia when he read about AIT's troubles in the *Financial Times.* He had been following AIT, a large local employer, for years.

22. Goodley, "If AIT's Broke, Is Hicks in Time to Fix It?"

23. Anonymous, "AIT Group Sees GPB 1.1M Rev, Pft Shortfall."

24. Anonymous, "AIT Put Up for Sale," *Investors Chronicle* (June 19, 2002).

EXHIBIT 11.5

AIT'S ESTIMATED PROFITS FOR YEAR ENDING MARCH 31, 2002

	£ Millions
Profit Estimate as of 5/16/02	**6.7**
Disallowed as of 5/31/02	−1.1
Profit as of 5/31/02	5.6
Disallowed as of 6/13/02	−4.3
Estimated Profit as of 6/13/02	1.3
Estimated Profit after Tax as of 7/18/02°	**−8.6**

Source: Anonymous, "AIT Group PLC," *Multex Global Estimates* (May 16, 2002); and casewriter.

Note: ° Includes impact of revenue restatements recommended by Ernst & Young.

EXHIBIT 11.6

AIT'S DAILY CLOSING STOCK PRICE JANUARY 2, 2002, THROUGH JUNE 18, 2002

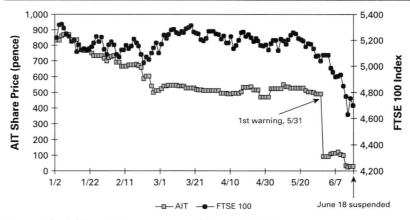

Source: Adapted from Datastream, accessed January 29, 2003.

"I'd never bought shares," he said, "but I was impressed with what Richard [Hicks] was doing." Randall was an executive vice president at Remec, a defense electronics firm that had bought the wireless masthead amplifier company, Airtech, that he had turned around.

The timing was fortuitous. His contract with San Diego-based Remec was expiring and the self-confessed turn-around guy—"I like to do things that are difficult"—was ready for something closer to home, where he was building an oak-timbered house. His builder, who was also working on a project for Hicks' brother, put the two together. Said Randall:

> We arranged for a half-hour meeting on June 25, that became five hours. The bank was set on selling the company because it was scared that it wouldn't get its money back. I kept thinking there must be room for rescue

rights here. All we needed was a broker and some venture money. And I knew where we could find both.

Hicks recalled:

I had returned from my trip in late March and things went very bad very fast. When the investment bankers first started talking about selling the company, I put my hand up and said, 'Aren't there any alternatives?' and was given to understand that no, there weren't any. But I very much wanted to save the company; there were sixteen years of my life tied up in it as well as the jobs in the community. I almost didn't call Nick; my brother gave me the number and everyone had been giving me numbers of some guy they knew that could save the company and after 100 of these, you get a little burned out. Nick's was 101, but as soon as we started talking, I knew this was perfect; he was talking about investing so I knew he was serious, and he had a proven track record in turn-around situations.

"The first thing I did," said Randall, "was send Hardy Smith an e-mail saying 'Help!'" Smith and his firm, Bessemer Venture Partners (BVP), had backed Randall at Airtech and regarded him as "one of our best CEOs ever." On June 26, Smith was en route to a meeting with his colleagues, Rob Stavis and Jeremy Levine, to talk about a different transaction (see Exhibit 11.7 for bios). He brought up AIT, based on Randall's three-page sketch of the deal, which envisioned a core investor group that included himself, Hicks, and BVP investing £6 million, £3 million of which would go in immediately to hold the company while it raised £6 million in a new share offering, of which the core group would take half, for a total injection of £12 million.

Although the concept was outside BVP's early stage focus, it matched a strategy that Stavis had been pursuing, as he explained:

In the current market, you can do one of two things. You can seed new technology that will blossom in three to five years, or you can look into distressed assets. Currently, many companies have invested millions of dollars into building software packages—some are worthless, some are very valuable assets. We had to determine into which category Portrait fell. If it turned out to be interesting, we still were concerned that AIT needed significant financial restructuring—typical buyout work—that was not our forte.

Levine added:

But AIT was, in many ways, a start-up situation. It had a product in beta—Portrait, with a half-installation, and no cash on its balance sheet. At the same time, it had an installed product that generated a steady income stream. If we could make Portrait work, we would have picked up a great product for pennies on the dollar.

"What we'd been looking for," Stavis said:

was a deal with a hook. For us, the hook was Nick. Here was a seasoned, trusted CEO to inject. Moreover, the technology addressed the financial services sector, where I was comfortable.

The timing was uncertain. The board could not set an official deadline for bids because AIT, as a public company, could always be purchased in a hostile takeover. Nonetheless, UBS Warburg, the investment bank, was running an accelerated sales

EXHIBIT 11.7

BIOS OF JEREMY LEVINE AND ROB STAVIS

Jeremy Levine, Principal

Jeremy joined Bessemer Venture Partners' Larchmont, New York, office in 2001. He focuses on software and infrastructure opportunities and manages BVP's investments in Thinq, Mobility, and Voyant. Prior to joining Bessemer, Levine was vice president of operations at Dash, an Internet software publisher.

Levine joined Dash from AEA Investors, a private equity firm specializing in leveraged and management buyouts, where he specialized in consumer products, specialty chemicals, and light industrials in the United States and Europe. Earlier, as a management consultant with McKinsey and Company, he helped *Fortune* 500 financial services and consumer products companies address challenges in strategy and technology.

Levine graduated from Duke University with a B.S. in computer science and economics.

Rob Stavis, Partner

Rob Stavis joined Bessemer in July 2000 as a venture partner in the firm's New York investment office, located in Larchmont, New York. He primarily focuses on early stage investments in financial services technologies and business process automation.

Prior to joining Bessemer, Stavis was a private equity investor, managing a portfolio of private equity interests in a variety of industries including telecommunications, software, technology, gaming, and restaurants.

Until July 1998, Stavis was the cohead of global arbitrage trading for Salomon Smith Barney. Stavis served as a member of the firm's operating committee, risk management committee, and the control and compliance committee. He was involved in the transition of Salomon Brothers during mergers with Travelers and then Citicorp. Additionally, he served as chairman of the firm's recruiting committee. Stavis' group managed a balance sheet of more than $100 billion, investing in arbitrage opportunities worldwide using a highly quantitative, computer modeling-oriented approach. He has published numerous articles on derivatives pricing and risk management.

Stavis holds degrees from the Engineering School of the University of Pennsylvania and the Wharton School of Management.

Source: http://www.bvp.com, accessed April 21, 2003.

process, and any party that wanted to be considered in that process had to submit a bid by Monday, July 8. Said Stavis:

> The big challenge was whether we could understand what we were getting into fast enough. It was incredibly complicated—old product, new product, new business model, existing deals which most early stage companies never have. We had to understand the accounting and that was enough to really give us pause. Here we were, in the post-Enron age, looking at investing millions of dollars in a company that had admitted its accounting was screwed up!

In his efforts to save the company, Hicks had also contacted the Arbib family, the founders and largest shareholders of Perpetual, an investment and mutual fund company that was Henley's largest employer. Amvescap had recently bought the firm for £1.3 billion. The Arbibs asked their former main board director and vice president of information technology, Geoff Probert, to review AIT's Portrait package. A product demonstration on Sunday, June 30, convinced Probert that he and the Arbibs should join the core group.

DUE DILIGENCE

At the same time that the core group was forming, BVP started its due diligence. The process began on Friday, June 28, when Levine delayed his trip to a family reunion to go to Meriden, Connecticut, the headquarters of AIT Group-USA, the former IMA. Levine and Stavis had decided that the Connecticut trip would provide background data with a minimal investment of time and money. Levine left the meeting intrigued:

> They were very smart guys. I saw a demonstration of the Portrait product and was very impressed, especially because it was conducted by business analysts rather than engineers. The progress that was being made in converting IMA's EDGE customers to Portrait was also encouraging. I did learn about some curious deals—it was vague, but it gave me a base to start asking questions.

BVP's Smith had left for a board meeting in Europe on Thursday, June 27. During a layover at Heathrow, he met with Hicks, Randall, and Tim Oldridge, a partner with the law firm of Taylor Joynson Garrett (TJG, now Taylor Wessing), one of the few UK law firms to combine an early stage investment practice with considerable public company expertise. This was the first time that the group—less the Arbibs—had met. Said Smith, "It helped us lay out the general approach for the deal and the diligence and take the pulse of the team."

On July 2, Levine arrived in Henley to begin due diligence in earnest. He had a week to determine whether BVP should invest almost $5 million. Based on his initial research and the meeting with AIT-USA, he had a list of questions to address. He said, "I arrived with a sense of what I needed to focus on. I knew we couldn't know everything, but we had to know what could really hurt us."

One decision had to be made very early in the process. Because AIT was an ongoing concern and not a start-up, it had reams of contracts, leases, and other documents that would have to be examined before the core group knew what it would be acquiring in an investment. The investors therefore had to commit to hiring the lawyers at TJG to read every document available for potential bidders. Said Smith, "This was a big decision. We didn't know if we'd get the deal, or even want it, yet we were hiring very expensive legal assistance."

TJG's Tim Oldridge, the lead lawyer, dispatched a ten-person team to AIT's data room. He said:

> Jeremy [Levine] pointed out specific areas he wanted us to look at—employment contracts, banking agreements, acquisitions, mergers, joint ventures, licenses, patent deals, and any pending litigation, along with real estate. We needed to understand what was going on, and the scope for changing anything the core group could not live with. We read everything and made brief summaries.

Levine moved into one of the conference rooms at AIT's headquarters. Another room in the building served as the data room, holding all the documents for inspection. He explained:

> This was very convenient. I had easy access to the data and a good view of the other bidders. And it gave me a presence on site. I ate in the cafeteria, and I got to know the people.

First, Levine talked with each executive. "I wanted to get their perspective on what had happened and how things worked," he said.

The AIT staff was aware that Hicks was trying to save the company. It seemed highly likely that the other bidders would take it into receivership to wipe out the impending liabilities of roughly £10 million from leases and the remaining sums due to IMA over the rest of the year.

The core group presented a challenge for UBS Warburg, the investment bank coordinating the sale. Charged with getting the best price for the company, it was also supposed to ensure that all bidders had equal information. Yet the core group planned to invest in the company, rather than to purchase it, which created needs for different data.

The List

Over dinner on July 2, Levine, Smith, and Geoff Probert, for the Arbib family, assembled a list of five criteria that had to be satisfied before they would feel comfortable making a bid, assuming that the customers supported AIT and the Portrait product. Hicks, they knew, was already committed to saving his company.

The list read:

1. Accounting issues run to ground.

2. The model of the business going forward works with enough headroom for error.

3. Hicks' role is defined and appropriate.

4. Confidence in the Portrait product.

5. The deal is good enough.

With the tight timeframe imposed by the bank, each of the items would have to be pursued in parallel.

Preamble: Customer Support for AIT and Portrait

Levine had already started making customer calls. Tracy Isacke, director of alliances and marketing, and Alistair Rowley in sales supplied Levine with a comprehensive list of customers, partners, resellers, and firms that had evaluated AIT's product but purchased elsewhere. Isacke said:

> I liked him [Levine]. I had turned to some of my contacts from my tenure on the board at Xerox to see if I could put anything together to save the company, and by now, it was clear that the only way to keep it as a going concern was the core group.

Levine called upon a part-time contractor for BVP, who happened to be in London on other business, to help with customer calls. The references were glowing. Levine recalled:

> From these calls, we learned that AIT had a very strong reputation among large customers, something that most start-ups lack. The customers wanted the company to survive. They truly felt that AIT had worked with them, rather than imposing an external framework on their business processes the way that some other providers did. But they had been unnerved by this situation. A bank's front-end system is its heart, and to think that the company that supports this might collapse is pretty scary.

Even companies that had signed up with other vendors usually did so reluctantly, often citing AIT's inability to provide global support rather than shortcomings in the product.

Accounting Issues

Along with customer calls, Levine took the lead in delving into the details of AIT's accounting:

> I became obsessed with touchable revenues. What could we count on for revenues going forward? How fast would they come in? And here was where we ran into the difference between a take-over/turnaround situation and an early stage venture investment. Early stage companies don't have accounts, except maybe for QuickBooks. AIT had fifteen years of financials, the last five as a public company. Early stage companies don't have customers or contracts either, or if they do, there may be two or three. AIT had seventy customers and real estate leases and contracts with resellers—a whole room full of data.

To understand the details, Levine interviewed AIT veterans—Tracy Isacke of alliances, Alistair Rowley in sales, and Gareth Bailey, CFO at the time. Recalled Isacke:

> It was intense. We were getting in at 6:30 A.M. and leaving at 11 at night. Jeremy knew what he needed to know and kept asking questions in a clever way. He'd start, 'Help me understand . . .', or 'I don't quite get this yet . . .' and he wouldn't leave the subject until he understood exactly what was going on.

Rowley said:

> I realized that the investors wouldn't be working so hard unless they were investing for the long term. That was a relief, as I'd dealt with some UK venture folks before and it was like being savaged by a dead sheep.

Touchable Revenues

After talking with customers and other partners, Levine and Rowley took a hard look at the revenue forecast. Working from the "worst case" projections, Levine further backed down the probability that prospects would actually buy:

> The most likely prospects had 75 to 100 percent ratings. And that would have been realistic if this hadn't happened. But we had to back them all down and move the revenue streams out in time, because the customers told me that they were rattled. If this had been an isolated situation, it would have been one thing, but after two years of software companies imploding, customers were skittish.

As a result, anticipated revenues were set at £22 million, 30 percent lower than the company's earlier worst-case expectation of £33 million, and almost half the expected case of £40 million. Levine said, "About £16 million of this came from maintenance fees and current engagements that would be very difficult to terminate. Even though AIT had won some good contracts in tough competition, we weren't going to count on anything that wasn't basically in the door."

Other Accounting Issues

Levine kept digging:

> I felt that we really needed to understand the balance sheets and customer contracts, as well as the deals that the AIT-U.S. people had mentioned. I rapidly realized that I was out of my depth. AIT had changed CFOs six

months before, the previous CFO had left, and Matt White, the CFO who was coming on with Nick [Randall], was still working out his exit from Remec. So when I first arrived, I said, "We need forensic accounting help." Even though I kept saying this, by the end of Friday, we still didn't have forensic accounting help. And the bid had to be presented on Monday.

Levine learned that accounting support was still lacking at the daily wrap-up meeting on the evening of Friday, July 5. Although the core group was willing to pay whatever was necessary, the challenge lay in finding the accountants, as financial experts in high-tech contracts were scarce, especially on the day after a major U.S. summer holiday. Levine called Stavis at 1 P.M. New York time and explained the situation. Stavis said:

> I tried to contact a friend at Ernst & Young (E&Y) who wasn't in the diligence practice, but could possibly give us a start. He wasn't in. So I went to the Web site and started calling offices, moving west. No one was in—it was voicemail after voicemail. At last I found an executive assistant in the Chicago office who really wanted to help. I told her to take out a piece of paper and write a message, something like, "Bessemer Venture Partners, which does a great deal of business with the firm, is working on a time-sensitive deal that requires some forensic high-tech contract work in London over the weekend. Can you help?" I then asked her to go down the halls and read it to any partner she found. An hour later, she called me back. Amazingly enough, the Chicago office of E&Y specialized in high-tech forensic accounting and two of their best guys had just moved to London. I simply couldn't believe it. I got their number, Jeremy got them, and they spent the weekend at AIT.

The E&Y accountants studied AIT's books and found nothing of concern. Among the host of customer contracts, however, they found five instances of license sales to third-party installers where they recommended a restatement of revenue. All were signed between September 2001 and March 2002, and each followed a similar pattern. AIT sold the partner a number of licenses at a discounted price for which the partner paid up front, and AIT promised to purchase a certain value of services over a period of time on a "take-or-pay" basis. AIT was contractually obliged to pay the agreed-upon amount to its partner, regardless of whether it actually used the services. With rising demand, the contracts would have benefited both parties, but if demand did not materialize as expected, AIT would have had its own installation force sitting idle while the partner did the installations, or it would have to pay for services it did not consume.

The deals took the following form: AIT sold an installer £1 million worth of licenses for its Portrait software for £650,000, a 35 percent discount. The installer paid £325,000 in March 2002, and the balance in January 2003. AIT committed to use £1.3 million of the partner's services over the coming fiscal year. AIT then credited the entire £650,000 as revenue received in fiscal 2002 (ended March 31, 2002) and ignored the possibility that the services could become a liability, believing that it would take them in the normal course of business. For the installer, which had a 50 percent margin on services, this was a wash. The deal gave AIT some up-front cash, an implicit commitment from the installer, and a chance to train it on Portrait, but at what could be a punishing price if the services it had committed to take were unneeded.

The UK Generally Accepted Accounting Principles had no set rules for revenue recognition for software companies, which made this treatment technically legal.[25] It was, however, aggressive. The E&Y report commented, "Irrespective of the specific accounting rules, accounting is meant to reflect the economic reality of a business transaction." Correspondingly, the team recommended that the license fees match the service commitments made, essentially reducing fiscal year 2002 revenues by £6.5 million to £36.2 million. Backing out the contribution of IMA, true AIT revenues were £31.8 million, down 6 percent from 2001's £33 million and in line with the decline in the industry as a whole.

As the core group had already known about these contracts, the fact that E&Y found nothing else untoward was comforting. "In a way," said Levine, "it was a good outcome. We had been afraid that we might have overlooked something else. Instead, it was just these five."

The core group already knew about another situation, too. AIT had participated in the founding of an outsourced customer call center that used Portrait. AIT had lent the start-up £3.4 million, of which £1 million had been used to buy a Portrait license. This amount was listed on AIT's books as revenue in 2002. The entire loan, however, appeared highly unlikely to ever be repaid. In turn, this meant that the £1 million could not be treated as revenues but as a partial payment of a debt.

A Good Deal

At the same time that Levine was sorting through contracts and sales forecasts, Randall, the incoming CEO, was working with Guy Peters, the broker from Old Mutual Securities, to create a deal that would save the company and provide meaningful returns to the core group. Peters explained:

> It was a very complicated situation—you can't just put equity money into a public company, even if it's been suspended. You have to comply with the market rules, company law, and the guidelines laid down by the largest institutional investors, which meant that you generally have to offer a significant proportion of the new shares first to the existing shareholders (a rights offering) before offering them to other investors.[26] The process usually requires an extraordinary general meeting (EGM) to approve the sale. All this takes time. So the core group would have to loan the company money in the meantime pending the requisite approvals.

Randall added, "But we didn't want to loan anything until we knew, one, that we would win the deal, and two, that it was even a deal we wanted."

As the diligence continued to expose liabilities and reduce expected revenue, the amount needed to refinance AIT grew. Randall's initial e-mail to Smith had proposed

25. Similar accounting treatments had occurred in the United States as well, although not in the software industry, which had strict revenue recognition rules. Some Internet firms were known to book advertising sales as revenue without reporting the commitments they had made to buy ads elsewhere. Another example occurred with Global Crossing and other telecommunications firms, which employed bandwidth swaps in the same manner, crediting revenues from bandwidth they "sold" without noting the concomitant purchases they would make.

26. In the United Kingdom, a public stock offering could take one of several forms. A "public offering" referred to any sale of shares to the public through any mechanism; a rights offering gave existing shareholders a right to purchase a certain number of shares at a certain price; and a firm placement offered shares to public entities, usually institutional investors, which committed to purchasing a certain amount.

a total investment between £10 million and £12 million, with £6 million from the core group. It now became obvious that AIT would require closer to £20 million (see Exhibit 11.8 for sources and uses of funds). Early on, Old Mutual's Peters had suggested the structure of a private deal followed by a public one: a £6 million loan from the core group to cover AIT's operating expenses, later to be converted into stock. The core group could not participate in a rights offering because, except for Hicks, the members were not current shareholders. The loan would hold the company until a public offering in the range of £11 million could be arranged. These shares would be offered first to existing shareholders, each of whom would receive the right to purchase a certain number of shares at 10.5 pence each. Despite the recent tumble in the share price, the discount between its last close at 38.5 p and the new share price of 10.5 p seemed enough to generate some interest from existing investors. The core group's £6 million bridge loan would convert to shares at a price of 5 pence, and the group would purchase an additional £2.5 million of shares in the public offering at 10.5 pence. Peters felt he could sell the £11 million of shares.

At this point, a number of differences between investing in public and private companies and investing in the United States and the United Kingdom became apparent. The core group wanted its loan to be senior to AIT's bank loan. The executives and Hicks, however, had lent the company £1.35 million of their own money, junior to the bank. BVP's Stavis, who handled the eventual negotiations with the bank on the matter said, "It's a business culture difference—in the U.S., new money is always senior to old."

Other differences arose. In a private deal, investors just injected money into a company. In a UK-quoted company, any new shares issued for cash (beyond a preauthorized level) first had to be offered to existing shareholders before they could be offered to new investors, unless the existing shareholders approved an alternate deal. In private deals, an investor naturally received the right to appoint a board member. BVP would have two seats on AIT's five-member board and Probert would have one. In a UK public company, this was highly unusual and difficult for Peters to explain to other potential investors.

EXHIBIT 11.8

ANTICIPATED SOURCES AND USES OF FUNDS

Capital Raised by Company	Amount
Interim financing (from core group)	£6,000,000
Firm placing (core group)	2,500,000
Total from Core Group	**8,500,000**
Public offering	10,500,000
Debt for equity swaps	1,500,000
Total Financing	**20,500,000**
Transaction fees	(1,500,000)
Payment on directors' loans	(650,000)
Payment to bank	(3,000,000)
Net to company	**£15,350,000**

Sources: AIT Group Annual report for year ending March 2002 and casewriter.

The speed of the process and the company's dire financial straits meant that the core group had to provide interim financing before it knew if the shareholders would approve the deal at the extraordinary general meeting. In addition, BVP's Levine commented, "Every day that went by, we were incurring more fees."

The Model Works Going Forward, with Headroom for Error

The current CFO, Gareth Bailey, and Matt White, the future CFO, with input from Levine, built a very complex model to test the impact of different assumptions on the company's future cash position. This became central to the next phase of the diligence—determining whether the company was raising enough money. The model fed pricing discussions that were taking place with Peters, fee negotiations with UBS Warburg and the law firms, contract renegotiations with partners and landlords, and cost-cutting measures that would be enacted at AIT. While many of these would not be implemented until the core group knew whether its bid had been accepted, the model directed the diligence efforts. Levine explained, "The model gave us an idea of where to look next. We knew what we could count on coming in. Now we had to minimize what was going out." Here, the work of the legal team from Taylor Joynson Garrett was particularly helpful in determining whether AIT had any scope for renegotiation.

The lawyers from TJG had not been working alone. "A typical early stage deal," said Levine, "has about ten documents. AIT had a roomful, and five law firms." One firm represented the nonexecutive directors who were concerned about their liability in the FSA investigation, one represented the company in the purchase negotiations, TJG represented the core group, and another law firm, replaced by yet one more, was working for AIT and its executive directors. They had been running up fees at the rate of £14,000 per day.

Levine shared the results of his model with everyone involved (see Exhibit 11.9 for projections). Said Tracy Isacke, director of alliances:

> It was a shock at first, to see the numbers [revenues and contracts] so low. You could push back and he'd explain his assumptions and you ended up agreeing that where he ended up was pretty much the right place. He put his numbers together and he didn't change anything.

Levine noted:

> It was comforting to people that I put things on paper. It showed them what I was thinking. With in-depth interviews where you pick and probe, people feel very exposed. When you write up a summary and share it with them, it's comforting; they can trust that you've understood what they told you. And their feedback helped me test my assumptions.

Confidence in Portrait

The Arbibs' Geoff Probert took on the task of assessing Portrait:

> I sat in on some of Jeremy [Levine]'s interviews, and I was confident that I didn't have to duplicate his work. He and Hardy [Smith] were so thorough that the Arbibs and I felt that, if it was good enough for them, it was good enough for us. So I focused on the software. In my experience, a system that can work across a company's existing database information, permit changes to the database structures, and allow the definition of new

EXHIBIT 11.9a

HYPOTHETICAL PROJECTED INCOME STATEMENT FOR AIT, POSTINVESTMENT

	Year Ending 3/31/03	Year Ending 3/31/04	Year Ending 3/31/05	Year Ending 3/31/06
	£'000	£'000	£'000	£'000
Revenues				
License sales	5,606	13,408	19,818	33,764
Product maintenance	2,996	1,297	2,422	5,236
Services & support	13,429	14,709	16,911	19,788
Total revenue	22,030	29,413	39,151	58,788
Nonexceptional Costs				
Total nonexceptional costs (including payments under lease obligations)	34,026	24,353	31,978	48,639
EBITDA Pre Exceptionals	(11,995)	5,060	7,173	10,149
Exceptional Costs				
Transaction costs	1,957	—	—	—
Redundancy and reorganization	2,153	—	—	—
Writedown investments	2,447	—	—	—
Other writedowns	979	—	—	—
Total exceptionals	7,536	—	—	—
EBITDA Post Exceptionals	**(19,531)**	**5,060**	**7,173**	**10,149**
Depreciation & Amortization	1,852	1,897	2,043	2,251
Interest	495	225	196	196
Profit before Tax	**(21,879)**	**2,939**	**4,933**	**7,701**
Corporation Tax				
Profit after Tax	**(21,879)**	**2,939**	**4,933**	**7,701**

Source: Casewriter.

products within the database without requiring substantial rewrites is the Holy Grail for business software developers. And Portrait did it.

BVP also arranged for a technical expert from Extraprise, one of its portfolio companies and a systems integrator that worked closely with Siebel Systems, to attend a product demonstration. Probert recalled, "He was very excited about the product, too. What with the customer assessment and the outside corroboration, we felt that we really had a viable product, assuming we could save the company." Probert was sufficiently impressed with the product and the rescue team that he agreed to serve on AIT's main

EXHIBIT 11.9b

AIT'S HYPOTHETICAL PROJECTED CASH FLOW

Note: Due to the forward-looking nature of projections and the applicable UK regulatory requirements, we are not able to reproduce the actual projections in question. Accordingly, the data below have been prepared specifically for this case study; they are hypothetical and do not represent the actual projections of AIT.

Year End March (£ *millions*)	2002/03E	2003/04E
EBITDA pre exceptional items (from exh. 9a)	−£12.0	£5.1
+Costs for redundancy and reorganization°	−2.2	0.0
+Corporate tax paid	0.0	0.0
=Gross operating cashflow	−14.2	5.1
(Increase)/decrease in current assets†	−£3.9	−£3.6
+Increase/(decrease) in current liabilities‡	0.5	0.2
=Change in net working capital	−3.4	−3.4
Capital expenditures	−£0.6	−£0.7
Cash flow	−£18.2	£1.0

Notes:

° This is the only exceptional charge likely to result in immediate cash outflow.

† Change in current assets does not include shifts in cash balances.

‡ Change in current liabilities does not include portion of long-term debt due within one year.

Sources: Butt & Robertson, "AIT Group: Performing strongly in Turbulent Times," *Dresdner Kleinwort Wasserstein Research* (May 27, 2002); and casewriter.

board as its director of software, and to draw no pay, aside from a performance-related bonus, for the first nine months.

Hicks' Position

Of all the members of the core group, Hicks' position was the most unclear. Nick Randall was clearly the CEO-in-waiting; Probert and BVP's Smith, Levine, and Stavis the investors. Hicks, on the other hand, was an insider from the beginning, but also a member of the outside rescue group. Levine said, "Richard [Hicks] had bought us a seat at the table, but he didn't have a clear role. For a time it was unclear who was in charge—the old CEO was shell-shocked, the new one wasn't in yet."

Hicks agreed:

This was a strange situation. I hadn't been on the front lines for a long time. All the executives were running around helping various bidders and supplying information, while the potential bidders went trolling through all our data. I didn't know anything about refinancings or rescue rights. So I did some cash flow management and basically tried to keep the faith, and convince people—customers and employees—that AIT would continue.

Because of Hicks' long history with the firm, he had built personal relationships with the bank and other parties. He commented, "BVP definitely put orders of magnitude more effort into the due diligence process than I'd ever expected." After a series of conversations with Randall, the incoming CEO, the two agreed that Hicks would be executive chairman, essentially, as Hicks described it, "keeper of the flame. This is a very special company that got terribly fat, but I'm hoping it can survive."

THE LETTER TO THE BOARD

The bid letter was due to the board of directors by 5 P.M. on Monday July 8. On Sunday, the core group held a meeting with everyone involved in the diligence effort, including the legal team, the Ernst & Young accountants, and BVP's Levine. One of the lawyers from TJG said:

> The time pressure was great. We had reviewed vast quantities of documents and I had less than an hour to tell the core investor group what they needed to know. A customary diligence report would be hundreds of pages long, detailing what we had seen, what we wish we'd seen, and why the client can't sue us. For this key briefing, I spoke from a bundle of notes.

In the bid letter, the core group proposed injecting £20.5 million into the company. The core group would invest a total of £8.5 million, £6 million as a loan that would convert to shares and an additional £2.5 million purchase of shares outright. This would be accompanied by approximately £11 million raised through a combination of a firm placement with other institutional investors and a rights offering, in addition to £1 million to £2 million of debt-for-equity swaps with various creditors. The precise composition of the package, beyond the core group's participation, was somewhat flexible. The group emphasized that the board must decide quickly. "We were afraid that there might be other bidders," said Randall. "And particularly concerned about a trade sale, possibly to Chordiant."

Here the group hit a hurdle. The board did not want to accept anything but a full proposal, and the core group could not complete a full proposal without knowing if it had won the deal, which would then allow it to restructure the company's obligations. By July 10, no other credible bidder had emerged and the board awarded the deal to the core group.

MAKING IT WORK

BVP's Levine said, "Now that we had won the deal, it became a lot of negotiating. In a way, it was less fun."

Isacke, AIT's director of alliances, differed:

> We had established what was wrong, now we were going to fix it. Jeremy [Levine] hadn't dwelled too long on what had gone wrong—we had tried to do what was best for the company and what we'd had directions to do—but it had been painful.

Levine commented, "It was like we had this bright shiny apple of £20.5 million. And everyone kept taking bites out of it."

Bites at the Apple

The costs that Levine had included in the model did materialize, and were often larger than anticipated. Severance costs of reducing AIT's workforce from almost 500 to 200 approached £3 million. The company, in keeping with UK custom, had a fleet of seventeen company cars under leases that were difficult to break. The real estate leases were long-running and had limited break clauses.

A number of deals had to be renegotiated. These included equipment leases, the IMA purchase agreement, and the installer deals, but the most pressing was the bank loan. BVP's Stavis said, "In conversations with stockholders, everyone was really steamed that the bank was going to get out of this whole, when it had let the situation get so far out of control." After a series of conversations, the bank agreed to convert between £1 million and £2 million of debt to equity in exchange for an upfront payment of £3 million.

The bank was reluctant to grant seniority to the first £2 million of the core group's £6 million loan. It was willing to negotiate, though, because AIT had few assets. "The executives had gone in junior with their money," said Stavis:

> so the bank didn't see why we should be any different. We kept holding the fact that the company was running out of money over the bank's head, and the company kept getting these stays of execution—once it was a tax refund. In the end, though we did get seniority.

AIT's Isacke and BVP's Levine took up revising the reseller deals. Isacke said:

> It was sort of good cop/bad cop. Jeremy [Levine] would take a very hard line and I'd jolly the partner along convincing them that this was the best we could do. I'd think we had everything ironed out and then Jeremy would throw in something new and we'd be back at it. But in the end, we had better contracts for most of them.

The Pricing

"The biggest bite of the apple," said Levine, "was the way the price fell." Peters, the broker, had felt confident that he could sell the step-up of 5 pence/10.5 pence. When he and Randall started meeting with institutional investors, though, they encountered fierce resistance.

"We had thought that it was such a discount from its last trading position that there'd be no problem," said Peters:

> What we found, though, was that the old investors were furious. They wanted to know exactly what had gone wrong and whom they could blame. And new investors, distressed securities experts, were not happy about the instant 2× return for the core group.

A week into the process, Peters suggested to the core group that they reprice the deal to 3.5 pence and 6 pence (see Exhibit 11.10 for cap table). BVP's Stavis said:

> That really made us reconsider if we wanted to do the deal. We could get out, with about three weeks invested and about £500,000 in fees. In fact, at the end of every day, Hardy [Smith], Jeremy [Levine], and I would ask each other if we still wanted to do this. And the answer kept being yes.

While Peters was on the road raising money with Randall, the incoming CEO, he was also working with the lawyers at TJG to gain regulatory approval of the deal and nursing a severely broken hip. Because AIT had been part of the Official List, it was subject to certain disclosure requirements. AIT's anticipated relisting on the less stringent and tax-preferred Alternative Investment Market (AIM) reduced but did not eliminate the regulations to which the company had to conform. Hovering in the distance was the FSA investigation and how that might affect the company. A senior banker had

EXHIBIT 11.10

SUMMARY CAPITALIZATION TABLE, 3.5P/6.0P DEAL

	Shares	£ Invested	Price/ share	Percent Fully Diluted Ownership
Core group				
Interim loan converted	171,428,571	£6,000,000	£0.035	36.3%
Shares from firm placement	41,666,667	2,500,000	0.060	8.8%
Option grants and existing shares	24,166,667	—	0.060	5.2%
Core investor group subtotal	**237,400,262**	**8,500,000**		**50.3%**
Pre-existing shares	17,790,237	—	—	3.8%
Public offering	176,529,945	10,500,000	0.060	37.4%
Equity for debt swaps	14,093,985	1,500,000	0.060	3.0%
Option pool (excluding core group grants)	26,000,000	—	—	5.5%
Subtotal others	**234,414,167**	**£12,000,000**	**—**	**49.7%**
Fully diluted total°	**471,814,429**	**£20,500,000**	**—**	**100.0%**
	—	—	—	—
Total option pool size	42,500,015	—	—	9.0%
	—	—	—	—
Weighted price to core group	**£0.042**	—	—	—
Price to new investors	**£0.060**	—	—	—
Pricing step-up	**41.7%**	—	—	—
	—	—	—	—
Post-money valuation	**£28,308,866**	—	—	—

Sources: Company information and casewriter. Numbers are approximate.

Note:

° A 15:1 reverse split would immediately follow the closing, bringing the price per share to £0.525 for the conversion shares and £0.90 for the public offering.

Fully diluted ownership would be:

BVP and affiliates: 19%

Management: 19%

Arbib Group: 12%

Total investor group ownership: 50%

observed, "The FSA is not in the business of putting companies out of business, but to track down wrongdoers." BVP's Smith concluded that AIT's brand-new management and board, along with its complete cooperation with the agency, made the investigation more likely to cause distraction than anything else.

The structure of the deal required various waivers from the UK regulatory authorities. The £6 million convertible loan would normally require shareholder approval before the money was committed, because of the involvement of Hicks, a shareholder and board member, and the rules of the UK Listing Authority that governed transactions between public companies and their directors. Given AIT's financial straitjacket, the listing authority made an exception and waived that requirement. In addition, another agency, the Panel on Takeovers and Mergers, sanctioned a "Rule 9" waiver. This regulation, which was part of the UK Takeover Code and applied to all UK public companies, required any group acquiring more than 30 percent of a company's shares to make an offer for 100 percent. Subject to approval by AIT's shareholders at an extraordinary general meeting (EGM), this "concert party" rule was waived after each member of the core group disclosed his previous transactions in AIT shares, his seats on the boards of other companies, and a certain amount of personal detail.

Another issue involved timing. Once the price was agreed upon, a circular had to be prepared and sent to all shareholders and anyone else who might invest through the public offering. This essentially served as a prospectus, and described the company, its financial condition, and the investment proposition. At least twenty-three days had to elapse between the distribution of the circular and the EGM where the offering would be approved. Only then could the shares be issued and sold.

"And then," said BVP's Levine, "the price problem came back." Not only were the investors unhappy about the price, but the overall value of the UK financial markets, especially the broad-based FTSE All-Share index, had fallen steadily over the period (see Exhibit 11.11). After approaching twenty institutional investors with the 3.5p/6p

---

EXHIBIT 11.11

MOVEMENT IN UK MARKETS BETWEEN JUNE 18, 2002, AND JULY 18, 2002

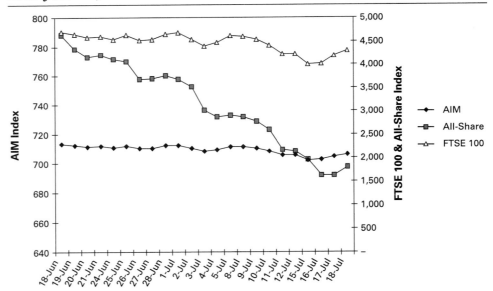

Sources: http://www.ftse.com and http://www.londonstockexchange.com, accessed April 22, 2003.

Note: AIT had been listed on the London Stock Exchange's Official List, and was part of the All-Share index until trading in its shares was suspended on June 18, 2002. It planned to relist on the AIM. The FTSE 100 is the index of the 100 leading companies in the United Kingdom; the All-Share represents almost 99 percent of the United Kingdom's total market capitalization and aggregates the FTSE 100 (large cap), FTSE 250 (midcap) and FTSE Small Cap indices; and the AIM index tracks the smaller, growing firms listed on the Alternative Investment Market.

deal, Peters said, "It became clear that we couldn't raise enough money that way. We were short about £4 million."

Incoming CEO Randall recalled:

> We were meeting with a well-known investor who said he would invest £2.5 million on behalf of his funds, and there were three or four other investors who would follow his lead, but only if there wasn't a step-up. He was concerned that the core group could make money while the other investors were still in a losing position. He said he didn't mind us getting more if the company did well. If this had been at the beginning, we might not have listened, but this was the end and we wanted to stop this process and get on with the real business of turning the company around. So we called BVP back in the States.

THE PRICE PROBLEM

Levine and Stavis looked at each other. "So what do you think?" asked Levine.

"Early on, OMS said something about warrants," said Stavis, "and the Arbibs seemed OK about them. Why don't you figure out how many three-year warrants with a 3.5p exercise price we'd need for a corresponding deal?" As Levine left the office, Stavis called after him, "Really, do you think we've found everything?"

12

A Note on Valuation in Private Equity Settings

The valuation of private companies, especially those in the earlier stages of their life cycle, is a difficult and often subjective process. Early stage companies typically forecast a period of negative cash flows with highly uncertain—but tantalizing—future rewards. This cash flow profile is very sensitive to the valuation assumptions made.

This note will discuss a variety of valuation techniques that can be used in private equity settings. The intention is to provide a practical tool kit to be used when tackling cases in the second and third modules of *Venture Capital and Private Equity*. Much of the background theory will be glossed over; the focus will be on the essential underlying mechanics of each method and a discussion of strengths and weaknesses. The references at the end of this note provide more detailed information on the various valuation techniques discussed.

This note addresses the comparables, net present value, adjusted present value, venture capital, and options valuation methods. We also discuss the use of Monte Carlo simulation employing the Crystal Ball software package to enhance these valuations. The following five sections are each dedicated to one valuation method. Each section has a corresponding appendix with a detailed example of the method.

1. COMPARABLES

The use of comparables often provides a quick and easy way to obtain a ballpark valuation for a firm. When searching for comparables, we seek other firms that display "value characteristics" similar to those of the company we are interested in. These value characteristics include risk, growth rate, capital structure, and the size and timing of cash flows. Often, these value characteristics are driven by other underlying attributes of the company which can be incorporated in a multiple. For example, the anticipated cash flows for a new health maintenance organization (HMO) might be accurately predicted by the number of members it has enrolled (see the example in Appendix 12.1).

John Willinge (MBA '96) prepared this note under the supervision of Professor Josh Lerner as the basis for class discussion. It supersedes an earlier note, "A Note on Valuation in Venture Settings," HBS No. 295–064.

There are, however, many potential problems with the use of comparables for private companies. (The strengths and weaknesses of each method are summarized in Exhibit 12.1.) First, it is often difficult to ascertain what valuations have been assigned to other privately held firms. It may consequently be impossible to compare our firm to

---

EXHIBIT 12.1

STRENGTHS AND WEAKNESSES OF VARIOUS VALUATION METHODS IN PRIVATE EQUITY SETTINGS

Method	Strengths	Weaknesses
1. Comparables	• Quick to use • Simple to understand • Commonly used in industry • Market based	• Private company comparables may be difficult to find and evaluate • If using public company comparables, need to adjust resulting valuation to take into account private company's illiquidity
2. Net Present Value	• Theoretically sound	• Cash flows may be difficult to estimate • Private company comparables (β and capital structure) can be difficult to find and evaluate • WACC assumes a constant capital structure • WACC assumes a constant effective tax rate • Typical cash flow profile of outflows followed by distant, uncertain inflows is very sensitive to discount and terminal growth rate assumptions
3. Adjusted Present Value	• Theoretically sound • Suitable (and simple to use) in situations where the capital structure is changing (e.g., highly leveraged transactions such as leveraged buyouts) • Suitable in situations where the effective tax rate is changing (e.g., when there are NOLs)	• More complicated to calculate than the NPV method • Same disadvantages as NPV method except overcomes the shortfalls of the WACC assumption (i.e., constant capital structure and tax rate)
4. Venture Capital	• Simple to understand • Quick to use • Commonly used	• Relies on terminal values derived from other methods • Oversimplified (large discount rate "fudge factor")
5. Asset Options	• Theoretically sound • Overcomes drawbacks of NPV and APV techniques in situations where managers have flexibility	• Methodology is not commonly used in industry and may not be understood • Real world situations may be difficult to reduce to solvable option problems • Limitations of Black-Scholes model

the companies that are the most similar. Second, because accounting and other performance information on private firms are often unavailable, key ratios may not be calculable, or other important impacts on valuation may be missed. Finally, the valuations assigned to comparable firms may be misguided. Periodically, whole classes of firms have been valued at prices that seem unjustifiable on a cash flow basis.

Sound judgment should consequently drive the use of comparables. One must search for potential measures of value that can be sensibly applied from one company to the next. In public markets, common ratios are (1) the share price divided by the earnings per share (the P/E ratio), (2) the market value of the firm's equity divided by total revenue, and (3) the market value of the firm's equity divided by the shareholder's equity on the balance sheet (market-to-book ratio). These ratios, however, may be misleading. Consider the price-earnings ratio. The earnings (profit after tax) reflect the capital structure of the company, since earnings are after interest expenses and taxes. Common sense would therefore tell us that when comparing two companies with similar characteristics except for substantially different capital structures, it would be more appropriate to use a multiple based on earnings before interest and taxes (EBIT). By using this latter comparable, we compensate for the differing capital structures of the two entities. This is because EBIT ignores the different levels of interest expense incurred by the two companies. (Of course, the use of EBIT ignores the interest tax shields associated with these capital structures, which we may wish to factor into the comparisons.)

Accounting-based comparables, such as those mentioned above, are clearly less suitable in a private equity setting where companies are often unprofitable and experiencing rapid growth. One must therefore look for other sensible measures of value. For example, in an Internet business a good indicator of value may be the number of subscribers enrolled by a company. A valid proxy for the value of a biotechnology firm may be the number of patents awarded. In a gold exploration company, a typical measure of value is the number of ounces of gold indicated by initial drilling results. These are just a few examples of nonfinancial, industry-specific measures that can be used to estimate the value of a firm.

Interestingly, a recent study suggests that industry-specific multiples have strong explanatory power for the offering prices of IPOs. In contrast, accounting-based multiples, such as the price-earnings ratio and the ratio of the market to book value of equity, were found to have little predictive ability. The reason is that among young, publicly traded firms in the same industry, accounting-based multiples vary substantially.[1]

Another issue related to the use of public market comparables to value private companies is the marketability of the equity. Because shares in private firms are typically less marketable than those of publicly traded firms, it may be appropriate to apply a discount for illiquidity. The size of the proper discount will depend on the particular circumstances. Surveys suggest, however, that discounts for lack of marketability used in practice fall within a very narrow band, often between 25 percent and 30 percent.[2]

2. THE NET PRESENT VALUE METHOD

The net present value (NPV) method is one of the most common methods of cash flow valuation. (Others include the equity cash flow and capital cash flow methods. the adjusted

---

1. M. Kim and J. Ritter, "Valuing IPOs," unpublished working paper, Sloan School of Management, Massachusetts School of Technology, 1996.
2. S. Pratt, *Valuing a Business: The Analysis and Appraisal of Closely Held Companies* (Homewood, IL: Dow Jones-Irwin, 1996).

present value method discussed in the next section is a variation on the capital cash flow method.) This section briefly visits the basics of the NPV method.

The NPV method incorporates the benefit of tax shields from tax-deductible interest payments in the discount rate (i.e., the weighted average cost of capital, or WACC). To avoid double-counting these tax shields, interest payments must not be deducted from cash flows. Equation 12.1 shows how to calculate cash flows (subscripts denote time periods):

$$CF_t = EBIT_t \times (1 - \tau) + DEPR_t - CAPEX_t - \Delta NWC_t + other_t \qquad (12.1)$$

where:

$$
\begin{aligned}
CF &= \text{cash flow} \\
EBIT &= \text{earnings before interest and tax} \\
\tau &= \text{corporate tax rate} \\
DEPR &= \text{depreciation} \\
CAPEX &= \text{capital expenditures} \\
\Delta NWC &= \text{increase in net working capital} \\
other &= \text{increases in taxes payable, wages payable, and so forth}
\end{aligned}
$$

Next, the terminal value should be calculated. This estimate is very important as the majority of the value of a company, especially one in an early stage setting, may be in the terminal value. A common method for estimating the terminal value of an enterprise is the perpetuity method.

Equation 12.2 gives the formula for calculating a terminal value (TV) at time T using the perpetuity method, assuming a growth rate in perpetuity of g and a discount rate equal to r. The cash flows and discount rates used in the NPV method are typically nominal values (i.e., they are not adjusted for inflation). If forecasts indicate that the cash flow will be constant in inflation-adjusted dollars, a terminal growth rate equal to the rate of inflation should be used:

$$TV_T = [CF_T \times (1 + g)] \div (r - g) \qquad (12.2)$$

Other common methods of terminal value calculation used in practice include price-earnings ratios and market-to-book value multiples, but these shortcuts are not encouraged! The net present value of the firm is then calculated as shown in Equation 12.3

$$(12.3)$$
$$NPV = [CF_1 \div (1 + r)] + [CF_2 \div (1 + r)^2] + [CF_3 \div (1 + r)^3] + \ldots + [(CF_T + TV_T) \div (1 + r)^T]$$

The discount rate is calculated using Equation 12.4:

$$r = (D \div V) \times r_d \times (1 - t) + (E \div V) \times r_e \qquad (12.4)$$

where:

$$
\begin{aligned}
r_d &= \text{discount rate for debt} \\
r_e &= \text{discount rate for equity} \\
\tau &= \text{corporate tax rate} \\
D &= \text{market value of debt} \\
E &= \text{market value of equity} \\
V &= D + E
\end{aligned}
$$

If the firm is not at its target capital structure, however, the target values should be used for $D \div V$ and $E \div V$.

The cost of equity r_e is calculated using the familiar capital asset pricing model shown in Equation 12.5:

$$r_e = r_f + \beta \times (r_m - r_f) \tag{12.5}$$

where:

r_e = discount rate for equity

r_f = risk-free rate

β = beta, or degree of correlation with the market

r_m = market rate of return on common stock

$(r_m - r_f)$ = market risk premium

When determining the appropriate risk-free rate (r_f), one should attempt to match the maturity of the investment project with that of the risk-free rate. Typically, we use the ten-year rate. Estimates of the market risk premium can vary widely; for the sake of the course, 7.5 percent can be assumed.

For private companies, or spin-offs from public companies, betas can be estimated by looking at comparable public firms. The beta for public companies can be found in a beta book or on the Bloomberg machine. If the firm is not at its target capital structure, it is necessary to "unlever" and "relever" the beta. This is accomplished using Equation 12.6:

$$\beta_u = \beta_t \times (E \div V) = \beta_t \times [E \div (E + D)] \tag{12.6}$$

where:

β_u = unlevered beta

β_t = levered beta

E = market value of equity

D = market value of debt

An issue arises where there are no comparable companies. This often occurs in entrepreneurial settings. Common sense is the best guide in this situation. Think about the cyclical nature of the particular firm and whether the risk is systematic or can be diversified away. If accounting data is available, another way is to calculate "earnings betas," which have some correlation with equity betas. An earnings beta is calculated by comparing a private company's net income to a stock market index such as the S&P 500. Using least squares regression techniques, the slope of the line of best fit (the beta) can be calculated.

Strengths and Weaknesses of the Net Present Value Method

Estimating firm values by discounting relevant cash flows is widely regarded as technically sound. The values should be less subject than comparables to distortions that can occur in public and, more commonly, private markets.

Given the many assumptions and estimates that have been made during the valuation process, however, it is unrealistic to arrive at a single, or "point," value for the firm. Different cash flows should be estimated under "best," "most likely," and "worst" case assumptions. These should then be discounted using a range of values for WACC and the terminal growth rate (g) to give a likely range of values. If you can assign probabilities to each scenario, a weighted average will determine the expected value of the firm.

Even with these steps, the NPV method still has some drawbacks. First, we need betas to calculate the discount rate. A valid comparable company should have similar financial performance, growth prospects, and operating characteristics to the company being valued. A public company with these characteristics may not exist. On a similar note, the target capital structure is often estimated using comparables. Using comparable companies to estimate a target capital structure has much the same drawbacks as finding comparable betas. Third, the typical start-up company cash flow profile of large initial expenditures followed by distant inflows leads to much (or even all) of the value being in the terminal value. Terminal values are very sensitive to assumptions about both discount and terminal growth rates. Finally, recent finance research has raised questions as to whether beta is the proper measure of firm risk. Numerous studies suggest that firm size or the ratio of book-to-market equity values may be more appropriate.[3] Few have tried to implement these suggestions, however, in a practical valuation context.

Another drawback of the NPV method is in the valuation of companies with changing capital structures or effective tax rates. Changing capital structures are often associated with highly leveraged transactions, such as leveraged buyouts. Changing effective tax rates can be due to the consumption of tax credits, such as net operating losses, or the expiration of tax subsidies sometimes granted to fledgling firms. Under the NPV method, the capital structure and effective tax rate are both incorporated in the discount rate (WACC) and assumed to be constant. For this reason the adjusted present value method (Section 3) is recommended in these cases.

MONTE CARLO SIMULATION

When calculating values using spreadsheets, we arrive at a single, or "point," estimate of value. Even when undertaking sensitivity analysis, we simply alter variables one at a time, and determine the change in the valuations. Monte Carlo simulation is an improvement over simple sensitivity analysis because it considers all possible combinations of input variables. The user defines probability distributions for each input variable, and the program generates a probability distribution describing the possible outcomes.

One such package, which shall be described here and used in class, is Crystal Ball.[4] The first step is to set up the base case spreadsheet. We then define the assumption and forecast variables. We will determine the effect of changes in the assumption cells on the value contained in the forecast cell. Assumption cells contain variables such as the discount rate, terminal growth rate, and cash flows. Assumption cells must contain numerical values, not formulas or text. Probability distributions are used to define the way in which the values in the assumption cells vary. Crystal Ball has a suite of probability distributions to choose in describing the behavior of each variable. The user needs to select an appropriate distribution, and estimate the key parameters (e.g., mean and standard deviation).

Assumptions can be defined by highlighting one variable at a time and using the command Cell Define Assumption. Similarly, the forecast is defined by highlighting the cell with the valuation calculation and using the command Cell Define Forecast. A simulation is then generated using the command Run Run. To create a report, use the command Run Create Report. A summary of the report for the NPV valuation performed

---

3. For an overview, see Eugene F. Fama and Kenneth R. French, "The Cross-Section of Expected Stock Returns," *Journal of Finance* 47 (1992): 427–465.

4. Crystal Ball is a personal computer simulation package produced by Decisioneering, Inc., 1515 Arapahoe Street, Suite 1311, Denver, CO 80202. Its phone is 800-289-2550 or 303-534-1515; its fax, 303-534-4818; and address on the World Wide Web, http://www.decisioneering.com.

in Appendix 12.2 is shown in Exhibit 12.2. It shows the probability distribution for the value of the subsidiary, Hi-Tech. The report also indicates that the assumptions were defined as normal distributions with means equal to the values initially contained in the cells, and standard deviations set at +10 percent of the mean.

The availability and simplicity of simulation packages make them a useful tool. Simulation allows a more thorough analysis of the possible outcomes than does regular sensitivity analysis. An additional benefit is that simulation packages allow the user to consider the interrelationships between the different input variables; as the manual

---

EXHIBIT 12.2

SIMULATION REPORT PRODUCED BY CRYSTAL BALL USING DATA FROM APPENDIX 12.2

Statistics	Value
Trials	500
Mean	562
Median	535
Mode	–
Standard Deviation	194
Variance	37,485
Skewness	0.89
Kurtosis	4.05
Coeff. of Variability	0.34
Range Minimum	162
Range Maximum	1,296
Range Width	1,134
Mean Std. Error	8.66

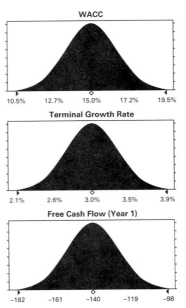

Forecast: Net Present Value

500 Trials — **Frequency Chart** — **10 Outfitters**

$ Millions

Assumptions

Assumption: WACC

Normal distribution with parameters:
Mean	15.0%
Standard Deviation	1.5%

Assumption: Terminal Growth Rate

Normal distribution with parameters:
Mean	3.0%
Standard Deviation	0.3%

Assumption: Free Cash Flow (Year 1)

Normal distribution with parameters:
Mean	−140
Standard Deviation	14

describes, it is easy to define correlations between the various explanatory variables. One must remember, however, that in reality the shapes of distributions, and interrelationships between variables, can be very hard to discover. As sophisticated as the output reports look, the adage about a model being only as good as the assumptions behind it still applies.

3. THE ADJUSTED PRESENT VALUE METHOD

The adjusted present value (APV) method is a variation of the NPV method. APV is preferred over the NPV method when a firm's capital structure is changing or it has net operating losses (NOLs) that can be used to offset taxable income. (An example demonstrating the APV method can be found in Appendix 12.3.)

The NPV method assumes that the capital structure of the firm remains constant at a prespecified target level. This is inappropriate in situations such as leveraged buyouts, where initially the capital structure is highly leveraged, but the level of debt is reduced as repayments are made. In this case, the "target" capital structure changes over time. A way of illustrating this issue is by considering a LBO firm with an ultimate target capital structure of zero; that is, after a certain period it aims to have paid off all its debt. Under the NPV method, the discount rate (WACC) would be calculated using an all-equity capital structure. This ignores the fact the firm has been levered up. APV overcomes this drawback by considering the cash flows generated by the assets of a company, ignoring its capital structure. The savings from tax-deductible interest payments are then valued separately.

The NPV method also assumes that the firm's effective tax rate, incorporated in the WACC, remains constant. This is inappropriate where a firm's effective tax rate changes over time. For example, it is typical for a start-up company to have incurred NOLs before it attains profitability. Under certain circumstances, these NOLs can be carried forward for tax purposes and netted against taxable income. APV accounts for the effect of the firm's changing tax status by valuing the NOLs separately.

Under APV, the valuation task is divided into three steps. First, the cash flows are valued, ignoring the capital structure. The cash flows of the firm are discounted in the same manner as under the NPV method, except that a different discount rate is used. We essentially assume that the company is financed totally by equity. This implies that the discount rate should be calculated using an unlevered beta, rather than the levered beta used to compute the WACC used in the NPV analysis. The discount rate is calculated using the capital asset pricing model shown in Equations 12.5 and 12.6.

The tax benefits associated with the capital structure are then estimated. The net present value of the tax savings from tax-deductible interest payments have value to a company and must be quantified. The interest payments will change over time as debt levels are increased or reduced. By convention, the discount rate often used to calculate the net present value of the tax benefits is the pretax rate of return on debt. This will be lower than the cost of equity. Conceptually this is sensible. The claims of debt holders rank higher than those of ordinary shareholders and therefore are a safer stream of cash flows.

Finally, NOLs available to the company also have value which must be quantified. NOLs can be offset against pretax income and often provide a useful source of cash to a company in its initial profitable years of operation. For instance, if a company has $10 million of NOLs and the prevailing tax rate is 40 percent, the company will have tax savings of $4 million. (Note, however, that this ignores the time value of money. The net present value of the NOLs will only be $4 million if the firm has taxable income of $10 million in its first year. If the NOLs are used over more than one year, then discounting will reduce their value to some amount less than $4 million.)

The discount rate used to value NOLs is often the pretax rate on debt. If you believe that the realization of tax benefits from the NOLs is certain (i.e., the firm will definitely generate sufficient profits to consume them), then use the risk-free rate. If, however, there is some risk that the firm will not generate enough profits to use up the NOLs, then discounting them by the pretax rate of corporate debt makes sense.

4. THE VENTURE CAPITAL METHOD

The venture capital method is a valuation tool commonly applied in the private equity industry. As discussed, private equity investments are often characterized by negative cash flows and earnings, and highly uncertain but potentially substantial future rewards. The venture capital method accounts for this cash flow profile by valuing the company, typically using a multiple, at a time in the future when it is projected to have achieved positive cash flows and/or earnings. This "terminal value" is then discounted back to the present using a high discount rate, typically between 40 percent and 75 percent. (The rationales for these very high target rates are discussed below.)

The venture capitalist uses this discounted terminal value and the size of the proposed investment to calculate her desired ownership interest in the company. For example, if the company's discounted terminal value is $10 million, and the venture capitalist intends to make a $5 million investment, she will want 50 percent of the company in exchange for her investment. This assumes, however, that there will be no dilution of the venture capitalist's interest through future rounds of financing. This is an unrealistic assumption, given that most successful venture-backed companies sell shares to the public through an IPO.

The underlying mechanics of the venture capital method are demonstrated by the following four steps. (An example demonstrating the venture capital method can be found in Appendix 12.4.) The method starts by estimating the company's value in some future year of interest, typically shortly after the venture capitalist foresees taking the firm public. The "terminal value" is usually calculated using a multiple: for example, a price-earnings ratio may be multiplied by the projected net income in the exit year. (See the discussion of comparables in Section 1.) The terminal value can of course be calculated using other techniques, including discounted cash flow methods.

The discounted terminal value of the company is determined by, not surprisingly, discounting the terminal value calculated in the first step. Instead of using a traditional cost of capital as the discount rate, however, venture capitalists typically use a target rate of return. The target rate of return is the yield the venture capitalist feels is required to justify the risk and effort of the particular investment. The formula for calculating the discounted terminal value is shown in Equation 12.7:

$$\textit{Discounted Terminal Value} = \textit{Terminal Value} \div (1 + \textit{Target})^{\textit{years}} \qquad (12.7)$$

Third, the venture capitalist calculates the required final percent ownership. The amount of the proposed investment is divided by the discounted terminal value to determine the ownership necessary for the venture capitalist to earn her desired return (assuming that there is no subsequent dilution of her investment).

Finally, she estimates future dilution and calculates the required current percent ownership. Equation 12.8 would be the correct answer if there were to be no subsequent "rounds" of financing to dilute the venture capitalist's interest in the company.

As we have seen, venture-backed companies commonly receive multiple rounds of financing, followed by an IPO. Hence, this assumption is usually unrealistic. To compensate for the effect of dilution from future rounds of financing, she needs to calculate the retention ratio. The retention ratio quantifies the expected dilutive effect of future rounds of financing on the venture capitalist's ownership. Consider a firm that intends to undertake one more financing round, in which shares representing an additional 25 percent of the firm's equity will be sold, and then to sell shares representing an additional 30 percent of the firm at the time of the IPO. If the venture capitalist owns 10 percent today, after these financings her stake will be $10\% \div (1+0.25) \div (1+0.3) = 6.15\%$. Her retention ratio is $6.15\% \div 10\% = 61.5\%$.

$$\textit{Required Final Percent Ownership = Investment} \div \textit{Discounted Terminal Value} \qquad (12.8)$$

The required current percent ownership necessary for the venture capitalist to realize her target rate of return is then calculated using Equation 12.9:

$$(12.9)$$

$$\textit{Required Current Percent Ownership = Required Final Percent Ownership / Retention Ratio}$$

Strengths and Weaknesses of the Venture Capital Method

A major criticism of the venture capital method is the use of very large discount rates, typically between 40 percent and 75 percent. Venture capitalists justify the use of these high target returns on a number of grounds. First, they argue that large discount rates are used to compensate for the illiquidity of private firms. As discussed in Section 1, equity of private companies is usually less marketable than public stock, and investors demand a higher return in exchange for this lack of marketability. Second, venture capitalists view their services as valuable and consider the large discount rate as providing compensation for their efforts. For example, they provide strategic advice, credibility, and access to specialized intermediaries such as lawyers and investment bankers. Finally, venture capitalists believe that projections presented by entrepreneurs tend to be overly optimistic. They submit that the large discount rate compensates for these inflated projections.

Financial economists suggest that although the issues raised by venture capitalists may be valid, they should not be addressed through a high discount rate. They propose that each of the "justifications" should be valued separately using more objective techniques. First, they argue that the discount for lack of marketability makes sense, but that the estimated premium is far too large: there are numerous investors with long-run time horizons, including endowments, foundations, and individuals. Second, financial economists contend that the services provided by the venture capitalist should be valued by determining what that would have to be paid to acquire equivalent professional services on a contract basis. Once the fair market value of the services provided was determined, shares equal to this value could be given to the venture capitalist. Finally, financial economists submit that discount rates should not be inflated to compensate for the entrepreneurs' overly optimistic projections. They argue that judgment should be applied to determine the likely values of various scenarios and the probability that they will occur. This will result in unbiased estimates of the cash flow of the firm.

The use of high discount rates suggests an element of arbitrariness in the venture capitalist's approach to valuing a company. A better process is to scrutinize the projections and perform reality checks. This involves asking a number of questions. What has been the performance of comparable companies? What share of the market does the company need to meet its projections? How long will it take? What are the key risks? Are contingency plans in place? What are the key success factors? This type of analysis is far more meaningful than just taking the entrepreneur's pro formas and discounting them at a very large rate.

5. OPTIONS ANALYSIS

In some cases, it is appropriate and desirable to use option pricing techniques to value investment opportunities. Discounted cash flow methods such as NPV and APV can be deficient in situations where a manager or investor has "flexibility." Flexibility can take many forms, including the ability to increase or decrease the rate of production, defer development, or abandon a project. These changes all affect the value of the firm in ways that are not accurately measured using discounted cash flow techniques. One form of flexibility that is of particular interest to the venture capitalist is the ability to make follow-on investments.

Private equity-backed companies are often characterized by multiple rounds of financing. Venture capitalists use this multistage investment approach to motivate the entrepreneur to "earn" future rounds of financing and also to limit the fund's exposure to a particular portfolio company. Often, the first right of refusal for a later stage of financing is written into the investment contract.

The right to make a follow-on investment has many of the same characteristics as a call option on a company's stock. Both include the right, but not the obligation, to acquire an asset by paying a sum of money on or before a certain date. As we shall see, this flexibility is not readily accounted for by discounted cash flow techniques. By way of contrast, option pricing theory accounts for the manager's ability to "wait and then decide whether to invest" in the project at a later date.

To illustrate the drawback of using NPV flow methods when pricing options, consider the following simplified example. A project requiring an investment of $150 today is equally likely to generate revenues next year, that—discounted to today's dollars—total $200, $160, or $120. Consequently, the project will have a net present value of $50, $10, or −$30. The expected return is $10 [= ($1/3$) × (50 + 10 − 30)].

Now consider an investor who has the ability to delay his investment until period 1.[5] By delaying investing until he obtains further information, he can avoid investing when revenues will only be $120. Essentially, by waiting and gathering more information, the investor modifies the expected return profile from [$50, $10, −$30] to [$50, $10, $0]. The option to delay investing is worth $10, the difference between the new expected NPV of $20 [= ($1/3$) × (50 + 10 + 0)] and the earlier $10 expected value.

This section introduces a developing area in finance. For the purposes of brevity a basic knowledge of option pricing theory (at the level, for instance, of Brealey and Myers) is assumed. Readers are referred to the references at the end of this note for further literature on option pricing techniques.

VALUING FIRMS AS OPTIONS

The Black-Scholes model values European options using five variables as inputs. For an option on a stock, these comprise the exercise price (X), the stock price (S), the time to expiration (t), the standard deviation (or volatility) of returns on the stock (σ), and

---

5. We assume the net present value of the investment in today's dollars is still $150, whether the investment is made in Period 0 or Period 1.

the risk free rate (r_f). Using these variables, we can value the right to buy a share of a company's stock at some future point. We can evaluate a firm's decision to invest in a project using a similar framework. The equivalents are shown in Table 12.1.

Once the input variables have been estimated, the value of the option can be calculated using a Black-Scholes computer model or a call option valuation table.

REDUCING COMPLEX PROBLEMS TO OPTIONS ANALYSES

Real-world decisions can be difficult to reduce to mathematically solvable problems. There is often great value, however, in attempting to simplify these types of problems. For example, the right to abandon the development of a gold mine is similar to a put option. A finance lease gives the leaseholder both the right to cancel the lease by paying a fee (a put option), and the right to purchase the asset for a fixed price at the end of the lease (a call option). This note will consider only the solution of call options using the Black-Scholes formula for European options (which can only be exercised at the end of the period).

Table 12.1 describes the five inputs necessary to value an investment option by a firm. The approximation of four of the variables (X, S, t, r_f) is fairly intuitive and is illustrated in the example in Appendix 5. The process of estimating the fifth variable, the standard deviation (σ), merits further discussion. One way to estimate the standard deviation is to look at the stock price volatility for businesses with assets comparable to the project or company under consideration. These are, for instance, available on the Bloomberg machine. An important point is that volatilities estimated using this method will require adjustment to take into account the leverage of the comparable company. Remember that leverage amplifies risk, and hence comparable companies with higher leverage than the project under consideration will have higher risk. As a guide, volatilities of 20 percent to 30 percent are not unusually high for single companies, and many small technology companies have volatilities of between 40 percent and 50 percent.

STRENGTHS AND WEAKNESSES OF USING OPTION PRICING TO VALUE INVESTMENT OPPORTUNITIES

Option pricing theory is useful in situations where there is the "flexibility" to wait, learn more about the prospects of the proposed investment, and then decide whether

TABLE 12.1

FINANCIAL AND FIRM OPTION VARIABLES

Variable	Financial Option	Firm Option
X	Exercise price	Present value of the expenditures required to undertake the project
S	Stock price	Present value of the expected cash flows generated by the project
t	Time to expiration	The length of time that the investment decision can be deferred
σ	Standard deviation of returns on the stock	Riskiness of the underlying assets
r_f	Time value of money	Risk free rate of return

to invest. As discussed, opportunities that incorporate flexibility will consistently be undervalued using discounted cash flow techniques.

There are at least three concerns associated with the use of option pricing methodology. First, it is not well known to many business people, particularly in the private equity community. As with most "new technologies," it may be difficult to convince associates and counterparties that its use is valid. A second drawback of the option pricing methodology is the difficulty of reducing real-world opportunities to simple problems that can be valued. While the models can accommodate cases where the firm pays dividends or where the option can be exercised early, the calculations may be more complex. Option pricing used inappropriately can inflate values achieved using other methods, thereby falsely justifying projects that would otherwise be rejected. Finally, some situations may not be appropriate for the Black-Scholes formula. For instance, the exact pricing of a series of call options that are nested (i.e., where one cannot be exercised before the other one is) is a difficult problem. In these cases, it may be best to use simulation techniques.

FOR FURTHER READING

R. Brealey and S. Myers, *Principles of Corporate Finance* (New York: McGraw-Hill, 1991).

T. Copeland, T. Koller, and J. Murrin, *Valuation: Measuring and Managing the Value of Companies* (New York: John Wiley & Sons, 1991).

European Venture Capital Association, "The EVCA Performance Measurement Guidelines," Zaventum, Belgium, EVCA Venture Capital Special Paper, 1994.

E. Fama and K. French, "The Cross-Section of Expected Stock Returns," *Journal of Finance* 47 (1992): 427–465.

S. Fenster and S. Gilson, "The Adjusted Present Value Method for Capital Assets," Harvard Business School note No. 294-047, Harvard Business School Publishing, 1994.

R. Higgins, *Analysis for Financial Management* (New York: Irwin, 1992).

S. Kaplan and R. Ruback, "The Valuation of Cash Flow Forecasts: An Empirical Analysis," *Journal of Finance* 51 (1995): 1059–1093.

M. Kim and J. Ritter, "Valuing IPOs," Unpublished working paper, Sloan School of Management, Massachusetts Institute of Technology, 1996.

T. Luehrman, "Capital Projects as Real Options: An Introduction," Harvard Business School note No. 295-074, Harvard Business School Publishing, 1995.

S. Pratt, *Valuing a Business: The Analysis and Appraisal of Closely Held Companies* (Homewood, IL: Dow Jones–Irwin, 1996).

R. Ruback, "An Introduction to Capital Cash Flow Methods," Harvard Business School note No. 295155, Harvard Business School Publishing, 1995.

D. Siegel, J. Smith, and J. Paddock, "Valuing Offshore Oil Properties with Option Pricing Models," *Quarterly Journal of Economics* 103 (1988): 473–508.

APPENDIX 12.1

SAMPLE VALUATION USING COMPARABLES

The fifty-year-old chairman and major shareholder of Private Health, a private regional Health Maintenance Organization (HMO), is considering selling his stake in the company and retiring. He has asked Private Health's chief financial officer (CFO) to calculate the value of the firm by the following morning. The two main options that he is entertaining are the sale of his interest to an Employee Share Ownership Plan (ESOP) and to one of the firm's publicly traded competitors. The CFO regularly receives research reports from investment bankers eager to take the company public. From these reports she is able to compare the following information for Private Health and two public HMOs operating in the same region. Data are for the 1995 financial year (amounts in millions of dollars unless indicated):

	Private Health	Happy Healthcare	Community Health
Balance Sheet			
Assets	$160	$300	$380
Long-Term Debt	5	100	0
Net Worth	80	120	175
Income Statement			
Revenues	350	420	850
EBITDA	45	55	130
Net Income	30	20	75
Market Data			
Earnings per Share ($/share)	3.00	0.67	2.14
Price-Earnings Ratio (times)	N/A	21.00	14.50
Shares Outstanding (m)	10	30	35
Number of Members	500,000	600,000	1,100,000

From the above information, the CFO was able to calculate the following multiples and implied valuations for Private Health:

	Happy Healthcare	Community Health	Average	Private Health Implied Value ($M)
Price-Earnings Ratio	21.0	14.5	17.7	533
Market Value/EBITDA	7.64	8.37	8.00	360
Market Value/Sales	1.00	1.28	1.14	399
Market Value/Book Value of Equity	3.52	6.21	4.86	389
Market Value/Member	700	989	844	422

The CFO felt that on an overall basis the multiples gave a good indication of the value of Private Health but that it was overvalued on a P/E multiple basis. She believed this was because Happy Healthcare (long-term debt to total assets of 33 percent) was substantially more leveraged than Private Health (3 percent). Valuing Private Health using Community Health's P/E ratio of 14.5 gave an implied valuation of $435 million. Based on her analysis, she was confident that the value of Private Health was in the range of $360–435 million if sold to a public company. If the shares were sold to an ESOP, she believed that, because of the company's private status, it would be appropriate to assume a discount of 15–20 percent, or a valuation of $290–360 million.

APPENDIX 12.2

SAMPLE VALUATION USING THE NET PRESENT VALUE METHOD

Lo-Tech's shareholders have voted to cease its diversification strategy and refocus on its core businesses. As a part of this process, the company is seeking to divest Hi-Tech, its start-up high-technology subsidiary. George, a venture capitalist, has been approached by the management of Hi-Tech, which wants to purchase the company. He decides to value Hi-Tech using the NPV method. George and Hi-Tech management have agreed on the following projections (all data are in millions of dollars):

	Year 1	Year 2	Year 3	Year 4	Year 5	Year 6	Year 7	Year 8	Year 9
Revenues	100	140	210	250	290	380	500	650	900
Costs	230	240	260	275	290	310	350	400	470
EBIT	−130	−100	−50	−25	0	70	150	250	430

The company has $100 million of NOLs that can be carried forward and offset against future income. In addition, Hi-Tech is projected to generate further losses in its early years of operation that it will also be able to carry forward. The tax rate is 40 percent. The average unlevered beta of five comparable high-technology companies is 1.2. Hi-Tech has no long-term debt. Treasury yields for ten-year bonds are 6.0 percent. Capital expenditure requirements are assumed to be equal to depreciation. The market risk premium is assumed to be 7.5 percent. Net working capital requirements are forecast as 10 percent of sales. EBIT is projected to grow at 3 percent per year in perpetuity after Year 9.

George first calculated the Weighted Average Cost of Capital (WACC):

$$\text{WACC} = (D \div V) \times r_d \times (1 - \tau) + (E \div V) \times r_e = 0 + 100\% \times [6.0 + 1.2 \times (7.5)] = 15\%$$

He then valued the cash flows, which showed the company had a net present value of $525 million. As suspected, all the value of the company was accounted for in the terminal value (the present value of the cash flows was $(44) million and the present value of the terminal value $569 million, giving a net present value of $525 million).

The terminal value was calculated as follows:

$$TV_T = [CF_T \times (1 + g)] \div (r - g) = [233 \times (1 + 3\%)] \div (15\% - 3\%) = \$2,000$$

George also performed a scenario analysis to determine the sensitivity of the value of Hi-Tech to changes in the discount rate and the terminal growth rate. He developed a scenario table shown in the attached spreadsheet.[6]

George's scenario analysis gave a series of values ranging from $323 million to $876 million. Clearly this large range did not provide precise guidance as to Hi-Tech's actual value. He noted that the cash flow profile of negative early cash flows followed by distant positive cash flows made the valuation very sensitive to both the discount rate and the terminal growth rate. George considered the NPV method a first step in the valuation process and planned to use other methods to narrow the range of possible values for Hi-Tech.

6. Sensitivity analyses can be easily undertaken using the Microsoft Excel command Data Table.

(Continues)

APPENDIX 12.2 *(Continued)*

WACC Calculation

Tax Rate	40.0%
Rm – Rf	7.5%
EN	100.0%
Bu	1.2
10 Year Treasury Bond	6.0%
WACC	15.0%

Cash Flows

Terminal Growth Rate	3.0%

Year	0	1	2	3	4	5	6	7	8	9
Revenues		100	140	210	250	290	380	500	650	900
Less: Costs		230	240	260	275	290	310	350	400	470
EBIT		−130	−100	−50	−25	0	70	150	250	430
Less: Tax		0	0	0	0	0	0	0	26	172
EBIAT		−130	−100	−50	−25	0	70	150	224	258
Less: Ch. NWC		10	4	7	4	4	9	12	15	25
Free Cash Flow		−140	−104	−57	−29	−4	61	138	209	233
Discount Factor		0.870	0.756	0.658	0.572	0.497	0.432	0.376	0.327	0.284
PV (Cash Flow)		−122	−79	−37	−17	−2	26	52	68	66

PV (Cash Flows)	(44)	
Terminal Value		2000
PV (Terminal Value)		569

<u>Net Present Value and
Sensitivity Analysis</u>

PV (Cash Flows)	(44)
PV (Terminal Value)	569
Net Present Value	525

		WACC		
		13%	15%	17%
Terminal	2%	699	476	323
Growth	3%	778	525	355
Rate	4%	876	583	391

Tax Calculation

EBIT	−130	−100	−50	−25	0	70	150	250	430
NOLs Used	0	0	0	0	0	70	150	185	0
NOLs Added	130	100	50	25	0	0	0	0	0
Tax	0	0	0	0	0	0	0	26	172
Beginning NOLs	100	230	330	380	405	405	335	185	0
Ending NOLs	230	330	380	405	405	335	185	0	0

Net Working Capital (10% sales)

Beg NWC		10	14	21	25	29	38	50	65
End NWC	10	14	21	25	29	38	50	65	90
Ch. NWC	10	4	7	4	4	9	12	15	25

APPENDIX 12.3

SAMPLE VALUATION USING THE ADJUSTED PRESENT VALUE METHOD

Vulture Partners, a private equity organization specializing in distressed company investing, was interested in purchasing Turnaround. Mr. Fang, a general partner at Vulture, used the following projections to value Turnaround (all data are in millions of dollars):

	Year 1	Year 2	Year 3	Year 4	Year 5
Revenues	200	210	220	230	240
Costs	100	105	110	115	120
EBIT	100	105	110	115	120
ΔNWC	3	3	4	4	5

Turnaround had $220 million of NOLs, which were available to be offset against future income. At the beginning of Year 1, the company had $75 million of 8 percent debt, which was expected to be repaid in three $25 million installments, beginning at the end of Year 1. The tax rate was 40 percent. Mr. Fang believed an appropriate unlevered beta for Turnaround was 0.8. The ten-year Treasury Bond yield was 7.0 percent and the market risk premium 7.5 percent. Net cash flows were forecast to grow at 3 percent per year in perpetuity after Year 5. Mr. Fang performed the following steps.

Mr. Fang employed the APV method to value Turnaround and, as such, used the cost of equity as the discount rate:

$$\text{Cost of Equity} = r_f + b_u \times (r_m - r_f) = 7.0 + 0.8 \times (7.5) = 13.0\%$$

Cash flows and the terminal value were both calculated in the same manner as under the NPV method. Mr. Fang arrived at a terminal value of $690 million using the perpetuity method (assuming a growth rate of 3 percent per annum).

Mr. Fang then calculated the interest tax shields by multiplying the interest expense for each period by the tax rate of 40 percent. The interest expense was calculated using the debt repayment schedule. The present value of the interest tax shields, equal to $4.2 million, was determined by discounting each year's interest tax shield at the pretax cost of debt.

To value the tax shields from the NOLs, Mr. Fang first determined the taxable earnings for each period and hence the rate at which the NOLs would be utilized. By subtracting the interest expense on debt from taxable earnings (EBIT), he determined the amount of NOLs that would be used each period. The NOL tax shields were then calculated by multiplying the NOLs consumed each period by the tax rate. Mr. Fang discounted the NOL tax shields at the pretax cost of debt. The present value of the NOLs was equal to $77 million.

The sensitivity analysis showed the likely valuation range for Turnaround to be on the order of $650 to $750 million. The range of values indicated that the valuation was reasonably sensitive to both the discount and terminal growth rate assumptions.

(Continues)

APPENDIX 12.3 *(Continued)*

Discount Rate Calculation

Tax Rate	40%	Rm – Rf	7.5%
10 Year Treasury Bond	7.0%	Bu	0.8
Discount Rate (Unlevered)	13.0%		

Step 1: Value Cash Flows

Terminal Growth Rate 3.0%

Year	0	1	2	3	4	5
Revenues		200	210	220	230	240
Less: Costs		100	105	110	115	120
EBIT		100	105	110	115	120
Less: Tax		40	42	44	46	48
EBIAT		60	63	66	69	72
Less: Ch. NWC		3	3	4	4	5
Net Cash Flow		57	60	62	65	67
Discount Factor		0.885	0.783	0.693	0.613	0.543
PV (Cash Flow)		50	47	43	40	36
PV (Cash Flows)	217					
Terminal Value						690
PV (Terminal Value)						375

Step 2: Value Interest Tax Shields

Beginning Debt		75	50	25	0	0
Repayment (End of Year)		25	25	25	0	0
Ending Debt		50	25	0	0	0
Interest Expense		6.0	4.0	2.0	0.0	0.0
Interest Tax Shield		2.4	1.6	0.8	0.0	0.0
Discount Factor	8.0%	0.926	0.857	0.794	0.735	0.681
Present Value		2.2	1.4	0.6	0.0	0.0
Net Present Value	4.2					

Step 3: Value NOLs

EBIT		100	105	110	115	120
Interest Expense		6.0	4.0	2.0	0.0	0.0
EBIT less Interest Expense		94	101	108	115	120
NOLs Used		94	101	25	0	0
Beginning NOLs		220	126	25	0	0
Ending NOLs		126	25	0	0	0
NOLs Used		94	101	25	0	0
NOL Tax Shield		38	40	10	0	0
Discount Factor	8.0%	0.926	0.857	0.794	0.735	0.681
Present Value (NOL)		35	35	8	0	0
Net Present Value (NOLs)	77					

Step 4: NPV and Sensitivity Analysis

PV (Cash Flows)	217
PV (Terminal Value)	375
PV (Tax Shields)	4
PV (NOLs)	77
Net Present Value	673

WACC				
		12.0%	13.0%	14.0%
Terminal	2%	692	635	589
Growth	3%	739	673	619
Rate	4%	798	718	655

APPENDIX 12.4

SAMPLE VALUATION USING THE VENTURE CAPITAL METHOD

James is a partner in a very successful Boston-based venture capital firm. He plans to invest $5 million in a start-up biotechnology venture and must decide what share of the company he should demand for his investment. Projections he developed with company management show net income in year seven of $20 million. The few profitable biotechnology companies are trading at an average price-earnings ratio of fifteen. The company currently has 500,000 shares outstanding. James believes that a target rate of return of 50 percent is required for a venture of this risk. He performs the following calculations:

$$\text{Discounted Terminal Value} = \text{Terminal Value} \div (1 + \text{Target})^{\text{years}} = (20 \times 15) \div (1 + 50\%)^7 = \$17.5 \text{ million}$$

$$\text{Required Percent Ownership} = \text{Investment} \div \text{Discounted Terminal Value} = 5 \div 17.5 = 28.5\%$$

$$\text{Number of New Shares} = 500{,}000 \div (1 - 28.5\%) - 500{,}000 = 200{,}000$$

$$\text{Price per New Share} = \$5 \text{ million} \div 200{,}000 \text{ shares} = \$25 \text{ per share}$$

$$\text{Implied Pre-money Valuation} = 500{,}000 \text{ shares} \times \$25 \text{ per share} = \$12.5 \text{ million}$$

$$\text{Implied Post-money Valuation} = 700{,}000 \text{ shares} \times \$25 \text{ per share} = \$17.5 \text{ million}$$

James and his partners are of the opinion that three more senior staff will need to be hired. In James's experience this number of top caliber recruits would require options amounting to 10 percent of the common stock outstanding. Additionally, he believes that, at the time the firm goes public, additional shares equivalent to 30 percent of the common stock will be sold to the public. He amends his calculations as follows:

$$\text{Retention Ratio} = [1 \div (1 + .1)] \div (1 + .3) = 70\%$$

$$\text{Required Current Percent Ownership} = \text{Required Final Percent Ownership/Retention Ratio}$$
$$= 28.5\% \div 70\% = 40.7\%$$

$$\text{Number of New Shares} = 500{,}000 \div (1 - 40.7\%) - 500{,}000 = 343{,}373$$

$$\text{Price per New Share} = \$5 \text{ million} \div 343{,}373 \text{ shares} = \$14.56 \text{ per share}$$

APPENDIX 12.5

SAMPLE VALUATION USING OPTION PRICING

Sharon Rock, a famous venture capitalist, was considering whether to invest in Think-Tank, Inc., a company owned and managed by Mr. Brain. ThinkTank had developed a new product that was ready to be manufactured and marketed. An expenditure of $120 million was required for the construction of research and manufacturing facilities. Rock was of the opinion that the following projections developed by Mr. Brain and his associates were justifiable (all data are in millions of dollars):

	Year 0	Year 1	Year 2	Year 3	Year 4	Year 5
Cash Flow except CapEx	0.0	0.0	0.0	10.0	25.0	50.0
Capital Expenditures	−120.0	0.0	0.0	0.0	0.0	0.0
Total Cash Flow	−120.0	0.0	0.0	10.0	25.0	50.0

Rock performed a NPV valuation using a discount rate (WACC) of 25 percent and a terminal growth rate of 3 percent. She was unimpressed with the resulting valuation of −$11.55 million.

After thinking more carefully, Rock realized that the investment could be broken into two stages. The initial investment, which would need to be made immediately, would be $20 million for R&D equipment and personnel. The $100 million expenditure on the plant could be undertaken any time in the first two years. (Whenever the project would be undertaken, the present value of the plant construction expenditures would total $100 million in today's dollars.) Rock decided that the option to expand should not be valued using discounted cash flow methods, for she would only pursue the opportunity if the first stage of the project were successful. The expansion opportunity could more validly be considered as an initial $20 investment bundled with a two-year European call option and priced using the Black-Scholes model.

The easiest variables to estimate were the time to expiration (t) and the risk-free rate (r_f), being two years and 7 percent, respectively. The exercise price (X) was equal to the present value of the investment to build the plant, or $100 million. The stock price (S) was estimated by discounting the expected cash flows to be generated by the underlying assets associated with the expansion opportunity. Using a discount rate of 25 percent and a terminal growth rate of 3 percent per year, S was calculated as worth as $108.45 million in Year 0. The only Black-Scholes input variable remaining to be calculated was the standard deviation (σ). Rock found this difficult to estimate but proceeded to look at some comparable companies. She estimated that the value of σ was likely to lie in the range of 0.5 to 0.6.

Using this data Rock then calculated the Black-Scholes European call option to be worth between $38.8 and $43.7 million. The total net present value of the project, equal to the cost of the first stage investment and the value of the call option (the stage 2 opportunity), was therefore between $18.8 and $23.7 million [= −$20 million + $38.8 to $43.7 million].

Based on this analysis, Sharon Rock decided to invest in ThinkTank on the provision that she would be granted first right of refusal on any subsequent rounds of financing.

13

A Note on European Private Equity

INTRODUCTION

About 27 billion Euros were invested by European private equity funds in companies during 2002, making Europe the second most developed private equity market after the United States (see Exhibit 13.1).[1] But important differences remain between the various European nations. The largest and most developed private equity market in Europe is the United Kingdom, followed by fast-growing France (Exhibit 13.2).

Until very recently, over 90 percent of European private equity funds were devoted to buyouts or other later-stage investments. Although the term "venture capital" in Europe is synonymous with private equity, true venture capital (i.e., early stage investments) did not come into its own until the late 1990s. While the venture capital industry seems to have substantial opportunities for growth, some observers argue that the buyout market may in fact be *too* developed in some European countries, and that a dramatic fall in fund-raising and investments is likely.

This note will discuss the trends in European private equity through mid-2003, comparing private equity in Europe with the U.S. industry wherever possible.[2] It will also highlight differences among the European countries. It focuses entirely on Western Europe, and does not consider the emerging private equity industries in such nations as Poland and Russia.[3]

1. This case presents all tabulations in Euros (and its predecessor, the ECU, or European Currency Unit). During 2002, one Euro equaled on average U.S. 95 cents. The tabulations do not include investments in Europe by American private equity funds, which the European Venture Capital Association (EVCA) estimates totaled approximately several billion Euros in 2002.

2. Unless otherwise noted, the analysis is based on numerous interviews with European and American private equity professionals, as well as an analysis of the database of the Centre for Management Buyout Research (CMBOR) at the University of Nottingham and the publications of the European Venture Capital Association and Initiative Europe.

3. These countries, among others, are discussed in Josh Lerner and Gonzalo Pacanins, "A Note on Private Equity in Developing Countries," Harvard Business School note No. 297-039.

Professor Josh Lerner and Reynir Indahl and Eric Zinterhofer (MBA '98) prepared this note as the basis for class discussion.

EXHIBIT 13.1

**TOTAL PRIVATE EQUITY INVESTMENT
(BILLIONS OF ECUs OR EUROS)**

	Venture Capital	Buyouts and Other Private Equity	Total
1984	0.15	0.36	0.51
1985	0.35	1.02	1.37
1986	0.33	1.07	1.40
1987	0.34	2.50	2.84
1988	0.43	3.02	3.45
1989	0.42	3.85	4.27
1990	0.35	3.77	4.12
1991	0.32	4.31	4.63
1992	0.28	4.42	4.70
1993	0.20	3.92	4.12
1994	0.31	5.13	5.44
1995	0.32	5.23	5.55
1996	0.44	6.35	6.79
1997	0.71	8.94	9.65
1998	1.62	12.84	14.46
1999	3.24	21.87	25.11
2000	6.66	28.30	34.96
2001	4.18	20.15	24.33
2002	2.92	24.73	27.65

Source: European Venture Capital Association, *EVCA Yearbook* (Zaventum, Belgium: EVCA, 2003) (and earlier years).

PRIVATE EQUITY FUNDS IN EUROPE

European private equity has gone through cycles similar to those in the United States. A boom in the late 1980s was followed by a bust in the early 1990s. The late 1990s saw an extraordinary recovery. Fund-raising—fueled by the increasing interest in Europe by U.S. institutional investors—far surpassed earlier levels (Exhibit 13.3). This increase in fund-raising was largely due to the strong returns that the European funds have delivered to investors—the returns from all European private equity funds have averaged 24.9 percent between 1995 and 1999—as well as concerns about the degree of competition in the U.S. market.[4] The late 1990s were years of strong growth in the volume of deals as well, with the activity in many markets exceeding the levels of the late 1980s. The first years of the 2000s saw a rapid decline in venture capital activity, but continued strength elsewhere.

We will first consider the patterns in buyouts. While the aggregate trends may be similar to those in the United States, many striking differences exist between the individual European countries and the United States. The United Kingdom had almost the

4. Venture Economics, *Investment Benchmark Reports: European Private Equity* (Newark, NJ: Venture Economics, 2000). All reported returns are capital-weighted averages.

EXHIBIT 13.2

PRIVATE EQUITY INVESTMENT BY COUNTRY (MILLIONS OF ECUs OR EUROS)

	Venture Capital	Buyouts and Other Private Equity	Total
1995			
Austria	0	1	1
Belgium	6	105	111
Denmark	3	27	31
Finland	8	26	34
France	27	824	851
Germany	89	577	666
Greece	3	5	8
Ireland	1	18	19
Italy	45	209	253
Netherlands	76	391	467
Norway	5	115	120
Portugal	4	51	55
Spain	18	145	163
Sweden	6	79	86
Switzerland	1	48	48
United Kingdom	28	2,605	2,633
Total	321	5,225	5,546
2002			
Austria	27	119	146
Belgium	109	250	359
Denmark	138	103	241
Finland	99	357	456
France	493	5,358	5,851
Germany	561	1,945	2,506
Greece	13	32	45
Ireland	28	77	105
Italy	65	2,561	2,626
Netherlands	201	1,521	1,722
Norway	83	118	201
Portugal	10	59	69
Spain	106	862	968
Sweden	249	1,219	1,468
Switzerland	132	180	312
United Kingdom	600	9,785	10,385
Total	2,919	24,729	27,648

Source: European Venture Capital Association, *EVCA Yearbook* (Zaventum, Belgium: EVCA, 2003); and earlier years.

Note: Total includes several smaller nations in Western Europe not broken out individually.

EXHIBIT 13.3

**TOTAL PRIVATE EQUITY FUND-RAISING
(BILLIONS OF ECUs OR EUROS)**

1986	1.88
1987	2.95
1988	3.48
1989	5.11
1990	4.58
1991	4.19
1992	4.21
1993	3.43
1994	6.69
1995	4.40
1996	7.96
1997	20.00
1998	20.34
1999	25.40
2000	48.02
2001	40.01
2002	27.53

Source: European Venture Capital Association, *EVCA Yearbook* (Zaventum, Belgium: EVCA, 2003); and earlier years.

---

same level of investment in 2002 than the United States, compared on a per capita basis, while most Continental European markets had far less (Exhibit 13.4). (Similar patterns appear in the size of the public market relative to GDP.) These differences, however, may be declining with time. In particular, France has experienced rapid growth. Furthermore, the level of private equity in the United Kingdom may be above a sustainable level and may fall in coming years; the dramatic increase of capital under management and the emergence of high-yield debt issues have led to a setting where there is highly competitive bidding for deals.

Historically, European buyout funds grew out of financial institutions, although many of these have lately gone through management buyouts themselves and become independent. Some of the largest and most prestigious independent European funds are offshoots from financial institutions, including Doughty Hanson (Charterhouse and Westdeutsche Landesbank), BC Partners (Barings), Industri Kapital (Skandinaviska Enskilda Banken), and Cinven (the Government Coal Board Pension Fund). Other top-tier funds are still operated as subsidiaries, including Charterhouse and DMG Capital. The United Kingdom was the cradle of European private equity, and most of the top-tier players are of British origin. The industry's capital is increasingly concentrated among a few organizations: the top fifteen firms increased their share of the funds consistently over the past decade.

Continental markets have been less consistent. The driver behind the growth of German LBOs in the 1990s was the new focus on shareholder value that has forced companies to spin off companies as a part of their restructuring and refocusing efforts.

EXHIBIT 13.4

PRIVATE EQUITY INVESTMENTS PER CAPITA, 1999 (ECUs OR EUROS)

	Venture Capital	Buyouts and Other Private Equity
Austria	3.33	14.69
Belgium	10.58	24.27
Denmark	25.56	19.07
Finland	19.04	68.65
France	8.20	89.15
Germany	6.80	23.58
Greece	1.18	2.91
Ireland	7.00	19.25
Italy	1.13	44.62
Netherlands	12.48	94.47
Norway	18.44	26.22
Portugal	0.99	5.84
Spain	2.58	20.97
Sweden	27.98	136.97
Switzerland	18.33	25.00
United Kingdom	10.12	156.58
All Europe	*7.46*	*63.21*
United States°	*23.42*	*107.39*

Source: European Venture Capital Association, *EVCA Yearbook* (Zaventum, Belgium: EVCA, 2003) and International Monetary Fund, *International Financial Statistics* (Washington, International Monetary Fund, 2003).

° The U.S. calculation uses fund-raising data rather than investment figures. In some cases, the capital may have been invested in another country.

Another reason for the German growth has been the increasing frequency of succession issues among the Mittelstand companies (the Mittelstand companies are small- to medium-sized family business, many of which were started after the Second World War). These perceived opportunities have led to widespread optimism among German buyout organizations and to the entry of numerous new groups. Nonetheless, by 2001, many investors were becoming disillusioned with the difficulty of this market and were scaling back their activities in Germany.

France and Italy have been erratic. The uneven nature of these markets has been attributed to the lackluster performance of some high-profile deals in the 1990s, as well as the difficult regulatory environment, especially in France. France experienced a major rebound in activity in 2002, due to a few large transactions. Whether this surge in activity will be sustainable is an open question. Probably the most developed buyout industries outside the United Kingdom are the Dutch and Swiss markets. In both cases, the presence of a strong private pension system has facilitated the raising of funds from local sources. Among the Nordic countries, Sweden has been the only country with a steady transaction flow, although lately Finland has experienced a surge in activity. Denmark and Norway have been more erratic with a limited stream of deals, which is attributed to the many small- to medium-sized family companies and difficult ownership rules.

Most of the new entrants on the Continent are United Kingdom–based private equity organizations, along with some American firms. It remains unclear how successful these new entrants will be. It is more challenging to do deals on the Continent than in the United Kingdom or the United States. Accounting standards, government regulations, and union contracts inhibit due diligence and limit the ability to turn around underperforming businesses. Management culture has been another obstacle. While financial incentives commonly work well in the United Kingdom and the United States, these are less emphasized on the Continent, especially in Germany; numerous observers suggest that German managers put a higher priority on community standing and cooperation at the work place. Hence, some buyout firms have found it challenging to identify managerial talent who can lead their new acquisitions and make the difficult operational improvements needed. This reluctance, however, appears to be rapidly easing.

On the venture capital side, similar changes have happened on a much more accelerated time frame. As Exhibit 13.1 makes clear, in its earliest years, the European private equity industry had a significant representation of venture capital investments. Over time, however, the venture capital portion dwindled dramatically. The shrinking representation of venture capital investments reflected their poor performance. Between 1980 and 1994, for instance, the average mature large buyout fund in Great Britain boasted a net return of 23.1 percent and the average mid-sized buyout fund had a return of 14.7 percent. Meanwhile, the typical venture fund had a net return of 4.0 percent over the same period.[5] As a result, most venture capital specialists were unable to raise new funds, and generalist investors (such as Apax and 3i) shifted to an emphasis on buyouts.

This situation began reversing itself around 1997. The shifting attitudes were in part triggered by American venture groups, particularly East Coast–based organizations such as General Atlantic and Warburg Pincus. Attracted by the modest valuations of European technology and biotechnology start-ups relative to their American counterparts, general partners increasingly began traveling to Europe to invest in portfolio companies. This trend accelerated at the end of the decade, as American groups such as Benchmark and Draper Fisher Jurvetson began targeting large amounts of capital (sometimes in dedicated funds) for European venture investments. The trend was also helped by the superior performance of venture investments in the last years of the decade. In fact, by the end of 1999, the ten-year performance of venture capital funds (17.2 percent) was almost indistinguishable from that of buyout ones (17.5 percent).[6] (Generalist funds performed significantly more poorly, with 9.5 percent rate of return over this period.)

Meanwhile, European-based funds also became more active. The increase in activity was manifested in three ways. First, groups that had been active for a number of years, such as Atlas Ventures, were able to raise significantly larger amounts of funds. Second, new entrants—in many cases modeled after American groups—became increasingly active. (Examples include Amadeus in the United Kingdom and Early Bird in Germany.) Finally, generalist funds increased their allocation to venture capital again: for instance, over the late 1990s, 3i moved from a 15 percent allocation to technology investments to a 40 percent share.

5. See "European Performance Surveyed—A Tentative First Step," *European Venture Capital Journal* (December 1996): pp. 3–6.

6. Venture Economics, *Investment Benchmark Reports: International Private Equity* (Newark, NJ: Venture Economics, 2000).

This pattern reversed itself again in the early 2000s. Many of the new venture groups—facing worthless portfolios and little chance of raising new funds—exited the business. Many other groups returned to solely emphasizing buyout activities. The historical disparity between venture and buyout returns reappeared in Europe, with venture funds returning 4.4 percent between mid-1998 and mid-2003, while buyout funds earned 10.8 percent.[7]

THE EUROPEAN PRIVATE EQUITY CYCLE

Fund-raising

The key sources for European private equity funds have traditionally been segmented by national boundaries. Private equity groups would raise funds from banks, insurance companies, and government bodies in their own country, with little involvement of other investors. The one exception was the United Kingdom, where fund-raising has had a strong international flavor—with a heavy involvement of U.S. institutional investors—since the earliest days of the industry.

These barriers are now breaking down, as Exhibit 13.5 reports. The changes are being driven by two factors. First, institutional investors—particularly in the United

EXHIBIT 13.5

GEOGRAPHIC SOURCES OF NEW PRIVATE EQUITY

	Same Country	Other European Country	Outside Europe
1985	92.0%	2.7%	5.3%
1986	91.9	3.8	4.3
1987	77.1	9.0	13.9
1988	79.8	11.1	9.1
1989	67.6	8.0	24.4
1990	71.0	14.0	15.0
1991	77.0	13.0	10.0
1992	83.5	7.7	8.8
1993	81.1	7.2	11.7
1994	73.1	7.0	19.9
1995	77.2	11.6	11.2
1996	71.8	11.4	16.8
1997	49.2	17.3	33.5
1998	52.1	16.8	31.1
1999	57.1	21.3	21.6
2000	52.4	20.7	26.9
2001	47.0	18.4	34.6
2002	50.0	21.1	28.9

Source: European Venture Capital Association, *EVCA Yearbook* (Zaventum, Belgium: EVCA, 2000); and earlier years.

---

7. Venture Economics, http://www.ventureeconomics.com, accessed November 3, 2003.

States—are becoming increasingly interested in European funds. Second, many international private equity firms are becoming much more active in Europe. American firms such as Chase Capital Partners, Kohlberg Kravis Roberts (KKR), and Texas Pacific Group (on the buyout side), Accel, Benchmark, and General Atlantic (on the venture side), and Carlyle (on both the venture and buyout fronts) have entered Europe in one way or another in recent years.

A consequence of these changes is the increasing presence of investment advisors, sometimes called gatekeepers. (These are firms that advise investors, primarily large institutions, about their private equity investments or directly manage their holdings.) In the United States, this is a very well developed market: firms as Abbott Capital, Adams Street, and Cambridge Associates have built strong franchises assisting pension funds and endowments with private equity investments. Gatekeepers and advisors in Europe have been few, reflecting both the immature nature of the private equity market as well as the lack of large institutional investors with appetite for private equity. Several of the large United States private equity advisors and gatekeepers are currently entering Europe, attracted by pension reforms in Europe as well as an increasing allocation to European private equity by European and American institutional investors. Local advisors are also gaining an increasing following.

One challenge to institutional investors in selecting investments is that there appears to be less strategic differentiation between European private equity firms than between those in the United States. In the United States, private equity players have increasingly focused on developing a niche or a specialty, while in Europe the niches are just emerging. For instance, Doughty Hanson, dubbed the KKR of Europe, has achieved considerable success by undertaking large transactions with a heavy reliance on financial engineering and little operating involvement.

Investing

Competition for buyout transactions is intense in Europe, especially in the United Kingdom. According to the Centre for Management Buyout Research at the University of Nottingham, private equity firms in recent years have involved in close to 60 percent of all mergers and acquisition activity in the United Kingdom, far above the 15 percent to 20 percent range seen in the United States. Most of the deals in the United Kingdom are initiated through auctions. Investment banks have made the United Kingdom auction process very efficient; there is little opportunity to buy firms for below their market value. On the Continent, the process is less efficient. For instance, in Germany and France, personal relationships with lawyers and accountants are important sources of deals for private equity investors. But increasingly, large Continental firms are sold to private equity groups through auctions as well.

The companies that are purchased by European private equity funds are primarily subsidiaries of conglomerates or family businesses. Unlike the United States, buyouts of public companies are rare. One reason for this is the stringent corporate control rules in some countries; for instance, in France, interest expense of debt can only be deducted if 95 percent or more of the equity is acquired, which is difficult to accomplish in the case of a public firm with widely scattered holdings.

In the early years of the European private equity industry, a management buyout (MBO) transaction was typical. The existing management team initiated a typical buyout. The managers would negotiate with the parent, hire an intermediary to represent them, and find a buyout firm that would provide the equity. Accounting firms were until recently the intermediary of choice to either auction or "shop around" a firm.

During the 1990s, the leading investment banks entered the auction market, and the role of the accountants has been reduced to due diligence work (they continue to play a role in the auctioning of smaller deals). On the Continent, lawyers and accounting firms appear to continue to manage more deals than investment banks.

While many American private equity groups seek to initiate and control transactions themselves, United Kingdom buyout firms have often been described as "process integrators." For example, buyout firms involve investment banks, accounting firms, and lawyers to support them in preparing the bid, assembling the capital structure, and undertaking the due diligence. A management consulting firm is then involved to improve firm operations after the acquisition. A strong tie to intermediaries may be an important competitive advantage in Europe: Doughty Hanson is reported to have derived a significant part of its deal flow through PriceWaterhouseCoopers in Germany.

As a result of this environment, buyout firms often find it difficult to identify proprietary deal flow—that is, transactions that are reviewed by only one private equity group. Until recently, this was not too troubling for the major private equity groups, as most investments were syndicated by a number of these groups. (The lead investor would collect a fee from the other participants and could be confident that the other investors would reciprocate in subsequent transactions.) As the size of private equity funds has increased, relationships have become less collegial, and syndication less frequent.[8]

These changes have had three consequences. First, private equity organizations have become much more aggressive in initiating transactions. There has been an increase in management buy-ins (MBI) and investor buyouts (IBOs), where an outside management team or a private equity firm initiates the deal, and the existing management team may or may not play a role. Second, the reliance on intermediaries for the identification and management of transactions appears to be declining. Alchemy, Industri Kapital, and CVC, among others, are reported to rely more on internal resources rather than outsourcing. Finally, larger buyouts have become more common. It is increasingly common to see pan-European deals, which are often financed at least in part with high-yield debt.

There have also been substantial differences between the way that venture capital investment is undertaken in the United States and Europe, though these are gradually diminishing. Many European venture capitalists have traditionally had financial or consulting backgrounds, rather than operating experience. Perhaps as a result, the relationships between venture capitalists and portfolio companies have tended to be much more distant, with a greater emphasis on an assessment of financial performance than on hands-on scrutiny.[9]

Another difference relates to the geographic distribution of investments. As in buyout investing, there has been a strong tendency to invest in the same country as the fund is located. The reluctance to co-invest reflects both the legacy of legal and regulatory barriers to such transnational investments (now greatly reduced) and the very distinct business cultures that characterize many European nations. As Exhibit 13.6 reports, while this pattern is gradually changing, localization of investment remains an important part of the landscape.

A third difference is the size of transactions. While the past few years have seen a dramatic increase in the size of a typical venture capital transaction in the United States,

8. Similar behavior is seen in many other economic settings. For an overview, see Jean Tirole, *The Theory of Industrial Organization* (Cambridge, MA: MIT Press, 1989), chapter 6.

9. See, for instance, the case studies presented in Gavin Reid, *Venture Capital Investment: An Agency Analysis of Practice* (London: Routledge, 1998).

EXHIBIT 13.6

GEOGRAPHIC DISTRIBUTION OF PRIVATE EQUITY INVESTMENT

	Same Country	Other European Country	Outside Europe
1987	89.7%	3.0%	7.3%
1988	92.3	4.3	3.4
1989	87.9	8.9	3.2
1990	86.6	10.8	2.6
1991	90.6	6.5	2.9
1992	89.0	7.9	3.1
1993	89.4	7.3	3.3
1994	86.5	11.3	2.2
1995	87.9	9.3	2.8
1996	83.7	12.5	3.8
1997	80.5	17.0	2.5
1998	76.8	16.8	6.4
1999	77.3	17.7	5.0
2000	72.7	20.1	7.2
2001	71.3	23.3	5.4
2002	75.7	21.5	2.8

Source: European Venture Capital Association, *EVCA Yearbook* (Zaventum, Belgium: EVCA, 2003); and earlier years.

European investors have not followed suit. For instance, even during the boom year of 1999, the typical seed or early stage transaction in Europe was only about one-tenth the size of the average venture capital financing in the United States.[10] The result, some observers claim, is that European start-ups find it challenging to compete in the many winner-take-all competitions that characterize many segments of high technology.

Exiting

A sale to a corporate acquirer—also known as a trade sale—is the most common form of exit, both in the United Kingdom and on the Continent. The United Kingdom has an advantage over the other European countries in terms of exit, since it has a well-developed capital market. Even when a private equity group sells a company to a corporate acquirer, having the option to take the firm public helps insure an attractive sale price.

The lack of a developed capital market on the Continent has been a particular challenge to smaller, venture-backed companies. Over the past two decades, there have been a variety of efforts to create liquid markets for venture-backed firms in Europe. In the early 1980s, many European nations had pushed to develop secondary markets.

10. This comparison is based on European Venture Capital Association, *EVCA Yearbook* (Zaventum, Belgium: European Venture Capital Association, 2000), and National Venture Capital Association, *National Venture Capital Association Yearbook* (Newark, NJ: Venture Economics, 2000). The U.S. tabulation excluded buyouts funded by venture capital organizations.

These were designed to be more hospitable to smaller firms than the primary exchanges in these countries, which often had rigorous listing requirements (e.g., high levels of capitalization or extended records of profitability were required). At the same time, they sought to retain many of the regulatory safeguards for investors that were found in the major exchanges. (In addition, a number of countries had lightly regulated third-tier markets.) The secondary markets allowed venture capitalists to successfully unwind their positions. Their success, in turn, generated new investments in venture capital.

After the October 1987 decline in world equity prices, IPO activity in Europe dried up, as it did in the United States.[11] But unlike the United States, which recovered with a hot IPO market in 1991, in Europe there was no recovery. In 1992–93, there were 432 IPOs on the NASDAQ; on European secondary markets (with 30 percent of the number of listed firms), there were only thirty-one. In some countries, the decline in IPO activity was even more extreme: only five companies listed in Germany's two secondary stock markets in 1992–93; none listed in Denmark's between 1989 and 1993. Consequently, European private equity investors found IPOs of firms in their portfolios to be much more difficult to arrange, and were more likely to exit firms through trade sales. Trading volume in European markets for small-capitalization firms had also lagged. The ratio of total transaction volume to end-of-year market capitalization was 21 percent in European secondary markets in 1992; for the NASDAQ, the corresponding ratio was 138 percent.

One response to these problems was the EASDAQ market. The European Venture Capital Association developed the concept of a new pan-European public market for growing companies with international operations after observing the difficulties in other exchanges. EASDAQ had been designed after the liquid and generally efficient NASDAQ market in the United States and began operations in 1996. EASDAQ hoped to become an effective financing route for those companies that could not afford or simply wanted to avoid their nation's primary markets.

EASDAQ, however, was a failure. Only several dozen firms had listed on the new exchange. In many of these cases the firms cross-listed on NASDAQ or another established exchange. In almost all of these cases, the bulk of the trading took place elsewhere, where transaction costs were considerably lower. In addition, EASDAQ soon attracted competition for a variety of sources. Many national exchanges reestablished or upgraded their second-tier markets. Ultimately, NASDAQ acquired the European exchange and then closed it.

The most successful of these challengers was EuroNM, a coalition of five new equity markets. In 1999, the number of technology firms listed on that exchange doubled, and their capitalization grew to 35 billion Euros. The most successful of these new markets was the Neuer Markt, the German small-capitalization exchange. One aspect of this exchange that many believe contributed to its success was its strict disclosure and listing standards, which equaled or exceeded those seen in the NASDAQ market. This contrasted sharply with the British small-capitalization Alternative Investment Market and many other European second-tier markets, which have had modest disclosure standards. Nonetheless, after experiencing dramatic price declines and diminishing liquidity, the Neuer Markt was shuttered in 2003.

11. This paragraph is drawn from Graham Bannock and Partners, *European Second-Tier Markets for NTBFs* (London: Graham Bannock and Partners, 1994).

ISSUES FACING EUROPEAN PRIVATE EQUITY INDUSTRY

Many challenges face the European private equity industry today. In this final section, two of these concerns will be highlighted. These are likely to continue to be important issues in the years to come.

First, as the market becomes more competitive—particularly in the United Kingdom—there will be a need for the majority of private equity players to focus on adding value to their holdings beyond financial engineering. Numerous European private equity firms in Europe today are grappling with the need to build their competence in helping portfolio firms with their operations. Developing such skills is unlikely to be easy for many groups, whose partners have a primarily financial orientation.

Second, many of the British and American private equity organizations are expanding into other European countries. This is driven by the maturity of the British and American markets, the seemingly attractive opportunities on the Continent, and the pressure to deploy the increasingly large equity funds that they are raising. But numerous challenges are associated with growing from a one-office small fund to a larger multinational one. Among the issues are how to provide incentives across countries and offices, how to govern each office's decision processes, and how to implement the expansion. For instance, how should the carried interest be split if the French deal team wants the German deal team to help a French portfolio firm enter Germany? If the German team is highly productive, but the French office does not do any deals for a year, who should get compensated and in what way? How can a team used to working in the United Kingdom break into the German buyout market, given both their lack of business relationships and the different business practices?

14

Brazos Partners:
The CoMark LBO

On a snowy day in late November 2001, Randall Fojtasek[1] and Patrick McGee, partners in Brazos Equity Fund, LP, could smell the barbecue that had been brought in for lunch at their Dallas headquarters. "Another lunch spent working on the CoMark buyout," Fojtasek remarked. "Do you think this should be an asset or a stock deal?"

McGee looked up from the papers he was reviewing. "More to the point, will we be able to get it financed? In this financing market, if the banks don't think the revenue model is sustainable, it won't matter if it's asset or stock. In the meantime, let's eat."

Brazos Equity Fund was a middle market leveraged buyout (LBO) group, founded in 1999 by two former Hicks Muse principals, Jeff Fronterhouse and Patrick McGee, along with Randall Fojtasek, the ex-CEO of one of Hicks Muse's portfolio companies. It had access to a total of $400 million in capital: $200 million raised from such organizations as Aetna, Mellon Ventures, First Union, Fleet Boston, Morgan Stanley Dean Witter, and the University of North Carolina, and $200 million in potential co-investments from its limited partners. The fund's strategy emphasized buyouts of companies valued between $25 million and $250 million, with demonstrable cash flow and good management located throughout the United States but with a particular emphasis on Texas and the Southwest, a region surprisingly underserved by LBO firms.

The CoMark deal was important for several reasons. For one, it fit exactly in Brazos' "sweet spot"—a reasonably priced company with solid cash flow, good management, and a well-defined niche in building modular structures. As an operation owned by two families, it matched another of Brazos' strengths. Fojtasek had run his family's business for years, taking it through several LBOs as he increased operating income from $12 million to $44 million and getting a unique understanding of both the operational and

---

1. Pronounced "FOE-ta-shay."

Senior Research Associate Ann K. Leamon prepared this case under the supervision of Professors Josh Lerner and Felda Hardymon. HBS cases are developed solely as the basis for class discussion. Cases are not intended to serve as endorsements, sources of primary data, or illustrations of effective or ineffective management.

the familial issues involved.[2] In addition, the first-time fund had yet to close a deal, and while this was not unusual in 2001, the partners were feeling some pressure.

"We can't sit on the sidelines," said McGee, returning to the conference room with a plate heaped with ribs and beans. "We've got to put this money to work, but we have to make good investments. CoMark looks perfect, but we've got to be sure about the deal and the model, and hope the lending market cooperates."

THE U.S. LBO INDUSTRY

For the U.S. buyout industry, the late 1990s looked very different from the go-go years of the 1980s that had inspired books like *Barbarians at the Gate* and films like *Other People's Money*. As venture capital generated triple-digit returns, the 35 percent returns from even such august LBO firms as Thomas H. Lee and Hicks, Muse, Tate & Furst looked dowdy indeed (see Exhibit 14.1a for comparative returns). In fact, buyouts even failed to offer a premium over more liquid public investments such as the S&P 500 (see Exhibit 14.1b).

LBO firms made money by buying established companies, fixing them or selling off various portions and eventually selling the enterprise itself. Usually these transactions were funded by significant amounts of debt—as high as 95 percent in the late 1980s.[3] As long as the company could carry the debt, selling the healthy parts or improving performance would generate sufficient cash to yield average returns of 26 percent. When the company was sold, the bank loan would be repaid and the excess went to the partners in the fund.

EXHIBIT 14.1a

COMPARATIVE INTERNAL RATES OF RETURN FOR VARIOUS PRIVATE EQUITY FUNDS, THROUGH SEPTEMBER 30, 2001

Fund Type	Number	Average	Cap. Wtd. Avg.	Pooled Avg.	Max.	Upper Quartile	Median	Lower Quartile	Min.
Early/Seed VC	450	21.0	11.8	21.5	729.6	25.2	8.5	–2.6	–90.9
Balanced VC	387	13.1	8.9	16.0	273.1	18.2	7.8	0.2	–91.4
Later Stage VC	183	13.5	2.6	17.0	212.6	19.8	6.8	–2.2	–72.7
All Venture Capital	1019	16.7	8.7	18.0	729.6	20.6	8.0	-0.9	–91.4
Small Buyouts	169	13.2	11.4	23.5	243.9	20.5	11.6	0.1	–44.7
Med. Buyouts	87	9.2	9.2	19.3	83.4	20.9	7.2	–3.7	–74.3
Large Buyouts	91	-3.0	–5.7	10.9	60.1	13.6	0.0	–12.4	–100.0
All Buyouts	416	7.6	–1.2	15.8	243.9	18.5	7.2	–3.4	–100.0
Buyouts & Other Private Equity	485	7.2	–0.8	14.9	243.9	17.9	7.2	–3.3	–100.0
All Private Equity	**1508**	**13.6**	**2.4**	**16.8**	**729.6**	**19.7**	**7.8**	**–1.9**	**–100.0**

Source: Adapted from Thomson Financial Venture Economics/NVCA, http://www.venturexpert.com, accessed March 12, 2002.

Note: Cap. Wtd. Avg.: Capital Weighted Average, Pooled Avg: Pooled Average, Max.: Maximum, Min.: Minimum

---

2. For more on Randall Fojtasek, see Sam Hayes and Josh Lerner, "The Fojtasek Companies and Heritage Partners: March 1995," Harvard Business School Case No. 297-046.
3. Amy Tsao, "The Second Coming of LBOs," *Business Week* (March 16, 2001).

EXHIBIT 14.1b

RETURNS TO VENTURE CAPITAL, S&P 500, AND BUYOUTS, 1984–2000

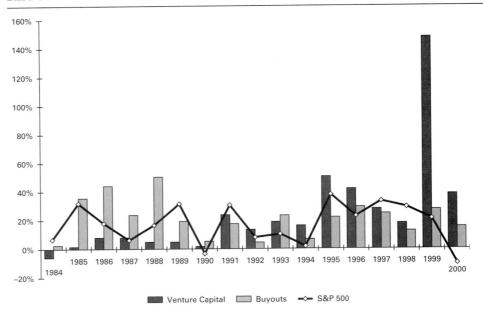

Sources: Adapted from Venture Economics, *Investment Benchmark Reports,* various years; and Datacomm database, Thomson Financial.

A number of trends had made the buyout business more challenging in the 1990s. The 1980s had seen a number of underproductive and underleveraged firms that were ripe for efficiency-increasing measures, such as assuming more debt, which had tax advantages due to the deductibility of interest, motivating management through the then-novel concept of incentive stock option plans, and splitting off or closing uncompetitive or distracting divisions of the firm. By the early 1990s, though, companies had learned the lessons of the '80s, and adopted higher rates of operating leverage and stock option plans to align the interests of management and stockholders. In addition, productivity in the United States grew at an annual rate of 3.1 percent between 1995 and 2000, giving buyout firms little scope for value-added increases. Such productivity growth also increased companies' earnings and thus their initial purchase price, which left less opportunity to realize gains on exit. The senior managing director at one buyout firm observed, "Corporate America is generally more efficient than in the 1980s. There are not as many [situations] where you can just cut expenses and capital expenditures and . . . realize a great return on investment. You have to be prepared to add value in some way."[4] In fact, by the end of the 1990s, only 24 percent of returns came from increased leverage for the acquired company and 43 percent from increased operating value, while in the 1980s, 40 percent had come from leverage and 34 percent from operation improvements.[5]

4. David Ying, quoted in Robert Pease, *Asset Alternatives Research Report: Strategies for Successful Buyout Investing* (Wellesley, MA: Asset Alternatives, 2001), p. 27.
5. Pease, *Asset Alternatives Research Report,* p. 40.

The very structure of the U.S. economy had made life more difficult for buyout funds. Companies with solid, leverageable assets, such as manufacturing firms, had become less common as the economy shifted toward services.

Even when a buyout firm found a good target, obtaining the necessary leverage to complete the deal was a challenge. Generally, two types of leverage were used: first on the balance sheet came senior debt, provided by financial institutions such as insurance companies and commercial banks, and beneath that, subordinated debt. This could consist of high-yield (junk) bonds, issued in the name of the acquired company, or privately placed debt, which was usually privately placed unsecured debt with an equity conversion feature. In the 1980s, the high-yield bond market provided leverage as high as eight or nine times equity. During the 1990s, although the volume of high-yield bonds issued soared to four times the level of 1989, leverage multiples were much more restrained.

The market for senior debt had not grown to the same extent. The savings and loan scandal in the early 1990s inspired the government to tighten regulations on the senior lending market and created a significant degree of risk-aversion among lenders, also constraining the multiples at which companies could be levered. Another constraint on the issuance of senior debt was the consolidation of the banking market. According to one study, only thirty-six unique commercial lenders existed in the senior debt market in 2000, down from more than 100 in 1993.[6]

This changed the typical financing structure for a buyout deal significantly and reduced the possible returns. The average equity contribution to a buyout increased from 18 percent in 1987 to 38 percent in 2000, while senior debt fell from 56 percent to 33 percent. With the increasing sophistication of target company sellers, the field was more challenging than ever.

The year 2001 had been no exception to that trend. Fund-raising had fallen to $35 billion, from 2000's $63.5 billion. (See Exhibit 14.2 for LBO market trends.) Funds complained that good companies were harder to find than ever, partly because leverage was difficult to obtain, but also because sellers were sitting on the sidelines waiting for valuations to recover. One noted fund, Thomas H. Lee Partners, did just one deal in twenty

EXHIBIT 14.2

LBO MARKET TRENDS

	1992	1993	1994	1995	1996	1997	1998	1999	2000	2001
Total Fund-raising ($B)	6.7	8.2	13.2	19.0	22.8	19.1	57.2	39.0	63.5	35.4
Transaction Volume ($B)	9.6	11.0	13.0	20.9	29.0	29.7	41.0	63.4	39.0	23.0
Number of Transactions	270	255	228	272	277	275	306	386	283	153
Purchase price as a multiple of EBITDA	NA	5.4×	6.5×	7.0×	7.1×	8.6×	8.3×	7.4×	6.7×	5.5×°
Average equity contribution excl. rollover equity[†]	22.0%	25.2%	26.2%	23.7%	22.9%	26.7%	28.1%	31.6%	33.9%	35.1%

Sources: Josh Lerner, "Acme Investment Trust: January 2001," Harvard Business School Case no. 202-055, p. 15; and various articles in *Buyouts,* January 7, 2002.

Notes:

° Estimated from Leslie Green, "Multiples Down But Should Strengthen," *Buyouts* (February 18, 2002).

† Adapted from Robert Polenberg et al., *Q1 2002 Leveraged Buyout Review* (Standard & Poor's, April 2002), p. 7.

6. Pease, *Asset Alternatives Research Report,* p. 39.

months. Nonetheless, some firms had closed significant funds in 2001. Kohlberg Kravis Roberts, famed as performing the biggest LBO on record when it paid $31 billion for RJR Nabisco in 1989, closed a $6 billion fund; Blackstone Capital Partners closed on $4 billion; and CSFB's DLJ Merchant Banking Partners III closed on $2.2 billion, which put its total fund at $5.4 billion. Six other funds had a first close above $1 billion.[7]

Increasingly, buyout funds were moving away from the megabuyouts that had made the industry its name. New strategies included investing in the less-efficient small-company segment, establishing a specialty investment focus, developing operating expertise to aid the companies after acquisition, and diversifying geographically (particularly into Europe, which was seen as having many of the buyout characteristics of the United States in the 1980s) and into broader areas of private equity, such as venture capital and mezzanine financing.[8]

Brazos Partners

Fojtasek, Fronterhouse, and McGee had founded Brazos (named for a Texas river) in late 1999 (see Exhibit 14.3 for bios). Fronterhouse and McGee had worked together at Hicks Muse, which Fronterhouse joined in 1991 and McGee in 1994, and they had met Fojtasek when Hicks Muse purchased his company. Fojtasek's experience was a perfect complement to Fronterhouse and McGee. In 1993, at age twenty-nine, he had become president and CEO of his family's firm, Fojtasek Companies (which later became Atrium Companies), a major building materials manufacturer. By 1995, he had increased its revenues by 54 percent to $83 million. He then negotiated its LBO by Heritage Partners, a Boston-based private equity firm. Remaining as president and CEO, he guided the firm as it made a number of acquisitions and went through two additional buyouts, by Hicks Muse in 1996 and finally by GE Investments in 1998, when the firm had approximately $400 million in revenues.

McGee explained their reasons for forming Brazos:

> While at Hicks Muse, our mandate was to pursue transactions where we could deploy anywhere from $100 million to $500 million of equity, with a preference for the $200 million to $300 million range. Consequently, we were not focusing on smaller opportunities, many of which had better overall valuation parameters and, in fact, were in our own backyard.

Fojtasek's was one of those, McGee noted:

> Atrium [Fojtasek's firm] was a perfect example. It was a great little company when Heritage Partners bought it in 1995. In 1996, when Hicks Muse made an equity investment of $32 million, it was really the last deal they did of that size. Selling Atrium in '98 to GE Investments for an annual return of over 50 percent further supported the thesis that smaller companies in traditional businesses can yield superior returns if you just focus on the fundamentals of the business and its industry.

Brazos targeted firms with enterprise values between $25 million and $250 million, solid management teams and well-defined niches.

Texas offered unique advantages as well. Said McGee:

> Texas is the eleventh largest stand-alone economy in the world and has the third largest universe of public and private midmarket companies in the

---

7. Leslie Green, "Fund-Raising Hardly Compares to Last Year," *Buyouts* (January 7, 2002), p. 1.

8. Pease, *Asset Alternatives Research Report*, p. 15.

EXHIBIT 14.3

BIOGRAPHIES OF BRAZOS PARTNERS

Randall S. Fojtasek

Fojtasek has extensive operating and acquisition experience. Mr. Fojtasek was formerly with Atrium, a manufacturer of building products. He joined Atrium in 1989 and from 1993 to 1999, Fojtasek served as president and chief executive officer. During his tenure as CEO, he was responsible for eleven transactions representing approximately $700 million in transaction value. Revenues increased from $99 million to $401 million, and EBITDA increased from $12 million to $44 million. Fojtasek also was responsible for negotiating and completing three recapitalizations with private equity sponsors: Heritage Partners, Hicks Muse, and GE Investments. The realized IRR for these investments is 80.6 percent.

Jeff S. Fronterhouse

Fronterhouse has extensive private equity and buyout investing experience. Fronterhouse was formerly a principal at Hicks, Muse, Tate & Furst. He joined Hicks Muse in 1991 and was instrumental in executing more than thirty transactions that together exceeded $3 billion in transaction value. His activities extended to the consumer, manufacturing, media, and services sectors in the United States and Latin America. Prior to joining Hicks Muse, Fronterhouse specialized in mergers and acquisitions for The First Boston Corporation from 1987 to 1989.

Patrick K. McGee

McGee has extensive private equity and buyout investing experience. McGee was formerly a principal at Hicks, Muse, Tate & Furst. He joined Hicks Muse in 1994 and was instrumental in executing sixteen transactions exceeding $4.5 billion in transaction value. His activities extended to the media, technology, financial, manufacturing, and services sectors in the United States, Latin America, and Europe. Prior to joining Hicks Muse, McGee was employed for seven years in the investment banking division of Merrill Lynch, most recently in the firm's media and telecommunications group in New York.

Source: Brazos Partners.

---

nation. But, fortunately for us, there are very few buyout groups here—only about a dozen. Most are in the Northeast and California. Of the twelve in Texas, a number are energy-specific. There's Haas Wheat and Hicks Muse, of course, but they play in a different part of the pool. So the competition for traditional midmarket buyouts in this region is very limited. While we're not restricting ourselves geographically, it just makes sense for us to concentrate on the area that we know and where we're known to find our deals.

Most deals, the partners felt, were driven by relationships and thus likely to be local. In an inefficient market with inefficient pricing, even local deals offered the potential for outsized returns. At the same time, buyout firms had to offer real value. Fojtasek said, "Capital is viewed as universally available. The question is what value you add. Before, if a buyout fund could create scale in an industry, it could probably be successful. Today, you need to be able to grow the company and its cash flow organically and efficiently, while leading the industry as you go."

McGee agreed and pointed out another way that Brazos could add value:

When we formed Brazos, we also needed another point of differentiation, another alternative to offer sellers, so we developed the Generation Transfer Transaction[SM] (GTT[SM]). The GTT[SM] is a tax-efficient structure that provides liquidity as well as continued operating control for the owner along with a flexible capital structure to accommodate future growth. As we execute the strategy, we can leverage Randall's unique background of experience in operations and acquisitions of a family business, which complements the extensive private equity experience that Jeff and I have.

The GTT[SM] was modeled on the Private IPO structure, which had been developed by Heritage Partners, the initial purchasers of Fojtasek's company. This structure solved the common situation in family-owned businesses when the founder had become more risk averse, given the concentration of the family's net worth in the business, while parts of the second generation had different goals, either wanting to expand the business and or to diversify their assets. In a GTT[SM], the owners would reinvest a sum that enabled them to maintain 50.1 percent of the common stock of the new company. With a GTT[SM], the managers achieved some liquidity of their holdings, while still retaining the powerful incentives of significant equity ownership. Since the transaction was considered an exchange of securities, the cash reinvestment would not be taxed until the new shares were liquidated. The investors could be the entire family, or, more often, just those family members who would remain actively involved in the business after the transaction.

Brazos would buy 49.9 percent of the common stock and a block of preferred shares with attached warrants for the purchase of common stock. Brazos would also arrange the senior debt financing for the balance of the purchase price. While the family controlled 50.1 percent of the voting rights, it would hold between 35 percent and 50.1 percent of the economic ownership of the firm, depending upon the future financial performance of the company.

The GTT[SM] ensured that the family would control the firm for a specified period of time, as long as it met certain performance targets. If performance fell short of the targets, Brazos would own more of the firm and thus receive a greater percentage of the eventual purchase price when it was resold. Brazos as a minority owner also had protections such as significant board representation, supermajority rights to block major changes, and, in the case of severe underperformance, the right to take control of the board.[9]

McGee noted, "The GTT[SM] is not the only type of transaction we do. We are also traditional majority investors in businesses. Often, in fact, the GTT[SM] transactions turn into outright sales, as the seller becomes comfortable with Brazos and the way we view a partnership with the family and the management team."

Brazos had also developed a strategic relationship with Maverick Capital. Maverick, a large hedge fund that traded large-cap public equities and had an average annual return in the high 20 percent range, would use its network and public-market relationships to help Brazos research industries, conduct diligence and, in some cases, source deals. The individual portfolio managers at Maverick had invested $25 million in the fund.

In addition to the $200 million that Brazos had raised, certain limited partners had expressed a desire to provide up to an additional $200 million for co-investments in Brazos' transactions. In any investment, the fund would get the first "strip" of equity. Brazos would then offer any additional amounts to the outside limited partners (LPs). This helped the fund stretch its resources, as McGee described:

> With a $200 million fund, we have a technical concentration limit of 20 percent, capping an equity investment in a single transaction at around $40 million. This co-investment relationship comes into play if we encounter a situation that requires, say, a $50 million equity commitment. In this case, the fund would invest $30 million or so and we would offer the remainder to those investors who have expressed a desire to participate on a co-investment basis.

9. Drawn from company information; and Hayes and Lerner, pp. 9–10.

In an environment where some transactions might require more equity, this relationship allowed a smaller fund to buy larger companies.

McGee did not feel that any one fund posed a particular competitive threat. "Our biggest competitor," he said, "is the seller opting not to do anything because the valuation or timing is not right."

When Brazos first began fundraising in December 1999, its most significant competition was another sector of the private equity world, venture capital, and its stratospheric returns. Even in this environment, the fund held a first close of $150 million in April 2000 and a second close of $50 million in April 2001. It was the result, Fojtasek said, of:

> . . . eighteen months of meetings. Fund-raising is one of the biggest barriers to entry in this business. It requires stamina and relationships. We were unique because we could mitigate much of the first-fund bias through our connection with Maverick, the combination of operating and financial experience, our position in the market, my family business experience, and Jeff and Patrick's private equity expertise as well as their successful record at Hicks Muse, but we still struggled. At the end of the day, a first-time fund is *very* hard to raise.

By the end of November 2001, Brazos had not closed any buyout transactions. One deal had been in the final negotiating stages when the company turned away from private equity to the mezzanine market for a different solution to their capital needs.

THE COMARK DEAL

Finding the Deal

The proposed LBO of CoMark Building Systems, a manufacturer of modular commercial buildings, came to Brazos in early August 2001 through an investment bank that was also an LP in the fund. The banker had already shown the deal to a different buyout group that had been unable to arrange the necessary financing. Fojtasek noted, "We can only assume that the other group had structured a quick deal with the seller and sent the investment bank's book around to a group of lenders without looking at it very carefully. Based on that, the lenders declined so the firm couldn't do the deal. As a result, the investment bank brought the opportunity to us and asked if we wanted to take a look at it."

Although McGee and Fojtasek were initially skeptical, they met with the management, reviewed the book, and became intrigued. "It was right in our own backyard, so the due diligence was easy," said Fojtasek. "Also, it was a traditional manufacturing business, an area in which we had significant investing and operating experience." The partners realized that they had to understand the business. "The bottom line," said McGee, "was that the investment bank's offering memorandum did a poor job of describing CoMark's product and the solution it provided for the customer. We had to develop our own perspective and investment thesis. Then, to raise outside financing, we had to rewrite the entire book to better articulate the company's value proposition and the sustainability of its cash flow."

Mike Bowers and Jim Clayton, CoMark's founders, were both in their late fifties, and their children were not interested in taking over the business. They did not have the capital resources to expand, and they wanted to diversify their personal estates, as the stock of CoMark made up almost their entire portfolio. Bowers, with an MBA from Wharton, was a talented operator and a classic entrepreneur. He was still excited by entrepreneurship and wanted to directly supervise daily operations, especially sales and marketing. He felt that the company's revenues could reach $100 million in the near future but he knew additional capital was necessary to get there. While he wanted to take some of his money off the table, he still wanted to continue his involvement in the business. Clayton, on the other hand, a very seasoned operations and manufacturing executive, was ready to slow down. The opportunity was unusual, according to Fojtasek:

> We were in an uncompetitive situation, which was rare. We had time to turn over every rock, to talk to customers, to learn it all, and then to decide. Usually, the time frame is very compressed, we have less certainty and that makes us more risk averse. Here we could address the uncertainties instead of just closing the door. Had the situation been different, we might not have moved forward.

McGee and Fojtasek spent all of August and September, including meetings via cell phone while on vacation, understanding CoMark's business. McGee recounted:

> The founders are tremendous entrepreneurs and over the past several years, have really built a great business. But, like many founding entrepreneurs, the knowledge to run the business was in their heads—not in a manual or with other members of the management team. It took us many hours and multiple sessions to download this information and decipher the nuances of the business. It was during this process that we realized these guys were critical to the success of the business and consequently, at the end of the day, our structure would need a significant rollover investment from Mike and Jim, as well as other terms to keep them focused on the operation.

Relations between the parities were congenial. McGee said, "Having Randall on the team was terrific. Not only did he understand the nuances of a closely held manufacturing business, but a division of Atrium was one of the company's suppliers."

Industry Background

Commercial modular buildings were a $3.1 billion industry in 2000. The industry was highly fragmented and regionalized; 268 manufacturers existed nationwide, with average sales of $11.6 million. The products could be used in a variety of applications, including dormitories, offices, classrooms, daycare facilities, medical and dental clinics, and even some churches, banks, and retail establishments (see Exhibit 14.4 for pictures).

Modular buildings offered several advantages, chief among which was the speed with which they could be constructed and put in place. Modular structures took between forty-five and ninety days from order to occupancy, as opposed to close to six months for preengineered steel structures and up to a year for site-built facilities. They also could be relocated (although in reality few were), providing temporary space where needed, and they could be leased. This last was extremely important, as payments could go through operating rather than capital budgets. Another distinct advantage for the modular buildings was cost, which ranged between $30 and $60 per square foot, half to three-quarters of the cost of other structures.

Manufacturers followed one of two business models. Almost 100 firms, including CoMark, were integrated manufacturers, with their own manufacturing facility and sales force. The other model, used by more than 200 firms, was an independent manufacturer that only built the structures and then sold them to a dealer, which would lease the buildings to the end-user.

EXHIBIT 14.4

TYPICAL MODULAR COMMERCIAL BUILDINGS

Administrative Offices, Taos, New Mexico

Fort Hood

High School, Dallas, Texas

Dormitories at Fort Eustis, Virginia

Source: Brazos Partners.

CoMark, and the rest of the industry, defined output in terms of "floors," conceptually the footprint of one building segment.[10] Buildings rarely exceeded two stories in height, but they could be composed of a number of connected floors placed horizontally. Modular buildings of three or more floors were more complicated to construct and to assemble on the site, but this segment was growing, while the smaller modular office (one or two floors) market was flat to shrinking. Modular buildings (three or more floors) were also more likely to either be sold outright or leased long-term, while the smaller units generally had short-term leases.

CoMark Building Systems, Inc.

CoMark, a specialty manufacturer of commercial modular buildings, was founded in 1989 by Jim Clayton and Mike Bowers. CoMark's major customers were government, education, and the private sector. As of September 2001, CoMark's revenues were $35

10. As an example, the trailers used as headquarters on construction sites were considered the typical size of one floor plate.

million, with an adjusted EBITDA (earnings before interest, taxes, depreciation, and amortization) of $10.6 million, on track for $37.3 million in annual revenue and $10.9 million in annual EBITDA. The backlog of unfilled orders had risen to $12.6 million in revenue, as opposed to $7.3 million for the same time the year before (see Exhibit 14.5 for financials).

CoMark sold to three major market segments: government agencies (the armed forces, postal service, Bureau of Indian Affairs, Immigration Service, and Forest Service); education; and private entities (churches, medical centers, and the like) (see Exhibit 14.6 for revenue by market segment and number of firms). Government sales generated 73 percent of 2001 revenues, with 22 percent from education and the balance from the private sector. Education sales, which often were put to competitive bid, typically yielded the lowest margins because of simpler design requirements. CoMark was also increasing its share of the faster-growing, and higher-margin, modular building (3+ floor) market.

CoMark assembled its buildings in two 65,000-square-foot buildings on its fourteen-acre site in DeSoto, Texas (just outside Dallas). Unlike other manufacturers, which ran units down the production line front to back, CoMark ran them side by side, an innovative and efficient approach. Completing a floor took five days, and all of them were built to uniform commercial building codes. When they came off the line, the building sections were placed on wheels and trucked to the site, where the building was assembled and inspected by a local engineer. (See Exhibit 14.7 for construction process.)

CoMark sold directly to the end-user, emphasizing a close connection between the sales person and the customer, with the same person involved in every step of the sales and production process. Direct sales conferred significant benefits, including pricing power when competing with dealers, the ability to tailor a solution to an end-user's needs, higher

---

EXHIBIT 14.5

HISTORICAL FINANCIALS FOR COMARK

($ in millions)	1998	1999	2000	Sept. '01 LTM	2001E
Revenue	$11.7	$15.6	$30.0	$35.0	$37.3
Gross Margin	$3.2	$5.1	$11.4	$14.9	$15.3
Adjusted EDBITDA	$1.7	$3.3	$8.1	$10.6	$10.9
EBIT	$1.4	$2.9	$7.7	$10.4	$10.7
Capital Expenditures	$0.1	$0.1	$0.1	$0.1	$0.1
Balance Sheet Items at End of Year					
Net Working Capital (excluding Cash)	$1.0	$0.5	$2.3		$2.9
Cash	$0.7	$2.0	$1.2		$0.0
Total Debt	$0.0	$0.0	$0.0		$25.0
Shareholders' Equity	$2.0	$2.7	$3.8		$15.0
Sales Personnel	2	4	7	13	13

Source: Brazos Partners.

Note: LTM = Last Twelve Months, E = Estimated.

EXHIBIT 14.6

REVENUE BY MARKET SEGMENT, 1998–2002P

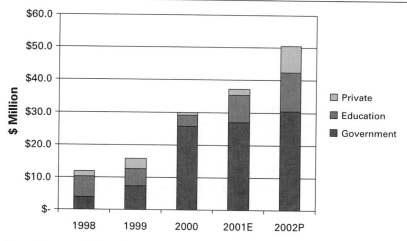

Source: Company information.

EXHIBIT 14.7

LATERAL CONSTRUCTION TECHNIQUE

Building section in progress

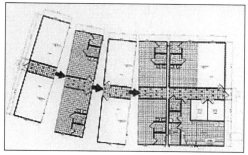

Source: Company information.

gross margins, and greater control over all aspects of the project. Almost 40 percent of its government end-users and 12 percent of its education end-users were repeat purchasers.

Between 1999 and 2000, CoMark's total revenue had doubled as sales to government agencies tripled. This was due to several changes. After years during which the sales force consisted of Bowers and his wife, two other salespeople were added in 1999, and the force grew to seven in 2000 with a further increase to thirteen in 2001. The company also instituted "CoMark University," a six-month sales training course for all salespeople. In addition to the usual techniques of finding opportunities and upselling, the course trained salespeople to assist in the design, specification, and costing of projects, helping them understand the entire production process.

CoMark could fill orders both by building the structures itself and by brokering the business out to smaller operators. Brokered buildings carried margins that were half those of self-manufactured jobs, but the process allowed CoMark to handle jobs without expanding its capacity. The company would try to broker out the lower-margin jobs, handling high-margin projects, usually for the U.S. government, in-house. To ensure that brokered buildings adhered to CoMark's quality standards, a company representative would be at the manufacturer's site throughout the construction process.

CoMark would also broker big government contracts if it lacked the capacity to meet the delivery date. A few of these small subcontractors required down payments at the start of the project with the balance on completion. CoMark would install the building and was paid fifteen days later. In most cases, though, the subcontractor did not require the down payment. From its start in brokering in 2000, CoMark had grown that aspect of its business to $12.5 million in revenue.

"Selling to the government is not an easy business," said Fojtasek:

> It took Bowers four or five years and a significant amount of trial and error to crack that code, but now it's a competitive advantage for the company. CoMark made its name in dormitories, so when a military base is calling up troops and needs to house them in ninety days, they can comfortably call CoMark for the solution. Think of it as spot-market housing. In addition, the company can arrange the sale as an operating lease, meaning that the expense can flow through the operating budget of the base and not be considered a one-time base capital expenditure.

Between 1998 and 2001, CoMark's production of floors had almost doubled, to 697 from 368. Sales per production employee had almost tripled, from $89,000 to $252,000 (see Exhibit 14.8). Part of this was due to the company's greater comfort level with the lateral production technique, but it was also due to incentives. CoMark had instituted a program that increased a production employee's pay for the week by $1 an hour if that person was at work on time every day that week. In addition, if certain production goals were met for the week, additional hourly bonuses would be paid. Consequently, the average hourly pay moved from $8 in 1998 to $11 in 2001 under this system, even as total direct labor cost as a percent of sales declined.

McGee said:

> Once we figured out how it worked, we were excited about the business. For instance, the old bank book counted the government as one customer. But really, the company was selling to a number of agencies (i.e., different customers) within the government, each with its own purchasing agents, budget, and space requirements. You had to look at each end-user as unique. This solved the perceived customer concentration issue.

EXHIBIT 14.8

FLOORS AND SALES PER PRODUCTION EMPLOYEE, 1998–2002P

	Floors	Sales per Production Employee ($000s)	# Production Employees
1998	368	$89	131
1999	465	125	125
2000	564	198	121
2001E	697	252	116
2002P	878	254	136

1998 to 2001E Compound Annual Growth Rate

Floors Produced	24%
Sales per Production Employee	41%

Source: Company information Note: P = Projected, E = Estimated.

Fojtasek agreed:

> It was a good company in a good industry and was selling to the government effectively. It had an extremely efficient production process that could be replicated in other markets or even internationally. If you can create critical mass in a fragmented industry like this one, you can create significant equity value. We don't produce returns for our investors by selling off parts of the business; we make returns from growing the business and operating it more efficiently.

Another attractive quality, McGee and Fojtasek felt, was CoMark's recession resistance. "It has diverse market segments and end-users," McGee explained, "and modular buildings are low-cost and flexible, which are good characteristics in a downturn. In addition, some of CoMark's major customer segments—government and education—are by nature recession-resistant."

By the end of September, Brazos and CoMark had come to financial terms and issued a letter of intent (LOI), which meant they agreed on the value. The parties next had to deal with contingencies and get the deal financed. During October, the accountants, legal team, and consultants performed due diligence on CoMark, including a nine-month audit and an environmental review.

THE NATURE OF THE TRANSACTION

The private equity group and the company had engaged in intensive conversations from August through October. Not only had many of Brazos' initial reservations about the company been resolved, but the investors had also identified a variety of ways in which they could add value to the firm.

These suggestions had several dimensions. First, Fojtasek saw that the company needed capital to grow and take advantage of expansion opportunities in the Southeast and Southwest. "Capital expenditures were less than $500,000 per year, which was more than adequate to maintain current sales levels. To grow, however, we would need to invest more in production capacity and further develop the sales force." More importantly, he and McGee knew that to take the company to the next level, they had to supplement the management team and begin a transition for Clayton and Bowers. "Mike [Bowers] was acting as the CEO, CFO, and VP of sales and marketing for the business. We had to find a way to make him more efficient and free him up to think strategically. The first order of business was to hire a CFO and eventually a CEO who could institutionalize the business for our exit."

But before the transaction could proceed, a number of important issues about its structure had to be resolved.

Price

The price was not a matter of debate. The founders wanted $40 million. Fojtasek said, "They were very pragmatic guys. They wanted certainty. Our concern was that they were projecting EBITDA of an unsustainable level. We needed a structure to address that." The lack of flexibility in regard to price reflected the fact that CoMark's owners had no urgent need to sell the firm. "Our biggest competition," said Fojtasek, "was the seller deciding not to do anything. We had a number of options as far as structuring the deal, but the question was whether the structure would meet the needs of Brazos as well as the selling shareholders."

While there was not much flexibility in regard to price, Brazos had suggested a minor modification to address the sustainability of EBITDA. The fund offered to purchase the company for $38 million in cash at the closing, with a deferred $2 million payment for each of the next two years if CoMark hit its 2002 and 2003 EBITDA projections (see Exhibit 14.9 for projections).

Determining comparable valuations was difficult. CoMark's business model was fairly unique because it was an integrated manufacturer that had its own sales force and produced the product in its own facility. No public companies were considered integrated manufacturers in the same sense. The closest comparables were Modtech Holdings, which specialized in the lower-margin education sector, and Williams Scotsman, a private firm that was more of a dealer than a manufacturer. Another public comparison, Miller Building Systems, had been purchased in 2000 by Coachman Industries, a maker of RVs and modular buildings (see Exhibit 14.10 for comparables).

Financing

The various parties generally agreed upon their respective contributions to the transaction. In particular, the two founders agreed to contribute capital to the transaction in two important ways, through the provision of seller financing and the reinvestment of capital into the company. This allowed a satisfactory deal to be structured despite the relatively modest financial contribution from the banks. (See Exhibit 14.11 for a summary of the capital structure after the closing of the proposed transaction.)

In structuring the proposed transaction, the Brazos partners asked the banks to assume a modest amount of debt. The team structured the loan as a $16 million senior term loan, at a rate expected to be the London InterBank Offering Rate (LIBOR) plus 425 basis points, or approximately 6.25 percent, and a $10 million working capital revolver. McGee said, "We were looking for 1.5× EBITDA, which really got the banks interested. Yet, given the tenuous bank market, we wanted to cast our net as wide as possible, so

EXHIBIT 14.9

BRAZOS' PROJECTED FINANCIALS FOR COMARK

($ in millions)	2002	2003	2004	2005	2006
Revenue	$50.5	$56.0	$60.9	$64.8	$ 69.1
Gross Margin	$18.9	$21.0	$22.8	$24.1	$25.7
Adjusted EBITDA	$14.7	$16.3	$17.7	$18.8	$19.9
EBIT	$14.4	$16.0	$17.3	$18.3	$19.4
Capital Expenditures	$0.5	$0.5	$0.5	$0.5	$0.5
Balance Sheet Items at End of Year					
Net Working Capital (excluding Cash)	$5.3	$5.8	$6.3	$6.8	$7.1
Cash	0.0	0.0	3.7	14.4	26.1
Bank Loan	10.6	4.0	0.0	0.0	0.0
Seller's Note	9.7	10.5	11.3	12.2	13.2
Total Debt	20.3	14.5	11.3	12.2	13.2
Shareholders' Equity	$22.5	$31.1	$40.8	$51.4	$62.8

Source: Company information.

Notes: These projections are based on numbers provided by the firm's management. It assumes the transaction is undertaken via a stock purchase. The debt figures assume that the senior debt is paid off by 2004. The debt associated with the seller's note continues to increase due to accrued interest. Yield on the 10-year Treasury bond was 4.65 percent in November 2001. Interest on the bank debt averaged 6.25 percent and the sellers' note carries a rate of 8 percent.

we contacted fifteen relationship banks and had positive replies from six. We have whittled it down to two leads and will choose between them."

Before they began approaching banks, the partners had realized that one prerequisite to financing the transaction would be the development of a new investment memorandum, or "bank book," for potential lenders. "Everyone was impressed with the depth of our understanding of the business," said Fojtasek. During the fall, McGee and Fojtasek worked with the CoMark founders to hone their presentation. In the first two weeks of November, Fojtasek recounted, "It was a steady stream of banks coming in. We'd give the three-hour presentation, take them to tour the facility, then they'd get back on the plane and go home."

By the end of November, Brazos was receiving term sheets. The banks would take the deal to their credit committees and, with approval, negotiate a commitment letter. After executing a purchase and sale agreement, the deal would close.

The other critical source of financing, aside from Brazos and the banks, was the managers of the firm themselves. Brazos asked the sellers to provide two sources of financing. First, the founders were asked to reinvest $4 million of the purchase price in the form of equity. This step—which meant that the founders retained 27 percent

EXHIBIT 14.10a

COMPARABLE COMPANIES AS OF THE END OF 2000

	Comark Building Systems Inc.	Miller Building Systems Inc.	Modtech Holdings, Inc.	Williams Scotsman Inc.°
City	Desoto	Leola	Perris	Baltimore
State	Texas	Pennsylvania	California	Maryland
Ownership	Private	Private	Public	Private
Sales ($Mil)	30.0	17.5	234.7	432.1
Sales % Growth Past Year	93.0	NA	40.4	NA
Assets ($Mil)	6.6	NA	187.7	NA
Description of Business	Wooden & steel framed modular buildings	Modular office components	Modtech Holdings, Inc. is a modular building manufacturer, designer, and wholesaler, providing modular classrooms in California and commercial and light industrial modular buildings in the Southwest and Mountain region.	Lease Rents & Wholesales Mobile Offices & Modular Buildings
# of Employees	150	100	1,540	1,200
Equity Market Value ($Mil)	NA	NA	96.8	NA
Outstanding Debt ($Mill)	00.0	NA	38.5	NA
Beta	NA	NA	0.93	NA

Sources: Adapted from http://www.globalabb.onesource.com, accessed February 8, 2002; and company information.

Notes: ° Williams Scotsman figures are for the parent, Williams Holdings, which is also privately held.

The yield on the ten-year Treasury bond was 4.65 percent in November 2001.

NA = Not available.

of the equity of the firm—would help ensure that the management was strongly motivated to make the investment succeed.[11]

Brazos also proposed an increasingly common option in midmarket buyouts, a subordinated seller note. To get the deal done, Clayton and Bowers provided a 10-year, 8 percent subordinated seller note, which served two purposes. It gave Brazos the leverage needed to meet its return threshold and it would keep the founders involved. Not only would they be motivated by their earn-outs and their substantial equity stakes, but they would also receive the seller note.

11. The 27 percent stake did pose one tax difficulty. Brazos had originally proposed to purchase 80 percent of the firm, but the management team resisted, as it wanted to retain a larger stake. Had management been willing to sell an 80 percent stake and to make such an election, under Section 338(h)(10) of the Internal Revenue Code, Brazos could have treated the sale as an asset sale for tax purposes, even if it had actually purchased the firm's equity. For a discussion, see Mark J. Silverman, "Section 338(h)(10)," *Practicing Law Institute—Tax Strategies for Corporate Acquisitions, Dispositions, Spin-Offs, Joint Ventures, Financings, Reorganizations and Restructurings, 2001* (New York: Practicing Law Institute, 2001), p. 41.

EXHIBIT 14.10b

MODTECH HOLDINGS DETAILS

Key Financials ($M)	Dec. 31, 2000 $M	% Chg	Dec. 31, 1999 $M	% Chg	Dec. 31, 1998 $M	% Chg
Total Assets	187.7	11.2%	168.7	103.6%	82.9	21.5%
Total Long-Term Debt	23.6	−26.3	32.0	N/A	0.0	N/A
Total Debt	38.5	−1.3	39.0	N/A	0.0	N/A
Working Capital	17.2	52.7	11.2	−78.5	52.1	43.1
Book Value	122.1	10.3	110.7	70.0	65.1	35.5
Total Revenue	234.7	40.4	167.2	31.0	127.6	−4.8
Net Income	10.4	24.2	8.4	−49.3	16.5	27.1
EBIT	24.6	29.5	19.0	−28.0	26.4	21.8
EBITDA	28.3	31.4	21.6	−22.1	27.7	20.1
Operating Cash Flow	2.1	−85.5	14.4	−56.2	32.8	1,507.1

Financial Ratios	Dec. 31, 2000		Dec. 31, 1999		Dec. 31, 1998	
Asset Turnover	1.3	−0.9%	1.3	−21.3%	1.7	−35.6%
Receivables Turnover	8.8	−15.6	10.5	41.8	7.4	−12.0
Inventory Turnover	24.1	−3.6	25.0	7.2	23.3	−11.9
Interest Coverage	4.9	−8.8	5.4	−95.8	129.0	496.4
Long-Term Debt/Total Equity	0.1	−33.7	0.2	N/A	0.0	N/A
Quick Ratio	0.8	6.1	0.8	−74.2	3.0	82.7
Current Ratio	1.4	−1.7	1.4	−63.7	3.9	40.8
Return on Equity (%)	8.9	−6.2	9.5	−67.3	29.2	−28.8
Return on Assets (%)	5.8	−12.4	6.7	−69.5	21.9	−14.0

Margins(%)	Dec. 31, 2000		Dec. 31, 1999		Dec. 31, 1998	
Gross Profit Margin	15.4	−9.6%	17.1	−27.0%	23.4	17.5%
Operating Margin	10.4	−5.6	11.1	−43.7	19.7	22.5
Pre-Tax Margin	4.4	−11.5	5.0	−61.3	13.0	33.5
Net Profit Margin	4.4	−11.5	5.0	−61.3	13.0	33.5

Market Data	Dec. 31, 2000		Dec. 31, 19999		Dec. 31, 1998	
Price ($)	7.3	20.8%	6.0	-60.7%	15.3	−21.8%
Shares Outstanding	13.3	1.6	13.1	33.1	9.9	0.5
Market Value ($mm)	96.8	22.8	78.8	−47.7	150.5	−21.4

Source: Adapted from http://www.globalabb.onesource.com, accessed February 8, 2002.

Brazos believed that this option was preferable to the most frequent alternative, a mezzanine note, for three reasons. First, the mezzanine players sought returns of about 20 percent, which would decrease Brazos' returns. Second, going to the mezzanine market added a layer of complexity to the deal. Finally, whether anyone would actually want to provide the loan, given the difficult financing environment, was open to question.

EXHIBIT 14.11

PRO FORMA TRANSACTION OVERVIEW

Items	$ Million
Total Enterprise Value	38.0
Fees and Expenses	2.0
Total Purchase Price°	**40.0**
Senior Bank Debt	16.0
Seller Note	9.0
Total Debt	**25.0**
Brazos Equity	11.0
Management Equity	4.0
Total Equity	**15.0**
Total Financing Raised	**40.0**
Total Cash to Sellers	**25.0**

Source: Brazos Partners.

Note: ° Does not include potential earn-out payments of $2 million at the end of Years 1 and 2.

Structure

Originally, the seller had proposed a stock sale: the private equity group would purchase 73 percent of the equity in the firm from the management team. Over time, however, Brazos became increasingly aware that structuring the transaction as an asset sale was preferable. Convincing the management team of the virtues of this option, however, was proving to be challenging.

Management's reluctance to consider an asset sale was understandable. If the managers sold 73 percent of their equity in a stock transaction, they would have to pay capital gains on that portion.[12] (See Exhibit 14.12 for a summary of the tax implications of the two purchase options.) This would translate into a tax obligation of $6.2 million, which was 20 percent (the capital gains rate) of the difference between the $32.5 million of proceeds (the $38 million purchase price less the $4 million reinvested in the firm and a $1.5 million value assigned to the real estate) and 73 percent of the cost basis in the firm, or $1.3 million.

If, on the other hand, the transaction were structured as an asset sale, the tax obligation would be substantially higher. The $4 million that the management team reinvested in the firm would no longer be treated as a tax-free exchange of securities. Rather, the management team would have to pay capital gains on the entire gain realized from

---

12. The cost basis of the company was modest, about $1.8 million; CoMark was structured as an S-corporation and was not a capital-intensive company. An S corporation was a firm that was structured like a corporation but taxed like a partnership. Consequentially, no taxes were paid at the corporate level; all obligations instead "flowed through" to the individual shareholders. Because all of the shareholders of an S corporation must be individuals, trusts, estates, or tax-exempt charitable organizations, at the time of the Brazos investment CoMark would be converted into a C corporation, the form of virtually all major corporations in the United States.

EXHIBIT 14.12

FINANCIAL AND TAX IMPLICATIONS OF THE TWO TRANSACTION ALTERNATIVES

Calculation of Capital Gains Tax Obligation

($ in millions)

	Stock Purchase Option[°]	Asset Purchase Option[°]
Total Pre-tax Proceeds[†][‡]	$34.0	$38.0
Less Real Estate[§]	1.5	1.5
= Total Company Proceeds	**32.5**	**36.5**
Less Cost Basis[‖] (73% for stock/100% for asset)	1.3	1.8
= Capital Gains	**31.2**	**34.7**
Capital Gains Taxes @ 20%[#]	6.2	6.9

New Basis of Management's Equity Holding

	Stock Sale Option	Asset Purchase Option
Old Basis	$1.8	$1.8
Less Basis Used in Capital Gains Tax Calculation	1.3	1.8
Plus Basis of New Investment[°°]	0.0	4.0
= New Basis in Stock	**0.5**	**4.0**

Source: Company information.

Notes:

[°] Assumes 73 percent of the stock purchased from seller in the stock purchase option and 100 percent of the assets purchased in the asset purchase option.

[†] Does not include potential earn-out payments of $2 million at end of Years 1 and 2.

[‡] Under the asset purchase option, the $4 million reinvestment would be made on an after tax basis.

[§] Prior to the sale, the real estate was owned by the firm's founders, not CoMark itself.

[‖] For the purposes of this analysis, assumes that the basis in the assets and the basis in the stock is the same at $1.8 million.

[#] In neither scenario would the entire tax burden be due immediately, as the capital gain on the seller note is deferred until it is retired. Excludes consideration for state taxes, if any.

[°°] Under the stock sale basis, the equity purchase would be treated as a tax-free exchange of securities.

the transaction. This would be 20 percent of the difference between the $36.5 million of proceeds (the $38 million purchase price less the $1.5 million of real estate) and the entire cost basis of the assets of the firm, or $1.8 million. In all, this approach would translate into an immediate tax obligation for the founding team of an additional $700,000.

But the asset purchase method also contained a substantial tax advantage for the firm. Both structures would generate $34.7 million in goodwill (the difference between the purchase price and the cost basis of the assets and the real estate). This goodwill could not be depreciated for tax purposes if the purchase was structured as a stock transaction. But if the deal was structured as an asset sale, the goodwill could be depreciated over fifteen years. At an assumed 40 percent tax rate, this reduced taxes (in nominal dollars) by over $900,000 annually over fifteen years. "With an EBITDA of $11 million, " said Fojtasek, "this becomes real money."

Brazos was convinced that this transaction would be beneficial not just to the private equity investors, but also to CoMark's management team. The founders were skeptical, however, that the benefits would outweigh the initial tax disadvantages. As McGee said, "We have to convince them that the incremental benefits of the asset deal were greater than the $700,000 tax hit."[13]

TAKING STOCK

Darkness had covered Dallas, showing slow-moving headlights as drivers picked their way home over unaccustomedly icy streets. "I'll say one thing—an asset deal will certainly help our cause with the banks," McGee observed.

Fojtasek shook his head. "I think they were more worried about the recurring revenues. We've covered that one."

"What I'm concerned about," said his partner, "is that if we push the asset deal, the sellers will just decide to do nothing. How can we make it attractive and easy for them?"

---

13. Structuring the transaction as an asset sale was also favorable to Brazos because of liability considerations. In a stock purchase, Brazos would also be assuming all the liabilities associated with CoMark. Brazos' exposure would be greatly reduced in an asset sale. (Of course, even if the private equity group assumed the legal liabilities in a stock purchase, the purchase agreement could require the sellers to make various warranties as part of the sale.)

15

Montagu Private Equity

I never really knew a thing about buyouts until I did this one.
—Chris Masterson, CEO of Montagu Private Equity

In mid-March 2003, Christopher Masterson, CEO of newly named Montagu Private Equity, was about to brief his colleagues on the status of a management buyout. In his twenty-year career in private equity, Masterson had done hundreds of buyouts. This one, though, was different—it was his own firm.

Until a year before, his group of twenty-five had handled all the European private equity (PE) investment for HSBC, with $800 billion in assets the world's second-largest financial services organization.[1] Masterson's group specialized in midmarket buyouts, deals that required between £50 million and £500 million in total funding, or £2.5 million or more in equity. Between 1994 and 2001, the HSBC Private Equity Partnership Scheme (the Scheme), which Masterson's group operated, had invested £870 million ($1.3 billion) in fifty-five companies, exited thirty-one of those positions, and realized a 30 percent composite internal rate of return (IRR) net of all fees. The Scheme was not a formal limited partnership fund arrangement but a series of discretionary co-investment agreements with ten institutional limited partners (LPs). In March 2002, though, HSBC had committed $750 million to U.S.-based AEA Investors.[2] This was a move that Montagu had not anticipated.

Masterson and his team faced a dilemma. In February 2002, the month before HSBC decided to back AEA, Masterson's group had held the first closing of a £1.2 billion ($1.8 billion) fund. HSBC had committed £600 million to the effort. The relationship with the bank had proved very helpful in raising the fund, as the PE group shared the parent's prestige, history, and aura of dependable conservatism. Montagu also had exclusive rights to any appropriate deals that came through the bank's extensive network. Although AEA

---

1. All $ figures are U.S. dollars.
2. Erik Portanger, "HSBC Is Latest to Turn Its Back on Turnarounds," *The Wall Street Journal* (March 19, 2003), p. C10.

Professors Felda Hardymon and Josh Lerner and Senior Research Associate Ann Leamon prepared this case. HBS cases are developed solely as the basis for class discussion. Cases are not intended to serve as endorsements, sources of primary data, or illustrations of effective or ineffective management.

had focused on the United States, it had done some European deals, and a $750 million commitment to its new fund might renew its interest in the Continent. Montagu might find itself bidding against AEA for an asset, setting up conflicts of interest.[3]

In the year since that announcement, Masterson had been exploring his group's options with HSBC. At today's meeting, he would present the draft agreement to his colleagues. He knew there was a lot at stake. The group was currently negotiating four deals, with one that would probably cost about £800 million, far outstripping Montagu's usual limit of £500 million. As part of HSBC, Masterson would have been less concerned about exceeding the ceiling by 60 percent. Now, though, he and his team had lost that safety net. In addition, retaining the team was very important. If one or two left, the remaining partners could still argue that the organization was fundamentally unchanged. But if a larger number pulled out, the new group might have difficulty maintaining the confidence of the LPs. Another issue was whether Montagu could continue to differentiate itself in the market without the connection to HSBC. "When you have the HSBC seal on your card," Masterson mused, "everyone knows you have the firepower to do a deal. There's built-in credibility in belonging to the bank. What will replace it?"

Masterson thought again about the terms of the buyout from HSBC. Was this the right option? Was the price right? What, really, were they buying in purchasing an asset management company? Finally, did the relationship with HSBC give them something intangible, something that they were not aware of, the loss of which would make the independent Montagu worth far less than it had been as part of the group?

EUROPEAN PRIVATE EQUITY[4]

In Europe, private equity had historically leaned more toward buyouts than venture investing. After a brief fling with venture capital in the late 1990s and early 2000s, that balance had reasserted itself by 2002. European PE funds overall had raised €27.5 billion ($26.1 billion) in 2002, of which 66 percent was earmarked for buyout activity. This reflected a sharp fall from the level of the year before, when €40 billion ($35.9 billion) was raised (see Exhibit 15.1 for European fund-raising and investment figures). In addition to the change in stage, the industries of interest had shifted from high tech to more customer-facing firms.[5]

As the NASDAQ slump that started in 2000 dragged on, PE activity throughout Europe had similarly slackened. By early 2003, though, a number of factors had coalesced to revive buyouts, even as venture investing remained fairly quiet. In addition to the ability of buyout firms to continue to raise money, an increasing number of well-priced opportunities appeared on the market. Throughout Europe, conglomerates, whether state-run or private, were slimming down. In some cases, European Union directives forced countries to break up national monopolies. In others, companies that had overexpanded, such as the United Kingdom's Invensys and the French Vivendi, sold off profitable divisions to preserve the core business.[6] Another impetus sparking buyout activity was a set of proposed finance regulations known as Basel II, which defined

3. Portanger, "HSBC Is Latest to Turn Its Back on Turnarounds."

4. For a more comprehensive view of European private equity, see Reynir Imdahl, Eric Zinterhofer, and Josh Lerner, "A Note on European Private Equity," HBS Case No. 299-017. Note that "Europe" refers to the Continent and the United Kingdom.

5. Data from "Official EVCA European activity figures," European Private Equity & Venture Capital Association press release, June 4, 2003, http://www.evca.com, accessed August 28, 2003.

6. Benjamin Beasley-Murray, "Public Woe, Private Gain," *Global Finance*, http://globalf.vwh.net (September 1, 2003), accessed September 1, 2003.

EXHIBIT 15.1

FUND-RAISING AND INVESTMENT, 1992–2002, FOR BUYOUT-RELATED ACTIVITY IN NORTHERN AND WESTERN EUROPE

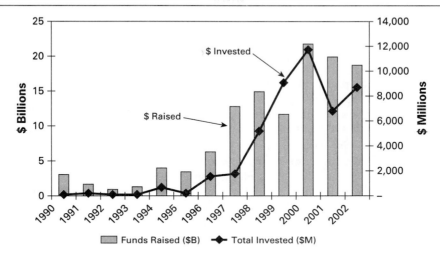

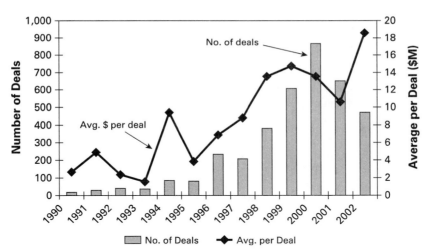

Source: Adapted from Venture Economics, http://www.ventureexpert.com/, accessed November 3, 2003.

capital adequacy rules for banks. Due to its size, this was not an issue for HSBC. Other banks, however, found that compliance with these regulations required them to reduce their riskier lending operations, usually to family-owned and small businesses, which were then willing to be purchased.[7] A few years before, competing firms in the same industry would have been interested in acquiring these operations, often at healthy valuations, but depressed stock prices and, sometimes, crushing debt loads made such

---

7. Charles Pretzlik, "Basel II Rules 'Could Cost €10 bn in Finance,'" *The Financial Times* (August 25, 2003), p. 19; and Lisa Bushrod, "Small but Well Formed," *European Venture Capital Journal* (May 1, 2003), p. 1.

trade sales, especially the mega-deals above €1 billion, less feasible. Thus, the buyout operators found a far more open field.[8]

By 2002, many sellers had also reset their expected prices to match the reduced market.[9] One example of this occurred in December 2001 when Diageo of the United Kingdom sold Burger King to Texas Pacific Group for $1.5 billion, 30 percent less than the price agreed at the start of negotiations.[10]

Europe, however, could not be viewed as a single buyout entity. Activity varied between countries. The United Kingdom had traditionally led both in terms of the number of deals and the value at which they were completed, but the Continent was catching up. In 2002, the United Kingdom still led in the number of deals, but its total had declined slightly from 2001, to 613, while continental Europe's total rose to 528.[11] Driven by several huge deals in excess of €1 billion—the sale of the French electric company LeGrand (€4.9 billion) to Kohlberg Kravis & Roberts and the public-to-private transformation of the paper-packaging manufacturer Jefferson Smurfit led by Madison Dearborn Partners (€3.2 billion)—the Continent registered total and average deal values higher than those of the United Kingdom.[12] The Continent's total enterprise value of €38.7 billion far outpaced the United Kingdom's €25 billion, as did the average amount per deal of €86.5 million compared with €45.4 million.[13]

Overall, corporate divestitures made up 40 percent of European buyout activity in 2002.[14] Family businesses, where changes were often triggered by succession issues, generated only 12 percent to 20 percent of the deals.[15]

Along with sellers, investors had also adjusted their expectations. One survey by Alt Assets, a PE information firm, found that investors expected annual returns close to 17 percent over the next five years, down substantially from the historic returns of 30 percent but termed "juicy" in comparison to public market levels.[16]

To achieve these returns, however, firms had to exit their positions, and exits were proving difficult. The public markets were practically closed to initial public offerings (IPOs), making trade sales (purchases by other companies) or secondary buyouts (sales of companies from one PE firm to another) more common. In both 2001 and 2002, a sad fourth exit option became more widely used, as 44 percent of all European exits had been through bankruptcy, as opposed to IPOs, trade sales, or secondary buyouts.[17] Into such uncertain times, Montagu planned to make its debut.

8. Lisa Bushrod, "European Buyouts Fight Back," *European Venture Capital Journal* (March 1, 2003).

9. Angela Sormani, "European Buyouts Fight Back," *Buyouts* (March 3, 2003), p. 1.

10. Beasley-Murray, "Public Woe, Private Gain."

11. "Annual Statistics," Centre for Management Buy-out Research, http://www.nottingham.ac.uk (March 30, 2003), accessed August 28, 2003.

12. Bushrod, "European Buyouts Fight Back"; Jefferson Smurfit Group, http://www.smurfit.ie; and Beasley-Murray, "Public Woe, Private Gain."

13. Sormani, "European Buyouts Fight Back."

14. "Mid market Buy-outs Boom," Centre for Management Buy-out Research, http://www.nottingham.ac.uk (March 30, 2003), accessed August 28, 2003.

15. Laetitia Mowat, "Deal Frenzy Expected." Press release from Deloitte & Touche, http://www.deloitte.com, accessed August 28, 2003.

16. Beasley-Murray, "Public Woe, Private Gain."

17. "Buy-out Exit Trends," Centre for Management Buy-out Research, http://www.nottingham.ac.uk/business/cmbor, accessed November 3, 2003.

MONTAGU PRIVATE EQUITY

The name of Montagu had withstood tumultuous times in the past. It had first been used in 1853 for a London bullion dealer[18] and merchant bank, Montagu & Samuel. The United Kingdom's Midland Bank purchased Montagu & Samuel (then called Samuel Montagu & Co.) in 1974 and merged it with the bank's own PE outfit, which had been founded in 1968. The new organization was renamed Midland Montagu Ventures. When HSBC bought Midland Bank in 1992, the PE unit became Montagu Private Equity and then, in 1995, HSBC Private Equity.[19] Once the current buyout was complete, the organization would resume the name of Montagu Private Equity.

Reflecting on the name changes in 2000, Chris Masterson had said, "We wanted that label [the HSBC name] and the concomitant credibility . . . the HSBC name effectively gives entrée to any boardroom on the globe and that, of course, is hugely valuable."[20]

Since 1968, Montagu under its various names had acquired thirty-five years of experience in the European PE market.[21] Its first external effort, the HSBC Private Equity Partnership Scheme, was launched in 1994, not as a concrete fund with a certain amount raised but rather as a series of discretionary co-investment agreements with ten institutional investors. Between 1994 and 2001, the Scheme had invested a total of £870 million in fifty-five opportunities. Montagu/HSBC had contributed £326 million of the total. The portfolio had seen thirty-one exits by the end of 2001 for a composite IRR of 30 percent net of all fees (see Exhibit 15.2a for comparative returns, Exhibit 15.2b for valuation, Exhibit 15.2c for investments, and Exhibit 15.2d for sectors).

Montagu focused on deals with enterprise values between £50 million and £500 million, in companies that had solid management teams and growth records and were located in western or northern Europe and the United Kingdom. The majority were management buyouts (MBOs) and buy-ins (MBIs), situations where a management team purchased either the entirety of an enterprise or a substantial share of it, while some were institutional buyouts (IBOs), in which a PE investor group bought a company with limited participation from the management team. In a few situations, Montagu would provide acquisition or expansion financing. One such deal involved Innovex, a provider of testing services to the pharmaceutical industry. In 1993, Montagu supplied the company with £5.3 million in acquisition financing; Innovex provided testing services to the pharmaceutical industry. After a Montagu-led recapitalization three years later, Innovex merged with Quintiles, a U.S.-based company, yielding Scheme investors a 544 percent IRR net of carry.

Another important Montagu deal was the MBO of a French steel company, Manoir. Montagu led Manoir's £65 million MBO in 1997. Less than two years later, it was sold to an institutional investor for an IRR of 80 percent.

The Caradon transaction illustrated Montagu's working methods. Montagu structured, arranged, and led the £496 million IBO of Caradon PLC's plumbing division in 2000. Caradon had conducted a competitive auction for the business, which included

18. Precious metals trader.

19. Portanger, "HSBC Is Latest to Turn Its Back on Turnarounds"; Lisa Bushrod, "HSBC PE Reverts to Montagu Name," *European Venture Capital Journal* (April 1, 2003); and *HSBC Group Fact Sheet* (August 2002).

20. Lisa Bushrod, "Happy to Be Captive," *European Venture Capital Journal* (October 1, 2000).

21. For simplicity, this case will refer to the organization known as Midland Montagu, Montagu, HSBC Private Equity, and Montagu Private Equity as "Montagu."

EXHIBIT 15.2a

COMPARATIVE RETURNS

Indicators	Returns
HSBC Scheme—IRR net of all fees	**30.0%**
FTSE All Share Total Return°	14.0
European Private Equity—Buyouts†	26.2
European Private Equity—Generalist Partnerships†	17.8
European Private Equity—All Private Equity†	25.8
UK Private Equity—Mid-MBO‡	22.1
UK Private Equity—Large-MBO‡	26.4
UK Private Equity—Generalist‡	32.3
UK Private Equity—Total‡	27.2

Source: "The HSBC Private Equity European LP: Information Memorandum, May 2001," private document, May 2001, p. 4.

Notes:

° Between August 18, 1994, and December 29, 2000.

† Source is European Venture Capital Association data, five years to December 31, 2000.

‡ Source is British Venture Capital Association data, five years to December 31, 1999.

EXHIBIT 15.2b

VALUE OF SCHEME PORTFOLIO

	(in £ million)
Total Invested (since inception, 1994)	**870**
—from HSBC	*326*
—from Scheme investors	*544*
Less cash returned as of Dec. 31, 2000	(600)
Net cash invested as of Dec. 31, 2000	270
Value of current portfolio (at market)	**569**

Sources: Adapted from "The HSBC Private Equity European LP: Information Memorandum, May 2001," private document, May 2001, p. 4; and casewriter.

market leaders in showers, bathroom fixtures, boilers, and radiators. Montagu felt that it won the deal due to its extensive research into the sector, combined with its industry contacts, expertise in financial structuring, and what the firm described as "our reputation for delivery." Slightly more than a year later, Montagu sold two divisions and refinanced the remaining organization (still named Caradon Plumbing), recouping its entire investment.

The relationship with HSBC was symbiotic. The bank referred deals to the PE group and, in many cases, the PE group made money with them. Yet Montagu was only a tiny portion of HSBC's activities. The net gain from the Scheme to HSBC was £150

EXHIBIT 15.2c

HSBC PRIVATE EQUITY SCHEME INVESTMENTS, 1994–2000

	Realized Investments (in £ millions)					Unrealized Investments (in £ millions)		
Company	Deal Size	Deal Type	Year	Multiple	Company	Deal Size	Deal Type	Year
Innovex	82	Acq. Finance	1996	4.9×	TMD Friction	438	IBO	2000
A M Paper	145	IBO	1997	2.0×	Cardon Plumbing	496	IBO	2000
Harwich	77	IBO	1997	1.9×	Strix Group	122	MBO	2000
ANC	50	MBO	1995	2.3×	Auto Windscreens	98	MBO	1998
TM Group	173	MBO	1995	2.1×	Xtrac	69	IBO	2000
CRP Holdings	70	MBO	1998	1.5×	ColArt	101	IBO	1999
Manoir Industries	66	MBO	1997	2.9×	Lyndale Foods Newco	66	IBO	1999
Sterling Organics	40	MBO	1995	1.9×	Cintex Group	38	IBO	1999
EJA Engineering	31	MBO	1996	2.4×	Crompton	84	IBO	2000
Lyndale Foods	16	MBI	1996	3.7×	Flagship Foods	174	IBO	1999
Schaffner	83	MBO	1996	1.9×	Ashbourne Pharmaceuticals	32	IBO	1999
London United	26	MBO	1994	2.9×	Erikem	172	MBI	1996
London General	32	MBO	1994	1.8×	HCT Shaping Systems	39	MBI	1998
BCH Vehicle Hire	140	MBO	1995	1.8×	TM Group	184	Development Capital	1998
Avocet Hardware	78	MBO	1997	1.5×	M&M Medical	34	IBO	1999
CentreWest	27	MBO	1994	1.8×	Manro	38	MBO	1996
Corner	20	MBO	1994	2.3×	Prize Food Group	61	MBI	1997
Metric Group	16	MBO	1997	1.6×	Abbey Hospitals	12	MBI	1997
IRO-Memminger	62	MBO	1995	2.1×	British Federal	11	MBO	1995
Transport Research	14	MBO	1996	1.6×	Coal Products	122	MBO	1995
Belfast Airport	35	MBO	1994	3.0×	Elifin SA	58	MBO	1997
Melville	14	MBO	1994	2.4×	Thermopol	11	MBO	1995
SPIG	5	MBO	1994	2.1×	Trader Media Group	276	MBO	1998
Xtra-Vision	12	Acquisition	1994	1.7×	Clinphone	10	MBO	1997
Eco Bat Technologies	184	MBI	1996	1.3×				
Warrior Group	104	MBI	1997	1.1×				
United Texon	134	MBI	1995	1.2×				
Croydon Land/Estates	58	Privatization	1994	1.1×				
Morris Mechanical	11	MBO	1994	1.3×				
Pioneer	9	MBO	1994	1.4×				
Elysia	6	IBO	1995	1.3×				
Total				**2.0×**				

Source: "The HSBC Private Equity European LP: Information Memorandum, May 2001," private document, May 2001, p. 7.

Note: MBO = management buyout, MBI = management buy-in, IBO = institutional buyout.

EXHIBIT 15.2d

HBSC SCHEME INVESTMENT SECTORS

Sector	% of Total
Engineering/Manufacturing	45%
Chemicals/Pharmaceuticals/Health	13
Auto/Transport	11
Food/Retail	10
Support Services/Financial	4
Electronics	4
Paper/Printing	6
Energy/Property	7

Source: HSBC.

million over eight years and paled in comparison to the bank's annual profit after taxes, which exceeded £4 billion in 2002.

Masterson explained:

> HBSC felt it had to be involved in private equity to be a global financial institution. And it understood that the best way to do PE investing is with a group of experienced PE specialists who were trusted both in the industry and throughout the organization. We managed PE investing not only on behalf of the HSBC group but also for the upper managers, who participated in the fund. Over time, we built up a track record both as good deal makers and as good guys. People throughout the bank didn't hesitate to hand on deals to us when they found them.

HSBC had avoided the situation that plagued other large banks at the end of the 1990s, in which the organizations had taken large amounts of equity in pre–initial public offering placements for private companies. While the banks had enjoyed soaring valuations in the rising market, they had suffered severely when the market turned. Due in part to problems with their PE portfolios, Citigroup's share price had fallen 31.9 percent and JP Morgan Chase's 78.4 percent between January and October of 2002, while HSBC's stock price had fallen 6.7 percent.[22]

HSBC Private Equity European LP

In May 2001, Montagu began raising funds for a true limited partnership fund, the HSBC Private Equity European LP, aimed at "unquoted equity investments including management buyouts, management buy-ins, development capital, corporate restructurings, corporate joint ventures, and public-to-private transactions" in the European private equity "middle market," where required financing ranged from £50 million to £500 million and equity amounts were £2.5 million or more.[23] Industries of interest included a variety of industrial and service companies but not technology or high growth.

---

22. Erik Portanger, "No Fads, Please," *The Wall Street Journal* (October 28, 2002), p. A1.

23. "The HSBC Private Equity European LP: Information Memorandum, May 2001," private document, May 2001, p. 2.

Most of the investors from the previous Scheme participated, HSBC contributed half of the target £1.2 billion, and Montagu recruited seven new investors.

Montagu was based in London with offices in Manchester, Paris, Dusseldorf, and Stockholm. Its target markets included the United Kingdom, France, Germany, and the Nordic region. In addition to Montagu's buyout activities in Europe, HSBC had private equity efforts in Asia, India, South America, North America, and Canada, along with a venture operation, HSBC Ventures, that made equity investments of up to £2 million in small companies.[24] Montagu's Masterson sat on the Asia fund's advisory committee, but Montagu itself invested only in northern and western Europe.

The fund's prospectus emphasized Montagu's close links with HSBC, stating, "The Partnership will be HSBC's primary investment vehicle for all investment opportunities that meet the Partnership criteria and are introduced to Montagu and/or the HSBC Group."[25] Montagu's board included three HSBC executives and six Montagu executives, and all decisions would be unanimous (see Exhibit 15.3 for selected biographies). HSBC generated leads for Montagu throughout its operations. Masterson pointed to

EXHIBIT 15.3

SELECTED BIOGRAPHIES OF MONTAGU EXECUTIVES

Chris Masterson, Chief Executive

Masterson joined Montagu in 1991 and has more than eighteen years' experience of investing in unquoted companies. He read psychology at University College, London, and has an MBA from Manchester Business School. He worked for 3i for four years and subsequently was a founding shareholder of Castleforth Fund Managers.

Phil Goodwin, Head of UK Investment

Goodwin joined Montagu from 3i, where he had twelve years of private equity experience and was 3i's local director in Manchester. He gained a first in PPE at Oxford and started his career with a spell at Unilever.

Nigel Hammond, Head of European Investment

Hammond joined Montagu in 1995 after spending five years with 3i. A graduate in civil engineering, he started his career with Pannell Kerr Forster, where he qualified as a chartered accountant.

David Farley, Finance Director

Farley joined Montagu from JP Morgan, where he had fourteen years' investment banking experience and was responsible for its leveraged buyout business. A graduate in mathematics at Bath, he first worked as an engineer with British Aerospace before qualifying as a chartered accountant with KPMG. In addition to his role as finance director, Farley is head of portfolio management.

Vince O'Brien, Director

O'Brien joined Montagu in 1993 from Coopers & Lybrand and has worked in the private equity industry for more than fifteen years. An Oxford graduate in modern history and a qualified chartered accountant, he sits on Montagu's investment committee and is responsible for fund-raising and all aspects of investor relations. He became a member of the Council of the British Venture Capital Association in 2001.

Source: Montagu Private Equity.

24. "The HSBC Private Equity European LP: Information Memorandum, May 2001," private document, May 2001, pp. 16–24, passim.

25. *Ibid*, p. 10.

the synergies in one deal, the buyout of a division of the German firm BBA, saying, "An individual within the bank had lunch with the head of BBA's frictional materials division and called us to say that the business was potentially for sale. That kind of lead is like gold dust."[26] Between 1994 and 2000, the majority of the Scheme's life, HSBC had referred 20 percent of Montagu's deals (see Exhibit 15.4 for all sources of deals). In just the two years of 1999 and 2000, 45 percent of Montagu's investments had been referred by HSBC's network.

Masterson and his colleagues also had a close relationship with HSBC's senior executives. Masterson explained:

> As long as we didn't abuse it, we could access their network to get into almost any boardroom in Europe. For instance, we knew that one firm was shopping a division. Everyone knew it. But no one could get in to see the CEO. He simply did not want to deal with PE firms; he thought we were a bunch of bandits. The CEO of HSBC at the time got us in to see him. Now that does a lot for us. It gives us gold-standard credibility. I told the vendor that everyone knew he was selling the business, we even knew which investment bank he'd retained. All the PE firms had the same LPs, the same sources of debt, and we were looking for the same return. The only difference was who was serious about doing the deal. I walked him through all the models we'd run on public data to derive an offer price. Finally, I said, "Look, give us formal access to the management team, give us your operating numbers going forward. As long as they stand up, the number we quote here is the number we'll pay. Skip the hassle of conducting an auction and the potential embarrassment if it fails. Go with us and we'll do a fair, painless deal." We ended up doing the deal without ever issuing a formal book to the world and spilling the company's operating secrets to its competitors. And the reason we could do that was that I was part of a global organization and could be relied upon.

EXHIBIT 15.4

DEAL SOURCES

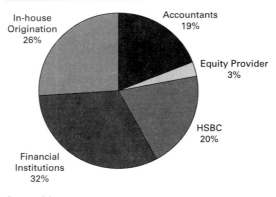

In-house Origination 26%
Accountants 19%
Equity Provider 3%
HSBC 20%
Financial Institutions 32%

Source: Montagu.

26. Bushrod, "Happy to Be Captive."

The link with HSBC also conveyed the impression that a deal would indeed get done. "You don't have to prove you have money when you're part of HSBC," Masterson continued. "With billions in assets and £4 billion in profits after taxes, whether you have money is not even a question."

Furthermore, Montagu's relationship with HSBC allowed it to offer the convenience of "one-stop shopping" to its targets, as one organization could provide everything from asset management to corporate finance, underwriting services, and working capital lines.

At the same time, Montagu knew that its relationship with HSBC could raise concerns with prospective limited partners. The fund's prospectus specifically stated:

> In no circumstance will the Partnership invest in or take over a problem loan or investment from anywhere within the HSBC group (including Montagu) unless the circumstances are disclosed to the Investors' Committee and considered by Montagu to represent a valuable investment opportunity. . . . No investee company will be required to use HSBC Group derived facilities if facilities are available elsewhere on better terms. . . . Montagu maintains appropriate Chinese Walls in relation to the flow of information with all other entities within the HSBC Group.[27]

Masterson, too, was well aware of potential conflicts, commenting, "The HSBC group always competes at arm's length with other candidates to provide additional services to our portfolio companies."[28]

LPs often raised other concerns about institutional funds. One was the potential for talented corporate PE practitioners to leave the less-lucrative compensation scheme of their parent to set up an independent shop where they could keep all the fees and carry. Masterson rejoined, "Look at our pedigrees. We're corporate guys. Yes, we like a bit more freedom and a bit more compensation, but we have them here."

Another worry involved the possibility that the in-house PE group might be blocked from doing a deal that an important bank customer wanted, or that might compete with such a customer. Yet because HSBC's management could invest in Montagu, it had an incentive to hand good deal leads to the in-house group. It was then up to Montagu to win the deal.

Montagu's Investment Philosophy

Montagu felt that it had built its track record in the middle market by finding and backing the right CEO. Masterson said, "At one of our corporate retreats, Phil Goodwin, head of UK investment, said, 'We've done good deals and we've done bad deals. Why not do more of the good deals?' Like so many really profound things, it appears totally obvious. But when we looked at our deals through that lens, we could see that the most important indicator of success was that we knew and trusted the CEO."

Montagu specialized in corporate spinouts and family businesses, and made only occasional forays into secondary buyouts, deals where a PE firm purchased a company from another PE firm. Yet it was not doctrinaire. David Farley, finance director (CFO) and director of the portfolio, said, "We say we don't do secondaries. Well, we did a secondary recently. But the difference was our confidence in the management team. By rolling their entire gain into our deal, and taking no cash out, they were buyers and not partial sellers. The alignment of interest made all the difference."

27. "The HSBC Private Equity European LP: Information Memorandum, May 2001," p. 12.
28. Bushrod, "Happy to Be Captive."

Masterson explained:

> We work with incumbent CEOs who've been in the business for a long time, made a career, and assembled a team. Sometimes they've only been at that particular firm for a few years, but they're long-term industry players. We may add a new CFO, but often the CEO and the CFO are a team and have built the firm. In a spinout, they're usually a little bitter and feel ignored; their division may have been drained of cash to sustain less profitable units that are nearer and dearer to the heart of the headquarters group. Or they feel misunderstood. They have a fire about them, a drive to succeed. It's like describing a rhino to a blind person; when you're in the room with one, you know it.

The relationship with the CEO was central. Masterson continued, "If we aren't supremely confident in the CEO, we won't buy the business. We win deals because we have the confidence to pay the most, and we'll pay the price if we have confidence in the people that we're backing. You can't just buy a business and arbitrage it anymore."

Montagu chose its deals carefully. "Our skill set is demonstrated by our track record," Masterson said.

> Choosing high-quality incumbent management is actually a lowest risk strategy. Rather than parachuting someone in, we look for incumbent management that is number one or two in the niche. We need that because we exit through trade sales, and who better to build a company and take it to the next level than the driven guy with a business plan who's been constrained from implementing it by a distant and uninvolved head office? But the plan isn't enough—execution is the key. We have developed this into a laser focus. We had been looking at 100 different things; now we just look at whether the business is leverageable—at no more than 65 percent debt-to-equity—and that it's a mature northern European business in our price range. And then the rocket fuel is an equity-owning CEO.

As an example, Masterson pointed to one of the Scheme's deals, the 1998 buyout of Auto Windscreens from the Heywood Williams Group for £98 million. This company was the second-largest automotive glass replacement and repair company in the United Kingdom and Republic of Ireland. He explained:

> This was a perfect business for us. These guys knew the parking lot of the UK, Scotland, and Wales. We have lots of different makes of car and thus a lot of different windscreens [windshields]. They were savvy managers and knew how to manage the inventory. In addition, windscreens are a grudge purchase—no one wakes up in the morning and wants to buy one for fun. So it's not particularly cyclical. The CEO of the parent was not interested in automotive stuff, and here these guys wanted to KILL their number one competitor in the industry. They were ready to go out on their own.

In 2001, RAC Group PLC bought the business from Montagu, for a 27 percent IRR and 1.8× multiple.

Montagu also did a number of family-business transactions and had developed an unusual approach, as Masterson described:

> We go into these in a very open way. Most of the time, you've got the founder who wants to get some liquidity, some of the family wants to be involved, some doesn't. You don't know what they want. So we ask them, right up front. And it's disarming for them. They know everything about

their industry, but then they come down here to London and into our building that looks like the Sistine Chapel, and they're nervous. They've never done a buyout before. And for us to ask them what they want—and it's very rarely just money—is extremely powerful. It puts the ball in their court. We position our offer that, as long as it's reasonable, we'll give them what we want. And we usually can do it.

In February 2002, Montagu held its new fund's first close. The next month, Masterson learned that HSBC would be providing 70 percent of AEA's newest fund. "The elephant," he said, "had rolled over and wounded the mouse severely. The question was what we were going to do about it."

The Negotiations

Masterson and his team decided first that he would handle the negotiations with HSBC. As CFO Farley said, "The rest of us were obviously keenly interested in what was going on, but we had a business to run. We were finishing the fund-raising for the new fund, we were doing deals, and someone had to mind the store. You have to have someone lead the deal; it would have been a disaster if we were all in there."

The Montagu executives decided they had three options: they could lobby HSBC to reconsider its strategy; they could walk in as one and quit; or they could try to work something out. Masterson said, "We were very aware that HSBC had contributed 50 percent of our funds. It wasn't like some other groups, which ended up out on their own and didn't even know if they could raise money. We had a fund, we had a portfolio. We had a good relationship with HSBC and wanted to continue it. We just weren't sure how we'd arrange all this."

Masterson's counterpart in the negotiations was Ian Cotterill (pronounced Cott-RELL), the chief operating officer in the Investment Banking and Markets division of HSBC. His responsibilities included accounting, operations, and oversight of the PE interests. Cotterill was on Montagu's board and knew all the details of the organization. Initially, he was not convinced that AEA and Montagu could not coexist. Cotterill said:

> AEA had a long history of introducing private investors to the private equity asset class. As we wanted to introduce the bank to this constituency, the relationship was an important strategy for us. We proposed that Montagu would get first refusal on any deals that HSBC generated; only then would they go to AEA. We also considered constructing legal agreements that disclosed the entire situation and having each investor sign, therefore holding HSBC blameless—but every time you approach the LPs, it becomes an opportunity for a negotiation. What with the press coverage on conflicts of interest between merchant and investment banking, and the general trend in the industry toward independent management companies, we finally agreed that an MBO made the most sense [see Exhibit 15.5].

Even within HSBC, a PE group had been an uncertain fit. Cotterill went on: "Montagu had always operated more independently than the other groups. This was a small group of individuals that had a different compensation scheme and they were highly entrepreneurial. They were very well-liked and well-respected within the organization; it's simply that if anyone was a candidate for an MBO, it was they."

Simply disbanding the group and returning the funds raised was one option. In such a strategy, the Montagu partners would lose their cohesiveness and the 30 percent of their carry that was not vested. If they violated their noncompete agreements, they

---

EXHIBIT 15.5a

SAMPLE OF PRIVATE EQUITY SPIN-OUTS FROM FINANCIAL INSTITUTIONS

Date	Parent	Spin-out	Assets Under Management	Purchase Price (for Equity)
March '03	HSBC	Montagu Private Equity	£1.5 billion	Undisclosed°
Feb. '03	Deutsche Bank	DB Capital Partners	Later stage portion of €3.5 billion portfolio	€ 1.5 billion†
Feb. '03	Zurich Financial	Gresham		Undisclosed‡
June '01	HSBC/Credit Commercial de France§	Charterhouse Securities	£1.0 billion‖	£127 million§
April '01	CSFB	Phoenix Equity Partners (fka DLJ European Private Equity Ltd)#	£500.0 million‖	Undisclosed
Dec. '00	Merrill Lynch	Mercury Private Equity (now HG Capital)	£700 million‖	Undisclosed, but included fee sharing on old portfolio
May '00	NatWest Bank	Bridgepoint Capital (fka NatWest Equity Partners)	£522.0 million‖	Undisclosed
1999	Electra Investment Trust	Electra Partners°°	£1.1 billion	£14.5 million cash, total max. payment after shared fees of £64.0 million††

Source: Casewriter.

Notes:

° Caroline Merrell, "Management Team Buys CDC from HSBC," *The Times* (June 21, 2001), p. 26.

† William Hutchings, "Consortium Puts €1.5B behind DB Capital MBO," *eFinancial News* (February 21, 2003).

‡ Zurich invested £265 million in Gresham's new fund after the spin-off. Source: Nicola Hobday, "Zurich to Spin off PE unit," *Daily Deal* (September 10, 2002).

§ HSBC acquired Charterhouse as part of its takeover of Credit Commercial de France SA and subsequently sold it to the management team. Source: Hobday, "Zurich to Spin Off PE Unit."

‖ Dataquest database, accessed August 8, 2003.

DLJ had bought Phoenix, with £133 million under management, in April 1997 for approximately £50 million.

°° Nicholas Lockley, "Baring Private Equity Seeks Buy-out from ING," *The Financial News* (April 16, 2001).

†† Christa Fanelli, "Electra Partners Nabs EURO1B for Fund," *Buyouts* (May 7, 2001); and *Electra Investment Trust Annual Report* (September 30, 2003).

---

would forfeit the vested portion of the carry. HSBC would be left with a portfolio that had to be managed.

"I wanted us to maintain a strong connection with HSBC," said Masterson. "That's why I suggested they only sell us 80.1 percent of the firm. We needed each other. We needed to figure out a way to make it happen."

What Is a Management Company Worth?

The challenge, both Cotterill and Masterson agreed, was setting a value on the management company. Cotterill said, "We started off by breaking down where we make money on private equity. We determined that it came through management fees and

EXHIBIT 15.5b

SAMPLE OF PURCHASES OF EQUITY SHARE IN PRIVATE EQUITY FIRMS

Date	Purchaser	Firm Purchased	Assets Under Management in Purchased Firm	Purchase Price	Implied Valuation
Feb. '01	CalPERS	Carlyle	$170 billion	$175 million (for 5%)	$3.5 billion[*]
July '99	Putnam Investments	Thomas H. Lee Co.	$6 billion	$250 million (for 20%)	$1.2 billion[†]
Feb. '99	Credit Suisse Group	Warburg Pincus Asset Management	$22 billion	$650 million (for 100%)	$650 million[‡]
July '98	American International Group	Blackstone Group	$6.1 billion	$150 million (for 7%) + $1.2 billion in future funds	$2.2 billion[§]

Source: Casewriter.

Notes:

[*] Kara Scannell, "Deals and Deal Makers," *The Wall Street Journal* (February 2, 2001), p. C15.

[†] Erica Copulsky, "Thomas Lee Co. Gets $250 million—Twice—in Its Deal with Putnam," *Investment Dealers' Digest* (July 18, 1999), p. 1.

[‡] Bill Hall and Jane Martinson, "Credit Suisse Arm Buys US Fund Group," *The Financial Times* (February 16, 1999), p. 19.

[§] John Authers, "AIG to Invest $1.2bn in Blackstone," *The Financial Times* (July 31, 1998), p. 29.

investment gains, and arrangement fees net of the usual operating costs and the costs of failed deal efforts [broken deal costs]."

Masterson and Cotterill came to a shared conclusion: "Excluding investment gains, the management company itself wasn't worth much."

Montagu had net assets of £300,000 from desks, computers, and other items. Its balance sheet was complex, as Montagu had managed third-party funds since 1994 and also invested directly for HSBC. The previous investments had been funded from HSBC's balance sheet, matched with co-investments from third parties through the Scheme. Montagu had historically charged a management fee of 2 percent of invested (as opposed to committed) capital, as it had not raised money for a fund due to the Scheme's deal-by-deal approach. HSBC, as Montagu's parent, had not paid fees. Carry was 15 percent with no hurdle. The existing portfolio from the Scheme was worth £569 million. It would need ongoing management and attention, and it also ensured the continuing interest of the 10 LPs from the Scheme.

The new £1.2 billion fund had a different structure. Outside LPs paid 2 percent fees on the £600 million they committed. The LPs could, however, terminate these commitments if they lost confidence in Montagu's ability to perform without HSBC. Carry was 15 percent with no hurdle, paid on a deal-by-deal basis, and the Montagu executives could invest an additional 6 percent in the sweet equity (common stock) of a deal.

When Montagu was part of HSBC, the fee stream from the third-party money covered the base salaries for Montagu staff. Outflows such as broken deal costs and bonuses came from HSBC's balance sheet. Arrangement fees on successful deals, which were paid by the target company, were inflows that had gone entirely to HSBC.[29]

29. Industry norms for these fees ranged from 0.5 percent to 1.5 percent of the enterprise value.

"The portfolio was really difficult to value," said Masterson. He added:

> The management company's value lies in the portfolio, and that's a function of our track record. The track record came from the team. Therefore, we had to keep the team together. But the value of the management company also depends on the deal we strike with HSBC and whether that allows us to continue as a viable entity.

Cotterill and Masterson modeled the management company's income streams over time, making assumptions about the changes in the cost structure when the group was independent. In particular, the group's overhead would fall, as it would no longer share the cost of HSBC's overhead. Projecting these sums seven years out,

---

EXHIBIT 15.6

MONTAGU STRUCTURE, PRE- AND POST-MBO

Prior to MBO

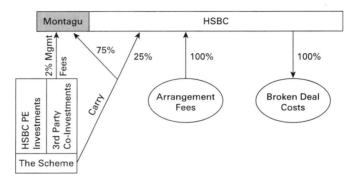

Post-MBO

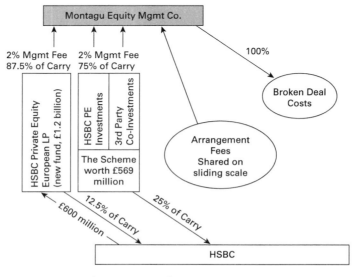

Source: Casewriter from Montagu information.

as a function of the funds the firm could raise and the structure used to raise them, gave a predicted income for the management company. Profits were more difficult to determine, as they depended on the costs incurred. Investment gain would depend on the level of investments.

Negotiations

Masterson started from the point of view that the team was effectively being laid off and therefore should be paid severance. He suggested that HSBC should pay Montagu £3 million. Cotterill promised to come up with his own suggested valuation.

To avoid conflicts of interest, Cotterill and Masterson decided that HSBC should pay the same fees as other LPs on both the old portfolio and the new fund going forward. Montagu would manage the old portfolio under contract. HSBC's share of the old portfolio was converted into a limited partnership vehicle that stood alongside the LP interests from the Scheme. The existing management contract with third-party investors in the Scheme (2 percent fee and 15 percent carry without a hurdle calculated on a deal-by-deal basis) was extended to include HSBC (see Exhibit 15.6).

HSBC's relationship with the new fund also changed. In the prospectus, the bank would have invested in each deal pro rata and in parallel with the fund, up to a total investment on its part of £600 million.[30] Now the arrangement was much more like a classic fund, in which HSBC had committed £600 million that would be called down as needed. HSBC paid fees on its committed capital and on the old portfolio, which was valued at the lesser of cost or net asset value.

The details of the final agreement also needed to be worked out. The two tried to create a structure that would not redistribute wealth between the two groups. Cotterill said, "Masterson's business depended significantly on HSBC's continuing commitment. We were really arguing about shades of gray."

Shades of Gray

Some of the most vexing shades of gray included carry, office space, and the split of arrangement fees. Management fees would cover the expenses of establishing the organization and the ongoing operating costs. Montagu's expenses before bonuses ranged between £14 million and £16 million. Any profits from the management fees would be split 80/20 between Montagu and HSBC, reflecting the ownership percentages.

Carry

Carried interest on the new fund was 15 percent of the capital gain. Prior to the MBO, 75 percent had gone to the individual who was the lead investor in the transaction and 25 percent to HSBC. Masterson suggested that 100 percent of the carry on post-MBO investments should go to Montagu. Cotterill pointed out that this violated the spirit of the "no major change" rule. After three weeks of discussions, the two agreed that 12.5 percent of the carry on new investments would go to HSBC.

Arrangement Fees

It was assumed that broken deal fees (cash outflows for expenses incurred in deals that Montagu lost) would equal arrangement fees (cash inflows from the fees paid by companies that Montagu purchased). Previously, HSBC had received 100 percent of the arrangement fees but also been liable for 100 percent of broken deal fees. With its 20

---

30. "The HSBC Private Equity European LP: Information Memorandum, May 2001," p. 11.

percent ownership, HSBC would now have received 20 percent of the fees. Instead, Masterson and Cotterill agreed to split them on a sliding scale. The first £5 million of cumulative fees stayed on Montagu's balance sheet as a rainy day fund should the firm suffer a string of broken deals. When total cumulative arrangement fees for the life of the fund were between £5 million and £7.5 million, HSBC would receive 20 percent. It would receive 30 percent of amounts above £7.5 million.

Fringe Benefits

Determining the details of benefits, Cotterill said, "was not real science—it was more haggling over bits of money." Chief among these was Montagu's office space. At the time of the negotiations, Montagu occupied elegant quarters on the first floor of Vintner's Place, an ornate building directly on the Thames Riverfront path. Cotterill said, "It wasn't in either of our interests for them to leave the building." HSBC agreed to pay Montagu's rent for three years on lower floor space, both easing Montagu's transition and helping its own property management group.

Masterson worked with HSBC to replicate the benefits that Montagu's staff had enjoyed, either in cash or in substance. He said, "Normally, you don't think about insurance or cars. But in an MBO, you need to."

Governance

HSBC kept two seats on Montagu's investment committee, held by Cotterill and Christopher Gill, HSBC's head of credit and risk. Deals no longer required unanimous approval, however. Cotterill explained, "The other LPs would have been worried if we had veto power. And we still have a card to play. If we really don't like a deal and Montagu ignores our concerns, we may have second thoughts about investing in its next fund."

Wrapping It Up

Once the deal was completed, Masterson had to find the money to make the purchase. He said, "It was one of those odd moments when you realized things have changed. In the past, we would have gone to HSBC and they would have given us the money. When we made investments, the bank would front the money that we wired, giving us time to make the capital calls from our LPs.[31] But this wasn't the case anymore."

Masterson approached the Bank of Scotland, which was an investor in the fund and had a long history of working with PE firms, both as an experienced investor and as provider of customized funding solutions to funds and management companies. David Lyall, director of funds management, said:

> Our investment rationale centered on the strong historic investment track record of the Montagu team operating within the HSBC Group. The strength and depth of the team was backed by strong infrastructure and governance support that came with being part of a large banking group. The HSBC relationship also provided 50 percent of Montagu's investment capital and strong deal flow to the private equity business. This was important, as we had not only invested for returns on equity but also to be in a better position to

---

31. In PE funds, LPs committed capital but did not write a check for the full amount when the fund closed. As the general partners (GPs) completed deals, they would "call down" capital from the LPs. Often, a time lag ensued between the deal's close and the GP's receipt of the LP's money. The time lag could occur not only because the LP had to make arrangements to wire funds, but also through the bookkeeping necessary for the GP to compute the amount each LP owed to the fund.

supply acquisition financing debt to the firm's investments. All in all we viewed this as a great investment proposition.

The news of the spin-out initially raised concerns that our original investment rationale would be diluted. As investors, we were comforted by the fact that they still had a good relationship with HSBC and the whole team was sticking together. Our pedigree as a knowledgeable lender in such situations presented further opportunities to strengthen our relationship with Montagu.

The Bank of Scotland established a £60 million bridging line for Montagu, in addition to supplying the purchase price and a working capital facility. Lyall explained:

Because we've been seriously involved in this business for quite a while and have over £1 billion with 100 funds and sixty-five managers, we really understand how private equity firms work. We have developed a suite of lending products that help general partners manage the business end of their operations. For example, we know how much time it takes LPs to meet their capital calls—the bridging facility therefore helps Montagu to fund an investment with certainty prior to calling on their LPs. By investing with them, we were betting on their deal-doing ability. By banking them, we were betting on their strength as a business.

Montagu then had to receive approval from all the investors, investees, syndicate partners, and banks with which it had done deals currently in its portfolio. In all, 400 entities had to approve the transaction. Said Masterson, "No one balked." Elaborated Matt Lyons, an investment manager, "We called our portfolio companies and were prepared for the worst. Without exception, they didn't miss a beat. The reaction was, 'If nothing's changed, why are you bothering us?'"

The group also received blanket indemnity from HSBC on the portfolio investments (protection against unexpected asbestos claims, for instance) and on claims against the management company.[32] Finally, Montagu needed approval from the Financial Services Authority, the United Kingdom's stock market regulator. Because it was a pre-existing entity, the process only took five months as opposed to the year or more that approving a new entity would have required.

THE ANNOUNCEMENT

Masterson looked again at the agreement that he knew by heart. It had been the hardest year of his life. He knew it had been equally difficult for his staff, especially since they were all deal makers themselves and had forced themselves to keep their hands off this most personal of all transactions. He hoped they would be pleased with it. He planned to give them three months to question, protest, or complain; thereafter he wanted their uncompromising loyalty and commitment. If things worked out as he hoped, that commitment would be well rewarded.

32. An indemnity was required because the portfolio assets were held in Montagu's balance sheet when Montagu was a subsidiary of HSBC. In the previous thirty years, in excess of £8 billion had passed through that balance sheet. This transaction moved those assets to a limited liability partnership controlled by HSBC. The indemnity assured Montagu and its LPs that they would not be made liable for unexpected claims (asbestos, for instance) based on the past portfolio.

16

Metapath Software: September 1997

On September 29, 1997, John Hansen called together his board to debate an interesting choice that his company had to make. Hansen—the CEO of Metapath Software Corp., a Seattle-based provider of software and services to wireless carriers—had two offers to describe to his board.

The first was an offer to be acquired by CellTech Communications, a wireless products company that had only recently gone public. Under the terms of the deal, Metapath's shareholders would at closing receive common stock in CellTech valued at $115 million. CellTech at that time had a market capitalization of approximately $260 million. The second offer was from a consortium of investors led by Robertson & Stephens Omega Fund (RSC) and Technology Crossover Ventures (TCV) to buy $11.75 million of stock at a $76 million premoney valuation. While the price seemed generous for a private company of Metapath's stage, the terms of the preferred stock the funds were proposing to buy were much stricter than the terms of the stock owned by existing shareholders.

For Metapath's shareholders, CellTech's offer had much to commend it: near-term liquidity at an attractive price, without the dilution of further financings and an IPO. And the terms on the financing proposed by RSC could make a sale of the company extremely dilutive to the founders in the event of a sale further down the road. However, Hansen and his board believed Metapath had great potential as an independent public company—probably greater than CellTech—and wondered whether the two businesses made sense together.

HISTORY OF METAPATH

Metapath (formerly called Securicor Wireless Networks, or SWN) was formed in January 1995 out of a joint venture with Securicor Telesciences Inc. (STI) and a consulting company, Networks Northwest, operated by Hansen himself. The mission of SWN was to build a software product that allowed wireless carriers—that is, operators of wireless

Senior Lecturer Felda Hardymon and Bill Wasik prepared this case as the basis for class discussion rather than to illustrate either effective or ineffective handling of an administrative situation.

telephone networks—to see exactly what calls were on their networks at any point in time. The company began with a single contract, with US West New Vector Group, the cellular arm of the large telephone company US West. Despite sluggish sales early on, SWN rebuffed an offer by Securicor Telesciences to purchase the company in February 1996, opting to go it alone. In addition to taking new capital from their existing investor, Bessemer Venture Partners, they brought in two new firms, Norwest Capital and U.S. Venture Partners, and bought out STI's position.

The company had continued to make good progress in developing its business. Soon after the Norwest/USVP financing, the company closed a mammoth $19 million order with Sprint and also beefed up its product offering. By the time of the CellTech offer in September 1997, Metapath's revenue had grown to $6.4 million in the preceding quarter, representing three large customers.

Hansen felt that Metapath was emerging as the premier company in its market space and would have an excellent chance of going public within the next two years. Recent public offerings for vendors to wireless service operators had gone well, and the market was paying three to five times revenue for such companies.

In his discussions with analysts at major investment banks that underwrite technology IPOs, Hansen had come away with two requirements for Metapath to be salable as a public company. One was that Metapath needed to attract more customers. As it stood, Metapath's revenue was all concentrated in four accounts, and the analysts feared the dependence on these few key customer relationships would make Metapath seem too risky an investment. The other requirement was that Metapath smooth out its quarter-to-quarter revenues, which had been choppy. Hansen's plan assumed that both of these problems would be worked out in a year.

With that in mind Hansen and his board embarked on raising enough money to see them through to cash break-even and, ultimately, an initial public offering.

RSC'S OFFER

Hansen and his CFO, Paul Bialek, contacted several late-stage and mezzanine funds to solicit their interest in a Metapath financing. Over time, two funds emerged as candidates to lead the round—Robertson Stephens Omega Fund (RSC) and Technology Crossover Ventures (TCV). In the subsequent discussions, RSC emerged as being quicker to provide specific term sheets and so most of the negotiations took place with the partners at RSC. Subsequent to a term sheet being settled the company invited TCV to join with RSC and the existing insiders to form a $11.75 million round. Originally the company wanted to limit the round to $10.75 million but the appetite around the table was such that to include everyone it was agreed to expand the round by $1 million.

The term sheet is Exhibit 16.1.

Unlike investors in public stocks, venture capital investors usually purchase preferred stock in the private companies they fund. The chief attribute of such stock is its liquidation preference—in the event of a sale or liquidation of the company, the holder of the preferred stock has a right to receive consideration equal to the face value of the stock (that is, equal to the cost basis of the stock) in preference to all other shareholders. Venture capitalists insist on such stock for a simple reason: since the management of a private start-up company typically owns "founder's stock" with little or no paid principal, nearly any sale of the company—even one at a price below that paid by their venture investors—will provide the management with an attractive return on their investment.

Accordingly, venture capitalists typically insist on convertible preferred stock, where in the event of a liquidation the shareholder has the option of either converting to common stock at a predetermined ratio or invoking the liquidation preference

EXHIBIT 16.1

TERM SHEET PRESENTED TO JOHN HANSEN BY ROBERTSON, STEPHENS ON SEPTEMBER 22, 1997

Issuer	Metapath Software Corporation (the "Company")
Amount	$10,750,000
Security	Series E Convertible Preferred Stock ("Series E Preferred").
Price per Share	$6.00 (the "Original Purchase Price"). The Original Purchase price represents a fully diluted share count (12,497,928) for an approximate pre-money equity valuation of $75 million.
Investors	New investors led by Omega Ventures II, Crossover II and other funds managed by Robertson, Stephens & Company (together "Omega") will invest $5.0 million. Existing investors (Bessemer, Norwest, and USVP) will invest $4.5 million. Partners of Wessels, Arnold & Henderson will invest $250,000. Integral Capital partners will invest $1.0 million. If Integral does not invest both Omega and existing investors will each invest another $500,000.
Board Representation	The size of the Board of Directors will be increased to six to accommodate an experience industry executive who is acceptable to the Company and holders of Series E Preferred.
Board Observation Rights	A representative from Omega shall have the right to attend all meetings of the Board of Directors in a nonvoting advisory capacity and shall be entitled to receive all information given to board members, consult with and advise management of the Company on significant business issues and shall have the right to examine Company records. Such rights will terminate upon the closing of the Company's IPO.
Dividend only in	Holders of Series E Preferred receive an accruing 8 percent dividend to be paid the event that either Series A, B, C, or D dividends are paid.
Liquidation	Upon any liquidation of the Company, the holders of Series E Preferred shall be paid out of the assets of the Company an amount equal to the purchase price plus any accrued but unpaid dividends. The remaining proceeds will be used to pay the holders of all other Preferred shareholders an amount equal to their purchase price plus any accrued but unpaid dividends. After all obligations to preferred shareholders are met, the remaining assets of the Company shall be distributed on a pro rata basis to all common and Series E preferred shareholders on an as-converted basis.
Redemption Rights	Same as Series D. However, the Company will not have the option to redeem the Series E Preferred.
Registration Rights	The holders of Series E Preferred will be entitled to one demand registration and will have full piggy-back rights on all public offerings.
Other Terms	Similar to Series D Preferred except where changes are necessary to accommodate specific circumstances of Series E Preferred.
Closing	The closing will be subject to usual closing conditions including satisfactory completion of Omega's due diligence. Anticipated closing is October 6, 1997.
Exclusivity	From the date of the acceptance of this term sheet, until thirty days thereafter, the Company shall not solicit, nor engage to solicit, offers related to the financing of the Company from other parties and shall not "shop" the term sheet.
Expenses	Company will reimburse Omega its reasonable legal and due diligence expenses. The current maximum estimate is $15,000.

and receiving the entire principal up front. This protects venture investors in the event of a "cheap sale" by management: if you're going to get rich, the argument goes, at least give me my money back first.

All in all, Metapath had raised $9.6 million to date in four rounds of financing, summarized in the table in Exhibit 16.2. The first two "rounds" occurred simultaneously, at the founding of the company in January 1995, when STI and Bessemer supplied the initial funds for the venture. In addition to common stock, the two entities were each awarded redeemable preferred stock that was unable to convert into common. In fact, the stock looked a lot like debt: it paid a dividend, and the principal—essentially all of the funds STI and Bessemer contributed, the common having been purchased at a nominal amount—had to be repaid starting in five years, after which it had to be returned in three annual payments. STI insisted on such a structure (often called a "straight redeemable, cheap common" structure) because it was uncomfortable with investing nonredeemable equity—even equity with a liquidation preference—in a start-up company. The third and fourth rounds, which together constituted $8 million of the $9.6 million invested in the company, were both standard convertible preferred stock instruments.

What worried Bialek and Hansen was that Robertson Stephen's proposed instrument was a participating convertible preferred stock (PCPT). Like a convertible preferred stock, a PCPT has a conversion rate at which the holder can convert from the preferred into common equity. This conversion rate sets the "price" of the offering. Moreover, in the event of a qualified public offering, the stock automatically converts into common stock. And like a standard convertible preferred stock, a PCPT carries a liquidation preference.

But a PCPT differs from a convertible preferred in that in the event of a sale, even though the holder has received the face value in consideration, he still has a right to "participate" in further consideration as if he had converted into common stock. Therefore, unlike a convertible preferred, where the holder has to choose between taking his consideration based on his liquidation preference or taking his consideration based on his percentage of ownership after conversion to common equity, the holder of a PCPT does not have to choose. He gets both his liquidation preference and his equity participation.

To see an example of this, let's assume that two firms (A and B) each buy 10 percent of a company (WidgetCo) for $1 million, but A is issued convertible preferred stock and B is issued participating preferred stock. Some time later, WidgetCo is sold to Consolidated Widget for $20 million in cash. At the time of the sale, A has the option of either converting to common stock or invoking its liquidation preference, that is, demanding the return of its $1 million and forgoing its "participation" in the cash distribution to the common shareholders. In this case, clearly A will convert to common stock; after conversion, A's position is worth 10 percent of $20 million, or $2 million a healthy step-up from its initial investment.

But B does not have to make any such choice. Under the terms of its stock, B receives its $1 million as a liquidation preference, and then B also participates in the cash distribution, that is, receives its share of common stock as well. So B receives $1 million, plus 10 percent of $19 million (the remaining cash proffered for the company), for a total of $2.9 million. (A's stake, one will note, is in fact only $1.9 million—10 percent of the value has been paid out in B's liquidation preference.)

EXHIBIT 16.2

SUMMARY OF METAPATH'S FINANCING HISTORY TO DATE

	A	B	C	D
Date	January 20, 1995°	January 20, 1995°	September 30, 1995	April 30, 1996
Amount	$600,025.00	$999,975.00	$1,000,002.00	$7,000,00.00
Participants	Securicor Telesciences	Bessemer Venture Partners	Bessemer Venture Partners	Bessemer, U.S. Venture Partners, Norwest Venture Partners
Price/Common Share	$1.05†	$1.05†	$1.05	$1.62
In Event of Liquidation or Sale	Paid out after Series C and D, pro rata with Series B	Paid out after Series C and D, pro rata with Series A	If not converted, paid out after Series D	If not converted, paid out first
In Event of IPO	Gets redeemed	Gets redeemed	Converts to common	Converts to common
Voluntary Conversion to Common	Not convertible	Not convertible	Convertible with > 66⅔% vote of round	Convertible with > 80% vote of round
Dividend	Immediate quarterly payments of LIBOR + 1%	After January 1, 2000, annual payments of 8% face value	After January 1, 2000, annual payments of 8% face value	After January 1, 2000, annual payments of 8% face value
Mandatory Redemption?	Yes: 3 equal annual increments beginning January 17, 2000	Yes: 3 equal annual increments beginning January 17, 2000	No	No
Antidilution	Yes	Yes	Yes	Yes
Demand Registration Rights	Demand rights granted upon request of > 50% of Series A–D	Demand rights granted upon request of > 50% of Series A–D	Demand rights granted at the earliest of (a) July 31, 1999; (b) six months after IPO; or (c) the request of > 50% of Series A–D	Demand rights granted at the earliest of (a) July 31, 1999; (b) six months after IPO; or (c) the request of > 50% of Series A–D

Notes:

° Note that A and B are the same round (January 20, 1995) wherein the company sold nonconvertible redeemable preferred stock packaged with common stock. The only difference between A and B is the dividend policy: the stock owned by Securicor Telesciences paid a current dividend and the stock owned by Bessemer did not. This was the result of the original three-way negotiations between the founders, Securicor Telesciences and Bessemer that originally capitalized the company. In all other respects, the stock from the original capitalization held by Bessemer and Securicor Telesciences was identical.

† The price per share of a round composed of packaged securities, in this case a nonconvertible redeemable preferred packaged with common stock, is calculated by the total amount invested divided by the number of common shares received. Usually some low value is assigned to the common shares; in this case for every $1 of face value of preferred stock the investor bought, he also bought a common share for 5¢, hence the "price per common share" is $1.05.

(Note that had Consolidated Widget gone public in a qualified offering, both A and B would have been forced to convert to common stock and would each own an equal amount of the company. In that case, the difference between their preferences is erased.)

Hansen had tried to negotiate the participating feature away. He offered to lower the price from $6 per share to $5.50 per share if RSC agreed to drop the participating feature. RSC countered that the participating feature was necessary to protect it in the event of a sale of the company at a small step-up from the current round. Such a sale would provide quite attractive returns to management and the earlier shareholders—who enjoyed a significantly lower cost basis—but leave RSC with little more than it put in. Besides, RSC pointed out, the company's plans were to go public at a significant step-up from this round, in which case the PCPT would be forced to convert to common stock with no additional payout.

THE CELLTECH OFFER

In the midst of soliciting the round of financing, Metapath had received an unsolicited offer to be acquired by CellTech for $115 million in common stock (see Exhibit 16.3). This had been a surprise to the management, who knew CellTech as a vendor of wireless technology that was largely hardware based. The two companies had some contact because Metapath's newest product integrated with one of CellTech's products.

A report, written by an investment banking analyst and released in the summer of 1997, assessed CellTech's market opportunity as follows:

> The key growth driver for CellTech's services is the increasingly competitive nature of the telecommunications industry. Increasing competition will force wireless service providers to demand value-added solutions that provide a competitive advantage and that differentiate their service offerings from others. Now solutions will enable wireless service providers to compete on new features and total service offerings instead of price alone. . . .
>
> CellTech is uniquely positioned to fulfill these needs by providing open access to its platform and leveraging its [technical] expertise. . . Access to the CellTech platform will provide other [application providers] with a physical connection to wireless service providers and access to real-time data.
>
> CellTech's long-term strategy is to be the leading provider of value-added solutions to wireless telecommunications carriers. As part of its strategy, management plans to: 1) maintain the Company's leadership in its current product market; 2) expand its market share in domestic markets; 3) pursue international market opportunities; 4) leverage the CellTech platform to provide new low-cost, value-added solutions; and 5) provide superior customer support.

A merger with CellTech would provide some distinct operating benefits to Metapath. As Exhibits 16.4 and 16.5 show, Metapath's sales and marketing infrastructure was still embryonic; as Exhibits 16.6 and 16.7 suggest, CellTech, which was selling solutions to the same customers, already had a fully formed marketing and domestic sales organization. (Like Metapath, CellTech was just beginning the process of building an international presence.) Also, despite the fact that CellTech's and Metapath's respective

EXHIBIT 16.3

TERM SHEET PRESENTED TO JOHN HANSEN BY CELLTECH COMMUNICATIONS ON SEPTEMBER 25, 1997

This draft term sheet outlines some of the principal terms of Alpha's potential acquisition of all of the capital stock of Zenith by means of a merger of a wholly owned subsidiary of Alpha ("Alpha Sub") with and into Zenith. This draft term sheet is for discussion purposes only and is not binding. In addition, this draft term sheet does not address all of the material terms of the potential transaction, which will only be addressed after all due diligence has been completed and a definitive agreement between Zenith, Alpha, and Alpha Sub has been executed.

Structure of Acquisition	Merger of Alpha Sub with and into Zenith, with Zenith being the surviving entity.
Merger Consideration	Pursuant to the merger, Alpha would issue or reserve for issuance shares of and options on Alpha Common Stock in exchange for all of the shares, options, and warrants of Zenith. The aggregate number of shares issued or reserved for issuance by Alpha ("Merger Consideration") would be equal to $115,000,000.00 divided by the average closing stock price of Alpha's common stock over the five trading day period ending two trading days prior to closing; provided that a collar would exist such that in no event would the average closing stock price used in such calculation vary by more than 5 percent relative to the average closing stock price as of the day immediately preceding execution of definitive agreements. For purposes of calculating the number of shares of Alpha Common Stock to which Zenith shareholders, option holders, and warrant holders would be entitled, the exchange ratio ("Exchange Ratio") would equal the Merger Consideration divided by the "Total Zenith Shares," subject to any adjustments required on account of any applicable liquidation preferences. The "Total Zenith Shares" would be equal to the sum of the Zenith common shares outstanding plus all the Zenith common shares that would be issued upon the conversion or exercise of Zenith securities convertible into or exercisable for common stock (including but not limited to, all vested and unvested employee stock options, warrants, and convertible preferred stock).
Treatment of Zenith Employee Stock Options	Zenith's outstanding stock options would not be accelerated by virtue of this transaction (beyond mandatory, nondiscretionary acceleration provisions, if any, currently described in Zenith's option plans) and will be rolled over into Alpha stock options (with identical vesting) such that each Zenith stock option would be converted into an Alpha stock option exercisable for a number of shares equal to the existing number of shares multiplied by the Exchange Ratio (subject to the effect of any liquidation preference). The new exercise price would be equal to the existing exercise price divided by the Exchange Ratio (subject to the effect of any liquidation preference).
Marketability of Shares	Subject to compliance with securities laws and pooling and tax requirements. Alpha would provide shares of Alpha common stock to Zenith initially through exemption from registration, and would amend the Investors' Rights Agreement with certain of Alpha's investors (originally executed with Alpha's venture capital investors) such that existing holders of Zenith registration rights would become parties to the Investors' Rights Agreement.
Lock-up of Alpha Stock underwriters	All shares of Alpha Common Stock received by Zenith shareholders in the merger will be subject to a lock-up for a period of up to ninety days as required by in connection with any public offerings by Alpha
Employee Issues	Key employees of Zenith as may be identified during the due diligence process (collectively the "Key Employees") will enter into a three year noncompete/nonsolicitation agreement with Alpha.
Closing Conditions	Conditions to Closing, (or, in particular cases, execution of definitive agreements) would include, among other things: • Completion of due diligence to the satisfaction of Zenith. • The transaction being accounted for as a pooling of interests business combination.

(Continues)

EXHIBIT 16.3 (CONTINUED)

TERM SHEET PRESENTED TO JOHN HANSEN BY CELLTECH COMMUNICATIONS ON SEPTEMBER 25, 1997

- The transaction being a tax-free reorganization.
- No material adverse change in Zenith between execution of a Merger Agreement and closing.
- Receipt by Alpha of a satisfactory legal opinion, dated as of the closing.
- Execution of employment and noncompete and nonsolicitation agreements by Zenith Key Employees.

Survival of Representations and Escrow Provision	Representation and warranties would survive closing by one year. An escrow of 10 percent of the shares issued in the transaction would be established to support the representations and warranties.
Fees and Expenses	All legal, broker or finder fees incurred by Zenith or its shareholders in connection with the transaction would be deemed to be expenses of the shareholders, and would be borne by the shareholders of Zenith and would not become obligations of Alpha or Zenith.
Timing	Alpha and its legal and financial advisors would begin their due diligence review of Zenith as well as negotiation of definitive agreements promptly. The parties would seek to execute definitive agreements as soon as practical.
Board Representation	Alpha agrees to use good faith efforts to obtain the approval of its Board of Directors to nominate an individual designated by a majority of the Zenith stockholders (which person must be acceptable to Alpha's Chairman and must have prior relevant experience) to serve one three year term on the Alpha board of Directors.
Voting Rights/Proxy	Selected insiders and other shareholders of Zenith would agree to vote for this transaction, and would grant Alpha an irrevocable proxy to vote the shares owned by such shareholders with respect to any matter requiring a Zenith shareholder vote.
No Other Negotiations	Zenith would immediately enter into an agreement under which, for a period ending six weeks from the date of such agreement (the "Expiration Date"), Zenith would not, directly or indirectly, through any officer, director, affiliate, or agent of Zenith, or otherwise, take any action to solicit, initiate, seek, entertain, encourage, or support any inquiry, proposal, or offer form, furnish any information to, or participate in any negotiations with, any third party regarding any acquisition of Zenith, any merger of consolidation with or involving Zenith, or any acquisition of any material portion of the stock or assets of Zenith.
Confidentiality	This Term Sheet and related discussion would not be disclosed by Zenith or any of its representatives.

technologies were quite different—Metapath's products largely consisted of software running on standard server platforms in the wireless switching office, while CellTech's products were mostly hardware-based and installed in the field with the cellular base stations—Hansen felt that some of CellTech's engineers could potentially be useful to Metapath's development group.

Just by the numbers, the CellTech deal had other immediate merits. A valuation of $115 million was certainly attractive for a company with a revenue run-rate of $25.6 million. Moreover, the transaction would give the existing shareholders liquidity in the near future (after a ninety-day lockup, plus whatever restrictions regular securities rules might place on the stock). This was quite tempting for Metapath's investors given that, even with stellar execution, the company was over a year away from its own IPO. Also,

EXHIBIT 16.4

METAPATH SOFTWARE CORPORATION—QUARTERLY INCOME STATEMENTS ($000's), PREPARED AS OF SEPTEMBER 30, 1997

	Quarter Ended				
	3/31/97 Actual	6/30/97 Actual	9/30/97 Actual	12/31/97 Forecast	Total Forecast
Revenue					
System sales	3,412	4,598	4,738	3,072	15,820
Service	792	1,560	1,697	2,405	6,453
Total revenue	4,204	6,158	6,435	5,476	22,273
Cost and Expenses					
Cost of systems sales	1,134	1,243	1,189	807	4,373
Service & implementation	1,231	1,331	1,398	1,456	5,416
Product development	1,191	1,392	1,573	1,571	5,727
Sales	530	774	718	906	2,928
Marketing	343	502	519	627	1,990
General & administrative	892	966	805	889	3,551
Total costs & expenses	5,321	6,208	6,201	6,256	23,985
Operating income (loss)	(1,117)	(49)	234	(780)	(1,712)
Other					
Interest income	18	20	10	71	120
Interest expense	(45)	(91)	996)	(98)	(330)
Other, net	0	0	0	0	0
Income before taxes	(1,144)	(120)	149	(806)	(1,921)
Income tax expense	0	0	0	0	0
Net Earnings (Loss)	(1,144)	(120)	149	(806)	(1,921)

unlike in an IPO, a stock sale like the CellTech deal would not dilute the ownership of the existing shareholders.

In the end, Metapath's board members were left asking themselves how Cell-Tech's stock would perform over the next twelve to eighteen months. This was a difficult question to answer, as the company had gone public only a few months prior and thus had little history as a public stock. One of Metapath's board members had been an investor in CellTech and had a mixed opinion of the company. But in the three months leading up to the offer for Metapath, the stock had traded up from its IPO price of $15 per share to the $19–22 range.

Also, financial analysts seemed to be bullish on the stock. Another analyst report on CellTech from the summer of 1997 ended as follows:

> Due to the Company's large addressable market opportunity, rapid forecasted growth in EPS, technology leadership and conservative financial policies, we believe the shares could trade between 40×–45× forward earnings. This suggests a near-term price target between $21–24 per share.

EXHIBIT 16.5

METAPATH SOFTWARE CORPORATION—BALANCE SHEET ($000'S), CURRENT MONTH AND PREVIOUS MONTH, PREPARED SEPTEMBER 30, 1997

	As of 9/30/97	As of 8/31/97
Assets		
Current assets:		
Cash	557	950
Accounts receivable	846	635
Inventory		
WIP	807	905
Spare parts	920	944
Prepaid expenses	415	424
Total current assets	3,545	3,857
Property & equipment	5,376	5,033
Accumulated depreciation	(1,288)	(1,162)
Property & equipment, net	4,088	3,871
Total Assets	7,633	7,728
Liabilities & Shareholders' Equity		
Current liabilities:		
Accounts payable	1,754	1,385
Accrued liabilities	429	365
Deferred revenue		
System revenue	3,365	3,736
Maintenance revenue	1,465	1,753
C/P of long-term obligations	2,576	1,446
Total current liabilities	9,590	8,685
Long-term obligations	2,247	2,366
Total liabilities	11,837	11,051
Preferred stock—Class A	61	61
Preferred stock—Class B	976	976
Stockholders' equity:		
Preferred stock—Class C	2	2
Preferred stock—Class D	7	7
Common stock	6	6
Additional paid-in capital	6,363	6,357
Accumulated loss	(11,619)	(10,733)
Total shareholders' equity	(5,241)	(4,361)
Total Liabilities & Equity	7,633	7,728

EXHIBIT 16.6

CELLTECH COMMUNICATIONS—QUARTERLY RESULTS OF OPERATIONS (IN THOUSANDS)

	Quarter Ended					
Revenues	31-Mar-96	30-Jun-96	30-Sep-96	31-Dec-96	31-Mar-97	30-Jun-97
System revenue	0	4,825	6,038	8,906	8,882	11,022
Service revenue	159	336	405	654	1,010	1,184
Total revenues	159	5,161	6,442	9,559	9,892	12,206
Cost of revenues						
Cost of system revenues	46	5,035	5,617	8,045	8,135	8,142
Cost of service revenues	232	607	596	699	902	769
Total cost of revenues	277	5,642	6,213	8,745	9,036	8,911
Gross profit (deficit)	(119)	(481)	229	815	856	3,295
Operating expenses						
Research and development	1,034	1,295	1,369	1,720	1,503	1,753
Sales and marketing	905	1,304	1,494	2,141	1,683	1,939
General and administrative	617	695	632	874	1,078	1,062
Total operating expenses	2,556	3,294	3,495	4,736	4,264	4,755
Operating loss	(2,674)	(3,775)	(3,266)	(3,922)	(3,408)	(1,459)
Interest income (expense), net	79	(20)	(163)	(136)	(3)	50
Loss before income taxes	(2,595)	(3,794)	(3,429)	(4,057)	(3,411)	(1,409)
Income taxes	1	0	1	3	2	2
Net loss	(2,596)	(3,794)	(3,430)	(4,060)	(3,413)	(1,411)

Longer-term, we believe the Company will be able to maintain its rate of earnings growth by internally developing new products and extending its expertise and product offerings through acquisition. Based on preliminary 1999 EPS estimates of $0.80 per share, we believe a twelve to eighteen month price target above $30 is appropriate.

While Hansen was not sure how much weight to give to the valuation estimates in the analyst report, he was struck by the positive consensus of observers in the financial community about the prospects for CellTech's stock.

EXHIBIT 16.7

CELLTECH COMMUNICATIONS—BALANCE SHEETS (IN THOUSANDS)

	31-Dec-95	As of 31-Dec-96	30-Jun-97
Assets			
Current assets:			
Cash and cash equivalents	7,691	18,544	11,419
Short-term investments	2,128	2,667	10,642
Accounts receivable	894	3,592	3,396
Inventories	2,406	10,112	12,308
Prepaid expenses	123	90	747
Total current assets	13,241	35,004	38,513
Property & equipment, net	1,973	2,636	3,061
Other assets	181	325	397
	15,395	37,966	41,971
Liabilities and stockholders' equity			
Current liabilities			
Accounts payable	368	3,728	1,381
Accrued expenses	785	2,721	3,524
Notes payable (current portion)	241	1,961	2,072
Capital lease obligations (current portions)	48	311	412
Deferred revenue	1,178	4,880	12,072
Total current liabilities	2,620	13,600	19,461
Notes payable	1,138	4,111	3,142
Capital lease obligations, noncurrent portion	119	668	653
Total liabilities	3,876	18,379	23,255
Stockholders' equity			
Convertible preferred stock, $.001 par value	5	10	11
Common stock, $.001 par value	0	1	1
Additional paid-in capital	27,238	49,178	53,130
Accumulated deficit	−15,724	−29,602	−34,427
Total stockholders' equity	11,519	19,587	18,715
	15,395	37,966	41,971

17

A Note on Private Equity Securities

IN THE BEGINNING, THERE WAS COMMON STOCK

Common stock is the basic unit of ownership. It does not carry any special rights outside of those described in the company charter and bylaws. It gives the holder ownership, but that ownership is subordinated to 1) all government claims (read "taxes"), 2) all regulated employee claims (e.g., pension obligations), (3) all trade debt (accounts receivable), 4) all bank debt, and 5) all forms of preferred stock. Specifically, were the company liquidated—or sold in an asset sale—the common shareholder stands behind all of those other stakeholders before getting the residual value, that is, what's left after all other obligations are satisfied.

Typically, venture capitalists do not buy common stock. The fundamental reason is illustrated by the following example:

Joe Flash has a great idea for a new Internet company and goes to his local venture capitalist, Rex Finance. Joe and Rex agree that $1.5 million will fund the project to the next big value accretion point, and they further agree to a 50.05/49.95 split, with Joe holding the majority stake. But contrary to standard venture practice, perhaps because the competition to finance Joe's deal is so great, Rex agrees to an all common stock structure. Therefore, immediately after the closing, the company has an implied enterprise value of $3 million (since the market price that Rex paid was $1.5 million for 49.95 percent), one employee (Joe), one class of tangible assets (cash) and some intangible assets (Joe's PowerPoint slides and a business plan).

On the day of the closing as they walk out of the lawyers' office, Joe bumps into his old friend, John Terrific, who is vice president for business development of WooWee!, a public Internet company valued in the market at just over $12 billion. WooWee! needs ideas and talent to maintain the promise of its "full" market valuation, so John pulls Joe

Senior Lecturer Felda Hardymon and Professor Josh Lerner prepared this note as the basis for class discussion.

aside and offers him $2 million for Joe's new company. Seeing a quick return on the hours he put in writing his business plan, and realizing WooWee! will use its considerable resources and market clout to enter the market ahead of him should he decline their offer, Joe accepts the offer.

How is the pie divided? Joe and Rex each get $1 million from WooWee! So in a matter of minutes, Joe's investment goes from $0 (sweat equity) to $1 million, while Rex's investment goes from $1.5 million (cash) to $1 million. Rex was powerless through the whole process; and WooWee! was able to recruit Joe and own his idea for a mere $500,000 since they end up with the $1.5 million (less the legal fees) that was in Joe's company. How could Rex have avoided this disaster?

Most venture securities have three features, any one of which would have saved Rex from having to explain to his partners how he lost $500,000 in an afternoon:

1. Preferred stock.

2. Vesting of founder, management, and key employee shares.

3. Covenants and supermajority provisions.

This note will briefly discuss each with the major variations commonly used in practice.

Key to all of these structural features is the concept of the entrepreneur earning his equity through value creation. In this example, Rex valued Joe's company based on its potential value, not on its current tangible value. In a perfect, frictionless world, Rex's money might be metered into Joe's company precisely in proportion to value being created and to the expenses incurred. But in the real world, entrepreneurs need to finance ahead of their expenses. Moreover, value is created in lumps coincident with important events like first proof of product feasibility, first customer shipment, and major successes in the marketplace, and so on. Venture capital exists to bridge between such value accretion events; at the same time, the entrepreneur's stake should not be perfected until he or she has delivered on the promised value. This is the basis of most deviations of typically used venture securities from common stock. In the above example, Joe had not *earned* his equity interest at the time of the WooWee! buyout, and that violated the principle of reward for performance.

Preferred Stock

Preferred stock has a *liquidation preference* over common stock: that is, in the event of sale or liquidation of the company, the preferred stock gets paid ahead of the common stock. There must be a face value to preferred stock, which is the amount that gets paid to the preferred stock before moving on to paying the common stock. Generally, the face value of a preferred stock in a private equity transaction is the cost basis the venture capitalist pays for the stock. If in the original example Rex had invested his money in Joe's company in the form of preferred stock, then when WooWee! purchased Joe's company, Rex's $1.5 million would have been returned to him through a redemption of the preferred stock. But how would the remainder $500,000 been divided? That leads to the variations of preferred stock used in private equity transactions.

Redeemable Preferred

Redeemable preferred, sometimes called "straight preferred," is preferred stock that has no convertibility into equity. Its intrinsic value is therefore its face value plus any dividend rights it carries.[1] In most ways it behaves in a capital structure like deeply subordinated debt. Redeemable preferred stock always carries a negotiated term specifying when it *must* be redeemed by the company—typically, the sooner of a public offering or five to eight years. It is used in private equity transactions in combination with common stock or warrants. For example, had Rex agreed with Joe to the same 50.05/49.95 split, but had specified that his investment would be in the form of a redeemable preferred stock with $1.5 million face value plus 49.95 percent of the common stock, then the WooWee! transaction would have first redeemed out the straight preferred stock ($1.5 million to Rex) and the remaining $500,000 would have been split proportionally to the ownership of common stock ($250,000 each to Rex and to Joe).

Had the company gone on to a successful public offering, Rex could have expected his initial $1.5 million investment to be returned through a redemption of the redeemable preferred without affecting his basic ownership position held in common stock. He would, in effect, be getting his money back *and* keeping his investment. This aspect of "double-dipping" is sometimes troubling to entrepreneurs. Moreover, when a material portion of the proceeds of a public offering is used to redeem out a venture capitalist's preferred stock, the public market value of the company can be adversely affected. These negatives of the redeemable preferred[2] led to the use of convertible preferred stock in private equity transactions.

Convertible Preferred Stock

Convertible preferred stock is preferred stock that can be converted *at the shareholder's option* into common stock. This forces the shareholder to choose whether he will take his returns through the liquidation feature or through the underlying common equity position. Clearly, if the value being offered for the company exceeds the implied total enterprise value at the time of the investment, then the shareholder will convert the preferred stock to common stock in order to realize his portion of the gain in value.

---

1. Generally, venture securities carry no dividends, or defer dividends considerably out into the future, because venture capitalists are capital-gains oriented. In fact, many venture partnerships do not grant a carried interest to the general partners on dividends received. Moreover, dividends can limit the ability of a growth company to raise capital since it raises the question: "Why are you returning cash to your shareholders when you need it to grow?" Finally, dividends create an asymmetry of rewards between the preferred shareholders (typically the investors) and the common shareholders (typically the founders, management, and key employees), which in turn leads to a misalignment of incentives between investor and company. Large public companies often issue preferred stock with high dividends, which are themselves preferential to common stock dividends, in order to attract certain classes of investors who desire high-income streams. The use of preferred stock in venture securities is based on the preference value and the "earn out" principle and should not be confused with this common use of preferred stock in large public companies. We will not discuss dividends in this note since they generally do not play a large role in venture securities.

2. One might suggest a solution to this problem of assigning more of the value of the unit to the common stock. However, it is accepted practice to assign as much value as possible to the preferred. There are three reasons for this practice: 1) Tax deferral—Since redemption of preferred stock is simply a return of capital with no associated gain, there is no tax on redemption. Moreover, since the preferred is much more likely to be redeemed before the common is sold, then putting more value in the preferred portion of the unit defers tax. 2) Security—The preference is protection from the common receiving value before it is earned and so it makes sense to put as much in that instrument as possible. 3) Pricing employee incentive shares—In declaring a fair market value for incentive stock option exercise prices or for employee purchase plans, a board of directors wants as low a share price as possible in order to embed as much value as possible in the incentive shares. Since these incentive plans use common stock as their underlying equity, the board can use the "cheap common" part of the transaction as the basis of a low share price.

In our example, if Rex had proposed a convertible preferred stock, then he would have received his original $1.5 million investment back from the redemption of the unconverted preferred and Joe would have gotten the residual $500,000. Rex would have left his preferred stock unconverted since converting the preferred to common would have left him with 49.95 percent of the proceeds ($1 million) and in a loss position. Clearly, if WooWee! had chosen to pay more than $3 million for Joe's company, Rex would have had an incentive to convert to common stock in order to enjoy his portion (49.95 percent) of whatever premium over the $3 million implied enterprise value that WooWee! was offering.

Conceptually, convertible preferred allows the entrepreneur to "catch up" to the investor after the investor's initial investment is secured. Therefore, convertible preferred stock differs from the redeemable preferred plus cheap common as follows:

Portion of Proceeds Received by Investor

Amount of Proceeds	Redeemable Preferred	Convertible Preferred
Up to face value of preferred (FV)	All to investor	All to investor
From FV to implied enterprise value (IEV) at time of investment	FV plus common equity proportion of increment over FV to investor	FV only to investor
Above IEV	FV plus common equity proportion of increment over FV to investor	Common equity proportion to Investor

In general, the public markets expect companies to have simple capital structure using only common stock and debt. Therefore, underwriters nearly always insist that all preferred stock be converted coincident with an initial public offering. To avoid a round of negotiations wherein investors demand to be compensated for their conversion to common, convertible preferred stock routinely contains a *mandatory conversion term* specifying that the company can force conversion as part of an underwritten IPO of a certain (negotiated) size and price. The size is usually large enough to ensure a liquid market (recently these terms tend to specify a $30 million or larger offering) and the price is negotiated to be high enough to ensure that it is in the venture capitalist's clear interest to convert (recently these terms tend to specify at least a factor of three increase in share price from that at the time the investment).

Convertible preferred stock naturally led to the idea that the conversion ratio need not be fixed. Many convertible preferred stocks contain *antidilution provisions* that automatically adjust the conversion price down if the company sells stock below the share price that the investor has paid.[3] The rationale for these provisions is that the company is presumably selling at a lower price (a "down round") because of underperformance. By having an automatic adjustment, the investor is less likely to oppose or forestall a dilutive financing to take on much needed capital when the company needs it most or when the private equity markets are difficult.[4]

---

3. The adjustment mechanism is a negotiated term and can range from complete adjustment ("full ratchet") to one based on the size of the round and the size of the price decrease ("weighted average formula"). Some antidilution provisions apply only below a certain negotiated price level, and some except smaller financings.

4. While antidilution provisions became prevalent based on adjusting the conversion ratio of convertible preferred stock, venture capitalists have applied the concept to the redeemable preferred structure by having the company issue free common shares in a down round according to similar formulas. Other antidilution structures include the use of payable-in-kind dividends should the company miss its targets.

Anecdotally, private equity deals in the 1970s tended to be of redeemable preferred structure, reflecting the paucity of capital available and the need to get it back as soon as possible to do more deals. As venture capital became more institutionalized during the 1980s, the market became more competitive and convertible preferred became the standard security. As the pattern of multiple private venture capital rounds became prevalent, later round players who were paying significantly higher prices than early round players insisted on having preferred stock with liquidation preferences over *both* common stock and lower-priced preferred stock.[5] This trend accelerated in the 1990s as later round investors paid higher and higher prices. These investors insisted on structures that gave them more participation in the returns reaped from the early sale of private companies at prices that gave astonishing returns to the early stage investor but considerably less returns to the later stage investor who had paid a high price expecting an exit in the hot public markets. The structure that satisfies this need is participating convertible preferred stock.

Participating Convertible Preferred Stock

Participating convertible preferred stock is convertible preferred stock with the additional feature that in the event of a sale or liquidation of the company the holder has a right to receive the face value *and* the equity participation as if the stock were converted. Like a convertible preferred, these instruments carry a mandatory conversion term triggered on a public offering. The net result is an instrument that acts like the redeemable preferred structure while the company is private and converts to common on a public offering.

A key companion term to a participating convertible preferred is the specification of when the participation term is in effect. Usually, the term reads, "in the event of sale or liquidation," and it often goes on to define liquidation as being any merger or transaction that constitutes a change of control. As a result, in a merger transaction between two private firms where the private surviving merged company issues new preferred stock in exchange for the preexisting preferred stock, these clauses may be triggered. This may set off a demand from the holders of the participating convertible preferred for both new preferred stock equal in face value to the old preferred stock plus a participation in the common equity of the new company. All of this can occur without any true liquidity event.

The driver behind the recent acceptance of participating convertible preferred is the willingness of later stage investors to pay very high prices if the terms include a participation feature. If the company goes public, the highly dilutive participating feature goes away.[6] Therefore, companies and their current shareholders feel confident issuing such instruments when the public market is hot and a public offering appears feasible if the company has any business success at all.

---

5. In the case of sharply increasing share prices in multiple private rounds, the later round players hold the same relationship to early round players that early round players hold to the founders in the initial financing. If the first financing is at $1 per share (that is $1 per *common equivalent share*—the price of the convertible preferred divided by the number of share into which it converts), and the later financing is at $5 per share, then the early round investors as well as management would be delighted with an offer to purchase the company for $4 per share. Unless the later round investor had a liquidation preference, he would lose money in such a transaction just as Rex lost money in our starting example.

6. Later stage, high-priced financings are almost always large, so the participating feature can be quite dilutive to management and existing shareholders.

To summarize the various preferred structures:

Portion of Proceeds Received by Investor

Amount of Proceeds	Redeemable Preferred	Convertible Preferred	Participating Convertible Preferred
Up to face value of preferred (FV)	All to investor	All to investor	All to investor
From FV to implied enterprise value (IEV) at time of investment	FV plus common equity proportion of increment over FV to investor	FV only to investor	FV plus common equity proportion of increment over FV to investor
From IEV to public offering	FV plus common equity proportion of increment over FV to investor	Common equity proportion to investor	FV plus common equity proportion of increment over FV to investor
Above public offering	FV plus common equity proportion of increment over FV to investor	Common equity proportion to investor	Common equity proportion to investor

Vesting

The concept of vesting is simple. It holds that an entrepreneur's stock does not become his or her own until he or she has been with the company for a period of time, or until some value accretion event occurs (e.g., the sale of the company). Typically vesting is implemented over a time period (currently, four years on the East Coast, three years on the West Coast), and the stock "vests" (i.e., the entrepreneur obtains unqualified ownership of the shares) proportionately over that time period. For administrative purposes, stock vesting usually occurs quarterly, occasionally annually, and maybe even monthly.

In our example, suppose Rex had eschewed preferred stock entirely but had insisted that Joe's shares vest proportionately over four years (1/16th per quarter). Then when the WooWee! transaction occurred, Rex could have insisted the company buy back Joe's stock at cost (probably a nominal 1¢ per share) and theoretically received the entire $2 million of proceeds. Of course, since Joe likely would have objected to receiving no proceeds from the sale to WooWee! and since WooWee! wanted to acquire Joe's talents and wished to see that Joe was a happy WooWee! employee, the transaction may have been called off under those conditions. Having foreseen this situation, Rex may have agreed to a partial acceleration of Joe's vesting in the event of acquisition.[7] If that agreement called for 25 percent acceleration, then the proceeds would be split 12.5 percent to Joe (25 percent of 50.05 percent) and the remainder to Rex.

7. Often venture terms allow for a 25 percent to 50 percent acceleration of vesting for certain managers on acquisition based on the theory that 1) many managers lose their job in an acquisition and it is not fair for those who have created the value to lose a big portion of it by the very act of perfecting that value for the shareholders, and 2) it is better to have the cooperation of management and key employees in the event of a potential acquisition, and acceleration acts as an incentive to get the deal done. Of course, acceleration acts *against* the interest of the acquiring company, which may have to spend stock option shares to remotivate the acquired employees who have had the benefits of acceleration. It also acts against the interest of the nonmanagement shareholders by effectively adding shares to the pool of shares to be bought. The fixed negotiated share price is therefore divided among more shares. For these reasons, acceleration usually is restricted to a few employees and often is only partial.

In general, preferred stock structures do a better job of implementing the "reward for performance" principle since they rely on the investment's terminal value. Furthermore, vesting is contractual: potential events and situations must be anticipated and written down if vesting is to do the same job as preferred stock. However, vesting does perform the very important function of preventing an employee from leaving and taking with him value disproportionate to the time he was employed at the company. Vesting creates the "golden handcuffs" that motivates an employee to stay when other opportunities call. If a company is doing well and a key employee holds valuable options or stock that would be lost if the employee left before a certain date or event, then the possibility of an early departure is greatly diminished.

Vesting also performs the function of returning shares to the incentive stock pool from employees who in some sense "haven't finished the job," thereby providing incentive stock for their replacements. This allows companies to budget their incentive stock by position or task with some assurance that they are somewhat protected from turnover. Similarly, vesting protects morale by assuring employees that those who leave will not benefit as much as those who stay behind and create value.

Covenants

Maybe the most basic way venture capitalists protect their investments is through covenant provisions. Covenants are contractual agreements between the investor and the company and fall into two broad categories: positive covenants and negative covenants. Positive covenants are the list of things the company agrees to do. They include such things as producing audited reports, holding regular board meetings and paying taxes on time.

In addition to the positive commitments, the preferred equity agreements also contain numerous covenants and restrictions that serve to limit detrimental behavior by the entrepreneur. Certain actions are expressly forbidden or require the approval of a supermajority of investors. For instance, sales of assets are often restricted. Any disposal of assets above a certain dollar value or above a certain percentage of the firm's book value may be limited without the approval of private equity investors. This prevents the entrepreneur from increasing the risk profile of the company and changing the firm's activities from its intended focus. It also prevents the entrepreneur from making "sweetheart" deals with friends.

The private equity investors are also often concerned about changes in control. The contracts may state that the founders cannot sell any of their common stock without approval of the private equity investors or offering the securities to the private equity investors. Similarly, restrictions may prevent a merger or sale of the company without approval of the investors. Transfer-of-control restrictions are important because venture capitalists invest in people. If the management team decides to remove its human capital from the deal, venture capitalists would want to approve the terms of the transfer. Control transfers may hurt the position of the private equity investor if they are done on terms that are unfavorable to earlier investors.

The purchase of major assets above a certain size threshold may also be forbidden without approval of private equity investors. This restriction may be written in absolute dollar terms or may be written as a percentage of book value. The wording is usually broad enough to cover purchases of assets or merger of the firm. Restrictions on purchases may help prevent radical changes in strategy or wasteful expenditure by the entrepreneur. Many such strategy changes could have detrimental effects on the value of the private equity investors' stake.

Finally, the contracts usually contain some provision for restricting the issuance of new securities. Almost all documents contain a provision that restricts the issuance of senior securities without the approval of previous investors. Many documents alter the restriction to include securities on the preferred equity level or any security issuance. Usually, a majority of preferred shares must vote in favor of such an issue. Restricting security issuance prevents the transfer of value from current shareholders to new security holders.

Often negative covenants are coupled with supermajority voting provisions wherein the company agrees not to do certain things unless a greater than 50 percent majority of shareholders (or in some cases, the board) agrees. So, for example, if Rex had insisted in the original deal that the company could only be sold if two-thirds of common shares agreed in a shareholder vote, then he would have had a veto over the WooWee! transaction, and presumably would have had the negotiating leverage to insist on an acceptable deal.

A few frequently encountered covenants are somewhat different from the positive and negative ones considered above. Many contracts also contain mandatory redemption rights. These are rights of the private equity investors that allow them to "put," or sell at a predetermined price, the preferred stock back to the company. Essentially, the venture capitalists can force the firm to repay the face value of the investment at any time. This mechanism can often be used to force liquidation or merger of the firm. The mandatory redemption provisions are often included for two reasons: 1) most venture partnerships have a limited life so they must have some mechanism to force a liquidity event before the partnership expires, and 2) mandatory redemption clauses help prevent "lifestyle companies," that is, companies that exist only to provide a good living to the management but do not accrete value to the investors. By demanding redemption the investors can get their money back, or in the event there isn't enough money available in the company, force a negotiation to create a liquidity event.

A contract usually explicitly states the number of board seats that venture capital investors can elect. Typically, in companies that are venture backed from the beginning, private equity investors control the board, or at least the board has a majority of outside (i.e., nonmanagement) directors where the investors at least have approval rights over those seats not held by them or the management. Even if the private equity investors do not own greater than 50 percent of the equity, the contracts may allocate control of the board to venture capitalists. The board control serves as an important check on management that may try to exploit minority shareholders. Similarly, in any future initial public offering, an outsider-dominated board lends credibility to the firm.

All in all, the most frequent use of covenants is to effectively disconnect control on important issues from owning a majority of the equity. Price and control then become separate items for negotiation. Control issues implemented through covenants and supermajority voting provisions can be settled quite specifically and therefore appropriately to each side's concerns. For example, management often has stronger concerns about operational matters than financing ones, while investors' concerns are typically the reverse. A negotiated set of covenants can leave investors minimally involved in determining operating policy but heavily consulted and involved in financial strategy.

18

Endeca Technologies (A)

On September 4, 2001, Steve Papa, CEO and founder of Endeca Technologies, could hear a construction worker nailing a "Commercial Real Estate Available" sign to a building across the street from his office in Cambridge, Massachusetts. This had become routine, as hundreds of early stage technology companies failed to raise additional growth capital. The words of his vice president of marketing, Steve Sayre, warred with the sound of the construction. "I know the board is actively working on the C round," Sayre said. "We'd better get this funding closed; I don't think the NASDAQ is going to hold up." Papa knew that his CFO shared Sayre's concerns. To an even greater extent, so did he (see Exhibit 18.1 for NASDAQ values), because not only had the NASDAQ fallen, but so had the number of venture deals and the amount of money invested in them (see Exhibit 18.2).

That afternoon, he and the board of his infrastructure software firm would have to decide between two term sheets, both raising $18 million but with very different impacts on the company's current owners and customers and on the way the company would be governed. One was an insider-led round at 98.5¢ per share that brought in a major potential customer; the other, which had arrived in the previous forty-eight hours, was priced at $1.25 per share and had a new lead investor but was likely to exclude the customer. Making the situation more awkward, Papa had verbally accepted the inside terms a week before, pending board review. "In this market," he thought, "I guess I'm lucky to have any term sheet at all, let alone two. I just wish it hadn't been so hard, and that they'd come in at the same time."

Endeca, then called Parallel Networks, had been founded in the summer of 1999 with seed funding from Bessemer Venture Partners (BVP) and several other firms. The first institutional round (the B round) took place in December 1999 with BVP and Venrock Associates participating. As a hot deal in a hot market, competition among venture capital (VC) firms had driven the pre-money valuation from $17 million to $27 million,

Professors Felda Hardymon and Josh Lerner and Senior Research Associate Ann Leamon prepared this case. HBS cases are developed solely as the basis for class discussion. Cases are not intended to serve as endorsements, sources of primary data, or illustrations of effective or ineffective management. Some names and numbers have been disguised.

EXHIBIT 18.1

NASDAQ COMPOSITE INDEX AND NASDAQ COMPUTER INDEX, JANUARY 2, 2001, TO AUGUST 31, 2001

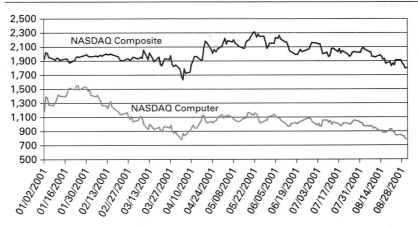

Source: Datastream, Thomson Financial, accessed April 22, 2002, and http://www.nasdaq.com, accessed April 22, 2002.

EXHIBIT 18.2

VENTURE TRANSACTIONS AND AMOUNTS INVESTED, 1999–2001

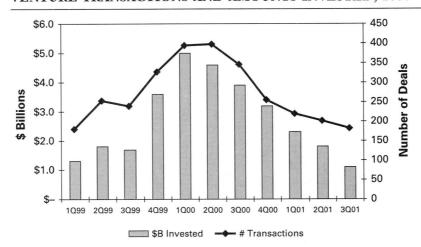

Source: Adapted from PriceWaterhouseCoopers, "Money Tree Survey, 3Q 2001," (October 15, 2001); and http://www.pwcmoneytree.com, accessed November 21, 2001.

with a post-money close at $35 million. Although the Series C round had been slated for November/December 2000, Papa had noted the increasingly difficult financing environment and managed to make his funds last for eighteen months, rather than the anticipated twelve.

The company had hit every milestone on its original plan. Its product had been installed at several marquee customers, including Tower Records and one of the world's largest asset management companies, and it was about to be in trials at Putnam and a major investment bank—Dean Stanley Goldman Credit Partners (DSGCP). A veritable who's who of potential customers was seriously considering the technology. Papa expected that $7 million would take his company to break-even, and he knew his management team was strong enough to keep the firm on track. He had started looking for $10 million in Series C funding in March 2001, and he had reduced the pre-money several times from $90 million to $60 million to, finally, $25 million. (For context, Akamai, a publicly traded technology company, had seen its market capitalization fall from $30 billion at the time of Endeca's Series B round, to $300 *million* at the time of Endeca's Series C, a decline of 99 percent.) It had been a depressing and exhausting battle even to get a term sheet.

Papa looked around the room at the other board members and observers: Hardy Smith from BVP; Steve Walske, former CEO of Parametric Technologies; Jim Baum, Endeca's president and COO, also from Parametric Technologies; and Mike Tyrrell, a general partner at Venrock (see Exhibit 18.3 for ownership and investment). Papa knew that BVP and Venrock would contribute $5 million each in the insider deal. BVP had indicated its willingness to participate at a similar level in the outsider deal, and Venrock would undoubtedly invest its pro-rata or more.

While the outsider-led deal offered a higher price, DSGCP, the potential customer, had been interested in investing but only at a lower valuation. Was the higher valuation

---

EXHIBIT 18.3

ENDECA'S CAPITALIZATION POST-SERIES A AND POST-SERIES B

(All numbers in millions)	Post Series A		Post Series B	
	$ in round	Cum. Shares	$ in round	Cum. Shares
BVP	0.65	0.86	5.60	4.67
Venrock	—	—	2.10	1.43
Ampersand	—	—	—	—
Others	1.15	1.51	0.40	1.79
Total Management Pool°	—	16.00	—	16.00
Total	**1.80**	**18.37**	**8.10**	**23.88**
	—	—	—	—
Post-Money	**$13.96**	—	**$35.10**	—
After additions to pool before Series C†	—	—	—	25.38

Source: Endeca.

Notes:

° Total Management Pool includes all common shares, and awarded and unawarded options.

† Just before the term sheet for the C financing round arrived, 1.5 million shares were added to the common pool.

worth the possible loss of DSGCP's involvement, especially since it was well known both to the company and in the industry? DSGCP would be a passive investor, thus keeping intact a board and governance structure that had worked extremely well. In addition, the outside investor wanted to put closing off for a week and change the investor counsel. Endeca had enough cash for another month of expenses. Was a higher price worth the risks and disruptions?

BACKGROUND

Endeca was founded in the summer of 1999, just after Papa finished his MBA. As he explained:

> We observed that information delivery on the Internet was still stuck in the 1970s. Given my background at groups building other large-scale Internet infrastructures [Papa was employee number fourteen at Inktomi and involved in the early Akamai team's business strategy], I knew there had to be a better way, and after several person-years of research we believed we had found it.

Endeca solved one of the most vexing problems of modern business—how to scale an enterprise's information architecture across any type of enterprise data. Large firms, whether Internet-based or old-line, maintained many databases with overlapping, inconsistent, or unrelated information. Endeca used advanced mathematical theory to build a taxonomy of items and item attributes that linked all the legacy databases, allowing questions to be answered in real time. With this "metarelational database," a user could incrementally define a very precise search ranging over a vast amount of data. Tower Records used Endeca's Technology in its online store, allowing customers to search its entire inventory of music and videos by a host of attributes. While many new technologies could search on item attributes, Endeca allowed a user to build a real-time search that honed in on the target, avoiding both floods of meaningless responses and no results at all.

Even more impressive was the technology's capacity for "drill down" information retrieval. For instance, an analyst could identify mutual fund customers with investment plans, and then drill down to determine assets by age group, gender, and even industry. As its test case, the Endeca team had used wine data, as wine was categorized in a number of different ways—country of origin, grape, mouth feel, price, and year—and the data was readily available.

In September 1999, Papa raised a seed round of $1.8 million. Hardy Smith had learned of the deal and put in $650,000, explaining to his partners, "I'm simply interested in the option value." The round had been filled out by Monarch Capital, the original backer of Inktomi, Papa's former employer; Sun Technology Ventures, a European VC; and some angels.

Hard on the heels of the seed financing, Papa raised a Series B round of $8.1 million. BVP's Smith offered to lead the deal at $17 million pre-money. On Christmas Day 1999, Papa stopped by Smith's home to show him his family's present—a real straitjacket—and tell him about a new development. At a trade show that fall, Papa had met a partner from a well-known West Coast VC firm. Learning that the Series B was open, the firm sent an aggressive term sheet setting the pre-money valuation at $30 million. By December 31, 1999, Smith and Papa had agreed to a $27 million pre-money valuation, for a post-valuation of $35.1 million. BVP took $5.6 million, for 19.5 percent ownership, and Venrock joined with $2.1 million, for 6 percent of the company. Venrock's Mike Tyrrell had recently come from Spyglass (which had commercialized the Mosaic browser), where he had been executive vice president of corporate development. Papa himself had connections with Venrock, where he had served a summer internship while at Harvard Business School. Tyrrell said:

> Venrock thought very highly of Steve [Papa], especially for his entrepreneurial drive and his deep technical knowledge. He was one of those guys that we always want to back. In fact, Venrock usually invests for 15 percent or more of a company; that we would participate with a lower ownership level was a testament to our respect for Steve.

In a memo to his partners, Smith commented:

> This is a high-risk, high-return deal. . . . But we can change the world with this deal and the work they are doing is so substantive that the barriers to entry will be high. I'd rather go for the home run when the need is so clear rather than hang back and try to catch on later.

"At the time," recalled Papa,

> we were talking about a pre-money for the C round in the hundreds of millions of dollars. Our plan was to have a fast ramp, close big customers early, and be back in the market in November. From the vantage point of January 2000, you have to realize, a $200 million pre-money made sense, especially if you had customers and a product. To put it in context, Akamai had a $30 billion market cap then versus the $300 million it had at the close of our Series C. Our key deliverables in this scheme were getting a beta version of the package with a customer, and building out the management team.

In the interim, though, the VC environment turned sour after the NASDAQ's swoon in April 2000. Smith explained:

> Steve [Papa] recognized that the glory days were over and started managing the company on a much more conservative basis. He concentrated on getting the product out and in shape to ship to customers, even as he built the team. A complete management team was going to be a prerequisite to any Series C financing.

Over the course of 2000 and 2001, Papa assembled an impressive group. The board had set aside a significant option pool, believing that a top-rate management team would be essential to the company's success. In addition to David Gourley, chief technology officer, who was one of the original software architects at Inktomi, other significant additions were Steve Walske, the former CEO of Parametric Technologies, who joined the board; Gary Vilchick, the CFO from Spyglass, who took the same position with Endeca; Mark Watkins, a senior software development executive with Parametric, who joined as vice president of software development; James Baum, previously executive vice president with Parametric, who joined as president and COO; Steve Sayre, the vice president of marketing, who had headed marketing for the Lotus division of IBM; and Chris Reisig, the vice president of sales, who had run Parametric's Asian and European operations, known for their sales prowess (see Exhibit 18.4 for the management team). As Papa said:

> Hiring good people may take longer up front, but it's essential if our business is going to scale to more than $100 million in revenue. One of the biggest mistakes we could make is hiring a management team that limits the long-term potential of the company. Having an experienced CFO in Gary [Vilchick] was essential in this turbulent financial environment, which was why he was one of my first hires.

EXHIBIT 18.4

ENDECA'S MANAGEMENT TEAM AS OF AUGUST 2001

Steve Papa, Chief Executive Officer

Steve Papa is a founding partner of Endeca and has helped shape several pioneering Internet service infrastructures. An early employee at Inktomi, Papa was the business lead in charge of creating the company's infrastructure caching business, which grew to make up 60 percent of Inktomi's revenues. He was also part of the original business team at Akamai. In addition, Papa was a venture capital associate with Venrock Associates, the venture capital arm of the Rockefeller family, and was responsible for managing NCR/Teradata's $500 million high-end enterprise computing system product line.

Papa holds an MBA from Harvard Business School and a BS in operations research and economics from Princeton University.

James Baum, President and COO

James Baum is the former executive vice president and general manager of Parametric Technology Corporation's (PTC) Windchill Business unit and brings more than eleven years of experience in software operations and product development to Endeca. As EVP and GM at PTC, Baum was responsible for all aspects of profit and loss, product strategy, product development, marketing, operations and services. Prior to that he was executive vice president of engineering, research and development at PTC, where he was responsible for all of PTC's product strategy and development. Baum also defined and executed PTC's acquisition strategy related to identification of target companies, technical due diligence, and organizational integration.

Baum holds a MS in engineering from Rensselaer Polytechnic Institute and a BS in engineering from Worcester Polytechnic Institute.

David Gourley, Chief Technology Officer

A founding partner of Endeca, David Gourley brings extensive development experience to the company, having helped implement and deploy the technology behind several of the largest Internet infrastructures in use today. Gourley was on the founding development team at Inktomi, where he helped build Inktomi's search engine infrastructure and went on to help build Inktomi's Internet infrastructure cache. At Inktomi, Gourley led several key customer deployments, including the deployment of AOL's cache infrastructure, one of the highest trafficked Internet infrastructures in the world.

Gourley holds a BA in computer science from the University of California at Berkeley.

Gary Vilchick, Chief Financial Officer

Gary Vilchick brings more than twenty-five years of experience in corporate finance and management to Endeca. Prior to joining Endeca, Vilchick was executive vice president and CFO of Spyglass, Inc., the company well known for commercializing Mosaic, the browser that launched the Internet revolution and became the technical foundation for Microsoft's Internet Explorer. During his five years as an executive at a public Internet company, Vilchick grew the company and led it through the announced $2.5 billion merger with OpenTV. He has also held senior level positions with Pitney Bowes, GK Technologies/Penn Central Corporation, and Rainess & Company.

Vilchick is a certified public accountant and holds a BS in accounting and finance from the University of Rhode Island.

(Continues)

In November 2000, the company shipped its first production system, a mutual fund evaluator, to a large asset management company. Installation took a few weeks, as the product required some customization to run across the installed databases. Even though it handled a small (5,000 records) database, the package provided immediate benefits to the users and showed that the basic technology worked and could be implemented at a customer's site without excessive cost.

EXHIBIT 18.4 (CONTINUED)

ENDECA'S MANAGEMENT TEAM AS OF AUGUST 2001

Chris Reisig, VP of Sales

Chris Reisig brings over ten years of sales and operations experience to Endeca. Reisig most recently worked for Mirror Image Internet, where he served as vice president of international sales and operations, expanding the company's international sales and operations organization in just one year. Prior to Mirror Image, Reisig held the positions of divisional vice president of European major accounts and divisional vice president of Asia Pacific sales and operations at Parametric Technology Corporation, where he managed a sales and support organization of more than 400 people and combined annual revenues in excess of $300 million.

Chris holds a BA in English from St. Bonaventure University.

Steve Sayre, VP of Marketing and Business Development

Steve Sayre brings nearly twenty years of software industry marketing experience and expertise to Endeca. As senior vice president of worldwide marketing at Lotus Development, a wholly owned subsidiary of IBM, Sayre had a key role in the growth of Lotus Notes from half a million to over 50 million users. While at Lotus, he was named to IBM's senior management group. Sayre has also held marketing and management positions at General Electric, Cullinet Software, and Easel Corporation, which he helped lead to a successful IPO.

Sayre holds a MBA from University of Pennsylvania's Wharton School of Business and a BA and MA from Tufts University.

Mark Watkins, VP of Software Development

Mark Watkins brings over fifteen years of executive level experience managing growth in both start-up development groups and multinational engineering organizations. Prior to joining Endeca, Watkins was vice president at Parametric Technology Corporation, where he was responsible for a multinational development team delivering Web-based enterprise applications. Mark has also held senior positions at Evans & Sutherland Computer Corporation and is a seasoned technical advisor on matters pertaining to mergers and acquisitions.

Watkins holds an MS in mathematics from the University of Utah and a BA in mathematics from the College of William & Mary.

Source: Endeca.

PREPARING FOR THE C ROUND

Although Papa was stretching his money, he knew he would have to raise more. As he said:

> With the slowdown in Enterprise IT spending, we realized in early 2001 that we'd have to go back in the market. We started talking with a number of possible strategic partners and potential investors on an informal basis. My board—Steve [Walske] and Hardy [Smith]—was very supportive of the effort, even though we had cash through October.

Walske observed, "The environment was bad and getting worse. Trying to get ahead of a slide like that is like trying to catch a falling knife. In an up market, your idea of a company's valuation is likely to lag the market; in a down market, it's easy to overprice."

Smith was more optimistic:

> I've been through bad cycles before. Even though the market was down, this was a good company. It was executing, it had a product that worked and was deployed at a marquee customer already, and everyone we talked to wanted to be our partner—that's how big the hole was in the market. There

may not always be money in the market for everyone, but there's got to be money out there for good firms.

The financing environment for software firms had reached its peak in the first half of 2000, when almost $10 billion was invested in close to 800 companies. By the time Papa and his board were trying to set a price for the C round, both the number of transactions and the amounts invested had been falling steadily for three quarters (refer to Exhibit 18.2). The NASDAQ was 60 percent off its March 2000 high, and experts were concerned about the economy falling into a mild recession.

At the same time, though, the behavior of both venture capitalists and the technology market was hard to forecast. Venture capital firms had raised unprecedented sums in 1999 and 2000, with a number of top-tier firms closing billion-dollar funds (see Exhibit 18.5 for venture funds raised). Although venture investment was down, the firms would have to put this money to work at some point. As Papa said, "All these venture capitalists were sitting on piles of money and getting a management fee for it. How do you justify a management fee if you're not doing anything?"

Spending on technology was another area of uncertainty. Since 1992, technology spending had increased at rates at least twice that of inflation, and, in a number of years, 15 percent to 20 percent (see Exhibit 18.6). Papa explained, "It seemed pretty likely that we could count on continued spending at the previous rate, although no increase."

At the meeting in February 2001, Walske and Papa asked Smith what BVP would contribute to the C round. Smith asked, "At what price?" Papa described the situation:

> By that time, I'd faced the fact that no one was going to give me a $200 million valuation. Even with a product installed at a major financial firm, with firms like AOL, Putnam, Tower Records, and Dana Farber considering our software for everything from customer relationship management to cancer research, I wasn't going to get $200 million pre. So I was looking to my board to give me an idea of the price we should take out in the market.

Smith drew a graph on the whiteboard in the conference room (see Table 18A).

EXHIBIT 18.5

VENTURE FUNDS RAISED 1997–2Q 2001

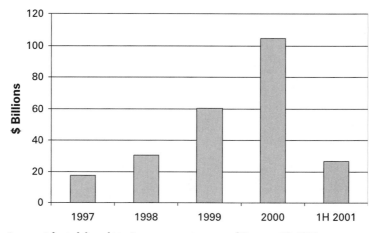

Source: Adapted from http://www.nvca.org, accessed January 25, 2002.

EXHIBIT 18.6

TECHNOLOGY SPENDING 1992–2000

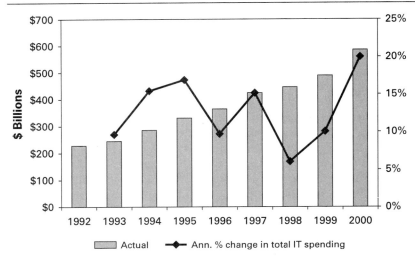

Source: Adapted from Bruce Tempkin et al., "Tech Recovery in 2003: A Different Beast," *The Forrester Brief* (October 24, 2001).

TABLE 18A

BVP'S CONTRIBUTION RELATIVE TO PRICE OF ROUND

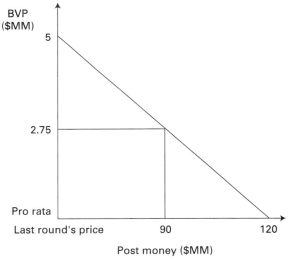

Source: Casewriter.

He explained, "It comes down to this. Assuming that we're raising $10 million, if the post-money is going to be $120 million, BVP will do pro rata but not more. At the last round's price, we'd put in $5 million, well above pro rata. It's a continuum—at $90 million, we'd put in an additional $2.75 million."

WHAT IF YOU GIVE A ROUND AND NOBODY COMES?

Papa, with his board's agreement, decided to go into the market at an $80 million pre-money valuation, looking for $10 million. The B round had closed at $35 million, so this was, as Papa said, "a nice step-up but one that was justified by the progress we had made." Smith felt that it was a good starting point.

Venrock's initial response, though, was not encouraging. When offered the chance to participate in a $10 million round at $80 million pre-money, Tyrrell demurred:

> We liked the company, and we thought Steve [Papa] was doing all the right things—he had assembled a great team, the product offering was quite differentiated and it had real traction with customers. But my partners and I had turned down many similar-stage West Coast deals because of valuation in this market and we had to be consistent here. We'd certainly participate up to our pro rata to be supportive—but for anything more than that, the valuation had to be in line with current market conditions.

"That meant," continued Papa, "that we were in the market seeking $6 million or $7 million with a $3 million to $4 million commitment from our insiders. We figured that the strategic investors were a good option."

The strategic investors to which Papa referred were also potential customers for Endeca's software. They included AOL/Time Warner, Morgan Stanley, and DSGCP, among others. The sales cycle for enterprise software usually lasted two or three months, and the economic uncertainty in the first half of 2001 had stretched it even further. As these firms had been evaluating Endeca's software for several months, they were well acquainted with the company.

Some of these prospective customers already had been actively considering an investment in Endeca. One of them had wanted warrants in exchange for signing up as an early customer. Several were quite far along in the sales process with Endeca. "What it came down to," said Walske, "was that everyone loved the idea of the product, and the fact that it really did what it said it would, but with all of the uncertainty in the capital markets, no one wanted to invest at that price."

Papa also pursued financial investors: "By this time we knew we were pushing the market on price. We knew we had a good company, though, so we went to some of the sector-specific venture capitalists, like Sweden's Investor AB [now Investor Growth Capital], RRE, Capital One's North Hill, and E°Trade Capital."

Most of these were interested enough in the deal to begin due diligence. Investor AB was especially intrigued and did serious research on the company. Another firm that looked at the deal in June was Ampersand Ventures, a Massachusetts-based group with a highly diversified portfolio that had recently increased its allocation to information technology (IT). Endeca did not entirely fit Ampersand's typical style: it preferred to be the first institutional investor in a company, and Endeca's database/infrastructure market also did not match Ampersand's IT target. Nonetheless, Ampersand had long-standing connections with

Endeca through its management team—Walske had worked at Ampersand in the early 1980s and eventually joined its advisory board; Jim Baum, Endeca's president, was being recruited to the board of directors of one of its portfolio companies; and Marc Dulude, an Ampersand operating partner, was a personal investor in Endeca and had previously worked with Baum. On the basis of those relationships, Charlie Yie and Stuart Auerbach of Ampersand visited Endeca. Yie said:

> We really liked the looks of the management team, but we had the sense that the price was too high relative to current market and the profile of the situation just didn't fit our sweet spot. Since they didn't have a financing in hand yet, we told them to keep talking to us, but not to make us a priority.

In the end, the strategics were willing to invest in support of the product, but they could not supply the amount of money required. Many confessed that they had their hands full with challenges from their own internal VC units. None of the financial investors was interested. "We had a resounding 'no' on the basis of price from the financial players," said Smith.

By the end of June 2001, Papa said:

> I had thrown the $90 million post out the window and was offering the company at $60 million. We were still looking for $10 million. Then it was like walking down a rotted staircase—first 90, then 60, and suddenly we were talking "$40 million to $60 million." And there were still no takers.

In early July, Papa had an indication from AOL Time Warner that the company would put in $2 million if Endeca had an outsider-led term sheet. "I was ecstatic," said Papa. "After all, AOL had been a great early customer reference for Inktomi; I had no doubt that they would be equally helpful for Endeca." AOL's insistence upon an outsider-led term sheet stemmed from its experience in leading rounds for start-ups. After a few situations where the valuation had turned out to be aggressive, AOL's management had stipulated that its internal venture group should only participate in market-based deals led by outsiders.

Smith was in London when Papa relayed the news. "The first thing I did," he said,

> was call Lehman Brothers. I told them that we had AOL and we needed an outside term sheet. With $2 million from Lehman and AOL, and $4 million from the insiders, we could get the round done.

Smith also called RRE, which had turned down the deal earlier due to the price. Papa called DSGCP. "We were motivated," admitted Smith. "We wanted a term sheet, any term sheet, at any price."

No one sent a term sheet. DSGCP and RRE both said that they thought the market for the company, given its revenues, was roughly $25 million pre-money. DSGCP had earlier made a verbal offer of $20 million, based on very financially oriented later-stage analysis, rather than an early stage option-based approach.

Finally, Smith explained, "I called Bruns Grayson at ABS Ventures [the venture arm of Alex Brown] and told him we had AOL lined up." Papa, meanwhile, called 5Paces Venture Capital, a new firm in Atlanta, Georgia. Both were extremely interested.

"At last," said Smith, "we had traction. ABS understood the deal and showed enthusiasm. Walske and I both knew the main investors, Bruns Greyson and Bill Burgess, because they had been the investment bankers for Parametric's IPO some years earlier."

A TERM SHEET AT LAST

At the beginning of August, ABS made an offer at just under $18 million pre-money, pricing the company at less than its Series A value (70¢ per share, as opposed to the A round's 76¢ per share and $1.47 in the B round).[1] In addition, the new investors insisted on halving the burn rate and implementing a go-slow strategy. Papa said, "This gave us all some real concerns. In addition to avoiding the devastation to morale with a potential headcount reduction, we also wanted to ensure that the employees' stock options retained significant value after all the hard work they had done to get us where we were."

As it became clear that the deal would be less than $1.47 per share, Smith opened the subject of antidilution measures. Antidilution terms required the company to issue make-up shares or adjust a conversion price downward for existing investors if the company sold shares at a lower price later. The B round investors had "Weighted Average Antidilution," which was based on a formula that took into account the size of the new round and the difference in the new and the old prices.[2] "Full ratchet" antidilution, the alternate method, meant that the company had to grant enough shares to make the previous higher-priced round equal to the lower-priced current round.[3] The ABS term sheet would give the C round investors a lower cost basis than that of the insiders and trigger the antidilution clause in the term sheet.

Smith wanted to protect Bessemer's interests with a full ratchet, and Papa could see his point:

> What it came down to was fairness. Smith had put a ton of time into this company, he'd been a mentor to me, and I could see his reasons for wanting to change the antidilution on the B round to full ratchet. It was looking like the price of BVP's participation, which was going to be important if we were to get the deal done.

Smith elaborated:

> My partners and I love this company and have been committed to backing it from the beginning. But the hard truth was—as my partners pointed out—that the market was driving the price and our strong participation would be key to getting the round done. We had seen similar situations on several West Coast deals and, as a firm, decided we would only participate in such deals if we received full antidilution protection.

1. Just before the term sheet for the C financing round arrived, the common pool was increased by 1.5 million shares, bringing the total number of shares to 25.38 million.

2. For example, a venture capitalist who had bought 1 million shares of a $4 million round at $2 per share with weighted average antidilution protection would receive roughly an additional 20 percent (approximately 200,000 shares) if the company later raised $8 million at $1.50. The calculation for the effective price per share would be: [(total money in last round × price per share in last round) + (total money in current round × price per share of current round)] ÷ (money in both rounds), or [($4,000,000 × $2) + ($8,000,000 × $1.50)] ÷ ($4,000,000 + $8,000,000), or $1.67 as the weighted average price, which would then be applied to the shares purchased in the previous round. The venture capitalist would end up with 1,197,605 shares, rather than the 1 million held originally.

3. With full ratchet antidilution protection, our same venture capitalist who had bought 1 million shares at $2 per share would have the right to an additional free 333,333 shares if the company sold shares at $1.50/share [((2.00 ÷ 1.50) − 1) × 1,000,000] in the future. The venture capitalist would then have 1.33 million shares, just as if the $2 million had been invested at the new price of $1.50 per share.

Renegotiating terms from a previous deal was not unheard of, especially in a changing market. In the past, with a rising market, accepted term sheets could be trumped; the same could happen as the market moved in the opposite direction. Smith pointed out, "Our B round term sheet was renegotiated when the other group submitted theirs!"

In a phone conversation during the weekend of August 11, Smith and Tyrrell observed that a full ratchet and the $25 million pre-money valuation would allow Venrock to increase its position substantially, receiving ownership commensurate to the value it had added. It would also ensure that the team's current operating plan continued and kept the value of the employees' stock options significant. The two venture capitalists decided to offer an inside round at 98.5¢ per share, which turned out to be roughly $25 million pre-money. They would share the $10 million, with Venrock taking more to increase its ownership, and leave the round open for another $5 million, getting the deal done at $15 million with an option to close as high as $18 million. They had the term sheet on Papa's desk on Monday, August 13.

Papa turned down the ABS deal and agreed to take the Venrock/BVP offer to the board. Everyone agreed to show the last $5 million to the financial and strategic investors that had turned it down at higher prices, leaving $3 million for AOL Time Warner should it choose to participate. The most interested prospect was DSGCP, which was already evaluating Endeca's software. At $25 million, it was interested enough to request the entire $5 million but still needed approval from its investment board.

During the negotiations with DSGCP, Papa realized that the ratchets had created a problem—even though the pre-money valuation was roughly $25 million, the effect of the full ratchets for the series B investors made the price to an outsider effectively $28 million (see Exhibit 18.7 for prices of other deals in the sector). He explained:

> I was showing the documents to DSGCP and they were OK with $25 million, although they really preferred $20. And then they saw the number at the top— 'Hey, what's this $28 million?' and I had to explain about the ratchets and that $25 million was the pre-ratchet pre-money. I was afraid we would lose them on this, and I really wanted them in the deal. I thought their combination of financial expertise and experience as a customer would be very helpful.

Papa also continued to talk to other investors who had seen the deal, including Ampersand. On Tuesday, August 14, with the Venrock/BVP deal on his desk, Papa had a long-delayed meeting with the partners at Ampersand. Yie said:

> All the partners were very impressed with Endeca. It didn't quite fit our screen, but it had good people and the potential for a big market. When Steve [Papa] said he had a term sheet, the time had come for Ampersand to make its move or not.

Smith, Tyrrell, and Papa all had indicated that, given the choice, it was better for the company to have strategic investors in the deal, not another financial player. "I had no track record with Ampersand," said Papa. "We had a tight time frame, they didn't know me and I didn't know them. I really didn't want to scare them off, even though we could only get them in the deal if DSGCP decided not to participate."

On Wednesday, Yie spoke separately with both Smith and Tyrrell, learning the deal's details. He then spoke with Papa. "Initially," Yie explained, "we suggested that we could match the Venrock/BVP deal."

Papa said:

> Basically, I had to tell Ampersand that we could only make room for them if, by the day of the board meeting, they gave us a term sheet that offered

EXHIBIT 18.7

SAMPLE FINANCING HISTORIES OF DATABASE SOFTWARE COMPANIES

Name	Round	Stage of Development at Round	Close Date	$ Millions Raised	Post-Money Value ($ Millions)
Avaki	1	Product in Beta Test	Feb. '01	16.0	25.0
Callidus Software	Seed	Product development	Feb. '97	1.0	2.7
	1	Shipping product	Jan. '98	4.0	13.0
	2	Product in Beta Test	July '98	5.8	26.0
	3	Shipping product	Feb. '99	12.0	55.1
	4	Shipping product	Nov. '99	13.6	133.6
	5	Shipping product	March '01	40.0	100.0
ClearForest	Seed	Startup	Aug. '98	1.0	NK
	1	Shipping product	Dec. '99	7.8	25.0
	2	Shipping product	Feb. '01	14.0	48.5
Entopia	Seed	Startup	Sep. '99	1.3	3.0
	1	Product development	Jan. '00	1.3	NK
	2	Product development	Sep. '00	18.0	48.0
High Tower Software	1	Product development	July '98	1.9	4.0
	2	Shipping product	Sep. '00	10.9	25.0
infoShark	1	Shipping product	March '98	2.0	NK
	2	Shipping product	July '99	4.5	14.0
	3	Shipping product	Feb. '01	6.0	25.0
Ipedo	Seed	Product development	June '00	1.0	NK
	1	Shipping product	Feb. '01	7.0	20.0
Kanisa	1	Product development	Feb. '99	10.3	22.0
	Corporate	Shipping product	March '00	15.0	90.0
	2	Shipping product	June '00	18.0	168.0
	3	Shipping product	Aug. '01	30.1	NK
LexiQuest	1	Shipping product	Jan. '97	6.0	NK
	2	Shipping product	Aug. '98	4.0	NK
	3	Shipping product	Feb. '99	15.0	35.0
	4	Shipping product	June '00	25.0	94.8
Modulant	1	Shipping product	Feb. '01	15.5	26.0
Neartek	1	Shipping product	Oct. '99	21.0	NK
	2	Shipping product	Feb. '01	26.0	86.0
NOCpulse	1	Product development	April '00	12.0	24.0
	2	Shipping product	July '01	8.1	32.1
OuterBay Technologies	1	Shipping product	Aug. '01	19.0	31.0
Phonetic Systems	1	Shipping product	Feb. '99	1.2	NK
	2	Shipping product	Dec. '99	7.0	NK
	3	Shipping product	Dec. '00	37.5	110.0

(Continues)

EXHIBIT 18.7 (CONTINUED)

SAMPLE FINANCING HISTORIES OF DATABASE SOFTWARE COMPANIES

Name	Round	Stage of Development at Round	Close Date	$ MMs Raised	Post-Money Value ($ MMs)
PointBase	1	Product in Beta Test	Feb. '99	3.6	NK
	2	Shipping product	Sep. '99	7.0	NK
	3	Shipping product	Aug. '00	25.0	100.0
QUIQ	Seed	Shipping product	Sep. '99	0.3	NK
	1	Shipping product	Sep. '99	3.0	10.0
	2	Shipping product	Aug. '00	15.0	46.0
Radik Software	1	Product development	March '00	2.0	11.0
	2	Product development	Dec. '00	11.5	33.5
Simile Software	Seed	Shipping product	Jan. '99	3.3	NK
	1	Shipping product	June '00	17.0	45.2
	2	Shipping product	Open°	3.0	NK
Softface	1	Product development	Dec. '99	1.5	6.3
	2	Shipping product	March '01	6.0	14.7
	3	Shipping product	Open°	10.4	30.5
Torrent Systems	Seed	Startup	Nov. '94	0.6	2.8
	1	Product development	June '96	3.2	10.2
	2	Product development	April '97	1.5	17.5
	3	Shipping product	Dec. '97	5.3	19.8
	4	Shipping product	March '01	12.0	39.7
Verilytics	1	Shipping product	Nov. '00	26.0	140.0
Vyant Technologies	1	Product development	March '00	6.0	15.0
	2	Shipping product	Dec. '00	30.0	92.0
WhizBang! Labs	3	Shipping product	April '00	20.0	120.0
Xythos Software	1	Shipping product	Jan. '01	6.2	20.2

Source: Adapted from http://www.venturesource.com, accessed April 30, 2003. Companies are a sample of those defined as "Database Software," the sector that includes Endeca.

Note: ° Company was in the market but had not yet closed the round at the time of the case. NK = Not known.

---

to lead an alternate deal at a significantly higher price. Otherwise, it would be unfair to the insiders who had been extremely supportive throughout the entire process.

Yie commented:

I thought we had come a long way as a partnership when we decided to match the Venrock/BVP term sheet—after all, Endeca's fit was marginal from a profile standpoint. But learning that we needed to come up with something higher became the critical test of our interest in the deal because we thought that the Venrock/BVP term sheet fully valued the company. This clearly gave us pause but after some intense discussion among ourselves we decided to come up with a higher offer. Once we made this decision, we fast-tracked the due diligence. Reaching this conclusion was much easier because we'd known Steve [Walske] for so long—when he vouched for Papa and Reisig, the information was coming from a trusted source. Furthermore, we had also had an opportunity to get to know Jim Baum well over the previous year and thought very highly of his management skills.

On August 16, Yie and Auerbach started the due diligence.

Papa felt that the Venrock/BVP deal had some advantages, observing, "It was a good deal, given the unrelenting erosion of the markets. I felt it would cement the relationship with DSGCP, which was really important, and maintain a board and investor lineup that had been extremely effective." Investor counsel, managed by Smith, was already drafting the closing papers. Late on Wednesday, August 29, Yie submitted a term sheet offering to lead the round with $8 million at $1.25 per share and full ratchet protection for the Series B investors. The effective pre-money, with ratchets, was $32.9 million. Papa said:

> At that price, I knew that DSGCP and maybe even Venrock would have trouble. This was a real dilemma—I felt extremely uncomfortable going back to DSGCP with yet another higher valuation, and Venrock had really supported us when we needed it. Mike [Tyrrell] had stepped up to the plate to get this round done, and I didn't know how Venrock would react. It was great to get the price, but was it going to be worth the cost?

Nonetheless, the offer was a substantial step up, and he had to consider it:

> Then the phone lines heated up. Since it was August, of course I couldn't easily get in touch with Mike [Tyrrell] or Hardy [Smith]. I finally tracked down Mike on Thursday and asked if Venrock would participate in the higher deal. He said he'd have to talk with his partners. I didn't get Hardy until Friday, but when I asked him the same thing, he said that Bessemer would participate in either one.

To get up to speed, Ampersand also wanted to delay closing by a week, from September 7 to September 14. "Our cash balances weren't where I wanted them to be and I really didn't want to delay this any further," said Papa. "But what can happen in a week?"

THE MEETING

As the board meeting began, Papa looked again at the two term sheets (see Exhibit 18.8) and the resulting capitalization (see Exhibit 18.9). The $18 million was twice as much as he had estimated the company needed to break even, but with the market uncertainty extending the sales cycle, he wanted to be sure. He had to admit he was worried. If he turned down the Venrock/BVP offer and then the Ampersand deal fell through before closing, he could not be sure of lining up a third deal before the fume date (see Exhibit 18.10 for the timeline). The Venrock/BVP deal was a sure thing, with DSGCP very likely to come along. Ampersand added a huge amount of uncertainty to the situation. He knew that Vilchick, the CFO, and Sayre in Marketing just wanted to close on the money, on time. Papa and Baum also wanted to get back to business and put the distraction of raising money behind them. And yet the Ampersand deal would give his employees the morale boost of having escaped a down round, and he knew that in the venture business, you were only as good as your last round. Which deal should he recommend?

EXHIBIT 18.8

HISTORICAL DATA ON THE TWO FINANCING ROUNDS AND THE TWO OPTIONS FOR ROUND C

(All numbers in millions)	Post–Series A		Post–Series B		Post-Series C—Venrock/BVP deal		Post-Series C—Ampersand deal	
	Total $ Invested	Cum. Shares	Total $ Invested	Cum. Shares	$ Invested in round	Cum. Shares	$ Invested in round	Cum. Shares
BVP	0.65	0.86	5.60	4.67	5.00	—	3.50	—
Venrock	—	—	2.10	1.43	5.00	—	6.50	—
Ampersand	—	—	—	—	—	—	8.00	—
Others	1.15	1.51	0.40	1.79	8.00	—	——	—
Total Mgmt. Pool°	—	16.00	—	16.00	—	17.50	—	17.50
Total	**1.80**	**18.37**	**8.10**	**23.88**	**18.00**	—	**18.00**	—
(shares post-addition)†	—	—	—	25.38	—	—	—	—
Post-Money	$13.96	—	$35.10	—	—	—	—	—

Source: Endeca.

Notes:

° Total Management Pool includes all common shares, and awarded and unawarded options.

† Just before the term sheet for the C financing round arrived, 1.5 million shares were added to the common pool.

EXHIBIT 18.9

THE TWO TERM SHEETS, ABRIDGED

Item	Venrock/BVP Term Sheet	Ampersand Ventures Term Sheet
Amount and Security	Up to $18,000,000 in Series C Convertible Preferred Stock (the "Series C," together with Endeca's Series A Convertible Preferred Stock, the "Series A," and Series B Convertible Preferred Stock, the "Series B," the "Preferred") Minimum closing: $10,000,000. Later closings allowable for up to sixty days from initial closing.	$18 million for Series C Convertible Preferred Stock (the "Series C Stock"), at a purchase price of $1.25 per share, convertible into shares of Common Stock of the Company.
Purchasers		The investment will be made by the following entities or their affiliates (the "Purchasers") in the amounts indicated: —Ampersand Ventures: $8M —Current Investors: $10M —Total: $18M
Price	The Series C will be sold at $0.985 per share. Each share of Series C converts into one share of common stock (subject to antidilution adjustment and stock splits) at the holders' option.	
Redemption	The Preferred shall be redeemed in equal quarterly installments from January 1, 2008, through December 31, 2010. *NB: Series B will be modified to conform to Series C mandatory redemption.*	Each holder of Series C Stock may elect, at such holder's option, to have the Company redeem up to a maximum of 33.3 percent, 50.0 percent, and 100 percent of the outstanding shares of Series C Stock held by such holder on each of the fifth, sixth, and seventh anniversary dates, respectively, of the Closing, at a price of $1.25 per share, plus any accrued but unpaid dividends. If any shares are eligible for redemption in one year and the holder of Series C Stock chooses not to have such shares redeemed in that year, he may elect to have them redeemed in a later year, provided that such election must be made not later than the seventh anniversary of the Closing.
Voting Rights	The Preferred votes as if converted.	On all matters submitted to a vote of holders of Common Stock generally, holders of Series C Stock shall be entitled to exercise a number of votes equal to the number of shares of Common Stock into which shares of Series C Stock then held by such holder are convertible on the appropriate record date. Holders of the Series A, Series B, and Series C Preferred Stock (together, the "Preferred Stock") shall vote with holders of Common Stock as a single class on all matters submitted to a vote of the Common Stockholders.

(Continues)

EXHIBIT 18.9 (CONTINUED)

THE TWO TERM SHEETS, ABRIDGED

Item	Venrock/BVP Term Sheet	Ampersand Ventures Term Sheet
Liquidation Preference	The Series C has a liquidation preference equal to its original purchase price, payable upon a merger, sale, or liquidation of Endeca. *NB: Series A and B will be modified so that the Series C ranks on parity with the Series A and Series B.*	In the event of any liquidation, dissolution or winding up of the Company, the holders of Series C Stock shall receive an amount per share of Series C Stock equal to its purchase price, plus any accrued but unpaid dividends, before any payments to holders of the Series A, Series B, Common Stock or other capital stock of the Company. If the assets of the Company available for distribution upon liquidation are not sufficient to pay to each holder of Series C Stock $1.25 per share plus any accrued but unpaid dividends, such assets shall be distributed pro rata among the holders of the Series C Preferred Stock on the basis of the number of shares held by each holder thereof. The merger or consolidation of the Company into or with another corporation or the sale of all or substantially all of the Company's assets shall be deemed to be a liquidation of the Company unless the holders of 60 percent of the shares of the Series C Preferred Stock then outstanding elect otherwise by giving written notice thereof to the Company at least fifteen days before the effective date of such event.
Mandatory Conversion	The Series C must convert to common stock upon consummation of an underwritten public offering of at least $10,000,000 at a price of at least ___/share (split adjusted). *NB: Series A and Series B will be modified to conform with Series C on mandatory conversion.*	Each share of Series C Stock will be convertible, at any time, at the option of the holder, into shares of Common Stock, at a conversion price of $___ per share (subject to adjustment as described below), plus the payment of all accrued but unpaid dividends. The Company may require the conversion of all (but not less than all) of the Series C Stock in the event of a firm commitment underwritten public offering of Common Stock of the Company at a price which equals or exceeds $___ per share in which the net proceeds received by the Company equal or exceed $___ million.
Antidilution	Broad weighted average protection (i.e.: adjustment to conversion price) for issuance of shares at a price below the Series C common equivalent share price (except to employees *or* under a Board approved stock incentive plan) in a financing of at least $200,000 for the holders of Series C on a common equivalent basis in future offerings only if investor participates pro rata to common equivalent position.	The Series C shareholders shall be entitled to full ratchet anti-dilution protection only if that shareholder participates pro-rata to their common equivalent position in that financing. The conversion price and the number of shares of Common Stock into which shares of Series C Stock are convertible shall also be appropriately adjusted to reflect stock splits, stock dividends, reorganizations, reclassifications, consolidations, mergers or

(Continues)

EXHIBIT 18.9 (CONTINUED)

THE TWO TERM SHEETS, ABRIDGED

Item	Venrock/BVP Term Sheet	Ampersand Ventures Term Sheet
Antidilution *(Continued)*	Existing Series B will be price adjusted to convert at \$.985/share and will be modified to have weighted average anti-dilution identical to Series C.	sales and similar events. There will be no adjustment in the conversion price upon the issuance of up to _____ shares of Common Stock (or options to acquire such shares) to employees of the Company under the Company's Incentive Stock Plan. Concurrent with this financing, the conversion price of the Series B Stock will be adjusted to the Series C share price of \$1.25 per share.
Negative Covenants (Venrock/BVP) **Covenants and Restrictions (Ampersand Ventures)**	The approval of 66 percent of face value of the Preferred is required for the following (i) organic changes outside the normal course of business, (ii) the sale, liquidation or merger of Endeca, (iii) any increase in Board seats or a change in election procedures, or (iv) the issuance of any equity security senior to Series C.	The Purchase Agreement for the Series C Stock will contain customary covenants and restrictions and will specify certain actions which may be taken by the Company only with the consent of the holders of 60 percent of the outstanding shares of Preferred Stock (except that altering, changing or amending the preferences or rights of any individual series of preferred stock will require the consent of 60 percent of the outstanding shares of that series) including, without limitation: authorizing, creating or issuing any debt or equity securities (except for the issuance of shares (or options to purchase the same) reserved for issuance to employees of the Company); merging with or acquiring another entity or selling substantially all of the assets of the Company; paying dividends on or making other distributions with respect to any securities other than the Preferred Stock; engaging in any business other than the business engaged in by the Company at the time of the Closing or described in the Business Plan or otherwise making any substantial deviation from the business strategy contained in the Business Plan; increasing or decreasing the number of directors constituting the Board of Directors; repurchasing or redeeming any securities, except for repurchases under restricted stock agreements with employees previously approved by the Board of Directors; transferring, by sale, license or otherwise, any intellectual property rights of the Company.

(Continues)

EXHIBIT 18.9 (CONTINUED)

THE TWO TERM SHEETS, ABRIDGED

Item	Venrock/BVP Term Sheet	Ampersand Ventures Term Sheet
Representations and Warranties	Standard.	The Company will make representations and warranties in the Stock Purchase Agreement customary in transactions of this kind including, without limitation, representations regarding due incorporation, qualification and standing, charter documents and by-laws, corporate power, enforceability of the Stock Purchase Agreement and related agreements, subsidiaries, capitalization, authorization, due issuance, use of proceeds, litigation, contracts and commitments (including contracts between key employees and prior employers), financial statements, subsequent developments, title to assets, proprietary information and environmental matters.
Financial Statements	Annual audit by a nationally recognized firm plus monthly actual versus plan and prior year, plus annual budget sixty days before beginning of fiscal year to holders of more than 3,000,000 split-adjusted shares. All recipients of financial statements must execute nondisclosure agreement acceptable to Endeca's counsel.	The Company will submit unaudited financial statements to holders of at least 3,000,000 shares of Preferred Stock not later than sixty days after the close of each fiscal quarter and not later than thirty days after the end of each month. including income statements, balance sheets, cash flow statements, summaries of bookings and backlogs, and comparisons to forecasts and to corresponding periods in prior years. Audited annual financial statements shall be provided not later than ninety days after the end of each year. Not later than thirty days after the start of each fiscal year, the Company shall provide an annual Operating Plan prepared on a monthly basis and, promptly after preparation, any revisions to such Operating Plan. The Company will promptly provide other customary information and materials, including, without limitation, reports of adverse developments, management letters, communications with stockholders or directors, press releases and registration statements.
Registration Rights	Pooled with Series A and B. Two (2) demand registrations, subject to $5 million *and* 100,000 share trigger, unlimited piggybacks, and evergreen S-3 if requested and possible. All of the above shall be at Endeca's expense.	1. The holders of the Series C Preferred Stock shall be entitled to two demand registrations on Form S-1 or S-2, or any successor forms, at the Company's expense, exercisable upon request of holders of not less than 50 percent of the outstanding Series C Preferred Stock. A registration will not count for this purpose (i) unless it becomes effective and holders are able to sell at least 50 percent of the shares sought

(Continues)

EXHIBIT 18.9 (CONTINUED)

THE TWO TERM SHEETS, ABRIDGED

Item	Venrock/BVP Term Sheet	Ampersand Ventures Term Sheet
Registration Rights (*Continued*)		to be included in the registration, or (ii) if the Company elects to sell stock pursuant to a registration statement at the same time. There will be no piggybacking on such registrations without the consent of the participating Preferred Stock stockholders. 2. The holders of the Series C Preferred Stock shall be entitled to unlimited registrations on Form S-3, or any successor form. 3. The holders of the Series C Preferred Stock shall have unlimited piggyback registration rights at the Company's expense, with priority over all other selling stockholders. 4. The Company shall not grant registration rights to any other party without the consent of 60 percent of the holders of the Series C Preferred Stock.
Dividends		Dividends shall accrue on each share of Series C Preferred Stock when and as declared by the Company's Board of Directors, and shall be payable before the payment of any dividends with respect to any other Series of Preferred or Common Stock and in the event of a liquidation, dissolution or winding up of the Company.
Options and Vesting	Additional pool for future employees of _____ shares set aside with vesting of four years straight line with a one-year blackout. Endeca will have a right of first refusal on all employee shares vested prior to a public offering. Employees may transfer shares to immediate family, trusts, and the like.	
Employee Agreements	Proprietary Information Agreements must be obtained from all employees and Non-Compete Agreements must be obtained from all key employees. The agreements must be in a form satisfactory to the Board.	The Founders and Key Management of the Company shall enter into agreements in a form satisfactory to the Purchasers, (i) not to compete with the Company and (ii) not to induce, directly or indirectly, employees of the Company to terminate their employment with the Company, during the term of their employment and for a period after termination of their employment. All employees and consultants of the Company shall execute standard nondisclosure and assignment of inventions agreements with the Company in form satisfactory to the Purchasers.
Closing	ASAP subject only to completion of definitive legal documents acceptable to all parties.	On or before September 14, 2001. The Stock Purchase Agreement will contain customary closing conditions, including satisfactory completion of legal due diligence review.

Source: Endeca.

EXHIBIT 18.10

TIMELINE

Date	Event
3/01	Set price of $80 million pre-money.
5/01	Price falls to $60 million pre-money.
5/15/01	Price falls to $40 million to $60 million pre-money.
6/01	DSGCP makes verbal offer at $20 million pre-money.
7/1/01	AOL expresses interest in investing $2 million if an outsider leads the deal.
7/12/01	ABS makes contact.
8/1/01	ABS submits term sheet at 70¢ per share.
8/13/01	Venrock/BVP deal submitted to Papa, $25 million pre-money ($28 million including ratchets).
8/14/01	Endeca management presents to Ampersand team.
8/15/01	Ampersand expresses "strong interest."
8/16/01	Ampersand begins due diligence.
8/20/01	BVP begins legal process for closing.
8/29/01	Ampersand's term sheet arrives at $32.9 million pre-money ($1.25 per share).
9/4/01	Endeca's board meets.

Source: Endeca.

19

Chengwei Ventures and the hdt* Investment

On a bright warm day in late October 2001, Bo Feng, partner of Chengwei Ventures, a Chinese venture capital firm, gathered with the management team of hdt° in the thirty-second floor conference room looking out over Shanghai's tiled rooftops to the skyscrapers beyond. Feng had strongly encouraged the creation of hdt°, which had come about through the merger of one of Chengwei's portfolio businesses, T2 Technologies, with iTOM, another venture-backed start-up. He firmly believed in the future of the merged company, even though the integration had taken longer than expected and the group was still trying to decide on a business model. "We don't have forever," he warned the four others in the room.

Chengwei Ventures had been founded in 1999 by Feng and Eric Li. Backed by $60 million from Yale University, Sutter Hill Investments, the University of Michigan, Sandford Robertson (founder of the Robertson Stephens investment bank), and the Power Corporation of Canada, Chengwei was one of the first independent venture capital (VC) funds to operate in China. Global funds, such as Walden, Atlas, Softbank, and AIG, had started branch offices as the market had opened, and government-sponsored funds existed in every province, but Chengwei was rare in its independence. Among venture capitalists, though, its concerns were all too common. Feng explained, "VC is the same everywhere; you have to find good companies and grow them."

T2 Technologies and iTOM were both venture-backed high-tech start-ups founded by the new crop of Asian entrepreneurs. T2, founded by Ji (Jim) Wang, operated on the Doubleclick model, providing database management, customized ad-serving, and performance measurement services to corporate Web sites. iTOM, led by twenty-four-year-old Hao (Jerry) Wang (no relation), had been backed by Hong Kong-based Tom.com, the major Asian Internet portal, and provided Web site design and creative marketing services for such clients as Motorola, Sony, and Intel. They had merged in February 2001.

Senior Research Associate Ann K. Leamon prepared this case under the supervision of Professors G. Felda Hardymon and Josh Lerner. HBS cases are developed solely as the basis for class discussion. Cases are not intended to serve as endorsements, sources of primary data, or illustrations of effective or ineffective management.

Both Jim and Jerry felt the merger made sense, saying, "T2 was scalable but had no customers; iTOM had customers but couldn't scale. So this brought two halves together." Actually making the halves work together had been challenging, but, in Feng's opinion, not unusually so. "We face the same challenges facing any venture capitalist—personnel, management, marketing—in a context that's just coming together."

Choosing the business model had proven tricky. Just after the merger, the company had focused on providing technology-based marketing solutions, such as customer insight, digital content, and relationship data management services, with revenues from stand-alone solution software and consulting projects. Now the team was considering a different approach, providing integrated enterprise-level solutions to help companies enhance their marketing effectiveness. Revenues would come from packaged solutions that covered everything from building the Web site through providing the marketing infrastructure, automation, and applications.

In its current form, the company had reached a 12 million renminbi (RMB) (U.S. $1.45 million) annual run rate. "If we change the model and get it wrong, we've blown up a perfectly good little company," worried Feng silently. "If we can get this right, though, we'll have a powerhouse."

CHINA

The People's Republic of China (PRC), roughly the size of the United States, boasts a civilization at least 5,000 years old. It is organized as thirty-one provinces, taking into account four municipalities with province-level status and five "autonomous regions." Hong Kong and Macao made up two additional "special administrative regions" (see Exhibit 19.1 for map). With 1.3 billion inhabitants in 2001, it was the world's most populous nation, with most of the population crowded in the fertile eastern 20 percent of the country.[1]

Vast disparities existed within the huge nation. In 2000, the PRC had a gross domestic product of $1 trillion (for comparison, GDP of the United States was $10 trillion, Japan's was $4.8 trillion, and Germany's $1.9 trillion).[2] The national average gross domestic product per capita, excluding Hong Kong and Macao, was $735, which made China poorer than Indonesia. On the provincial level, though, the story was very different. GDP per capita ranged from $280 in Guizhou (on a par with Bangladesh) to Shanghai's $3,400 (Turkey or South Africa), and Hong Kong's $22,990, which was above Great Britain.[3] The economy still had strongly rural, with 499 million of the labor force of 712 million living in rural areas. Almost 25 percent of these country-dwellers, however, worked in nonfarm occupations, primarily factories in the provinces.[4] From a Western marketing perspective, then, despite the sheer number of its inhabitants, the real Chinese market was limited to the inhabitants of the major cities, or about 250 million people.[5]

On most developmental measures, China scored better than other East Asian/Pacific countries and even better than other lower-middle income nations. Life expectancy, at seventy years, was higher, as were literacy rates and access to clean water;

1. Dominic Ziegler, "China: Now Comes the Hard Part," *The Economist* (April 6, 2000), http://www.economist.com, accessed September 21, 2001.

2. The Economist Intelligence Unit (hereafter EIU), "EUI Country Profile 2001: China," http://lib.harvard.edu:2713/ report_dl.asp?mode=pdf&valname=CPBCNC, p. 31, accessed April 2, 2002.

3. Ziegler, "China: Now Comes the Hard Part."

4. The EIU, "EUI Country Profile 2001: China," p. 30.

5. Anonymous, "What Would Mao Think?" *The Red Herring* (October 2000), http://www.redherring.com, accessed January 2, 2002.

EXHIBIT 19.1

MAP OF PEOPLE'S REPUBLIC OF CHINA

Source: Casewriter.

infant mortality was lower. China had 65 million cell phones in use by July 2001, 22 million Internet users, and three Internet service providers.[6] The total number of Internet users was probably underestimated, as many accessed the Internet through "Net cafés." By contrast, the United States had 86 million cell phone users[7] and 93 million home Internet users as of August 2000.[8]

China's recent history had been tumultuous. After centuries of imperial rule that kept it closed from the rest of the world, the Kuomintang (KMT) under Sun Yat-sen (and later Chiang Kai-shek) rebelled in 1911. A brief period of instability became war between the U.S.-backed KMT and the Soviet-backed Chinese Communist Party (CCP) led by Mao Zedong. By 1949, the CCP controlled the mainland, having driven the KMT to the island of Taiwan. Mao set up a centrally planned economy, in which all businesses were owned by various levels of government, whether national (state owned enterprises, or SOEs), provincial, or local. After Mao's death in 1976, Deng Xiaoping became the

6. *Ibid.*

7. U.S. Census, http://www.census.gov/statab/www/part3.html#social, accessed January 2, 2002.

8. U.S. Census, http://www.census.gov/prod/2001pubs/p23-207.pdf, accessed January 2, 2002.

new leader and recognized that his nation was stagnating, even as the surrounding Asian tiger economies were charging ahead.[9]

In an impressive balancing act, Deng began to introduce elements of a market economy while maintaining tight political control. His economic reforms liberalized agriculture, allowed private ownership, and encouraged a small degree of foreign investment. If farmers or workers in a factory produced more than the specified quota, they could sell the surplus on the private market. Local governments could establish and invest in small enterprises. Rural incomes soared by 17 percent annually between 1978 and 1985. On the international front, the most significant change occurred in 1980, when foreign direct investment was authorized in four special economic zones. In 1984, fourteen more coastal cities were added to the list, and in 1990, an all-out free-for-all occurred as every city scrambled for foreign investment, regardless of its official designation.[10]

During the 1980s and 1990s, the PRC continued to experiment with free-market reforms. The special zones, and, to a lesser extent, the provinces themselves, could adapt or supersede national laws as they saw fit. If the adaptation, known as a principle, proved successful, the national government might incorporate it into the national laws. In the meantime, a veritable crazy quilt of regulations had evolved, many of which worked at cross-purposes to one another and any of which could be invoked as a bureaucrat felt necessary.[11]

The PRC took another major step in 1990 when the first two stock exchanges opened in Shanghai and Shenzhen, listing about 800 state-owned enterprises (SOEs). Because the government continued to hold roughly 70 percent of their shares, the liquidity on these exchanges was fairly shallow.[12]

In 1997, the business environment in the PRC took another turn toward a market economy. In the 15th Party Congress, leader Jiang Zemin announced further easing of the restrictions on foreign investment. Although greater foreign investment was now allowed, the business environment in China was still a work in progress. Legal institutions, in particular, were embryonic, making contracts sometimes difficult to enforce. Banking institutions were also still developing. Other business regulations, such as the fact that all shares were to have equal power, made the granting of preferred stock difficult. Yet still other challenges had little to do with regulation; for instance, concerted marketing campaigns were unknown, and credit card usage extremely low.[13] Although China had adopted the International Accounting Standards in 1993 for all SOEs, small firms still used what one observer called "shoe-box accounting."

Even in 2001, with its accession to the World Trade Organization (WTO) and the granting of permanent Normal Trade Relations status with the United States, China stood with one foot in the eighteenth century and one in the twenty-first as it made the transition to a market economy. Despite high tech and the Internet, and broadband cables laid in subway tunnels beneath Beijing, personal connections, as embodied in the concept of *guanxi*, were particularly important. These governed Chinese business relationships—one would prefer to do business with a family member, then a friend, then an acquaintance, and only last with a foreigner. This was not nepotism, but a response to the fact that China did not yet have a rules-based economy; transactions were not based on contracts nearly as much as personal agreements that could not be verified or

9. Michael Roberts, "AsiaInfo," *HBS Case No. 800-179*, p. 4.

10. The EUI, "EUI Country Profile 2001: China," p. 15.

11. Ying Liu, John Tan, and Zheng Yin, "New Margin Venture Capital," unpublished MBA paper for Venture Capital and Private Equity, April 30, 2001.

12. Ziegler, "China: Now Comes the Hard Part."

13. CIA, *The World Factbook*, http://www.cia.gov/cia/publications/factbook/geos/ch.html, 2001, accessed January 3, 2003.

enforced through the public sphere. *Guanxi* meant that one did business with people whose background, assets, and status were well known and who could be personally pressured to hold to an agreement. Experts anticipated that the importance of *guanxi* would decline as formal contract law became more established in China.[14]

Venture Capital in China

Private equity arrived in China concurrently with the government's establishment of the Shenzhen Science & Technology Industrial Park in June 1985, but it did not really take off until over a decade later. In 2000, China and Hong Kong together had 32 percent of the capital under management in Asia ($29.3 billion) and 313 funds, or 22 percent of the total.[15] The lion's share of this, however, was Hong Kong's. At the same time, though, the mainland had seen a dramatic growth, albeit from a small base. The number of venture capital firms in China had grown from four in 1996 to 121 in 2000, with new funds raised increasing from $311 million in 1996 to $2.1 billion in 2000. China's total private equity pool was $5.2 billion in 2000, up 39 percent from $3.7 billion the year before, due to China's steady 8 percent growth rate and its accession to the WTO. Major contributors of funds included corporations (of which a large number were SOEs), followed by banks and government agencies (see Exhibit 19.2). In a departure from previous years, only 44 percent of the funds were raised outside China, reflecting the government's renewed commitment to direct investment to nurture the reform process.[16]

The Chinese government initially provided, directly or indirectly, almost all the venture capital funds raised domestically, which was not unusual in Asia—Singapore and Taiwan jump-started their VC industries by either providing funds or directly investing in start-ups. The challenge came from the intellectual environment of VC, which required

---

EXHIBIT 19.2

SOURCES OF VENTURE CAPITAL IN CHINA

Source	% of Total ($5.2 billion)
Corporations°	45%
Banks°	21%
Government Agencies	17%
Insurance Companies	7%
Pension Funds	5%
Private Individuals	4%
Others	1%

Source: Adapted from Asian Venture Capital Association, *The 2002 Guide to Venture Capital in Asia,* 13th ed., (Hong Kong: AVCJ Holdings, October 2001), p. 42.

Note: ° These include state-owned enterprises.

---

14. Ziegler, "China: Now Comes the Hard Part."

15. Asian Venture Capital Association, *The 2002 Guide to Venture Capital in Asia,* 13th ed. (Hong Kong: AVCJ Holdings, October 2001) p. 42.

16. *Ibid.,* p. 43.

ruthless competition where start-ups either succeeded or went bankrupt. In China, bankruptcies were rare and mismanagement itself rarely punished.[17] The head of Shanghai's venture capital agency, Shanghai Venture Capital Corp., said that success required learning to feel "like it's our money and not the government's money at all."[18]

Gradually, however, nongovernmental domestic entities became involved in VC. In July 2001, Legend Holdings, China's largest computer maker, announced a RMB 200 million ($24 million) venture capital fund for information technology start-ups.[19] Foreign sources of funds had also become more significant: New Margin, run by Bo Feng's brother Tao, had raised its second fund of $88 million from government and private sources throughout Asia, while its first $22 million fund had been supplied entirely by the Chinese government.[20] In 2000, twelve china-targeted funds, two of which were Chinese, raised $957 million; in 1995, five funds, all international, raised $486 million.[21] (See Exhibit 19.3.)

Early stage (seed and start-up) venture investments comprised 44 percent of disbursements in 1999, with the vast majority of all private equity investments (93 percent)

EXHIBIT 19.3

VENTURE CAPITAL POOL IN CHINA, 1991–2000

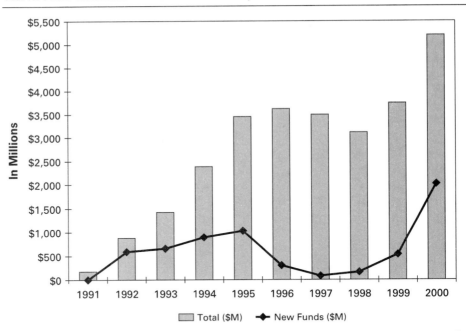

Source: Adapted from Asian Venture Capital Association, *The 2002 Guide to Venture Capital in Asia*, 13th ed., (Hong Kong: AVCJ Holdings, October 2001), p. 42.

---

17. Henry Sender, "China Tries Venture Capitalism," *The Asian Wall Street Journal* (January 3, 2001), p. N1.

18. Yuda Hua, quoted in Sender, "China Tries Venture Capitalism."

19. Anonymous, "China: Legend to Set Up Venture Capital Fund," *World Reports—Asia Intelligence Wire* (July 4, 2001).

20. Anonymous, "What Would Mao Think?"

21. *Asian VC Journal*, p. 48.

in China-based companies. The most popular areas of investment were consumer-related and infrastructure, with computer related/Internet, manufacturing, and utilities also receiving attention.[22] On an investment per company basis, though, heavy manufacturing ($20 million) came in a close second to infrastructure ($30 million), with transportation ($9.5 million), consumer-related ($9.2 million), and telecommunications ($8.2 million) the next three (see Exhibit 19.4).

In comparison, 22 percent of U.S. venture capital investment ($13.1 billion) went to early stage investments in 1999, with online-specific efforts receiving the bulk of that, 43 percent or $25.3 billion. Communications, Computer Software, Other Products, and Medical/Health Related sectors followed.[23]

Exits were difficult, even with the establishment of the stock exchanges. Theoretically, both trade sales and listings, in China, Hong Kong, or on NASDAQ, were options. Listing on the Shanghai exchange, though, was almost prohibitive for young firms. While NASDAQ high-fliers such as AsiaInfo and Sina.com had generated eye-popping

EXHIBIT 19.4a

CHINA'S PRIVATE EQUITY DISBURSEMENTS BY INDUSTRY, 2000

Industry	$ Invested (millions)	% of Total	# of Companies	% of Total	$/Company (millions)
Infrastructure	$512	12.2%	32	3.2%	$16.00
Consumer Products/Services	$421	10.0%	76	7.5%	$5.54
Telecommunication	$340	8.1%	76	7.5%	$4.47
Information Technology	$314	7.5%	136	13.4%	$2.31
Computer Related	$311	7.4%	112	11.0%	$2.78
Electronics	$289	6.9%	72	7.1%	$4.01
Medical/Biotechnology	$283	6.7%	63	6.2%	$4.49
Service—Nonfinancial	$263	6.3%	39	3.8%	$6.74
Manufacturing—Heavy	$249	5.9%	19	1.9%	$13.11
Construction	$215	5.1%	21	2.1%	$10.24
Transportation/Distribution	$187	4.4%	36	3.5%	$5.19
Utilities	$186	4.4%	36	3.5%	$5.17
Manufacturing—Light	$146	3.5%	36	3.5%	$4.06
Financial Services	$132	3.1%	20	2.0%	$6.60
Travel/Hospitality	$126	3.0%	32	3.2%	$3.94
Other	$113	2.7%	124	12.2%	$0.91
Retail/Wholesale	$85	2.0%	56	5.5%	$1.52
Textiles and Clothing	$33	0.8%	29	2.9%	$1.14
Total	**$4,205**	**100%**	**1,015**	**100%**	**$4.14**

Source: Adapted from Asian Venture Capital Association, *The 2002 Guide to Venture Capital in Asia*, 13th ed., (Hong Kong: AVCJ Holdings, October 2001), p. 42.

22. AVCA, *The 2002 Guide to Venture Capital in Asia*, 13th ed., p. 54.

23. National Venture Capital Association, *The 2001 National Venture Capital Association Yearbook* (Arlington, VA and Newark, NJ: Thomson Financial/Venture Economics, 2001), p. 30.

EXHIBIT 19.4b

U.S. PRIVATE EQUITY DISBURSEMENTS BY INDUSTRY, 2000

Industry	$ Invested (millions)	% of Total	# of Companies	% of Total	$/Company (millions)
Online Specific	$48,062.6	46%	2,459	45%	$19.55
Communications	17,713.8	17	567	10	31.24
Computer Software & Services	14,407.4	14	962	18	14.98
Other Products	5,360.5	5	303	6	17.69
Medical & Health Related	3,628.8	4	341	6	10.64
Semiconductor & Other Electronics	6,161.6	6	239	4	25.78
Consumer Related	1,667.1	2	141	3	11.82
Computer Hardware	2,297.1	2	147	3	15.63
Biotechnology	2,770.8	3	180	3	15.39
Industrial/Energy	1,423.8	1	76	1	18.73
Total	**$103,493.5**	**100%**	**5,415**	**100%**	**$19.11**

Source: NVCA, *The 2001 National Venture Capital Association Yearbook* (Arlington, VA and Newark, NJ: Thomson Financial/Venture Economics, 2001), p. 30.

returns, they were rare. Said Feng, "We don't spend a lot of time thinking about exits. If we have a good company, we can list it in Hong Kong or on NASDAQ, or it will be a great candidate for a trade sale. But right now, we're just trying to build the companies." A second Chinese exchange, modeled after NASDAQ, had long been in the offing; in October 2001, the government had announced its indefinite postponement. The difficulty in exits for firms that might have wished to do so had pushed up the value of China's private equity portfolios to $3.4 billion from $3 billion the year before.[24]

CHENGWEI VENTURES

Chengwei Ventures was founded in 1999 because its founders felt that they could fill a distinct hole in the market. Both founders, Eric Li and Bo Feng, were Shanghai natives. Both had spent significant time in the United States and gravitated to private equity deals in Asia. Li had come to California in 1986, where he studied computer science at UC Berkeley and joined Perot Systems. After earning an MBA from Stanford, he did private equity deals with Orchid Asia and then founded an investment business focusing on China, doing mostly LBOs.

Feng, the son of a senior government official, had left China in 1987 to study filmmaking in San Francisco. In 1993, he met Sanford Robertson of Robertson Stephens (RSC) and joined the firm's Asia team. Because RSC did not have a clear business model for Asia at the time, Feng spent two years visiting thousands of companies in China. "The key problems," he explained,

> were that there were no pure technology companies—they were all conglomerates, no clear lines of ownership—because of all the years of state

24. AVCA, *The 2002 Guide to Venture Capital in Asia*, 13th ed., p. 46.

ownership, and no entrepreneurial talent. In all that time, I met two true entrepreneurs, the founders of Sina.com, Wang Zhidong, and AsiaInfo Holdings, Edward Tian and James Ding."

Feng helped RSC raise a $20 million private placement for AsiaInfo, then left RSC in 1997. After a short period with ChinaVest, as the Beijing chief representative doing equity research, he established Roberston Feng Investment Banking in 1998 with Robertson. "This was a difficult position for me," he said. "People were investing in Chinese transactions, especially Internet-related ones, at outrageous valuations and with questionable entrepreneurs. I concluded I could do better as a principal investor than as an agent."

Li had been having similar thoughts in conversations with his mentor, G. Leonard Baker of Sutter Hill Ventures. One night over their quarterly dinners, when they usually discussed history, a mutual interest, Li confided that his partner wanted to raise another fund to do more investments in traditional industries. "I've found I just like startups," he admitted. Baker took him to Sutter Hill, which decided to lead an investment in Li's nascent fund. Baker then asked, "Who will be your partner? VC is lonely work."

Robertson had introduced Li and Feng in 1995 while Li was at Orchid Holdings. In his investment business, Li had been one of Feng's clients. Li explained, "I thought of everyone I knew and narrowed the list to four and talked with all of them and decided on Bo."

Li and Feng named the fund Chengwei, Chinese for "becoming," in recognition of the emergence of Chinese venture capital, and began raising funds in November 1999. Their connections with Robertson and Baker generated significant interest from organizations that did not customarily invest in first-time funds: Yale (Sutter Hill's biggest investor and on whose investment committee Baker sat), Stanford University, Sutter Hill, and Power Corporation of Canada, which had a long history of investing in China and was also a limited partner in Sutter Hill. The fund raised $60 million. Chengwei was structured as a typical U.S. limited partnership but registered in the Cayman Islands. Sutter Hill's participation was on a no fee/no carry basis; the other LPs paid a fee and the general partners received carry in the low 20 percent range.

Chengwei's investment philosophy tended to focus on software and services companies (see Exhibit 19.5 for Chengwei's mission statement). While the central idea was the same as in the United States—find good young companies and grow them—Li and Feng faced unique challenges. "Chinese entrepreneurs need a great deal of assistance in building world-class companies," Feng explained, adding:

> Most entrepreneurially oriented business people here don't have any hands-on experience. There's also very little formal business training. There's a shortage of trained executives, whether CEOs or midlevel managers, who can come in and hit the ground running. You have U.S.-trained Chinese nationals who often lack the network and knowledge of local conditions. Local managers generally lack professionalism and broad experience—they don't have a keen understanding of the importance of meeting deadlines, for instance. Our ideal person is often a Chinese national who has worked for the Chinese division of a multinational. And it's terribly hard to recruit them now, because all we can offer is our equity and that's not worth as much as it once was, compared to the steady salary and benefits of a multinational. We call it the "iron rice bowl." Eric and I are less concerned about deal flow than about entrepreneur flow. People have to be opportunistic and quick-moving; you can't be analytical here because there's nothing to analyze. We find in our business; if you wait to find enough information to analyze Chinese industry trends, it will be too late to start a company.

EXHIBIT 19.5

CHENGWEI VENTURES' MISSION STATEMENT

Chengwei Ventures invests in early stage technology companies in greater China.

Our Entrepreneurs

We are first and foremost in the business of backing people. Our entrepreneurs are the center of our universe and we exist to enable them to build great companies. We see ourselves as partners and cofounders with our entrepreneurs in launching and developing businesses.

Our General Partners

The general partners of Chengwei Ventures are local venture capitalists. We are all natives of Shanghai with experience in Silicon Valley. Our professional backgrounds enable us to add significant value to our entrepreneurs in general management, finance, and global networking.

Our Investors

Our lead investor and partner, Sutter Hill Ventures, is one of the earliest venture capital firms in Silicon Valley and has backed some of the most successful companies in the U.S. high-tech industry. Mr. Sanford Robertson, founder of Robertson Stephens & Co., is a lead individual investor. Most of our limited partners are leading institutional investors and Silicon Valley entrepreneurs. We bring the core capital and know-how of the Silicon Valley knowledge economy to be invested in China's entrepreneurial companies.

Our Executives

It takes three kinds of people to succeed in venture capital: great entrepreneurs, exceptional technical talents, and capable professional managers. China has an abundance of the first two and a real shortage of the last one. So one of Chengwei Ventures' most important activities is developing a network of executives with experience managing businesses who have the desire to seek an entrepreneurial path

Source: http://www.chengwei.com, accessed January 11, 2002.

Nonetheless, Chengwei did extensive due diligence before investing. Feng joked, "We probably break up more firms than we invest in; we'll discover severe flaws in their business models and they'll just throw up their hands." Much of the information centered on the entrepreneur—could he afford the venture, did his lifestyle allow for it, did he know the market and the hole he was trying to fill.

Part of the challenge was the lack of financial statements. Feng said, "It's shoe-box accounting. When you have no revenues, you don't need to account for them. Besides, it's China. There are no accounting rules to speak of. Some stores still do their accounts on abacuses."

All investments were structured as Cayman Island corporations, avoiding many of China's unsettled legal issues and allowing the firms to issue preferred stock, which was illegal in China. Feng and Li served on the boards of their companies and split responsibility quite clearly, with each having his own companies. They often had to step in and directly restructure their investments. "This is our real distinction," said Feng. He continued:

> We can provide hands-on assistance with long-run strategy, with achieving goals, while most of the other funds, like Softbank and IDG, are almost index funds. They'll throw money at a company and then sit back and hope

something good happens. You can't do that in China today. All the local venture capitalists can really offer is their government connections, which again isn't much help if you're a company that doesn't know what it's doing and doesn't have a decent management team to do it.

As of October 2001, Chengwei had made twelve investments. Six were early stage, with Chengwei the lead investor (see Exhibit 19.6). They were all in Shanghai or Beijing, not only because these cities were the loci of entrepreneurial activity, but also because it allowed the partners to use their time more efficiently.

T2 TECHNOLOGIES AND ITOM

hdt° had been formed in February 2001 from the merger of two companies, T2 Technologies of Shanghai and Beijing-based iTOM. Chengwei had seeded T2 and then joined with New Margin, run by Feng's brother, Tao, in a second round. Feng explained:

> "I met Jim [Wang, the founder] back in 1998. He came to me because I'd invested in Stockstar, an online trading business, and he was involved in a rival effort, Websoft, which was backed by IDG. Jim felt that it wouldn't succeed, so I helped him sell his shares—you have to realize, it's unusual for people to switch jobs in China—and start T2 to do online information gathering. We'd had a lot of meetings in the interim; I knew he was smart, he just had to come up with something that we could make a business."

T2 developed the Textclick Ad Alliance, an affiliated online advertising and market research network. Revenues were generated by serving targeted ads within the Textclick network, on the idea of the Doubleclick model. In addition, the T2 iPanel

---

EXHIBIT 19.6

CHENGWEI FUND I PORTFOLIO

Company	Date Acquired	% of Company Purchased in Round	Industry
A	1/28/2000	10%	Internet
B	2/28/2000	20	Internet
C	5/23/2000	1	Technology Service
D	5/30/2000	33	Software
E	5/31/2000	9	Industrial Software & Service
F	8/23/2000	22	Software/Systems Integration
T2 Tech.	9/12/2000	35	Software
E	10/10/2000	9	Industrial Software & Service
G	10/30/2000	48	Systems Integration
H	11/14/2000	34	Software
I	2/8/2001	NA	Telecommunications
hdt°	5/25/2001	NA	Software
hdt°	5/31/2001	NA	Software

Source: hdt°.

module collected information about the behavior of Web site visitors—number of pages viewed, ad click-through statistics, purchasing habits, and the like—for which clients would pay a subscription fee. iPanel also offered an online focus group network service that delivered customized questionnaires to participating members and tracked their responses, allowing marketers to test their brand concepts or marketing campaigns before launch. Finally, T2 provided data mining services to help clients refine and target their marketing campaigns.

"The problem was," Jim Wang said, "that it wasn't really a business. It was just sort of tech excitement. We could do this neat thing, serving ads to Web site visitors, but we didn't know how to generate real revenues from it."

There were other problems, as Feng elaborated. "Textclick wasn't easy to use and Jim, while he's a fantastic programmer, isn't especially customer savvy. He basically had a college dorm room tech business."

iTOM was a different situation. Feng had met Jerry Wang in the same week he met Jim Wang:

> I was visiting a company where the founder and Jerry were doing a presentation for me. Halfway through, I felt that Jerry was smarter than the founder and said to him that if he ever wanted to talk about an idea, to call. A week later, Jerry came to see me. He had lots of good ideas but no substance. I had him study a business plan with Jeff, my assistant.

In March 2000, Jerry Wang cofounded iTOM, the one of the first Web site design and interactive marketing agencies in Asia. iTOM developed interactive and digital content along with portal software, with backing from Tom.com, a Hong-Kong-based Internet "megaportal" that provided the Chinese mainland with information and entertainment, in the model of America Online. Tom.com was a subsidiary of Hutchison Wampoa Ltd., partly owned by Li Ka-shing, one of the world's richest men, whose son, Richard Li, was involved with Pacific Century CyberWorks Ltd. (PCCW), a major provider of telephone, wireless, and broadband services in Hong Kong and much of Asia. Jerry Wang freely admitted he was

> right in the center of the bubble. I had money from Tom.com and I was spending it—the best office space in Beijing, fancy desks, the works. Then Bo asked if I had a business model, and how I was going to scale this thing, and I gave him a blank stare. Bo said if I ever decided to pursue a real business, I should come see him.

Unlike T2, iTOM did not want for customers. "It's easy to find good programmers in China," said Jerry:

> It's hard to find creative people. I had the right customers—Intel, Sony, Nippon Paint—but not the right business. I got there through other contacts, sort of one-removed. So if Jim had a college-dorm-room tech business, I had a college-dorm-room creative business.

Said Feng:

> I kept thinking that there had to be something that we could do to leverage the strengths of these two firms. Yes, T2 could scale but scaling zero doesn't get you far. And iTOM had revenues and customers but wasn't scalable in that model; it needed more emphasis on software, something replicable, and less on design.

The Merger

In November 2000, Feng introduced Jim Wang and Jerry Wang at a dinner. "On the escalator afterward," he recounted, "I said that the two companies should merge. My assistant thought I had food poisoning." The two CEOs had not gotten along well; Jim admitted, "I almost left several times because I thought Jerry was too young and inexperienced and artsy." By January 2001, though, the two had accepted the idea.

Actually merging the companies required four months. Tom.com's share of iTOM had to be bought out, as did New Margin, which owned part of T2; they had to find a CEO and to settle the economics for each partner. Geography did not help either: T2 was headquartered in Shanghai, iTOM in Beijing.

Building the executive team was a challenge. Bin (Ben) Zheng, the vice president of operations for T2, had been brought in to strengthen T2's sales and marketing before the merger. During the merger, Feng, Jim and Jerry realized that he had significant managerial skill and involved him in the daily issues. "Ben kept everyone talking," said Feng. "And that was a huge contribution. There were still a lot of times when Jim walked out of board meetings. But since his company still couldn't find a customer, he kept coming back."

The interim CEO was Darwin Tu, who had spent ten years in the United States. After four years in school, first at the University of California at Berkeley for an MSA and then master's in marketing and statistics at Stanford University, he had done database marketing for the financial services industry and then was an early member of Digital Impact, an e-marketing startup that went public on NASDAQ. He had met Eric Li at Stanford and was asked to consult on the merger at the start of 2001.

This solved the immediate CEO problem. "Darwin is very good at strategy," said Feng. "He was the perfect guy at the time. Jim became the chief technical officer and Jerry the president and chief marketing officer." (See Exhibits 19.7a and 19.7b for biographies.)

Tu said:

> We realized that there really isn't any marketing here in China, just advertising. We decided to focus on providing e-marketing solutions, especially to state-owned enterprises, which are huge and have never had to market

---

EXHIBIT 19.7a

BIOGRAPHIES OF hdt° TEAM MEMBERS

Darwin Tu, CEO

Client Services and Strategy Consulting at Digital Impact; Project and Product Management at Fair Isaac. Darwin has masters' degrees in statistics and business administration from Stanford University and the University of California at Berkeley, respectively.

Jerry Wang, President and CMO

Strategic development cooperator for Macromedia in China and cofounder of iTOM. He was responsible for iTOM's strategy, business, and technology development. Jerry has a BA in marketing and advertising from Shanghai's Tongji University.

Jim Wang, CTO

A guru in Internet technologies. Cofounder of Textclick.com and T2 Technologies, Jim has a BS in computer software from Shanghai's FuDan University.

EXHIBIT 19.7b

BIOGRAPHIES OF CHENGWEI PARTNERS

Bo Feng, Cofounder and Managing Partner

Feng was born and raised in Shanghai. He went to the United States as a college student and studied film at San Francisco State University. He joined Robertson Stephens & Co. in 1993 and built the firm's investment banking business in China. Feng was instrumental in the development and financing of two of the most successful high-tech start-ups in China: AsiaInfo.com and Sina.com. He served as a board director on AsiaInfo in 1997–1999. He also founded Robertson, Feng Technology Associates, an investment bank, with his mentor and partner, Sanford Robertson. He cofounded Chengwei Ventures in 1999.

Feng loves golf and soccer and prefers fast cars.

Eric X. Li: Cofounder and Managing Partner

Li was born and raised in Shanghai. He went to the United States as a college student and graduated from University of California at Berkeley. In 1990, he joined Perot Systems Corporation, a start-up systems integration company founded by Ross Perot, as one of its earliest members. He also worked in investment banking for J. P. Morgan. He attended Stanford Business School and received his MBA degree in 1995.

Li returned to China in 1995 with Orchid Asia Holdings, an investment fund he cofounded, and made significant investments in traditional industries in the Asia Pacific region. He cofounded Chengwei Ventures in 1999.

An avid reader and amateur historian, Li prefers quiet evenings of reading and contemplation.

Yang Dong Shao: Managing Partner

Shao was born and raised in Shanghai. He studied economics at Fudan University for two and half years before transferring to Columbia University, where he earned his BA in economics and mathematics with honors. He joined Salomon Brothers in New York City in 1993 in its investment banking division, where he specialized in debt and equity financing in global capital markets as well as mergers and acquisitions. He attended Stanford Business School and earned his MBA degree in 2000.

Shao is an avid golfer and bridge player.

---

at all. We wanted to develop platforms for e-commerce. While there are lots of U.S. firms that do that, it's entirely different in China. Instead of credit cards for online purchases, there's a complex invoicing process. We were selling stand-alone solution software, so clients could mix and match what they needed, or hire us as consultants to help them create a solution.

Feng was closely involved in the business model development. "I kept pushing Darwin to get to profitability. Great ideas are fantastic, but we needed revenues."

"Part of the challenge," said Jim,

was that we had to keep the old companies going even as we built this new one. So even as we were working out the details of the merger, T2's Textclick network had reached 100,000 member sites, and iTOM had done major work with Nippon Paints, providing it with the content management software that created a centralized technology platform to support all of its Web sites.

In its business plan, hdt° observed that the market for technology-based marketing solutions was immense, especially given the immaturity of the e-marketing market. In March 2001, 48 percent of Chinese enterprises owned neither a Web site nor a registered domain name, 9 percent had registered a name but had not established a Web site, while 7 percent had a Web site but had not registered a domain name. Only 36 percent of China's corporations had Web sites with established, registered domain names, and only 12 percent of these updated their sites daily. Almost two-thirds of the major sites offered audio and interactive content, and of these, over half outsourced their production. In short, the market for Web-development providers was expected to grow at 90 percent in 2001, with the market for online design, publishing, and development reaching RMB 1.1 billion ($132.3 million). The hdt° team felt it could get 1 percent of the market for 2001, or RMB 13 million ($1.6 million) (see Exhibit 19.8 for business plan excerpts and Exhibit 19.9 for projections).

hdt* IS BORN

In April 2001, T2 and iTOM officially became hdt°, providing a broad range of services that included market research, portal integration, and promotion and database marketing. Through the spring and summer, the new company did such projects as helping Legend Computers (China's IBM) introduce its brand online and relaunching Sony's Sonystyle.com Web site, a significant business-to-consumer e-commerce platform in China. With Microsoft, hdt° delivered a prototype interface for interactive television services, and with Research International, the firm launched a product that allowed

---

EXHIBIT 19.8a

hdt°'S MISSION STATEMENT

To serve our market by helping clients understand, and intelligently serve theirs. To this end, we will design, develop and deploy products and services that help professional marketers in China:

- **GENERATE** powerful technology-based market strategies.
- **LEVERAGE** cutting edge communication and information technologies to build unforgettable brand experiences.
- **MASTER** customer management techniques that drive overall business performance by creating lasting, individualized relationships.
- **MAXIMIZE** marketing ROI with reporting management tools that provide measurable results.

EXHIBIT 19.8b

EXECUTIVE SUMMARY FROM hdt° BUSINESS PLAN

hdt° creates intelligent, technology-based marketing solutions that change the way companies and their markets interact. We intend to become China's leading supplier of products and services that combine technology, textbook fundamentals, and relentless creativity to maximize return on the marketing dollar. We help professional marketers leverage technology to mobilize campaigns that fuse market intelligence, strategy, Web development, online promotion, and email based marketing activities into integrated efforts that drive sales, build brand, and improve overall business performance.

Source: hdt°.

EXHIBIT 19.9a

PROJECTIONS FOR hdt° (APRIL 2001–DECEMBER 2001)

Items (in RMB 1,000s)	April–June	July–Sept.	Oct.–Dec.	Total
Total Revenue	2,550	4,100	6,600	13,250
Expenses				
Salaries, Benefits, & Training	2,229	2,415	2,577	7,221
Rent, Furniture, & Equipment	1,464	744	744	2,952
Marketing & Sales	389	447	453	1,289
Administration	330	330	339	999
Other	71	36	32	139
Total Expenses	4,483	3,972	4,145	12,600
Net Income (Loss)	**(1,933)**	**128**	**2,455**	**650**

Source: hdt°.

Notes: $1 = RMB 8.28, as of November 2001.

Historical performance figures are not available.

EXHIBIT 19.9b

HEADCOUNT PROJECTIONS FOR hdt°

Function	April–June	July–Sept.	Oct.–Dec.
R&D	18	20	20
Sales & Services	28	37	42
Marketing & Administration	14	16	18
Total	**60**	**73**	**80**
Number of Projects	7	10	14

Source: hdt°.

Pepsi to conduct its first online employee survey in China. It also hosted the Intel/Macromedia Flash Film Contest, which attracted more than 4,000 Chinese-language entries from around the world, marking a significant milestone in the development of China's interactive industry. In October, hdt° signed contracts with China Railway Communications Corp. and China Netcom to develop enterprise portals for broadband applications. In the five months since the merger was officially completed, revenues had risen 500 percent, to RMB 5 million ($604,000).

Feng commented, "We need a new CEO. Darwin was terrific in the early days, but now we need someone who can grow this." While they looked for the new CEO, Tu had become the chief strategist and Feng was acting CEO. He continued:

> The other issue is the business model. Right now, we're going into companies that know what they need and just need us to implement it—like Pepsi and Sony. The big multinationals. But even bigger than the multinationals

are the SOEs. They don't have a clue about Web sites. It's not that they have Web sites and they're not collecting customer data. They don't have Web sites and they don't even know who their customers are, let alone collecting data on them. And yet, is it worth the risk? Catering to the multinationals is something we know how to do. The SOEs are a different situation and they're part of the old China. Do they even want to come into the new China?

China is at a remarkable point in its history. It had a world-leading economy but when the industrial revolution came along, the economic fundamentals changed so dramatically that all of the advantages it had accumulated in agriculture became drawbacks. Now it stands with one foot in the eighteenth century and one in the twenty-first. If we can make the leap, we will lead the world.

He knew that hdt° had to find a business model that would serve as a similar bridge, to carry both it and the country into the twenty-first century.

20

A Note on Private Equity in Developing Countries

The past several years have seen two striking patterns in private equity activity in the developing world. The first of these has been a dramatic increase in activity, followed by a pronounced decline. The second has been a shift in the composition of investments toward more early stage investments.

These shifts in fund-raising volume have been fueled largely by institutional investors based in the United States. The reasons for the growth in activity during the early and mid-1990s are several. Among them was the rapid growth of many developing nations and, in many of them, the relaxation of curbs on foreign investments. Perhaps equally important was the perception by many institutional investors in the mid-1990s that the returns from private equity investments in the United States were likely to decrease. Over the last years of the decade, however, these two perceptions shifted and private equity fund-raising in developing countries suffered as a result.

A second profound change has been in the mixture of private equity invested. Until very recently, private equity investing in developing countries was overwhelmingly focused on later-stage investments (e.g., buyouts, infrastructure, and mezzanine transactions). In the late 1990s, true venture capital transactions, particularly relating to the Internet and telecommunications, became much more frequent, a pattern that has continued (though at a somewhat reduced intensity) into the 2000s.

While comprehensive data is hard to come by, an example may help illustrate these patterns.[1] Fund-raising by private equity funds based in China climbed from $16 million in 1991 to over $1 billion in 1995, with the single largest source being U.S. institutions. It then fell to an average annual level of $183 million in the years 1996 through 1998. Fund-raising rose sharply in the late 1990s, only to fall again in the 2000s. Meanwhile, the share of private equity investment devoted to seed and start-up firms (as opposed to mezzanine, restructuring, and infrastructure companies or projects) increased

---

1. No single directory captures private equity activity in the developing world. The Chinese data is drawn from Asian Venture Capital Journal, *The Guide to Venture Capital in Asia: 2003 Edition*, Hong Kong, Asian Venture Capital Journal, 2003 (and earlier editions).

from 2 percent in 1992 to 43 percent in 2000. These patterns have been repeated in regions as diverse as South America, Eastern Europe, and the India subcontinent.

This note seeks to identify some of the key challenges and opportunities that private equity investors in developing nations face. The first section presents a broad overview of some of the key reasons why developing nations are a potentially attractive investment environment for institutional investors and private equity funds. The note then considers the "private equity cycle." Sections II through IV examine the process from fund-raising through investing to exiting, contrasting developing and developed nations. The opportunities that make private equity in developing countries attractive are highlighted, as well as the potential risks.

It is worth cautioning that this note only tries to identify broad patterns. This discussion should not blind the reader to the substantial heterogeneity in the private equity industries of various developing countries. A key reason for these differences, of course, is that developing nations differ from one another along many dimensions. Please bear this caution in mind as you read through this note.

I. WHY INVEST IN DEVELOPING NATIONS?

In this section, we will discuss two sets of rationales for the growth of private equity activity in the developing world.[2] The first relate to the changes in the developing nations themselves. Many have undertaken radical reforms. External changes—for example, technological innovations—have also helped make these nations more attractive arenas for investment. The second set relates to the changing conditions in the developed nations. Many institutional investors have been skeptical that attractive returns that have recently characterized venture capital and leveraged buyout investments in many developed nations can be sustained, and are looking for new arenas in which to invest.

The Increasing Attractiveness of Developing Nations

Much of the interest in private equity investing in developing nations must be attributed to their economic progress over the past decade. A critical impetus to much of this progress, in turn, has been the economic reforms adopted by many of these nations. The pace at which capitalism has rolled through developing economies is breathtaking. It is easy to forget that as recently as fifteen years ago, only one billion of the world's citizens were in capitalist economies. Today, three times that number is in economies that are strongly capitalist in orientation.[3]

While a detailed discussion of these changes is beyond the scope of this note, it is worth noting a few of these reforms. One of the most substantial macroeconomic shifts was the 1989 Brady Plan. This allowed several Latin American countries to restructure their external debt. The enormous reduction in debt service led to a substantial boost in the economic health of these markets. The successful reform process

---

2. According to the World Bank, developing nations are those countries that have either low- or middle-level per capita incomes; have underdeveloped capital markets; and/or are not industrialized. It should be noted, however, that the application of these criteria is somewhat subjective. For instance, Kuwait appears on many lists of developing nations despite its high per capita gross domestic product. The reason for its inclusion lies in the income distribution inequality that exists there, which has not allowed it to reach the general living standards of developed countries.

3. For a provocative discussion of these changes from a practitioner perspective, see Lucy Conger, "Interview—Garantia launches Brazil Equity Fund," *Reuters News Service*, September 26, 1995.

led to an increase in major investors' confidence in developing nations: as seen, for instance, in the increase in the market prices of these nations' debt.

Other macroeconomic reforms were initiated by the developing nations themselves, though often with the prodding of such international bodies as the International Monetary Fund. One arena for such reforms has been major tax reforms. Many developing countries realized that one way to fuel the economy is by lowering taxes on capital gains, thereby encouraging equity investment and stock market growth. Likewise, in many nations, restrictions on foreign investment—which often prohibited investments in particular industries, stipulated that foreign investors needed to hold a minority stake, or limited the repatriation of profits—have been relaxed. Finally, several developing nations have made great progress in improving their accounting and disclosure standards. These changes have served to lower the costs of investing in these nations, as well as to diminish the information asymmetries that foreign investors face.

Other drivers of the economic progress of developing nations have been external. An example is the lowering by many developed nations of many tariff and nontariff barriers to imports from developing nations. Both exports and imports by developing nations increased more than threefold between 1987 and 2001.[4] A second example is technological change. Thanks to innovations in information and communication technologies, investors in developed countries—whether corporations or institutions—can better monitor their investments. A substantial decline in inflation-adjusted transportation costs has also made greater trade and investment feasible. These trends have led to spectacular growth in many of the developing nations. While the developed economies grew at an inflation-adjusted annual rate of 3.6 percent between 1990 and 2000, emerging market economies grew at 5.1 percent.[5]

The Decreasing Attractiveness of Developed Nations

A second critical factor in the growth of private equity investing in developing countries has been the perception of diminishing investment opportunities in the developed nations, particularly the United States. The pool of private equity under management in the United States has grown from $4 billion in 1980 to over $300 billion at the end of 2003. This growth has largely been attributable to the relaxation of the formal and informal curbs that limited private and pension funds from investing in private equity.

This growth, many institutional investors argue, has had three deleterious consequences. First, the increase in the size of many private equity funds has led to an alteration in the incentive structure of these funds. In particular, the management fees charged by private equity investors have remained relatively constant, averaging about 2 percent (typically calculated as a percentage of capital under management). But since the capital managed per partner has increased dramatically, this has meant that these fees have become a significant source of income. Many investors fear that the incentive provided by the share of the profits reserved for the private equity investors has consequently become less effective. Second, many private equity organizations have encountered strong demand when they seek to raise new funds. This allowed them to negotiate partnership agreements without the many covenants that previously protected investors in these funds. If an institution insisted on the inclusion of a particular form of protection, the venture capitalists could simply exclude it from the transaction. Finally, many institutional investors argue that the current market is characterized

4. International Monetary Fund, *International Financial Statistics Yearbook* (Washington: International Monetary Fund, 2002).

5. *Ibid.*

by an imbalance between the supply of capital and attractive investments. Many argue that this has led to unjustifiable increases in valuations, or, more colloquially, the phenomenon of "money chasing deals."

These concerns have led to institutional investors, particularly in the United States, to consider more favorably private equity funds specializing elsewhere. One focus has been continental Europe, which has lagged both the United States and United Kingdom in the supply of private equity. But the low inflation-adjusted growth rates in many European nations have led many institutions to also focus on the developing nations.

Why Private Equity?

In view of the above patterns, it may not be surprising that institutional investors have been investing in a broad array of asset classes in developing nations. Institutional holdings of both public equities and corporate and government debt have increased sharply in recent years. But a particular focus of interest recently has been international private equity funds.

This interest is illustrated by a 2001 survey of seventeen of the largest institutional investors conducted by Goldman Sachs and Frank Russell Capital. It found that international private equity had increased from representing 0 percent of all alternative investments in 1992 to 17 percent in 2001.[6]

Institutional investors frequently justify their interest in private equity funds in developing nations by highlighting the similarities to venture capital in the United States. Like venture capital investments, many companies in developing nations are characterized by great uncertainty, difficult-to-value assets, and substantial information asymmetries. In the developing world, a venture capital–like style of investment should consequently yield attractive returns.

II. THE PRIVATE EQUITY CYCLE: FUND-RAISING

In many respects, private equity in developing and developed countries is similar. In both settings, professional investors provide equity or equity-linked capital to privately held firms. Another key element is the ongoing involvement of the private equity investor in monitoring and assisting the company. Where private equity in developing countries differs is in its implementation. The next three sections will highlight some of these differences.

Fund Structures

The fund structure standard in developed countries is the limited partnership. The general partners are the individual venture capitalists (or an investment management firm controlled by these individuals). The general partners are in charge of raising, making, monitoring, and exiting the investments. In return they are paid a management fee plus a share of the profits. The limited partners are prohibited from playing an active role in managing the investments and usually enjoy tax benefits. For instance, taxes are typically paid not at the fund level, but rather by the individual general and limited partners. This enables tax-exempt investors to avoid almost all tax obligations.

This limited partnership structure has served as a model for many private equity funds in developing countries. For instance, virtually all of the funds focusing on Latin

6. Goldman, Sachs & Co. and Frank Russell Capital, Inc., *2001 Report on Alternative Investing by Tax-Exempt Organizations*, (2001).

America have been structured along the lines of U.S.-style limited partnerships.[7] A major issue for venture capital funds in Asia, however, has been the general lack of legal structures that allow the establishment of limited partnerships.

Without the ability to form a limited partnership, many Asian venture capital funds are structured as corporations. This corporate structure puts several limitations on the limited partners' ability to ensure that the fund will dissolve at the end of a stated period (e.g., ten years). With the corporate structure, it is easier for the general partners to prolong the fund's life. Since the forced liquidation—and the consequent need for general partners to return for additional funds—is one of the most powerful control rights exercised by limited partners, it is not surprising that this has been a major concern.

Capital Sources

The financing sources for private equity funds in the developing nations have largely been the same ones who invest in private equity funds based in the United States: pension funds, corporations, insurance companies, and high net worth individuals. To date, U.S.-based organizations have made up the bulk of these investors. European investors are gradually increasing in importance.

Several additional parties, however, have played an important role in the raising of private equity funds in developing nations. These have included U.S. foreign aid organizations like the U.S. Agency for International Development (USAID), quasi-governmental corporations like the Overseas Private Investment Corporation (OPIC), and multilateral financial institutions like the International Finance Corporation (IFC). Their role has been twofold. First, USAID and IFC have invested in funds directly. Rather than serving as traditional limited partners, however, they have typically provided financial support through long-term loans or direct grants. Second, these agencies have provided guarantees to private investors that they will receive some or all of their capital back. OPIC has been particularly aggressive in providing such guarantees.

The track record of these public efforts has been somewhat mixed. A recent internal critique at USAID[8] argued that of all the funds that it had supported over the past two decades, only one—the Latin American Agribusiness Development Corporation (LAAD)—had proven over time to be sustainable. Furthermore, it argued, this fund had become sustainable only by shifting from equity funding to more conventional agribusiness lending.

The critique attributed this poor performance to two factors. First, the government bodies often chose the wrong investors to invest in or guarantee. In many cases, the implementing institution had little or no previous experience as a private equity investor. The funds' ability to attract the right individuals to manage the portfolios was often been limited by government restrictions on the compensation of the investors. A second problem was the excessive constraints on the implementers. Many private equity funds were given very narrow mandates, such as the agricultural sector, and businesses that were either very small or owned by women. Since the number of potential investments was somewhat limited at best, the sustainability of the funds was severely impacted by these restrictions. In other cases, the government bodies conducted lengthy reviews of potential investments, and consequently the funds lost the opportunity to participate in

---

7. Lorenzo Weissman, "The Advent of Private Equity in Latin America," *The Columbia Journal of World Business* 31 (Spring 1996): 60–68 (this information is on page 68).

8. James W. Fox, "The Venture Capital Mirage: An Assessment of USAID Experience with Equity Investment," Working paper, Center for Development Information and Evaluation, U.S. Agency for International Development (Washington, 1996).

attractive deals. It should be noted, however, that it would have been very difficult to obtain attractive returns from private equity investments in most developing nations during the 1970s and 1980s, even under the best of circumstances.

One capital source that is likely to become increasingly important for private equity funds is retirement savings in the developing nations themselves. East Asian nations have very high savings rates, often about 30 percent of gross domestic product. These high rates partially reflect the younger average age in developing countries, as well as cultural differences. While many of these individual savings are invested informally in the privately held businesses of relatives and friends, little has been directed into institutional private equity funds.

These patterns are likely to change in future years. Leading the way has been Chile, which has privatized much of its retirement savings. Pension funds have already helped to finance privatization programs in Chile, taking equity positions of between 10 percent and 35 percent in privatized firms. As the funds have grown, regulators have increasingly widened the fields in which they can invest. Several are considering initiating private equity investment programs.[9]

III. THE PRIVATE EQUITY CYCLE: INVESTING

The investment process in developing and developed nations is often very different. In this section, we will discuss four aspects of these differences: the types of deals that are considered, the process by which companies are identified and evaluated, the structuring of the investments, and valuation.

Types of Investments

Private equity funds in developed nations undertake a diverse array of potential transactions. Venture capitalists in the United States usually target high-technology sectors of the economy, while buyout firms focus on more mature firms in a variety of industries that need to restructure or combine. By way of contrast, funds in developing nations have until recently targeted already-established firms in traditional industries.

Typical investments by developing country private equity funds fall into four broad categories. The first are privatizations. The World Bank estimates that eighty countries in recent years have made privatization a primary public-policy concern. More than 7,000 large-scale privatizations have been undertaken, at an annual rate of $25 billion per year.[10] Many of these newly privatized enterprises are undercapitalized and desperately need to modernize. The simple distribution of shares to employees or others will not solve their need for financing. In many cases, the national capital markets are still not well developed, and access to international markets is limited to the largest firms. Consequently, governments and the private sector are turning to private equity to fill the investment gap.

A second market opportunity has been corporate restructurings. Globalization has inspired increased competition for many businesses in developing countries: lower trade barriers and new regulatory frameworks have forced companies to refocus their activities. Furthermore, the transfer of technologies and techniques from developed nations

9. For a general overview, see Jim Freer, "The Private Pension Path," *LatinFinance* (July/August 1995): 34–38; for a specific discussion of future investment plans, see Felipe Sandoval, "CORFO Targets Small and Medium Enterprises," *Chile Economic Report* (Summer 1995): 2–9.

10. These statistics are from William L. Megginson, Robert C. Nash, and Matthias van Randenborgh, "The Financial and Operating Performance of Newly Privatized Firms," *Journal of Finance* 49 (1994): 403–452 (the information is on page 404).

has provided new challenges, which existing management has often not been capable of meeting. Consequently, many private equity investments in developing nations have focused on either (1) purchasing and improving the operations of established firms or business units, or (2) consolidating smaller businesses to achieve large, more cost-effective enterprises.

The final two categories of private equity investors are largely unique to the developing world. The first of these is investments in strategic alliances. In many cases, major corporations have made strategic investments (acquisitions, joint ventures, and alliances) in developing countries without a detailed knowledge of the business environment or their partners. To address these information gaps, corporations have increasingly welcomed private equity funds as third-party investors. The private equity investor is expected to provide much of the informed monitoring of the local partner that the corporation finds difficult to undertake.

A final class of investment has been infrastructure funds. Most infrastructure projects in the developed world have been financed through the issuance of bonds. In some developing nations, particularly in Asia, private equity funds have financed major projects, such as bridges, docks, and highways.

There are several reasons for the reluctance of private equity investors in developing nations to make the kinds of early stage, technology-intensive investments that U.S. venture capitalists specialize in. First, of course, in many markets trained technical talent and the necessary infrastructure (e.g., state-of-the-art research laboratories) are scarce. Second, in many nations intellectual property protection is weak, or the enforcement of these rights questionable. Thus, even if one was able to develop a successful product, it is unclear how rapid imitation could be avoided. A third factor is the difficulty in exiting these investments (discussed in more detail below). Finally, many investors argue that investing in a developing country is already a very risky act. To take on additional business risk would be imprudent. Consequently, they concentrate on mature enterprises with established track records.

In recent years, true venture capital investments have become more common in developing nations. These have fallen into three broad categories. The first set have sought to provide services to developing countries that are already available in the developed nations, such as investments in business-to-business exchanges and online auction sites geared to a particular region. The second category has sought to link the human capital in developing nations with labor-starved Western corporations. The leading examples of these types of transactions have been in India, where numerous software firms have received venture backing to provide programming services to American and European corporations. The final—and still rarest—set of transactions has sought to commercialize technology originating in developing countries for sale in the global marketplace.

Deal Identification and Due Diligence

The screening of investments is a major focus of private equity funds in developed nations. Typically, a venture capitalist in the United States receives several hundred times more proposals than he could invest in. Funds develop broad criteria to quickly select the deals that will be subject to in-depth evaluation later on.

In developing countries, private equity investors have to be more opportunistic, since the number of attractive investments is lower. While deals are identified from the same sources—e.g., other entrepreneurs and business intermediaries like lawyers and accountants—most investors take a much more active strategy. They exploit tight relationships among business and social groups in the region. This often gives them a first-mover advantage over outside investors without such ties.

The criteria employed by private equity investors are similar in developed and developing nations. In interviews, both sets of investors place management as the overriding factor in the success of any venture. Many speak of the need for "chemistry" among venture capitalists and the entrepreneur, and seek to evaluate the management team's commitment, drive, honesty, reputation, and creativity. Other criteria—such as the size of the market, the threat of obsolescence, and the ability to exit the investment—are also similar.

In evaluating potential deals, however, private equity investors in developing nations emphasize two sets of risks often not encountered in developed nations. The first of these is country risk. A revolution, for instance, might lead to the nationalization of foreign investments. A more common threat, however, is the potential costs of rent-seeking behavior. The highly regulated infrastructure sector is usually of great concern to investors because politically motivated regulatory changes can directly affect cash flows. Investors need to carefully analyze the institutions and legal framework as well as industry regulations. One very visible example of the potential costs of this behavior was the Enron Dabhol project in India. In this case, the recently elected government of Maharashtra, a state in India, canceled the power plant contract of Enron for the largest proposed foreign investment in India. Accused of bribery and overcharging, Enron agreed to renegotiate the contract even though it claimed already to have spent $300 million on the unfinished plant.[11] Working to limit these dangers, however, may be government's concerns about the reputational consequences of such actions: that is, the potential of their actions to deter future private investment and to invite criticism from multilateral financial organizations.

A second concern is exchange rate risk. While this is hardly unique to developing countries, the Mexican peso devaluation dramatically demonstrated the volatility of these markets. A major devaluation of a developing nation's currency could lead to a sharp drop in the returns enjoyed by its U.S. investors. Ways to mitigate this risk include entering into currency swaps, the purchase of options based on relative currency prices, or the purchase of forward currency. Since the nature and timing of the future payments is usually unknown to private equity investors, however, this poses some real challenges. While hedging tools have attracted increasing interest, their actual use by private equity investors in developing nations appears to be very limited.

Deal Structuring

The choice of financing vehicle also differs between developed and developing markets. Investors in developed nations use a variety of instruments, including common and several classes of preferred stock, debt, and convertible preferred. These financial instruments allow the private equity investors to stage investments, allocate risk, control management, provide incentives to executives, and demarcate ownership.

In many developing countries, private equity investors primarily use plain common stock. This reflects several factors. First, in several countries, especially in Asia, different classes of stock with different voting powers are not permitted. Thus, investors must seek other ways in which to control the firm. These are often of extreme importance,

---

11. For an overview, see Jonathan Bearman, "Death of Enron's Dabhol LNG Project Sends Shockwaves Through Industry," *Oil Daily* 45 (August 9, 1995): 1 ff.

since most of the companies are family owned or controlled. Such control rights allow the venture capitalists to step in during such messy controversies such as a dispute between two sons as to who should succeed the father as president.

A new study shed light on this issue by analyzing a sample of 167 transactions from a wide variety of private equity groups in developing countries.[12] It assesses deal structures, and how they vary with the nature of the nations in which the investments are made. The paper finds a number of patterns:

- Unlike in the United States, where the use of convertible preferred securities is ubiquitous, in developing nations a much broader array of securities are employed. Protections of private equity investor rights that are standard in the United States are encountered far less frequently.

- The choice of security employed appears to be driven by the circumstances of the private equity group and the nation. Investments in common law nations (e.g., those such as India, whose legal system was based on the United Kingdom's) and by private equity groups based in the United States and United Kingdom are considerably less likely to employ common stock or straight debt, and more likely to employ preferred stock.

- Transactions in common law nations are generally associated with more contractual protections for the private equity group, such as antidilution provisions. Private equity groups attribute the absence of these terms in other nations to the difficulties of enforcing these provisions in court.

- In nations where the rule of law is less well-established, private equity groups emphasize large equity holdings. They are likely to make the size of their equity stakes contingent on the performance of the company and to have the majority of the firm's equity if the investment encounters difficulties.

- Larger transactions with higher valuations are seen in common-law countries.

Pricing

Significant differences also appear in the pricing of transactions in developed and developing nations. Reflecting the later stage of most investments, the types of spectacular returns seen in U.S. ventures such as Digital Equipment, Genentech, and Netscape have traditionally not often been encountered. As William Hambrecht, chairman of the San Francisco–based investment bank Hambrecht & Quist, points out, "Asian investing success in baseball terms is characterized by double and triples, not the occasional home run characteristic of U.S. venture capital."[13] This traditional pattern is changing, however, as venture investments become more commonplace: examples including Star-Media in Latin America and Infosys in India.

Venture capitalists' assessment of the value of a company in a developing nation is often problematic. Challenges abound at many levels. For instance, many developing countries lack timely and accurate macroeconomic and financial information. Sometimes macroeconomic variables published by central banks are manipulated by governments to portray a healthier economy. These uncertainties—combined with political

---

12. Josh Lerner and Antoinette Schoar, "Private Equity in the Developing World: The Determinants of Transaction Structures," Unpublished working paper, Harvard University and MIT.

13. Wendi Tanaka, "Advising the Asia Investor: Experts Say It May be a Gold Mine, but No Quick Rewards," *The San Francisco Examiner* (September 20, 1994), p. D1.

and regulatory risks—may make it extremely difficult to draw up reasonably accurate projections. The uncertainty increases further since most private companies, especially family-run businesses, do not even have audited financial statements. Furthermore, accounting principles and practices, although improving, are still very different from Western standards.

IV. THE PRIVATE EQUITY CYCLE: EXITING

Perhaps the most vexing aspect of venture investing in developing nations has been the difficulty of exit. The fortunes of private equity investors in the developed world have been largely linked to those of the market for initial public offerings (IPOs). Studies of the U.S. market suggest that the most profitable private equity investments have, on average, been disproportionately exited by way of IPOs. In both Europe and the United States, there has been a strong link between the health of the IPO market and the ability of private equity funds to raise more capital.

Private equity investors in developing countries cannot rely on these offerings. Even in "hot markets" where large foreign capital inflows are occurring, institutional funds are usually concentrated in a few of the largest corporations. Smaller and new firms typically do not attract significant institutional holdings, and have much less liquidity.

An illustration of these claims is India, which saw over 2,000 IPOs between January 1991 and April 1995. Despite the volume of IPOs, the public market has not been an attractive avenue for exiting private equity investments. The bulk of these offerings appear to be bought by individual investors, who purchase them at huge discounts (the typical share trades on the day of its offering at 106 percent above its offering price). After the offering, trading appears to be very thin for most offerings. For instance, 18 percent of the offerings do not trade on the day immediately after the offering (most of these apparently never trade again). It would be very difficult for a private equity investor to liquidate a substantial stake in a young firm through this mechanism.[14] The situation in many other emerging markets, which lack the infrastructure of settlement procedures, payment systems, custodial or safekeeping facilities, and regulations is even bleaker.

Consequently, private equity investors in developing countries have tended to rely on the sale to portfolio firms to strategic investors. This can be problematic, however, when the number of potential buyers is small. The purchaser can exploit the private equity investor's need to exit the investment, and acquire the company for below its fair value. This is particularly likely to be the case when the firm invests in a strategic alliance: the only feasible purchasers are likely to be the other partners in the alliance.

Several private organizations have tried to develop creative approaches to the exiting problem. Examples include the listing of the shares on an exchange in a developed country, and the acquisition of a similar firm in a developed country (which is subsequently merged with the firm in the developing nation). This is likely to be an area for continued innovation in the years to come.

V. LOOKING FORWARD

The future of private equity in the developing world remains highly uncertain. But there are reasons to be optimistic. While the interest on the part of U.S. institutional investors

14. Ajay Shah, "The Indian IPO Market: Empirical Facts," Working paper, Centre for Monitoring the Indian Economy (Bombay, 1995).

remains rather variable, the increasing involvement of leading private equity organizations in investments in developing nations should increase the quality of the deal selection and management. The evolution of institutions such as national securities exchanges, regulatory agencies, banking systems, and capital markets suggest that the difficult problem of exiting investments may eventually be addressed.

Perhaps most persuasively, the types of environments where private equity funds have thrived in the United States are quite similar to developing nations: the investors have specialized in financing illiquid, difficult-to-value firms in environments with substantial uncertainty and information asymmetries. In short, it would not be surprising if the private equity industry in developing nations slowly matures, with the investment cycle becoming increasingly similar to that of developed nations.

FURTHER READING

Aylward, Anthony (1998), *Trends in Venture Capital Finance in Developing Countries*, International Finance Corporation, Washington.

Asian Venture Capital Journal (2003 and earlier years), *Asian Venture Capital Journal*.

Asian Venture Capital Journal (2003), *The Guide to Venture Capital in Asia: 2003 Edition*, Asian Venture Capital Journal, Hong Kong.

Asset Alternatives (2001 and earlier years), *Latin American Private Equity Analyst*, Wellesley, Massachusetts.

Carter, Laurence W. (1996), *IFC's Experience in Promoting Emerging Market Investment Funds*, Washington, International Finance Corporation.

Chotigeat, T., et al., "Venture Capital Investment Evaluation in Emerging Markets," *Multinational Business Review* 5 (Fall 1997): 54–62.

Dale, William B., and Richard N. Bale (1958), *Private United States Venture Capital for Investment in Newly Developing Countries*, Industrial International Comparative Studies, Investment Series, #2, Development Center, Stanford Research Institute, Menlo Park, California.

Folta, Paul H. (1999), "The Rise of Venture Capital in China: Context and Cases for Newcomers and Skeptics," *China Business Review* 26 (no. 6): 6–15.

Foust, Dean, Karen L. Miller, and Bill Javetski, "Special Report: Financing World Growth," *BusinessWeek*, (October 3, 1994): 100–103.

Fox, James W. (1996), "The Venture Capital Mirage: An Assessment of USAID Experience with Equity Investment," Working paper, Center for Development Information and Evaluation, U.S. Agency for International Development, Washington.

Fretz, Deirdre, "Emerging Markets' Push for Private Equity," *Institutional Investor* 29 (October 1995): 319–320.

Lerner, Josh, and Antoinette Schoar (2003), "Private Equity in the Developing World: The Determinants of Transaction Structures," Unpublished working paper, Harvard University and MIT.

Mitra, Devashis, "The Venture Capital Industry in India," *Journal of Small Business Management* 38 (April 2000): 67–78.

Sagari, Silvia B., and Gabriela Guidotti (1992), "Venture Capital: Lessons from the Developed World for the Developing Markets," Discussion Paper No. 13, International Finance Corporation, Washington.

Schwartz, Larry W., "Venture Abroad: Developing Countries Need Venture Capital Strategies," *Foreign Affairs* 73 (November–December 1994): 14–19.

Sedelnick, Lisa, "Sector Funds Surge," *LatinFinance* (December 1995): 13–16.

Weissman, Lorenzo, "The Advent of Private Equity in Latin America," *The Columbia Journal of World Business* 31 (Spring 1996): 60–98.

The Private Equity Cycle: Exiting

The third module of *Venture Capital and Private Equity* examines the process through which private equity investors exit their investments. Successful exits are critical to ensuring attractive returns for investors and, in turn, to raising additional capital. But private equity investors' concerns about exiting investments—and their behavior during the exiting process itself—can sometimes lead to severe problems for entrepreneurs.

We will employ an analytic framework very similar to that used in the first module of the course. We will not only seek to understand the institutional features associated with exiting private equity investments in the United States and overseas, but also to analyze them. We will map out which features are designed primarily to increase the overall amount of profits from private equity investments, and which actions seem to be intended to shift more of the profits to particular parties.

WHY THIS MODULE?

At first glance, the exiting of private equity investments may appear outside the scope of *Venture Capital and Private Equity.* It might seem that such issues are more appropriate for courses that focus on public markets. But since the need for an ultimate exit from the investments shapes every aspect of the private equity cycle, this is a very important issue for both private equity investors and entrepreneurs.

Perhaps the clearest illustration of the relationship between the private and public markets was seen during the 1980s and early 1990s. In the early 1980s, many European nations developed secondary markets. These sought to combine a hospitable environment for small firms (e.g., they allowed firms to be listed even if they did not have an extended record of profitability) with tight regulatory safeguards. These enabled the pioneering European private equity funds to exit their investments. A wave of fundraising by these and other private equity organizations followed in the mid-1980s.

After the 1987 market crash, initial public offering activity in Europe and the United States dried up. But while the U.S. market recovered in the early 1990s, the European market remained depressed. Consequently, European private equity investors were unable to exit investments by going public. They were required either to continue to hold the firms or to sell them to larger corporations at often-unattractive valuations. While U.S. private equity investors—pointing to their successful exits—were able to raise substantial amounts of new capital, European private equity fundraising during this period remained depressed. The influence of exits on the rest of the private equity cycle suggests that this is a critical issue for funds and their investors.

The exiting of private equity investments also has important implications for entrepreneurs. As discussed in the first module, the typical private equity fund is liquidated after one decade (though extensions of a few years may be possible). Thus, if a private equity investor cannot foresee how a company will be mature enough to take public or to sell at the end of a decade, he is unlikely to invest in the firm. If it were equally easy to exit investments of all types at all times, this might not be a problem. But interest in certain technologies by public investors seems to be subject to wide swings. For instance, in recent years "hot issue markets" have appeared and disappeared for computer hardware, biotechnology, multimedia, and Internet companies. Concerns about the ability to exit investments may have led to too many private equity transactions being undertaken in these "hot" industries. At the same time, insufficient capital may have been devoted to industries not in the public limelight.

Concerns about exiting may also adversely affect firms once private equity investors finance them. Less scrupulous investors may occasionally encourage companies in their portfolio to undertake actions that boost the probability of a successful initial public offering, even if they jeopardize the firm's long-run health: for example, increasing earnings by cutting back on vital research spending. In addition, many private equity investors appear to exploit their inside knowledge when dissolving their stakes in investments. While this may be in the best interests of the limited and general partners of the fund, it may have harmful effects on the firm and the other shareholders.

THE FRAMEWORK OF THE ANALYSIS

The exiting of private equity investments involves a diverse range of actors. Private equity investors exit most successful investments by taking them public.[1] A wide variety of actors are involved in the initial public offering. In addition to the private equity investors, these include the investment bank that underwrites the offering, the institutional and individual investors who are allotted the shares (and frequently sell them immediately after the offering), and the parties who end up holding the shares.

Few private equity investments are liquidated at the time of the initial public offering. Instead, private equity investors typically dissolve their positions by distributing the shares to the investors in their funds. These distributions usually take place one to two years after the offering. A variety of other intermediaries are involved in these transactions, such as distribution managers who evaluate and liquidate distributed securities for institutional investors.

---

1. A Venture Economics study finds that a $1 investment in a firm that goes public provides an average cash return of $1.95 in excess of the initial investment, with an average holding period of 4.2 years. The next best alternative, an investment in an acquired firm, yields a cash return of only 40 cents over a 3.7-year mean holding period. See Venture Economics, *Exiting Venture Capital Investments* (Wellesley, MA: Venture Economics, 1988).

This module will examine each of these players. Rather than just describing their roles, however, we will highlight the rationales for and impacts of their behavior. We will again employ the framework of the first module. We will seek to assess which institutions and features have evolved to improve the efficiency of the private equity investment process, and which have sprung up primarily to shift more of the economic benefits to particular parties.

Many of the features of the exiting of private equity investments can be understood as responses to many uncertainties in this environment. An example is the "lock-up" provisions that prohibit corporate insiders and private equity investors from selling at the time of the offering. This helps avoid situations where the officers and directors exploit their inside knowledge that a newly listed company is overvalued by rapidly liquidating their positions.

At the same time, other features of the exiting process can be seen as attempts to transfer wealth between parties. An example may be the instances where private equity funds distribute shares to their investors that drop in price immediately after the distribution. Even if the price at which the investors ultimately sell the shares is far less, the private equity investors use the share price *before* the distribution to calculate their fund's rate of return and to determine when they can begin profit-sharing.

THE STRUCTURE OF THE MODULE

This module begins by exploring the need for avenues to exit private equity investments. We will examine the role of venture capitalists and other actors, both in the reasonably well-developed—but still problematic!—U.S. market, as well as overseas. As described above, the inability to exit investments has been a major stumbling block to the development of the private equity industry outside of the United States. We explore the perspectives of and implications for private equity investors, entrepreneurs, firms, limited partners, and the specialized distribution managers that they hire. Once again, we will seek to assess which behavior increases the size of the "pie" and which actions simply change the relative sizes of the slices.

FURTHER READING ON EXITING PRIVATE EQUITY INVESTMENTS

Legal Works

Joseph W. Bartlett, *Equity Finance: Venture Capital, Buyouts, Restructurings, and Reorganization* (New York: Wiley, 1995), chapter 14.

Michael J. Halloran, Lee F. Benton, Robert V. Gunderson, Jr., Keith L. Kearney, and Jorge del Calvo, *Venture Capital and Public Offering Negotiation* (Englewood Cliffs, NJ: Aspen Law and Business, 1997 and updates), volume 2.

Jack S. Levin, *Structuring Venture Capital, Private Equity, and Entrepreneurial Transactions* (Boston: Little, Brown, 2000), chapter 9.

Practitioner and Journalistic Accounts

Paul F. Denning and Robin A. Painter, *Stock Distributions: A Guide for Venture Capitalists* (Boston: Robertson, Stephens & Co. and Testa, Hurwitz & Thibeault, 1994).

European Venture Capital Association, *Venture Capital Special Paper: Capital Markets for Entrepreneurial Companies* (Zaventum, Belgium: European Venture Capital Association, 1994).

Venture Economics, *Exiting Venture Capital Investments* (Wellesley, MA: Venture Economics, 1988).

Numerous articles in *Buyouts, Private Equity Analyst,* and *Venture Capital Journal.*

Academic Studies

Christopher B. Barry, Chris J. Muscarella, John W. Peavy III, and Michael R. Vetsuypens, "The Role of Venture Capital in the Creation of Public Companies: Evidence from the Going Public Process," *Journal of Financial Economics* 27 (October 1990): 447–471.

Bernard S. Black and Ronald J. Gilson, "Venture Capital and the Structure of Capital Markets: Banks versus Stock Markets," *Journal of Financial Economics* 47 (March 1998): 243–277.

Daniel Bradley, Bradford Jordan, Ivan Roten, and Ha-Chin Yi, "Venture Capital and IPO Lockup Expiration: An Empirical Analysis," *Journal of Financial Research* 24 (2001): 465–493.

Hsuan-Chi Chen and Jay Ritter, "The Seven Percent Solution." *Journal of Finance* 55 (1999): 1105–1131.

Douglas J. Cumming and Jeffrey G. MacIntosh, "A Cross-Country Comparison of Full and Partial Venture Capital Exits," *Journal of Banking & Finance* 27 (2003): 511–548.

George W. Fenn, Nellie Liang, and Stephen Prowse, "The Private Equity Market: An Overview," *Financial Markets, Institutions, and Instruments* 6 (#4, 1997): 1–26.

Paul A. Gompers and Josh Lerner, "Venture Capital and the Creation of Public Companies: Do Venture Capitalists Really Bring More Than Money?" *Journal of Private Equity* 1 (Fall 1999): 15–32.

Paul A. Gompers and Josh Lerner, *The Venture Capital Cycle* (Cambridge: MIT Press, 2004), chapters 14-20.

Steven N. Kaplan, "The Staying Power of Leveraged Buyouts," *Journal of Financial Economics* 29 (October 1991): 287–313.

Tim Loughran and Jay R. Ritter, "The New Issues Puzzle," *Journal of Finance* 50 (March 1995): 23–51.

William C. Megginson and Kathleen A. Weiss, "Venture Capital Certification in Initial Public Offerings," *Journal of Finance* 46 (July 1991): 879–893.

21

Apax Partners and Xerium S.A.

One bright day in early October 2002, Tom Gutierrez, CEO of Xerium S.A., looked up from the cluttered conference table at the others in the meeting: Michael Phillips and Korbinian (Korby) Knoblach of Apax Partners, a global private equity firm; Michael Collins, Xerium's retired CEO; and several bankers. They had met in person or over the phone almost every day since April, when they first put Xerium up for sale. Apax had purchased Xerium from its corporate parent in 1999, and after three years of audited financials and a performance that had dramatically exceeded the initial plan had decided to sell the company. But the process had not gone as planned, and the parties involved now faced a difficult decision.

Xerium was a global company headquartered in Westborough, Massachusetts, with thirty-eight facilities worldwide. Its plants made "clothing" and "rolls," consumable inputs to the papermaking process. Clothing was the highly engineered fabric belt that carried the paper through various stages of the forming process. Rolls included two products: spreader rolls, the small curved rolls that stretched and smoothed the paper and clothing on the machines; and roll coverings, synthetic or natural products that coated the mammoth metal rolls themselves (up to twelve meters long and two meters in diameter and weighing 100 tons). Both products needed frequent replacement and, while a small component of the price of paper, directly affected its quality and were essential to running the machines, which could cost $500 million apiece. Xerium was a solid, steadily growing company, as sales of its products were tied to the amount of paper produced and not to the price at which it sold. While paper prices were notoriously cyclical, paper production increased with global gross domestic product growth, which averaged 3 percent per year.

In October 1999, Apax had purchased Xerium (then named BTR Paper Technology) for $750 million (excluding $33 million in fees)—$700 million in cash and the balance in a performance payment. Since then, Xerium's performance (4.5 percent compound annual growth in revenues and 8.4 percent in earnings before interest, taxes, depreciation, and amortization, or EBITDA) made it an attractive sale prospect. As there had been little recent activity in the mergers and acquisitions market, investment

Professors Josh Lerner and Felda Hardymon and Senior Research Associate Ann Leamon prepared this case. HBS cases are developed solely as the basis for class discussion. Cases are not intended to serve as endorsements, sources of primary data, or illustrations of effective or ineffective management.

banks and private equity firms might be interested in any new prospect. Furthermore, the high-yield debt market was stable, facilitating any financing. Phillips knew that Apax could use a quick return to bolster the performance of its Apax Europe IV fund. He wanted to sell the company, but only at the right price, something between six and seven times EBITDA. In April 2002, Apax had formally solicited bids for the company, specifying a minimum offer of $1 billion.

Now that the field of 40 initial bidders had been narrowed to two, no one in the conference room liked the result. The one all-cash bid, $960 million, was less than Apax's minimum target of $975 million. The one at $1 billion only reached that amount through payment-in-kind dividends. Both prices were likely to drop as the buyers hammered away at performance projections. Gutierrez said, "It seems to me that we have three options. Michael [Phillips], you and Apax could take the best offer on the table. Second, we can call some of the groups that didn't make the cut and see if we can rekindle their interest. Or we could refinance the company ourselves. I don't know about you, but I'm starting to get really excited about the growth prospects and cost savings we've identified. Maybe we are leaving money on the table if we sell now."

Phillips knew that a refinancing would probably allow Apax to extract its full cost basis or a bit more from the company, while sharing in future potential gains. As the paper industry was emerging from one of its cyclical slumps, Xerium's sales were likely to grow substantially. A sale at the target price would yield 2 or 2.1 times Apax's investment. But a clean early exit would also send an important, reassuring signal to the investors in Apax IV. What was the wisest course to pursue?

THE PLAYERS

Apax Partners[1]

Apax Partners was one of the first global private equity firms.[2] Its "balanced portfolio approach" meant that it was active in everything from early stage investments to buyouts. By 2002, its partners advised on investment pools with a total of $12 billion in equity. The firm had more than 180 investment professionals operating out of offices across Europe, Israel, the United States, and Japan.[3] Apax's early stage practice focused on six major sectors: information technology, media, retail and consumer, financial services, healthcare, and telecommunications. Its buyout operations were separate and would consider opportunities in any sector. Recent large transactions had included the acquisition of Yell (British Telecom's yellow pages) and Damovo (Ericsson's division specializing in sales and services of corporate telecommunication solutions).[4]

Apax had a complicated history. In 1969, Alan Patricof had founded Alan Patricof and Associates in the United States. The firm became a thriving private equity operation. Three years later and completely independently, Ronald Cohen and Maurice Tchénio had established MMG, a firm that provided corporate financial advice to and

---

1. This section informed by Josh Lerner, Felda Hardymon, Antonio Alvarez-Cano, and Borja Martinez, "Apax Partners and Dialog Semiconductor: March 1998," in Lerner and Hardymon, *Venture Capital & Private Equity: A Casebook, Vol. II* (New York: John Wiley & Sons, 2002), pp. 177–178.

2. In classical Greek, *apax* meant something that occurred once and only once. The name was chosen to symbolize both the group's unique role and its full integration across activities and frontiers.

3. Apax, http://www.apax.com/history, accessed December 31, 2003.

4. *Ibid.*

invested in high-growth businesses from offices in Chicago, Paris, and London. In 1977, the two organizations joined forces in an entity named MMG Patricof. Alan Patricof and Associates continued to operate in the United States; MMG Patricof did European mergers and acquisitions consulting work and began to establish a presence in European private equity. MMG Patricof renamed itself Apax Partners in the mid-1980s. Apax raised its first pan-European fund in 1999. Two years later, in 2001, Alan Patricof and Associates and Apax merged their U.S. and European operating companies under the name Apax Partners.

Apax described the reason for its global orientation as follows: "As the global economy becomes more and more developed, it is our view that those private equity firms that operate on a global basis will be able to spot emerging trends early, support the growth of global companies and use the world's stock markets most effectively."[5] Apax Europe V, a €4.4 billion ($4.1 billion) pan-European multistage, multisector private equity fund, had closed in March 2001. The preceding pan-European fund, Apax Europe IV, had closed in April 1999 at €1.8 billion ($2 billion) and had been fully invested by June 2001.

By late 2002, Apax, like all other private equity firms, was struggling with the protracted global downturn. While it was admittedly too early to draw firm conclusions on performance, median internal rates of return (IRRs) to European private equity overall had slumped since the mid-1990s (see Exhibit 21.1 for returns to European private equity over time). Returns had not always been so bleak—one Apax fund showed an 85 percent IRR—but 1999 vintage funds, of which Apax IV was one, were contending with the difficult exit environment and poor performance from their early stage investments.[6] Phillips observed, "An early exit from Xerium, which was doing well, would be helpful for Apax IV."

EXHIBIT 21.1

MEDIAN RETURNS TO EUROPEAN PRIVATE EQUITY BY VINTAGE YEAR

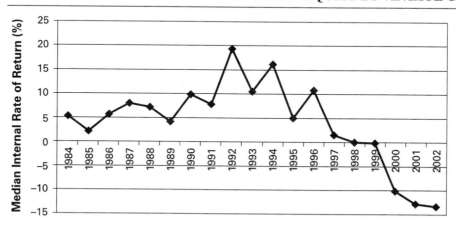

Source: Adapted from Venture Economics, http://www.venturexpert.com, accessed January 9, 2004. Data are calculated as of June 30, 2003.

5. *Ibid.*

6. John O'Donnell, "Apax Goose Stops Laying Golden Eggs," *The Sunday Times* (May 4, 2003).

Xerium

Xerium S.A., was initially BTR Paper Technology (BTRP), a division of a UK-based engineering and process control conglomerate that was founded in 1798 and had changed its name numerous times until taking British Tyre and Rubber (BTR). Exactly what BTR stood for continued to vary with the times, but the initials did not change. In 1976, BTR acquired two companies that made rolls and roll coverings, disposable inputs for the papermaking industry, and established a subsidiary, BTR Paper Technology, or BTRP. A few years later, BTRP acquired a paper machine clothing maker, establishing a position as a supplier of two crucial inputs to the industry (see Exhibit 21.2 for a diagram of a paper machine and where these products are involved). Although other continuous-process industries such as textiles and fiberboard used similar products, the paper industry was by far the biggest consumer.

By the 1990s, BTRP had expanded to a worldwide presence, both through acquiring other companies and by establishing its own manufacturing plants, some under license (see Exhibit 21.3 for the acquisition history and Exhibit 21.4 for a map). It also invested in research and development to create more highly engineered and thus higher margin products.

BTRP developed an extremely decentralized organization. Its eighteen offices in seventeen countries operated thirty-eight plants almost independently, using the brand names Weavexx for North American clothing, Huyck for non-U.S. clothing, Stowe-Woodward for roll covers, and Mount Hope for spreader rolls. The head office of BTRP, in Westborough, Massachusetts, contained ten people.

From 1965 through 1993, CEO Owen Green led the parent BTR through hectic acquisition activity, took it public in 1982, and headed its unprecedented 1991 hostile takeover of Hawker-Siddeley, a troubled aircraft manufacturer known for its work

---

EXHIBIT 21.2

ROLLS AND CLOTHING IN PAPER MACHINES

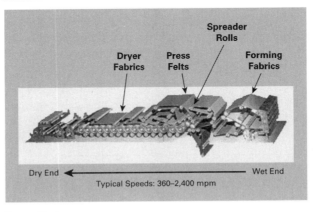

Source: Xerium.

EXHIBIT 21.3

BTRP'S ACQUISITION HISTORY TO 1999

Year	Division	Company	Location°	Sales ($MM)†
1976	Rolls	Stowe Woodward/Mount Hope	U.S.	NA
1980	Clothing	Huyck	U.S.	170
1980	Rolls	Becker	Germany	13
1988	Clothing	Nortelas	Brazil	11
1988	Rolls	Nokia	Finland	14
1989	Rolls	Irga	Italy	14
1990	Rolls	Boetcher	Germany	4
1990	Rolls	Plastex	Germany	5
1990	Clothing	Niagara-Lockport	Canada	86
1995	Rolls	Wittler	Germany	10

Source: Apax Partners.

Notes:

° Primary location.

† Sales of the most recent full year before acquisition.

EXHIBIT 21.4

BTRP'S LOCATIONS AS OF 1999

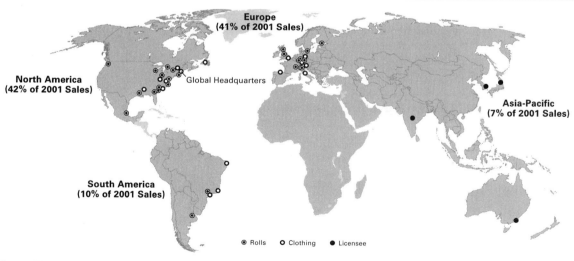

Source: Xerium.

during World War Two.[7] Recalled Michael Collins, former Group CEO of the paper division (see Exhibit 21.5 for Collins' biography):

> Green believed in a very flat organization. He created a very unique culture, with lots of little aphorisms, such as, "Sales is vanity, profits are sanity." It was a very detail-oriented company; every group CEO was expected to have a deep understanding of the business operations. And there was a clear, organization-wide understanding that every year was to be an improvement on the one before. The budget wasn't called a spending plan but a profit plan. It may not seem like a big thing, but it really made a difference.

In 1998, after Green had been succeeded by two different CEOs, BTR merged with its rival, engineering and controls giant Siebe. The merged company changed its name first to BTR/Siebe and then to Invensys. It was, general opinion held, "one of the most value-destroying mergers in history."[8]

Collins commented, "It became very clear that Invensys had to sell assets. It had enormous debt and was hemorrhaging cash. Because BTRP was a solid, cash-generating division, we knew it would be sold early." Late in 1998, Invensys decided that BTRP was "noncore" and engaged Morgan Stanley to find a buyer for the organization.

THE BUYOUT

Michael Phillips, a partner in Apax's office in Munich, Germany, and a member of the leveraged transactions team, was aware of the action around BTRP (see Exhibit 21.6 for his biography). He said, "In this business, we generally know what's going on. If the first time we hear of a transaction is when we receive the book [the seller's presentation of the business to be sold], we're in trouble. That's very rare. We'd heard the rumors about BTRP being on the market but had discounted them. In fact, when we were offered the chance to bid, we turned it down because it wasn't in our direct field of interest."

Shortly thereafter, in late 1998, Phillips received a call from a former Apax corporate finance expert who had become a global mergers and acquisitions advisor. This

---

EXHIBIT 21.5

BIOGRAPHY OF MICHAEL COLLINS

Michael Collins is the nonexecutive chairman of Xerium S.A., the corporate parent of a thirty-eight-plant global operation that manufactures consumables for the paper industry. Since September 2003, he has also been chairman and CEO of Damovo S.A., a telecommunications integrator with operations in nineteen countries. From 1993 through 2002, Collins served as group president of BTRP, having joined BTR in 1980. During his career at BTR, he was chief executive of eight different groups, at one point simultaneously managing four groups with 13,000 employees and combined revenues of $1.3 billion. Prior to joining BTR, he was president of Becton-Dickinson, a U.S. medical devices manufacturer. He holds a degree in chemistry and physics from London University.

Source: Apax.

---

7. Information from http://premium.hoovers.com/subscribe/co/boneyard/factsheet.xhtml?COID=42398, accessed December 30, 2003.
8. "Mea culpa, Invensys . . . ," *Investors Chronicle* (April 25, 2003).

EXHIBIT 21.6

APAX TEAM BIOS

Michael Phillips, Leveraged Transactions, Germany

Michael Phillips joined Apax Partners in 1992, focusing on leveraged transactions, buyouts and investments in retail and consumer. A graduate in engineering chemistry from Queen's University in Kingston, Canada, Phillips also holds an MBA from INSEAD, where he graduated with distinction.

Upon graduating from University, he worked at Ciba Geigy Canada Ltd. as a manager in the plastics additives division. He then spent three years at OTTO Holding Ltd. in Cologne, one of Germany's largest waste management companies, as the general manager of an operations subsidiary.

Korbinian Knoblach, Leveraged Transactions, Germany

Korbinian Knoblach is a member of the leveraged transactions team, specializing in business and financial services. Before joining Apax Partners in 2002, Knoblach attended the University of Regensburg and Tulane University in New Orleans, Louisiana, and graduated with distinction from the Leipzig Graduate School of Management.

During his studies, Knoblach undertook internships in private equity (Apax Partners), mergers and acquisitions (Donaldson, Lufkin & Jenrette), management consulting (Roland Berger Strategy Consultants), and the automotive industry (Siemens Automotive).

Source: Apax, http://www.apax.com, accessed February 11, 2004.

---

individual had a mandate to sell Wangner-Finckh, a German-based family-owned maker of paper industry consumables with 1998 revenues of roughly $70 million and EBITDA close to $13 million. Phillips commented:

> Normally, we wouldn't have been interested because family businesses are challenging and Wangner-Finckh was too small to be a stand-alone investment. But we knew BTRP was in play. Although neither of them interested us separately, the synergies of the two together were significant. Wangner had great engineering and would be a perfect fit with BTRP to expand its European presence. BTRP had been underinvested because Invensys was draining its profits to service the debt, but it was highly profitable and had great management.

In addition to its European market presence, Wangner also had information on a historically opaque industry. Few clothing and rolls makers were public, limiting the information that Phillips and his team could access before declaring their formal interest in BTRP. Wangner, however, had a wealth of information and insights across the industry and even into BTRP itself.

It was also clear that BTRP would be sold. "With revenues of $450 million per year," Phillips explained, "BTRP was too small for an initial public offering [IPO]. And because the sector wasn't hot, the price would not be high."

In early 1999, the Apax team formally entered the bidding process for BTRP. Apax created two teams and ran the acquisitions of Wangner and BTRP simultaneously. "We knew there wouldn't be an auction for BTRP," said Phillips. "It was in the paper industry, which is not an exciting sector, there were a limited number of consolidation options, and it wasn't hugely scalable. It wasn't glamorous. It was a solid, cash-generating company growing 3 percent to 5 percent per year."

After the initial flurry of activity, only three other firms were interested: CVC Capital Partners, Doughty Hanson, and Bain Capital.[9] None seemed particularly threatening to Apax, as Phillips explained:

> CVC, for instance, was capacity constrained. It wasn't really focused on BTRP but was bidding on another Invensys asset and wanted to be perceived as serious. Bain did little business in Europe and wouldn't be able to execute a global buyout. In fact, both of these had contacted us to see if we'd be willing to team up, as neither was well-positioned regarding the asset. Lastly, through the interaction with Wangner-Finckh, we knew Doughty Hanson wasn't a serious contender.

"So within a month," Phillips continued, "we had all good signs. We had good insights, a good asset, a distressed seller, and no real competition in the deal. As soon as we started due diligence, things got better. BTRP had high cash assets and potential cost savings, we identified ways to increase profits at Wangner, and the deal was still uncontested."

The process of due diligence was intense. Along with research, the team made site visits, met management, and did financial and market analysis. BTRP's decentralized structure both helped and hindered the work. Phillips explained:

> It wasn't a company really but a group of separate operating units. BTRP Canada ran Canada, BTRP Argentina ran Argentina. There were no group-wide control systems, just a collection of individual country accounts. The headquarters made pro-forma statements as if a company existed. This made it very difficult to do the analysis of the physical business units. We had to take the pro forma, disaggregate it to the country level, and then reaggregate it. There were big exchange movements during the three years that constituted history, so even merging accounts or standardizing them in a single currency during the period was complex. Our ability to produce consistent results was, to say the least, limited. But the advantage was that this further reduced the enthusiasm of our competitors. Not only was the time investment significant, but we incurred huge fees for financial and legal due diligence, something in the neighborhood of $3 million. We learned from the market how much our competitors were willing to spend on due diligence. In effect, we out-due-diligenced and outspent the competition.

One of the reasons Apax was willing to make the investment was that Invensys needed to sell. "A big risk is always that the vendor decides not to go through with the transaction," said Phillips. "One reason we were willing to spend so much time and money on due diligence was that we knew we had a distressed vendor. Invensys needed cash desperately. The CEO had to sell something by year's end."

The Apax team bid $1 billion as a starting figure. It was, as Phillips explained,

> the way these things work. The investment bank tells you what you need to bid to be part of the transaction. Then during due diligence, you learn more and more and develop a credible alternate business plan. With our deep insight into valuation details and industry trends, we could argue against the business plan that the bank and the company had devised. For one thing, no one had transparent audit accounts for the past. We had a solid defensible

---

9. Richard Rivlin and Peter Thal Larsen, "Four in Running for Invensys Paper Unit," *The Financial Times* (July 1, 1999), p. 27.

base case very different from that of the company. Yet we also knew we could build the business. We knew the company better than the vendor. We even had an estimate of group pension liabilities, which Invensys didn't have.

The items that reduced Apax's opening bid fell into two categories. Some were financial issues, such as pension liabilities and deferred capital expenditures, which reduced the final price but did not benefit Apax or anyone else, as they were true financial costs that would have to be borne. The others were differing assumptions about the business plan. By viewing potential growth opportunities conservatively and taking a sober view of future challenges, Apax built a business plan that contained lower projections than Invensys' base case.

Collins, the group president of BTRP at the time, commented:

> Management is always torn in a buyout. The information given the bidders often embellishes the company's potential, increasing its value and the price the vendor can get. The management is in the middle, because potential sellers are wooing you to get your information and the vendor is urging you to support the official position. The biggest issue is that you don't want to make promises you can't keep. If you support a price that burdens the company with debt, it's not fair to the employees who have to work in such constrained circumstances. While vendors may argue that it's "pain that goes away," it's not fair to anyone if you set unrealistic expectations.

The quality of prospective buyers varied. Collins recalled, "Apax was extremely thorough. Some bidders were so casual that they hadn't even decided what questions were important before they showed up. People who didn't understand the business were worried about the margins; they didn't see how they could be sustained."

Apax's thoroughness showed in the final purchase price of $750 million. This included the cost of the company, $651 million, and of paying off $99 million of debt. The total consideration, including fees of $33.1 million and $7.6 million of cash injected into the business, came to $790.7 million. The deal was structured as an asset sale. Sources of financing included $510 million of senior debt, $170.7 million of equity, and $110 million in seller financing. Invensys provided an interest-bearing subordinated note of $50 million and received a $60 million earn-out contingent on very high performance. The earn-out, however, was not included in the computed purchase price. Invensys also reinvested $18 million for a 10 percent share in the new company. The deal closed in October 1999, six months after Apax had started its due diligence (see Exhibit 21.7 for details).

The mechanics of the deal were complex, as each of the seventeen operating units was purchased individually and the debt held on the balance sheet of each country's office, to be written off against goodwill. The transaction was structured as tax-advantageously as possible given each country's regulations. Phillips said, "We did upstream mergers, downstream mergers, whatever was most tax-efficient." The holding company was headquartered in Luxembourg to ensure that profits could be repatriated tax-free.

A few months later, Apax completed the acquisition of Wangner and merged it into BTRP, renaming the entity Xerium. The sellers, the Wangner family, received 10 percent of the combined company. Including the refinancing of $10 million of existing debt, Wangner was valued at $87 million, or 6.8× EBITDA. BTRP, for contrast, was valued at 5.0× EBITDA. Wangner's higher valuation stemmed from assumed cost synergies and avoided capital expenditures. Including these reduced the multiple to 4.6. Unlike BTRP's management, Wangner's management did not receive a stake in the new business (see Exhibits 21.8a and 21.8b for schematic and details), but the company's owners did. At

EXHIBIT 21.7

STRUCTURE OF APAX'S PURCHASE OF BTRP

Uses of Cash	$ million	Sources of Cash	$ million	Comment
Total Enterprise Valuation	**750.0**	**Total Debt**	**620.0**	
~Net Debt	99.0	**Total Senior Debt**	**510.0**	
~Purchase price for 100% of equity	651.0			
		A Senior Facility	300.0	LIBOR + 200 bps
		B Senior Facility	110.0	LIBOR + 250 bps
		C Senior Facility	100.0	LIBOR + 300 bps
		Subordinated Debt	**110.0**	All held by seller, some contingent.
		Total Equity	**170.7**	
		~Shareholder's Loan ~(10% coupon)	138.7	From all investors except management.
Transactions Cost	**33.1**	~0% Interest Loan	30.9	From all investors pro rata to equity.
Cash Injected into Business	**7.6**	~Nominal Capital	1.1	Held by all investors.
		Shares of the total Equity		
		+ BTRP Mgmt	$2.2	7.0%
		+ Invensys	$18.2	10.0%
		+ Apax	$150.3	83.0%
Total Uses of Financing	**790.7**	**Total Sources of Financing**	**790.7**	

Source: Apax.

Note: At the time of the buyout, the ninety-day LIBOR rate was 5.25 percent. BPS = basis points, 1/100 of 1%.

the end of this merger, Invensys owned 10 percent of the combined business, the Wangner family 10 percent, BTRP's management 6 percent, and Apax the balance.

SELLING XERIUM

By April 2002, the market environment looked favorable for selling BTRP (now Xerium). Xerium, in turn, looked like a good sales prospect. The Apax team had already refinanced it once, repaying some of the high-coupon debt.[10] The company had also acquired two small rolls companies since the merger with Wangner (see Exhibit 21.9).

The old decentralized structure had remained. The head office had grown to sixteen people as Xerium took on tasks such as treasury, tax, human resources, and risk management that had previously been handled by Invensys. Collins, who had been on

10. Lisa Bushrod, "Xerium," *European Venture Capital Journal* (December 1, 2002), p. 1.

EXHIBIT 21.8a

POSITION OF XERIUM AFTER WANGNER ACQUISITION

Items	$ millions	Items	$ millions	Ownership
Total Enterprise Valuation	**$837.5**	**Total Debt**	**$680.0**	
~Purchase price	$706.6	~Senior Debt	$570.0	
~net debt	$109.0	~Sub Debt	$1,10.0	
~Wangner purchase of newco	$21.9			
Transactions Cost	**$39.0**	**Equity**	**$207.7**	
		~Shareholders' loan	$172.1	
Cash Injected into Business	**$11.2**	~0% Interest loan	$34.4	
		~Nominal Capital	$1.1	
		+ *BTRP Mgmt*	*$2.2*	*6.3%*
		+ *Invensys*	*$19.7*	*10.0%*
		+ *Apax*	*$163.8*	*73.7%*
		+ *Wangner*	*$21.9*	*10.0%*
Total Uses	**$887.7**	**Total Sources**	**$887.7**	

Source: Apax.

the verge of retiring when Apax purchased BTRP, had recruited Tom Gutierrez from another Invensys division in August 2001 to take his place as CEO. Gutierrez had run BTR's sensors business and later worked for Collins running the electronics division, moving eventually to lead the $3 billion power systems unit (see Exhibit 21.10 for his biography). He said, "Michael [Collins] and I have the same approach to business. He wanted to turn Xerium over to someone who shared his view of a lean profit-focused operation with a thin organizational structure. After I joined the firm, I spent six months traveling the world with him to learn the business."

Xerium had out-performed Apax's business plan substantially (see Exhibits 21.11a and 21.11b). EBITDA had reached $160 million for the year ending December 2001, up over 8 percent since 1998, its last full year with Invensys. The company had restructured, closing plants and selling some businesses. Phillips observed, "It's the private equity effect. When people can earn big bonuses for hitting targets, they tend to hit them."

In selling Xerium, Apax faced an unusual conundrum. Gutierrez said:

> The first time around, Apax got a good deal because it could create value in the company. But deals are highly contextual. You have to have an angle to add value, and you must not overpay. The problem here was that the company had performed so well that no one could see the upside. And it wasn't glamorous. You wouldn't get high-tech type growth. But you would get 3 percent annual growth, cash generation, technological leadership, and the ability to survive in downturns. You wouldn't be able to buy it cheap and restructure it because it was already running very well.

EXHIBIT 21.8b

ACQUISITION OF BTRP AND WANGNER

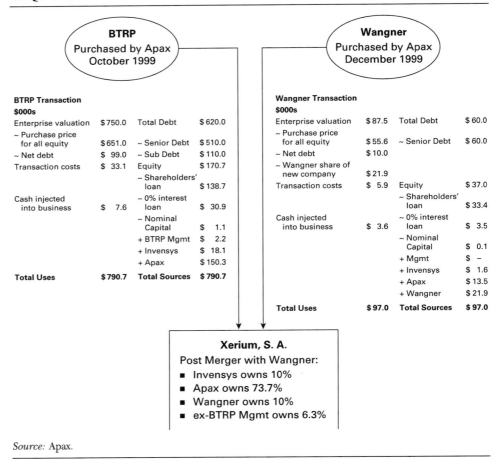

BTRP Transaction $000s			
Enterprise valuation	$ 750.0	Total Debt	$ 620.0
~ Purchase price for all equity	$ 651.0	~ Senior Debt	$ 510.0
~ Net debt	$ 99.0	~ Sub Debt	$ 110.0
Transaction costs	$ 33.1	Equity	$ 170.7
		~ Shareholders' loan	$ 138.7
Cash injected into business	$ 7.6	~ 0% interest loan	$ 30.9
		~ Nominal Capital	$ 1.1
		+ BTRP Mgmt	$ 2.2
		+ Invensys	$ 18.1
		+ Apax	$ 150.3
Total Uses	**$ 790.7**	**Total Sources**	**$ 790.7**

Wangner Transaction $000s			
Enterprise valuation	$ 87.5	Total Debt	$ 60.0
~ Purchase price for all equity	$ 55.6	~ Senior Debt	$ 60.0
~ Net debt	$ 10.0		
~ Wangner share of new company	$ 21.9		
Transaction costs	$ 5.9	Equity	$ 37.0
		~ Shareholders' loan	$ 33.4
Cash injected into business	$ 3.6	~ 0% interest loan	$ 3.5
		~ Nominal Capital	$ 0.1
		+ Mgmt	$ –
		+ Invensys	$ 1.6
		+ Apax	$ 13.5
		+ Wangner	$ 21.9
Total Uses	**$ 97.0**	**Total Sources**	**$ 97.0**

Xerium, S. A.
Post Merger with Wangner:
- Invensys owns 10%
- Apax owns 73.7%
- Wangner owns 10%
- ex-BTRP Mgmt owns 6.3%

Source: Apax.

EXHIBIT 21.9

XERIUM'S ACQUISITIONS SINCE APAX PURCHASED BTRP

Year	Division	Company	Location°	Sales ($MM)[†]
1999	Clothing	Wangner	Germany	67
2001	Rolls	Trelleborg	Sweden	6
2002	Rolls	Robec	Germany	3

Source: Xerium.

Notes:

° Primary location.

† Sales of the most recent full year before acquisition.

EXHIBIT 21.10

BIOGRAPHY OF TOM GUTIERREZ

Tom Gutierrez joined Xerium in 2001 after working for Invensys for five years. He served as CEO of Invensys Power Systems (1999–2001), a $3 billion multinational business, where he executed three major acquisitions and significantly improved profitability. Prior to being appointed CEO of Invensys Power Systems Group, he served as CEO of Exide Electronics (1997–1998), a subsidiary of Power Systems, which achieved 30 percent profit growth in his first year. He was also the group chief executive of BTR Sensor Systems Group (1995–1997) and COO of Pulse Engineering (1992–1994). Gutierrez has more than thirty years of experience in product development, manufacturing, marketing, sales, and general business management. He received his BSEE from Florida Institute of Technology in 1972.

Source: Xerium.

EXHIBIT 21.11a

XERIUM'S FINANCIAL RESULTS (BASED ON MANAGEMENT NUMBERS)

$ millions	2000	2001	2002
Total Sales			
Jan 2000 Plan at 1999 Exch. Rates	515.3	524.4	533.7
Jan 2000 Plan at 2002 Exch. Rates	459.1	467.3	475.7
Actual at 2002 Exch. Rates	492.2	495.9	513.5
Actual versus Plan	*7.2%*	*6.1%*	*7.9%*
EBITDA			
Jan 2000 Plan at 1999 Exch. Rates	163.6	173.0	178.3
Jan 2000 Plan at 2002 Exch. Rates	146.1	153.9	158.6
Actual at 2002 Exch. Rates	158.0	157.5	167.0
Actual versus Plan	*8.2%*	*2.3%*	*6.6%*
Credit Statistics			
Total Debt/EBITDA	3.3x	3.0x	
EBITDA/Cash Interest	3.4x	3.8x	
Debt (millions)	$560.0	$475.0	

Source: Xerium.

The Industry and Competitors

All was not well in the paper industry. It had been in a protracted slump since the beginning of 2000. While paper prices did not affect Xerium's sales directly, the resulting cash constraints would incline paper manufacturers to curtail production, shut down machines, and extend the use of clothing and rolls beyond their recommended life, thus indirectly reducing sales of rolls and clothing.

EXHIBIT 21.11b

XERIUM'S PROJECTIONS AS OF END OF 2001

($ millions)	1999A	2000A	2001A	2002E	2003E	2004E	2005E
Sales	453.8	492.2	495.9	513.5	535.8	559.5	587.2
% growth		*8.5*	*0.8*	*3.5*	*4.3*	*4.4*	*4.9*
Variable Contribution	267.6	293.6	287.9	305.4	318.5	332.7	348.5
% margin	*59.0*	*59.7*	*58.1*	*59.5*	*59.4*	*59.5*	*59.3*
EBITDA	133.9	158.0	157.5	167.0	177.6	188.3	199.3
% margin	*29.5*	*32.1*	*31.8*	*32.5*	*33.2*	*33.6*	*33.9*
Depreciation & Amortization	57.5	59.9	52.4	51.2	50.8	52.3	52.6
Capital Expenditures	46.4	38.0	32.2	36.0	41.0	41.0	41.0
Working Capital as a % of Sales	40.0%	36.6%	35.9%	34.4%	34.0%	34.0%	34.0%
Free Cash Flow	92.2	136.1	135.3	122.3	131.1	140.9	147.4

Source: Xerium.

Compounding the pricing pressure on Xerium, the paper industry was consolidating. Three significant mergers had occurred since Xerium's acquisition. At the same time, other trends increased the need for Xerium's products and put a premium on its research and development efforts. New machines ran faster (up to 2,400 meters per minute), putting extreme stresses on the clothing and roll coverings. New paper types, such as those using recycled products, required different types of consumables, as did the effort to make higher quality paper from lower quality raw materials.

Despite the dismal macro environment, which pressured sales and orders, Xerium's market share of clothing had grown from 12 percent in 1999 to 14 percent in 2001, while its share of the rolls business had risen from 45 percent to 46 percent. Part of this was due to its acquisitions, but much stemmed from its research and development efforts. Capital expenditures had run at roughly 8 percent of annual sales from 1993 to 1998, 50 percent higher than the level of major competitors. The company was exceeding its profitability targets due to restructuring and product price increases, made possible both through its own innovative products and the ongoing consolidation in the clothing and rolls business.

Xerium's two product groups had very different characteristics. While both comprised a very small proportion of the cost of paper and were crucial to its final quality and the ability of producers to use their expensive machines, clothing was considered a commodity and rolls a specialty item. Clothing was part of "cost of goods sold" and thus purchased centrally through the customer's central office. To differentiate itself, Xerium had invested heavily in research and development, developing two- and three-ply products that generated margins dramatically higher than commodity one-ply clothing. It also focused on the high-margin "forming fabrics" and "press felts" rather than low-margin "dryer felts."

Roll coverings, on the other hand, were considered the domain of individual maintenance departments, and the primary focus was not on price but reliability and quality. Given the rolls' cost and specificity (there were no standard paper machines), a plant would have only one backup for each roll. Should the backup roll fail while the original roll was getting a new cover, the entire machine would shut down, at a cost of $10,000 per hour. The sheer size and weight of the rolls meant that most of their maintenance had to be performed on site, a clear advantage for Xerium's roll companies with their thirty locations worldwide. While the fragmentation and regional nature of the rolls business meant that most contracts were negotiated directly with the plant in question, Xerium had the only two centrally negotiated preferred supplier contracts in that sector. Xerium also bundled mechanical services with its roll re-covering and would do routine maintenance on the internal workings of the rolls while they were off the machine and conveniently accessible. This helped the paper makers avoid using multiple suppliers and paying transportation charges.

Xerium had leading positions in both of its markets (see Exhibit 21.12 for competitor financials). It was tied with J. M. Voith, a paper-machine maker with a clothing division, for the number two position in the clothing market behind Albany International (NYSE: AIN), which had a 30 percent share. In rolls, Xerium led the world market with its 46 percent share, over twice that of Voith's 21 percent.[11]

Xerium's performance had allowed it to pay down its acquisition-related debt ahead of schedule. By the time Apax was considering its sale, Xerium had paid an extra $77 million and reduced its total debt to $475 million by the end of 2001, bringing its leverage to 2.5× EBITDA.

The Sales Process

Apax began the sales process in January 2002 with a beauty contest. Gutierrez described it saying:

> In a single day, a bunch of banks come through to tell you what they think the company is worth, how they'd market it, and why they're the best group

---

EXHIBIT 21.12

COMPETITORS' FINANCIALS

($ millions)	Albany International	J. M. Voith
Est. 2002 Sales	$816.0	$3,226.9
1-Year Sales Growth	–2.5%	6.8%
Est. 2002 Net Income	$49.0	$62.4
1-Year Net Income Growth	52.2%	–28.3%
Est. Long-term Debt (YE 2002)	$221.7	$652.3
Beta	0.9	NA
Market Capitalization	$1,037.2	NA

Sources: Adapted from OneSource and Hoover's.

Note: NA = Not Available.

---

11. Xerium information.

for the job. Morgan Stanley's UK branch had handled the original deal for the vendor, so we chose them because they already had a background with the business. That's extremely important; you have to be sure the bank understands the business. We spent about two months building the selling case—even as I was still learning the details of the business. We prepared the presentation and the financials, and the bank developed the preliminary marketing pitch for the asset [the teaser]. We agreed on the groups that would receive the book. We didn't, for instance, want any competitors because they're likely to raid the data room, learn your secrets, and never get serious. It was pretty clear even then that only another financial group would buy the company. This process took about two months.

In addition to the book, the process and presentation were important. Gutierrez went on:

Coming from the high-tech industry, I understood the process. To present effectively, you have to have sales skills, presentation skills, and the ability to think on your feet when you're asked tough questions. The buyers bring experts and consultants to chip away at your story and drive down the value of the business. As the vendor, you may have a really good operations team that can't present, or a team of very polished presenters that don't know the business. Neither works. The key is to build the presentation to include the entire management team, because it would look funny if key people weren't there, but you showcase the people who have the best blend of business understanding and presentation skills. We prepared for presentations and practiced answers to questions for quite a while.

The teaser, sent in April 2002, generated forty responses. One reporter commented, "The Xerium sale is already attracting interest on Wall Street."[12] The valuations ranged between $850 million and $1.2 billion; a sale at the upper end of the range would give Apax a 50 percent IRR.[13] The forty contenders were reduced to seven based on their reputation, their credibility, and the likelihood they would actually complete the deal. These received the full book, full access to the management team, site visits, and the presentation. Gutierrez explained, "You can't really handle more than seven serious bidders. It's incredibly time-consuming." By July 2002, the group of seven had fallen to two, a New York–based investment bank consortium and a U.S. conglomerate.

Gutierrez said, "If you just give one buyer an exclusive, you could be left standing at the altar and then have to generate interest from groups you'd jilted in the past." Neither of the two deals was perfect. The one bid that came in above $1 billion included preferred-payment-in-kind notes;[14] the "clean" deal offered $960 million. And the financial markets were falling.

OPTIONS

Gutierrez said, "At this point, we really had to consider our options. We had not even thought of recapitalizing the company at the beginning. Apax wanted to get out. But now I was really up to speed with the business, and it seemed we had some options."

---

12. Jeremy Adams, "Apax Hopes to Sell Xerium," *The Financial News* (April 2, 2002).

13. *Ibid.*

14. That is, notes that paid interest in more of the company's debt.

Refinance and Try Later

The paper industry downturn had been substantial and almost exactly coincided with Apax's ownership of Xerium. "If we could grow market share and margins in a downturn," mused Gutierrez, "what could we do when this turns around?" Analysts projected that the paper industry would start to recover in 2003. In addition, the company could take advantage of some of the growth and cost-cutting opportunities that the management team had identified in preparing for the bidders' questions. Another possibility included making acquisitions of complementary businesses or of competitors that would consolidate Xerium's position as number one and two in its markets. While future acquisitions to its dominant position in the rolls market might bring up antitrust concerns, Xerium could either expand into other paper industry consumables or acquire its competitors in the clothing industry, where it had held periodic talks with some of the smaller makers. Yet refinancing would not give Apax IV the same boost as a sale. One could also wonder how long the "buyout phenomenon" would maintain the management's enthusiasm for hard work and cost cutting.

Nonetheless, there was nothing to guarantee that a buyer would offer a better price next time. Apax's Phillips said, "It's just not glamorous. Buyers get confused between its products and the paper industry. Yet Xerium has high margins and it's part of a small group of producers in a wonderfully stable market. Financial buyers, though, just don't get excited about something that grows at 3 percent to 5 percent per year and won't ever grow at 10 percent like a software firm."

If Apax did recapitalize, it needed to have a capital structure that gave the company sufficient cash flow. The cash flow would be used to pay down the existing debt, repay the $50 million vendor loan to Invensys, and repay the shareholder loans with their 10 percent coupons.[15] Phillips estimated that Xerium's debt would rise from $425 million to $775 million. Part of the question, then, would be how much of the higher-interest but nonamortizing[16] senior A debt should be in the package as opposed to lower-coupon, but amortizing,[17] senior B and C (see Exhibits 21.13a, 21.13b, 21.13c, and 21.13d for one possible refinancing scenario). Refinancing, Phillips estimated, would pay out 1.2 times the original investment. This was a far cry from the return of more than 30 percent that Apax would have received from a sale at anything above $975 million.

GO BACK TO THE WELL

Contacting nonfinalist buyers had some allure. For one, they knew the company to a certain degree, so Xerium's team would not be starting from scratch. Some of them even called from time to time. Yet going through the process took vast amounts of management time. Gutierrez said, "Reopening the process would be hideous. During 2002, the management team did very little but handle the selling process. If we hadn't been so decentralized, I think it would have sunk the business. If we assume a multiple of seven and figure that our profit fell by $5 million due to management distraction, our investors lost $35 million in enterprise value."

15. Shareholder loans were given by all investors except management. This helped to create "sweet equity" for managers, as they invested on the same terms in the nominal equity of the company but did not have to give a shareholder loan, which gave them a relatively higher stake in the company.

16. A nonamortizing loan requires the payment of interest only until a due date, when the principal must be paid.

17. An amortizing loan requires the payment of interest and principal over its life.

EXHIBIT 21.13a

XERIUM'S BALANCE SHEET IN OCTOBER 2002

Item	Amount ($ millions)
Assets	$711.3
Cash and Equivalents	50.8
Net noncash working capital	206.3
Total Assets	**$968.4**
Total current liabilities	$109.2°
Total provisions	4.9°
Long-term liabilities	
~Long-term senior debt	**448.5**
Senior A	*229.2*
Senior B	*115.5*
Senior C	*103.8*
~Other long-term debt	68.7°
Shareholder Loans	**264.5**
~10% loans	*231.6†*
~0% loans	*32.9°†*
Vendor note	67.8
Equity (retained earnings)	4.8
Total Liabilities and Equity	**$968.4**

Source: Apax.

Notes: ° Unchanged after possible refinancing.

  † Because Xerium is a Luxembourg-based entity, the capital structure is euro-dominated. The balance on the shareholder loans is higher here than in Exhibit 21.8a due to exchange rate movements between the euro and the dollar.

  The Luxembourg corporate tax rate as of October 2002 was 30.38 percent, the long-term corporate bond rate was 5.15 percent, and the risk-free rate on the ten-year Belgian government bond, which Luxembourg used as its long-term benchmark bond rate according to the 2002 EIU Country Commerce Report on Luxembourg, was 4.6976 percent.

It was a distinct option, though. The third-best bidder, which had dropped its bid from $1 billion to $900 million when it thought it was Apax's only option, kept calling. Xerium was continuing its strong performance, and the paper industry rebound was getting closer every day.

A Bird in the Hand . . .

The final clean bid, after intensive due diligence, was likely to fall to $935 million.[18] The company would have endured ten months of total management distraction and was going to pay $30 million in fees regardless of which option was chosen. If Apax exited at $40 million less than its asking price, would that be the worst possible option?

18. Benjamin Wottliff, "Paper Blow to Invensys Windfall," *Sunday Business* (October 20, 2002), p. 1.

EXHIBIT 21.13b

XERIUM'S PROPOSED FINANCING IN 2002

Facility	Amount ($ millions)	Coupon	Maturity
Term Loan A	$302.0	LIBOR + 2.25%	Amortizing over seven years ending 2009
Term Loan B the	$150.0	LIBOR + 2.75%	Amortizing over eight years ending 2010: 1% per annum for the period 2003–2009 and remainder in two installments in 2010
Term Loan C	$150.0	LIBOR + 3.25%	Amortizing over nine years ending 2011: 1% per annum for the period 2003–2010 and the remainder in two installments in 2011
Total Senior Term Debt	**$602.0**		
Mezzanine Term Loan Facility	$122.1	LIBOR + 5.00% Cash + 6.00% PIK°	Bullet repayment in 2012
Existing Cash	$50.8		
Total Funded Debt	**$774.9**		
Revolving Facility	$50.0	LIBOR + 2.25%	$10M cancelled after thirty months; $40M final maturity in 2009. Not used but arranged at the same time.

Source: Xerium.

Notes: The amortization period is the time during which payments of principal and interest must occur.

° PIK (payment in kind) is interest in the form of additions to the debt; that is, the interest will accrue and be added to the debt at a rate of 6.0 percent per year. This amount will be capitalized at the end of each month (and thereafter accrue interest) and will be paid on the final repayment or prepayment of the facility.

EXHIBIT 21.13c

USES OF REFINANCING

Uses of Refinancing	$ Millions
Refinance existing bank debt	448.5
Transaction cost	31.9
Repay vendor note	67.8
Repay 10% shareholder notes	231.6
Net impact of interest and exchange rate movements	−4.9
Total Uses	**774.9**

Source: Apax.

EXHIBIT 21.13d

TRANCHE ALLOCATION ACROSS CURRENCIES/COUNTRIES

Country	Denomination	Senior A	Senior B	Senior C	Mezzanine	Total
U.S.	US$	63%	58%	33%	0	45%
U.S.	Euro	0	0	67%	0	14%
Canada	Canadian $	6%	22%	0	0	7%
Italy	Euro	7%	20%	0	0	7%
Austria	Euro	7%	0	0	0	3%
Luxembourg	Euro	17%	0	0	46%	15%
Luxembourg	US$	0	0	0	54%	9%
Total (US$ millions)		**302.0**	**150.0**	**150.0**	**122.1**	**724.1**

Source: Apax.

THE FINAL EXIT

One question everyone had was the final exit for Apax. Gutierrez commented, "We know Apax is not a long-term owner. An exit is problematic. We can't go public with the public markets as they are, and we're too big to be purchased by a paper company. Where do we go except to another private equity house?"

Former CEO Michael Collins said, "We need to find this company a home somewhere. It would be a great holding for a family office. It's a good, cash-generating company, but it's paid $77 million in takeover transactions fees over the past three years. That can't continue."

22

The Exxel Group: March 2001

The conference room table was covered with detailed reports; the air was thick with the smoke of Cuban cigars. Outside, downtown Buenos Aires glimmered brilliantly in the afternoon sun. But Juan Navarro and Carlos Oris de Roa had little time to enjoy the spectacular view. Within the hour, the two men were leaving on a journey that would be critical to the disposition of the private equity group's most successful investment to date.

The men were traveling to Paris—the headquarters of the French supermarket conglomerate Carrefour—to discuss Exxel's stake in the Argentine retailer Norte. Since the purchase of Norte a little more than four years before in a $440 million transaction, Exxel had enjoyed considerable success in improving both revenues and margins at the retailer. In September 1998, the private equity group had undertaken a complex transaction with Promodès, a major French retailer that was subsequently acquired by Carrefour. This deal entailed the immediate sale of 49 percent of the company, as well as a complex series of put and call options. Exxel had reached the point where it could now exercise the option to sell its remaining stake in Norte immediately, or else wait as long as another eighteen months to do so. More generally, the transaction raised questions about the challenge of undertaking private equity without a liquid market for initial public offerings.

THE ARGENTINE ECONOMY[1]

Argentina was in 2001 the second largest country in South America, with a population of nearly 37 million. The nation had a 95 percent literacy rate, and its per capita

---

1. This and the following section draws in part on Alex Hoye and Josh Lerner, "The Exxel Group: October 1995," Harvard Business School case No. 297-068. Unless otherwise noted, the sources of this section are Daniel Artana and Fernando Navajas, *Stabilization, Growth and Institutional Build-Up: An Overview of the Macroeconomics of Argentina, 1991–1995*, Buenos Aires, Fundacion de Investigaciones de Economicas Latinoamericanas, 1995; Economist Intelligence Unit, *Country Report: Argentina*, London, Economist Intelligence Unit, 2000; and Republic of Argentina, Ministry of Economy, Public Works and Services, *Economic Report*, Buenos Aires, Republic of Argentina, various years.

Professor Alberto Ballve of IAE (Universidad Austral) and Professor Josh Lerner prepared this case. We thank Gustavo Herrero of the HBS Latin American Research Center for his assistance. HBS cases are developed solely as the basis for class discussion. Cases are not intended to serve as endorsements, sources of primary data, or illustrations of effective or ineffective management.

gross domestic product (GDP) of about $7,500 was the highest in Latin America by nearly a factor of two.

While these achievements were impressive, Argentina's economic history had been characterized by substantial missed opportunities. In 1910, Argentina ranked ninth among the world's nations in wealth, with a per capita GDP only $30 below that of France.[2] But its highly remunerative trade with Western Europe—especially exports of grain, wool, and beef—dwindled after World War I, the victim of restrictive trade policies of Europe and the United States.

These difficulties were exacerbated after 1945, as the country turned to a protectionist economic policy and was beset by both economic and political chaos. After many years of military dictatorship, the nation returned to democracy in 1983 when the ruling military junta yielded power after a costly war with Great Britain. The political transformation, however, did not produce economic stability. By 1989, when Carlos Menem was elected president, the nation was gripped by hyperinflation with rates nearing 5,000 percent (see Exhibit 22.1 for macroeconomic data). Hyperinflation created an environment where businesses succeeded through financial management rather than productivity advances.

Modern Argentine economic policy was launched in 1991, when Economy Minister Domingo Cavallo, a Harvard-trained economist, implemented a monetary plan. The Convertibility Law ensured that the money supply was fully backed with foreign currency and fixed the Argentine peso as worth exactly one U.S. dollar. The inflation rate dropped rapidly. Concurrently, Menem and Cavallo implemented a series of policies, sanctioned by the International Monetary Fund, to privatize businesses, reduce trade barriers, create private pension funds as part of a reform of the social security system, and deregulate industries and capital markets. For instance, in 1994, Argentina, Brazil, Paraguay, and Uruguay had formed a trading bloc called the Mercosur.

These bold steps had a substantial effect. The country's per capita GDP grew at an annual rate of almost 6 percent between 1991 and 1997; total imports and exports, at a rate over 15 percent. The capitalization of the stock market rose from $650 million in January 1991 to $63.2 billion in October 1997. This reflected not only an increase in security prices, but also new listings of privatized companies. (To cite one example, the oil enterprise YPF was the world's fifth largest initial public offering [IPO] at the time of its issue, with a market capitalization of $3.04 billion.) These offerings were frequently purchased by overseas investors: a June 1994 estimate suggested that foreigners held between 50 percent and 60 percent of the outstanding float on the Argentine market, and between 20 percent and 25 percent of total capitalization.[3]

But the growth of the Argentine economy was far from even. For instance, with the devaluation of the Mexican peso in December 1994, foreign direct investment in

---

2. In 2000, France's per capita GDP was $21,819. Detailed economic histories of Argentina include Carlos F. Diaz Alejandro, *Essays on the Economic History of the Argentine Republic* (New Haven: Yale University Press, 1970); Paul H. Lewis, *The Crisis of Argentine Capitalism* (Chapel Hill: University of North Carolina Press, 1992); and Laura Randall, *An Economic History of Argentina in the Twentieth Century* (New York: Columbia University Press, 1978).

3. The stock exchange was capitalized at $37 billion in early March 2001. This represented approximately 15 percent of GDP versus 74 percent in the United States at the same time. Market capitalization and trading volume were heavily concentrated among a few large firms and recently privatized companies; while most companies traded with great infrequency. Furthermore, recent new exchange listings had been largely reserved for large corporations and privatizations. The four largest companies accounted for 58 percent of market capitalization and 85 percent of trading volume in June 2000. There had been a total of eighteen initial public offerings (IPOs) between January 1990 and March 2001 in Argentina, almost all of which involved banks, energy concerns, and utilities.

EXHIBIT 22.1

ARGENTINE MACROECONOMIC DATA

	Inflation Adjusted GDP Change (%)	Per Capital GDP ($)	Consumer Price Index Inflation (%)	Average Exchange Rate (Peso per $1)	Money Market Rate (%)	Deposit Rate (%)	Exports ($ billions)	Imports ($ billions)	Average Unemployment (%)	Population (millions)
1985	−6.6	6,227	600.0	0.00006	1,161	630	10.4	5.6		30.32
1986	7.3	6,584	81.9	0.00009	135	95	9.1	7.0		30.77
1987	2.6	6,659	174.8	0.00021	253	176	8.7	8.4		31.22
1988	−1.9	6,438	387.7	0.00087	524	372	12.2	7.9	3.1	31.67
1989	−6.2	5,958	4,923.9	0.04233	1,387,179	17,236	10.0	5.0	7.1	32.11
1990	0.1	5,883	1,341.9	0.48759	9,695,422	1,518	14.6	6.5	6.3	32.55
1991	8.9	6,324	84.0	0.95355	71	62	14.6	11.2	6.0	32.97
1992	8.7	7,198	17.5	0.99064	15	17	15.4	18.8	7.0	33.37
1993	6.0	6,706	7.4	0.99895	6	11	16.3	20.9	9.3	33.67
1994	7.1	7,484	3.9	0.99901	8	8	19.2	21.5	10.7	34.18
1995	−2.8	7,457	3.4	0.99975	9	12	21.0	20.1	15.9	34.60
1996	5.5	7,729	0.2	0.99966	6	7	23.8	23.7	16.3	35.22
1997	8.1	8,211	0.5	0.99950	7	7	26.4	30.5		35.67
1998	3.9	8,275	0.9	0.99950	7	8	26.4	31.4	14.1	36.12
1999	−3.4	7,744	−1.1	0.99950	7	8	23.3	25.5	15.5	36.58
2000	−0.5	7,700°	−0.9	0.99950	8	8	26.3	25.1		37.00

Sources: Compiled from various International Monetary Fund and Argentine government reports.

Note: ° Approximate number.

Argentina virtually ceased. Deposit in domestic banks and domestic branches of international banks dropped by 19 percent, a "bank run" of greater magnitude than the one the United States suffered during the Great Depression. Within a few months, the broader impacts of the crisis (dubbed by Argentines the "Tequila Effect") were readily apparent; for instance, unemployment rates reached 18.4 percent in May 1995.

While the effects of this shock were short-lived, the same could not be said for the recession triggered by the Russian financial crisis of August 1998. Once again, investors lost confidence in developing markets, and Argentina was soon beset by substantial capital outflows. Investors' fears were exacerbated by the substantial public debt incurred by the Argentine government, which raised the specter of default. Furthermore, the decision of Argentina's largest trading partner, Brazil, to devalue its currency in January 1999 made it increasingly difficult for Argentina to export its products.

At the beginning of 2001, the Argentine economy was in the midst of a deep recession, which had already extended for thirty-four months. The economy was still highly dependent on agricultural and energy commodity exports and the spread between Argentine and U.S. government securities (an indicator of country risk) was reaching unprecedented heights. In addition, most Argentine companies were constantly constrained in their growth due to the unavailability of debt financing at reasonable costs and the lack of demand for stock offerings. The new administration of President Fernando de La Rua had initiated a variety of efforts to invigorate the economy, and the International Monetary Fund had led a $40 billion rescue package to stave off a public debt default, but these steps had been inadequate to restore investor and consumer confidence.

PRIVATE EQUITY IN LATIN AMERICA

Private equity investing in Latin America grew out of the debt crises of the 1980s.[4] Many global banks, having lent aggressively to Latin businesses and governments in the 1970s and early 1980s, found themselves with substantial portfolios of nonperforming loans by the late 1980s. Meanwhile, many of these institutions faced increasing regulatory scrutiny in the United States and elsewhere. Eager to clean up their balance sheets, many of these banks agreed to convert loans into equity stakes. One of the first outsiders to make equity investments in private Latin firms was George Soros in the late 1980s. A few others followed.

Many of the early private equity investments in Latin America, however, encountered severe difficulties. An example was a $34 million fund organized by a U.S. investment bank in 1990 to invest in Chile. More than $9 million was invested in a private cemetery, a project that collapsed (with a total loss to the investors) six months later when it was discovered that its regulatory permits had been obtained illegally. It was not until the early successes of the Exxel Group (see below) and the Brazilian fund, G.P. Capital Partners (a private investment firm created and managed by the partners of Banco de Investimentos Garantia, today CSFB Garantia), as well as the general improvement in macroeconomic conditions, in the mid-1990s that Latin American private equity markets began attracting considerable attention (see Exhibit 22.2).

---

4. The discussion of the evolution of the Latin American private equity market is based on "Crisis? What Crisis? Mexican Woes Fail to Dent Interest in Latin Funds," *Private Equity Analyst* 5 (February 1995), pp. 1, 4, 9; Victoria Griffith, "The Advent of Venture Capital," *LatinFinance* (March 1996), pp. 46–49; Lorenzo Weissman, "The Advent of Private Equity in Latin America," *Columbia Journal of World Business* 31 (Spring 1996), pp. 60–68; and assorted other press accounts.

EXHIBIT 22.2

LATIN AMERICAN PRIVATE EQUITY FUND-RAISING, 1992–2000

	Amount Raised				
Year	Buyout	Mezzanine	Venture Capital	Total	Largest Fund Raised in Year (size in $ millions)
1992	$107	$0	$0	$107	Argentina Private Equity Fund I [Exxel] [$47]
1993	100	0	22	122	Latin American Capital Partners [BEA] [$36]
1994	847	0	0	847	G.P. Capital Partners [$500]
1995	827	0	0	827	Argentina Private Equity Fund II [Exxel] [$150]
1996	1,516	0	0	1,516	Supermarket Holdings, L.P. [Exxel] [$215]
1997	3,317	0	39	3,556	AIG-G.E. Latin American Infrastructure Fund [$1,013]
1998	3,664	0	0	3,664	CVC Opportunity Equity Partners [$1,100]
1999	1,131	225	194	1,750	Darby Latin American Mezzanine Infrastructure Fund [$225]
2000	1,536	0	1,101	2,637	J.P. Morgan Latin American Capital Partners [$677]

Source: Compiled from Holly Johnson, "Total Raising Hits $2.6 Billion; Venture Firms Provide Boost," *Latin American Private Equity Analyst* 1 (January 2001), pp. 1, 14–16; and assorted press accounts.

Note: The largest fund is determined using all funds that had a final closing in a given calendar year.

These funds followed a variety of templates. While the original pioneers had been country-specific funds, many subsequent groups such as Advent International, Darby Overseas Investments, and Westsphere Capital Management, raised funds for the entire continent. In a number of cases, the U.S. Overseas Private Investment Corporation, a quasi-governmental corporation that provided loan guarantees and other incentives to U.S.-based private equity organizations active in the developing world, facilitated the fund-raising efforts. The first generations of funds almost exclusively focused on buyout investments. During the late 1990s, however, fund-raising by venture capital funds—typically focused on Internet-related investments—surged.

By the end of 2000, however, disillusionment about Latin American private equity had set in.[5] Not only had the volume of overall fund-raising declined, but numerous "franchise funds" had encountered severe difficulties accessing capital. For instance, Hicks, Muse, Tate & Furst Latin America Fund II, which had originally set a $750 million target, had a first closing of only $125 million after almost a year of marketing.[6] Many limited partners expressed concerns that the region seemed gripped by an endless series of political and economic crises. One manifestation of these crises was the almost total absence of a market for Latin American IPOs, with the exception of a few transactions at the height of the Internet bubble. The lack of liquidity meant that many private equity groups were sitting with large portfolios of unexited investments.

5. See the discussion in Holly Johnson, "Fund Raising Totals $2.6 Billion; Venture Firms Provide Big Boost," *Latin American Private Equity Analyst* 5 (January 2001), pp. 1, 13–16; and Holly Johnson, "Private Equity's Future in Region Remains Cloudy," *Latin American Private Equity Analyst* 5 (May 2001), pp. 1, 15–16.

6. In interviews in December 2000, the fund's principals suggested that they would be able to ultimately raise $300 million. See "Hicks, Muse Lowers Target for Latin American Fund," *Latin American Private Equity Analyst* 5 (January 2001), p. 10.

The disillusionment was also a consequence of poor management by the private equity groups themselves. In particular, a number of funds affiliated with U.S. investment banks (or begun by former investment bankers) had specialized in taking minority stakes in Latin American firms, often with neither board representation nor effective control rights. These investors often found it difficult to exit their investments, since the firms' management resisted going public and few corporate acquirers were interested in a minority equity stake. Even when the private equity group had received contractual protections, such as registration rights, frequently the ability of investors to enforce these provisions in the courts was questionable. Many of the funds that had encountered difficulties were seeking to operate simultaneously in a number of countries. In many cases, the oversight and coordination of the multiple offices was lacking.

THE EXXEL GROUP

Initial Steps

The Exxel Group was one of the pioneers of Latin American private equity. The private equity group was founded in 1991 by Juan Navarro, who at the time was chairman of Citicorp Capital Investors S.A. (CCI), Citicorp's private equity investment vehicle in Argentina.

Both Navarro's father and his grandfather had been leaders of Uruguay's medical and scientific establishments. His mother's family held influential positions in the Argentine scientific and banking communities. After briefly attending university in Uruguay, where he found the curriculum to be steeped in leftist ideology and of little interest, Navarro moved to Argentina. While completing his education, he joined an Argentine bank in which his mother's family had major role. In 1980, seeking greater challenges, Navarro joined Citibank's Argentine subsidiary. He spent the next six years as a banker in Buenos Aires and New York City.

Navarro's involvement in the private equity industry began in 1986, when he identified the opportunity to develop this new business within Citibank. Prior to assuming this position, Navarro spent several months with Citicorp Venture Capital in New York. The group's chairman, William Comfort, had shared many valuable insights into the private equity process.

Between 1987 and 1991, Navarro directed CCI's involvement in more than a dozen substantial investments in Argentine entities. He saw that the unprecedented political and economic changes taking place in the country in the late 1980s, coupled with market globalization, would have a significant and long-lasting effect on privately held companies, as well as on government-owned companies subject to privatization.

In 1991, Navarro decided the time was right to undertake an effort of his own. He was motivated by four beliefs. The first two related to the overall economic environment. First, the recent reforms, he believed, had led to a turning point for the Argentine economy. They would create numerous attractive investment opportunities as many established conglomerates restructured and family businesses struggled to adjust to the newly competitive environment. Second, the public and private equity of Argentine firms was attracting increasing attention from overseas financial investors, who previously had little interest in these securities. Local firms had previously financed themselves largely through other means, among which were direct investments from multinational partners and bank loans.

Navarro's second set of motivations for beginning his own fund was derived from his observations of the private equity industry. He noted that most successful private equity organizations in the United States were not affiliated with a major financial institution. He believed that free-standing organizations avoided many of the conflicts of interest and internecine battles that plagued groups affiliated with major investment and commercial banks. Finally, he was convinced there was an opportunity to build a franchise as a buyout fund geared to Argentine firms. Because of the early stage of the market, it would be possible to pioneer this effort as a free-standing organization, rather than as a subsidiary of a major financial institution.

In planning his effort, Navarro was guided by several principles:

- The new fund would invest in buyouts, recapitalizations, privatizations, and mergers of Argentine firms. Given that returns were uncertain enough in these later-stage investments in the region, Navarro believed that venture-oriented or early stage operations were impractical. Rather, Navarro would seek to build on his unique strength: his ability to originate deals, based on his strong ties with local business community, and then to add value to these enterprises.

- The group would be an independent organization with strong U.S. ties. The strong connections to U.S. financial institutions and institutional investors would bring credibility to the private equity group. The ties with U.S. institutions would also allow Navarro and his partners to help the firms in their portfolio in ways that they could not otherwise. In order to create a fund that was attractive to U.S. investors, Navarro sought to "clone" a U.S. buyout fund: e.g., using the same partnership structure and law firms.

- He would develop a network of service providers to complement the work of his partnership. In 1990, Argentine lawyers, accountants, bankers, and notaries[7] were not familiar with the workings of and philosophy behind the U.S. buyout industry. Thus, Navarro resolved to focus his energies not only on the development of his own organization, but on the cultivation and education of a network of intermediaries and service providers.

To implement this vision, Navarro sought to leverage his resources. First, he recruited an advisory board that included some of the leading lawyers, bankers, and businessmen in Buenos Aires. This group gave an immediate credibility to the new fund. Second, he attracted a management team of experienced professionals including Jorge Demaria, the former Argentine undersecretary of privatizations who would play a key role as the fund's second-in-command, Marcelo Aubone, Jorge Romero, and several other former colleagues from CCI, management consultants from McKinsey & Company, and former senior executives. (Exxel's management team in March 2001 is listed in Exhibit 22.3.)

The Evolution of the Group

One of the first decisions Exxel took was to select a U.S. bank to solicit investments from institutional and individual investors. For its first two funds, Navarro selected Oppenheimer & Company to play this role. (Oppenheimer's Private Equity Group had raised capital for funds in areas as diverse as Chile, India, and Israel). The first fund, the Argentine Private Equity Fund I, L.P., closed in April 1992 with $46.8 million. The initial fund had largely been raised from sophisticated individual investors in the United States as well as the Brown University Endowment, Batterymarch Financial Advisors,

---

7. Most key documents in Argentina needed to be notarized. Becoming a notary there required several years of special practice after obtaining a law degree.

EXHIBIT 22.3

THE EXXEL TEAM

The following investment professionals, as well as Juan Navarro, formed Exxel's management team:

Jorge Demaria

Jorge Demaria, age fifty, joined Exxel in 1991. He is a restructuring and turnaround specialist with an extensive business operations experience in a wide range of industries. He was an exclusive business advisor to Citicorp Capital Investors S.A. from 1987 to 1991, where he evaluated more than 100 investments. From 1985 to 1987, Demaria served in the Argentine Government as Undersecretary of Privatizations. Prior to that, he was a senior partner in the management consulting firm Tanoira, Demaria y Asociados. During the 1970s, Demaria held corporate planning and operations positions at Liquid Carbonic S.A. and Bridas S.A. At age twenty-seven, he became chief executive officer of Magnasco, one of the largest dairy companies in Argentina at that time, after leading the takeover of the company. Demaria holds a Ph.D. degree in economics from the University of Buenos Aires and has attended graduate courses in sociology and mathematics.

Marcelo Aubone

Marcelo Aubone, age fifty-seven, joined Exxel in 1991. He was a senior officer at Citicorp Capital Investors S.A. from 1988 to 1991. At Citicorp, he led several teams that participated in major Argentine privatizations. From 1986 to 1988, he was chief financial officer of a leading industrial company. Before that, Aubone was a senior manager at Banco Ganadero and Banco Río, with responsibilities in corporate finance. Aubone has a law degree from Universidad Católica Argentina, where he also attended graduate courses in political science.

Jorge Romero

Jorge Romero, age fifty-two, joined Exxel in 1991. He has extensive experience in leveraged finance, placement of high yield bonds, and syndication of bank debt. Romero worked at Citicorp in Buenos Aires for five years in the strategic, planning, corporate and trading departments. He later became a shareholder and a member of the board of directors of Banco Mariva, a wholesale banking institution in Argentina. He was also a member of the board of directors of the Argentine Private Banks Association. Romero is a certified public accountant, with a degree from the University of Buenos Aires.

Carlos Oris de Roa

Carlos Oris de Roa, age sixty, joined Exxel as a member of its executive committee in 1997. He has a demonstrated track record in establishing strategic direction, managing operations and creating value in companies across diverse business sectors. From 1993 to present, Oris de Roa held executive board–level positions in several of Exxel's portfolio companies, including Poett San Juan S.A., Supermercados Norte S.A., Fargo S.A., and Devoto Hnos. S.A. Prior to that, Oris de Roa was president of Compañía Continental S.A., executive vice president of Continental Milling Co., and general director of Finagrain S.A. of Geneva, Switzerland. Oris de Roa has degrees in business administration from Universidad Católica Argentina and from Columbia University.

F. Horacio Crespo

F. Horacio Crespo, age fifty-six, joined Exxel as a member of its executive committee in April 2001. He is one of the most experienced professionals in the area of mergers and acquisitions, international structuring and financial instruments in Argentina. Crespo has worked with Exxel on all major transactions since 1991. In addition, he has also worked with the federal government of Argentina to create the legal framework required for developing securitization, leasing and derivatives in the country. Prior to joining Exxel, Crespo held several executive positions in PricewaterhouseCoopers, including partner in charge of tax and legal services for

(Continues)

EXHIBIT 22.3 (CONTINUED)

THE EXXEL TEAM

F. Horacio Crespo *(Continued)*

Latin America, member of the Global PwC Tax and Legal Executive Committee, and partner in charge of the tax and legal area of Coopers & Lybrand Argentina. He was also a member of the Argentine Coopers & Lybrand Executive Committee from 1992 until 1999. Prior to joining Coopers & Lybrand, Crespo was the founding partner of one of the most prestigious local tax and consulting firms in Argentina, which merged with Coopers & Lybrand in 1992. Crespo also has extensive teaching experience and is a tenured professor of taxation at the Universidad Católica Argentina. Crespo is a certified public accountant, with a degree from the University of Buenos Aires.

Miguel Blanco

Miguel Blanco, age fifty-four, joined Exxel in 1997. From 1982 to 1997, he was a partner and member of the executive committee of Coopers & Lybrand, Argentina. He was involved in major Argentine privatizations and in the initial public offering processes, both in Argentina and the United States, for several of Coopers & Lybrand's clients. Blanco has actively participated in the definition of Argentine accounting and auditing standards and is the chairman of the Accounting and Auditing Standards Committee of the Argentina CPA Board. He has extensive teaching experience as a professor at the University of Buenos Aires and Universidad Católica Argentina. Blanco is a certified public accountant, with a degree from the University of Buenos Aires.

Mirta Carballal

Mirta Carballal, age fifty-eight, joined Exxel in 1994. She heads the financial control, tax planning, and reporting functions that are involved in the takeover process and the ongoing monitoring activities of Exxel's portfolio companies and holding company structures. Prior to joining Exxel, Carballal was the financial controller of Xerox Corporation (Argentina) for ten years. Prior to Xerox, she served many years at Ford Motor Company (Argentina) as a member of a team in charge of acquisitions. Carballal is a certified public accountant with a degree from the University of Buenos Aires.

Marcelo Chao

Marcelo Chao, age thirty-four, joined Exxel in 2000. Previously, he was a partner at Hermes Management Consulting, where since 1995 he led several projects involving Exxel acquisitions and portfolio companies, especially in the retail and consumer good sectors. From 1992 to 1995, Chao was vice president of Citibank in Buenos Aires, managing commercial and credit relations with corporate clients, and from 1991 to 1992 he worked for McKinsey & Co. Chao is a certified public accountant and holds a degree in business administration from Universidad Católica Argentina.

Alejandro Montagna

Alejandro Montagna, age thirty-four, joined Exxel in 1999. From 1997 to 1999 he was involved in a number of projects involving Exxel acquisitions and portfolio companies at Hermes Management Consulting. Montagna worked for The Boston Consulting Group in the Paris and Buenos Aires offices from 1996 to 1997. From 1991 to 1994, Montagna worked for Terrabusi, a leading Argentine food manufacturer, where he was an assistant to the chief executive officer and was responsible for the development and implementation of all industrial expansion projects. Montagna holds an MS degree in industrial engineering from the University of Buenos Aires and an MBA from Harvard Business School.

Martin Steinweg

Martin Steinweg, age thirty-five, joined Exxel in 1999. Prior to that, he was a partner at Hermes Management Consulting, where, since 1996, he led a large number of projects involving Exxel acquisitions and portfolio companies. From 1994 to 1996, Steinweg worked for McKinsey &

EXHIBIT 22.3 *(CONTINUED)*

THE EXXEL TEAM

Martin Steinweg *(Continued)*

Co. in Argentina, Chile and Brazil, and between 1990 and 1994, he held senior positions in the treasury departments of Exxon Chemical in Houston and Esso Argentina. Steinweg, a German citizen, has a degree in business administration from the University of Belgrano and an MBA degree from Columbia Business School. He also completed executive programs at Northwestern University and at INSEAD (Europe).

Terence A. Todman

In addition to this management team, Ambassador Terence A. Todman, age seventy-five, acts as a senior advisor to the firm and is a member of its board of directors. Todman is a retired U.S. Foreign Service officer who holds the personal rank of career ambassador, a lifetime title. He was ambassador to Argentina (1989–93), to Denmark (1983–89) to Spain (1978–83), to Costa Rica (1957–77), to Guinea (1972–75), and to Chad (1969–72). In 1977, he was assistant secretary of state for Inter-American Affairs.

Oppenheimer & Company, and Rockefeller & Company (the Rockefeller family office). In this initial fund, Oppenheimer served as the general partner and the Exxel Group as the investment advisor.

In subsequent funds, Exxel's funds assumed a more traditional flavor. Exxel was able to raise capital from some of the largest and most prestigious institutional investors. These included the insurers Aetna and Allstate; the endowments of Columbia University, Princeton University, and MIT, the Ford Foundation, and the Wellcome Trust; a financial advisor, the Common Fund; the pension funds of AT&T and General Motors; public pension funds such as those of California (CalPERS) and Oregon; and commercial and investment banks such as Deutsche Bank, Chase, and Citigroup. Similarly, it took over the management of the fund, ultimately retaining Merrill Lynch in a traditional placement agent role for its funds.

Exxel's fund-raising history is listed in Exhibit 22.4. Because its partnership agreement limited the amount that could be invested in any one transaction to a set portion of the fund—typically 25 percent—Exxel had frequently raised companion funds to finance individual transactions. These funds raised a substantial amount of equity, but instead of being invested in a range of transactions, they were devoted to a single transaction.

By February 2001, Exxel had invested, through capital and debt funding, $4.8 billion in seventy-three companies (through twenty-four platform investments and forty-nine follow-on acquisitions) in a wide range of industries. These transactions are summarized in Exhibit 22.5.

Fund Operations

Critics sometimes denigrated Exxel as a purely financial investor, which sought to generate profits by "flipping" investments to foreign investors who were willing to overpay for transactions.[8] Whatever the merits of this characterization of the fund in its earliest

---

8. For representative discussions of Exxel's operations, see Brian Caplen, "Exxel's Gauchos Play for High Stakes," *Euromoney* (November 1998), pp. 24–29; and Miriam Bensman, "The Henry Kravis of Argentina," *Institutional Investor* 31 (August 1997), pp. 107–114.

EXHIBIT 22.4

EQUITY FUNDS ORGANIZED BY EXXEL

Name of Fund	Size ($ MM)	Closing Date	Objective
The Argentina Private Equity Fund I, L.P. (" Fund I")	46.7	April 1992	Diverse
The Argentina Private Equity Fund II, L.P. ("Fund II")	150.0	February 1995	Diverse
Credit Card Holding Co-Investment, L.P.	88.5	November 1995	Argencard S.A.
Supermarkets Holding, L.P. S.A.	215.0	November 1996	Norte
Exxel Capital Partners V, L.P.	866.8	October 1997	Diverse
Exxel Capital Partners 5.5, L.P.	154.5	March 1999	Diverse
Freddo Holdings, L.P. S.A.	66.0	March 1999	Freddo
Mercosur Supermarkets, L.P. S.A.	97.0	May 1999	Devoto Hnos.
Entertainment Depot, L.P.	243.2	July 1999	Musimundo S.A.
Total Capital Raised	1,927.7		
Exxel Capital Partners VI, L.P.	850.0°	In progress	Diverse

Source: Exxel.

° Exxel Capital Partners VI, L.P., was still being raised in February 2001. Closings to date had totaled $480 million. Exxel expected to complete the fund-raising process in the second quarter of 2001. The group anticipated that the final size of the fund would be about 25% smaller than Exxel Capital Partners V.

EXHIBIT 22.5

INVESTMENT PORTFOLIO

Company Name	Date(s) of Acquisition	Industry	Revenues (US$ MM)
Poett San Juan S.A.°	Jan. 1993	Manufacture and sale of branded household cleaning products: Ownership: 100%	80
La Papelera del Plata S.A.†	July 1993	Manufacture and sale of branded tissue paper products. Ownership: 23% with joint control of 69%	92
Emdersa‡	March 1993 & Aug. 1996	Electric power distribution in the provinces of San Luis, La Rioja and Salta. Ownership: 88%	160
Bestov Foods S.A.§	Jan. 1994 & May 1995	Pizza Hut restaurants Ownership: 60%	13
SPM‖	Nov. 1994	Prepaid medical services (HMOs and hospitals). Ownership: 89%	200
Argencard S.A.#	Nov. 1995	Credit card network administrator and processor in Argentina and Uruguay and the exclusive licensee of MasterCard in both countries. Ownership: 56%	205

(Continues)

EXHIBIT 22.5 (CONTINUED)

INVESTMENT PORTFOLIO

Company Name	Date(s) of Acquisition	Industry	Revenues (US$ MM)
Supermercados Norte S.A.	Nov. 1996	Largest supermarket chain in Argentina Ownership: 100%	2,300
Blaisten S.A.°°	Oct. 1997	Home improvement retail chain Ownership: 100%	100
Fargo S.A.††	Oct. 1997	Branded bakery products. Ownership: 100%	155
Interbaires S.A.‡‡	Dec. 1997	Operation of Airport Duty-Free Shops. Ownership: 80%	120
EDCADASSA§§	Dec. 1997	Operation of Airport Customs Warehouses. Ownership: 45%	80
OCA S.A.‖‖	Dec. 1997	Private postal service courier. Ownership: 100%	285
Havanna S.A.##	Feb. 1998	Branded confectionery products. Ownership: 70%	40
IBG S.A.°°°	Feb. 1998 & Nov. 1998	Marketing and retail of leading apparel products Ownership: 93%	120
Musimundo S.A.†††	May 1998	Music and consumer electronics retailer. Ownership: 100%	320
Devoto Hnos. S.A.‡‡‡	July 1998	Largest supermarket chain in Uruguay. Ownership: 49%	230
Freddo S.A.§§§	March 1999	Gourmet ice cream producer and retailer. Ownership: 100%	30
Bodegas y Viñedos López S.A.‖‖‖	June 1999	Premium wine producer and marketer. Ownership: 33.3%	40
LatinStocks.com###	Aug. 1999	Internet financial services. Ownership: 58%	Start-up
Sports Management Company°°°°	Jan. 2000	Sports management Ownership: 79%	15
Mirácula††††	Jan. 2000	E-commerce solutions Ownership: 20%	Start-up
Nexxy Capital‡‡‡‡	Feb. 2000	Internet incubator Ownership: 70%	Start-up
Integralco§§§§	Oct. 2000	Contract catering Ownership: 80%	60

Sources: Corporate documents and press accounts.

Notes:

° Poett is the result of a build-up strategy implemented by Exxel through the merger of five consumer-goods companies, which were successively acquired from January 1993 to January 1994: (i) Ciabasa, a branded household detergent manufacturer with prestigious but underinvested brands; (ii) Papelera Mar del Plata, a regional tissue paper company; (iii) Poett, the market leader in the branded air freshener market, with additional strong brands in other categories such as insecticides, all-purpose cleaners, and toilet deodorants; (iv) Daniel Chozas' brands leaders in the tissue napkin market and the food wrappings category; and (v) YPF Household Division; license to use the YPF umbrella brand in the household product industry and distribution rights for such products in more than 3,000 YPF gas stations. The company was sold in December 1995 for $95 million to Clorox and Unilever.

(Continues)

EXHIBIT 22.5 (CONTINUED)

INVESTMENT PORTFOLIO

Notes *(Continued)*:

† Exxel jointly controlled La Papelera del Plata S.A. with other two family groups, each owning a 22.9 percent interest for a total ownership of 68.7 percent. Sold at a modest loss in March 1996.

‡ Emdersa is the result of the merger of three electric power distribution companies acquired by Exxel: Edesal S.A., acquired in March 1993, serving the province of San Luis; Edelar S.A., acquired in May 1995, serving the province of La Rioja; and Edesa S.A., acquired in July 1996, serving the province of Salta. Unión Fenosa, the second largest utility in Spain, and Exxel's partner in Emdersa, held a 12 percent ownership in the company. In March 1999, Exxel sold 100% of Emdersa to GPU International (U.S.), including Unión Fenosa's 12 percent ownership for $435 million.

§ Bestov Foods S.A. was liquidated in June 1998 and the investment was written off.

‖ SPM is the result of a build-up and merger strategy executed by Exxel through five acquisitions in the HMO and hospital sectors: (i) Galeno S.A., (ii) Life S.A., (iii) Keranis S.A.; (iv) Jockey Club S.A.; and (v) TIM S.A.

Argencard S.A. owns 100 percent of MasterCard Uruguay, 100 percent of Posnet S.A., a point of sale network system, 12.75 percent of Red Link S.A., one of the two ATM networks in Argentina, and 100 percent of Clearing de Informes, the leading credit bureau in Uruguay.

** Exxel is executing a build-up strategy in Blaisten S.A., having acquired 100 percent of Cisilotto Hnos. S.A. and Casa Nine S.A.

†† Fargo holds a 65 percent market share in the industrialized bread market, reaching 42,000 points of sale on a daily basis. The company is expanding its product mix and has recently acquired the Antojos bakery chain.

‡‡ Interbaires S.A. has the exclusive right, until the year 2010, to operate the duty-free shops in all the Argentine International Airports. The remaining 20 percent owner is the Argentine government.

§§ EDCADASSA has the exclusive right, until the year 2009, to operate the customs warehouses in all Argentine international airports. Exxel has the operational control of the company as per the company's by-laws. The remaining 55 percent owner is the Argentine government.

‖‖ OCA S.A. acquired 100 percent of SKYCAB S.A., 100 percent of OCASA Internacional, 100 percent of Tiempost S.A., the leading private postal services company in Uruguay, and 100 percent of Patria, an air cargo freight company.

Havanna S.A. produces and commercializes four major product categories with its leading brand Havanna and is the exclusive distributor of the prestigious Italian coffee brand Illy. Havanna sells its products through both company-operated and franchised stores and is implementing a strategy to launch its products in the United States and Europe.

*** International Brandgroup (IBG) is the leading marketer and distributor of premier global apparel products in Argentina and the Mercosur region. IBG holds the exclusive licenses to distribute Lacoste, Polo Ralph Lauren, Kenzo, Armani, Gap, Banana Republic and Guess? clothing and accessories, in addition to its own proprietary brands, including Paula Cahen d'Anvers and Coniglio, among others. In addition, the Company is securing approximately twenty additional licenses for leading international luxury brands that will be sold through Palacio Duhau, the most exclusive fashion department store in Buenos Aires.

††† Musimundo is the leading music and consumer electronic retailer and one of the top three players in books. The company is executing an aggressive expansion plan by opening stores throughout Argentina and expanding into neighboring countries. In addition, Musimundo launched its e-commerce operations through Musimundo.com in September 1999.

‡‡‡ Exxel is executing an expansion strategy in Devoto, by new store openings and follow-on acquisitions. In May 1999, Devoto acquired 100 percent of the supermarket chain Dumbo S.A., becoming the largest supermarket chain in Uruguay. In June 2000, Exxel sold 51 percent of Devoto to Casino Guichard Perrechon (France) while maintaining control and management responsibility for the company.

§§§ Freddo S.A. produces and commercializes branded gourmet ice cream through its specialty-store chain in Argentina, Chile, and Uruguay.

‖‖‖ Exxel is executing a build-up strategy in the premium wine sector.

LatinStocks is an Internet financial services company combining financial research with on-line trading capabilities that it is currently developing. AOL Latin America owns 10 percent of the company. Exxel exited LatinStocks at a substantial loss in February 2001.

**** Exxel is developing a leading position in the large and fast growing sports industry in Latin America. The Sports Management Company is focusing initially on soccer, the dominating professional sport in the region. The company's business divisions include operations of professional soccer clubs in Argentina, Brazil, and Uruguay, as well as sports marketing and player representation.

(Continues)

EXHIBIT 22.5 *(CONTINUED)*

INVESTMENT PORTFOLIO

Notes *(Continued)*:

†††† Mirácula offers an easy, fast, and inexpensive e-commerce solution to small and medium-size companies in Brazil, and it is expanding to Argentina.

‡‡‡‡ Nexxy Capital is an Internet project accelerator developed in Brazil with the objective to select and develop business opportunities in the Web in Latin America, providing financial support to young entrepreneurs. The company is screening more than 1,200 projects as well as developing its regional expansion to Argentina.

§§§§ Grupo Integralco is the leading operator in the Argentine contract catering market. The Group consists of three companies that cover all segments of the market with nationwide coverage and has centralized commercial and corporate functions.

years, over time the Exxel Group had developed a well-articulated and distinctive approach to assessing and overseeing transactions.[9]

The process by which Exxel selected investments evolved gradually. At the beginning, the search for potential investments was done on the basis of suggestions provided by investors and analyses of commercial databases. Over time, the group undertook a systematic effort to analyze each sector's situation and trends, then moving down to the Latin American region and, finally, to the Argentine level. Once Exxel determined that a market was attractive, target companies were thoroughly analyzed from strategic, operating, and financial perspectives. The location of these analytic activities had also changed over time. As Navarro noted,

> At the beginning, we enlisted an army of professionals to work on business analysis, but, later, we realized it was not the structure we needed. We decided to "outsource" several tasks. For example, we helped set up an external consulting company which now provides us with these services. The group consists now of only a few executives, almost all directors, with very little support. For any activity that requires it, we prefer to hire consultants. It may be more expensive, but we have no overhead.[10]

In March 2001, Exxel had a total of thirty-five staff, of whom twenty were professionals.

While the level of staffing had been reduced, progressively greater attention had been paid to the operations of the Exxel Group's portfolio firms over time. Discussing the changing allocation of his time, Navarro noted:

> At the beginning, I spent 80 percent of my time making key contacts with the partners, potential investors in the funds, and focusing on organizational issues, constantly looking for ways to ensure the team had the necessary skills to reach maximum effectiveness. For the last two years, the recession

9. Exxel's purchase in December 1997 of private postal service OCA and the trucking firm Villalonga Furlong, which also controlled concessions to the duty-free shops and other services at Argentine airports, also generated considerable controversy. The deal announcement caused an outcry in the press and the legislature because the business was alleged to be controlled by Alfredo Yabrán, who had been accused by Domingo Cavallo of being an organized crime boss and to have bribed public officials extensively. Exxel was forced to engage in a broad publicity and lobbying campaign to address the concerns that the deal generated.

10. Originally, the consulting firm Hermes had agreed not to work for other clients without Exxel's permission. (Exxel, in turn, committed to use a set amount of the group's services.) Over time, the relationship was loosened.

forced us to focus more on operations in order to maintain company valuations. Now, operations take up 80 percent of our time.

In overseeing transactions, Exxel operated under the premise that companies in all countries tend to converge in format and strategy. As a result, the Exxel mangers relentlessly pushed firms to generate scale economies in order to compete in an increasingly globalized market. Moreover, the group set goals for operational margins using industry averages from the most developed economies, and it similarly assessed the firms' strategic positioning relative to leading firms around the globe.

This greater attention to operations manifested itself in a number of ways. One example was the increased emphasis on the provision of support services. Small teams handled fundamental support tasks for the portfolio companies, through their direct intervention or using outsourced service providers. For instance, the administrative area, run by Miguel Blanco, used a consistent accounting system across the portfolio firms. This group had six auditors who frequently visited companies to identify control issues and were allowed to call any member of the Executive Committee whenever they identified a problem. This area also provided support for information technology and facilitated bulk purchases of more than one hundred goods and services across portfolio firms. Other centralized support areas related to corporate finance, human resources, and media and institutional relations.

The firm also encouraged cooperation between the firms in its portfolio. At the same time, the firms were free to act according to their best business judgments. For instance, Exxel's portfolio company IBG was interested in selling its clothing in Norte's stores. With Exxel's encouragement, the two firms negotiated a three-month trial. When IBG did not generate enough sales, the experiment was abandoned.

At the heart of the process was the six-person executive committee. In meetings held every other month, this body monitored the achievement of strategic objectives, investments, and the financial targets indicated in each portfolio firm's annual budget. Companies throughout the group were also monitored through daily and weekly visits.

Another key activity for committee members was to keep in permanent contact with local and international actors in the industries where Exxel had active investments, identifying potential exit strategies and partnership opportunities. The private equity group found that in a number of instances, serious discrepancies had appeared between the prices at which entities were valued in the Argentine market and valuations that foreign acquirers were willing to pay. Often, foreign acquirers had been deterred by the modest scale of Argentine firms and by their poor operating performance. By purchasing, consolidating, and improving firms, Exxel could overcome these barriers. In some instances, the group "tailored" companies' offerings to match the lines of business of specific prospective acquirers.

Exxel applied the same disciplined approach to understanding its investment failures. Two early disappointments—La Papelera del Plata and Bestov Foods (which controlled Pizza Hut franchises in the region)—instilled in Exxel's managers a conviction about the necessity of taking a controlling stake in its portfolio firms. An Internet company, LatinStocks.com, invested in at the height of the technology bubble and sold at a loss thereafter, underscored their focus on later-stage investments.

Exxel's senior managers anticipated continued evolution in future years. While raising its most recent fund, Exxel Capital Partners VI, the group announced its intention to commit 40 percent of its capital to Brazilian investments. (To date, Exxel had just done some small transactions in this nation.) To this end, the firm anticipated opening an office in Sao Paulo.

NORTE SUPERMARKETS

Norte, founded in 1964, was a supermarket chain concentrated in the greater Buenos Aires area. At the time of the initial buyout, it was the third largest supermarket chain in Argentina, and its revenues and profitability had grown sharply since the transaction.

The Original Transaction

In February 1996, Exxel had initiated conversations with the Guil family about the possible sale of Norte. The firm's founder, Alberto Guil, expressed interest in selling all of the company, as long as the transaction was done at a multiple of earnings equal to that at which publicly traded Argentine supermarkets traded. Guil, despite having founded the firm and being solely responsible for its operations, held only 25 percent of its equity. (His relatives held the remainder.) Having recently remarried, he was eager to both scale back his involvement and increase his liquid wealth. Exxel considered Norte as an attractive buyout target for several reasons. One set of rationales related to the industry itself; the other, to the specific situation of the firm.

The first set of considerations related to the industry dynamics. Exxel and its consultants had extensively researched this sector, concluding that it presented substantial opportunities. The highly fragmented Argentine grocery industry was, dominated by *almacenes,* small family-run shops. These facilities, which typically had between 50 and 150 square meters of floor space, offered neither extensive selection nor attractive prices. While the first self-service supermarkets were introduced into Argentina in the 1980s, *almacenes* still played an extensive role. Purchases at supermarkets and hypermarkets (large facilities, frequently found in Europe, which sold groceries, clothing, and other household items) had only risen from 35 percent of total consumer grocery purchases in 1990 to 42 percent in 1995. Not only were the numbers in the United States and Europe were much higher, but the comparable figure for Chile was 64 percent and for Brazil 85 percent. Similarly, within the supermarket sector, the industry was much less concentrated than in the major developed countries: most firms had modest market shares. As part of its assessment process, Exxel did extensive econometric modeling to understand the likely evolution of the Argentine supermarket sector. This shed light on the questions such as whether supermarkets or hypermarkets would emerge as the dominant retailers in Argentina.

The second set of rationales related specifically to Norte. Six factors were identified as critical by the deal team. First, the firm had invested heavily in superstores (facilities with greater than 2,000 square meters of floor space), and was recognized as the leader in this rapidly growing sector. Second, its facilities were located in prime areas of the Buenos Aires metropolitan area, the densely populated region that was home to nearly one-third of Argentina's residents. Third, the firm had a strong brand name, and was recognized both for the quality of its offerings and the competitiveness of its prices. Next, the firm had recently invested in a new distribution center, which management believed was the most advanced in Argentina. The firm had invested extensively in information technology, to allow it to track sales and more efficiently stock shelves. Fifth, the firm had had low management turnover and had rotated its key managers across the different stores, which provide a depth of experience and perspective that many competitors lacked. Finally, as a family owned firm, it faced substantial capital constraints, which precluded the full pursuit of profitable investment opportunities.

At the same time, the private equity group identified a number of significant risks:

- Perhaps most fundamentally, this was to be a large purchase, considerably greater than the $150 million Argentina Private Equity Fund II, L.P., that the group was managing at the time. To complete the transaction, the firm would need to access a considerable amount of debt and additional equity financing. Furthermore, if Norte were to access international debt markets, it would need to borrow in dollar-denominated debt. While the Argentine peso had been pegged to the dollar in recent years, were Argentina to devalue its currency, the increase in the debt load might be substantial.

- Second, it was clear that if the firm were to be purchased, it would have to be at a significant valuation. While Exxel projected that it could substantially grow revenues and profitability (see Exhibit 22.6), others expressed doubts. After all, Norte was still run by its founder, Alberto Guil, one of the most respected figures in the Argentine industry. The extent to which further operating improvements could be wrung from the Norte facilities remained unclear.

- Finally, the industry dynamics were changing. In particular, major international retailers such as Carrefour and Wal-Mart had entered the market. Such giant competitors could price their goods aggressively, which could depress Norte's margins.

After weighing these considerations, Exxel decided to proceed with the purchase of Norte. Including fees and expenses (approximately $29 million) and the assumption of debt of $31 million, the firm paid a total of $440 million in the transaction. The purchase price represented 8.6 times the earnings before interest, taxes, depreciation, and amortization (EBITDA) at the time. Thus, in November 1996, Norte was (indirectly) acquired by a new Cayman Island–based corporate entity, Supermarkets Holding (SUHO) Co.[11]

The purchase price was financed almost equally through debt and equity. The debt was initially raised through a senior secured long-term loan of $130 million and a bridge financing of $90 million. The long-term debt from a consortium of banks consisted of two equal tranches. The first was a three-year note on which the interest rate was LIBOR (London Interbank Offer Rate) plus 3.25 percent; the second, a four-and-a-half year note whose rate was LIBOR plus 4.25 percent. The bridge financing from Merrill Lynch, with an initial rate starting at LIBOR plus 6.5 percent and steadily escalating, was anticipated to be a short-term financing source, which would rapidly be refinanced through a public offering or private placement.

Because the Argentina Private Equity Fund II, L.P., was constrained to putting no more than 25 percent of its capital, or $37.5 million, into a single deal, it was necessary to raise additional equity capital. To do this, the fund established a Cayman Island–based partnership, Supermarket Holdings, L.P. This fund raised $180 million from existing limited

---

11. By adopting this "off-shore" structure, Exxel ensured that non-Argentine investors would face neither any Argentine tax obligations on the capital gains from the investment nor any obligations from Argentina's personal property tax. Unlike Argentina or the United States, the Cayman Islands imposed neither corporate nor income taxes, nor any taxes on the gains from or sales of limited partnership interests. The actual acquisition was made by a special purpose Argentine corporation called "Supermarket Acquisition, S.A.," which was wholly owned by SUHO Co. This vehicle was the one that issued the debt, and was later merged with Norte. This additional holding company was employed so that the debt financing could be arranged before the purchase of Norte closed.

EXHIBIT 22.6

SUMMARY HISTORICAL AND PROJECTED FINANCIAL OPERATING DATA OF NORTE IN NOVEMBER 1996 (U.S. DOLLARS IN MILLIONS)

| | Actual Results | | | Projected Results | | | |
| | Fiscal Year Ended June 30, | | | Fiscal Year Ended June 30, | | | |
Income Statement Data	**1994**	**1995**	**1996**	**1997**	**1998**	**1999**	**2000**
Net sales	$787.2	$ 855.9	$991.5	$1,153.8	$1,378.3	$1,716.7	$2,065.3
Gross income	158.8	167.9	194.1	228.4	276.8	346.6	418.5
Selling and administrative expenses (excluding directors' fees)	(126.1)	(142.1)	(160.1)	(190.5)	(214.2)	(257.7)	(297.1)
Directors' fees	(5.9)	(6.8)	(1.3)	—	—	—	—
Operating income	26.8	19.0	32.7	37.8	62.6	88.9	121.4
Interest income (expenses)	1.2	5.3	0.6	(18.0)	(20.1)	(17.8)	(13.9)
Other income (expenses), net	(0.2)	1.1	0.5	(1.1)	0.7	0.9	1.0
Income tax	(9.5)	(7.6)	(8.7)	(8.6)	(15.9)	(24.5)	(35.5)
Net income	$18.4	$17.8	$25.1	$10.1	$27.3	$47.4	$72.9
EBITDA	$20	$28.3	$46.0	$65.9	$90.4	$118.8	$152.4
Operating and Balance Sheet Data							
Stores at beginning of fiscal year	17	18	20	24	26	31	36
New stores interior	0	0	2	0	3	3	2
New stores Greater Buenos Aires	1	2	3	2	2	2	2
Stores closed	0	0	0	0	0	0	0
Stores at end of fiscal year	18	20	24	26	31	36	40
Total square meters of selling space	33,058	43,228	62,559	71,429	91,429	111,429	127,429
Capital expenditures	$29.0	$71.4	$54.8	$31.6	$62.0	$65.8	$60.2
Change in net working capital (positive figures represent cash inflows)	NA	NA	8.6	9.4	13.2	21.0	21.2
Debt outstanding	0.0	31.9	39.6	236.1	210.6	185.1	167.9

Source: Supermercados Norte.

Note: The yield on the ten-year U.S. Treasury bond rate in November 1996 was 6.20 percent. The spread between these bonds and dollar-denominated Argentine government bonds of approximately the same maturity was 4.4 percent. The short-term rate for loans in pesos to top-tier corporations was 10.5 percent; the yield for the shortest-term peso-denominated Argentina federal government Treasury bills (Letes) was 7.13 percent. Norte's publicly traded competitor, Disco, had an equity market capitalization of $392.2 million in November 1996, with debt outstanding of $200.6 million. In the previous four quarters, Disco's revenue was $844.4 million; its EBITDA, $52.1 million; its net income, $21.0 million; and its beta, 0.43. We thank Professor Juan J. Cruces of the University of San Andrés for help in compiling this information. In making projections, it is reasonable to assume a 40 percent tax rate for Norte. Corporate interest payments were tax deductible under the Argentine tax code.

partners and some new investors. Thus, the total equity financing for the transaction was $215 million.[12] Exhibit 22.7 provides a schematic representation of the transaction.

12. While the equity was issued by the Cayman Islands entity, the Argentine company raised the debt. (The source of the remaining funds was excess cash on Norte's balance sheet.) Supermarket Holdings, L.P., was structured as a limited partnership, with Exxel serving as the general partner. Despite the fact that investors usually do not pay a carried interest for co-investments, Exxel was able to negotiate a carry from several of the co-investors in SUHO, L.P.

EXHIBIT 22.7

STRUCTURE OF NORTE IMMEDIATELY AFTER EXXEL PURCHASE (NOVEMBER 1996)

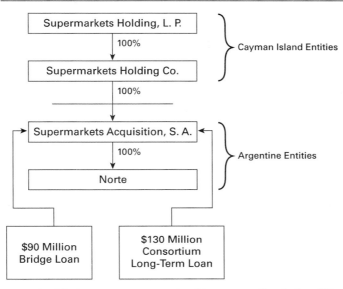

Note: The debt financing was soon replaced by a $220 million high-yield bond financing.

The Evolution of the Transaction

The firm moved rapidly to make its mark on Norte. These steps included operational and financial changes.

On the operational side, a major focus was increasing the quality of the goods offered at the store. For instance, the chain began purchasing live cattle, whose condition could be better assessed than already-dressed meat. Similarly, they arranged to purchase vegetables directly from farmers, rather than at the central market, where it appeared that a wholesaler who had a "special relationship" with the purchasing manager often provided inferior products. Exxel's partners were intimately involved in the negotiations, even for the disposal or sale of the hides and bones of the slaughtered animals. The results were an increase in both market share and profitability for Norte. Exxel also began building seven new stores, which would increase floor space by about 30 percent. (See Exhibit 22.8 for data on the changing market shares of Argentine supermarket firms, and Exhibit 22.9 for Norte's financial performance.)

Exxel carefully studied public records of U.S. buyouts of supermarket chains and also retained an executive from Sainsbury (a major grocery chain in the United Kingdom) to review Norte's operations. As a result of the research and consultation, Exxel adopted the compensation scheme used at Safeway (which had been bought out by Kohlberg Kravis Roberts): managers were rewarded based on a weighted average of the store's return on assets and an index of customer satisfaction. These conversations also led to the initiation of a variety of longer-range plans as well. These initiatives included the development of products to be sold under the Norte label (i.e., "private

---

EXHIBIT 22.8

EVOLUTION OF MARKET SHARE OF ARGENTINE SUPERMARKETS, 1998–2000

Chain	1998	1999	2000
Norte	15.9%	17.6%	17.7%
Carrefour	13.0	15.7	17.2
Disco	14.3	14.6	13.7
Coto	10.3	12.2	13.7
Jumbo	4.8	4.9	4.9
Wal Mart	4.4	4.5	4.5
La Anonima	3.6	4.4	4.7
Casino	3.1	3.9	4.7
Toledo	2.0	2.0	2.2
Dia	0.2	0.6	1.6
Eki	0.1	0.4	0.8
Others	28.3	19.2	14.3

Source: Compiled from CCR Information Resources, "Analisis Estrategico del Retail: Situacion Competitiva," unpublished presentation, 2001.

---

label" offerings), the continued upgrading of Norte's information systems, and the implementation of a customer loyalty program.

On the financing side, the firm first refinanced the outstanding debt obligations. The firm's offering of publicly traded debt (a seven-year maturity issue yielding 10.875 percent) met strong demand, so much so that the offering was expanded to $220 million. The success was even more extraordinary as it was the first "junk bond" offering to finance a leveraged buyout outside of the United States and Western Europe. (Even in Europe, only a few such transactions had been completed.) This transaction allowed the firm to retire both the bridge loan and the debt from the bank consortium.

The funds came, however, with restrictive covenants, such as the requirement that Norte's EBITDA be twice the size of interest payments. When the firm needed additional working capital in December 1997, it was consequently impossible for the firm to incur any more debt at the operating company level. As a result, SUHO Co. obtained a $100 million line of credit from Banco Galicia, which was then injected into Norte as an equity investment. This was again a groundbreaking transaction: the first loan of this size from an Argentine bank to a foreign holding company.

Only a year into the transaction, however, the question of exiting the investment arose. In late 1997, the French chain Casino approached Exxel, seeking to buy Norte. Not only was the proposed valuation attractive, but Exxel also realized that a strategic partner could help enhance the firm's logistics, marketing programs, and new store offerings. As a result, Exxel began discussions with a variety of international supermarket chains. Given the modest number of players in the industry and Exxel's extensive knowledge of the industry, the private equity group decided not to use an investment banker, but rather to negotiate the transaction itself.

Talks soon focused on four groups: Promodès; the Dutch firm Ahold, which already had a relationship with the Argentine chain Disco; another French chain, Comptoirs

EXHIBIT 22.9

SUMMARY OF HISTORICAL FINANCIAL OPERATING DATA OF NORTE (U.S. DOLLARS IN MILLIONS)

	Actual Reports			
	Fiscal Year Ended December 31,			
Income Statement Data	**1997**	**1998**	**1999**	**2000**
Net sales	1,103.5	1,374.8	2,143.7	2,037.0
Gross income	238.6	323.5	592.7	608.3
Selling and administrative expenses (excluding directors' fees)	(191.9)	(261.4)	(481.1)	(511.5)
Directors' fees	0.0	0.0	0.0	0.0
Operating income	46.8	62.0	111.6	96.8
Interest Income (expense)	(28.0)	(32.6)	(72.3)	(105.2)
Other income (expenses), net	(10.1)	(5.3)	(12.3)	(37.0)
Income tax	(5.5)	0.0	(9.3)	(4.3)
Net income	3.2	24.0	17.7	(49.8)
Goodwill amortization	(4.7)	(7.2)	(36.5)	(48.6)
Net Income after Goodwill amortization	$(1.5)	$16.9	$(18.7)	$(98.4)
EBITDA	67.4	92.2	178.6	173.7
Operating and Balance Sheet Data				
Stores at beginning of fiscal year	25	42	61	141
New stores interior	11	15	52	1
New stores Greater Buenos Aires	6	4	20	3
Stores closed	0	0	0	6
Stores at end of fiscal year	42	61	141	139
Total square meters of selling space	96,022	134,747	259,600	264,420
Capital expenditures	$146.7	$194.9	$173.7	$61.3
Change in net working capital	50.6	59.9	74.3	(100.2)
Debt outstanding	270.5	343.0	676.7	835.3

Source: Supermercados Norte.

Note: Norte's 1999 results include Tia as of January 1, although acquisition of Tia was made on January 31, 1999.

Moderne; and D&S from Chile. This task was greatly complicated by the instability that gripped the capital markets of the developing world after the Asian financial crisis in the fall of 1997. During the nearly twelve months that Exxel researched and negotiated a possible transaction, the key Argentine stock market index fell by 61 percent, and many Latin American supermarket shares fell even more substantially.

Despite these difficulties, Exxel succeeded in closing a transaction with Promodès in September 1998. In this transaction, Promodès agreed to pay $411.6 million for 49 percent of the equity in SUHO Co. This translated into an implied enterprise value of $1.25 billion, an equity value of $840 million, and a multiple of trailing EBITDA of 15.2×. (By way of comparison, publicly traded rival Disco was trading at a trailing

EBITDA multiple of 5.7×, and a portfolio of large publicly traded South American supermarkets at 6.4×.) This transaction is illustrated in Exhibit 22.10.[13] As part of the transaction, Promodès received four of the eight seats on Norte's board of directors, but the chairman of the board (appointed by Exxel) had double voting rights. Promodès was protected, however, by the requirement that the annual business plan and financial statements, as well as significant operating and financing decisions (e.g., asset sales and unanticipated debt issues), be approved by a supermajority of the board.

The transaction also had a number of complex features:

- As part of the transaction, Promodès had an option to purchase an additional 2 percent of Norte one year after the closing of the transaction. The purchase price (or, put another way, exercise price of the put option) would be determined by a formula: $0.02 \times [(11 \times EBITDA) -$ Norte's financial debt minus cash and marketable securities]. This purchase would give Promodè majority ownership, but Exxel was contractually guaranteed to control the investment until September 2001, unless it exercised it right to sell the firm to Promodès sooner. The EBITDA would be based on the period from October 1998 to September 1999.

- Exxel had the right to put the shares of Norte to Promodès, beginning in January 2001. This option could be exercised between January 2001 and September 2002. The purchase price would again be determined by a formula: $0.49 \times [(9 \times$

EXHIBIT 22.10

STRUCTURE OF NORTE IMMEDIATELY AFTER PROMODES TRANSACTION (SEPTEMBER 1998)

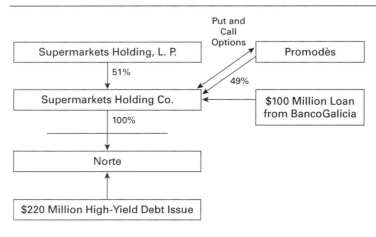

---

13. The Promodès investment was structured as one in SUHO Co., not Norte, because of Argentine tax law: an equity sale within two years of the buyout may have prevented to Norte from deducting the interest payments associated with the debt incurred during the transaction. In late 1998, Promodès swapped its holding in SUHO Co. for 49 percent of Norte. This swap was advantageous for two reasons. First, French regulators strongly discouraged companies from holding equity in holding companies in tax havens such as the Cayman Islands. Second, there was a significant accounting advantage to holding shares in the operating company. By holding shares in Norte, Promodès could consolidate Norte's results in its financial statement, which was attractive because of Norte's higher operating margins. The transaction after this swap is illustrated in Exhibit 22.11.

EXHIBIT 22.11

STRUCTURE OF NORTE IMMEDIATELY AFTER PROMODES SWAP

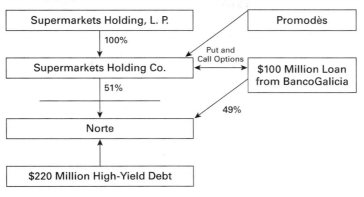

Source: Promodès.

EBITDA) – financial debt minus cash and marketable securities]. The EBITDA was calculated based on the previous four completed quarters: for example, if Exxel undertook the put on March 28, 2001, the financial results in calendar year 2000 would be used to calculate the price.

- If Exxel did not exercise the put, Promodès had the right to call the shares of Exxel between October and December 2002. The exercise price would be the same as in the Exxel put option.

This complex structure emerged from the differing perspectives of the parties:

- Exxel felt strongly that it did not want to hold an investment where it did not have a control position. Thus, it sought to ensure that it would retain control as long as it was involved. This transaction allowed the firm to retain control for as long as three years after the deal.

- Exxel also was concerned that Norte had considerable growth potential, which the private equity group wanted to be rewarded for. Thus, the flexibility as to when to exercise the put option, and the contingent aspect of the valuation in the second transaction, was also attractive.[14] Finally, the private equity group was well aware that shifts in strategy and direction by corporations were not uncommon. By structuring the transaction so the purchase price in the second transaction was lower than that of the initial deal, the danger that the corporation would balk when Exxel exercised its put was minimized.

- Promodès did not mind allowing Exxel to control the investment initially, as it was relatively unfamiliar with the Argentine market. By having a call option to ultimately purchase Exxel's equity in Norte, there was little danger that it would not ultimately achieve control.

14. It might be thought that Exxel and Promodès could have simply negotiated the purchase price at the time the put option was to be exercised. Exxel feared, however, that this type of situation could lead to a "hold-up problem," since there would only be one potential buyer at this point. (It was unlikely that any other retailer would be interested in a minority stake in a supermarket chain controlled by a rival.)

- By basing the purchase price on Norte's previous four quarters, rather than just the latest quarter, Promodès limited the temptation to artificially inflate the purchase price by cutting expenses to unsustainably low levels or raising prices to above market prices. Either of these actions would be likely to translate into declining customers and revenues well before the year was out.[15]

Four months later, in January 1999, the transaction shifted again, when Norte purchased Tia, the fifth largest supermarket chain in Argentina. The company was purchased for the sum of $720 million, or 15× EBITDA.[16] To finance the transaction, Norte issued $480 million of nonvoting, nondividend preferred stock issued to Promodès, used $50 million of available cash on its balance sheet, borrowed an additional $100 million in bank debt, and assumed $90 million in debt that Tia had already borrowed.

Reflecting the substantial contribution of Promodès to the transaction, Exxel's ultimate ownership stake was adjusted. In particular, the two parties decided that at the time Exxel exercised its put option, the preferred stock would convert into common shares. Rather than identifying a precise conversion ratio, the two firms chose to identify a range. If the EBITDA of Norte were high enough at the time of the exercise of the put option, Exxel would receive 30 percent of the purchase price. At a lower level, it would receive 35 percent, and in between the share would vary on a straight-line basis between these two targets. The cutoff points were larger each quarter, reflecting the anticipated growth of the firm. If the put option were exercised in March 2001, the respective cutoffs would be EBITDA in the previous four quarters of $205 million and $230 million. If the put option were exercised in September 2001 (immediately before control would revert to the corporation), the respective cutoffs would be $220 million and $250 million.

Reflecting the firm's rapid growth, there were additional debt issues in the next two years. In 1999, Norte issued $275 million in senior secured floating rate notes due in 2004. These were used to refinance the $90 million in Tia debt assumed with the acquisition and $100 million of debt taken on for the Tia acquisition, with the balance used to refinance short-term debt of Norte. In 2000, the firm replaced this offering (as well as $75 million in short-term debt) with $350 million in 10-year bonds denominated in Argentine pesos. To protect the foreign exchange risk, these bonds were convertible into common equity if there was a devaluation of the peso exceeding 10 percent *and* if at the time of the devaluation Exxel no longer was a shareholder of Norte.

The transaction underwent another dramatic shift in August 1999, when Carrefour announced its intention to acquire Promodès. Unlike Promodès, Carrefour had a substantial presence already in Argentina, with a 23 percent market share in 1999. The harmonious relationships between Exxel and its corporate partner became far more challenging, particularly as Norte's performance far outstripped that of the French retailer's stores during the difficult months of late 2000.

The Decision

Outside the conference room, the sun had begun its descent. Yet the men continued to debate the question of whether Exxel should exercise its option to put the shares to Carrefour immediately. By exercising the option early, Exxel would be relinquishing a considerable amount of "option value" that it would enjoy if it held the right until the last possible moment. Moreover, the De La Rua government had recently reappointed

---

15. In sale agreements of other firms in the Exxel portfolio, these incentive issues had been addressed by giving the corporation the right to call the firm six months before Exxel could exercise its put option.

16. Exxel did, however, achieve $80 million in operating synergies during the first year after the acquisition. Taking into account the synergies, the entry multiple was 5.6× EBITDA.

the architect of the Argentina's 1991 recovery, Domingo Cavallo, as economics minister. This move might suggest grounds for optimism about the nation's prospects.

On the other hand, there was the manner in which the exercise price was calculated. The price was based not on the current sales, but rather on the cumulative EBITDA in the previous four quarters. The Argentine economy had significantly weakened over the past four quarters, and retail sales in general (and at Norte) in particular had suffered (see Exhibit 22.12). If they waited, the purchase price might fall, as the good quarters of 2000 sales were by replaced by leaner and less profitable quarters in 2001.

Moreover, Exxel had extensive management challenges as it was. With their exposure to the Argentine retail sector, many of Exxel's portfolio companies had been hurt by the recession. Moreover, the scaling-up of the Brazilian effort would require considerable management attention. Thus, simplifying the portfolio had many virtues.

More generally, Navarro wondered about the future of private equity exits in the region. Would the structure of these types of transactions need to be refined to address problems that were unforeseen at the time the Norte deal was signed? More generally, would it be possible to sustain a robust private equity market without a market for IPOs?

EXHIBIT 22.12

INFORMATION RELEVANT TO PUT OPTION EXERCISE

| | Quarter Ending | | | | |
	3/31/00	6/30/00	9/30/00	12/31/00	
Norte:					
Sales ($ millions)	509.1	507.7	493.7	526.8	
EBITDA ($ millions)	41.4	37.1	35.5	59.7	
Total stores	141.0	140.0	138.0	139.0	
All Argentine supermarkets:					
% Change in prices from year earlier	–6.6%	–4.4%	–3.1%	–1.7%	
% Change in total revenues from year earlier	+0.7%	–2.9%	–4.4%	–6.4%	

| | Quarter Ending | | | | |
	3/31/99	6/30/99	9/30/99	12/31/99	
Norte:					
Sales ($ millions)	440.3	500.1	525.5	620.9	
EBITDA ($ millions)	30.4	46.5	41.6	52.1	
Total stores	122	123	142	141	
All Argentine supermarkets:					
% Change in prices from year earlier	–5.7%	–1.9%	+0.7%	+0.5%	
% Change in total revenues from year earlier	–4.8%	–5.3%	–5.8%	–6.0%	

| | Days of Month | | | | |
	1–7	8–14	15–21	22–8	29–31
Norte sales, January 2000 ($ millions)	33.4	38.2	36.4	35.1	17.4
Norte sales, January 2001 ($ millions)	32.6	34.1	33.8	32.8	13.6
Norte sales, February 2000 ($ millions)	41.7	39.1	37.4	40.0	5.5°
Norte sales, February 2001 ($ millions)	38.9	36.0	36.1	36.2	0.0[†]

Sources: Compiled from corporate documents and CCR Information Resources, "Analisis Estrategico del Retail: Situacion Competitiva," unpublished presentation, 2001.

Notes: ° February 2000 concluded on February 29.

[†] February 2001 concluded on February 28.

23

A Note on the Initial Public Offering Process

The process of taking portfolio firms public is very important for entrepreneurial firms and their financiers. While the claim of Black and Gilson that "a well developed stock market is critical to the existence of a vibrant venture capital market" may be overstated, there is clearly a strong relationship.[1] To be a successful entrepreneur, an understanding of the initial public offering (IPO) process is important.

This note summarizes the mechanisms by which firms go public. It highlights some of the key institutional features associated with these offerings and suggests some explanations for why the process works as it does. While we note differences across countries, our focus will be on the major industrialized country with the greatest volume of offerings, the United States. Although the note must of necessity summarize the complexity and details of these offerings, the Additional Information Sources suggest some references for those who wish to learn more about this often-mysterious process.[2]

WHY DO FIRMS GO PUBLIC?

Firms and their investors typically have several motivations for going public. At the same time, some real costs may also be associated with such a transaction. The relative importance of these competing factors may vary across time and circumstances.

---

1. Bernard S. Black and Ronald J. Gilson, "Venture Capital and the Structure of Capital Markets: Banks versus Stock Markets," *Journal of Financial Economics* 47 (1998): 243–277.
2. This discussion is based in part on a variety of sources, especially Jay R. Ritter, "Initial Public Offerings," in Dennis Logue and James Seward (eds.), *Warren, Gorham, and Lamont Handbook of Modern Finance* (New York: WGL/RIA, 1998); Josh Lerner, "ImmuLogic Pharmaceutical Corporation" (case series), Harvard Business School case Nos. 292-066 through 292-071, 1992; and Katrina Ellis, Roni Michaely, and Maureen O'Hara, "When the Underwriter is the Market Maker: An Examination of Trading in the IPO Aftermarket," *Journal of Finance* 55 (2000): 1039–1074.

Potential Advantages

One important motivation for going public is the need to raise capital. Many technology companies, such as new semiconductor manufacturers and biotechnology firms, require hundreds of millions of dollars to successfully introduce a new product. This kind of capital may be difficult to raise from other sources. Banks and other debt financiers, for instance, may consider the firm too risky to lend funds to. Meanwhile, even if a venture capital group was willing to finance such a company's initial activities, it might not be able to continue funding the firm until it achieved positive cash flow. For instance, most private equity groups are restricted to investing no more than 10 percent or 15 percent of their capital in a single firm. Thus, the need to raise capital to finance projects may be an important motivation to go public.[3]

A second motivation is the desire to achieve liquidity. Entrepreneurs are likely to worry about placing all their eggs in one basket and will seek to achieve diversification by selling some of their shares. Private equity investors are also likely to desire to liquidate their investments in a timely manner, whether through outright sales of the shares or through the distribution of the shares to their investors, in order to achieve a high rate of return.[4]

Achieving liquidity, however, is typically not done at the time of the IPO. This is because of the fears of investment bankers, who worry that if insiders such as entrepreneurs and board members are seen as bailing out at the time of the offering, new investors will be unwilling to purchase shares. (Insider sales at the time of the IPO are more common among private equity–backed firms in Europe.) Thus, they seek to prohibit or severely limit the sale of shares at the time of offering and to restrict any additional sales during a "lock-up" period. (In addition, the speed and timing of sales by insiders may be restricted by government regulations, as is the case in the United States.) After the lock-up period expires, however, insider sales are likely.

A third motivation is that going public may help the firm in its interactions with customers or suppliers. Being a public firm can help a firm project an image of stability and dependability. This is particularly important in industries where products do not represent a one-time purchase, but require ongoing service or upgrades. For instance, a corporation may be unwilling to purchase software to run a critical function from a small private firm that might soon disappear and not be available to offer upgrades or address problems. Enhanced visibility is a particularly important rationale for foreign technology companies seeking to break into the U.S. market, who have increasingly chosen to go public on the NASDAQ exchange in New York rather than on their local exchange.

Potential Disadvantages

At the same time, going public involves some real costs, which lead many firms to resist going public:

- The legal, accounting and investment banking fees from an offering are substantial, frequently totaling 10 percent of the total amount raised in the offering or more.

3. It should be noted that many firms raise far more in follow-on offerings than they do in their IPOs. But the IPO may provide important advantages: even if the firm does not raise all the financing that it needs in the initial offering, it is likely to find a follow-on offering to raise more equity substantially quicker to arrange and less expensive after it is publicly traded.
4. For more about private equity distributions, see "Rogers Casey Alternative Investments," Harvard Business School case No. 296-024.

- The degree of disclosure and scrutiny associated with being a publicly traded concern may be troubling, especially for a family business that has been run as a private firm for several decades.

- If a firm files to go public and the offering must be subsequently withdrawn, even due to factors beyond the company's control, some managers fear that the company may be "tainted." In particular, other investors may be reluctant to even consider investing in the concern, presuming that the reason that it was forced to withdraw its IPO was due to some ethical lapse or fundamental business problem.

Another complication is introduced by the fact that the market's appetite for new issues appears to vary dramatically over time. In particular, the volume of IPOs changes dramatically from year to year. These periods of high IPO activity appear to follow periods when stock prices have risen sharply. The bunching of offerings is even more dramatic when patterns are examined on an industry basis. During these periods, firms may find it significantly easier to sell shares in IPOs to investors.

WHAT IS THE IPO PROCESS?

The process by which firms go public is a complex one. This summary highlights the crucial steps along this journey.

First Steps

The first step in the going public process is the selection of the underwriter. Firms considering going public will frequently be courted by several investment banks. Among the criteria used by firms and their private equity investors to evaluate banks are the reputation of the research analyst covering the firm's industry, the commitments made to provide analyst coverage in the months or years after the offering, and the performance of past IPOs underwritten by the investment bank. One arena where investment banks very infrequently compete is in the pricing of the transactions. A fee of 7 percent of the capital raised, plus the legal and other costs borne by the bank, is standard across investment banks of both high and low caliber.[5]

In many cases, firms select multiple underwriters to manage the offering. These might include, for instance, a smaller investment bank that specializes in a particular industry and a larger bank with the ability to market equities very effectively. (For instance, many high-quality venture backed deals are underwritten by a technology specialist such as Hambrecht & Quist and one of the largest, most prestigious underwriters such as Goldman, Sachs or Morgan Stanley, termed "bulge bracket" bracket firms in Wall Street parlance.) Only one of the banks, however, will be designated as the lead, or book, underwriter. This firm will be responsible for the most critical function, the management of the records of who desires shares in the new offering and the allocation of the shares among investors. The managing or co-managing banks will in turn recruit other banks and brokerage houses to join the "syndicate," the consortium that will actually sell the offering to its clients. Thus, while only one to three banks will actually underwrite the offering, the number of financial institutions involved is actually much larger.

---

5. In some small offerings, less prestigious underwriters may demand warrants from the firm in addition to a fee in cash. In some of the very largest offerings, the fee may fall as low at 5 percent. For a detailed discussion, see Hsuan-Chi Chen and Jay R. Ritter, "The Seven Percent Solution," *Journal of Finance* 55 (2000): 1105–1131.

Even before the offering is marketed, the underwriter plays several important roles. These include undertaking due diligence on the company to ensure that there are no skeletons in the closet, determining the offering size, and preparing the marketing material. In collaboration with the law firm representing the firm, the investment bank will also assist in the preparation of regulatory filings.

In most major industrialized nations, permission from one or more regulatory bodies is required before a firm can go public. In the United States, these are the Securities and Exchange Commission (SEC) and state regulatory bodies. The review of the SEC focuses on whether the company has disclosed all material information, not on whether the offering is priced appropriately. In past years, state regulators occasionally sought to assess whether an offering was fairly priced. (To cite one example, Massachusetts regulators had in December 1980 initially barred the sales of shares of Apple Computer in the state, even though it was an operating profitable company, on the grounds that its IPO price was too high.) Since 1996, however, all offerings being listed on one of the three major exchanges have been exempt from state-level scrutiny.

The extent of the disclosure required varies with the size of the offering and the firm. Many nations have provisions for simplified filings for smaller firms, or for those that will be listed on one of the smaller exchanges. In the United States, for instance, firms going public with less than $25 million in revenues can use file Form SB-2 rather than the much more exhaustive S-1 statement, and those raising less than $5 million can file under Regulation A, which requires even less disclosure.

There may be other regulatory requirements as well. For instance, in the United States, the SEC designates the weeks before and after the offering as the "quiet period." The firm's ability to communicate with potential investors during this period (aside from the distribution of the offering document, also known as the prospectus, and formal investor presentations) is severely limited.

Marketing the Offering

As the firm undergoes regulatory scrutiny, the investment bank begins the process of marketing the offering. It typically circulates a preliminary prospectus, or "red herring" (so named for the disclaimers typically printed in red on the document's cover), to prospective institutional and individual investors in the firm. In many cases, the firm will also undertake a "road show," in which the management team describes the company's lines of business and prospects to potential investors.

The actual mechanism used to determine the price varies across countries. In the United States, "book-building" is the most frequently employed approach. In particular, the underwriter learns from potential investors how many shares will be demanded at each proposed price, which enables him to set the best price for the company. All indications of interest are recorded in a central "book" compiled by the lead underwriter. In many other countries, however, the share price is set before the information about demand is gathered (though a number of these countries, such as Great Britain and Japan, have recently adopted the U.S. system in hopes of stimulating IPO activity). Elsewhere, other systems are employed, such as formal auctions to determine the offering price.

Reputable investment banks in the United States typically undertake only "firm commitment offerings." In these transactions, unlike "best efforts" offerings, the investment bank commits to sell the shares to investors at a set price. This price, however, is not set until the night before the offering, so the actual risk that the investment bank runs of not being able to sell the shares is very small. This information gathered about demand proves invaluable during the "pricing meeting" on the night before the

IPO. In this session, the investment bank and firm bring together all the information about demand in order to determine the price at which the shares will be sold to the public. In determining a price, the bankers are also likely to factor in information about valuation of comparable firms, as well as discounted cash-flow analyses of the firm's projected cash flows.

The Day of the Offering and Beyond

Whatever valuation is set at the time of the offering, the share price is likely to increase on the next trading day. (On average, even the first trade of the stock is at a substantial premium to the IPO price.) While the median firm undergoes only a very modest increase in its price, a small but significant number of firms have experienced a significant jump in their share price after going public. This was particularly true in the late 1990s in the United States, where Internet companies such as Yahoo!, TheGlobe.com, and the Internet Capital Group have all experienced jumps of several hundred percent on their first day of trading. But more generally, these types of high returns have been observed on the first day of trading across many nations and time periods.

Several explanations have been offered for this frequently observed pattern of high first-day returns:

- One possibility is that the increase in price (or the discount offered to investors who purchase IPO shares) is necessary to attract investors. Otherwise, uninformed investors might fear that they would be taken advantage of in offerings: for instance, informed investors would purchase most of the shares of promising firms, while leaving them holding the bulk of the unpromising offerings.

- A second possibility is that there is a bandwagon effect at work. Once sophisticated institutional investors indicate interest in a stock by buying shares, other less sophisticated investors rush in to purchase shares.

- A third explanation is that the investment bank frequently has "market power." This view suggests that bankers deliberately set offering prices too low in order to transfer wealth to the select investors whom they let participate in the IPO. These investors, having reaped big returns on the first trading day, will presumably reward the bank by steering other transactions, such routine custodial services, to the bank.

Each of these explanations is likely to capture some, but not all, of the complex phenomenon of IPO pricing.

Another commitment made by underwriters in the United States is to stabilize the price in the days and weeks after the offering. Typically, the underwriter will try to prevent the share price from falling below the offering price. In undertaking this stabilizing activity, the investment bank will almost always employ the "Green Shoe" option, a complex feature named after the 1963 offering where it was first employed. Essentially, investment bankers reserve the option to sell 15 percent more shares than the stated offering size. The investment banker will often sell 115 percent of the projected offering size; for instance, if the firm announced its intention to sell 2 million shares, the investment bank would actually sell 2.3 million. If the share price rises in the days after the offering, the bank simply declares the offering to have been 15 percent larger than the size projected initially. If the share price drops below the initial offering price, however, the bank will buy back the additional 15 percent of shares sold. This will allow the bank to help fulfill its commitment to support the stock price (the purchase of the shares may drive up the share price) while profiting by disparity between the price at which it sold the shares and the lower price at which it repurchased them.[6]

The relationship between the underwriter and the portfolio company does not end in the weeks after the offering. Rather, at least in the United States, a complex relationship continues, with many points of interaction. These include the analyst coverage noted above, but also a variety of other roles.[7] In virtually all cases, a U.S. investment bank will serve as a market maker: a trader responsible for insuring orderly day-to-day transactions in a security (including holding excess shares if necessary). In fact, the lead underwriter is virtually always the most important source of market-making activities in the months after the IPO. Finally, the underwriter of the IPO continues to serve as a financial advisor in most cases: about two-thirds of the firms completing a follow-on offering in the United States in the three years after the IPO employ the same underwriter.

ADDITIONAL INFORMATION SOURCES

Barry, Christopher B., Chris J. Muscarella, John W. Peavy III, and Michael R. Vetsuypens, "The Role of Venture Capital in the Creation of Public Companies: Evidence from the Going Public Process," *Journal of Financial Economics* 27 (October 1990): 447–471.

Black, Bernard S., and Ronald J. Gilson, "Venture Capital and the Structure of Capital Markets: Banks versus Stock Markets," *Journal of Financial Economics* 47 (March 1998): 243–277.

Chen, Hsuan-Chi, and Jay R. Ritter, "The Seven Percent Solution," *Journal of Finance* 55 (June 2000): 1105–1131.

Gompers, Paul A., and Josh Lerner, *The Venture Capital Cycle* (Cambridge: MIT Press, 1999), Section III.

Halloran, Michael J., Lee F. Benton, Robert V. Gunderson, Jr., Keith L. Kearney, and Jorge del Calvo, *Venture Capital and Public Offering Negotiation* volume 2 (Englewood Cliffs, NJ: Aspen Law and Business, 1995).

Megginson, William C., and Kathleen A. Weiss, "Venture Capital Certification in Initial Public Offerings," *Journal of Finance* 46 (July 1991): 879–893.

Ritter, Jay R. "Initial Public Offerings," in Dennis Logue and James Seward (eds.), *Warren, Gorham, and Lamont Handbook of Modern Finance* (New York: WGL/RIA, N1998).

6. When the bank is particularly worried that the share price will drop, it may sell even more than 15 percent of shares that the "Green Shoe" option allows. Essentially, the bank has then constructed a "naked short" position: it must buy back the excess shares, whether the share prices rise or drop. If the share price falls, it will once again have supported the price more effectively while profiting from its trading strategy. If the share price rises, however, it will need to purchase the additional shares at a loss.

7. Perhaps not surprisingly, it has been shown that investment banks issue more buy recommendations on companies that they underwrite than on other firms and that these recommendations seem to be excessively favorable (relative to the firms' subsequent performance).

24

Between a Rock and a Hard Place: Valuation and Distribution in Private Equity

> To me, it is not rocket science to decide on a company's valuation.
> —Rick Hayes, CalPERS[1]

In the private equity organization, the limited partnership structure has long been the traditional organizational form. Above all, it handled the problems posed by the two defining characteristics of private equity (PE): illiquidity and uncertainty of opportunity. Management fees supported the general partners during the initial period of illiquidity; carried interest kept them closely involved in the success of the investments; and the blind pool with capital called down as investments were made responded to the uncertainty of opportunity. The manager who created value in the portfolio was rewarded very well.

For limited partners (LPs), though, investing in such a vehicle required a huge leap of faith. One LP described it as "investing in the future behavior of individuals based on a track record, but with no rights or protections." LPs might feel particularly exposed because a limited partnership structure was inefficient in encouraging accountability. With a fund life that typically lasted ten years, LPs had to wait a long time before they learned how much their investment would return. Short of drastic measures, their only feedback method was choosing not to invest in a following fund. In the interim, they had to trust that their general partners (GPs) would act honorably and responsibly if the fund encountered bad times. Said one LP, "It's like being in the jungle with a lion on top of you. You have to hope it's a friendly lion."

---

1. Testa Hurwitz & Thibeault, LLP, "Reporting Portfolio Valuations," unpublished slides from a conference, March 7, 2002.

Professors Felda Hardymon and Josh Lerner and Senior Research Associate Ann Leamon prepared this note as the basis for class discussion. Portions of this note are drawn from Hardymon, Lerner, & Leamon "The Plummer Endowment: The Distribution Question," *HBS No. 802-174* and Hardymon, Lerner, & Leamon, "The Valuation Conundrum (A)," *HBS No. 802-207.* The authors thank numerous experts for their help; errors are ours alone.

Nowhere was the need for partnership behavior more apparent than in the issues of valuation and distribution. Without clear guidelines and with myriad alternative ways to interpret situations and signals, issues around valuation and distribution became a tinderbox. How each party handled them—especially in a declining market—could set the tone for the relationship between GP and LP and even set the stage for whether or not that relationship would endure for the long term.

Valuation and distribution were not the glamorous heroics of fund-raising, investing, or exiting. They were, nonetheless, essential parts of the partnership's life involving as they did the details of valuing the portfolio and, when it became liquid, distributing the proceeds to the LPs. While these issues had existed since the start of the formal PE industry, valuation had become more noticeable and more contentious during the market slide that had started in 2000, while distribution had been a hot topic during the torrid pace of the boom of the late 1990s.

Of the two, valuation was receiving the bulk of the attention by 2002 and 2003, especially as public pension funds' portfolios fell under more intense scrutiny. Many PE firms valued their companies at the higher of cost or market value as determined by the most recent outsider-led financing round. This had led to happy surprises in a rising market, as companies would be refinanced or liquidated for more than their portfolio value. In the falling market of the early 2000s, surprises were not happy nor were they consistent, as different firms had different policies on revising their portfolio valuations. LPs had become keenly interested in the issue for a number of reasons, including portfolio diversification, budget projections, their own compensation, and pressure on the public pension funds to disclose interim performance statistics. In the winter of 2002, an LP/GP group had formed to study the idea, always floating in the background, of a common set of guidelines, such as those that the British Venture Capital Association had used since 1991. A year later, this group had issued valuation guidelines that met with varied responses. In the wake of lawsuits from disaffected LPs, even the Securities and Exchange Commission (SEC) had begun questioning the values that publicly traded PE firms such as MeVC had placed on their private company portfolios.[2]

The distribution of liquidated portfolio positions garnered less of the spotlight because they had become relatively rare. Initial public offerings (IPOs) of venture-backed companies had fallen from their height of 233 in 1999 to twenty-four in 2002, rising slightly to twenty-nine in 2003.[3] The number of mergers of venture-backed companies in the first three quarters of 2003 had fallen to 217, down 25 percent from the depressed level of the same period in 2002. The average price of these deals, however, had risen by $3 million to $19.7 million, from the year before—still far off the $29 million of 2001.[4] Meanwhile, the number of "reverse LBOs"—IPOs of firms that had previously undergone leveraged buyouts—fell precipitously. Despite the slow market, valuation and distribution were shared issues that, in one form or another, cropped up perennially in relationships between general and limited partners. They might shift in importance as the industry went through its cycles, but in the end, they were long-term, intractable questions that were not amenable to formulaic solutions. With the highly contextual nature of these issues, partnerships had to rely on teamwork and the goodwill of all parties to reach a resolution.

2. Robert Clow, "Mutual Funds Turn on Valuations as SEC Moves to Steady the Spin," *The Financial Times* (March 28, 2002), p. 27.

3. http://www.venturexpert.com, accessed February 24, 2004.

4. http://www.venturesource.com, accessed February 24, 2004.

THE LANDSCAPE IN 2003

For the PE industry, the early part of the twenty-first century constituted one colossal hangover after one heck of a party. The year 2000 had seen 629 venture capital (VC) firms raise $105 billion, and twenty-two funds each raised $1 billion or more. A total of 11,870 companies received $150 billion in investments,[5] and 684 exits yielded $120 billion.[6] Observed one veteran venture capitalist in early 2000, "I've just returned from a board meeting where we all flew down to Florida and met on the CEO's yacht. Now *that's* the top of the market."

He could not have been more correct. By 2002, VC activity had slipped below the levels of 1995. A mere $9 billion was raised. A total of 2,514 companies received $21.2 billion, and a mere 303 exits (twenty-four of them IPOs) yielded $12.2 billion.[7] The year had seen the unthinkable, as more than twenty VC firms, including such names as Kleiner Perkins, Charles River Ventures, Mohr Davidow, Accel Partners, and Mobius (formerly Softbank), returned funds from vehicles near or in excess of $1 billion to their LPs (see Exhibit 24.1 for funds and amounts given back). The venture capitalists cited reduced opportunities to invest their gargantuan funds and the lower prices prevailing in the market. Reducing fund sizes, though, also reduced the management fees the firm received. Some firms had even reduced the percentage fee that they charged or did not call down all of the fees to which they were entitled. Among the less frequently articulated arguments for these moves may have been the desire to placate LPs who were becomingly increasingly nervous as the interim valuations of their funds' portfolios continued to slide.[8]

Yet 2003 may have shown the start of a recovery. The amount of funds raised increased slightly, as 113 funds closed a total of $10.8 billion. This was on par with the industry's performance in 1995, when 173 funds had closed on $10.0 billion.[9] New Enterprise Associates accounted for over 10 percent of this amount by closing a $1.1 billion vehicle. Investments had fallen, to 1,884 companies receiving a total of $16.9 billion, but twenty-nine IPOs had occurred.[10] The number of mergers and acquisitions of venture-backed companies had fallen slightly, from 314 to 289, yet prices, where disclosed, had risen 20 percent to $63 million per deal.[11] (See Exhibit 24.2 for investments, commitments, and pre-money valuations over time.)

The LBO sector had suffered similarly, and also seemed to be recovering. The volume of fund-raising fell from $76.5 billion in 2000 to $25.6 billion in 2002, but inched up to $26.7 billion in 2003.[12] The total volume of transactions also fell sharply, from $56.7 billion in 1998 to $21.6 billion in 2002.[13] In the latter half of 2003, though, buyout transactions skyrocketed, buoyed by a number of multibillion-dollar deals to reach

---

5. http://www.venturexpert.com, accessed February 24, 2004.

6. http://www.venturesource.com, accessed February 24, 2004.

7. http://www.venturexpert.com and http://www.venturesource.com, accessed February 14, 2003.

8. Lawrence Aragon and Dan Primack, "Clawback Woes Hit Battery and Meritech," *Venture Capital Journal* (January 1, 2003), p. 1.

9. NVCA, "Venture Capital Fund Raising Picks Up in Fourth Quarter after Two Dormant Years," http://www.nvca.org (February 2, 2004), accessed February 24, 2004.

10. All data from NVCA yearbooks and press releases.

11. NVCA, "Venture-Backed Mergers and Acquisitions Benefitted from Rising Valuations in Fourth Quarter 2003," http://www.nvca.org (February 10, 2004), accessed February 24, 2004.

12. NVCA, "Venture Capital Fund Raising Picks up in Fourth Quarter after Two Dormant Years," http://www.nvca.org (February 2, 2004), accessed February 24, 2004.

13. The facts in this sentence and the remainder of this paragraph are from Standard & Poor's portfolio management data, *Q4 2002 Leveraged Buyout Review* (New York: Standard & Poor's, 2003).

EXHIBIT 24.1

FUND SIZE AND MANAGEMENT FEE CUTS IN 2002

Date	Fund Name	Old Size ($MMs)	New Size ($MMs)	Management Fee Cut ($MMs)	Other
May '02	Accel VIII	$1,600	$1,100		
Jun '02	Atlas VI	967	851		Restructured LP agreements
Dec '02	Atlas VI	851	600		
Jun '02	Austin Ventures VIII	1,500	850		
Jan '02	Barksdale Group				Disbanded
Dec '02	Battery V			$51	Given back in exchange for clawback removal
Nov '02	Bay Partners X	456	364		
May '02	Benchmark Europe	750	500		
July '02	BRM Capital Management II	253	153		
July '02	Carlyle European Venture Partners II	724	624		
May '02	Charles River XI	1,200	450		
Feb '02	ComVentures V	550		Yes	Cut fee from 2.5% to 2.0%
May '02	Crosspoint 2001				Did not close
Nov '02	Horsley Bridge Partners	2,100	1,600		Fund-of-funds
Mar '02	Kleiner Perkins X	627	471		
Dec '02	Meritech I	1,100		$45	
Jun '02	Meritech II	1,000	750		
Dec '02	Mobius (fka Softbank) VI	1,500	1,250		
Jan '02	Mohr Davidow VII	850	675		
July '02	Pacven Walden International	1,000	750		
May '02	Redpoint II	1,250	950		
Dec '02	Redpoint II	950	763		
Dec '02	Sevin Rosen VIII	875	600		
July '02	Spectrum Equity Investors Fund III	682.2		$27.5	Offset clawback
July '02	Spectrum Equity Investors Fund II	252.2		Yes	15% to 20% reduction in fees
Aug '02	TA Associates (3 funds)			$38	Offset clawback
Dec '02	Telecom Partners III	500	425		Cut mgmt. fees by 45%, will no longer invest in new companies
July '02	VantagePoint Fund IV	1,600		Yes	Reduced fees on 50% of fund
July '02	ViVentures II	633	494		
July '02	Worldview Technology IV	1,000	750		

Source: Casewriter through *The Daily Deal, Private Equity Week, The Venture Capital Journal,* and *Dow Jones* newswires.

EXHIBIT 24.2a

MONEY COMMITTED TO U.S. VENTURE CAPITAL FUNDS AND AMOUNTS INVESTED IN COMPANIES

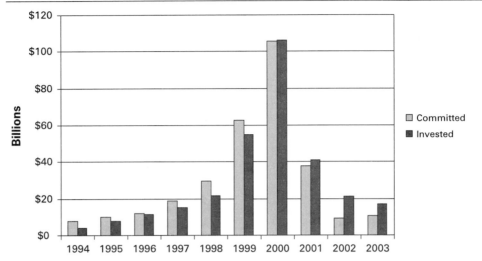

Source: Adapted from NVCA press releases and yearbooks.

EXHIBIT 24.2b

MEDIAN PRE-MONEY VALUATIONS FOR U.S. VENTURE-BACKED COMPANIES, 1997–3Q 2003

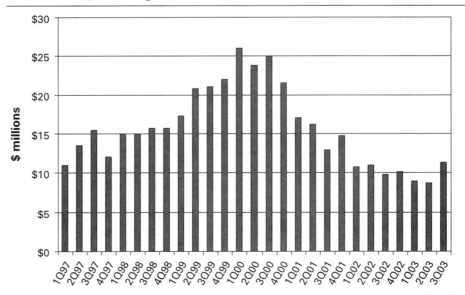

Source: Adapted from Venture One data, http://www.venturesource.com, accessed February 22, 2004.

$89 billion in disclosed value.[14] Exits had largely consisted of sales to other PE shops, with 2003 showing only 16 buyout-backed IPOs.[15] Although the fund-raising environment of 2003 was described as "tough," a number of well-known funds such as Hicks Muse were poised to enter the market in 2004.[16] Since 2000, though, lenders had sharply reduced the amount of money they would provide to buyouts.[17] LBO funds had had to put much more equity to work: the average share of equity in LBO deals climbed from 23 percent in 1996 to 41 percent in 2002. The deleveraging of these transactions translated into lower expected returns from successful investments.

SEARCHING FOR GUIDELINES

Valuation in the PE environment had always been a difficult issue, but especially so for VC. Without benchmarks such as public market pricing, a revenue-generating product, or even a close public comparable (after all, venture-backed companies were often doing something new and unusual and therefore were difficult to compare to existing public firms), external metrics were nonexistent. Valuation policies for private companies were rarely tied to the public markets in any formal way. Although private company valuations had historically appeared to follow trends in public markets, no precise relationship had been quantified or accepted for common use in the United States.

In the late 1980s, Bart Holaday of Brinson Partners (now Adams Street Partners) had urged his fellow venture capitalists to adopt a consistent valuation policy, and in 1990, the Ad Hoc committee of the National Venture Capital Association (NVCA) had proposed guidelines (see Exhibit 24.3). Although these were never formally adopted, they became the de facto standard approach. Because GPs were thought to have the best information about the company, valuation was their responsibility; the guidelines were to serve as a set of standards. GPs also were intimately acquainted with the private market as a whole, as they had a general sense not just of the value of their own companies but of what they would be willing to pay for those of other firms as well. Valuation was generally described as "more art than science" as it involved estimates of market development, technological progress, and company evolution in addition to more concrete pricing issues.

As companies became more like public entities—self-financing, for instance—they could be valued at discounts to their public comparables. Until then, companies were held at their book cost because "investment cost is presumed to represent value."[18] Cost was to be established through an outside-led round with a "sophisticated unrelated party" that was not a strategic investor. Strategics were seen as motivated by nonfinancial goals, and thus the valuation they placed on a company would be reduced by 50 percent. Companies would be marked up or down based on these transactions. If a first round had been priced at 50¢ per share and a second round at $2, as long as the second round was led by a sophisticated unrelated party, the entire holding could be marked up. The rule of thumb became "higher of cost or market unless impaired,"

14. Kenneth MacFayden, "LBO Firms Go on a Buying Binge," *Buyouts* (January 5, 2004).

15. Kenneth MacFayden, "Exit Markets Gaining Momentum," *Buyouts* (January 5, 2004).

16. Joe Christinat, "Q4 Fund Raising Tops First Three Quarters," *Buyouts* (January 5, 2004).

17. Dan Doron, "Multiples Rise amid Fierce Competition for Good Deals," *Buyouts* (March 3, 2003).

18. "Proposed Venture Capital Portfolio Valuation Guidelines (1989/1990)," National Venture Capital Association, unpublished document.

EXHIBIT 24.3

PROPOSED VALUATION GUIDELINES OF 1989–1990 OF THE NATIONAL VENTURE CAPITAL ASSOCIATION

Venture capital funds are required by generally accepted accounting principles to account for their investments in portfolio companies at value. There can be no single standard for determining value because value depends upon the circumstances of each investment. These valuation guidelines are intended to aid venture capital fund general partners in estimating the value of their investments.

Private Companies

1. Investment cost is presumed to represent value except as indicated otherwise in these guidelines.

2. Valuation should be reduced if a company's performance and potential have significantly deteriorated. Such reduction should be disclosed in the notes to the financial statements.

3. Valuation should be adjusted to equate to a subsequent significant equity financing that includes a sophisticated, unrelated new investor. A subsequent significant equity financing that includes substantially the same group of sophisticated investors as the prior financing should generally not be the basis for an adjustment in valuation.

4. If substantially all of a significant equity financing is invested by an investor whose objectives are in large part strategic, it is presumed that no more than 50 percent of the increase in the investment price compared to the prior significant equity financing is attributable to an increase in value of the company.

5. Valuation of a company acquired in a leveraged transaction should be adjusted if the company has been self-financing for at least two years and has been cash flow positive for at least one year. The adjustment should be based on P/E ratios, cash flow multiples, or other appropriate financial measures of similar companies, generally discounted by at least 30 percent for illiquidity. Such adjustment should occur no more frequently than annually and should be disclosed in the notes to the financial statements.

6. Warrants should be valued at the excess of the value of the underlying security over the exercise price.

7. The carrying value of interest bearing securities should not be adjusted for changes in interest rates.

Public Companies

8. Public securities should be valued at the closing price or bid price except as indicated otherwise in these guidelines.

9. The valuation of public securities that are restricted should be discounted appropriately until the securities may be freely traded. Such discount should generally be at least 30 percent at the beginning of the holding period and should decline proportionally as the restrictive period lapses.

10. When the number of shares held is substantial in relation to the usual quarterly trading volume, the valuation should generally be discounted by at least 10 percent.

Source: "Proposed Venture Capital Portfolio Valuation Guidelines (1989/1990)," National Venture Capital Association, unpublished document.

---

where "market" was the most recent independent round. Valuations should be reduced if "a company's performance and potential have significantly deteriorated."[19] An advisory committee might review the valuations, but this was usually limited to ensuring that the guidelines were correctly applied.

19. *Ibid.*

Firms had some latitude about whether to have their portfolio values audited. One VC firm did a random audit every year; others did not.[20]

Because the NVCA guidelines were never formally adopted, VC firms could use any valuation method that the partnership agreement allowed. A recent study by the Tuck School at Dartmouth found that roughly a third of the 561 firms that responded followed the proposed NVCA guidelines closely.[21] A larger number used some aspects of the guidelines, and almost three-quarters of the respondents felt that an industry standard was of some importance.[22] However, a small group of the surveyed firms indicated that "inefficiency and lack of transparency are good for the industry. . . . [A] standard would either be restrictive or uselessly vague."[23] An argument routinely heard in defense of the lack of a standard was, "It's better to be approximately right than precisely wrong."

The British Approach

In the early 1990s, the British Venture Capital Association (BVCA) had launched its own efforts to address venture fund valuation as the industry's performance had declined in that nation. With backing from a group of powerful LPs, the BVCA introduced measures designed to develop a set of performance benchmarks and a consistent set of valuation standards. These valuation standards tried to address one of the central issues of a declining market—the raising of funds based on values of portfolios that were inflated in the current environment. The guidelines, first announced in 1991 and refined in 1993, had been updated in 1997, when the PE industry in the United Kingdom became regulated by a new organization, the Financial Services Agency (FSA). Under the FSA, the BVCA became the self-regulatory body of the United Kingdom's PE industry, operating along the lines of the National Association of Stock Dealers (NASD) and Federal Accounting Standards Board (FASB) in the United States.[24]

In 2002, the BVCA proposed a new set of valuation guidelines that moved from the U.S. reliance upon cost to an approach based on fair value, or "the amount for which an asset could be exchanged between knowledgeable, willing parties in an arm's-length transaction."[25] The precise methodology to be used was defined over sixteen pages and was to be "appropriate . . . generally accepted . . . and [based] on market-based measures of risk and return. . . . Methodologies are to be applied consistently from period to period except where a change would result in a better estimate of Fair Value."[26] Preferred methodologies for valuing privately held companies included earnings multiples, the price of a recent investment, and net assets. Public companies could be held at their market price but discounted by 10 percent to 30 percent based on factors that would reduce liquidity, such as large holdings relative to the market or trading restrictions.[27] The European Venture Capital Association (EVCA) had adopted very similar guidelines.

20. Steven Brull, "Starting Over," *Institutional Investor* (June 2002), p. 81.

21. Colin Blaydon and Michael Horvath, "GPs Say Valuation Standard Is Important but Can't Agree on One," *Venture Capital Journal* (October 1, 2002), p. 1.

22. *Ibid.*

23. *Ibid.*

24. Jerry Borrell, "The Shape of Things to Come?" *Venture Capital Journal* (April 1, 2003), p. 1.

25. Lisa Bushrod, "New Valuation Guidelines for BVCA," *European Venture Capital Journal* (December 1, 2002), p. 1.

26. "New Reporting and Valuation Guidelines Exposure Draft," BVCA, http://www.bvca.co.uk, p. 37, accessed February 11, 2003.

27. *Ibid.*

Valuation in a Down Market

During the bull market of the late 1990s, the U.S. guideline of "higher of market or cost" had allowed for pleasant surprises when portfolio companies went public or were acquired, as the market value almost always exceeded the value at which the companies were listed in the portfolio. As one LP observed, "It was the world's worst time to try to establish guidelines." As the venture market came back to earth after March 2000, private companies, unable to go public, found themselves compelled to raise new rounds at valuations that had fallen sharply from previous levels. For instance, one company had built up the management team, progressed well on product development, and secured a significant initial customer contract when it went into the market in 2001 seeking $80 million at a $70 million pre-money valuation. Despite this progress, the year before it had raised $60 million at a $275 million pre-money value.[28] Nor had the situation changed a year later. IReady Corp., a computer networking start-up, closed a $19 million round in April 2002 but cut its post-money valuation from $120 million in its last round to $43 million.[29] It had little choice. As a senior partner at Mayfield, one of IReady's backers, said, "The consequence of not doing a down round is that you go out of business."[30] Clearly, the converse of pleasant surprises in an up-market was unpleasant ones in a slump.

These issues had also proven challenging for LBO organizations. Unlike venture-backed firms, which were typically refinanced on a twelve to eighteen-month basis, most LBOs were not refinanced until they went public years after the initial transaction. Groups could be tempted, therefore, to revalue the privately held firms in their portfolios. Doing so, however, could be a very subjective process; for instance, in many cases, dramatically different results could emerge when a price-to-earnings ratio or a market-to-book-value multiple was used to value the firm. Even seemingly conservative approaches could give misleading answers. Many groups argued that their valuations were conservative because they used the same multiples that they had used in the initial transaction. This assertion might be reasonable in a period of rising valuations, but the valuations of LBO transactions had fallen sharply to 2002, although 2003 saw the start of a recovery. However, if a deal had been done at 2003's average of 6.8 times earnings before interest, taxes, depreciation, and amortization (EBITDA), and multiples later fell back to 2001's 5.8, the conservatism of holding the company at its original 6.8 might be open to question.[31]

These difficulties were scarcely surprising. The private markets, despite the lack of formal correlation statistics, were influenced by the public markets—at least directionally. Most private companies looked to public enterprises to be their customers, partners, and acquirers. Falling public markets cheapened the stock that listed companies would use as currency for acquisitions and restricted their access to financing. This, in turn, made the public firms cut back on capital expenditures (often new technology from private companies) and generally concentrate on their core businesses. Any private company valuation method that did not take the volatility of public markets into consideration was doomed to be out of sync with true valuations.

While PE had always been a cyclical business, several aspects of the recent market had made the cycles more noticeable. Previous market declines had never been

28. Informal communication with Bessemer Venture Partners, May 17, 2002.

29. Brull, "Starting Over."

30. Kara Scanell, "Deals & Deal Makers: Start-ups Feel Pain of 'Down Round,'" *The Wall Street Journal* (February 4, 2003), p. C1.

31. Doron, "Multiples Rise amid Fierce Competition."

as spectacular as the one of 2000 through 2002, at least in terms of the amount of money and number of LPs and GPs involved. In addition, many participants—GPs and LPs alike—were new to venture investing and had never experienced the downside of the cycle.

In the PE environment, with high volatility, almost total illiquidity, and lack of transparency about true company performance until divestment, the stakes were high for both GPs and LPs.

Valuation from Many Perspectives

A GP walked a minefield when valuing companies. The interests of LPs had to be balanced with those of the firm and the individual partner. Keeping the value high made the portfolio look good, maintained the firm's internal rate of return (IRR), and pleased LPs. Writing down companies could lead LPs to decide not to renew commitments to future funds, or, in extreme cases, to request release from capital committed but not yet drawn down in a current fund. A poor IRR could prevent new firms from raising future funds.

In 2002, the valuation slide had directly and immediately affected a number of firms. Spectrum Equity Investors, TA Associates, and Battery Ventures, among others, had trimmed fees and returned money to LPs to avoid clawback. This term, included in almost every partnership contract, ensured that GPs would not have a larger share of returns than the partnership agreement stipulated. It was rarely invoked, but the conditions at the height of the market had set up the exact situation it had been designed to prevent.

Clawbacks worked in the following way: Consider a GP who raised a $100 million fund and made ten investments of $10 million each. Two investments liquidated early, for $50 million each, while the other eight stayed in the portfolio and were valued at cost. Assume that this fund employed a standard 80/20 percent split of capital gains between the LPs and GPs and followed the rule that distributions were divided between the GPs and LPs from inception.[32] When the first two investments were liquidated, the $20 million of invested capital was returned directly to the LPs. Of the $80 million in capital gains, 80 percent went to the LPs and $16 million (20 percent) to the GPs. These gains were paid out as the first two investments were exited, rather than after the fund had reached the end of its contractual life. The risk, however, was that the GPs would have over-distributed to themselves at the expense of the LPs if the remaining portfolio dropped in value. In our example, if the ultimate value realized from the remaining holdings of the portfolio was only $40 million (that is, 50 cents for each dollar invested), the GP would have over-distributed $8 million (20% × [$80 million – $40 million]) to itself.[33]

This could be complicated by "joint and several" clauses. These specified that each partner could be responsible for the entire amount of the clawback. If the GPs in the firm were a mix of senior partners who had invested their share of the $16 million, and younger partners who had spent their share on education for their children and a house, the entire $8 million owed the LPs might not be accessible. In the worst case, the junior partners might have to declare personal bankruptcy, the senior partners would cover the junior partners, and no one would be very happy.[34]

32. The different rules for liquidating PE portfolios are discussed in Josh Lerner, "A Note on Private Equity Partnership Agreements," HBS Case No. 294-084, and chapter 5 in *Venture Capital and Private Equity, A Casebook*, 3rd ed., (New York, NY: John Wiley & Sons, 2004.)

33. This problem could be avoided, of course, if the LPs first received all their capital back before there was any sharing of distributions, or if the distributions to the GPs were placed in an escrow account.

34. For top-tier firms raising funds after 1998, though, "joint and several" clauses had largely been replaced by "several" clauses, which specified that the partnership as a whole, not each individual partner, was responsible for the clawback. Additionally, the monies were repaid on an after-tax basis, bringing the net nominal value of the clawback to at most 50 percent of its gross amount.

Although GPs usually waited until the end of a fund's life to settle up with the LPs, betting that such imbalances would prove transitory, firms with 1999 funds were becoming more pessimistic about the eventual performance of their investments and opting to defray potential clawback liabilities early. Battery calculated that it would owe its LPs $44 million in clawback if its entire remaining portfolio lost all of its value. In exchange for the removal of the clawback term from that fund's partnership agreement, the firm offered to forego $51.4 million in fees. Spectrum had reduced fees on two funds by $27.5 million, while GPs at TA Associates wrote checks on their personal accounts to return $38 million to LPs.[35] In some cases, the LPs had agreed to remove the clawback term entirely; in others, the money returned was offset dollar for dollar against clawback obligations.[36] Overdistribution of funds and resulting issues around clawback were problems of both valuation and distribution. In the example above, the valuations could have changed for a number of reasons, including poor performance and exogenous changes in the private marketplace. Even if the company were valued correctly all along, clawback liabilities could occur because the distribution mechanism, to be discussed later, tried to get the money out to both parties as soon as possible. TA Associates had a unique approach to clawback; the firm settled up on an annual basis. The only way to solve the problem was the "real estate model," which returned 100 percent of capital to the LPs before distributing any carried interest, but that could cause other problems, including premature exits and risk aversion in investment choices.

Another situation that mixed valuation and distribution occurred when shares were actually distributed. Some partnership agreements stipulated that the relative split (the number of shares of the company received by the GP) was determined by the relative capital account balance of the GPs and LPs at the time of the distribution. Thus, the timing of valuation changes as well as their magnitude could directly affect a GP's compensation.

Interactions within a firm also complicated valuation. GPs could become emotionally tied to their companies and fear that writing them down would jeopardize the partnership's continued support. One firm addressed this issue by requiring that any company in the portfolio for more than four years would be written down to 25 percent of its value if it were still private. Said one partner, "It adds a conservative bias to a long-held position and reduces the possibility that we'll fall in love with our companies. In addition, it allows us to take the long view; the pressure is off so we're willing to hold it longer."

A new partner, especially one up for possible promotion, might be particularly reluctant to take a loss, and not without cause. One venture capitalist commented, "VC is a Darwinian world."[37] A number of VC firms had released partners, many new but some experienced, because they had been perceived as not contributing, or simply because the level of management fees was insufficient to support staff hired in a more affluent era. In 2002, Battery Ventures had let nine staff members go, including two partners, and Charles River Ventures had let go four partners and most of the staff of its Velocity unit, which had been created to nurture portfolio companies.

One venture capitalist commented that avoiding write-downs "is a fool's errand; it takes a short-term approach to a long-term issue." Even the annual audit of a partnership's books could force disclosures of overvalued companies.[38] The issue could arise

35. Mairin Burns, "The Clawback at Battery's Fund V," *The Investment Dealers' Digest* (December 9, 2002), p. 1.

36. Aragon and Primack, "Clawback Woes Hit Battery and Meritech,"

37. Sarah Lacy, "Investors Tougher on Big VC Firms," *Silicon Valley/San Jose Business Journal* (April 5, 2002), p. 1.

38. Eric Winig, "Reality check for VCs," *Washington Business Journal* (March 2, 2001), p. 3. Typically, however, accountants auditing the books of PE firms have accepted the firms' assessments of the value of the private firms in their portfolios and not sought to assess the reasonableness of the valuations.

with particular force for the venture arms of publicly traded firms (such as Oracle's venture effort or JP Morgan Partners),[39] when marking a portfolio to a depressed market could force the parent organization to show quarterly losses.[40]

A further complication for the GPs arose in the structures of recent deals. As the market slid, some firms had avoided down rounds by structuring complex deals with multiple liquidation preferences, participation, or other features.[41] A survey of San Francisco–area financings in the first quarter of 2002 had found that 62 percent gave senior liquidation preferences to their most recent investors, and over half of those had multiple liquidation preferences. All forty-five deals provided some antidilution protection, over 67 percent with weighted average and the balance with full ratchet.[42] Another study found that, while one liquidation preference had been the norm, three were now common, and six and seven were not unheard of.[43] These complex features moved the earlier investors further from realizing any gains. If, for instance, a Series C and a Series B round had been sold at $2 per share, but the C round carried a 3× liquidation preference and seniority, should the B round still be valued at $2 per share? If not, how should it be valued?

Discussing the practical impact of such terms, one venture capitalist gave the following example:

> We were invested in an e-commerce company that raised a round in July 2002. We had valued the company at, let's say, 1. A new investor offered 1.2, 20 percent more. We had actually considered writing the company down because it was in e-commerce, even though it was doing OK. So here's the new investor, offering an up round, but with gingerbread [complex terms]. So is the old round 1.2? 1? 0.8? How do we evaluate the gingerbread? It's great to get on the elevator, but what's the next floor? Not only is there no valuation algorithm that works in all situations, there's no valuation algorithm.

Even the public market did not necessarily assure consistent valuation. One example of the latitude that GPs could use in valuing securities appeared in a survey done by Peter Wendell of Sierra Ventures. When he founded the firm in 1982, Wendell wanted to establish a valuation policy. He surveyed a number of other venture firms regarding their approach to valuing the *public* securities in their portfolios. With two exceptions, Wendell found that most firms valued their public equities at about the same level as the firms were valued in the public marketplace. Those that held their equities at a level above the mean were all in the market raising a new fund. Those that valued their public holdings at a lower level were the investing arms of major family foundations and thus did not have to raise money on a regular basis.

Clarity, Consistency, and Conservatism

Given such variability in valuations of public securities, the range in private company valuations could hardly be surprising. All the while citing "clarity, consistency, and conservatism," firms might revisit portfolio valuations monthly, quarterly, semiannually, annually, or only when the company endured a "material adverse change" or closed a new financing. One survey found that 61 percent of its responding firms felt they were "more

---

39. The group formed from the merger of Chase Capital Partners and JP Morgan's PE group.

40. Britt Tunick, "An Evolutionary Battle," *The Investment Dealers' Digest* (March 19, 2002), p. 18.

41. For a discussion of these contractual provisions, see Felda Hardymon and Josh Lerner, "A Note on Private Equity Securities," HBS Case No. 200-027.

42. Tyson Freeman, "Survey Quantifies Severe VC Terms," *The Daily Deal* (June 7, 2002).

43. *Ibid.*

conservative" in their valuations than were their brethren.[44] Some firms never marked their companies above cost and routinely took "pro-active" markdowns if the outside market or the company's prospects worsened. Said a partner in a firm that followed such an approach, "We have had the same LPs for years. We don't have to prove ourselves. They expect us to be conservative."

Others felt that such pro-active markdowns were arbitrary and reactionary. One such firm felt that consistency required that the partners keep a telecommunications company at the high value set at its financing in 2000, despite the carnage in the external market. The GPs argued that the company had met all its milestones, although it was falling short of its revenue targets and would have to raise more money in 2003. Changing the valuation would mean a loss of historical consistency and the need to adopt a new policy. As a result, the VC firm chose not to change the valuation—unless the company had not found new financing by the end of the following quarter, in which case the GPs would mark it to zero, assuming that it would soon run out of funds.

Another company, Santera, was valued at 46¢ per share by Sequoia Capital and $4.42 by Austin Ventures, although the latter firm had a portfolio-wide "write-down reserve."[45] "But how much of that is allocated to Santera?" questioned an LP in a later conversation. To avoid such a situation, the CFO at one venture firm required that every GP contact the co-investors of each portfolio company to learn how they valued the company before releasing the report to LPs. Given the number of LPs with holdings diversified across a number of PE firms, many of whom syndicated their deals, significant valuation differences quickly became known.

In many cases, much of the impetus for valuation and revaluation came from LPs, who wanted to know the interim performance of their funds. One said, "Does this mean [PE firms] are telling me the value of our portfolio is $100 million when it's really worth $10 million?"[46] While the late 1990s had seen investors flocking to lock their money up for ten-year trips to triple-digit returns, the subsequent crash had left them curious or even nervous about what was going on, ignoring the long-held VC credo that "You can value your portfolio when you invest and when you exit. If you do it in between, you'll be wrong." But with the new LPs in PE, many of which managed public funds and had to report on a regular basis, the pressure for accurate interim valuations was intense. As one reporter observed, "GPs are spending almost as much time managing their LP relationships as their portfolio companies."[47]

With lots of money in venture portfolios and high volatility, valuation was an ongoing problem for LPs. Above all, they wanted "clarity, consistency, and conservatism" to ensure that they were allocating their assets correctly. Public stocks were also volatile, but they were liquid, meaning that those portfolios could be easily understood and rebalanced. Assets invested in venture firms were far less liquid and less transparent. Yet the effects of overallocation to that sector could be profound. Some foundations, required by law to distribute a certain percentage of their net asset value every year, could find themselves either over- or under-distributed if valuations were off by a significant amount. As one manager observed, "We got caught—a couple of billion dollars worth of unrealized gains evaporated, but we gave away real cash based on that." Other investors, such as endowments and pension funds, relied upon the valuations of

44. Blaydon and Horvath, "GPs Say Valuation Standard Is Important but Can't Agree on One."

45. Ann Grimes, "Deals & Deal Makers: VC Secret," *The Wall Street Journal* (November 4, 2002), p. C1.

46. *Ibid.*

47. Colin Blaydon and Michael Horvath, "What's a Company Worth?" *Venture Capital Journal* (May 1, 2002), p. 40.

the PE portfolios, sometimes smoothed over a few years, to determine their contributions to operating budgets. Said the manager of one endowment, "We really need accuracy. It's worse when we over-distribute, because that erodes the capital base. But under-distributing has its own costs in terms of scholarships we didn't fund or improvements we didn't make."

Write-downs also had costs to the fund managers themselves. Many reported to oversight committees and feared the impact of a large PE write-down on their returns and reputations. Managers of public pension funds and their elected superiors might be pilloried in the press or in future elections if seen to be risking employee pensions in investments that had lost money. Nor was this a mere fancy of an overactive imagination. The pressure for disclosure of the values of PE investments by public pension funds had forced the University of Texas and two big California pension funds to publish the interim IRRs and cash in/cash out positions of the funds they had invested in, and the picture was not pretty. A fund of funds might worry that decreased valuations from the funds in which it was invested might reduce its own LPs' willingness to invest again. On a personal level, many fund managers had their compensation or bonuses tied to their results, or even to the paper value of the portfolio—which might have a clause in the partnership document that required GPs to write down the value only if a down round occurred. The mantra of the experienced LPs was "clarity, consistency, and conservatism."

This was largely due to LPs' efforts to maintain a diversified portfolio of uncorrelated assets. Assessing the correlation of their individual PE holdings with other asset classes was difficult because the venture funds did not mark their portfolios to market on a regular basis. Some LPs, however, blamed the current downdraft in valuations on the pressure to mark to market, which had arisen from the accounting industry during the boom. By arguing against an illiquidity discount for private company stocks, even when they were in the six-month post-IPO holding period, some LPs perceived that accounting firms pushed their PE clients to mark their portfolios up.

Despite their unanimity about consistency and conservatism, LPs differed in their preferred methods for achieving it. Some suggested a strict adherence to valuations through third-party unrelated pricing and, in its absence, to cost, with interim revisions downward only. One LP wanted companies marked to a value that would realize a positive return going forward in any current environment. Some even differed on the use of discretion-based reductions. "The problem," said one, "is that you just have no idea where they're [the reductions] coming from."

Some LPs were more patient than others. Many, though, had begun PE investing in the late 1990s and were unaccustomed to the cyclical nature of the sector. Even the more experienced LPs might be annoyed with tardy adjustments and wildly varying valuations.

LPs also differed in their levels of sophistication as they dealt with the issue. Some large endowments ran databases that compared the values at which the different PE firms in which they had invested were holding the same company. This pressured the GPs to be, if not right, at least consistent.

CEOs

The valuation debate also affected the CEOs of portfolio companies. In essence, they were being asked to do more with less. To raise money in the early 2000s, companies were expected to have achieved milestones that, a few years before, would have been sufficient for an IPO. A company could go out to raise money with significant accomplishments, only to find that its value was half that of its previous round. A "down round" was tremendously demoralizing, as employees saw years of hard work resulting in a lower value for their stock option pool. Therefore, many GPs would do their best to support the company through bridge loans or inside rounds, aimed at keeping the paper value of the stock options at a reasonable level. In the end, the investors in early rounds might be "crammed" when new investors came in and imposed a new capital structure on the firm.

Sometimes valuations could affect all the parties to a transaction. One VC firm reduced the valuation of a portfolio company to 50 percent of cost, questioning its long-term viability. An LP who received the report released the supposedly private data. According to some in the industry, the company was in the midst of merger negotiations with an acquirer. Upon receiving the valuation data, the acquirer significantly reduced its offer price. In another example, Santera, the company with the wildly divergent valuations, was said to have lost a major potential customer when the article disclosing these differences appeared in *The Wall Street Journal*.

PROPOSALS

The current lack of standards had led to a "world turned upside down." LPs commented that the good funds had tended to cut their valuations first. "They don't have anything to prove," said one LP. "But it leads to the paradoxical situation that the good funds have lower valuations than the lesser ones." A GP said, "The NVCA-proposed guidelines worked well for ten years. But those ten years happened to coincide with the biggest venture run-up in history." Another observed, "There are standard ways to report an increase in valuation. . . . But when there's a decrease in valuation . . . there's no real standard."[48] He pointed to the variation in response, whether taking reserves against a company, reserves against a portfolio, or an outright decrease in valuation. One GP, frustrated by pressure from his LPs to write down the portfolio, had taken it all to zero, only to have his advisory committee threaten to do likewise with its capital contributions. One LP felt that there should be two sets of valuations: one holding the company at cost or less for the partnership's capital accounts and the other using more market-based indicators for performance presentations to investors. Clearly, there were no easy answers.

An industry conference in 2002 recommended five best practices:[49]

1. Maintain written valuation guidelines.

2. Have an internal committee to make valuation decisions.

3. Consult with co-investors on valuation issues.

4. Conduct a detailed valuation review with the advisory committee.

5. Reconsider the details of information given to all LPs.

The GPs' response to the issue generally depended on their previous methodology. The firms that had relatively stable LP bases and a long history of conservative accounting planned to "stay the course." Those that had marked up their valuations were considering changes and might have cut fund sizes and fees to avoid clawback.

---

48. Lindsay Jones, Advent International, in Carolina Braunschweig, "LPs Consider New Policy on IRRs," *Buyouts* (April 15, 2002), p. 1.

49. Testa Hurwitz & Thibeault, LLP, "Reporting Portfolio Valuations," unpublished slides from a conference, March 7, 2002.

The PEIGG

By 2002, LP concerns had raised the specter of regulation if the industry did not establish some sort of standards for disclosure and performance reporting. In February 2002, a group of LPs, GPs, buyout funds, and advisors created the Private Equity Industry Standards Board (PEISB) to study the issue and return guidelines for the valuation of investments and the reporting of information.[50] One of the group's earliest moves was to change its name to the much less official-sounding Private Equity Industry Guidelines Group (PEIGG).[51] In December 2003, the group published the results of its work only to find that industry groups such as the National Venture Capital Association declined to post them on their Web sites. Said one reporter, "The response has been tepid at best."[52]

In short, the PEIGG urged GPs to comply more closely with the U.S. Generally Accepted Accounting Principles' (U.S. GAAP) use of "fair value" in valuation.[53] U.S. GAAP defined fair value as "the amount at which an investment could be exchanged in a current transaction between unrelated willing parties, other than in a forced liquidation sale."[54] This meant, essentially, that GPs would have to determine the value of their companies based on the amount a willing purchaser would pay for them today, without reference to the original cost. While the GP still determined the valuation, which was to be reported on a quarterly basis, it was not longer automatically "cost or last round." Cost could still be used unless circumstances had changed sufficiently to make it differ from the company's fair value. Firms were urged to create semi-independent valuation committees to establish standards for each partnership, and co-investors in the same company were urged to come to a common valuation at which that company would be held in all portfolios.[55]

The guidelines aroused a great deal of comment. Some LPs were concerned that without an independent third-party review, GPs would write up investments.[56] Other observers observed that establishing fair market value was as much art as science, with no specific approved methodology. One observer commented, "The PEIGG blessed just about all known valuation approaches as appropriate in some circumstances. . . . It is hard to see how this would ever get us to the goal of consistency."[57]

On the GP side, Jim Breyer, managing partner of Accel Partners, commented that "to carry an investment at cost when the general partners know that cost is unfairly high is irresponsible and standards to move the industry to more aggressive write-downs from cost, or from previous write-ups, is very positive. The troubling issue is the suggestion that . . . there should be write-ups of portfolio company valuations without third-party validation."[58]

50. "Uniform Valuation and Reporting Guidelines for Private Equity," Investran, http://www.investran.com (December 10, 2002), accessed February 14, 2003.

51. Borrell, "The Shape of Things to Come?"

52. Carolina Braunschweig, "NVCA Balks at Valuation Standards," *Buyouts* (January 5, 2004), p. 1.

53. This discussion informed by PEIGG, "U.S. Private Equity Valuation Guidelines" and "U.S. Private Equity Valuation Guidelines: Frequently Asked Questions," (December 2003), http://www.peigg.org, accessed February 20, 2004.

54. PEIGG, "U.S. Private Equity Valuation Guidelines," (December 2003), http://www.peigg.org, accessed February 20, 2004.

55. *Ibid.*

56. Carolina Braunschweig, "NVCA Balks at Valuation Standards," *Buyouts* (January 5, 2004), p. 1.

57. Susan Woodward in Braunschweig, "NVCA Balks at Valuation Standards."

58. Cited in Carolina Braunschweig and Dan Primack, "Could PEIGG Affect the Buyout World?" *Buyouts* (December 15, 2003), p. 1.

Ironically, some observers had commented that one of the reasons that returns to PE could outperform the market was the very lack of transparency that now seemed so troubling. As demonstrated in the technology bubble, the asymmetry between the value that insiders and outsiders placed on a private company could generate unbelievable returns. Would better valuation and disclosure change that?

Some questioned the entire furor around valuations, arguing that PE was little different from real estate holdings, where multiple appraisers could place different values on a property, and that the entire situation was theoretical because all that mattered was the money eventually received. In the end, though, one GP observed, "I really hope to encounter this problem again, because that means we'll have gone through another huge market rise." And with that rise would come distributions and their attendant headaches.

STOCK DISTRIBUTIONS IN PRIVATE EQUITY[59]

As valuations fell, taking the industry into the new realm of clawbacks and fee and fund reductions, the number of distributions waned. During all of 2003, 29 venture-backed companies went public, and only 10.5 percent of the value of those distributions was in stock. This was down from the high of 68 percent in 2000 (see Exhibit 24.4 for cash versus stock distributions over time). Yet distributions were still occurring—even in 2002, when 18 percent of distributions had been in stock, one LP reported that stock had funded 80 percent of his organization's capital calls. The industry also vividly remembered the delirious days of 1999 and 2000, when over $70 billion had been distributed from VC-backed IPOs. GPs were still making stock distributions, and LPs still had to decide whether to hold or sell the securities. Despite the market decline, the decision still had extremely high stakes.

PE investors[60] typically did not sell shares when one of their portfolio companies went public in an IPO. Instead, they usually entered into a "lock-up" agreement with the investment bank underwriting the deal, in which they agreed not to sell shares for several (usually six) months. Ostensibly, this made the sale of shares to the public easier, since investors often feared that the share price would tumble if insiders sold large blocks of securities in the months after the IPO. Once they decided to liquidate investments in publicly traded firms, PE investors typically employed one of two approaches. The PE investor could sell the shares in the market and distribute the cash to the fund's investors, which included both GPs and LPs. Often, although less so in 2002, the PE investor distributed actual shares.

Three reasons explained the frequency of stock distributions. First, SEC rules restricted the size of sales by corporate affiliates (officers, directors, and holders of 10 percent of the firm's equity). Venture investors often qualified as affiliates because of

---

59. This section draws from Felda Hardymon, Josh Lerner, and Ann Leamon, "The Plummer Endowment: The Distribution Question," HBS Case No. 802-174, March 7, 2001.

60. Distributions are also important in buyout funds. A major university endowment that is a large buyout investor estimates that over 30 percent of the distributions from buyout funds are in the form of securities. Distributions are also controversial in this setting. For instance, in September 1994 Wasserstein Perella's merchant banking fund distributed its shares of Maybelline, which it had held since 1990. Five days later, Maybelline announced disappointing earnings, and its stock price dropped by 36 percent. In a highly unusual move, Wasserstein Perella bowed to the limited partners' protests and reduced the price at which the distribution was recorded (thereby sharply reducing its profits). See Yvette Kantrow, "Wasserella Fund Investors See Red Over Share Payout," *Investment Dealers' Digest* 60 (September 26, 1994), pp. 3–4.

EXHIBIT 24.4

THE ANNUAL VOLUME OF VENTURE CAPITAL STOCK AND CASH DISTRIBUTIONS

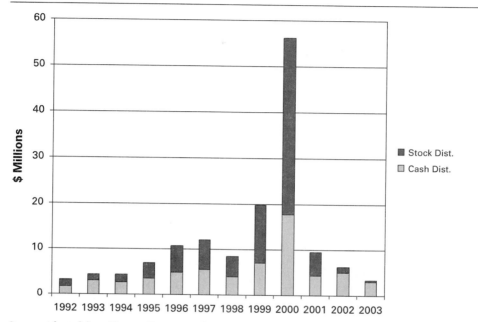

Source: Adapted from Venture Economics, http://venturexpert.com, accessed February 22, 2004.

their role on the board and their equity holdings (see Exhibit 24.5 for relevant securities law). The PE fund might hold a large fraction of the company's equity. Selling its entire stake could, consequently, take a long time. By distributing the shares to LPs (who were not considered affiliates and could therefore sell their shares freely), the PE investor could quickly dispose of a large stake.

Second, tax motivations provided an incentive for the GPs to distribute shares. If GPs sold the shares and distributed cash, the LPs and the GPs themselves were subject to immediate capital-gains taxes. The LP often included a mix of tax-exempt entities (e.g., pension funds, endowments, and foundations) and others that were not (individuals and corporations). These investors might have different preferences regarding the timing of the share sale. Furthermore, the PE investors themselves might wish to postpone paying personal taxes by selling their shares at a later date.

Finally, the PE investor might want to distribute shares due to concerns that selling shares to generate cash might depress their price. GPs had two reasons to worry about reducing the share price of a portfolio company that had gone public. First, outside fund trackers (e.g., Venture Economics and Cambridge Associates) and most LPs computed returns based on the closing price of the distributed stock on the day of distribution.[61] If a firm waited to sell the shares and return cash, the fund's return would

---

61. Many distributions are declared at 5 P.M. after the stock market has closed.

EXHIBIT 24.5

SECURITIES LAW RELEVANT TO VENTURE DISTRIBUTIONS*

Several SEC regulations are relevant to the distribution of stock by PE investors, especially Rules 144, 16(a), and 10(b)-5. The first governs trading in restricted and control stock; the second, reporting of insider transactions; and the third, insider trading around securities issues.

Restricted stock is defined as shares that (1) have not been registered with the SEC and (2) are acquired directly from the firm or an affiliate (such as an officer or director). Shares purchased by a PE investor from a private company generally meet these two tests. At the time of the case, restricted shares could not be sold for one year, except in the case of death of the owner. Between one and two years after the original issue, the shares could be sold, but only in a limited manner. Among the requirements were that the SEC must be notified of the sale, that the sale must be done through a broker who is a market maker, and that the volume traded in any three-month period could not be too large.[†] After two years, the shares could be traded freely.

In addition, Rule 144 restricts sales of control stock, even if it is not restricted. Control stock is defined as shares owned by individuals who are affiliates of a firm, such as directors, officers, and holders of 10 percent of the company's shares. Sales by these parties are allowed only under the same conditions as sales of restricted stock in the one to two years after the original purchase. In a long series of no-action letters, however, the SEC has made clear that distributions from affiliates to nonaffiliates (e.g., from a PE investor with a board seat to an institutional investor) are not subject to restrictions under Rule 144. Thus, distributions can be as large or small as the affiliate desires, and the recipient of the distribution can sell the shares as quickly as he desires.[‡]

Rule 16(a) states that affiliates of a publicly traded company must disclose their ownership of shares annually and any transactions monthly. This information is made available to the public through Forms 3, 4, and 5 (as well as through proxy filings). Provision 16(a)-7, however, explicitly exempts distributions of securities that (1) were originally obtained from issuers and (2) are being distributed "in good faith, in the ordinary course of such business." Thus, PE investors rarely report distributions to either the SEC or the public.

Rule 10(b)-5 is the general law limiting fraudulent activity "in connection with the purchase or sale of any security." More suits are brought under Rule 10(b)-5 than any other provision of the securities law. If several tests are met, private plaintiffs who have bought or sold shares can recover damages from the defendant. First, damages are available only under Rule 10(b)-5 to purchasers or sellers of the securities in question. Second, the plaintiffs must prove that the defendants had previous knowledge that their statements or actions were misleading. Third, it must be shown that the misrepresentations were not insignificant in nature, but rather "material." Fourth, the plaintiff must prove that he or she was actually misled by the deceptive statement or action on the part of the defendant. Fifth, there must be a causal link between the defendant's actions and the injury to the plaintiff. Finally, it must be shown that the defendant had a fiduciary duty to the shareholders of the firm. Not only are affiliates liable under this final requirement but so are "tippees": individuals who receive information about publicly traded firms from corporate insiders. In the landmark case *Dirks vs. SEC*,[§] the U.S. Supreme Court ruled that a tippee may be liable if the individual giving the tip (1) had a duty not to disclose the information and (2) stood to benefit in some tangible or intangible way from providing the tip.

(Continues)

be based on the dollars realized from the sale, which might be less than the market value at the time of the stock's distribution. A venture firm's return was its most important marketing tool when it sought to raise capital for a new fund. The distributed price might not be the actual price received (or even near it) when the LPs sold their shares. It could take two or three days, or even longer (six weeks at the height of the bubble), before the shares reached the LPs after a distribution was declared. If the market reacted negatively to the distribution, or if the price fell simply due to increased

EXHIBIT 24.5 (CONTINUED)

SECURITIES LAW RELEVANT TO VENTURE DISTRIBUTIONS[1]

While the SEC has not explicitly discussed the applicability of Rule 10(b)-5 to PE distributions, lawyers have applied the same principles that govern the interpretation of Rules 144 and 16(a). An interpretation widely accepted within the industry is that PE investors distribute investments in the normal course of the investment process. Consequently, a distribution does not convey information to the LPs. This presumption does not hold, of course, if the PE investor makes an explicit recommendation to either hold or immediately sell the shares. Otherwise, no presumption is typically made that an institutional investor that receives a distribution from a PE investor has received any information with those shares. Similarly, an institutional investor that observes that a PE investor has failed to distribute shares on which the lock-up period has expired has not received information from the PE investor.

Sources: Compiled from Harold S. Bloomenthal, *Going Public and the Public Corporation* (New York: Clark Boardman Callaghan, 1994); James Bohn and Stephen Choi, "Securities Fraud Class Actions in the New Issues Market," unpublished working paper, Harvard University, 1994; *Insider Trading and Short-Swing Reporting* (Chicago: Commerce Clearing House, 1992); and assorted other sources.

Notes:

° I thank Katherine Todd, formerly of Brinson Partners, and Robin Painter, Esq., of Testa Hurwitz & Thibeault, for helpful discussions of these issues. All remaining legal errors, however, are solely my fault!

† The volume sold by any party in a three-month period (including by relatives or any corporation or trust in which the party has a controlling interest) cannot exceed the greater of (1) 1 percent of outstanding shares or (2) the average weekly trading volume in the previous four weeks.

‡ If, however, the recipient of the distribution held a 10 percent stake in the company, then Rule 144 would apply. This is unlikely to be the case in distributions from venture funds, since there are usually several limited partners receiving the shares.

§ 463 U.S. 646, 103 S.Ct. 3255 (1983).

---

supply, actual returns to the LPs could be substantially less than calculated returns. In response to the LPs' concerns that GPs' performance numbers more closely reflect the actual performance of the stock, many GPs had adopted five-day average pricing in their reports. Another used a thirty-day post-distribution price, much to the annoyance of its LPs—"And what are we supposed to do with that?" asked one.

The second reason related to the GPs' compensation. Distributing higher-valued stock, rather than realized cash, returned more of the LPs' capital and hastened the day that GPs could start collecting carry without fear of clawback. The experiences of firms over-distributing early proceeds could make GPs even more interested in returning the LPs' capital.

The recent shift in distributions from stock to cash reflected the unrelenting market slide. Said one LP, "In the boom, we all looked like geniuses. Now, we all look like idiots. It used to be, if you sold, you got three times your cost back. If you held, it went up another 15 percent. Now, you just sell as fast as you can." From the perspective of the PE firm, selling the stock and returning cash very likely gave the LPs the best possible return and allowed the GPs to provide some extra services to the LPs, which were, one GP said, "the lifeblood of any partnership."

Many institutional investors could relate stories of shares that fell sharply in value after distribution, especially during the Internet bubble of 1999–2000. For example, the Internet toy retailer E-toys was valued at over $10.3 billion at its peak, with shares trading at $84 in October 1999. In December, when the lock-up from the IPO expired, the shares were still over $50. Several of the venture backers, including Highland Capital Partners and Bessemer Venture Partners, began distributing stock. Within two months the stock had fallen to under $20 per share, a drop of over 60 percent in sixty days. In March 2001, the company declared bankruptcy, and the equity was worthless.

But while the LPs of Bessemer and Highland were coping with a fast-falling stock price, those of Sequoia Capital, E-toys' lead investor, stood on the sidelines watching their shares lose value. Sequoia's GP, a member of E-toys' board, did not distribute Sequoia's 8 million shares; Sequoia was still holding the shares when E-toys declared bankruptcy.[62]

Sequoia was not alone in watching high-priced shares fall. The shares of high-flying technology company Akamai had dropped from a peak of $327 per share to $76 when the first lock-up expired in April 2000. In October, when Battery Ventures, one of Akamai's major investors, went to sell its shares, the price was down to $50 per share. As of January 2001, Battery still held 6 million shares, which were trading at $11.[63]

In another example, Crosspoint Venture Partners and Institutional Venture Partners (IVP) pursued different strategies when dealing with distributions from their portfolio company, Foundry Networks, a maker of Internet switching gear. Crosspoint distributed its 16 million shares to investors as quickly as possible in October 2000, when the price averaged $87. IVP distributed half its shares at $100 but still held 4 million shares in February 2001, valued at $10 each.[64]

Some PE firms held shares through the lock-up period and beyond. One GP said, "We may fund an A round at $1 and have an IPO at $12, but we'll work with that company until we have a share price of $100." In the recent market, this firm's LPs had requested that the firm distribute stock a little more quickly after the end of the lock-up.

Other firms might hold their companies' shares as a sign of support. "Many LPs interpret a distribution as a signal to dump the stock," said one GP. "That's not the case; we want to give them the opportunity to keep or sell. We're not public securities managers; we generally get out as soon as we can."

Another GP cited some exceptions to that approach: "There are a few exceptions. In biotech, for instance, companies go public but still require a lot of support until they really have achieved their full value. In those companies, we've maintained our holdings even after they've gone public, and these are coming to fruition. But by and large, when it's public, it's out of our sweet spot."

But there was one constituency that GPs uniformly advised to sell its shares: CEOs. One GP explained, "We're backing younger and younger people. They'll have 99.9 percent of their net worth tied up in one company. They have to liquidate some of it in an orderly way. And it can be hard to convince them to do it."

The decision to distribute stock was less a sign that the GPs had more or better information on its future performance than the natural rules of behavior and, to some degree, economics. GPs would naturally want to distribute stock that appeared to be increasing in value, not just to burnish their IRRs but also to reduce the damage to the stock price by increasing the supply. All GPs said that they tried to "distribute into strength." Yet the rules of economics dictated that increased supply, all things being equal, would reduce price, whether speaking of hog bellies or technology stocks. Distributing stock could compound the increased supply/reduced price dynamic if much

62. Luisa Kroll, "In the Lurch," *Forbes* (April 2, 2001), p. 54.

63. *Ibid.*

64. *Ibid.*

of that stock found its way into the hands of unsophisticated LPs who would promptly sell it. Even sophisticated LPs would be inclined to sell stock that came in small lots, as it was not worth their trouble to manage it. Yet unlike a typical situation where the supply and demand would come to equilibrium, a 1998 study of nearly 800 distributions showed more systematic evidence about the relationship between distributions and stock prices.[65] (See Exhibit 24.6 for the average stock price of firms, net of market returns,[66] from three months before to three months after distributions by venture funds. See Exhibit 24.7 for the returns for various subclasses of firms, including firms financed by older and younger PE organizations; companies taken public by high-, medium-, and low-reputation investment bankers; firms where the PE investor did and did not leave the board at the time of the distribution; and cases where the distribution was larger and smaller.) The stock price steadily fell after distribution.

This behavior was not seen, however, during the bubble of 1999–2000, when the prices for newly distributed stock tended to rise, rather than fall, after distribution. Anecdotally, this was said to occur because of pent-up demand for stock in companies that had received a lot of "street buzz." Suddenly the supply of the stock increased to the point that the big institutional buyers could purchase enough to reach their minimum holding levels.

EXHIBIT 24.6

THE NET-OF-MARKET RETURNS AROUND DISTRIBUTIONS

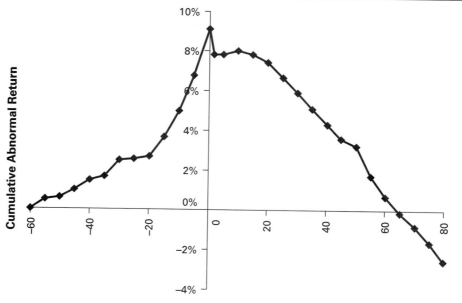

Day Relative to Distribution

Source: Adapted from Paul Gompers and Josh Lerner, "Venture Capital Distributions: Short- and Long-Run Reactions," *Journal of Finance* 53 (6) (December 1998): 2161–2183.

---

65. The results are presented in more detail in Paul Gompers and Josh Lerner, "Venture Capital Distributions: Short- and Long-Run Reactions," *Journal of Finance* 53 (6) (December 1998): 2161–2183.

66. Adjusted for the shift in the relevant stock index.

EXHIBIT 24.7

THE NET-OF-MARKET RETURNS AROUND DISTRIBUTIONS

The predistribution return is the return in the period from the sixth month prior to the distribution to the month before the distribution. The distribution window return is from the period from the day of the distribution to three days after. The post-distribution return is from the month after the distribution to twelve months after.

Sample	Pre-distribution Return	Distribution Window Return	Post-Distribution Return
Full Sample	14.2%	–2.0%	–6.8%
Venture Organization Age ≥ Median	15.4	–2.5	–8.3
Venture Organization Age < Median	12.7	–1.5	–5.0
High Underwriter Rank	10.2	–1.4	–0.1
Medium Underwriter Rank	15.8	–1.6	0.6
Low Underwriter Rank	14.1	–2.8	–12.9
Investor Does Not Leave Board	15.8	–2.1	–6.3
Investor Leaves Board of Directors	15.3	–2.8	–15.9
Distributions That Are Larger Than Median	16.4	–2.2	–6.7
Distributions That Are Smaller Than Median	10.9	–1.6	–4.3

Source: Adapted from Paul Gompers and Josh Lerner, "Venture Capital Distributions: Short- and Long-Run Reactions," *Journal of Finance* 53 (6) (December 1998): 2161–2183.

The distribution process often frustrated LPs and had done so for at least fifteen years, as a *Venture Economics* article from 1987 noted: "There are few venture capital fund management issues that evoke so much controversy as the timing and execution of stock distributions. Venture capital managers [and investors] differ in their philosophy as to when stock should be distributed and how those distributions should be handled."[67]

The distribution of shares posed a substantial administrative burden. Record-keeping and tax calculations were far more complex when shares were distributed. Also, it was often difficult to decide what to do with the shares. PE investors typically distributed shares with little notice, claiming that, under SEC regulations, LPs were safer if they were not advised of distributions in advance. The GPs explained that their behavior was due to the need to avoid providing information to hedge fund managers, who might short the stock and drive the price down before the distribution. In addition, distributions of young and obscure firms often came with little supporting information and few recommendations.

The bubble, though, had seen the emergence of a small industry that followed IPOs. Web sites such as IPOlockup.com tracked the announced IPOs and the time until their lock-ups expired. To confuse short sellers, GPs might distribute the stock in chunks rather than all at once. Some firms also took steps to ensure that their LPs understood the companies whose stock they were receiving. One firm in particular would bring in

67. Anonymous, "Stock Distributions—Fact, Opinion and Comment," *Venture Capital Journal* 27 (August 1987): 8.

the CEOs of its companies to have lunch with the LPs and make a presentation on the company's plans. "That way," said the GP, "my LPs understand what they're getting and make an informed decision about whether to sell or hold."

Dealing with Distributions

LPs had developed a number of distinct strategies for handling distributions. Several of these could be seen in the evolution of approaches taken by Harvard Management Corporation (HMC), the manager of the $19 billion Harvard endowment.[68] Kevin Tunick, one of the two managers of HMC's PE portfolio, which comprised over 15 percent of the Harvard endowment, described his initial approach as "Blow it all out"—HMC sold all of its distributions as soon as they were received. Most venture stocks dropped immediately after distribution, due in part to the modest size of the float, the share of the company that was actually available for trading prior to the distribution.[69] HMC's sales contributed to that drop, leading Tunick to conclude that HMC was losing too much value in the initial drop in the stock price. He next decided to change to a "maximizing dollar return" approach. In this approach, which Tunick described as "a trading play," he watched the behavior of the stock post-distribution and sold on the upswings. In practice, he was able to limit the loss of the stock's value to only a few percentage points relative to the day of distribution, but he held the distributed stock in the PE portfolio longer—on average thirty to forty-five days. Even though the method yielded proceeds within a few percentage points of the distributed value of the stock, Tunick found that "holding the stock in the PE portfolio for that longer period of time created a drag on the overall PE returns. In fact, the last year I used that method, merely holding those stocks in the PE portfolio reduced returns that year by nearly 2 percent."[70]

By 2002, HMC's PE managers, like those of many other PE groups, had developed a third, hybrid approach to PE stock distributions. They implemented a selling program immediately upon receiving the stock and liquidated the entire position in smaller increments over a few days. Typically the position was sold within five days.

Many large LPs with side-by-side public portfolios would use another approach and analyze each distribution internally. Often, this was equivalent to an automatic sell policy. In almost all cases, the sell-or-hold decision was made not by the officials responsible for venture investments but by the analysts handling publicly traded small-capitalization stocks. These analysts had their own lists of favorite stocks, which were unlikely to coincide with the stock distributions. Furthermore, the LP might have received only a small number of shares, which would further reduce the analysts' willingness to study the firms carefully.

Yet another method was to rely upon a stock distribution manager. These intermediaries received distributions from LPs and decided, with the LPs' input, on whether to sell or hold them. Examples of such firms included Shott Capital Management, S-Squared Technologies, Warburg Pincus, and T. Rowe Price. The enduring issue with using stock distribution managers was the problem of finding the appropriate benchmark against which to measure their performance. Since the manager did not actually

68. The discussion of HMC's approach is drawn from Hardymon, Lerner, and Leamon, "The Plummer Endowment: The Distribution Question," HBS Case No. 802-174.

69. One phenomenon that is not fully captured by Exhibit 24.6 is that in the days after the distribution, the bid/ask spreads will often become very wide for these stocks.

70. Note that in HMC's case, once cash was realized in the PE portfolio, it was "swept up" into the overall portfolio and no longer counted in the returns of the PE portfolio.

choose which security to buy but only which security to hold, there was no natural comparison benchmark. Moreover, such managers added fees to the PE portfolio.

During the late 1990s, though, these firms had become significant players in the distribution field. A managing director from Shott Capital Management said, "It used to be that the hardest thing was just getting people to pay attention to the issue. Now it's become a topic of discussion at the board level." Despite the fees that they charged, one distributing broker credited distribution managers with saving millions if not billions of dollars for LPs simply by maintaining a sense of objectivity about the company: "If you're the guy at the endowment and you go to all the meetings, you'll fall in love with the company." In addition, distribution managers tracked the distributions, the splits, and the mergers that occurred during the lock-up period and managed the attendant complexities for the client. Even in the down market, when the watchword was liquidation, distribution managers prided themselves on managing portfolios to maximize returns rather than minimize losses.

PE Distributions

Venture distributions followed a winding road from the announcement that a company had gone public at $12 per share to the arrival of money in the LP's pocket. First came the 180-day lock-up. Upon its expiration, or later, the PE investor would send a distribution notification to the LP. These notices detailed the amount of stock being distributed, the cost basis, the distribution value, and the restrictions to which it was subject. These might include volume restrictions if the size was more than 1 percent of the outstanding shares, if it had been held for less than two years, or if it needed to be de-legended.[71] The GP would have opened an account with a distributing broker (broker-dealer) and deposited the shares in it. The letter would request the LP to contact the broker with instructions about the action to take—sell, transfer to a custodian or distribution manager, or await instructions from another party. Brokers provided this service because they received the fee for executing the trade, which LPs frequently requested.

Even if the LP wanted the broker to sell the shares, there would be a delay as the physical certificate went to the transfer agent, who, with lawyers and the GP, would coordinate splitting large blocks of shares into smaller holdings for each LP. There might even be an additional delay—six weeks or more in the bubble—as the physical stock certificates made their way to the broker. If the stock was restricted by Rule 144, Rule 145, or Rule S-3, for example, the necessary paperwork had to arrive at the broker's office at the time that the sell order was given. Most brokers would then execute the trade, but settlement would be delayed. Many banks offered the service of trade execution in advance of finishing the paperwork, in effect lending the proceeds to the LP for a fee. Big institutions felt that it would be preferable to streamline the process rather than to cover over its inefficiencies with fees and loans.

Other players in the process aside from the investment banks that received the stock and tried to do most of the trades were the sales brokers who held the stock and did the trades; the brokers' 144 desks, who did the legal due diligence behind the stock and ensured that it met the SEC's filing requirements; and the transfer agents. During 1999 and 2000, the system had been stressed to its limits. One sales manager on the 144 desk remembered, "I got married during the summer of 1999. People were begging me not

---

71. The stock of private companies was stamped with a legend that prohibited it from being traded. Before it could be traded, each certificate had to be traded in for one without the legend.

to go on my honeymoon. We were handling twelve distributions a week. Everyone was simply clobbered by the volume, the splits, and the acquisitions."

Even as the transfer agents, distribution managers, and 144 desk people were working behind the scenes to clear the stock, the LPs were trying to decide what to do with it. In explaining his approach to handling distributions, the manager of a major endowment said, "We sell everything . . . eventually."

Especially since 2000, "eventually" had become somewhat closer to "immediately" for many LPs. Said one, "We really don't feel that we're being adequately rewarded for being long-term holders of small-cap tech companies. There may still be cases where the company has significant growth potential, but that's rare."

One LP cited three exceptions to its rule of selling distributions as soon as possible: "(1) if it is a very large distribution where putting the block up for sale would be problematic; (2) if the endowment is holding the stock or has held it in the past, we check to see if the public managers want it [in which case it is 'sold' to the public portfolio manager at the market price]; or (3) if it is on a watch list of stocks we may want to hold."

Another LP sold small distributions with one exception. If the stock was widely held by its venture firms, the institution might receive a number of small distributions of the same company, amounting to a position that would be worth its while to manage.

A few LPs pursued a strategy of selectively managing some of their post-distribution stocks. One that had such an approach explained its genesis:

> In 1986, we received the first Microsoft shares that the endowment ever owned. We held some of them, and they performed very well. In fact, had we held all of them until today, that single distribution would be worth billions. That experience and some other similar ones prompted us to start the program of selectively holding stocks. So far the strategy has worked. We track this "distributed portfolio" assigning a cost basis to the shares equal to the price on the day the shares are distributed. On that basis, this portfolio has been a net positive to the overall private equity portfolio.
>
> We are trying to improve on a blind sell policy by attempting to add value to the overall private equity portfolio return. One could measure this either by measuring the return on the "distribution" portfolio—which we do—and/or by measuring whether we are able to realize more value by holding these stocks than we would by selling them on distribution.
>
> The second key question I would ask is, how the heck do you do that? In other words, how do you decide which stocks to hold versus which to sell? One cannot easily reduce a complex decision process to a simple list of rules. Having said that, I can describe our process as boiling down to a few key essentials: (1) focus on the largest holdings and sell the rest, since the rule of winner-take-all applies here as everywhere in PE: all the returns come from the big winners; (2) focus on the number one players in their respective markets by looking for companies that can be long-term market leaders (again, most of the value accrues to the winners); and (3) focus on the portfolios of the best funds, since, in our experience, the best long-run post-distribution returns overwhelmingly come from a small handful of the best funds.

A selective hold strategy had become more challenging for another LP, as the manager observed:

> It will be a long time before tech companies have post-distribution appreciation potential. The public markets are smarter—and it makes it harder

to be a long-term holder. Fewer companies have legs post-distribution. At the same time, we know our GPs—some of them distribute stock as a regular pattern of moving it out, and with others, it's a definite vote on what they think the company's potential is.

One of the biggest challenges in maximizing post-distribution value, the LPs agreed, was that the GPs distributed the stock all on one day. "It's not a secret," said one. "The only question in today's market is whether the stock will rebound." One GP said that his firm tried to sell into strength, which had been easy in 2002, as its three exits had been in the stock of blue-chip companies. This GP was not alone in his desire to distribute into strength—almost all firms aspired to do so. The converse, however, was that they would hold a weakening stock, hoping to distribute once it stabilized. One LP complained:

> One of our GPs had a substantial position in a company that came off lock-up at 100. We received about 25 percent of it at 95. Sure, we'd rather have it at 100, but it's not a huge deal. Then they held the balance as it fell. It finally stabilized at 80. When we received the rest of the distribution, the price was 81. They said they didn't want to distribute a falling stock. Part of it was pride, but part was that they priced it at the ten-day average price before the distribution or the price at distribution, whichever was lower. The price had been falling when they first distributed it. My point is that I'd rather have it falling at 95 and maybe get out of the whole position at 90 than stable at 81. Who'd rather have 81 than 90? Not me!

PE firms almost never warned of an impending distribution for fear of signaling the short sellers in the market. In light of that, a major endowment had a number of rules it might follow: "We may push out pieces, maybe sell 25 percent a week in four weeks. We may accelerate if we're nervous, relax if we're not. We keep an eye on the volume; if that shrinks, we'll pull back. We don't want to impact the market in a negative way, and we have to be aware of who else is out there."

The other parties out there were a cause for concern. Many LPs would just sell small distributions—but if several PE firms made small distributions of thinly traded stock to their LPs, the market ended up coping with a large volume of sales. As a result, careful GPs with minor distributions to a number of inexperienced LPs might often liquidate the position themselves. Some LPs had begun evaluating their GPs on the price that they realized rather than the price at distribution, further encouraging the GPs to handle the sales themselves if they felt they could receive a better price.

Taking on this task, though, exposed the GPs to market and execution risk. Especially with thinly traded stocks, the risk of having the market change and torpedo even the best-planned strategy was significant. The opportunities for second-guessing any decision were endless. Often LPs, especially if they had their own sophisticated trading departments, were far better positioned to handle the mechanics of the operation than was a five-partner PE firm. By distributing stock rather than cash, one expert observed, the GPs mitigated the market risk to which they were subject—but shifted it to the LPs.

One phenomenon that had occurred during the bubble was the willingness of some VC firms to distribute stock that was still volume-restricted under Rule 144. Most LPs strongly encouraged their PE partners only to distribute stock that was immediately tradable. However, during 2000, one VC firm found that the fund had $2.8 billion in public equity. Not willing to incur that level of market risk, the GPs called their LPs and warned them that they would systematically distribute all their public stocks in regular increments (which turned out to be thirty to sixty days apart).

Although much of the stock was still subject to Rule 144, the LPs acquiesced, since they felt the distributions gave them a path to liquidity in an overvalued market. Commented one LP, "You have to understand that GPs didn't get into the business to manage public stock portfolios, but it's a big part of what they have to do."

One hotly debated issue was hedging. Yale University's endowment had started hedging the stocks in its PE firms' portfolios, or similar companies, before distribution.[72] This was abhorrent to GPs who did not want selling pressure on their stocks *especially* from LPs, who were ostensibly on their side. Other LPs wondered if such a strategy would be particularly effective.

ALL IN THE SAME BOAT

Where both valuation and distribution were concerned, the only consensus was that the two parties, GPs and LPs, must continue to experiment and try to find a balance that would satisfy both sides. A few firms cited strategies that seemed to move in the right direction—marking down companies to 25 percent after four years in the portfolio and using the five-day price average. Yet even then, ongoing goodwill was essential. The manager of a major endowment recalled, "In a down market, one GP did a distribution of a stock that was tanking. The five-day average was $5 per share. We got it at $2.50. We're smart enough to remember that." In the end, commented an LP, "GPs often eat their own cooking. It's up to them to make it work, or the entire asset class and all their companies will suffer."

---

72. Josh Lerner, "Yale University Investments Office: July 2000," HBS Case No. 201-048 (November 17, 2000).

The Private Equity Cycle: New Frontiers

The final module considers the future of the private equity industry. In the course of understanding the likely challenges that venture capital and buyout organizations will face over the next decade, we review many of the key ideas developed in *Venture Capital and Private Equity.* Rather than simply looking at more cases about the same private equity groups, however, the cases examine organizations that at first sight seem very different from the ones we considered previously.

WHY THIS MODULE? (1): THE FUTURE OF PRIVATE EQUITY

Economists studying the evolution of new industries in the nineteenth and twentieth centuries have noted a striking regularity: after a period of rapid growth, many industries go through a "shake-out," in which the competitive structure changes dramatically. Numerous firms drop by the wayside in these periods. Even when a considerable number of smaller firms survive, their role in the industry is frequently increasingly marginal. At the same time, a few firms frequently solidify their position as dominant industry leaders. Many of the victors from these periods of consolidation are frequently among the earliest firms active in the industry. The successful firms have managed in the past to adjust to industry changes. These established firms have often been joined by new entrants who, without the "baggage" of long-established industry practices, are particularly adept at exploiting the new industry dynamics.

The periods of rapid change in industry structure can be triggered by a variety of events. For instance, a new invention may be developed outside the industry that dramatically changes the cost of manufacturing products or providing services. As a result, the ideal size of the firm in the industry may become considerably larger. Firms that rapidly adopt the new innovation may grow quickly as a result, while those that do not may wither away.

Alternatively, such periods of rapid change may emerge because of the development of a dominant design, or a standard, in an industry. This standard might be technological (for instance, a software operating system) or organizational (e.g., Priceline's "reverse auction" approach to selling airline tickets) in nature. The firms that adopt can persuade their customers to adopt their new standard and can deter competitors from adopting their approach. They may be able to rapidly emerge as dominant factors in an industry, even if their approach is little better than alternative ones developed in the industry.

Yet another possibility is that these differences stem from changing market conditions. Firms often differ in their ability to adapt to rapid change, whether due to differences in the skill of management or historical happenstance. Furthermore, this adaptive ability may be self-reinforcing: once firms become good at responding to shifting events, they may find making subsequent adjustments easier to make. As we will argue below, the private equity industry today is in a period of profound change. These changes are likely to pose substantial challenges for many established private equity groups.

It is our belief that precisely such a shake-out period may be in store for the private equity industry in the next decade. To motivate our discussion of the revolutionary changes that may we believe will occur, it is worthwhile to step back in time. Investment banks in the 1960s found the established order that had characterized the industry for several decades overturned. The consequences for the competitors were profound. Both the experiences of the successful and unsuccessful firms during that period should be illustrative for today's private equity investors.

Between the Great Depression of the 1930s and the end of the 1950s, the structure of the investment banking industry was very stable. The status of the banks was sharply demarcated into several levels. Certain top-tier, or "bulge bracket," groups initiated most of the underwriting activity, and then syndicated transactions with their lower-status peers. The size of the allocations in the syndicated offerings (and the associated profits garnered) declined as one moved down the pecking order.

While the roles of the banks were well defined, in operation they were surprisingly similar. The size and scale of a bulge bracket and a middle-tier bank were not that different whether compared on underwriting volume, manpower, or scope. The ranking of the various banks was determined almost as much by social status and tradition as it was by the professional skills of the partners.

It might be thought that this would lead to many challenges, as lower-tier banks sought to move up the pecking order or new banks entered the industry. But there was surprisingly little such activity during the decades leading up to the 1960s. Observers attributed this inactivity to two factors. First, the lower-tier banks knew that challenging the established leaders would lead to them being cut out of subsequent syndicated transactions. While their share of the total profits in these transactions was modest, they did not believe that they could generate enough business by themselves to make up for this loss. Second, the most natural competitors, the large commercial banks, were barred by the Glass-Steagall Act of 1933 from entering the underwriting business.

This steady-state condition, however, began breaking down in the early 1960s. This was triggered by four separate changes, many of which may correspond to the shocks that simulated dramatic changes identified above as having led to shake-outs in a variety of periods:

- Underwriting and trading volume expanded dramatically during the 1960s. The expanding size of the "pie" increased the temptation for lower-tier groups and new entrants to challenge the bulge bracket firms because the profits to be garnered were so much larger. The increased volume also strained the existing systems at almost all the banks, which had been set up to accommodate far fewer transactions and trades.

- Corporate clients of the banks began demanding more sophisticated services. In particular, the merger wave of the 1960s led to a demand for advisory services, such as guidance on valuations and deal structuring, that had traditionally been extensively provided by investment banks.

- Regulatory changes led to increasing internationalization of the bond market. While U.S. investment banks had dominated the New York market for foreign bond issues, the relaxation of capital controls in the early 1960s led to the birth of a truly international EuroDollar market. European banks, particularly the German universal banks, emerged as formidable competitors in this new market.

- Regulatory pressures began eroding the pricing of brokerage transactions. Even before the "big bang" in 1975 (when the use of a uniform price schedule for commissions was abandoned), investment banks had come under pressure to modify their pricing schemes.

These external pressures had two consequences for the investment banking industry of the 1960s and 1970s. First, the established order of banks was disrupted. Second, the differentiation between top-tier banks and others was substantially enhanced.

It is instructive to compare the strategies of "winners"—those banks that moved substantially up the pecking order in these years—with those of the "losers." While the winners pursued very different strategies, each was predicated on rapidly responding to the industry's changing circumstances:

- New entrant Donaldson, Lufkin & Jenrette, sensing corporations' and institutional investors' demand for analytical tools, invested aggressively in building its stable of high-quality research analysts. It funded its expansion by completing an initial public offering in 1970, at a time when the overwhelming number of banks remained private partnerships.

- Merrill Lynch focused on servicing the large number of individual investors who were beginning to invest far more actively. The bank invested in building a truly national network of brokerages, at a time when the overwhelming number of retail brokers was regional or local in focus. At the same time, they aggressively invested in the technology to accommodate large trading volumes.

- Salomon Brothers, which had traditionally specialized in the bond market, realized the limitations of the numerous small securities houses that specialized in equity market-making activities. Sensing that a well-capitalized bank could far more effectively take the kind of risks that this activity entailed, it successfully moved into these markets, which had hitherto been shunned by the large investment banks.

Some of the leading investment banks, such as Morgan Stanley and Goldman Sachs, did respond to the changing environment. But other large banks did not. Many deferred investments in computer systems, for instance, and found themselves unable to keep up with the surge in trading volume in the mid-1960s. They often stuck to their core businesses, relying on traditional syndicated transactions rather than branching out into advisory services or the trading of novel securities. The consequences of these failures were in many cases quite abrupt. The bank Halsey, Stuart, for instance, fell from second in total underwriting volume in 1960 to thirteenth in 1965.

In addition to the changing order of investment banks, the differentiation among the banks increased substantially. For instance, the twentieth largest bank at the end of the 1950s had one-ninth the underwriting volume of the largest bank. By the end of the 1970s, the twentieth bank had one-fifteenth of the volume of the largest. The changes in the relative standing when measured by the number of investment professionals, net income, and the scope of activities were even greater. Also striking were the changes in the ways the banks were run. At the end of this period, the small banks remained largely informal organizations, with each banker largely operating autonomously. Within the largest banks, however, systematization had been instituted to a large degree: for instance, the processing of each proposed transaction was standardized and the risk of the bank's investment portfolio was periodically reviewed.

Our claim that these changes represent a road map for the private equity industry in the next decade may seem perplexing at first sight. After all, while the venture capital industry is in the business of funding innovation, the organizational innovation in this industry has been quite modest since the introduction of the limited partnership by Draper, Gaither & Anderson in 1958.

Despite the stasis in the private equity industry's structure over the past few decades, we are now seeing a convergence of changes in the industry that are reminiscent of the shifts that triggered the turmoil in investment banking. These include:

- The shifting mixture of investors in private equity funds. Universities, wealthy families, and corporate pension funds have long dominated these investments. But new investors are increasingly targeting this sector. In particular, public pension funds began heavily investing in private equity in the 1990s, more than a decade after their corporate peers. The large-scale entry of California Public Employees Retirement System into private equity investing is only the most visible manifestation of this phenomenon. These organizations, which often manage huge investment pools with very limited staffs, consequentially needed to make very substantial commitments to each fund they selected. Initially, they targeted buyout funds, which typically raised very large funds (and thus could accommodate large investments). But beginning in the late 1990s, these investors increasingly began targeting venture capital funds as well. More generally, a profound shift in the nature of long-term savings is under way in the United States. More corporate employees are managing their own savings in 401(k) and other defined contribution plans, rather than having their savings co-mingled with those of other investors in defined benefit plans. (The share of retirement savings in defined benefit plans, such as major corporate pensions, has fallen from 84 percent of all pension assets in 1980 to 70 percent in 1988 to about 58 percent today.) Individual investors increasingly desire to place some of their long-term retirement assets in illiquid investments like private equity, just as large pension plan managers have for the past two decades. These changing sources of capital are upsetting the traditional structure in the private equity industry.

- The rise in intermediation in the private equity marketplace. This second major change is a natural consequence of the first. Each of these new classes of investors is relatively inexperienced in these investments, which translates into a need for assistance in the investment process. Furthermore, the lean staffs of the public pension funds and the widely dispersed nature of individual investors suggests the demands for assistance will be continuing ones. We can point to numerous examples of these new investors leading to an increased emphasis on intermediation. The process of persuading a public pension fund to invest in a fund is frequently exhausting. In particular, in many instances, there are extensive reviews at both the staff and board levels, as well as by outside advisors. To address these demands, private equity groups that seek to raise large funds are increasingly turning to placement agents for assistance. These intermediaries prepare many of the marketing materials and assist in the raising of the fund. Among placement agents, the role of groups affiliated with large institutions such as investment banks has become increasingly prominent.

- The growing concentration of limited partner dollars. The third and final critical change in the environment has been the shifting allocation of investment dollars across private equity groups. The allocation of funds in the industry has traditionally followed a cyclical pattern. During boom periods, inexperienced and small groups have traditionally found it easier to raise money. Funds have gotten progressively less concentrated as the boom continued. Busts, when the level of fundraising has fallen, have been characterized by a "flight to quality." New private equity groups have found it difficult to raise funds during these years, as investors have concentrated on proven groups with established track records. During the boom period of the 1990s, however, a different pattern emerged. While numerous groups entered the industry, funds actually became more, not less, concentrated. In particular, the number of active groups increased from 374 in 1988 to 468 in 1993 to 727 in 1998. For instance, the share of venture capital controlled by the largest 5 percent of groups rose from 32.4 percent to 36.5 percent to 42.5 percent. It is likely that this increased concentration was in part a consequence of the entry of large state pension funds into venture investing and the role of intermediaries. In the more uncertain environment that followed the 2000 downturn in the private equity, this trend is likely to accelerate. Numerous examples demonstrate the disproportionate impact that the turbulent market conditions that followed have had on small and new groups. An illustration of the differential impact was the refinancing in early 2002 of a telecommunications equipment provider, which had closed a third financing round at a $500 million valuation in February 2000. While the company's prospects still seemed promising, the venture capitalist investors realized that they needed to assign the firm a sharply lower valuation to reflect the severe market correction. While the seasoned venture investors who had invested the bulk of their capital in the first and second rounds (which were at much lower valuations) were willing to reinvest, many of the investors who had invested for the first time in the third round were not. These hesitant investors included a number of marginal groups, which had begun investing in the past two or three years using as a "momentum" strategy: investing in companies about to go public in the hopes of quick capital gains. Once this strategy failed to work, they seemed frozen, unsure of how to proceed.

There is not a single "right answer" as to how to respond to these changing conditions. In this module, though, we will explore a variety of responses and seek to understand the strengths and weaknesses of each.

WHY THIS MODULE? (2): HYBRID PRIVATE EQUITY FUNDS

A second theme—which appears especially in the In-Q-Tel case—regards the challenges of undertaking "hybrid" funds. Since funds sponsored by corporate or government bodies are so different from traditional private equity funds, one may wonder why these organizations are considered in this volume. To be sure, these funds' goals are more complex than traditional funds: in addition to generating attractive financial returns, these efforts are seeking to more effectively commercialize internal research projects or to revitalize distressed areas.

There are three main reasons, however, for understanding these funds:

- First, this arena is likely to be an important one in the private equity industry in years to come. While the volume of these investments has been highly variable—considerably more so than the private equity industry in general—many corporations have incorporated venturing initiatives as permanent parts of their R&D strategy. Venture funds by public and non-profit bodies have attracted less attention, but have also been substantial. As recently as 1995, 40 percent of venture or venturelike disbursements in the United States—and more than half of early stage investments—came from public sources: those whose primary goal was not a high economic return. Nor has this activity been confined to the United States. Governments in dozens of countries have established significant public venture programs. In recent years, nonprofit organizations have also become increasingly active in encouraging and overseeing venture funds. Some of America's largest and most prestigious foundations, such as the Ford and McArthur Foundations, have been particularly active backers of community development venture funds. An interesting new trend has been the involvement of successful private equity investors, most notably Henry Kravis and his former colleague, George Roberts, as investors in and advisors to community development funds.

- Second, it is difficult to examine the issues faced in adapting the private equity model without thinking about the rationales for the key features of traditional private equity funds. In particular, in adopting the private equity model, features of independent funds have been adjusted or altered. In some cases, these changes have been benign; but in others, the consequences have been disastrous. By reviewing successful and failed modifications of the private equity model to serve the goals of corporate, public, and nonprofit organizations, we will gain a deeper understanding of how traditional funds work. During discussions, we will return repeatedly to the frameworks developed in the earlier modules of the course.

- Finally, corporate venture capital programs represent an interesting avenue for entry into the private equity field that relatively few students consider. The intense competition for jobs in traditional private equity organizations allows many funds to demand that new hires already have a demonstrated investment track record. Yet it is difficult to develop such a track record without a job in the industry. Corporations are often much more willing to hire candidates directly out of school. If one can make one's way into a corporate venture group, it can provide valuable experience and serve as a stepping-stone to a position at an independent private equity firm.

THE STRUCTURE OF THIS MODULE

Reflecting the fact that this is a review module, the cases do not seek to develop new conceptual frameworks. Rather, the emphasis will be on understanding several future paths along which the industry may evolve, and seeking to assess the likely implications for private equity groups.

As the reader reviews the cases in this module, however, it is also appropriate to consider where the same issues have surfaced earlier in the course. For instance, where have similar incentive problems to the ones faced by Battery emerged? Has the challenge of multiple investment objectives faced by In-Q-Tel been addressed elsewhere in the course? While the reporting issues that public private equity funds such as 3i face are partially a consequence of their special circumstances, how have similar issues affected the behavior of private equity groups elsewhere?

FURTHER READING ON THEMES FOUND IN THIS MODULE

Harvey Bines and Steve Thiel, "Investment Management Arrangements and the Federal Securities Laws," *Ohio State Law Journal* 58 (1997): 459–518.

Peter Eisenger, "The State of State Venture Capitalism," *Economic Development Quarterly* 5 (February 1991): 64–76.

Peter Eisenger, "State Venture Capitalism, State Politics, and the World of High-Risk Investment," *Economic Development Quarterly* 7 (May 1993): 131–139.

David J. Gilberg, "Regulation of New Financial Instruments under the Federal Securities and Commodities Law," *Vanderbilt Law Review* 39 (1986): 1599–1669.

Paul A. Gompers and Josh Lerner, *The Money of Invention* (Boston: Harvard Business School Press, 2001), chapters 7–10.

Steven Gordon, "Small Business Investment Companies: A Venture Capital Structure of Choice?" *Journal of Private Equity* 2 (Fall 1998): 45–55.

Josh Lerner, "The Government as Venture Capitalist: An Empirical Analysis of the SBIR Program," *Journal of Business* 72 (July 1999): 285–318.

Organisation for Economic Cooperation and Development, Committee for Scientific and Technological Policy, *Government Venture Capital for Technology-Based Firms* (Paris: OECD, 1997).

Charles M. Noone and Stanley M. Rubel, *SBICs: Pioneers in Organized Venture Capital* (Chicago: Capital Publishing, 1970).

Steven J. Waddell, "Emerging Socio-Economic Institutions in the Venture Capital Industry: An Appraisal," *American Journal of Economics and Sociology* 54 (July 1995): 323–338.

25

Battery Ventures

One evening in January 2002, Todd Dagres, senior partner at Battery Ventures, walked into the darkness gathering outside his office in Wellesley, Massachusetts. He noticed that the unseasonably warm weather had inspired the ornamental trees to put forth new shoots; some even looked as if they were about to bud. As he started his car and turned on the radio, a local newscaster mentioned the possibility of a freeze. Dagres thought about the venture climate, and how the unseasonable warmth of the late 1990s had given way to a recent freeze.

Dagres felt that his firm was more likely to survive frosty conditions than would its shrubbery. Battery was in the process of closing a second round of financing for Arbor Networks, one of its portfolio companies, and Dagres was pleased both with the company and with the way Battery had been involved with it. Thanks to his senior associate, Carl Stjernfeldt, and to other staff, Battery had been able to give Arbor significant support since leading its first round, allowing the young company to secure a term sheet for its second round at a higher valuation, despite one of the most difficult markets in years.

Battery differed from many venture capital (VC) firms by employing a number of analysts, associates, and venture partners to support the partners; in fact, the firm had a staff of sixty-seven, forty-four of whom were investment professionals. With offices in Wellesley and San Mateo, California, Battery Ventures invested primarily in early stage communications and software companies, although it occasionally did later-stage deals. The firm had made successful investments in such firms as Akamai Technologies, Allegiance Telecom, FORE Systems, and Qtera Corporation. In 2000, it had closed a $1 billion fund.

Battery's decision to staff up had been made in 1998, as VC firms found themselves able to raise more and more money, but ran up against constraints on partner time to investigate deals and pay appropriate attention to their portfolio companies. Over the intervening years, the firm had added analysts, who searched for deals; associates and senior associates, who did due diligence on prospective deals and maintained close contacts

Senior Research Associate Ann K. Leamon prepared this case under the supervision of Professors Josh Lerner and G. Felda Hardymon and with the assistance of Nitin Gupta (MBA '01) and Sameer Bharadwaj (MBA '01). HBS cases are developed solely as the basis for class discussion. Cases are not intended to serve as endorsements, sources of primary data, or illustrations of effective or ineffective management. Sections of this case were informed by "Battery Ventures," a paper written by Nitin Gupta and Sameer Bharadwaj as part of their MBA requirements.

with portfolio companies; and venture partners, who provided specialized recruiting, financing, and marketing help to the companies.

Dagres felt the structure had worked well, but, as he left the office, he had to admit that the current VC environment gave him some concerns. "What happens if you can't raise a $1 billion fund?" he wondered. "Are we locking ourselves into providing something that will prove to be a burden?" He also was aware that internal promotion opportunities might become more limited in the future. "Is this the right way to scale a firm?"

VENTURE CAPITAL IN 2002

Venture capital had been an important method of funding new businesses throughout the twentieth century. Over that period, it had gone through numerous cycles of boom and bust. While the 1990s had seen dramatic increases in the numbers of VC firms and in the sums they invested, the early 2000s had experienced a dramatic contraction (see Exhibits 25.1a and 25.1b). At the same time, however, the industry appeared to be approaching a substantial reorganization.

During the 1990s, private equity had become an accepted avenue of investing for groups that had previously avoided its perceived risk, primarily public pension funds and high-net-worth individuals. In May 2000, CalPERS (the California Public Employees' Retirement System) with $175 billion under management, increased its target for private equity from 4 percent to 6 percent, with the ultimate aim of 10 percent.[1] High-net-worth individuals, many of whom had made their money in venture-backed firms, had also significantly increased their investments in private equity. These new cash injections, combined with the continuing interest of long-time private equity players such as endowments and financial institutions, increased the pool of available funds by 3,000 percent over the

---

EXHIBIT 25.1a

NUMBERS OF VENTURE FUNDS AND FUNDS COMMITTED

Quarter	# of VC Funds	$ Billion Committed	$ Million (M) per Fund
Q4 '01	58	$4.60	$79
Q3 '01	59	6.90	116
Q2 '01	86	11.70	136
Q1 '01	114	17.40	152
Q4 '00	186	23.40	126
Q3 '00	129	28.60	222
Q2 '00	183	30.80	168
Q1 '00	165	21.80	132
Q4 '99	199	29.38	148
Q3 '99	107	11.81	110
Q2 '99	95	9.40	99
Q1 '99	89	9.18	103

Source: Adapted from National Venture Capital Association, http://www.nvca.org, accessed February 25, 2002.

---

1. Paul Gompers and Josh Lerner, *The Money of Invention* (Cambridge, MA: HBS Press, 2001), Chapter 10.

EXHIBIT 25.1b

VENTURE ACTIVITY 1995 THROUGH 2001

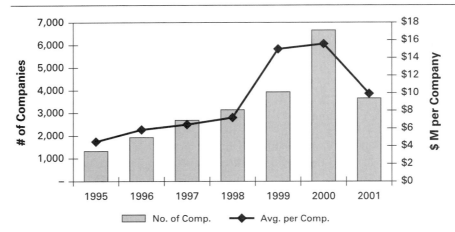

Source: Adapted from National Venture Capital Association, http://www.nvca.org, accessed February 25, 2002.

decade. Since 2000, though, fund-raising had dropped significantly, from 185 VC funds raising $31.74 billion in the second quarter of 2000 to a mere 46 funds raising $6.17 billion in the third quarter of 2001 (see Exhibit 25.2 for funds raised).[2]

Nonetheless, a number of firms had raised significant funds before the drought of 2001. Because of the relative inexperience of many of the new limited partners, the old pattern of boom times, in which many new venture groups would be funded, had not held true to the same extent during the 1990s. Although the number of VC firms in the industry practically doubled between 1988 and 1998, the concentration of funds among the top 5 percent of firms rose dramatically, as limited partners exhibited a "flight to quality" mentality (see Exhibit 25.3). The recent turbulence of the market only intensified this trend.

To succeed in such a crowded market, a firm had to join, or stay, in the top tier, by finding and backing the best deals. Once in the top tier, a firm could leverage its brand name by increasing its share of carried interest above the historical norm of 20 percent by and charging higher management fees. (Exhibit 25.4 shows those venture capital groups in 2000 whose share of carried interest was more than 20 percent.) As the market slowed in late 2000 and into 2001, however, the sustainability of these premiums was an open question.

During the boom, VC groups had pursued a number of initiatives to make themselves more attractive to entrepreneurs, as well. Some teamed with organizations that had other specialties—for instance, Accel Partners established a partnership with the leveraged buyout firm Kohlberg Kravis Roberts to offer comingled funds.[3] Others increased the size of their funds and expanded the scope of their investments. Yet another, Draper Fisher Jurvetson, raised two funds in excess of $600 million[4] and

2. National Venture Capital Association, http://www.nvca.org, accessed February 6, 2002.

3. Gompers and Lerner, *The Money of Invention.*

4. Charles R. Fellers, "DFJ Kicks Off 2001 with $1.4B in Funds," *Venture Capital Journal* (February 1, 2001), p. 22.

EXHIBIT 25.2

VENTURE ACTIVITY, 1990–2001

Year	Companies Funded	Total Invested ($M)	Average/ Company ($M)	Funds Raised ($M)	Total Raised ($M)	Internal Rate of Return		
						Upper Quartile	Average	Lower Quartile
1990	1,316	3,253.6	$2.47	$ 75	$2,550	27.9%	17.1%	0.5%
1991	1,086	2,429.8	2.24	41	1,488	26.2	18.1	6.6
1992	1,291	5,053.7	3.92	66	3,393	32.8	27.4	11.0
1993	1,150	4,903.9	4.26	93	4,115	34.7	24.3	3.6
1994	1,186	5,252.5	4.43	127	7,339	44.3	33.8	13.7
1995	1,321	5,456.7	4.13	146	8,427	71.5	46.6	10.4
1996	1,998	11,178.4	5.60	142	10,467	119.0	83.7	6.2
1997	2,697	17,405.9	6.45	191	15,176	121.9	80.1	10.9
1998	3,153	21,687.2	6.88	210	25,293	110.8	89.0	5.8
1999	3,962	59,531.0	15.03	209	37,464	105.1	68.6	1.5
2000	6,645	102,627.2	15.44	228	69,741	NA	42.0	NA
2001	3,679	36,536.8	9.93	142	40,600	NA	–23.1	NA

Sources: Compiled from National Venture Capital Association, http://www.nvca.org; Private Equity Analyst; and Venture Economics, http://www.ventureeconomics.com.

Notes: 2001 returns are through September 30, 2001.

NA = Not available

EXHIBIT 25.3

CONCENTRATION OF FUNDS AMONG TOP VC GROUPS

Year	Number of Venture Capital Groups	% of Funds Controlled by Top 5%
1988	374	32.4%
1993	468	36.5
1998	727	42.5

Source: Compiled from National Venture Capital Association, http://www.nvca.org.

affiliated itself with small early stage VC groups in areas "off the beaten track"—for example, the Pacific Northwest and Mid-Atlantic states. In exchange for up-front fees and a share of the ultimate profits generated by the funds, the Draper group helped the small firms raise funds and finance later-stage investments, which frequently exceeded the resources of the new groups.

VC firms in the late 1990s established a number of programs to nurture their start-ups. Incubator services provided office space to portfolio companies and a chance for them to learn from one another. Many firms established "entrepreneur in residence"

EXHIBIT 25.4

VENTURE CAPITAL ORGANIZATIONS CHARGING MORE THAN 20% CARRIED INTEREST

---

30 Percent Carried Interest

Accel Partners

Benchmark Capital

Charles River Ventures

Crosspoint Venture Partners

Idealab Capital Partners

Kleiner, Perkins, Caufield & Byers

Redpoint Ventures

25 Percent Carried Interest

August Capital Management

Battery Ventures

Bowman Capital Management

Brentwood Venture Capital

Crosspoint Venture Partners

Draper Fisher Jurvetson

Greylock Management Corp.

Hummer Winblad Venture Partners

InterWest Partners

Mayfield Fund

New Enterprise Associates

Palladium Venture Capital

Sequoia Capital

Sevin Rosen Funds

Sierra Ventures

Vantage Point Venture Partners

Source: Compiled from *Private Equity Analyst* and corporate documents.

---

programs, setting up an entrepreneur in the VC fund's own space, paying (usually) his salary while he decided on a venture in which the VC firm would invest. Others hired additional partner-level staff,[5] either specialists in areas such as recruiting, or successful former CEOs, who worked directly with portfolio companies and left deal making to the general partners.[6]

These "venture partners" were one approach to dealing with an increasingly obvious constraint in the venture capital organization—the scarcity of a general partner's

---

5. Some firms, including Battery, called these partners "venture partners." Others used the term "venture partners" to refer to deal-doing partners who received carried interest only on the companies in which they were invested, not on the entire fund's investments. In this case, the term "venture partner" will be used as Battery uses it, to refer to a non-deal-doing partner.

6. Gompers and Lerner, *The Money of Invention.*

time. This constraint also drove the increasingly large sums invested in each company. Firms had more money but partners did not have more time. A general partner at one tier-1 firm was sitting on the boards of eighteen companies, a less-than-optimal situation for all parties involved. As the market contracted in 2000, the situation became more dire. Battery's Dagres likened it to "Logan [airport] on a foggy day."[7] The holding time for portfolio companies almost doubled, to its historical average of five years; subsequent rounds were more difficult to raise; the companies needed more hands-on help in the difficult economy; and at the same time, many VC funds had raised large funds that needed to be invested, requiring that someone find new deals and manage new companies. One venture capitalist described it as "a train wreck." The venture train crashed into the reality of a twenty-four-hour day.

Indeed, the structure of VC firms had changed little since J. H. (Jock) Whitney, the founder of Whitney & Co., coined the term. Venture capital, one expert observed, "is a craft industry." A firm's uniqueness came, essentially, from the particular general partner who had found the deal and served as the face of the VC firm to the portfolio company.

General partners performed myriad roles, both for their own firms and for their companies, from raising funds and meeting with limited partners to finding deals, serving on boards, and providing informal advice. The demands from both the limited partners and the companies had become more intense by 2002, both in number and in complexity. Often, for instance, portfolio companies engaged in complicated alliances with large firms, involving complex and detailed negotiations. Along with new tasks came increased pressure on VC groups to provide top-quality assistance to their companies to help them survive in the tumultuous venture environment.

In the late 1990s, with public markets giving category leaders huge valuations, and venture firms raising larger funds with higher management fees, a venture firm could find itself in a virtuous cycle. Success brought it to the attention of more talented entrepreneurs. With the higher fees, it could expand and deepen its core capabilities for helping its investments (see Exhibit 25.5 for funds of more than $1 billion), whether through the services of venture partners or by arranging perks for the CEOs, such as CEO conferences or CEO side-by-side funds. The ability to raise higher fees also allowed VC firms to hire and, more importantly, retain talented general partners.

During 1999 and early 2000, a number of firms had adopted some variation of the value-adding services approach. Greylock offered some of its companies a service called Fast Forward, which included the services of specialists in finance, information technology, product development, and recruiting, along with free office space. Charles River Ventures had announced CR Velocity, a forty-person group to assist with such tasks as business planning, recruiting, and marketing. Mohr, Davidow Ventures had a staff of five partners who served as interim CEOs at its companies. Intel Corp.'s VC division had set up a protected Web site for its 600 portfolio companies, allowing them access to internally posted information on subjects such as human resources (getting a visa, setting up 401-Ks) and basic legal documents. Kleiner Perkins had hired a leading headhunter to help its companies recruit, and Bessemer Venture Partners had purchased a boutique executive search firm.[8] As a partner in one of the firms said, "Venture capital is no longer about the money. It's about the resources you bring to companies."[9]

---

7. Boston's Logan Airport was notorious for its delays on foggy days as planes stacked up waiting to take off or land.

8. Lynnley Browning, "Venture Capitalists: Venturing beyond Capital," *The New York Times* (October 15, 2000).

9. Donna Novitsky, partner in Mohr, Davidow, in Browning, "Venture Capitalists: Venturing beyond Capital."

EXHIBIT 25.5

FORMATION OF PRIVATE EQUITY FUNDS OF $1 BILLION OR MORE 1995–2001

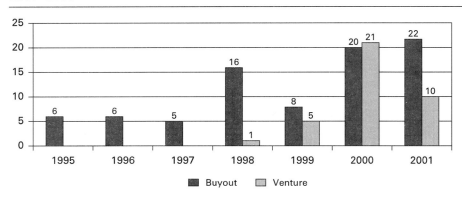

■ Buyout   ☐ Venture

Venture Capital Funds of Over $1 Billion

1998	Summit Partners V	$1.0 billion
1999	Benchmark Capital III	$1.0 billion
	Meritech Capital Partners	$1.1 billion
	Oak Investment Partners IX	$1.0 billion
	Softbank Capital Partners	$1.25 billion
	J.H. Whitney IV	$1.0 billion
2000	Accel VIII	$1.6 billion
	APA (Patricof) Excelsior VI	$1.1 billion
	Baker Communications Fund II	$1.1 billion
	Battery Ventures VI	$1.0 billion
	Kleiner, Perkins, Caufield & Byers X	$1.0 billion
	Lightspeed Venture Partners I	$1.0 billion
	Mayfield XI	$1.0 billion
	Meritech Capital Partners II	$1.2 billion
	Menlo Ventures IX	$1.5 billion
	New Enterprises Associates X	$2.2 billion
	Providence Equity Partners IV	$2.8 billion
	Redpoint Ventures	$1.25 billion
	Softbank Technology Ventures VI	$1.5 billion
	Sprout Capital IX	$1.6 billion
	St. Paul Venture Partners VI	$1.3 billion
	TA/Advent IX	$2.0 billion
	Technology Crossover Ventures IV	$1.7 billion
	THLee, Putnam Internet Partners	$1.1 billion
	U.S. Venture Partners VIII	$1.0 billion
	Vantage Point Venture Partners	$1.62 billion
	Weston Presidio Capital IV	$1.35 billion

(Continues)

EXHIBIT 25.5 (CONTINUED)

FORMATION OF PRIVATE EQUITY FUNDS OF $1 BILLION OR MORE 1995–2001

2001	Austin Ventures VIII	$1.5 billion
	Charles River Ventures XI	$1.2 billion
	Greylock XI	$1.0 billion
	Matrix VII	$1.0 billion
	Meritage Capital Partners II	$1.0 billion
	Oak Investment Partners X	$1.6 billion
	Spectrum Equity Investors	$2.0 billion
	Summit Partners VI	$2.1 billion
	Walden International Investment Group V	$1.0 billion
	Worldview Technology Partners	$1.0 billion

Sources: Compiled from various issues of *Private Equity Analyst* and adapted from Paul Gompers, Ann Leamon, and Josh Lerner, "Charles River Velocity," unpublished research, February 2001.

By mid-2000, though, the market had changed substantially. The plunge in the NASDAQ vastly reduced a VC firm's ability to exit its investments. With fewer exits, the number of portfolio firms increased, as promising new companies joined the current ranks. Many of the existing investments needed more funding, requiring more time and energy, while the entire portfolio was struggling to survive in a difficult environment (see Exhibit 25.6 for follow-on versus first rounds). The partners' attention had to be directed less toward attracting entrepreneurs than simply keeping companies alive. Given this new reality, some of the ambitions of these groups had been scaled back. Charles River cut a number of its Velocity staff. Greylock had held its Fast Forward Group's staff at the original number of two.[10] Few, if any, VC firms had divested their in-house recruiters, though.

Other firms responded to the market contraction by reducing the sizes of their funds. In early 2002, Mohr, Davidow announced that it would draw only 80 percent of the $850 million that had been committed to its seventh fund, saying, "We'd rather have [the fund] sized for [raising another], than to come to the end and say, 'Oops, sorry we didn't invest this.'"[11] That was just the latest move in that direction: Crosspoint Venture Partners declined to close on a just-raised $1 billion fund in early 2001. During that year, several smaller venture firms also returned funds, among them Octane Capital, which gave back almost half of its $265 million fund.[12]

BATTERY VENTURES[13]

Battery Ventures was founded in 1983 by Rick Frisbie, Bob Barrett, and Howard Anderson. As Dagres explained, "At that time, the firms in the area were TA and Summit,

10. Greylock, http://www.greylock.com, accessed February 7, 2002.

11. Bill Ericson, general partner, in Tricia Duryee, "Silicon Valley–Based Venture-Capital Firm Cuts Size of Latest Fund," *Knight Ridder Tribune Business News* (January 23, 2002), p. 1.

12. Matt Marshall, "San Jose, Calif.–Area Venture Capital Firm Cuts Size of Newest Fund," *San Jose Mercury News* (January 23, 2002), p. 1.

13. This section is drawn from Nitin Gupta and Sameer Bharadwaj, "Battery Ventures," unpublished MBA paper for Venture Capital & Private Equity Class, April 30, 2001.

EXHIBIT 25.6

FOLLOW-ON VERSUS FIRST FUNDING

	First ($ Millions)	Follow-on ($ Millions)	Total ($ Millions)	Follow-on as % of Total	
1980	$364	$280	$645	43%	
1981	721	594	1,314	45	
1982	685	1,108	1,793	62	
1983	1,080	2,066	3,146	66	
1984	1,055	2,286	3,341	68	
1985	1,183	2,222	3,406	65	
1986	1,590	2,467	4,057	61	
1987	1,553	2,900	4,452	65	
1988	2,199	2,678	4,878	55	
1989	1,930	2,770	4,700	59	
1990	967	2,295	3,262	70	
1991	582	1,882	2,464	76	
1992	2,116	2,943	5,059	58	
1993	1,528	3,362	4,889	69	
1994	2,359	2,904	5,263	55	
1995	2,295	3,177	5,471	58	
1996	5,516	5,696	11,211	51	
1997	7,255	9,958	17,213	58	
1998	9,134	12,848	21,981	58	
1999	19,873	39,499	59,372	67	
2000	34,398	69,096	103,494	67	
2001	10,021	30,516	40,537	75	

Sources: Adapted from Thomson Financial/Venture Economics, *2001 National Venture Capital Association Yearbook* (New York: Thomson Financial, 2001), p. 32; and Tracey Letterhoff and Kirk Walden, *PriceWaterhouseCoopers Moneytree Survey: Q4 and Full Year 2001,*" PriceWaterhouseCoopers/NVCA/Venture Economics, Q4 '01, http://www.pwcmoneytree.com/PDFS/mt_q4_01_report.pdf, accessed March 12, 2002; with casewriter estimates.

---

mostly doing later-stage deals. The founders saw an opportunity to do what they did, but on a smaller scale."

The firm established an affiliation with The Yankee Group, a high-technology market research organization at which Anderson had worked, which supplemented its research abilities and market expertise.[14] Battery's first four funds invested in a mix of early and later-stage companies, mostly in technology, with a concentration on early emerging firms. One reporter commented, "The firm typically seeks companies with a finished product and some revenue but in need of capital to accelerate its sales and marketing efforts."[15] Only in 1997 did the firm raise a fund specifically to invest in early

14. Georg Szalai, "Battery Ventures," *Venture Capital Journal* (February 1, 1999), p. 58.
15. *Ibid.*

stage firms. By then it had also developed its expertise in communications, software, and Internet/e-commerce. In 1999, Battery vaulted to prominence when its portfolio company, Akamai, went public at a price that soon hit $300 per share.

By 2002, Battery had invested in more than 130 companies worldwide. It managed more than $1.8 billion in capital and had closed a $1 billion fund in 2000 (see Exhibits 25.7a, 25.7b, 25.7c, and 25.7d). The firm expected to invest between $10 million and $40 million in forty or fifty companies, mostly in early stage deals but occasionally in later-stage transactions,[16] especially as the chaos in the technology market made big corporations eager to spin off struggling units. Dagres said, "You get a piece of a business at a very low price, bring in management, grow the business, and when the market comes back you sell it or take it public."[17]

Battery's Structure

During the 1980s, Battery's partners invested essentially without support, following the model of most of the industry. In 1991, the firm added associates who joined the firm after finishing their bachelor's degrees and spent two years simply finding deals. They spent the vast majority of their time (about 70 percent) searching for promising companies by attending trade shows, reading journals, and talking to their networks. Work on preliminary due diligence consumed the balance of their time. They were evaluated based on finding a certain number of deals per quarter, and were not involved in the postdeal process.[18]

Starting in 1998, the associate's role began to evolve. In part, this was due to the partners' time constraints. The firm had just closed its fourth fund at $200 million, yet still had only seven partners, the same number that had invested the previous $85 million fund (see Exhibit 25.8). Additionally, the partners became aware that the previous model, based on the quantity of deals originated, did not ensure deal quality.[19] To address this, the subpartner career ladder was enhanced to include analyst, associate, and senior associate levels. The analyst took on the old associate role of "dialing for deals." Associates became much more involved in predeal due diligence, and senior associates not only conducted predeal investigations but also worked with the company after the investment had been made. This ladder laid out a career path with promotion opportunities for talented employees, allowing an analyst to aspire to become a partner after seven or ten years.

Dagres noted:

> We get very involved with our companies. We have a board seat, we're usually the lead investor, and we generally own 20 percent or more. This requires us to have a broad organization. That meant that we were throwing money away by training associates for two years and letting them go. We started bringing associates in and promoting them to senior associate, then principal and partner. We have four partners who started off as associates.[20]

In 2002, Battery's organization included seven analysts on a two-year program; four associates on a three-year program; ten senior associates, who would stay at their

---

16. Gupta & Bharadwaj, "Battery Ventures," p. 2.
17. Raymond Hennessey, "Deals & Deal Makers: Bargain Bin: Venture-Capital Firms Find Opportunity in Struggling Units," *The Wall Street Journal* (December 26, 2001), p. C13.
18. Gupta & Bharadwaj, "Battery Ventures," p. 3.
19. *Ibid.*
20. Cited in Gupta and Bharadwaj, "Battery Ventures," p. 3.

EXHIBIT 25.7a

VENTUREONE PROFILE OF BATTERY VENTURES

Battery Ventures   *(last update November 2001)*

www.battery.com

Primary Office:

20 William Street, Suite 200   **Phone:** 781.577.1000
Wellesley, MA 02481   **Fax:** 781.577.1001

Other Offices:

901 Mariner's Island Boulevard, Suite 475   **Phone:** 650.372.3939
San Mateo, CA 94404   **Fax:** 650.372.3930

Firm Overview:

Type of VC Firm: Venture Capital   Year Founded: 1983
Total Assets under Management: US $ 1,816 Million
Parent Affiliation: The Yankee Group

148 Total Companies in Portfolio

Business Status	# of Companies	% of Total
Private	62	43%
Public	25	17
Acquired	40	28
Out of Business	18	12
	145	100%

Industries	# of Companies	% of Total
Information Technology		
Communications	43	30%
Electronics	11	8
Semiconductors	6	4
Software	51	35
Information Services	14	10
Healthcare		
Medical IS	1	1
Retail & Cons/Bus Prod/Srvc		
Retailers	1	1
Cons/Bus Products	1	1
Cons/Bus Services	17	12

Geographies	# of Companies	% of Total
California	48	33%
Massachusetts	38	26
Texas	12	8
Northeast	4	3
Mid-Atlantic	8	6
Southeast	12	8
Northwest	6	4
South	4	3
Midwest	10	7
West	3	2

Source: Adapted from VentureOne database, http://www.ventureone.com, accessed February 18, 2002.

EXHIBIT 25.7b

INVESTMENTS BY ROUND

Round Classes	# of Rounds	% of Total
Seed Round	3	1.0%
First Round	102	35.0
Second Round	78	26.0
Later State	82	28.0
Restart	11	4.0
Buyout	1	0.3
Debt/Non-Equity	11	4.0
Non-VC	6	2.0
Private Equity	1	0.3
	295	100.0%

Source: Adapted from VentureOne database, http://www.ventureone.com, accessed February 18, 2002.

Note: Based on all available Venture Source historical information through 4Q 2001.

EXHIBIT 25.7c

STATED INVESTMENT PREFERENCES

Industry Group	Industry Segment	Geographies	Round Preference
Information Technology	Software	US Territory	Seed Round
	Communications	Non-US	First Round
		Western Europe	Later Stage
Minimum Investment	US $3 million		
Maximum Investment	US $35 million		

Source: Adapted from VentureOne database, http://www.ventureone.com, accessed February 18, 2002.

EXHIBIT 25.7d

BATTERY'S FUNDS OVER TIME

Fund	Size ($M)	Stage	Date Closed	Avg. Investment per Company ($M)	Industry Focus
Battery Ventures	$35	Balanced	3/1/84	2.0	Communications
Battery Ventures II	42	Balanced	10/1/88	1.7	Communications
Battery Ventures III	85	Balanced	8/1/94	4.2	Communications
Battery Ventures IV, L.P.	200	Balanced	2/1/97	7.6	Communications
Battery Ventures V, L.P.	400	Early	5/1/99	6.9	Communications
Battery Convergence Fund	40	Balanced	7/1/99	1.6	Communications
Battery Ventures VI, L.P.	1,010	Early	5/1/00	NA	Communications

Sources: Battery Ventures, and adapted from VentureOne database, http://www.ventureone.com, accessed February 18, 2002.

EXHIBIT 25.8

BATTERY'S FUNDS PER PARTNER

Fund	Size ($M)	# Partners	Vintage	Avg. Investment per Company ($M)	Avg. $M/Partner	Avg. Companies/ Partner
Battery Ventures	$35	3	1984	2.0	$11.7	6
Battery Ventures II	42	5	1988	1.7	8.3	5
Battery Ventures III	85	7	1994	4.2	12.1	3
Battery Ventures IV, L.P.	200	7	1997	7.6	28.6	4
Battery Ventures V, L.P.	400	9	1999	6.9	44.9	7
Battery Convergence Fund	40	9	1999	1.6	4.5	3
Battery Ventures VI, L.P.	1,010	12	2000	NA	84.2	NA

Sources: Battery Ventures, and adapted from VentureOne database, http://www.ventureone.com, accessed February 18, 2002.

position one to three years; one principal, who had been with the firm for less than the duration of one fund; seven general partners; and five senior general partners (see Exhibit 25.9 for the organization chart). Analysts were recruited directly from undergraduate programs at Harvard, MIT, and Stanford. Although they had little work experience, they needed to have technical knowledge. Associates could be promoted from the analyst ranks or join after two years with another firm. At this point, they needed more domain knowledge, whether through education (undergraduate or graduate degrees) or work experience. Senior associates, who might come from the ranks of associates or directly from MBA programs, needed a combination of

EXHIBIT 25.9

ORGANIZATION CHART FOR BATTERY VENTURES, AS OF FEBRUARY 2002

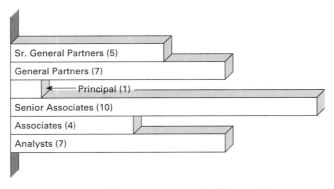

Sr. General Partners (5)
General Partners (7)
Principal (1)
Senior Associates (10)
Associates (4)
Analysts (7)

Sources: Casewriter and Battery Ventures. The balance of Battery's employees included five venture partners, an operating staff of nine, three entrepreneurs-in-residence, and clerical support.

business knowledge and domain expertise.[21] General partners could come from the senior associate staff, as had four of them, or from outside the firm. The hiring process was highly selective, as Battery evaluated its recruits based not only on intelligence, aggressiveness, competitiveness, technical aptitude, and experience, but also for their personalities and ability to fit into a culture that many described as "friendly" or "nice." (See Exhibit 25.10 for biographies of some Battery professionals.) As one senior associate said, "This is a group of genuinely nice guys."

EXHIBIT 25.10

BIOGRAPHIES OF SELECTED BATTERY INVESTMENT PROFESSIONALS

Partners

Thomas J. Crotty

Tom Crotty joined Battery in 1989. He focuses on the communications and e-commerce industries and is responsible for managing Battery's communications industry practice. Tom's investments include @stake Inc., Advanced Computer Communications (acquired by Newbridge Networks), Amber Wave Systems (acquired by U.S. Robotics), AnswerSoft (acquired by Davox), FaxSav Inc. (NASDAQ: FAXX), FORE Systems (FORE), Primary Rate Inc. (acquired by Xircom), RADNET (acquired by Siemens), SANgate Systems, and Witness Systems (WITS). Crotty began his venture capital career in 1986 when he joined Abacus Ventures, a partnership specializing in communications investments. He entered the technology business in 1980, joining IBM in the mainframe and minicomputer segments. Crotty received a BA in business from the University of Notre Dame and an MBA in finance from the University of Pennsylvania's Wharton School.

Oliver Curme

As manager of Battery's e-commerce investment group, Ollie Curme helps direct the firm's strategy in the software and e-business sectors. His major investments include Altra Energy Technologies, Aurum Software, Chordiant Software (CHRD), eCredit.com, HNC Software (HNCS), Infoseek (SEEK) and Pixelworks (PXLW). Prior to joining Battery in 1985, Curme was a lending officer in the High Technology Division of Bank of Boston. He holds a BS from Brown University and an MBA from Harvard Business School.

Todd Dagres

Todd Dagres focuses on opportunities in the communications and Internet infrastructure markets. Since he joined Battery in 1996, his major investments include Akamai Technologies (AKAM), Arbor Networks, Convergent Networks, EnvoyWorldWide, Equipe Communications, Predictive Networks, Qtera (acquired by Nortel), Redstone Communications (acquired by Siemens), RiverDelta Networks (acquired by Motorola) and XCOM Technologies (acquired by Level 3). He is an adjunct professor at the MIT Sloan School of Management, where he teaches a course titled "New Enterprise."

Michael Darby

Michael Darby joined Battery Ventures in 2000 and focuses on the communications and Internet infrastructure markets. From 1996 to 1999, he was director of business development at Cisco Systems, where he initiated and executed strategic investments, acquisitions, and partnerships. Some of Michael's investments included Akamai Technologies (AKAM), Portal Software (PRSF),

---

(Continues)

21. Gupta and Bharadwaj, "Battery Ventures," p. 3.

EXHIBIT 25.10 *(CONTINUED)*

BIOGRAPHIES OF SELECTED BATTERY INVESTMENT PROFESSIONALS

Michael Darby *(Continued)*

Silicon Spice (acquired by Broadcom) and Software.com (OPWV). He was also involved in Cisco's acquisition of companies such as Aironet Wireless Communications, Selsius Systems and Growth Networks. From 1994 to 1996, he was a vice president at the U.S. Russia Investment Fund, a $440 million early stage investment fund. Prior to 1994, he was at Booz Allen Hamilton. Michael graduated magna cum laude from Harvard University with a BA in economics. He also holds an MBA from the Stanford University Graduate School of Business.

Richard Frisbie

A founder of Battery, Rick Frisbie focuses principally on telecommunications services and the overall management of the firm. His investments at Battery include Allegiance Telecom (ALGX), Concord Communications (CCRD), Focal Communications (FCOM), Network Equipment Technologies, and Nextel Communications (NXTL). Frisbie serves on several portfolio company boards and has been a member of the board of directors of both the New England Venture Capital Association and the National Venture Capital Association. Frisbie spent six years in venture capital at UNC Ventures and two years in law at Hutchins and Wheeler. Rick holds a BA in government from Harvard College and a JD from Harvard Law School.

Morgan Jones

Morgan Jones joined Battery in 1996 and focuses on communications infrastructure, including optics, IP voice transport and services, broadband access and switching/routing platforms. He serves, or has served, on the board of directors of CenterForce Technologies, IP Unity, ipVerse, and Qtera and is an active contributor at Lara Technology. From 1992 to 1996, he was an officer in the U.S. Air Force. As lead engineer, he managed two significant start-up product developments totaling over $200 million in value. In this role, he gained product management and technical experience in the areas of data communication, wireless communication, software and client/server architectures. Prior to the Air Force, he was employed at Loral Data Systems developing mission management software for the Japanese Defense Agency. Morgan received an MS in electrical engineering from Stanford University in 1992, where he was the recipient of a National Science Foundation fellowship. In 1991, he graduated magna cum laude from Harvard University with a BS in engineering science.

Senior Associates

Neeraj Agrawal

Neeraj Agrawal joined Battery in 2000 and focuses on investments in enterprise software and Internet infrastructure. Most recently, he was a product manager at RealNetworks, leading Real's content integration strategy. Previously, Agrawal was part of the management team that launched SkyTV, News Corp.'s satellite television venture, in Latin America. At Sky, he focused on customer service, billing and MIS operations, and during his tenure, the subscriber base grew from zero to 50,000. Neeraj also worked as a management consultant at Booz Allen Hamilton and briefly as an investment banker in Merrill Lynch's Technology group. Neeraj holds a BS in computer science from Cornell University and an MBA from Harvard Business School. He is a board observer and is actively involved with Battery's investments in IBEX Process Technology and Bladelogic.

Sunil Dhaliwal

Sunil Dhaliwal joined Battery Ventures in 1998 and works in the Wellesley, Massachusetts, office, where he focuses on communications systems and services investments. Dhaliwal is a director of Storigen Systems and is a board observer at Storability and @stake. He has also been involved in Battery's investment in Akara. Prior to joining Battery, he worked in the High Technology Group at BT Alex. Brown, where he executed equity financings and mergers and acquisitions in the communications and software industries. He holds a BS in finance and international business from Georgetown University.

(Continues)

EXHIBIT 25.10 (CONTINUED)

BIOGRAPHIES OF SELECTED BATTERY INVESTMENT PROFESSIONALS

Carl Stjernfeldt

Carl Stjernfeldt joined Battery in 1999 and focuses on communications and European based investments. At Battery, he is a Board member at Red Sky Systems and an observer on the Boards of Arbor Networks, Cedar Point Communications, and Optium. From 1997 to 1998, he worked for Cambridge Technology Partners as a client partner and project manager. Prior to Cambridge, he held a number of operational roles with Summa Four developing telecommunications solutions for domestic and international service providers. Stjernfeldt holds a dual MS degree in electrical engineering from the Royal Institute of Technology (KTH) in Stockholm and Northeastern University in Boston, and an MBA from the MIT Sloan School of Management.

Associates

Julieann Esper

Julieann Esper joined Battery in 1999 and specializes in enterprise software investments, with particular expertise in supply chain management software, integration technologies and customer relationship management applications. She serves as a director on the board of Viewlocity and works closely with Optiant and ProfitLogic. Previously, she worked in the investment banking division at Advest, Inc., focusing on the software, semiconductor and electronics manufacturing services sectors. She graduated magna cum laude from Smith College with a BA in mathematics.

Scott B. Simpson

Scott Simpson joined Battery in 1998. He focuses primarily on the communications industry and has been involved with Battery's investments in ipVerse and Lara Technology. Scott graduated magna cum laude from Harvard College with an AB in history.

Analysts

Jessica Feldt

Jessica Feldt joined Battery's communications group in 2001. She graduated summa cum laude from Princeton University with an AB in economics and finance.

Benjamin A. Stingle

Benjamin Stingle joined Battery in 2000. He focuses primarily on software and Internet investments. Benjamin graduated cum laude from Harvard College with an AB in biology.

Source: Battery Ventures.

Principals and partners could also be hired from outside or promoted from within. Partners were limited to sitting on, at most, seven boards. Dagres explained, "This means that there are new guys that we've trained in our culture waiting in the wings. When my plate is full, there are new guys who can do deals, or I can move a deal that's running well off onto a senior associate. Then I have space to do a new deal."

At the same time, Battery split the firm administratively between software and communications. That meant, Dagres said, "The software guys don't have to explain complex software deals to communications experts, and communications guys don't have to explain comm deals to software guys." All the partners met as a group bi-weekly to approve deals, but the intense scrutiny would be done by the partners in the specialist groups.

Oliver Curme, another senior partner at the firm, commented:

> Most venture firms are collections of cowboys—four or five guys who're all outwardly focused. They do their own deals and they only get together to diversify risk and do some centralized administration. We're scaling Battery because, when you have a company, you want it to be the best or to do something no one has done before. I see an opportunity to build Battery into an institution that no one has built before. I see a way to change the venture capital market, and it's very clear to me.[22]

To fulfill this vision, Battery also added four venture partners (see Exhibit 25.11 for bios). Two, Dick McGlinchy and Rich Moore, provided marketing and communications

---

EXHIBIT 25.11

BIOGRAPHIES OF SELECTED VENTURE PARTNERS

Cornel Faucher

Cornel Faucher joined Battery in 2000 as a venture partner dedicated to assisting portfolio companies with executive search and staffing challenges. Most recently, he was a cofounder of a retained executive search firm, Lexington Associates. There, he leveraged his eighteen years of experience in senior management in the Internet, data networking, telecommunications industries to complete many high profile executive searches. Past positions include vice president of the Network Systems Division of PictureTel Corporation, where he spearheaded the company's entry into the Internet and e-commerce market. Prior to PictureTel, he was the vice president of product management for EIS International, a computer telephony integration company. Faucher holds an MBA from Suffolk University.

Dick McGlinchey

Dick McGlinchey joined Battery in 1999 to advise portfolio companies with critical marketing and sales strategies. He has a twenty-year history of helping some of the information technology industry's fastest growing and most successful companies such as Akamai Technologies, AT&T, Forrester Research, IBM, Lotus, Morgan Stanley Ventures, Powersoft and Symbol Technology. Prior to joining Battery, he was president and founder of Meridian Technology Marketing, the first technology marketing firm of its kind to offer a complete range of marketing services from high-level strategy development to tactical program management. In the mid-1980s, he cofounded McGlinchey & Paul, one of the most highly regarded press and analyst relations firms in the industry. In addition, he brings extensive international marketing experience to Battery with over fifteen years of successful marketing in major European markets. A 1972 graduate of Gannon College, he holds master's degrees in psychology from Kent State University and in journalism from Boston University.

Steve Terry

Steve Terry joined Battery Ventures in 2001 as a venture partner to assist Battery's portfolio companies in all aspects of capital markets activities. He has over ten years of experience working in the area of corporate finance. Most recently, he was an investment banking director at Credit Suisse First Boston's Technology Group specializing in communications software. Prior to this, he was with Robertson Stephens' Investment Banking Group within the Information Services and Convertible Securities practices. Earlier in his career he worked as an associate within Kidder Peabody's Mergers & Acquisitions Group and at Arthur Andersen as a member of its Corporate Finance Consulting Services practice. Steve has an MBA from the University of Texas and a bachelor's degree from Texas A&M University.

Source: Battery Ventures.

---

22. Cited in Gupta and Bharadwaj, "Battery Ventures," p. 4.

help to the portfolio companies; another, Cornel Faucher, assisted the firms with recruiting; and Steve Terry, the most recent addition, had joined the West Coast office in late 2001 to help portfolio companies arrange later rounds of financing. While Terry, McGlinchy, and Moore consulted directly with the firms, Faucher acted as a liaison to executive recruiting firms, educating them on the hiring firm's culture, reviewing resumes, and passing only the most likely candidates on to the company.

The Deal Process

Dagres ascribed Battery's high "batting average" (over 66 percent of its deals made money) to its deal process.[23] "We've set the organization up for due diligence. Any deal principal has to have deep domain knowledge. With a big organization, you have the ability to specialize."

Battery found deals through two avenues. In the first, partners or principals would find an opportunity and hand it to the associates and analysts for further investigation. In the second, teams of analysts and associates would study a sector in depth and look for promising companies by visiting trade shows, reading journals, and attending conferences. The team would take prospective deals to a senior associate, who would do further due diligence before taking it to the partners. A senior associate might also find, research, and present a deal to a partner.[24]

Depending on the senior associate's experience, a partner might or might not be involved in the deal research process. After due diligence, the team would prepare a hot-deal memo and an internal rate of return (IRR) analysis. They would present the deal at a staff meeting and, with approval from that body, take it through to final approval.[25]

Sometimes, after studying a market space, the team would find a significant hole that no companies appeared to be filling. In one case, the team drew up a business plan and formed a company, @stake, to provide Internet security.[26]

THE ARBOR DEAL

A typical example of Battery's process in action occurred in the firm's relationship with Arbor Networks, a provider of denial-of-service (DoS) protection technology.[27] Carl Stjernfeldt, a senior associate at Battery, described how he found the company:

> I had been looking at the larger market space of quality of service over the Internet. Because quality of service is one of the biggest reasons that voice over IP (VoIP) hasn't taken off, I began studying routing anomaly detection and correction. In the spring of 2000, I worked at a firm in that space and became very familiar with what was needed both in terms of service and what a company would have to provide to survive and thrive.
>
> I had learned that University of Michigan had some good research going on in this space, but no one could pinpoint who was doing it. So I sent a spam e-mail to all the professors in the mathematics, engineering, and statistics departments, probably forty-five people in all. I received about seven

23. Battery Ventures, http://www.battery.com, accessed February 1, 2002.

24. Gupta and Bharadwaj, "Battery Ventures," p. 4.

25. *Ibid.*

26. *Ibid*, p. 5.

27. In a denial-of-service attack, parts of the Internet backbone (computers that serve as routers and servers) are flooded with so many requests that they shut down. Arbor used this as a first application for its technology, as part of a strategy aimed at providing network security and availability products.

replies, all pointing me to Farnam [Jahanian, cofounder of what became Arbor Networks]. Finally a few days later, I received an email from him saying, "I guess you're looking for me."

Stjernfeldt's background fit well with Battery. While doing undergraduate work in his native Sweden, he had run a telecommunications firm doing work for Ericsson, then come to the United States and joined Cambridge Technology Partners, eventually working briefly with its in-house venture capital fund. He said, "I found that I liked the three-legged stool of VC: management, technology, and finance." While at MIT's Sloan School of Management, he had met Dagres, who had asked him to evaluate some technology deals. This led to an internship with Battery in the summer of 1999, when he learned that he liked the work and especially enjoyed the firm's culture. He joined Battery as a senior associate after completing his MBA in 2000. As Stjernfeldt said, "I saw the end of the bubble, but I never lived it. But if you can make good deals in the current environment, you can be a hero as things recover."

After tracking down Jahanian, Stjernfeldt arranged a conference call with him and his team for Friday, July 14. The following Tuesday, he arrived in Ann Arbor along with Ted Julian, a former analyst at Forrester who had been on the founding team of @stake. Julian, who had launched International Data Corporation's first Internet research service, had been investigating DoS protection technology with Stjernfeldt after leaving @stake shortly before.

Upon meeting with Jahanian and his colleague, Rob Malan, Stjernfeldt and Julian agreed:

> These were the only ones of all the groups we'd looked at that had the architecture to solve the problem. In addition, they were good guys. They had that midwestern down-to-earth quality. They were shrewd and realistic about their strengths and about their limitations.

Jahanian, now president of Arbor, had been a professor of computer science in the University of Michigan's College of Engineering since 1993, and a senior manager at IBM's research division for eight years before that. He was impressed with the Battery delegation:

> I had spent the previous fifteen years looking at scalability, availability, and security of Internet infrastructure. The prototype for our denial-of-service solution was already deployed by January of 2000 on a large regional service provider, and we had started looking into its commercialization by the spring of 2000. We'd filed patents and had begun discussions with the University of Michigan's Office of Technology Transfer about licensing the technology to Arbor. In addition, we'd started talking to venture capitalists through our existing relationships. The initial reaction was overwhelmingly positive. But when we talked with Carl [Stjernfeldt], I realized he'd done his homework. He had talked to other companies and to the researchers. When we had our first conference call, I'm not sure if he knew we were looking to commercialize the technology. He said he just wanted to talk about denial of service. I said I'd be happy to do so, but we were also exploring a commercialization path for our research technology. Three days later, he and Ted [Julian] came to our lab in Ann Arbor. I was extremely impressed with Carl's knowledge of the space. There was no question that he understood both the technology and the value proposition to customers.

Stjernfeldt also liked what he saw:

> We met Farnam and Rob [Malan, Arbor's co-founder and CTO], and realized there were seven others waiting in the wings—students and colleagues. These guys had the real solution. They had no ego. And Ted [Julian] had the marketing and public relations expertise that they needed (see Exhibit 25.12 for biographies of Arbor's team).

On Saturday, July 22, Stjernfeldt called Jahanian to ask if the team could present to the Battery partners. Stjernfeldt explained:

> Because I'd been studying the space, I knew that Arbor's product, a distributed noninvasive DOS solution, was what the market needed. In addition, they had an existing prototype that was running on MichNet, the Internet Service Provider for the greater Detroit area. It was an alpha version, and very much still a research project, but it was working.

Arbor was not the first firm in the market. "There were a couple of others," said Julian:

> Mazu had raised money from three highly respected investors and received some press. Though we knew Arbor had a superior architecture and suspected we were further along in its development, we couldn't know that for sure. While we were getting ready to launch the company, our competitors were already deploying their solutions in customer networks.

On Monday July 24, Battery submitted a term sheet. Dagres handled the term sheet negotiations while Stjernfeldt focused on continuing the due diligence. Julian, Stjernfeldt, and Dagres combined as the "Deal Team."

In December 2000, Arbor wrapped up an $11 million A round. Battery led the financing, with Cisco as a co-investor. Battery had two board seats. Dagres took one, and Mike Darby, a partner in the West Coast office, took the other board seat. Stjernfeldt explained, "Mike came to us from Cisco, where he was vice president of business development. Because Cisco is a channel as well as an investor, Mike's contacts are extremely helpful to the company."

Jahanian explained why his team chose Battery:

> Battery clearly understood the infrastructure space. They were strong both on the business and the technical side. And we liked the partners. Todd Dagres and Mike Darby each brought very unique expertise to our team. Todd had been involved in several successful Internet infrastructure companies with an enviable track record. I immediately clicked with him. Mike Darby brought a unique perspective as a former business development executive at Cisco. Carl has been engaged since day one. He's diligent and has a strong technical background.

Growing Arbor

Although the creation of the legal documentation took months, the Arbor and Battery relationship began shortly after the document was submitted. In September 2000, Julian became involved with the firm as chief strategist, working out of Battery's Wellesley offices. Arbor's business operations moved to Waltham, Massachusetts, while the engineering group stayed in Michigan.

EXHIBIT 25.12

BIOGRAPHIES OF ARBOR NETWORKS' FOUNDING TEAM

Dr. Farnam Jahanian, Chief Scientist and Cofounder

Farnam Jahanian brings to Arbor Networks over fifteen years of research and development experience and leadership in networking and distributed computing.

As a professor of electrical engineering and computer science and the director of the Software Systems Laboratory at the University of Michigan, Jahanian led pioneering research on the scalability, reliability and security of computer networks and distributed systems. His research efforts, aimed at developing new protocols and architectures for ensuring survivability and availability of network infrastructure in the presence of security attacks, hardware and software failures, and operational faults formed the basis of Arbor Networks' technology. Sponsors of Farnam's various research efforts at the University of Michigan include Cisco, DARPA, Hewlett-Packard, Hitachi, IBM, Intel, and the National Science Foundation.

Prior to joining the faculty at the University of Michigan in 1993, Jahanian was a research staff member at the IBM T. J. Watson Research Center, where he led several experimental projects in distributed and fault-tolerant systems. His research has had significant impact on commercial industry in several areas, including networking infrastructure, real-time computing, and highly available systems.

Throughout the course of his career, he has served on dozens of government and industrial panels, program committees, and editorial boards. He has written more than seventy published research papers and received numerous academic and research awards, including a National Science Foundation CAREER Award, the University of Michigan Amoco Teaching Award, and an IBM Outstanding Technical Innovation Award.

Jahanian holds a master's degree and a Ph.D. in computer science from the University of Texas at Austin.

Ted Julian, Chief Strategist and Cofounder

Ted Julian brings to Arbor a combination of in-depth knowledge of the security and networking markets and hands-on experience launching a start-up. He joined Arbor from @Stake where he was a company founder and VP of marketing. While at @Stake, the firm grew to over 130 employees and added to its Cambridge, Massachusetts, headquarters, offices in Raleigh, San Francisco, Seattle, and London. Prior to @Stake, Julian was a well-known industry analyst, first at International Data Corporation and more recently at Forrester Research.

Julian is a sought-after industry expert who appears regularly in the media ranging from TV appearances on CNN and ABC News to mainstream print media like *The Wall Street Journal* and *USA Today*. He is proud to have been named "Geek of the Week" by *The Boston Globe*. He holds a BS degree from Cornell University.

Dr. G. Robert Malan, Chief Technology Officer and Cofounder

Rob Malan brings more than ten years of research experience in computer networking and security to Arbor Networks. His thesis work at the University of Michigan formed the basis for Arbor Networks' technology, and he is the author of the company's patents. Malan transitioned technology from research prototype to product during his tenure in industry, which includes work at the IBM T. J. Watson Research Laboratory and at Hewlett-Packard.

Malan began his networking career working as a researcher on the Mach operating system project at Carnegie Mellon University. He has written eighteen papers published in top-tier computer security and networking journals and conference proceedings. He holds a Ph.D. and MSE in computer science from the University of Michigan and a BS in computer engineering from Carnegie Mellon.

Source: Battery Ventures.

During the fall of 2001, Arbor grew to fifty employees and was working on the next release of its technology. Its flagship product, Peakflow DoS, was a distributed, nonintrusive, scalable solution to the problem of network availability threats, like denial-of-service attacks, which plagued e-commerce firms and Internet service providers. It protected networks against availability threats, like DoS attacks and worms, both at the network core and at the edge, and did so without introducing new performance bottlenecks or additional points of failure. This last feature was key to its customers who were reluctant to add yet another device to their network if it might slow performance or cause a failure.

Starting in September, Battery worked with Arbor to create the business side of the firm. "At this point," Jahanian said, "Basically, we were a superb engineering team. We relied on Battery to help us build the business around our core strength."

With Jahanian as president, Julian as chief strategist, and Malan as CTO, the Arbor team turned to Cornel Faucher, Battery's recruiting venture partner, as well as Dagres and Stjernfeldt for help in filling out the management team. "Cornel's been a tremendous help," said Jahanian:

> We hired vice presidents of sales, operations, and finance in searches where he was actively involved in identifying Arbor's needs and recruiting the top talents to the company. Cornel has a very unique relationship with Arbor. He serves as Arbor's institutional memory for executive recruiting.

Julian credited Dick McGlinchey, the marketing venture partner, with making the product launch a success:

> We wouldn't have had such a great launch without him. Part of the credit, of course, goes to Farnam and Rob, who understood its importance and were willing to spend time and money on it. But for us, it was incredibly important—Asta had the momentum and Mazu had some press, so we had to make a big splash for our product before our competitors turned their initial awareness into the perception of leadership. With Dick's help, it really worked. We were barely three months old when we made the Ten to Watch lists at both Red Herring and Network World.

Stjernfeldt pointed out that the venture partners do not do the work for the companies. "The idea isn't that we do the work for them. It's not an incubator. We help them do the work, we don't do it for them." Part of the value of the venture partners, he felt, was their ability to save the companies money on fees from search firms and PR firms.

Stjernfeldt talked almost daily with Jahanian. "I raise the strategic issues to Todd—things like VP-level employee contracts, large capital expenditures, major stuff." Jahanian felt that Dagres and Darby were very accessible:

> I can talk with them easily about strategic issues between board meetings. It's common for someone from Arbor to be talking to someone at Battery on a daily basis. This has been very helpful for navigating the ship during the current economic climate. Arbor's track record during the last fifteen months is a testimony to the unique nature of our relationship.

Battery had been closely involved as Arbor raised its second round, in part because the company had decided to raise the funding without a CEO. Battery liked to have a new lead for a second round, along with a few new strategic investors. Dagres and

Stjernfeldt had worked with Arbor to assemble a list of potential investors, with notes about how to contact them. Stjernfeldt had helped the Arbor team create their pitch, then attended the first few meetings to give them feedback. As potential investors fell off the list, he helped identify others to add. He also served as the first check about Battery's response to various terms as term sheets were negotiated. Stjernfeldt said, "This was the first time I'd been involved in raising funds for a portfolio company, so I talked to Todd a lot."

Jahanian agreed: "Carl plays a unique role. He worries about the day-to-day things and acts as a point of contact to reach other Battery resources. He spends a lot of time working with the company and was instrumental in Arbor's successful B round."

While Dagres had identified his stand on various strategic issues, Stjernfeldt and Jahanian had handled the tactical and legal issues. Despite a financing environment described by some as a "nuclear winter," the firm had just signed a term sheet for an up round with a new lead investor.

GROWING BATTERY

Dagres felt that, if Arbor could survive in the current chilly climate, it would thrive once things warmed up. From a late starter, it had become the leader in its market. He had to think that some of that success came from the contributions of his firm.

He had to admit to some concerns. Battery's growth had added complexity to the firm. It had become a big firm and communication was more difficult. There were a lot of people to manage, even if the new mentorship program meant he only worked closely with a few. There were more processes to follow, more checklists. He knew the intensive due diligence process had cost the firm some deals, yet there had been others, like Arbor, where they had been able to move very fast. One of the concerns he had heard involved a "free rider" problem, whether other VC firms would use Battery's presence on a company's board to reduce their own input. In another version of that problem, others might hire away some of Battery's best associates and senior associates if Battery did not promote them quickly enough.

He had to admit he did not have all the answers. Yet, he thought:

> We want an organization that self-perpetuates, where analysts move up to be senior partners. If you are going to build a VC organization that will exist for a long time, you need to constantly bring people in and move them up. Most senior partners don't retire; their firm blows up. Instead of running Battery like a club, we're trying to build a company and that means we have to bring in the best people and grow. But our advisory board is concerned that this hasn't worked in the past because VC firms have their heyday and then people leave. Also, if you get too big too fast, your returns go down because inexperienced people start doing deals. So the big question is, can you have an organization that makes a lot of investments with a lot of people and still delivers top performance?[28]

28. Cited in Gupta and Bharadwaj, "Battery Ventures," p. 8.

26

Accel Partners' European Launch

On April 12, 2001, Kevin Comolli, managing general partner of Accel Partners' London office, looked up as Fearghal Ó Ríordáin, the firm's principal and the only other investment professional hired to date, threaded his way through the construction debris and sat down at the opposite desk. Ó Ríordáin said, "Cape Clear called. They're out of cash in six weeks and want to know if we're going to give them a term sheet."

Comolli sighed. Cape Clear was an Irish software firm founded by some of the top executives from one of Ireland's first technology superstars. It seemed to have all the features Accel sought—a strong team, a good technology in a new and growing space, and a defined path to revenues that included a strong focus on international growth. Yet he also had some doubts. This would be the fund's first investment, and the timing was not ideal. Accel Partners was still raising its European fund; Comolli was trying to recruit the team; he and Ó Ríordáin had just moved out of a serviced rental office and were trying to work in the middle of a construction zone; and they were still setting up the process for working with the California-based head office. On a macro level, the slide in the technology markets showed no sign of slowing and many U.S. firms had closed their European offices and cut their Europe-destined funds.

Nonetheless, Accel had persevered with its overseas effort. The U.S. parent firm had been founded in 1983 and focused on technology, software, and communications investments. It had raised a $1.6 billion eighth fund in 2000, primarily on its reputation as one of Silicon Valley's premier firms, having backed such successes as UUNET, Polycom, and RealNetworks.

As a result, the London office's first investment had a lot riding on it. It would be the proof of concept, indicating to potential limited partners, to the general partners in California, and to the team members Comolli was trying to recruit, the type of company that the team would be funding in the future. Comolli and Ó Ríordáin had been

Professors Felda Hardymon and Josh Lerner, and Senior Research Associate Ann Leamon prepared this case. HBS cases are developed solely as the basis for class discussion. Cases are not intended to serve as endorsements, sources of primary data, or illustrations of effective or ineffective management.. Some numbers have been disguised.

talking with Cape Clear for almost four months and liked what they knew. And yet, as Ó Ríordáin said to his colleague, "Can we have really found a world-beating technology company in Dublin?"

Comolli reflected, "We spent a lot of time putting together the investment approval process. Our U.S. colleagues support the investment, and it's the first we've ever shown them. We need to trust our own conviction, the process, and our partners."

Accel had also shown the Cape Clear deal to Greylock, another well-known U.S. venture firm, which had expressed interest in participating. Ó Ríordáin said, "I'm not sure about whether to include Greylock in the deal or not. How would we structure the deal to let Greylock in? And is this in our best interests and Cape Clear's?"

He went on, "Why don't I work out a valuation and two different deals, with and without Greylock? Then we can figure out what makes the most sense for everyone involved."

VENTURING IN EUROPE

By the first quarter of 2001, venture investing in Europe was in an uncertain state. The previous year had seen record-breaking amounts of money raised and invested, but the NASDAQ Europe Composite Index had followed its North American cousin in a steady slide beginning in March 2000. It had subsequently collapsed from a high of 82,000 to 14,000, and the London Stock Exchange's Alternative Investment Market (AIM) had plummeted similarly (see Exhibit 26.1). Many of the small venture firms that had sprung up over the past few years were struggling. Some experts were asking whether history was going to repeat itself.

U.S.-style venture capital (VC) had made an appearance in Europe in the mid-1980s, due in part to a hot venture market across the Atlantic. European banks also

---

EXHIBIT 26.1

EASDAQ AND AIM, 1999 TO MARCH 2001

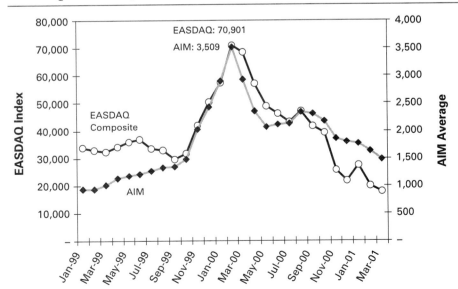

Source: Datastream, Thomson Financial, accessed October 28, 2002.

drove this activity, seeing it as a chance to found new companies that would be customers for their banking services. As a result, one expert commented, "The industry was staffed in completely the wrong way . . . with bankers and accountants. They were fine in terms of structuring the deals, but lacked the expertise to assess trends and technologies and to add value."[1]

This inexperience, coupled with the large amounts of money that were raised, meant that investors tended to do poor deals at high prices and often failed to establish solid corporate governance systems. Returns therefore lagged expectations, and the 1987 market crash annihilated the industry. Institutional investors, especially pension funds and insurance companies, fled the sector; European firms closed their VC operations; and U.S. firms closed or sharply reduced their European presence. Said one observer, "The Americans thought they'd show us how the game was played and instead had their heads handed to them."

The United States recovered in 1991, though, while Europe continued to languish. Part of the problem, many professionals believed, was the lack of an exchange analogous to the NASDAQ through which small private companies could go public. The London Stock Exchange closed its Unlisted Securities Market in 1994 after the number of listed stocks had fallen by 40 percent and its capitalization by 33 percent. A year later, the LSE established the Alternative Investment Market (AIM) as the exchange for small and growing companies—by 2002, 850 companies were listed.

Due in part to conflicting regulatory regimes, European countries established their own small-cap exchanges; Germany's Neuer Markt became the most popular as its disclosure requirements were the most stringent.[2] The European Venture Capital Association (EVCA) backed the establishment of the EASDAQ to serve as a European NASDAQ. In March 2001, it was acquired by NASDAQ and continued to operate as NASDAQ-Europe. In general, however, floating on NASDAQ continued to be viewed as the gold standard for venture-backed European firms throughout the 1990s. The inadequacy of the European small-cap markets forced investors to rely on exiting via mergers and acquisitions, often at undesirable valuations.[3]

The virtual collapse of European venture capital in the late 1980s gave the asset class a reputation for illiquidity that persisted into the middle of the next decade.[4] Venture capital in Europe returned to being synonymous with private equity, later-stage investing dominated by buyouts or transactions that involved a fair amount of financial engineering. The terms became used interchangeably, in contrast to the U.S., where VC referred to early stage deals and private equity implied later-stage or buyout investments. In addition, the long slump in European venture investment essentially removed the concept of venture funding from the general imagination.

By the end of the 1990s, though, conditions seemed riper for a solid VC recovery in Europe. All of the actors—investors, general partners, entrepreneurs, and even regulatory regimes—appeared to be aligning. The general public was becoming more aware of venture capital as a financing option. The fact that returns to private equity and VC

1. John Singer, Advent Capital, quoted in Rick Butler, "Europe Comes under Pressure to Perform," *Global Investor* (April 2000), p. 13.

2. Reynir Indahl and Eric Zinterhofer, "A Note on European Private Equity," in Josh Lerner and Felda Hardymon, *Venture Capital & Private Equity: A Casebook Volume II* (New York: John Wiley & Sons, 2002), p. 228.

3. Josh Lerner, "The European Association of Security Dealers: November 1994," in Josh Lerner, *Venture Capital & Private Equity: A Casebook,* 1st ed. (New York: John Wiley & Sons, 2000), p. 375.

4. Butler, "Europe Comes under Pressure to Perform."

funds had outpaced those on the London Stock Exchange by 10 to 20 percentage points persuaded institutional investors to come off the sidelines. A substantial pool of available capital began to accumulate as European institutions started allocating up to 10 percent of their assets to private equity and VC, and were joined by U.S. institutions seeking to diversify their portfolios. While the European allotment to the asset class was far from the 20 percent of some U.S. groups,[5] funds available for investment rose by 2.5 times between 1997 and 2000, from €18 billion to €44 billion.[6]

The technology boom of the late 1990s introduced other aspects of U.S. VC to Europe. General partners of European VC firms still tended to have strongly financial backgrounds, but many acknowledged the need for operational expertise. Although the European tech boom did not achieve the scale of that in the United States, it nonetheless gave rise to a number of successful companies that produced engineers and executives with a more entrepreneurial bent than had been the norm. Working for a startup, or starting one, had become more socially respectable. In addition, regulatory schemes were slowly being harmonized across Europe, tax rates for capital gains were falling, and stock options were becoming a more accepted form of compensation. Stock exchanges like the United Kingdom's AIM and Germany's Neuer Markt offered additional exit options, and a small number of support companies had sprung up to provide the accounting, human resources, legal, and other services that venture firms required.

Even as U.S. institutional investors began investing in European private equity funds, U.S. VC firms began entering Europe in droves. Some big firms, such as Advent, General Atlantic, and Benchmark, either established European operations for the first time or made their formerly opportunistic European investments more systematic. Atlas Venture had been operating in Europe since 1980, first as a branch of IDG Bank, a major Dutch institution, and later as an independent operation. The major European player was 3i, a UK-based venture capital and private equity firm, which extended its operations throughout Europe and into the United States and Asia. Small boutiques, such as Pond and Kennet, found novel ways of leveraging their European presence with U.S. connections. Pond, for instance, had offices in California and London but did no U.S. deals. The California office served only to keep a toe in the water. Kennet, established in Europe, teamed up with Broadview, a New Jersey–based investment bank with a private equity operation. The VC firm shared deal flow and did deals that were too small or young for the larger, later-stage partner.

The U.S. firms arrived for any of several reasons—to diversify, to avoid the competition that was bidding up deal prices at home, or to get a bargain on seed investments, as salaries, especially for engineers, were lower than in the United States. Given the language similarities, U.S. firms typically set up a general office in London. Some staffed these offices with local venture capitalists recruited from existing firms; others transplanted current employees; and yet a third option involved setting up a partnership with a local firm. All approaches presented their own challenges. The new recruits and even a partner firm, although they brought good local networks, might not be especially talented in VC as practiced by U.S. firms. The transplants, even if they were European nationals, often lacked a strong European network and could be perceived as brash outsiders with foreign ways. Partnerships, as long as the chemistry between the partners worked, were thought to have the best chance of success, although hard results could not yet be calculated. Benchmark and JP Morgan had used this approach

---

5. Butler, "Europe Comes under Pressure to Perform."

6. European Venture Capital & Private Equity Association, *2002 EVCA Yearbook* (Brussels, June 2002), p. 68.

and felt that it was successful. One venture capitalist observed, "What's important is that the two groups are working side by side and it's easy to learn from one another."

The organizational structure of the firms with European funds varied. With some, the European fund was separate from the others but offered the partners cross-carry, through which U.S. partners received a share of the returns from European deals, and Europeans received a share of the returns from the U.S. investments. Others created an entirely separate fund with its own carry. Even deal approval processes varied by firm. Some had marathon teleconferences across multiple time zones; others were fairly autonomous and held quarterly partner meetings.

Although most of the U.S. firms had little in the way of a network, they had substantial amounts of money and expertise and a brand-name cachet with limited partners, entrepreneurs, other VC firms, and potential customers and acquirers of portfolio companies. They could open doors in the United States, the world's largest market. Acquirers, customers, partners, and competitors were often U.S.-based and frequently venture-backed; the U.S. firms understood their culture and background. In addition, Europeans tended to view U.S. regulatory regimes and deal structures as the norm.

At the end of the 1990s, a number of early stage firms, both U.S. and domestic, were active in Europe. The amount of money available and the returns to be made inspired a host of entrants, just as it had a decade before. Most U.S. limited partners supported the European funds of the venture firms in which they had invested. A few, however, demurred. These felt that Europe did not offer sufficient diversification, as its returns were correlated with and lagged those in the United States. They also worried about the European venture market's concentration in the wireless and telecommunications sectors. Some viewed the European markets as less developed and European staff, both in portfolio companies and in the VC firms, as less experienced.

By the first quarter of 2001, though, the market appeared to have come firmly back to earth. One partner of a long-term European firm observed, "A large number of inexperienced people had far too much money and did really stupid deals. They overpaid for bad companies or even for good ones, and now the spigot's been turned off." Contrary to the usual situation, many firms that had raised their first funds in the late 1990s found themselves unable to raise additional money after the market crashed.

ACCEL ABROAD

Accel began its move into Europe in May 2000, when Kevin Comolli joined the firm, but the idea had already been circulating for some time. Jim Swartz, cofounder and general partner, explained:

> I'd always been interested in Europe. My first job was head of International Venture Capital for Citibank, although in those days, international meant we had three people in London, three in Canada, and two in Geneva. Also, Accel as a firm has a global orientation; its people have broad interests that aren't bounded by the North American continent. For example, when we formed Accel in 1983, we had a domestic and an international fund. In the late 1990s, we began looking for ways that we could grow, expand our scope, and increase our differentiation. We were seeing an increasing stream of really interesting technology companies coming from Europe and Israel to California. But ad hoc investments didn't seem to make sense—we felt we needed a comprehensive strategy. Besides, the time difference between Israel and the West Coast made managing those investments almost impossible from a logistical

standpoint. So as a firm we'd been thinking about establishing a European presence for quite some time.

At the same time, Kevin Comolli wanted to change careers. After fourteen years in Europe and the last four with Doughty Hanson in London, where he built the buy-out firm's European technology practice, he wanted to get closer both to early stage investing and to his family home in California. Contacting his Harvard Business School section-mate Jim Breyer, managing partner at Accel, he asked about California firms that might be interested in European operations. Comolli recounted, "We had this tremendous meeting of the minds about how to set it up." Swartz observed, "Jim Breyer had known [Comolli] from HBS [Harvard Business School], he had run remote offices of world-class firms, and we liked and trusted him. Basically, we all said, 'Here's the perfect guy to run this place—let's make it happen.'"

Together Swartz and Comolli created a memo of understanding in which they agreed on the organization and the approach to Accel's European operations. In May 2000, Comolli became a partner of Accel and moved from London to California for the next ten months. He had a lot to do: a legal fund entity to set up, a prospectus to write, money to raise, space to find, a team to staff, and investments to make. In addition, he had to learn how Accel ran its operations and how to both replicate its approach and adapt it to local conditions eight time zones away.

Support

Comolli felt strongly that the European effort needed the support of the entire Accel partnership. After meeting with the California office, he became comfortable that the entire partnership was behind the idea. In addition, two senior partners were willing to be involved in the operation. Swartz had just decided to reduce his commitments to Accel VIII to half-time and he offered to use the additional half-time for Accel Europe. Joe Schoendorf, another partner, had also decided to reduce his time with Accel's U.S. operations, but was willing to be involved with the London office.

During his ten months in California, Comolli established ties with the individual members of the partnership. He said, "If I was going to create another Accel, I had to know the culture. And they had to know and trust me. I spent a lot of time in those offices." Along with understanding the culture and decision-making methods, he also wrote the business plan and established the fund structure to make it tax-efficient for limited and general partners in the United States and elsewhere.

The European fund would focus on investing in European and Israeli companies in the networking and software sectors. In addition, it would also manage and co-invest in deals that Accel U.S. or even other U.S. firms found in Europe, providing on-site supervision that more distant investors would be hard pressed to supply.

Accel Europe planned to operate out of an office in London. Along with its logistical convenience, having the team in a single office provided significant operational benefits. Comolli explained:

> For good rigorous investment decision making, you need a critical mass of good people through which to circulate the opportunity. This is linked to our fundamental proposition of integration with Palo Alto [the California office]. If we were to set up satellite offices throughout Europe, for instance, we'd dramatically reduce our critical mass and the amount of critical thinking we can bring to bear on an investment opportunity. That would also make the integration with Palo Alto much more difficult as well.

Locating in London had another external benefit as part of Accel's approach to the market. "London is neutral financial territory," said Comolli:

> That means that all the firms can have a presence here without being seen to poach on someone else's preserve. We are trying to position ourselves as the partner of choice for local venture firms with portfolio companies that have global aspirations. We're trying to send an explicit message that we're not here to compete but to partner in situations where our domain knowledge, Silicon Valley ties, and business-building skills can complement a local firm's investment. We want to work together on deals and cooperate to make the companies successful.

The Fund

Accel decided to raise a separate fund for the European operations. This, Comolli and the partners felt, would bring a number of benefits:

- Choice for the current limited partners (LPs): The LPs would be able to control the geographic allocation of their investments. If they did not want to be in Europe, they could decline that fund and still remain in Accel's Fund VIII.

- The opportunity to attract a significant number of new European LPs: One of the goals of the new fund was to expand Accel's base of LPs. A number of the firm's existing LPs were European and invested through Accel in the United States. Accel wanted half of the LPs in the European fund to be new.

- A first-time fund buzz: Comolli felt that having a "quasi-first-time" fund would make the atmosphere more entrepreneurial and generate excitement and a sense of ownership among the European partners.

Comolli observed, "What we didn't anticipate was how much time it would take to educate new potential investors about the asset class. Of course, it would have helped if the markets had been better!" In addition, the terms of a top-tier Silicon Valley firm were not common in Europe, and therefore they required additional explanation to the potential LPs. On average, U.S. top-tier venture firms with funds of $500 million or more received 2.5 percent of the funds under management and carried interest between 25 percent and 30 percent. Non-U.S. venture capital and private equity firms with funds of the same size tended to charge management fees around 1.9 percent, and 20 percent carry.[7] Accel charged a 30 percent carry.[8]

In a chicken-and-egg situation, before Comolli could raise a fund, he had to have some idea of his staff and he had to write a prospectus. But before he knew what he could afford to pay his staff, he needed to know how much money he could raise. Before he could raise funds, he needed an address. To get an address and to understand what he could pay for space and how much space he would need, he needed to raise funds.

In October 2000, Comolli hired Fearghal Ó Ríordáin, an Irish engineer with an MBA from INSEAD, experience running large projects for Ericsson, and a summer internship in tech banking with Goldman Sachs (see Exhibit 26.2 for bios). Ó Ríordáin explained:

---

7. Josh Lerner and Felda Hardymon, *Venture Capital & Private Equity: A Casebook*, 2nd ed.(New York: John Wiley & Sons, 2002), chapter 5, pp. 69 and 72.

8. Data from *Private Equity Analyst* cited in Josh Lerner, Ann Leamon, and Felda Hardymon, "Battery Ventures," HBS Case No. 802-159, p. 15.

EXHIBIT 26.2

BIOGRAPHIES OF ACCEL EUROPE TEAM AS OF APRIL 2001

Kevin Comolli

Kevin Comolli is the managing general partner of Accel Partners, Europe. He has been active in international start-ups, general management, and venture capital investing for eighteen years.

Prior to joining Accel, Comolli was a London-based partner at Doughty Hanson & Co., a leading European private equity fund with over $3 billion under management, where he was responsible for the origination, execution, monitoring, and realization of pan-European transactions. Additionally, he was the founder of Doughty Hanson's technology fund initiative and has served on the boards of directors at companies in the United Kingdom, Germany, France, Italy, and The Netherlands.

Before joining Doughty Hanson & Co., Comolli served as executive director at Goldman Sachs International, where he was responsible for the solicitation and execution of a full range of investment banking services, including mergers and acquisitions, private equity investing, and equity and debt financing.

Earlier in his career, Comolli worked for Fanuc Robotics, the world leader in robotics. Fanuc develops and deploys full automation systems incorporating advanced hardware, software, and communications technology. Over his twelve-year career with Fanuc, he held various board, general management, sales, marketing, and engineering positions in Europe and the United States, including managing director, Germany; managing director, Italy; and vice president, Europe.

Comolli has lived in Europe the past thirteen years, including two years in Milan, five years in Munich, and six years in London. He speaks advanced German and conversational Italian, and he is an active member of the World Economic Forum.

In 1982, Commoli graduated with highest distinction from Northwestern University with a BS degree in engineering and mathematics. Later, he received his MBA from Harvard Business School through a full corporate scholarship from Fanuc Robotics.

Fearghal Ó Ríordáin

Fearghal Ó Ríordáin has considerable experience as a telecommunications design engineer and line manager with Ericsson, where he concentrated on wireless systems and equipment. At Ericsson, Ó Ríordáin led the development of software and hardware systems in a range of cellular wireless platforms in Scandinavia, Ireland, Germany, and North America.

Prior to joining Ericsson, Ó Ríordáin spent a number of years working in systems software at ESBI in Ireland and at CAE in Canada. More recently, he spent a brief period in the investment banking practice at Goldman Sachs International in London.

Ó Ríordáin received an M.Eng.Sc. in telecommunications and a BE in electrical Engineering with highest honours from the National University of Ireland. He holds an MBA with distinction from INSEAD.

(Continues)

In Europe, conventional wisdom generally holds that if you want to get into venture capital, you first go work for an investment bank like Goldman for five years to get experience with financial transactions and learn how to structure deals. Accel wanted just the opposite; they preferred an operational and engineering background, not a financial one.

In fall 2000, Comolli and Ó Ríordáin began raising funds, with a target of $500 million, an amount that Comolli felt could be sensibly deployed in the early stage market over a three- to four-year period. In December 2000, Accel Europe had its first closing at $250 million. Said Comolli:

> I have never worked so hard in my life as I did between May 2000 and our close. I was in the office at 6:30 or 7 A.M. and would leave at 10 or 11 at night, six days a week. I heard it all: "We're not interested in Europe." "We'll

EXHIBIT 26.2 (CONTINUED)

BIOGRAPHIES OF ACCEL EUROPE TEAM AS OF APRIL 2001

Jim Swartz

Jim Swartz has been active in venture capital since the early 1970s. Experienced in the operating needs of young companies, he particularly enjoys working with start-up teams that are defining new industries. He has served as a director for over forty successful companies and has been closely involved as lead investor with the emergence of numerous industry pioneering firms including Avici Systems, BroadBand Technologies, FastForward/Inktomi, FVC.com, Illustra/Informix, Medical Care America, Netopia, PictureTel, Polycom, Remedy Corporation, and Ungermann-Bass.

Current private company directorships include 2Wire, Comstellar Technologies, Gen3 Partners, InGenuity Systems, MetraTech, and Telera. In addition, Swartz is working closely with the Accel Europe team as a founder/mentor of Accel's European business.

Before founding Accel Partners, Swartz was founding general partner of Adler & Company, which he started with Fred Adler in 1978 after his tenure as a vice president of Citicorp Venture Capital. Early in his career Swartz worked as a management consultant, entering the venture capital industry in 1972.

Active in industry affairs, Swartz is a former director and chairman of the National Venture Capital Association and a former president of the New York Venture Capital Forum. He is a graduate of Harvard University with a concentration in engineering sciences and applied physics (he mostly remembers something about playing football) and holds an M.S. in industrial administration from Carnegie Mellon University.

Swartz's current interests include serving as chairman of the Swartz Foundation Trust and the Christian Center of Park City, Utah, and as a board member of the U.S. Ski and Snowboard Foundation and the Management Committee of the Salt Lake Organization Committee for the Winter Olympics of 2002 (SLOC). He is also a member of the board of advisors to Silicon Valley Community Ventures and the Western Governors University.

Source: Accel Partners.

see how the first fund does." "You don't have a team yet." "We'll just wait and see." I was back and forth across the Atlantic meeting with limited partners, interviewing potential employees, looking for office space. And all the time the markets were falling. It was absolutely exhilarating and exhausting.

Staff

Although staffing was contingent on the size of the fund, Comolli had to start hiring.

Ó Ríordáin spent a few months in California with Comolli, meeting the Accel partners and learning the firm's approach. He and Comolli returned to London in February 2001, working out of a serviced rental office. Comolli recalled, "We had to set up accounts for overnight mailing and for cabs and they all had to run off my personal bank account and my home address because serviced office space could not serve as an official company address."

After the fund held its first closing, Comolli began recruiting two more investment partners, Joe Golden and Kaj-Erik Relander. He said:

I knew it would be difficult to recruit these two if we didn't raise a fund of significant size. But if I didn't recruit people of their caliber, we'd never become the fund I wanted us to be. These guys were my dream team. So I started talking with them and hoped it would all come together.

Golden had lived in Europe for thirteen years, running various companies and, most recently, leading Cisco's European investment and acquisition group. Under his guidance, its investments had grown from zero in 1998 to €300 million in 1999 and €5 billion in 2000. Unhappy with the operational expertise of European venture capitalists—"We were investing in C rounds and I was rolling up my sleeves and doing things that the venture capitalists should have taken care of in the A round"—Golden was delighted to hear of Accel's European venture. He invited Swartz and Comolli for a visit to discuss a relationship like the one that Cisco enjoyed with Accel and other top venture capital firms in Silicon Valley. Soon thereafter, Comolli invited him to meet with the entire partnership as the prelude to a recruitment effort.

Relander was a Finn who also had significant operating experience. While at college, he had founded a company that sold Apple computers and created software for Apple databases. After selling it, he did management consulting, then spent six years doing deals for a Finnish venture capital firm that invested in technology. After earning his MBA from Wharton and the Helsinki School of Economics, he joined Telecom Finland (later Sonera), because he was curious about large companies. He served as CEO during its privatization. Comolli had cold-called him, hoping that he would be intrigued by the chance to come back to early stage work.

The Process

At the same time that he was recruiting people, finding space, and raising money, Comolli also had to create a process that integrated two offices on separate continents. The investment decision process required close communication, because although its most significant aspects were rigorous and formal (the due diligence, the investment proposal, and the approval meetings), another important component was informal and spur-of-the-moment. Through hallway meetings and quick questions, partners could help one another think through the investment opportunity and the deal structure.

Comolli and the California partners were committed to the idea of an integrated investment decision process. "The more focused minds you have on a project," said Comolli, "the better chance you have of identifying potential weaknesses and potential opportunities." Thus, the London partners would see the California deals and vice versa. The ties between the two offices went deeper than just the weekly investment meeting. They had regular offsite meetings alternating between California and London. The firm also held CEO summits to allow the portfolio companies to create networks not only among other companies in the portfolio but also with partners who might have complementary experience or contacts.

The depth of the integration philosophy, though, could be seen in the role of the investment committee. No investment occurred without a consensus. As Comolli explained, "It's not an up or down vote. We either all believe in the concept or we don't fund it."

The integration was intensified by cross-economics in the compensation system. The U.S. and European partners would split the carry and fees (after expenses) on the European fund, and Europeans shared in the carry on the U.S. Fund VIII. This, it was hoped, would align the interests of the groups.

Implementing integration on a daily basis had been a challenge. Even the times of meetings had proved a stumbling block. Traditionally, Accel's partners had met at 4:30 P.M. Pacific time on Mondays to review investment opportunities and discuss issues. At first, Comolli would join the meeting via audio conference, even though it began after midnight London time. Eventually, the California office changed the meeting to 8:00 A.M. Pacific time, allowing Comolli and Ó Ríordáin to participate during their workday.

Generating deal flow was another challenge. The firm's stated intention to do most of its deals in partnership with local venture capitalists required a delicate balancing act—could the group manage to find its own deals and still establish good relationships with local firms? By April 2001, Comolli and Ó Ríordáin had already received forty or fifty business plans. As Ó Ríordáin said, "It was hard, because we had this tension between wanting to invest in a company to test the model, and yet wanting to be sure the opportunity was really good."

The Deal Approval Process

The deal approval process was expected to be fairly straightforward and was similar on each side of the Atlantic. Having found a deal (which the Accel team called a project), a team would perform initial diligence, then present it to more senior partners for review. In the case of the European group, Jim Swartz and Joe Schoendorf filled this review role. A partner would take responsibility for leading the diligence on projects that passed this scrutiny, assessing the company's team and technology against a global standard and calling in other partners with suitable expertise as necessary. A potential European investee company might fly to California at this point to meet with domain experts in that office. When the team, along with the senior partners, had decided to recommend the investment to the entire partnership, the appropriate partners would create a formal investment recommendation. The candidate portfolio company and the project manager then presented to the entire partnership. For European companies, this meant another trip to California; U.S. firms would present in California with the London office listening to the conference call. After the presentation, the partnership would reach consensus on the investment decision. Most European deals would involve at least two trips to California.

Beyond the formal approval process, partners would also informally present possible investment opportunities in the weekly meetings of the separate software and network teams, a process called "socializing" the deal. Ó Ríordáin said, "When you present a project here, you'll get a thousand questions. It's not that people are out to get you, but these are questions that have to be answered before we make a decision." Comolli saw the approach as essential to the sense of cohesion between the two offices, saying: "It's important that everyone is behind the project. If it fails, it wasn't the individual investor as much as the entire partnership."

THE CAPE CLEAR INVESTMENT

Cape Clear Software Ltd. was founded in June 1999 by three executives from IONA Technologies, one of Ireland's first technology superstars. Established by college professors in 1991 and almost entirely self-funded, IONA was an application integration firm that had developed CORBA, a technology that linked disparate programs so they could work together. The company had raised $40 million in its 1997 NASDAQ listing.

David Clarke, Hugh Grant, and John McGuire were not members of the founding IONA team, but had joined the company between late 1994 and early 1996. Clarke and McGuire became senior product managers, and Grant was chief architect. By 1999, they were ready for something new, as Clarke explained:

> We felt that the challenges had changed; we weren't doing new things, just the same thing on a larger scale. In addition, we wanted to create something, and we felt that there were opportunities in the infrastructure software space

that weren't being filled. We had learned a lot from IONA and we left a lot of options on the table, but it was important that we go out on our own.

After their departure in June 1999, the trio spent three months studying the market to decide upon their product. Eventually they chose to focus on software that would facilitate the creation and integration of business applications on the Internet (later called Web services).

Cape Clear's product consisted of three parts, an XML (extensible mark-up language) business server, a set of tools, and a set of applications that would allow businesses to put their processes on the Internet. XML, a more powerful and flexible successor to HTML, was expected to revolutionize the ways that people accessed and integrated business software functionality. Previously, building new business applications and integrating them with existing systems had been expensive and time consuming and had required highly skilled (and hence scarce and expensive) technologists. With new products like Cape Clear's, less specialized individuals would be able to perform these tasks, allowing companies to be much more productive in their software application development efforts. Rather than writing pages of code to create a form in which one might enter a customer's name and address, a user simply selected the requisite code block for "Name" and "Address." By creating consistent forms throughout the business and with its business partners, a company could send purchase orders and pay bills electronically, saving time and avoiding mistakes in data entry.

Unlike IONA's founders, Clarke, McGuire, and Grant had decided to take venture funding. Clarke elaborated:

> The markets had completely changed by 1999. IONA had time to build a consulting model to support its product development. We were operating in a much more compressed timeframe, and the financing was essential. We also knew that our company would be focused on the U.S. even more than IONA had been. We did our entire customer due diligence there, and lots of market research. It was important that we eventually get backing from a U.S. firm. But it seemed to us in late 1999 that the U.S. venture capitalists weren't looking outside their boundaries. And it was important for us to stay in Ireland.

By January 2000, Cape Clear had a business plan and Clarke, the CEO, began raising money. A large number of individuals and angels were interested, but he avoided them, explaining:

> We knew we'd be raising additional money, because at this point we only wanted enough for a beta product and to raise the attention of the U.S. venture firms. We knew we needed to keep the cap table clean. We didn't want to have it all convoluted by strange early deals.

Cape Clear eventually took $1.5 million (€1.5 million)[9] from a local venture capitalist, John Flynn at ACT Venture Capital, and a U.S. equity analyst who had been impressed with the company. Clarke said, "We were looking for someone who understood what we were trying to do. And, although it may sound shallow, for a good personality fit. We figured we'd be spending a lot of time with these people and we ought to like them." In addition, Clarke saw ACT as a mentor going forward. "I had no experience in venture capital. I'd done some acquisitions for IONA, but never any venture capital. So we needed someone who could guide us."

---

9. Conversions are as of the period in question; in this case, €1 = $1.

Funding from the Irish government was another option, but Clarke turned it down. "In speaking with them, they seemed fairly bureaucratic, with lots of rules and paperwork. I wanted someone who would work with us, and I also feared that a U.S. venture capitalist might find it odd to have the government on the board."

Cape Clear also set up a subsidiary in California. "We wanted to have a presence in California, even if it was just an address," said Clarke. Cape Clear hired its first U.S. employee late in 2000.

In October 2000, the company grabbed headlines when two executives joined from IONA. Annrai (pronounced Onn-ree) O'Toole had been IONA's cofounder and CTO; Colin Newman had been the head of marketing. Both were ready to leave the company and, after some negotiation, joined Cape Clear as founders, investing in the firm. O'Toole said, "I'd worked with the Cape Clear guys before. I wanted to be in a startup again—I'd become strategic and missed being more closely involved. I had a sense that I had another ten years of living out of a suitcase left in me."

O'Toole came in as executive chairman, and Newman as senior vice president of marketing. They were considered founders and invested $1.5 million (€1.75 million)[10] between them, on the same basis as the original series A investors (see Exhibit 26.3 for the cap table). Clarke commented, "There were only twelve of us at the time, so it was easy to dilute everyone and make room for Annrai and Colin. I was relieved that we'd kept the structure so simple."

The executives tried to keep IONA's experiences in mind. "IONA was very focused on the United States," Clarke said. "We thought it had missed some opportunities. We wanted to stay aware of Europe, too." At the same time as they were completing the deal to bring on O'Toole and Newman, Clarke and his team encountered a small UK-based company that had developed an application server, which Cape Clear needed for its product. They decided to purchase the company rather than licensing someone else's

EXHIBIT 26.3

CAPE CLEAR CAP TABLE POST-SERIES A

	Shares	Price	Total Investment (€)	%
Founders Total (incl Newman & O'Toole Fdr shrs)	30,000,000			56.68%
ACT Current	11,502,114	0.218	€2,501,710	21.73
O'Toole & Newman Investment	10,226,778	0.218	€2,224,324	19.32
Vested Options	1,200,000			2.27
Additional Options				
Option Pool Total	1,200,000			2.27
Total	52,928,892			100.00%

Valuation Post Investment €11,512,034
Total Invested This Round €4,726,034

Source: Accel Partners.

10. Exchange rate of $1 = €1.17.

server. "Not only did it give us an important component of our package," Clarke explained, "but it gave us a footprint in England."

The product was scheduled for general release in December 2000, and Cape Clear decided to launch the fund-raising then, too. The company had received instant attention from U.S. venture capitalists when O'Toole and Newman joined, but, said Clarke, "We wanted to be sure we had everything together before we went out on the road. At the same time, we knew we wanted money from a Silicon Valley firm." O'Toole concurred: "IONA had never been plugged into the Silicon Valley network. This time I was determined that I'd be inside the tent looking out."

The team decided to raise $10 million to $20 million (€11 million to €22 million),[11] enough money to give the company real room to grow. Clarke explained, "Despite the tech[nology stock valuation] slide, things had gotten competitive in our space. We had a reputation as thought leaders and a definite lead on the market, but ever since Microsoft had come out with its support of SOAP[12] in March 2000, competition had become more intense." In addition, O'Toole had to have a crash course in venture capital, as he described, "I had worked on the IONA IPO, so I knew IPO language. But we were sitting there and David was talking about pre-money and post-money and I finally confessed that I didn't have a clue about what they were discussing."

On schedule, Cape Clear released the first version of its product, CapeConnect, in December 2000 and went out into the market. The company had grown to thirty employees, and it had revenues.

O'Toole and Clarke began meeting with venture capitalists, including Sequoia, Polaris, Lightspeed, and Warburg Pincus' European partners, soon afterward. They also received a call from Accel Partners' Fearghal Ó Ríordáin. Alan Austin, Accel's COO, had previously been with the same law firm that had helped Cape Clear set up its U.S. subsidiary, and he had learned of the company from his former colleagues.

In February 2001, O'Toole and Clarke met with Comolli, Ó Ríordáin, and Jim Swartz in Accel's temporary offices. Clarke remarked:

> I was struck by the difference between U.K. and U.S. venture capitalists. The U.K. venture folks wanted to know about finances—market sizing, revenue forecasts, cash flow forecasts. On the other hand, U.S. venture capitalists spent time drilling into the conceptual edifice. They wanted to know about how you thought about products, market, customers—your entire business philosophy. It seemed as if they were trying to gauge the depth of our understanding of the market place and how well we'd thought about how to enter it. They were less interested in defending a cash flow forecast than in the ideas of the operators.

Ó Ríordáin commented:

> In Europe, there are a lot of finance guys doing VC. Their attitude can often be to lock up the deal early and make a decision on whether or not they want to do it later. They give the term sheets up front and make the company sign on, then the venture capitalist does its due diligence. The VC firm can renegotiate, but the company can't. Accel's view is to develop a deep relationship with the company first, get to a point where you both know you want to spend the next number of years working on this project together and then agree the terms on which the deal will be done.

---

11. Prevailing exchange rate of $1 = €1.11.

12. An XML schema designed for modeling data calls on servers running various languages and protocols.

The Contenders

By the end of February 2001, Cape Clear had generated significant interest from both European and U.S. venture capitalists, but no term sheets. The company's cash would last through May. Warburg, where Clarke knew one of the partners, finally submitted an informal term sheet that offered to take the entire $20 million of the round. At the same time, Sequoia and Polaris had the team out for meetings. Sequoia especially seemed like a good match, as it had backed one of IONA's competitors and understood Cape Clear's approach and its people. Geography, however, turned out to be a stumbling block. O'Toole recalled, "Basically, Sequoia at that time wasn't interested in anything outside the 415/650 area codes [Bay Area and Silicon Valley]. As soon as they found out I had kids and a wife and wasn't interested in leaving Ireland, the interest died down."

Clarke added:

> It's important to us to be in Ireland from a social, financial, and cultural perspective. We had a clear idea of how it would work. We're not unreasonable; we're willing to travel. But they just didn't want to be involved in the complexity of an international deal.

Lightspeed pulled out for similar reasons. Clarke said, "They were a smaller firm; they weren't prepared to go abroad yet." Mayfield and Polaris, though, had become quite engaged. O'Toole commented:

> We really clicked with Polaris. Some of its partners had backed PowerSoft, and they saw us doing the same thing with enterprise software—basically democratizing it. Instead of having to go to a high priest to create an enterprise wide application, you could use CapeConnect.

Accel had introduced Cape Clear to Greylock's California office through Moshe Mor, who was an entrepreneur-in-residence at both Accel and Greylock. Mor brought the company to the attention of Aneel Bhusri, a Greylock partner who had been on the board of PeopleSoft, which had had a similar democratizing effect on human resources systems. Said Accel's Kevin Comolli, "We thought that Bhusri would click with them, and that Greylock would be able to contribute additional value and network contacts to the company." Clarke and O'Toole met twice with the Greylock partnership and had dinner with Bhusri and his partner, Bill Kaiser, in California. O'Toole said, "After that dinner, we knew we wanted to work with Greylock. We got to know Aneel and really liked him, and knew that he understood what we were trying to do." Soon afterward, Bhusri came to Dublin to meet the rest of the team and take a closer look at the operation.

While Greylock's focus on enterprise software and communications companies made it a good fit for Cape Clear, the firm had never invested outside the borders of the United States. As a result, said Clarke, "We would have to give it enough of the company to make it worth the pain of a board seat in Dublin. We knew that Greylock usually took no less than 20 percent in a company."

"By the end of March," said Clarke,

> we were starting to get nervous. We really liked Accel, we liked how they worked, that the London office was integrated into the California team. We liked Greylock. But we liked Mayfield too. Mayfield and Accel both wanted to lead the round. But no one had submitted a term sheet, and the quasi-term sheet that Warburg had given us had expired.

O'Toole elaborated:

> We really liked the integration between the two Accel locations. We didn't want a stand-alone European franchise of a U.S. venture capitalist, because

we wanted the benefits of the synergies. We preferred money from a U.S. firm without a European office to a franchised situation.

THE MEETING

In the first week of April, Clarke delayed his long-anticipated skiing vacation to go to California for a presentation to the full Accel partnership, the first time that Cape Clear had met with the whole group. Comolli had emphasized that Accel would bring both the European team and the U.S. resources, but to commit fully, the entire partnership would need to meet the group. Clarke said, "We'd already met with some members in California, but just on specific parts of the technology or the business plan."

After the meeting, Clarke went on his vacation, deciding that he would target other venture capitalists if Accel had not put in a term sheet by the end of the week. "We hoped the meeting would be a just a formality, but we weren't sure," he said. "It was our first time to meet Jim Breyer and some of the other general partners."

VALUING CAPE CLEAR

Ó Ríordáin stared at his computer screen, trying to decide where to begin to structure the deal. According to his due diligence and information from the California team, Cape Clear was easily six months ahead of any Web services company in the United States (see Exhibit 26.4 for actual and projected financials, and Exhibit 26.5 for competitor information). Accel wanted to lead the project, but he and Comolli very much wanted Greylock in the mix. The existing investor, ACT Ventures, needed to keep its ownership. Ó Ríordáin didn't want to dilute the option pool and demotivate the management team. What would be best for the company—and for Accel?

He thought it through once more. The company was not perfect, he admitted. He and Comolli had expressed reservations about its idea of selling the package as a download, rather than an enterprise-wide sale. For simplicity in a hoped-for IPO, it needed to be reorganized with a U.S. headquarters and R&D in Dublin, an idea he was not sure would be accepted. Swartz had suggested that O'Toole take the CEO position, which would mean that Clarke was likely to be demoted as well as diluted.

Ó Ríordáin prepared to draw up two term sheets, with and without Greylock. He knew the company was looking for $14 million to $20 million (€15.5 million to €22.2 million).[13] What would he need for a pre-money to make this work? What would adding Greylock do to the option pool? What would it mean for pricing and potential returns? And what did Greylock bring to the table? Ó Ríordáin forced himself to block out the stutter of nail guns in the background and to concentrate on the spreadsheet before him.

---

13. Exchange rate of $1 = €1.11.

EXHIBIT 26.4a

CAPE CLEAR'S ACTUAL AND PROJECTED CASH FLOW

	2000 Actual	2001 Estimated	2002 Estimated	2003 Estimated
(in euros)				
Loss before Tax	−2,552,037	−11,118,466	−10,828,314	9,628,677
Add back Depreciation	25,811	287,714	454,239	523,693
Fixed Assets purchased (Capital Expenditures)	−142,657	−876,950	−424,450	−145,950
Increase in Debtors (Accounts Receivable)	−56,230	−630,344	−1,699,151	−4,453,529
Increase in prepayments	−403,602	403,602	0	0
Increase in Other Current Assets	−160,009	160,009	0	0
Increase in Current Liabilities	788,875	574,465	395,281	689,208
Cash from Operations	**−2,499,849**	**−11,199,971**	**−12,102,395**	**6,242,098**
Directors Loan	-45,600	0	0	0
Ordinary Share Capital	0	0	0	0
Share Premium	57,026	0	0	0
Preference Shares	1,563,682	0	0	0
Funding from US/Ireland	2,878,687	0	0	0
Net Cash Movement	**1,953,946**	**−11,199,971**	**−12,102,395**	**6,242,098**

Source: Cape Clear.

Note: The projections assume that Cape Clear raised no additional financing (i.e., the impact of the B financing round is not considered).

EXHIBIT 26.4b

CAPE CLEAR'S ACTUAL AND PROJECTED INCOME STATEMENT

	2000 Actual	2001 Estimated	2002 Estimated	2003 Estimated
(in euros)				
Revenue	43,171	2,224,980	11,116,022	38,807,880
COS	9,256	354,307	1,839,860	6,701,680
Gross Profit	33,915	1,870,673	9,276,162	32,106,200
Total Expenses	2,585,952	12,989,139	20,104,476	22,477,524
Grants	0			
Pre-Tax Profit	−2,552,037	−11,118,466	−10,828,314	9,628,677
Taxes after loss carry-forwards[°]	0	0	0	0
Profit after Tax	**−2,552,037**	**−11,118,466**	**−10,828,314**	**9,628,677**

Source: Cape Clear.

Notes: The projections assume that Cape Clear raised no additional financing (i.e., the impact of the B financing round is not considered).

[°] As of 2003, Ireland's corporate tax rate would be 12.5 percent for most forms of corporate income.

EXHIBIT 26.4c

CAPE CLEAR'S ACTUAL AND PROJECTED BALANCE SHEET

(in euros)	Act. 2000 as of Dec. 31	Est. 2001 as of Dec. 31	Est. 2002 as of Dec. 31	Est. 2003 as of Dec. 31
Fixed Assets—net	131,110	720,347	690,558	312,815
Current Assets				
Debtors (accounts receivable)	56,230	686,574	2,385,725	6,839,254
Prepayments	403,602	0		
Other Current Assets	160,009			
Cash	1,980,008	−9,219,963	−21,322,358	−15,080,260
Total Assets	**2,730,959**	**−7,813,042**	**−18,246,075**	**−7,928,191**
Current Liabilities				
Purchase Ledger (accounts payable)	299,370	692,362	986,909	1,324,633
Accruals	410,500			
Leases	89,682	540,260	517,919	234,612
Deferred Revenue	0	0	76,500	683,100
Taxes Owed	11,816	153,211	199,787	227,978
Total Current Liabilities	**811,368**	**1,385,833**	**1,781,114**	**2,470,322**
Shareholders' Equity				
Ordinary Share Capital	1,860,918	1,860,918	1,860,918	1,860,918
Preference Share Capital	2,584,451	2,584,451	2,584,451	2,584,451
Share Premium	57,026	57,026	57,026	57,026
Retained Earnings	−2,582,804	−13,701,270	−24,529,584	−14,900,908
Total Liabilities & Shareholders' Equity	**2,730,959**	**−7,813,042**	**−18,246,075**	**−7,928,191**

Source: Cape Clear.

Note: The projections assume that Cape Clear raised no additional financing (i.e., the impact of the B financing round is not considered).

EXHIBIT 26.4d

CAPE CLEAR'S ACTUAL AND PROJECTED HEADCOUNT

	Act. 2000 as of Dec. 31	Est. 2001 as of Dec. 31	Est. 2002 as of Dec. 31	Est. 2003 as of Dec. 31
Business Units	21	68	81	81
Business Development	1	22	30	33
Customer Support/Training & Marketing	2	17	23	31
Corporate	5	15	21	23
	29	**122**	**155**	**168**
Consultants & Training Consultants	0	3	8	18
Total Headcount	**29**	**125**	**163**	**186**
Headcount by Location				
Dublin & UK	29	102	128	141
US	0	20	27	27
	29	**122**	**155**	**168**

Source: Cape Clear.

EXHIBIT 26.5

COMPETITOR INFORMATION

Company	Description	Founded	Pre-money Value at 2nd Round ($MM)	Amount Raised ($MM)	Current Status	2000 Revenue ($MM)	2000 Net Income ($MM)	Market Cap 4/01 ($MM)	Total Debt 4/01 ($ MM)	Beta
Webmethods[*]	Provides integration software solutions for Global 2000 corporations. The company's platform allows customers to link business processes, enterprise and legacy applications, databases and workflows both within and across enterprises. Emphasizes consulting services.	1996	$7.2	$3.6	IPO in 2/00, $35/share, $6.4 billion market cap.	$150.6	-$92.5	$1,140	$5.6	2.92
Bowstreet	Develops software and tools for Web Services Automation, designed to reduce the cost and complexity of creating and managing an infinite number of business-to-business applications. Not as user-friendly as Cape-Clear—still requires skilled minority to implement the system.	1998	$6.3	$7.6	Private	NA	NA	NA	NA	NA
Ariba[*]	Develops software to automate the procurement process in order to facilitate business-to-business electronic commerce. Offers "net marketplace" solutions and customized implementation.	1996	$14.0	$16.0	IPO in 6/99, $23/share, $3.8 billion market cap.	$236.0	-$555.4	$1,951	$0.8	2.51
BEA Systems[†]	Develops online transaction processing (OLTP) applications through professional consulting and technical training services. Provides e-business infrastructure; possible partner to Cape Clear.	1995	NA	$7.0	IPO in 4/97, $6/share, $341 million market cap.	$819.8	$17.1	$16,030	$573.9	1.99
IONA Technologies[‡]	Creates application integration software that allows disparate computer applications and systems to interact.	1991	None	None	IPO in 2/97. $18/share (ADR)[1], $137.6 million market cap.	$153.2	$14.2	$691	0.0	0.28

UK Benchmark bond (10 year): 4.78%

UK Treasury Bill (90 day, middle rate): 5.58%

Sources: DataStream, Venture Economics, http://www.venturexpert.com, accessed December 20, 2002; One Source, casewriter, and company information.

Notes:

[*] Results are adjusted to conform to calendar year.

[†] Fiscal year ended January 31; results are not adjusted.

[‡] IONA raised a small amount from individuals.

NA = Not available.

27

In-Q-Tel

Gilman Louie, CEO of In-Q-Tel, reclined in his desk chair and stared down at the Potomac River from In-Q-Tel's Arlington, Virginia, offices, as crew teams from area universities sculled gracefully past. It was April 2003, and a few weeks earlier, In-Q-Tel had completed the sale of one of its portfolio companies, Mohomine, Inc., a developer of data management software, to Kofax Image Products.

Founded in 1999 to acquire greater access to cutting-edge technologies on behalf of the U.S. Central Intelligence Agency (CIA), In-Q-Tel was a private, not-for-profit corporation funded entirely by appropriations from the federal intelligence budget. In-Q-Tel used a variety of "venture-enabled" approaches—equity, warrants and product development funding—to attract and build relationships with emerging companies. As its primary goal, In-Q-Tel sought to provide the CIA with solutions that would be supported by a competitive marketplace, not government funding. In this sense, it was less like a conventional venture capital fund and more like a corporate strategic venture fund.

In-Q-Tel had made more than forty investments since its founding. Approximately twenty-five of these deals had involved some form of equity investment and the remainder consisted of product development partnerships with firms like SRA, Booz Allen and Lockheed Martin. Typical investments ranged between $250,000 and $3 million because the company kept its investments small to maintain a diversified portfolio. After four years, In-Q-Tel had helped the CIA access emerging technologies: In-Q-Tel had seen more than 3,100 business plans and most of the firms it funded had never done business with the federal government before. Most importantly, the "return on technology"—In-Q-Tel's term for technology assimilation by its intelligence community clients—was high and increasing. In-Q-Tel had delivered dozens of technology pilots to the agency and made fifteen technology deliveries to the CIA in 2002 alone. The agency had recently adopted a couple of these for deployment to its technology infrastructure.

Because of In-Q-Tel's strategic successes, other government agencies had undertaken their own versions of that model. In-Q-Tel's board of trustees worried that other

Professors Josh Lerner and Felda Hardymon and Kevin Book (Fletcher School, '03), with assistance from Senior Research Associate Ann Leamon, prepared this case. HBS cases are developed solely as the basis for class discussion. Cases are not intended to serve as endorsements, sources of primary data, or illustrations of effective or ineffective management.

agencies' attempts to replicate the effort could potentially crowd the market, pose competitive risks, or erode In-Q-Tel's brand equity. As a result, the board had asked Louie to consider whether it might be time to expand In-Q-Tel's "limited partner" base to include other government agencies.

THE INFORMATION GAP AND THE VOLUME PROBLEM

The thinking behind In-Q-Tel derived from growing concerns on the part of intelligence community leadership that the CIA was getting cut out of the latest and most advanced technologies at a time when new intelligence priorities required it to improve its information infrastructure. In 1997, CIA director George Tenet recognized that the world order had shifted since the fall of the Berlin Wall. In a post–Cold War era where the United States remained the sole international superpower, America's new foes were nonstate actors who had learned to mobilize elements of American civilian infrastructure—like airplanes, cell phones, and the Internet—as strategic planning tools and offensive weapons. At the same time, with Internet use and wireless telephony proliferating at triple-digit growth rates, the immense quantity of available digital information simply overwhelmed the data management abilities of domestic intelligence agencies. Some intelligence community leaders characterized this information management challenge as the "volume problem."

In addition to the volume problem, the CIA suffered from an "information gap." Director Tenet and the head of the CIA's Directorate of Science and Technology, Dr. Ruth David, looked for the root cause of the volume problem and discovered yet another sea change: from the start of the Cold War through the beginning of the 1990s, the U.S. government had led the nation's investment in science, technology, and innovation, but recently the tables had turned. In the late 1990s, the venture capital asset class had risen to an all-time peak of popularity, fed by its extraordinarily high returns. Average fund size had grown by an order of magnitude, and hundreds of new players were rushing into the industry, supported by thousands of institutional investors eagerly seeking supernormal returns. Private industry now considerably outpaced the intelligence community—and the government as a whole—in innovation and technology spending. The explosive growth of the civilian Internet with the arrival of the World Wide Web brought two major shifts in the incentives facing innovators. First, the minds that would once have rushed to the doors of Sandia, Los Alamos, Livermore, and Oak Ridge national laboratories had been lured by the economic promise of Silicon Valley to pursue start-ups that focused largely on the consumer sector. Second, the small companies that once might have shared their cutting-edge technologies with the government despite stringent compliance terms and intellectual property controls now enjoyed an era of easy venture money with none of the encumbrances associated with doing business with the government. As a result, few small companies took the time to address the needs of the government sector, even though the defense and intelligence communities provided huge opportunities for qualified providers of information technologies.

SHORTCOMINGS OF EXISTING FEDERAL PROGRAMS

Although many federal programs to fund innovation and technology development had emerged during the latter half of the twentieth century, each of them put the intelligence community at a competitive disadvantage to the enormously successful private venture capital industry.

Small Business Innovation Research

In 1982, Congress passed the Small Business Innovation Development Act, creating Small Business Innovation Research (SBIR) set-asides for small companies competing for government contracts. First-round SBIR awards provided up to $100,000 so that small businesses could explore the feasibility of new technologies or innovations, and some companies qualified for additional awards of up to $750,000 to explore the commercialization potential of their technologies. But SBIR awards came with restrictions. To qualify for these set-asides, a company had to be for-profit, American-owned, independently operated, and composed of fewer than 500 employees. Companies applying for SBIR grants could submit proposals only for topics defined by any of the eleven government agencies that participated in the SBIR program, and only in response to published solicitations for bids; companies seeking funding for projects they initiated on their own were not eligible. In addition, only companies evaluating new technologies were eligible for SBIR assistance; existing products or innovations that had already been patented did not qualify for funding. The cumbersome SBIR application and approval process and the exclusion of products already under development deterred many of the technology companies that were producing software of interest to the intelligence community hoped to access. Many of the awards went to "SBIR mills" that had mastered the application process but did few commercialization activities.[1]

Advanced Technology Program

In 1988 the Omnibus Trade and Competitiveness Act established the Advanced Technology Program (ATP) under the Department of Commerce. Unlike SBIR, the ATP permitted private industry as a group to define the project space for "innovative technologies that promised significant commercial payoffs and widespread benefits for the nation."[2] ATP also broadened the scope of eligible participants, inviting "companies of all sizes, universities and non-profits" to participate in open, peer-reviewed competitions, although, like SBIR, ATP accepted proposals only in response to specific, published solicitations. Despite serving a broader franchise than SBIR, the ATP came with equally restrictive caveats, including rules that required companies to contribute to the costs of developing new technologies and the stipulation that ATP would not fund product development. Under ATP rules, private industry was responsible for all of the costs of commercialization, including product development, production, marketing, sales, and distribution.[3] Moreover, the program's focus on precommercial research was often self-defeating: young companies that rapidly moved from research to production were often scrutinized—and sometimes punished—by ATP program officials.[4]

DARPA

In 1958, the U.S. government created the Defense Advanced Research Projects Agency (DARPA), which had funded numerous highly successful space science and defense technology projects, including the computer network (ARPANET) that formed the

1. Josh Lerner, "The Government as Venture Capitalist: The Long-Run Effects of the SBIR Program," *Journal of Business* 72 (July 1999): 285–318.

2. Source is the NIST/ATP Web site, http://atp.nist.gov/atp/overview.htm.

3. *Ibid.*

4. Paul Gompers and Josh Lerner, *Capital Formation and Investment in Venture Markets: Implications for the Advanced Technology Program,* Report GCR-99-784, Advanced Technology Program, National Institutes of Standards and Technology, U.S. Department of Commerce, 1999.

foundation for the World Wide Web. But despite DARPA's successes, it was a project-based organization that moved deliberately and through a series of focused steps. DARPA planners made their best educated guesses at future military requirements—projects with long development cycles—and they looked exclusively at cutting-edge technologies to meet these requirements. Typical DARPA awards were in the neighborhood of one million to several million dollars. Unlike the "public venture" monies offered by SBIR and ATP, DARPA focused its investments exclusively on defense applications, not commercial ones, and exclusively toward new, leading-edge solutions rather than "best of breed" technologies or successful commercial endeavors likely to continue to capture market share with a dependable product.[5]

FFRDCs

Federally Funded Research and Development Centers (FFRDC) were set up to meet the defense needs of World War II. These programs were privately administered by universities and other non-profit institutions in cooperation with industrial firms. The FFRDC model provided incentives for private companies to participate in the development of new technologies by prohibiting the thirty-six centers from competing with private industry, limiting the possibility of the commercial diffusion of products developed under FFRDC programs. In addition, the close ties between FFRDCs and the elaborate federal bureaucracies governing their operations prevented them from moving quickly in response to new markets or product opportunities.

One important subset of FFRDCs was America's national laboratories. These well-funded programs in support of "pure research science" were fertile ground for the creation of groundbreaking technologies. But the advantages that the national labs offered in terms of scientific horsepower were offset by a near-total lack of commercialization support for the developers of new technologies.[6] Moreover, the financial opportunities of the dot-com and technology sectors drew the best and brightest away from the national laboratories and into Silicon Valley start-ups.

Challenges of Regulatory Compliance

Many smaller companies were deterred by the costs of compliance with the Federal Acquisition Regulations (FAR), the rules of government contracting. The FAR stipulated that federal contractors needed to maintain certain accounting and management systems to comply with federal oversight contracts, that the government was not allowed to take an equity stake in a private company, and that agencies seeking to fund contractors had to select firms that placed a heavy emphasis on identifying and articulating the government's needs—which could be a Sisyphian task given a slow-moving government bureaucracy and a fast-moving technology market.[7] As a result, lengthy procurements in accordance with the FAR often led to government assimilation of obsolete technologies.

Timing and "Year Money"

There was also the matter of fiscal timing. New entrepreneurs who had never done business with the government were unaccustomed to government funding processes,

---

5. Paraphrased from *Accelerating the Acquisition and Implementation of New Technologies for Intelligence: The Report of the Independent Panel on the Central Intelligence Agency In-Q-Tel Venture.* Business Executives for National Security, June 2001.

6. *Ibid.*

7. See S. Sorrett, S. Campos, and L. Campos, "Closing the Technology Gap: Bringing Technology from Outside the Government In," *The Procurement Lawyer* (Winter 2003), Exhibit 27.1.

which often depended on the timing of Congressional appropriations. The lengthy process of winning a government contract was an enormous opportunity cost in the form of time that an entrepreneur might otherwise have devoted to building an innovative technology. A further complicating factor was the fact that government contracts often required small commercial companies to develop technologies and products before a government requirement was ever written or published.

Turning a new technology into a successful company was usually multiyear process that often resulted in several years of unprofitable or money-losing performance before the new enterprise reached positive cash flow—losses that might have raised a red flag before the sharp eyes of budget-conscious agency heads. In the absence of "plus ups" (additional funds) during a fiscal year, government funding was on a single-year basis and new applications and awards would be required if further funding was desired in subsequent fiscal years. These added uncertainties created barriers to entry to the government market for capital-intensive early stage companies working in the fast-moving technology space.

EARLY BUSINESS MODEL

George Tenet and Dr. Ruth David recognized that the CIA was analogous to an information management enterprise staffed by knowledge workers. To succeed in its effort to protect the nation against new threats, the CIA would need to gain access to the most promising innovations in the information technology space. "The CIA needs to swim in the Valley," Tenet declared. The CIA wanted to make sure that it would know when new applications and technologies were developed, and equally important, the CIA wanted to manage the cost of its technology infrastructure and to make sure that newly acquired infrastructure did not become immediately obsolete. The cost of creating and maintaining one-off, customized applications far outstripped the cost of ownership of commercial, off-the-shelf (COTS) software. Not only were commercial software packages cheaper to purchase, but COTS software also tended to be updated more rapidly in response to the competitive marketplace.

Tenet commissioned Lockheed Martin CEO Norm Augustine to create a private, not-for-profit corporation to spend CIA money to facilitate the transfer of new technologies into the agency, particularly technologies in the areas of information management and Internet security. Augustine put together an all-star board of trustees (see Exhibit 27.1). Joanne Isham, who was the CIA's associate director of science and technology, recalled that the board helped the In-Q-Tel team overcome resistance within the agency to the fledgling concept:

> We believed that the formation of the board was critical to making the whole thing work. People in the agency didn't take us seriously until we threw out some of the names of the people we were hoping to get on the board. Buzzy Krongard [executive director of the CIA], who had been the chairman of Alex. Brown in Baltimore prior to joining the agency, knew many of these people and was instrumental in getting us started.

Jeffrey Smith, who served as the CIA's general counsel in 1995 and 1996 and had been retained as In-Q-Tel's outside counsel, added:

> Another big player was Michael Crow, who was at the time executive vice provost at Columbia at the time. He was picked because of his academic reputation, both for having done a wonderful job of taking technology at Columbia and spinning it out profitably and also from his work doing federally-funded research at universities. We brought Michael on and made him the acting president.

EXHIBIT 27.1

IN-Q-TEL BOARD OF DIRECTORS (APRIL 2003)

Lee Ault
  (chairman of the board) Former chairman and CEO of Telecredit, Inc.

Norman Augustine	Former chairman and CEO of Lockheed Martin, Inc.
John Seely Brown	Former director, Xerox PARC
Howard Cox	General partner, Greylock; chairman, National Venture Capital Association
Michael Crow	President, Arizona State University
Stephen Friedman	Senior principal, Marsh & McLennan Capital; former chairman, Goldman Sachs
Anita Jones	Professor, University of Virginia; former director of Defense Research and Engineering, U.S. Department of Defense
Paul Kaminski	President and CEO of Technovation, Inc; senior partner in Global Technology Partners; former undersecretary of defense for acquisition and technology
Jeong Kim	Former group president, Lucent Optical Networking; founder, Yurie Systems
John McMahon	Former deputy director of central intelligence; former president and CEO of Lockheed Missiles and Space Co.
William Perry	Former secretary of defense

Source: Compiled from In-Q-Tel documents and Business Executives for National Security, *Accelerating the Acquisition and Implementation of New Technologies for Intelligence: The Report of the Independent Panel on the Central Intelligence Agency In-Q-Tel Venture* (June 2001).

In February 1998, project Peleus came to life. The name would later be changed to In-Q-It, and finally to In-Q-Tel, inspired by the fictitious Q-Branch engineering outfit in Ian Fleming's James Bond stories. In the fall of 1999, the board chose as its CEO video gaming maven Gilman Louie, who had brought Tetris to the United States and worked for many years on the West Coast building software companies. Smith explained, "Gilman helped us look like a venture capital firm." But the question remained: how would the CIA get into private technology deals?

Key Inflection Points

When In-Q-Tel was first incorporated, the firm set out to be an integrator of commercial technologies, focusing its efforts mostly on the identification of promising products and early stage companies. In mid-1999, the company reoriented itself to become an incubator or "accelerator" for early stage companies, taking an active role in the development of solutions in cooperation with entrepreneurs. On September 30, 1999, the news broke with a front-page story in *The New York Times* and an editorial in *The Washington Post* that characterized the company as a venture capital fund. Business plans from eager entrepreneurs flooded into In-Q-Tel's Northern Virginia offices, and the firm found its final form. In-Q-Tel formalized an operations plan that included multiple modes of investment drawn from the private-sector VC world, including incubator funds, venture capital investments, strategic guidance to help companies to create products of import to the CIA, consulting services to portfolio companies, prototype laboratories, and a "think tank" component to assess the implications of new technologies and fast-moving trends.

From the federal government's point of view, using taxpayer money to make equity investments in private companies presented a completely new way of doing business. Previously, most of the intelligence community's technology requirements had been met internally or through a competitive bidding process that was often dominated by large systems integration companies. The In-Q-Tel Board worked to position In-Q-Tel's evolution into a strategic venture capital model as a way for the CIA to share risk with industry and with financial players. Louie explained:

> Basically, this model lets the agency "taste before they buy" and use other people's money to help make the goods. In our model, there wasn't enough money to solve all of the agency's problems under a direct procurement approach. $40 million wasn't going to get you that far. The strategy was to leverage the outside corporate strategic and conventional venture funds by joining up in a traditional syndicate model.
>
> As a result, the CIA didn't have to pick a single winner or loser. Now they could bet on three or four companies in a given product space without having to go through the process of a single procurement, which was good because it was very hard to pick winners in new technologies, and the cycle times were very short, particularly in the IT space.
>
> We bet in five to six spaces, twenty to twenty-five times per year. The best companies will rise to the top, and we can quickly vet out the ones that aren't so good, because the ones that aren't as good aren't going to get financial support. Even if we choose wrong, we will know what our competition is, so the agency will be able to make procurement decisions with better information.

Smith added:

> From the beginning, we had intended to invest in new and innovative companies and we had intended to use the capital markets and the venture industry as a way of getting into the deal flow, identifying technologies and taking equity positions. But one of the major legal questions was: could the government give appropriated money to a company knowing this company would then invest it in start-up companies? We got over that hurdle, although there were skeptics for some time.
>
> Beyond the legal issues, we had some resistance on Capitol Hill. The House and Senate Intelligence Committees supported In-Q-Tel, but there was a great deal of opposition from the appropriations committees, particularly the House Appropriations Committee. They were concerned about a "take the money and run" scenario, wherein In-Q-Tel would hit a home run and develop the next Microsoft, leaving the CIA with an equity stake worth a vast amount of money. Appropriators feared In-Q-Tel would pocket the money, so it wouldn't go to the benefit of the government, or worse, that the money would be used to fund secret CIA operations that Congress hadn't approved. It took us eighteen months to get past that issue.

The new model generated some concerns on the part of other organizations, including the intelligence community's traditional vendors—contractors and systems integrators—who feared In-Q-Tel might compete with their contracting relationships. Smith explained:

> We were contacted by an organization called the Professional Services Council, a trade association that represents a lot of the big systems integrators. Historically, the systems integrators have been opposed to FFRDCs because they believe the government was giving money to FFRDCs without competition. The Professional Services Council first heard about In-Q-Tel when they encountered an outdated document authored during the original planning stages that described the concept as an FFRDC. They went ballistic. We had to undertake a major effort in 1999 to persuade the systems integrators and contractors that not only was In-Q-Tel not an FFRDC, but that the firm could establish mutually beneficial partnerships with them.

Resistance to In-Q-Tel further diminished in September 2001 when hijackers armed with box cutters turned airplanes into highly efficient and destructive missiles. Even in the first hours that followed the attacks, journalists covering the tragedy questioned how the national intelligence infrastructure could have allowed such a thing to happen. An ensuing congressional inquiry suggested that the U.S. intelligence community had failed: various agencies had already collected data that potentially might have prevented the terrorist attacks, but due to the precise "volume problem" George Tenet had identified back in 1997, the U.S. government had failed to synthesize these data sources into actionable knowledge. American Airlines Flight 77 tore an ugly black gash in the side of the Pentagon, a scar that was clearly visible from In-Q-Tel headquarters, one mile upriver. Some In-Q-Tel employees witnessed the attack from their offices. Every day until reconstruction efforts ended, that vista reminded In-Q-Tel's employees of the unique set of opportunities and responsibilities associated with making investments in private companies to support national security. Whereas opportunity drove the first wave of business plans that flooded In-Q-Tel after the *New York Times* article in 1999, patriotism propelled the second wave of business plans that came two years later, after the terrorist attacks.

Value Proposition and Success Factors

The CIA had chartered In-Q-Tel to invest in commercially viable enterprises for a number of reasons. First, products targeted for the commercial market tended to be updated more often and to cost less than one-off, customized applications. Second, the CIA wanted to make sure that the companies producing the software and technologies it adopted would stay in business; it wouldn't help national security if a company that produced a critical piece of CIA infrastructure shut its doors. Third, In-Q-Tel hoped to earn a return on some of its investments. Although financial yield took a back seat to technology assimilation by the agency, an operations plan written in 1999 projected that the firm would receive a small portion of its funding from successful exits from its investments. This would further reduce the financial burden on the CIA and ensure that the proceeds from successes would help to fund other innovations of potential value to the intelligence community.

In-Q-Tel had performed well despite the dramatic downturn in the venture capital industry since the Internet bubble burst by creating value for multiple stakeholders. Entrepreneurs wanted In-Q-Tel to invest in their companies for several reasons. When In-Q-Tel was interested in a company, it signaled technical excellence to other VC firms, improving overall funding prospects. Moreover, In-Q-Tel's technology laboratory in Arlington, Virginia, provided an early beta-test environment to companies that produced technologies within its investment areas. Perhaps most importantly, In-Q-Tel gave young companies access to the intelligence community as a vertical market, reducing encumbrances typically associated with taking funding from, or doing business with, the federal government.

Conventional venture firms liked co-investing as syndicate partners with In-Q-Tel because of the firm's comprehensive due diligence practices. Like conventional venture funds, In-Q-Tel kept its venture team lean, staffing its Silicon Valley offices with about ten people who sourced candidate companies and executed the financial side of In-Q-Tel's investments. But unlike conventional funds, twenty-three technology professionals and consultants worked at In-Q-Tel's Northern Virginia offices, evaluating the technical integrity and potential compatibility of prospective firms' products for the CIA. Most of the technology team members had more than fifteen years' experience and many had come from the nation's top technology firms.

FIRM STRUCTURE AND OPERATIONS

In-Q-Tel was established as an evolving blend of corporate strategic venture capital, business, nonprofit, and government R&D models. To achieve its mission of identifying and delivering new technologies to the CIA and intelligence community, In-Q-Tel borrowed key elements from each model that enabled it to link the intelligence community to innovation in the commercial market, and bridge the potential disconnect between the government contractor and the venture capital worlds. As a private, independent, nonprofit corporation, In-Q-Tel could take equity positions in private companies. At the same time, In-Q-Tel was a government contractor, operating within the laws and regulations affecting the government contractors and the terms of its contract with the Agency. Using negotiated versions of the standard FAR patent and data-rights clauses, In-Q-Tel and the CIA developed a set of provisions that allowed companies to pursue commercial markets for their products while at the same time seeking favorable deals for the government. To support its dual mission, In-Q-Tel developed a bicoastal operation comprising more than forty full-time employees led by CEO Gilman Louie, with Mike Griffin serving as president and chief operating officer. Executive biographies are provided in Exhibit 27.2.

VENTURE TEAM

The firm's Menlo Park, California–based Venture Team consisted of about ten employees, including support staff, closely mirroring the model of a traditional VC or private equity group, where a small number of general partners and associates scouted deals, performed due diligence, prepared term sheets, and shepherded portfolio companies by sitting on their boards of directors. Viewed as a conventional venture capital organization, In-Q-Tel's Venture Team had three general partners: CEO Gilman Louie, managing partner/executive vice president Stephen Mendel, and partner Eric Kaufman. In addition, portfolio manager Joseph Addiego supported In-Q-Tel's portfolio companies in way similar to Battery Ventures' "venture partners"—in-house operating executives who provided professional services to that firm's portfolio companies. Four associates supported In-Q-Tel's general and venture partners.

EXHIBIT 27.2

IN-Q-TEL EXECUTIVE BIOGRAPHIES (APRIL 2003)

Gilman Louie, Chief Executive Officer

Gilman Louie, In-Q-Tel's chief executive officer, brings nearly two decades of diverse experience in strategic business development and product design. His career in the interactive entertainment industry included a number of pioneering moves, with successes such as the Falcon, an F-16 flight simulator, and Tetris, which he brought over from the Soviet Union. Most recently, Louie served as Hasbro Interactive's chief creative officer and general manager of the Games.com group.

Prior to joining Hasbro, Louie served as chief executive at a number of corporations, including Nexa Corporation, Sphere, Inc., Spectrum HoloByte, Inc., and MicroProse, Inc., which was sold to Hasbro in 1998. Louie has served on the board of directors of several corporations and groups, including Wizards of the Coast, Total Entertainment Network, Direct Language, and FASA Interactive. He is currently on the board of NewSchools.org, a nonprofit venture fund.

Louie completed the Advanced Management Program/International Senior Management Program at Harvard Business School, and he received his B.S. in business administration from San Francisco State University.

Michael Griffin, President/Chief Operating Officer

Griffin brings to In-Q-Tel nearly thirty years of experience in information and space technology and management of mission-driven organizations. He has supervised numerous large defense and aerospace programs of national significance ranging from leading NASA teams during the redesign of the International Space Station to pioneering research and development of complex weapons systems.

Most recently Griffin worked in private practice as an engineering and management consultant in the aerospace and defense industry. Prior to this, Griffin was executive vice president and chief executive officer of the Magellan Systems Division of Orbital Sciences Corporation. Before joining Orbital, he was senior vice president of Space Industries International and general manager of the Space Industries Division in Houston. Griffin previously served as both the chief engineer and the associate administrator for exploration at NASA, and at the Pentagon he served as the deputy for technology of the Strategic Defense Initiative Organization. He has also worked at the Johns Hopkins Applied Physics Laboratory, the Jet Propulsion Laboratory, and Computer Science Corporation.

Griffin has served as an adjunct professor at the University of Maryland, Johns Hopkins University, and George Washington University. He is the lead author of over two dozen technical papers, as well as the textbook *Space Vehicle Design,* and he is a registered professional engineer in Maryland and California. Griffin obtained his B.A. in physics from Johns Hopkins University, which he attended as the winner of a Maryland Senatorial Scholarship. He holds master's degrees in aerospace science from Catholic University, electrical engineering from the University of Southern California, applied physics from Johns Hopkins, civil engineering from George Washington University, and business administration from Loyola College of Maryland. He received his Ph.D. in aerospace engineering from the University of Maryland.

(Continues)

Technology Team

In-Q-Tel's Technology Team, led by senior vice president Joy Dorman, a thirty-year IT veteran, played a significant role in the successful adoption of the In-Q-Tel Model. From its offices in Arlington, the team took on the critical role of liaison between the agency and the venture capital community. They worked closely with agency staff in identifying capabilities, gaps, and needs and then transformed those needs into a technology vision for the agency's future. Based on that vision, the team collaborated with the West Coast venture team in devising an overall investment thesis for the company. The Technology Team had a wealth of experience with the average team member possessing fifteen to

EXHIBIT 27.2 (CONTINUED)

IN-Q-TEL EXECUTIVE BIOGRAPHIES (APRIL 2003)

Stephen Mendel, Managing Partner/Executive Vice President

As executive vice president of In-Q-Tel, Stephen Mendel is an integral member of the senior leadership of the company, working to implement the organization's strategic vision and refine the In-Q-Tel model. As managing partner of In-Q-Tel's Venture Group, Mendel directs the company's venture capital and investment strategy and manages In-Q-Tel's Menlo Park office.

Prior to joining In-Q-Tel, Mendel served in a wide variety of leadership roles in large public organizations and private technology start-ups. Stephen has served as vice chairman of Knowledge Revolution, CEO and president of AXS, CEO and president of Ithaca Software, executive vice president of Maxwell Communication Corporation-West, executive vice president of Spectrum-Holobyte, Inc. and executive vice president of MDL Information Systems. He has served as a member of the board of directors of AXS, Ithaca Software, Spectrum-Holobyte, Molecular Design, Opt4 Derivatives, Simmedia, Verso, Futurize Now, Knowledge Revolution, Intl.com, MarketScience, and Site Technologies.

Mendel's management style and business acumen have been recognized regionally and nationally. Under his leadership, Ithaca Software was recognized by *Inc.* magazine as one of the fastest growing private companies in America. He has been nominated to receive an Ernst & Young Northern California Entrepreneur of the Year Award, and he has spoken at numerous national and international conferences on topics ranging from entrepreneurship to exit strategies.

Mendel began his career as a lawyer at Feldman Waldman and Kline, where he represented and counseled business clients in corporate, securities, intellectual property, and commercial matters. He received his juris doctor with highest honors from Hofstra University and his B.A. degree in philosophy from the University of Rochester.

Source: In-Q-Tel Web site, http://www.in-q-tel.org.

twenty years' experience in both technical and executive roles, including significant experience as founders of technology start-ups. This experience provided the team with the expertise needed to evaluate the relevance and value of potential portfolio company technologies for agency needs. The team's reputation for providing rigorous, technical due diligence in support of In-Q-Tel investments was one of In-Q-Tel's key contributions to its relationships with the venture capital community.

In-Q-Tel Interface Center (QIC)

In 1999, Congress believed that In-Q-Tel's biggest obstacle would not be to find or invest in technologies, but to transfer In-Q-Tel's technologies to agency users. Dr. Ruth David also recognized the cultural challenges of working with the CIA, so she helped shape an organization within the agency that would be committed to working exclusively with In-Q-Tel: the In-Q-Tel Interface Center (QIC). The QIC oversaw In-Q-Tel's efforts and provided the junction point between In-Q-Tel's unclassified work and the classified work performed by the agency.

The QIC provided In-Q-Tel with an annual list of unclassified technology needs, or Problem Set, that outlined the investment spaces in which the firm would operate. The Problem Set also provided a cultural convergence point for In-Q-Tel employees irrespective of geographic locations and professional skill sets. Both the Venture and Tech Teams collaborated with the QIC to evaluate potential investments, and the QIC also played a critical role in transferring In-Q-Tel solutions to agency customers after investment.

Investment Thesis

The QIC collected information technology requirements across all of the agency's directorates and carefully abstracted, condensed, and translated them into target investment areas general enough to prevent unauthorized parties from "reverse engineering" the strategic intent of the CIA, but specific enough to ensure that In-Q-Tel would be able to make investments that served the agency's goals.

The original Problem Set defined by the QIC in 1999 contained four investment areas: information security, Internet, knowledge generation, and distributed architectures. These were subdivided and further refined for dissemination to In-Q-Tel. For example, the Internet investment area of the Problem Set targeted technologies to enable "open Internet use," "stealth use," "collaboration," "online, multimedia publishing," and "communications." Only technology requirements with commercial analogues were included in the Problem Set. Thus, while the CIA required technologies to prevent the tracing of agency traffic and to conceal the origins of data queries across the Internet, the QIC also determined that private business wanted to protect consumer privacy through anonymity in browsing and enable invisible business-to-business transactions.

The Problem Set evolved between 1999 and 2001 to include five areas, but it had remained stable since 2001. The current Problem Set consisted of geospatial technology, distributed data collection, security and privacy, knowledge management, and search and discovery. (The current problem set is presented as Exhibit 27.3.) Rather than changing in response to current events, such as the 2003 war in Iraq, the Problem Set was designed to provide In-Q-Tel with a clear investment framework. Occasionally, the venture team encountered new companies that had generated a great deal

---

EXHIBIT 27.3

CURRENT IN-Q-TEL PROBLEM SET (APRIL 2003)

Problem Set Area	Description
Distributed Data Collection	Focus on technologies that enable efficient and transparent management of devices ranging from health monitors to power grids to security systems (sensor networks that provide rapid insights and alerts via machine-to-machine communication).
Geospatial Technology	Focus on fully integrated analytic environments for geospatial and location information and services (fusing multiple data sources—maps, imagery, databases, location information and text—into a coherent picture).
Knowledge Management	Technologies that derive knowledge or insight from data repositories and streams through organization, retrieval, and presentation of relevant information.
Search and Discovery	Efficient search/retrieval of relevant content; mining areas of the Web inaccessible to ordinary search engines; quick assessments of content in multiple languages; visualization mechanisms/user interfaces.
Security and Privacy	Focus on mobile knowledge worker, online privacy of Internet users, adaptive information threat detection.

Source: In-Q-Tel Web site, http://www.in-q-tel.org.

of "buzz" with a technology that fell outside the Problem Set. An In-Q-Tel VP explained that profit motives did not skew investment choices in these instances:

> The three-legged stool of investment requirements provides a balanced approach to evaluating deals. We do, sometimes, make "predictive" investments—we say to our client, "This is something that we think the agency is going to need in a couple of years, based on what we know of the Problem Set."

An In-Q-Tel manager added:

> We make our own decisions, but the CIA plays a continuous advisory role in oversight of our portfolio choices. It would be foolish to ignore the interests of our investor and our primary customer.

Raising Investment Capital

When In-Q-Tel was founded, the CIA was designated as the exclusive provider of investment capital to the organization and every year since inception, In-Q-Tel had received an annual contract for between $30 million and $37 million from the CIA as a line item in the Directorate of Science and Technology budget. A 2001 study on In-Q-Tel commissioned by Congress recommended that the firm refrain from soliciting investment capital from other federal agencies or limited partners until it had demonstrated maturity and success in its CIA mission. Joanne Isham explained the rationale for controlling the size of In-Q-Tel's "limited partner" base:

> Once In-Q-Tel started getting traction, we began to get some pressure to open the firm up to other intelligence community agencies. I felt In-Q-Tel needed to build some credibility on its own before we expanded to include other agencies or to encompass other models. I wasn't sure that other agencies would appreciate how much political and intellectual capital the CIA and the director of central intelligence (DCI) had invested in In-Q-Tel. As a result, I kept In-Q-Tel internal to the CIA for the first few years.
>
> Moreover, at the five-year mark, we were going to have to determine whether In-Q-Tel was a good idea or a bad idea. If we had multiple agencies involved, I was afraid that we might fragment our support base when it came time to evaluate the project. But I always wanted In-Q-Tel to serve the broader intelligence community. I thought, "Why would you want to create competition by starting another firm?"

When Isham moved over to National Imagery and Mapping Agency (NIMA), which shared many information processing challenges with the CIA, she made the first move to expand In-Q-Tel's funding base.

> When I was selected as deputy director of NIMA, I knew I could be a trusted customer. Together with the CIA, we went to the DCI for approval to expand the model to include NIMA. We all felt this would be the process for other agencies going forward, too.

In mid-2002, In-Q-Tel initiated a pilot program whereby it received a small amount of money from the NIMA budget, and this trial was still ongoing. In-Q-Tel did not receive funding from any other sources, public or private, nor did the firm tap any external funding pools or side-by-side investment funds to supply capital for cash-intensive deals.

Deal Sourcing

In-Q-Tel built a network of more than 150 venture capital firms in order to gain access to promising technologies. In addition, the firm maintained affiliations with the nation's national laboratories and was planning to begin a university outreach program to explore the possibility of seeding new start-ups. Gilman Louie relied on his existing relationships with Silicon Valley venture capitalists to guide his investment decisions, but the firm received three-quarters of its new proposals through its Web site. Many of In-Q-Tel's portfolio companies heard about the firm through their contacts within government agencies and large government contractors. Some entrepreneurs sent their business plans to the company Web site, while others relied on contacts to schedule presentations in person.

Deal Structure

In-Q-Tel made equity and equity-like investments in privately-held public companies just like conventional venture capital firms. Although the media typically characterized In-Q-Tel as a venture fund, the firm employed diverse modes of investment in and involvement with its portfolio companies. A critical differentiator from venture funds was In-Q-Tel's use of strategic investments in existing companies—some of which were already public—either by funding product development for a specific technology, or through payments to larger companies for integration work. As an *incubator,* In-Q-Tel invested time and money to help entrepreneurs build out business plans and refine technology concepts. As a *venture capitalist,* In-Q-Tel employed equity investments, or equitylike vehicles (often warrants) to support the CIA's needs. Sometimes, In-Q-Tel operated as a *think tank,* aggregating subject matter expertise to help firms exploit fast-moving trends. Other times, In-Q-Tel operated as a *consulting firm,* helping organizations to identify undervalued assets and to create markets around products and services. (Exhibit 27.4 presents summary information describing twenty of In-Q-Tel's equity investments, and Exhibit 27.5 presents summary information concerning eight of In-Q-Tel's nonequity investments.)

In-Q-Tel occasionally made investments in public companies. For example, in March 2003, In-Q-Tel invested $1.53 million in a strategic product development partnership with Convera (NASDAQ: CNVR), a Vienna, Virginia–based search and discovery software provider, to fund enhancements of Convera's existing products to support specific requirements of the intelligence community. Because Convera was a public company, a company press release described the amount and purpose of In-Q-Tel's investment, as well as the structure of the deal, which took the form of two-year warrants to purchase 137,000 shares of Convera's common stock. The structure of most In-Q-Tel investments was usually not disclosed.

Irrespective of structure or mode, all In-Q-Tel deals had one feature in common: a work plan that linked the disbursement of investment monies to a portfolio company with that portfolio company's performance against mutually agreed on development goals. An In-Q-Tel venture associate noted:

> The development component is the focal effort of our deals. We will structure deals as development agreements with warrants attached to performance milestones. Essentially, with the achievement of each milestone, there is a warrant provision attached—effectively a call option for us.

In-Q-Tel usually took observer seats on the boards of its portfolio companies, although In-Q-Tel had taken full board seats at some companies. Typical investment size ranged

EXHIBIT 27.4

PARTIAL LISTING OF EQUITY INVESTMENTS (APRIL 2003)

Company	Brief Description	Problem Set Area
ArcSight	Enterprise Security Software	Security and Privacy
Attensity	Text Extraction Tools	Knowledge Management
Browse3D	3D Visualizaton Interface	Knowledge Management
Candera	Enterprise Storage Management	Security and Privacy
Decru	Storage Network Data Security	Security and Privacy
Graviton	Wireless Microsensor Networks	Distributed Data Collection
Intelliseek	Enterprise Intelligence	Search and Discovery
Keyhole	Geospatial Visualization	Geospatial Information Systems
Language Weaver	Machine Translation	Knowledge Management
MetaCarta	Geospatial Information Software	Geospatial Information Systems
Mohomine	Unstructured Data Analysis	Knowledge Management
NovoDynamics	Information Retrieval and Image Processing	Knowledge Management
Qynergy	Long Lasting Power Solutions	Energy Sources
Safeweb	Web-based Security/Privacy	Security and Privacy
SRD/Nora	Relationship Awareness	Knowledge Management
Stratify	Unstructured Data Analysis	Knowledge Management
Tacit	Expertise Automation	Knowledge Management
Traction Software	Enterprise Collaboration Tools	Knowledge Management
VitalContact	Real-Time Event Processing	Knowledge Management
Zaplet	Enterprise Collaboration Tools	Knowledge Management

Sources: Compiled from VentureSource database, In-Q-Tel documents, and media reports.

EXHIBIT 27.5

PARTIAL LISTING OF IN-Q-TEL'S NON-EQUITY INVESTMENTS (APRIL 2003)

Company	Brief Description	Problem Set Area
Convera	Enterprise Search/Retrieval	Search and Discovery
Divine/Northern Light	Search Solutions	Search and Discovery
Inktomi	Search Solutions	Search and Discovery
MediaSnap	Document Security Software	Security and Privacy
Open GIS Consortium	Standards body for GIS	Geospatial Information Systems
SAIC	Latent Semantic Imaging Project	Knowledge Management
SRA International	Speech Pattern Analysis Project	Knowledge Management
TruSecure	Internet Security Services	Security and Privacy

Sources: Compiled from VentureSource database, In-Q-Tel documents, and media reports.

between $250,000 and $3 million, distributed across various different investment rounds and across companies at various stages of development. Gilman Louie explained,

> In-Q-Tel invests in a range of technology solutions—from those poised to immediately deliver existing commercial products to those that will deliver breakthrough capabilities over the longer term.

Most of the time In-Q-Tel invested in syndication with other investment entities including Ford, Motorola, Siemens, Nokia, Oracle, and Sun and venture capital firms including Kleiner, Perkins; Merrill Lynch; Shell Ventures; Softbank; and Greylock. Third-party commercial investment by syndicate partners totaled more than $300 million. Sometimes In-Q-Tel led investment rounds and, rarely, it was the sole equity investor in a round. An In-Q-Tel venture associate noted,

> We have to be mindful about a couple of things because the size of our equity investments tends to be very small. We're sensitive about asking companies to open a full-blown round for us. Often we catch companies towards the tail end of a round, where there's enough equity left for us to make a small investment.

(See Exhibits 27.4 and 27.5 for information on equity and nonequity investments.) Occasionally, In-Q-Tel arranged strategic alliances between its portfolio companies including:

- The matching of Attensity's text extraction and link analysis software with software produced by Systems Research & Development's NORA, which identified "nonobvious relationships" between people, to build an engine that could mine large volumes of digital data for evidence of collusion.

- Envisaging a complete document exploitation system that included NovoDynamics, Mohomine, and Language Weaver. Kofax-Mohomine ingested hard copy documents and managed the workflow; NovoDynamics then performed optical character recognition for severely degraded documents, preparing them for Language Weaver's advanced machine translation.

Strategic alliances allowed the CIA to mix-and-match cutting-edge technologies to address complex information management goals, and strong alliances between similar and complementary portfolio companies also provided a measure of protection against the moribund IPO market. In order to ensure the sustainability of firms providing essential technology for CIA operations, In-Q-Tel could upgrade strategic alliances into outright mergers, or "roll-ups," to produce financially stronger firms, or firms more likely to be acquired or to go public.

Human Resources Factors

The substantial compensation packages available at the height of the dot-com bubble raised the price of skilled technologists and venture capitalists—the two main functional areas for which In-Q-Tel recruited. Thus the board of trustees used commercial market salaries as a baseline for In-Q-Tel's employee compensation program rather than the government pay scale. While the compensation levels were not set to bid personnel away from other companies, neither would compensation constitute a barrier for top talent to accept a position at In-Q-Tel.

In addition to In-Q-Tel's comprehensive compensation program, it also appealed to candidates by offering an opportunity to support national security, to enjoy interaction with cutting-edge technologies and to acquire the cachet of working with an intelligence organization while remaining in the private sector.

In-Q-Tel's compensation consisted of base pay, an annual incentive, and a long-term investment program; all were determined based on relevant market data in appropriate industries. The annual incentive plan (bonus) was based solely on performance. It was designed to focus, motivate, and reward In-Q-Tel employees for the achievement of specific annual goals and outcomes that advanced the firm's success in carrying out its mission for the CIA and the intelligence community.

The employee's annual incentive was tied to performance based on an annual "Performance Score," which rate In-Q-Tel's overall performance, and a scoring of the individual's performance. In-Q-Tel's score was based on the organization's achievements during the relevant fiscal year as determined by the board of trustees and advised by an annual review provided by QIC. Individual scores were recommended by each employee's manager, and approved by senior management.

At the height of the dot-com craze, most firms offered employee stock options (ESOP) but ESOPs were not permitted in a not-for-profit, non-stock corporation. To enable In-Q-Tel to compete in a labor market defined by equity-heavy compensation packages, the company structured an employee investment program (EIP)—a separately chartered LLC—as a co-investment vehicle to participate alongside In-Q-Tel investments. All In-Q-Tel regular employees participated in the EIP and participants could not choose their investments.

The company intended that the many components of the compensation package would align the incentives of In-Q-Tel staff with the long-term goals of the agency and the intelligence community.

In-Q-Tel's original operating plan had envisioned a one-to-three year career path for employees so that the company would be constantly infused by fresh blood and the latest industry knowledge. Jeffrey Smith observed:

> The idea for turnover came from the DARPA model, which had been successful in bringing in the best and the brightest to spend three years working on projects before moving on. It kept new blood coming in. We planned turnover for In-Q-Tel, but we have not had the turnover that we designed. We found that it was important to have stability, particularly at the top. On the technology end of things, however, it's important to have a high turnover, to have people coming out of industry and academia who really are the best and the brightest.

In-Q-Tel had been able to rely on the self-selection of candidates seeking the unique experience and training In-Q-Tel could provide, and the bleak employment picture in the venture capital industry since 2001 only reinforced the firm's value proposition.

RELATIONSHIP WITH PORTFOLIO COMPANIES

In-Q-Tel relied on the personal networks of its venture team to acquire new relationships with portfolio companies and to shepherd these companies through growth and rationalization. But In-Q-Tel's unique position as an interface to federal government and the intelligence community enabled the firm to provide its portfolio companies with marketing insights and strategic guidance to help them negotiate the complicated process of doing business with large, occasionally opaque government agencies, too.

SRD

One of the first companies In-Q-Tel funded was Las Vegas–based SRD, a producer of data analysis software for identifying "nonobvious" relationships. Jeff Jonas, SRD's founder and chief scientist, had written the Non-Obvious Relationship Analysis (NORA) package so casino industry clients could detect and thwart cheaters, but Jonas was interested in trying to sell NORA to the federal government for law enforcement and national security purposes. Jonas heard about In-Q-Tel in 1999 during a briefing he gave to the Critical Infrastructure Office in Washington. Jonas explained how In-Q-Tel's leverage of government relationships for deal flow led to the introduction:

> One of the people I briefed there said, "There's this guy I know who would like to hear about what you do" and they referred us to In-Q-Tel. We didn't submit our business plan through the Internet—we just gave our presentation in person and they were very impressed. We were the third company they funded.

Louie reflected on the early match-up with SRD:

> Jeff was a classic case study. Here was a guy who was running his company out of a checkbook. The question was: how would he grow his business and leverage our model to extend into the federal marketplace? He grew up as we were growing up. He had to suffer through our growth; both sides were learning at the same time.

Jonas emphasized In-Q-Tel's role in providing access to the federal marketplace and to federal technology strategists:

> It was very hard to be a West Coast company that had never done anything in Washington, with no visibility or awareness into sensitive federal organizations. You can't just show up from Vegas and say, "Do you want to buy a watch?" The intriguing part is that you end up being vetted, and you end up being introduced to people and places you don't otherwise get to see on your own.
>
> More than that, Gilman Louie went on the road and talked about his portfolio companies. He was able to get us on the radar screen of some prestigious think tanks like the Markle Foundation's Task Force on National Security in the Information Age, Center for Strategic and International Studies and the Center for Democracy and Technology. When you're in the business of doing what we do with billions and billions of rows of data, you absolutely have to have a proactive stance with regard to civil liberties. If you don't get that sorted out at the beginning, you get wrapped around the axle. By being involved with all of these groups we were sitting at the table contributing to thought leadership. As a result, we feel that we've made a valuable contribution on the privacy front and we're finding that a number of privacy advocates are seeing promise in our approach.
>
> Also, when we figured out how to correlate data that's anonymized for data sharing, within two or three days, In-Q-Tel got us in touch with former general counsels of the CIA, the National Security Agency and other agencies on a phone call strategizing how we could approach the new technology. Similarly, having interactions with In-Q-Tel's technology team gave us

confidence and made us feel that In-Q-Tel was smart. It's important to have a strategic partner that's bright.

Jonas recalled being very pleased that the In-Q-Tel model offered him intellectual property protections, both in a legal sense and also in a more practical sense:

> The technology that was funded by In-Q-Tel became part of a commercial product and not just for intelligence use. We were very concerned about IP implications. We wanted to make sure that our technology would never get "classified" for national security reasons. In-Q-Tel helped to allay our concerns about that.

Endeca

In-Q-Tel was working on a deal with Cambridge, Massachusetts–based Endeca, Inc., which produced software for data mining and search applications. Steve Papa, Endeca's chief executive officer, had approached In-Q-Tel as part of a broader development strategy for growing his company.

> We knew we had to get involved in the federal market. We believed that if we wanted to be a world-class software company in three years, 25 percent of our business was going to have to come from the federal government. We knew we had a product that could help the CIA with its mission, but we needed an intermediary. For Endeca to sell to an early adopter, we needed to understand the business problem of our client as well as our client did so we could show how we could help.
>
> But with the CIA, there was a need for security clearances and the secrecy would have made this impossible. It was impossible for small, innovative technology companies to sell into the agency. In-Q-Tel bridged that gap. The QIC enabled agency clients to become familiar with our technology.

Papa anticipated that working through In-Q-Tel would be somewhat challenging (as a sales intermediary, it would introduce a layer between Endeca and the end-user), but that the additional effort would provide a worthwhile return.

> One of In-Q-Tel's mission mandates is to prevent unclassified vendors and technology companies from divining the ultimate goals of the CIA, so we were concerned about the possibility that, during development, we might get a bug report without any context around it. However, we expect to be adding staff to support the CIA as a client, and In-Q-Tel has discussed helping us get security clearances for those employees working on the project.
>
> The fact is, a small company could have had fifty customers including blue-chip names and it wouldn't matter when it tried to pitch government agencies. Having a government reference client is very important, and the CIA is 10 percent of the market of the intelligence world.

Papa also expressed his sense that the In-Q-Tel model was particularly well suited for the CIA:

> In-Q-Tel's biggest advantage is dealing with the secrecy issue. With the Army, for example, there are fewer obstacles. The Defense Intelligence Agency handles procurement for top-secret Army projects, but for unclassified applications we could approach the client directly. Likewise, in many cases the applications in the CIA will be very different from other agencies' needs.

For example, if I had a satellite-driven application helpful for the National Security Agency [NSA, another intelligence agency], I would try to establish partnership with the large systems integrators that work with the NSA.

CHARTING THE COURSE AHEAD

In December 1999, Louie and In-Q-Tel's Board undertook a comprehensive examination of risks facing the young company. Louie had considered that In-Q-Tel's investments might not result in commercially successful technologies or, alternatively, that the CIA might not effectively assimilate technologies produced by In-Q-Tel's portfolio companies. To counter this risk, In-Q-Tel had focused its energies on proven or "near-proven" companies that conformed both to market intelligence gathered by In-Q-Tel and to the QIC Problem Set. On the organizational front, Louie and the board carefully crafted compensation to minimize the possibility that In-Q-Tel might suffer due to an inability to attract and retain key personnel. In-Q-Tel's founders had anticipated that the cultural inertia at the agency might limit the uptake of technologies into the CIA, and as a result, the requirements-gathering process and the QIC were developed to minimize conflicts and disconnects. And, due to the nature of In-Q-Tel's client and the Intelligence space, the firm undertook extremely stringent security policies to protect its data, physical location, and employees.

In-Q-Tel had considered its greatest financial risks in 1999 to be the possibilities that its portfolio investments might fail, that the government might cut off its funding, or that a government audit might mire the firm's operations in bureaucracy. Of course, nobody had considered the collapse of the dot-economy. When the bubble burst, IPO activity virtually halted, providing no opportunities for In-Q-Tel to exit any of its investments in a public offering. But despite macroeconomic reversals, the firm had performed very well at procuring new technologies for the agency. About half of In-Q-Tel's investments had been in knowledge management applications. Another quarter had gone to fund security and privacy technologies. The remaining areas—search and discovery, distributed data collection, and geospatial information systems—made up the balance of a portfolio of more than forty investments.

While In-Q-Tel was still somewhat short of the profitability goals it set for itself in 1999, the Mohomine transaction had demonstrated that the firm could generate returns from its investments. Moreover, the economy was starting to show signs of recovery. But other agencies were beginning to experiment with In-Q-Tel's model. In fall 2002, the Army put out a bid proposal to form a limited-purpose entity to fund private investment in mobile power devices for troops in the field, and the 2003 defense bill had allotted $25 million for this enterprise, now called OnPoint Technologies. The Office of Force Transformation was looking at its own ways to leverage private investment, and Congress had directed the Navy to study the applicability of venture capital models; the Navy was supposed to report its findings in just a few weeks. In-Q-Tel's five-year charter, which was due to expire in July 2004, provided for other limited partners including other government intelligence agencies and even private investors. Louie felt fairly confident that the CIA would renew In-Q-Tel's charter but he wondered whether the firm should expand its limited partnership base in the meantime to stave off potential competitive threats from other agencies, to drive greater profitability, or to increase the uptake of emerging technologies into the intelligence community.

Each time the expansion question had reared its head, Louie and the board had been forced to choose between diluting In-Q-Tel's personal expertise, organizational mindshare, and staffing bandwidth by accepting new assignments and risking the dilution of In-Q-Tel's brand by multiple competing entities entering its space. What would happen if other federal agencies copied the In-Q-Tel model? Would companies similar to In-Q-Tel erode the value of the firm's due diligence imprimatur? Would other agencies' private capital entities offer entrepreneurs better terms, or worse still, provide entrepreneurs with leverage to create an auction between multiple government strategic investors? Would the CIA continue to provide its annual appropriations to support In-Q-Tel if other alternatives arrived?

Louie had commented on the possibility that other agencies might turn to the In-Q-Tel procurement model:

> A little bit of competition could be useful because we can set up cooperative relationships, but a lot of them, done poorly, could disrupt the reputation of the model. You can imagine that, if Greylock gets four or five government funds calling on the same deal, it would drive them crazy! We are faced with striking that balance of knowing when to say "yes" to other agencies and when to manage expectations. This isn't just financial management in the venture capital sense; this requires a lot of organization and buy-in. Obviously, if we're offered money and we don't take it, the agency offering the money is going to want to do something else with it.

Dr. Ruth David, who in 1998 left the agency to become CEO of Anser, Inc., a not-for-profit research corporation, observed:

> Some agencies are thinking of funneling monies through In-Q-Tel, while others would prefer to establish entities specific to their missions. My view is that the In-Q-Tel model is still maturing—so having competitive models established by other agencies works to the good over the long haul.

Joanne Isham noted:

> The impact of proliferation of the model depends on the new firms' sponsors. Each agency has its own niche and its own network of companies and private funds that they deal with. How the entry of new firms might affect In-Q-Tel would depend on how the sponsoring firms view or treat the model.

Alternatively, expanding the limited partner base created issues of scale and efficiency. Louie noted:

> It's a tradeoff and it's not an easy one. In the past it was a conceptual debate, but now it's real. Other people are saying, "Well, you're successful with $40 million, what will happen if we do it with fifty times that amount?" But venture capital doesn't necessarily scale. Not all of the venture funds in the late 1990s were able to manage that transition.

Dr. Ruth David added:

> Expanding In-Q-Tel's scope to other agencies and other parts of the government makes a lot of sense. In-Q-Tel's deep understanding of the kinds of tools that are needed is certainly extensible to other departments. In addition, In-Q-Tel's portfolio companies are beginning to understand the mission needs of the agency and to develop products that would be useful to other intelligence community clients.
>
> I had originally proposed that In-Q-Tel serve the entire intelligence community, but there was a sense that starting with the CIA was appropriate for

a variety of reasons. When you're trying something totally untested, it's always best to start with a more discrete mission space.

The key issue around expansion will be targeting clients with similar needs, similarities in mission, or commonalities in the kinds of tools they employ. There are many other agencies that have comparable needs for advanced analytic tools, for example. Likewise, many interagency working groups are trying to figure out how to develop and enforce common standards and create common operating environments across agencies. Of course, I wouldn't suggest that In-Q-Tel try to take on every conceivable government mission at this stage.

Jeffrey Smith offered this perspective:

I think the consensus of the board and of the CIA is that we need to balance. We do not want to expand In-Q-Tel itself to such a degree that it can't cope. In other words, we fear that we will get too big, get too bureaucratic and we will be unable to do our jobs. I think that In-Q-Tel will need to stay reasonably small to be adroit.

Would expanding the limited partner base require Louie to hire more staff to address a broader Problem Set? Serving NIMA had required In-Q-Tel to create a separate, parallel process for gathering requirements. Isham noted:

NIMA has a different set of needs, thus we have our own process where we identify the technology roadmap and then flow requirements down to In-Q-Tel. Our Problem Set is very visual in nature and can therefore include In-Q-Tel; it could help us with a broader reach to industry and technologies.

Louie turned away from the window and back to his desktop computer, where he was writing his presentation for In-Q-Tel's board of trustees. Was it time to expand?

28

A Note on Corporate
Venture Capital

Corporations have had an enduring fascination with venture capital investments. Many organizations have seen venture capital as an intriguing alternative way in which to make investments, which offers a flexibility and speed that is very different from the traditional corporate capital budgeting and investment process. These appealing features have led many firms to experiment with corporate venture initiatives. These corporations have often discovered, however, that the implementation of such an effort is considerably more challenging than it appears from the outside!

This note provides a brief introduction to corporate venture investing. First, the historical evolution of these programs is reviewed. The special difficulties that these efforts face are then considered. Finally, we review the systematic evidence about the success of these programs, which suggests that despite the many difficulties they face, these programs have made valuable contributions and enjoyed real successes.

THE HISTORY OF CORPORATE VENTURE CAPITAL[1]

The first corporate venture funds began in the mid-1960s, about two decades after the first formal venture capital funds. The corporate efforts were spurred by the successes of the first organized venture capital funds, which backed such firms as Digital Equipment, Memorex, Raychem, and Scientific Data Systems. Excited by this success, large companies began establishing divisions that emulated venture capitalists. During the late 1960s and early 1970s, more than 25 percent of the *Fortune* 500 firms attempted corporate venture programs.

---

1. This history is based in part on Norman D. Fast, *The Rise and Fall of Corporate New Venture Divisions* (Ann Arbor: UMI Research Press, 1978); Robert E. Gee, "Finding and Commercializing New Businesses," *Research/Technology Management* 37 (January/February 1994): 49–56; and Venture Economics, "Corporate Venture Capital Study," unpublished manuscript, 1986; among other sources.

Professor Josh Lerner prepared this case as the basis for class discussion rather than to illustrate either effective or ineffective handling of an administrative situation.

These efforts generally took two forms, external and internal. At one end of the spectrum, large corporations financed new firms alongside other venture capitalists. In many cases, the corporations simply provided funds for a venture capitalist to invest rather than investing the funds itself. Other firms invested directly in start-ups, giving them a greater ability to tailor their portfolios to their particular needs. At the other extreme, large corporations attempted to tap the entrepreneurial spirit within their organizations. These programs sought to allow entrepreneurs to focus their attention on developing their innovations, while relying on the corporate parents for financial, legal, and marketing support.

In 1973, the market for new public offerings—the primary avenue through which venture capitalists exit successful investments—abruptly declined. Independent venture partnerships began experiencing significantly less attractive returns and encountered severe difficulties in raising new funds. At the same time, corporations began scaling back their own initiatives. The typical corporate venture program begun in the late 1960s was dissolved after only four years.

As was discussed in the first module of the casebook, funds flowing into the venture capital industry and the number of active venture organizations increased dramatically during the late 1970s and early 1980s. Corporations were also once again attracted to the promise of venture investing in response. These efforts peaked in 1986, when corporate funds managed $2 billion, or nearly 12 percent of the total pool of venture capital.

After the stock market crash of 1987, however, the market for new public offerings again went into a sharp decline. Returns of and fund-raising by independent partnerships declined abruptly. Corporations scaled back their commitment to venture investing even more dramatically. By 1992, the number of corporate venture programs had fallen by one-third and their capital under management represented only 5 percent of the venture pool.

Interest in corporate venture capital climbed once again in the mid-1990s, both in the United States and abroad. Once again, much of this interest was stimulated by the recent success of the independent venture sector; that is, the rapid growth of funds and their attractive returns. These corporate funds invested directly in a variety of internal and external ventures, as well as in funds organized by independent venture capitalists.

The increase in the scale of activity can be illustrated by some estimates by Venture Economics. The consulting firm believes that corporate investors accounted for 30 percent of the commitments to new funds in 1997, up from an average of 5 percent in the 1990–1992 period. Similarly, direct investments in the United States by these programs are believed to have risen from sixty-five investments totaling $176 million in 1995 to 936 transactions totaling $7.8 billion in 1999.[2] The years after 2000 again saw a rapid decline.

The most recent wave of corporate venturing activity was distinguished from earlier activity in several ways. First, the scale of activity has been considerably larger, with funds as large as $1 billion being established by firms such as Arthur Andersen and EDS. Second, the diversity of companies involved in these efforts has been greater, with many more services and traditional "old economy" manufacturers establishing such programs. (In earlier booms, activity was largely concentrated among high-technology firms.) Finally, many more firms outside the United States have participated in these efforts in recent years.

WHY IS CORPORATE VENTURE CAPITAL CHALLENGING?

This brief discussion makes clear that corporate involvement in venture capital has mirrored (perhaps even in an exaggerated manner) the cyclical nature of the entire venture capital industry over the past three decades. At the same time, numerous

2. Venture Economics, "Corporate Venture Capital Activity," unpublished tabulation, 2000.

discussions suggest that certain basic noncyclical issues also significantly influence corporate venture capital activity.

In particular, it appears that the frequent dissolution of earlier corporate venture programs was due to three structural failings. First, these programs suffered from a lack of well-defined missions.[3] Typically, they sought to accomplish a wide array of not necessarily compatible objectives, from providing a window on emerging technologies to generating attractive financial returns. The confusion over program objectives often led to dissatisfaction with the outcomes on the part of senior managers. For instance, when outside venture capitalists were hired to run a corporate fund under a contract that linked compensation to financial performance, management frequently became frustrated about their failure to invest in the technologies that most interested the firm. Instead, the venture groups were often perceived as selecting the investments that offered the highest financial return, independent of the benefits to the corporation.

A second cause of failure was insufficient corporate commitment to the venturing initiative.[4] Even if top management embraced the concept, middle management often resisted. R&D personnel preferred that funds be devoted to internal programs; corporate lawyers disliked the novelty and complexity of these hybrid organizations. In many cases, new senior management teams terminated programs, seeing them as expendable "pet projects" of their predecessors. Even if they did not object to the idea of the program, managers were often concerned about its impact on the firm's accounting earnings. During periods of financial pressure, money-losing subsidiaries were frequently terminated in an effort to increase reported operating earnings.

A final cause of failure was inadequate compensation schemes.[5] Corporations have frequently been reluctant to compensate their venture managers through profit-sharing ("carried interest") provisions, fearing that they might need to make huge payments if their investments were successful. Typically, successful risk taking was inadequately rewarded and failure excessively punished. As a result, corporations were frequently unable to attract top people (i.e., those who combined industry experience with connections to other venture capitalists) to run their venture funds. While this reluctance to offer incentive compensation is gradually easing, this remains a very real issue in many corporate venture programs today.[6]

All too often, corporate venture managers as a consequence adopted a conservative approach to investing. Nowhere was this behavior more clearly manifested than in the treatment of lagging ventures. As discussed in the second module of the casebook, independent venture capitalists often cease funding to failing firms because they want to devote their limited energy to firms with the greatest promise. Corporate venture

---

3. These problems are discussed in depth in the Fast volume cited above and in Robin Siegel, Eric Siegel, and Ian C. MacMillan, "Corporate Venture Capitalists: Autonomy, Obstacles, and Performance," *Journal of Business Venturing* 3 (1988): 233–247.

4. See the discussions, for instance, in G. Felda Hardymon, Mark J. DeNino, and Malcolm S. Salter, "When corporate venture capital doesn't work," *Harvard Business Review* 61 (May–June 1983): 114–120; Kenneth W. Rind, "The Role of Venture Capital in Corporate Development," *Strategic Management Journal* 2 (1981): 169–180; and Hollister B. Sykes, "Corporate Venture Capital: Strategies for Success," *Journal of Business Venturing* 5 (1990): 37–47.

5. These problems are documented in Zenas Block and Oscar A. Ornati, "Compensating Corporate Venture Managers," *Journal of Business Venturing* 2 (1987): 41–52; and E. Lawler and J. Drexel, *The Corporate Entrepreneur* (Los Angeles: Center for Effective Organizations, Graduate School of Business Administration, University of Southern California, 1980).

6. See, for instance, David G. Barry, "Some Venture Programs Sharing Gains with Corporate Workforce," *Corporate Venturing Report* 1 (July 2000): 1, 22–23.

capitalists have frequently been unwilling to write off unsuccessful ventures, lest they incur the reputational repercussions that a failure would entail.

HOW SUCCESSFUL HAVE CORPORATE VENTURING PROGRAMS BEEN?

The boom-and-bust pattern in corporate venturing has led many to conclude that corporate venture capital is inherently unstable and unlikely to be successful. But the actual historical track of these investments paints a quite different picture, one that challenges the conventional wisdom about corporate programs.[7]

When more than 30,000 investments into entrepreneurial firms by venture capital organizations over a fifteen-year period are examined, the pattern was striking. Investments by two types of organizations, independent venture partnerships and corporate funds, were compared. (Other hybrid venture funds, such as those affiliated with commercial and investment banks, are not used in this analysis.)

Far from being outright failures, corporate venture investments in entrepreneurial firms appear to be at least as successful (using such measures as the probability of a portfolio firm going public) as those backed by independent venture organizations. For instance, 35 percent of the investments by corporate funds were in companies that had gone public by the end of the sample period, as opposed to 31 percent for independent funds. It might be thought that the results are just a consequence of the fact that corporate groups often invest in later financing rounds. By this point in many firms, much of the uncertainty has been addressed and the probability of success is higher. But the results continue to hold up when controls for the age and profitability of the portfolio firm at the time of the original investment are added.

But the pattern of success is not uniform. The success of the corporate programs is particularly pronounced for investments in which there is strategic overlap between the corporate parent and the portfolio firm. The probability of going public by the end of the sample period, for instance, is 39 percent for this group. The success of investments when there is no overlap is much lower, particularly once the characteristics of the firm are controlled for.

These measures may be somewhat misleading. A corporate venture program may be strategically successful, even if the portfolio companies do not well: for instance, it may allow a firm to understand and head off a serious competitive threat to its core business. For instance, in 1980, Analog Devices established a corporate venture program, Analog Devices Enterprises (ADE), to generate both attractive financial returns and strategic benefits in the form of licensing agreements and acquisitions. By the time the program was suspended in 1985, Analog Devices took a $7 million charge against earnings. In 1990, with most of the portfolio liquidated, it took another $12 million charge. Of the eleven firms in ADE's portfolio, ten were terminated, acquired by other companies at unattractive valuations or relegated to the "living dead." Only one firm ultimately went public. In this case, ADE's stake was so diluted by a merger that it was worth only about $2 million at the time of the offering. At the same time, however, the program allowed Analog Devices, a manufacturer of specialized silicon-based semiconductors, to assess the threat that semiconductors based on an alternative technology,

---

7. This section is based on Paul A. Gompers and Josh Lerner, "The Determinants of Corporate Venture Capital Success: Organizational Structure, Incentives, and Complementarities," in Randall Morck, ed., *Concentrated Corporate Ownership* (Chicago: University of Chicago Press for the National Bureau of Economic Research, 2000), pp. 17–50.

gallium arsenide (GaAs), posed to its core business. Ultimately, this threat proved to be much smaller than originally anticipated, and many of companies failed. During this same period, Analog Devices' stock price climbed sevenfold, reflecting the improved prospects for silicon chipmakers.

But similar patterns emerge when the duration of the programs themselves is examined. The evidence suggests that corporate programs without a strong strategic focus are much less stable than those of independent funds. Many unfocused corporate funds cease operations after only a few investments, with the typical fund surviving for less than one-quarter the period of the average independent fund. Meanwhile, corporate funds with a strong strategic focus are almost as stable as independent funds.

In short, despite the many challenges that these efforts face, corporate venture capital programs can make a real difference!

ADDITIONAL INFORMATION SOURCES

Given the degree of interest in corporate venturing programs, there has been surprising little written about these efforts.

Nonetheless, there are several useful sources of information about these programs. First, there are two primary sources for data on these programs. The consulting firm Asset Alternatives (http://www.assetnews.com) publishes a helpful directory, the *Directory of Corporate Venture Capital Programs*. This includes profiles of the programs' objectives, key contact points, and representative investments. VentureOne's database tracks the progress of numerous corporate programs in addition to traditional funds.

In addition, occasional stories appear in more general publications such as *The Venture Capital Journal*.

Consulting and accounting firms periodically produce reports on the state of corporate venturing. Most of these, alas, are not particularly helpful. More useful for those interested in a particular program are the collections of news releases and press coverage about that program, which can be identified through careful searches in Lexis/Nexis, OneSource, and other business databases.

There are also a few academic studies:

Zenas Block and Oscar A. Ornati, "Compensating Corporate Venture Managers," *Journal of Business Venturing* 2 (1987): 41–52.

Norman D. Fast, *The Rise and Fall of Corporate New Venture Divisions* (Ann Arbor: UMI Research Press, 1978).

Robert E. Gee, "Finding and Commercializing New Businesses," *Research/Technology Management* 37 (January/February 1994): 49–56.

Paul A. Gompers and Josh Lerner, *The Venture Capital Cycle* (Cambridge: MIT Press, 1999), Chapter 5.

G. Felda Hardymon, Mark J. DeNino, and Malcolm S. Salter, "When Corporate Venture Capital Doesn't Work," *Harvard Business Review* 61 (May–June 1983): 114–120.

E. Lawler and J. Drexel, *The Corporate Entrepreneur* (Los Angeles, Center for Effective Organizations, Graduate School of Business Administration, University of Southern California, 1980).

Kenneth W. Rind, "The Role of Venture Capital in Corporate Development," *Strategic Management Journal* 2 (April 1981): 169–180.

Robin Siegel, Eric Siegel, and Ian C. MacMillan, "Corporate Venture Capitalists: Autonomy, Obstacles, and Performance," *Journal of Business Venturing* 3 (1988): 233–247.

29

3i Group PLC

On January 6, 2003, Brian Larcombe, CEO of 3i Group PLC, the United Kingdom–based venture capital and private equity firm, looked from his office window at the dome of St. Paul's across the Thames. He had just returned from the Christmas break and was preparing for the New Year's first meeting with his executive team. The past year, he thought, could only be described as a roller coaster. The collapse in the capital markets after September 11, 2001, and the Enron scandals had made life difficult despite some successfully exited investments. The company's results for the six months to September 2002 had shown a decline from the year earlier, but not as dramatic as the fall in the overall market. With £619 million in exits, showing a net gain of £118 million over the opening valuation, and strong cash flow, Larcombe could confidently describe the performance as "robust," and the results had been well received by the City,[1] which had particularly cheered the cash flow figures (see Exhibits 29.1a and 29.1b for results). Much of the performance, Larcombe felt, stemmed from the firm's international network, which allowed investors to select the best opportunities from a global pool. Larcombe was looking forward to his colleagues' input on using 3i's international strategy to continue to provide superior returns.

3i was unique among private equity firms. It had been founded in 1945 by the UK government and funded by a consortium of banks to provide capital for small and medium-sized businesses in the post–World War II rebuilding effort and to ensure that the country did not sink back into the pre-war economic depression. 3i was one of the few publicly owned private equity firms and one of the largest, with a portfolio valued at £5.1 billion ($7.3 billion), 2,606 portfolio companies, and 942 employees. It was one of the United Kingdom's leading companies and had held a place on the Financial Times Stock Exchange (FTSE) 100, the UK's large-cap stock market index, since shortly after it went public in 1994.

---

1. The UK investment community.

Professors Felda Hardymon and Josh Lerner and Senior Research Associate Ann Leamon prepared this case. HBS cases are developed solely as the basis for class discussion. Cases are not intended to serve as endorsements, sources of primary data, or illustrations of effective or ineffective management.

EXHIBIT 29.1a

CONSOLIDATED STATEMENT OF TOTAL RETURN FOR 3i GROUP

(in £ millions)	6 months to 9/30/02			6 months to 9/30/01			12 months to 3/31/02		
	Revenue	**Capital**	**Total**	**Revenue**	**Capital**	**Total**	**Revenue**	**Capital**	**Total**
Capital profits									
Net realized profits/(losses) over opening valuation		118	118		(5)	(5)		(39)	(39)
Net unrealized value movement in the period		(701)	(701)		(1,060)	(1,060)		(890)	(890)
Capital profits		**(583)**	**(583)**		**(1,065)**	**(1,065)**		**(929)**	**(929)**
Total operating income before interest payable	153		153	204		204	355		355
Interest payable	(52)	(3)	(55)	(59)	(3)	(62)	(114)	(6)	(120)
Administrative expenses	(53)	(23)	(76)	(63)	(23)	(86)	(121)	(50)	(171)
Amortization of goodwill	–	–	–	(2)	(72)	(74)	(2)	(71)	(73)
Cost of changes to organizational structure				(9)	(9)	(18)	(9)	(9)	(18)
Return before Tax and Currency Adjustment	**48**	**(609)**	**(561)**	**71**	**(1,172)**	**(1,101)**	**109**	**(1,065)**	**(956)**
Tax	(1)	2	1	(2)	8	6	(3)	4	1
Return for the Period before Currency Adjustment	**47**	**(607)**	**(560)**	**69**	**(1,164)**	**(1,095)**	**106**	**(1,061)**	**(955)**
Currency adjustment	1	(11)	(10)	–	(2)	(2)	(4)	(1)	(5)
Total Return	**48**	**(618)**	**(570)**	**69**	**(1,166)**	**(1,097)**	**102**	**(1,062)**	**(960)**
Total Return per Share									
Basic (pence)	7.8p	(101.3)p	(93.5)p	11.4p	(191.8)p	(180.4)p	16.8p	(174.5)p	(157.7)p
Diluted (pence)	7.8p	(101.0)p	(93.2)p	11.4p	(191.3)p	(179.9)p	16.7p	(173.3)p	(156.6)p

Source: 3i Group, http://www.3i.com/3i_interim_report_2002, accessed May 2, 2003.

EXHIBIT 29.1b

3i GROUP'S SUMMARY PERFORMANCE DATA, 1998–2002

(in £ billions)	Half Yr. as of 9/30/02[1]	Yr. Ended 3/31/02	Half Yr. as of 9/30/01	Yr. Ended 3/31/01	Yr. Ended 3/31/00	Yr. Ended 3/31/99	Yr. Ended 3/31/98
UK Portfolio valuation at 31 March/30 Sept	3.4	3.4	4.0	4.1	4.7	4.1	4.2
International Portfolio valuation at 31 March/30 Sept	2.0	1.7	2.4	1.7	1.3	0.5	0.3
Total Portfolio Valuation at 31 March/30 Sept	5.4	5.1	6.4	5.8	6.0	4.6	4.5
Share price (pence) at 31 March/30 Sept	431	787	700	1,122	1,318	626	598

Sources: 3i Group, "Report and Accounts 2002," March 31, 2002, p. 2; and 3i Group, "Interim Report for the Six Months to 30 September 2002," November 15, 2002, p. 2.

Note: 1. Half-year results are for March 31 to September 30.

To the outsider, 3i's structure was complex, consisting of 3i Group, the core operation that invested in privately held companies, and three funds managed under contract that invested in public companies. 3i also operated a number of side-by-side funds that invested third-party money in the Group's private company deals; three were currently investing, one was being raised, and four were fully invested. Starting in 1997, 3i had accelerated its international expansion and, by 2003, had 32 offices in fifteen countries (see Exhibit 29.2 for office locations). It was involved in deals across the entire private equity spectrum, from early-stage venture capital through growth investment

---

EXHIBIT 29.2a

3i'S OFFICES, 2002

Europe
Austria
 —Vienna
Benelux Countries
 —Amsterdam
Denmark
 —Copenhagen
Finland
 —Helsinki
France
 —Paris
 —Lyon
 —Nantes
Germany
 —Frankfurt
 —Berlin
 —Munich
 —Dusseldorf
 —Stuttgart
Ireland
 —Dublin
Italy
 —Milan
 —Padova
Spain
 —Madrid
 —Barcelona
Sweden
 —Stockholm
Switzerland
 —Zurich

UK
 —London (head office)
 —Aberdeen
 —Birmingham
 —Bristol
 —Cambridge
 —Glasgow
 —Leeds
 —Manchester
 —Reading

United States
 —Menlo Park, CA
 —Waltham, MA

Asia-Pacific
 —Hong Kong
 —Singapore

Sources: 3i Group, http://www.3i.com, accessed March 4, 2003; and 3i Group information.

EXHIBIT 29.2b

3i'S GEOGRAPHIC DISTRIBUTION AS OF SEPTEMBER 30, 2002

Country	Total Portfolio		New Investments (6 mo. ended 9/30/2002)
	£MMs	# Companies	£MMs
UK	3,390	1,552	248
Continental Europe	1,683	723	111
USA	200	73	31
Asia Pacific	80	26	3
Total	**5,353**	**2,374**	**393**

Source: 3i Group, http://www.3i.com/3i_interim_report_2002, accessed May 2, 2003.

and into mid-market buyouts, in sectors ranging from biotech and advanced technology to manufacturing and retailing (see Exhibit 29.3 for 3i's structure).

3i had surprised the industry in October 2001 when it cut its workforce by 18 percent, or 185 positions. Larcombe had looked at the drivers of the industry—"the capital markets, merger and acquisition activity, the technology spending plans of large corporations"—and "saw that they were all going down." The challenging conditions of 2001 inflicted a total loss, including net unrealized portfolio changes, of £960 million ($1.37 billion). Nonetheless, 3i was raising €3 billion ($3 billion) for its fourth European midmarket buyout fund. With a ten-year average compound return in the stock market of 13.8 percent, 3i outperformed its public market benchmarks (see Exhibit 29.4 for performance data). Larcombe knew that 3i would have to excel to deliver superior returns amidst the bloodbath of the current private equity scene. Along with a better offering than the competition's, it would have to derive real value from the network. He also knew that he had to motivate his staff by giving them a compelling vision of the future—not an easy task in the uncertainty that greeted the start of 2003.

Larcombe felt that the company was well positioned, due to its long history of private equity investing, the strength of the balance sheet, its dedicated staff, and the strategy of internationalization. In the period to September 30, 2002, its most recent half-year, 3i had capitalized on the early rebound in global economic activity. Its most noteworthy exit had been the sale of the discount airline Go! to EasyJet for £374 million ($534 million), a 156 percent return on a position held less than a year. Overall, 3i had realized £619 million ($1 billion) in the first half, but the year's later slump had reduced the portfolio's value. The external business environment had continued to be difficult, as capital markets had lower levels of merger and acquisition activity, initial public offerings had all but disappeared, and fund-raising had dropped significantly.

Yet this environment also conferred some benefits, as other firms succumbed to the same punishing conditions with which 3i contended (see Exhibit 29.5 for financials). The global network was in place and staffed, the infrastructure established. As he studied Christopher Wren's masterpiece, of which the architect had been so uncertain that he had built two smaller versions as test runs, Larcombe thought, "We're building something completely new for the venture capital industry. But we need to demonstrate that we can provide sustainable returns on this investment."

EXHIBIT 29.3

3i'S STRUCTURE

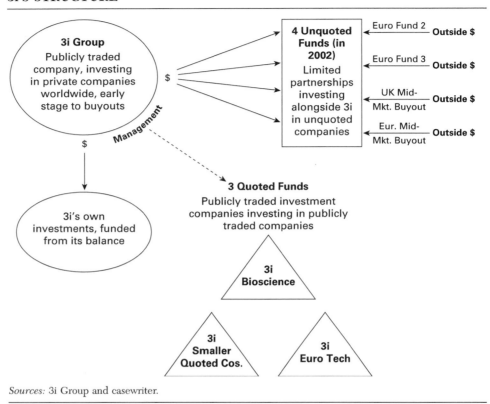

Sources: 3i Group and casewriter.

3i'S HISTORY[2]

3i Group plc, formerly known as Investors in Industry, was one of the oldest private equity groups in Europe. Its most direct predecessor, the Industrial and Commercial Finance Corporation (ICFC), was founded in 1945 to provide long-term capital for small and medium-sized firms and to help domestic industry recover from the ravages of World War II and the Great Depression. The Bank of England and the five major clearing banks at the time funded the effort with £10 million in equity ownership, in effect establishing a future competitor.[3]

ICFC used both debt and equity to fulfill its mandate. This was a tricky proposition, as assessing the long-term prospects of small, private businesses was not a widely

2. Drawn from 3i, "Fifty Years of Growth: 1945–1995," private document; Richard Coopey and Donald Clarke, *3i: Fifty Years of Investing in Industry* (Oxford, UK: Oxford University Press, 1995); and personal conversations.
3. Royal Bank of Scotland Group, Barclays Bank, Lloyds Bank, Midland Bank Group, and NatWest Bank Group.

EXHIBIT 29.4a

3i'S SHARE PRICE WITH FTSE 100

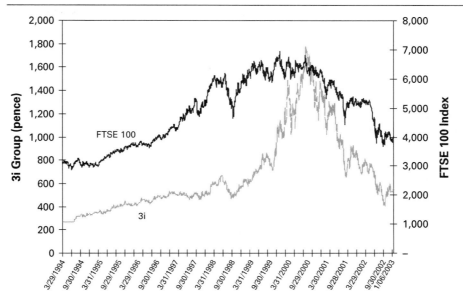

Source: Data from Datastream.

EXHIBIT 29.4b

3i GROUP'S COMPOUND ANNUAL RETURN (STOCK MARKET) VERSUS OTHER INDICES

(% for year ending March 31, 2002)	3i	FTSE All-Share	FTSE Small-Cap	S&P 500 Index	Russell 2000 Index
3 years	4.0	–1.7	10.5	–4.0	9.0
5 years	7.7	6.7	6.2	9.0	8.0
10 years	13.8	11.9	10.3	11.0	10.0

For years to September 30, 2002	3i	FTSE All-Share
3 years	–3.8	–11.1
5 years	3.0	–3.6
10 years	12.8	7.5

Sources: 3i Group, "Report and Accounts 2002," March 31, 2002, p. 2; 3i Group, "Interim Report for the Six Months to 30 September 2002," November 15, 2002, p. 2; Bill Barnard et al., "3i: Signposts and Destinations," Dresdner, Kleinwort, Wasserstein Research, June 2002, p. 6; and DataStream International, accessed August 30, 2002.

EXHIBIT 29.5a

3i GROUP'S CONSOLIDATED REVENUE STATEMENT

Year Ended March 31 (£ millions)	1994	1995	1996	1997	1998	1999	2000	2001	2002
Interest Receivable from Debt Securities, Etc.									
Interest receivable on loans and other fixed-income securities[a]	98	96	93	75	76	92	87	99	113
Fixed-rate dividends	31	32	36	50	56	42	34	21	19
Subtotal	**129**	**128**	**129**	**124**	**132**	**134**	**121**	**120**	**132**
Other interest and similar income	26	22	22	19	33	38	31	43	46
Subtotal Interest Income	**155**	**150**	**151**	**144**	**165**	**171**	**153**	**163**	**178**
Interest payable	−119	−110	−114	−99	−115	−110	−104	−117	−114
Net Interest Income	**36**	**40**	**37**	**44**	**50**	**62**	**48**	**46**	**64**
Dividend income from equity shares	62	69	82	96	104	83	117	123	111
Income from joint ventures	−1	−1	0	0	0	−1	−1	−2	9
Management fees receivable[b]	17	25	31	31	43	54	54	72	56
Other operating income	6	2	4	4	3	1	2	2	1
Total Operating Income[c]	**120**	**135**	**154**	**175**	**200**	**198**	**220**	**241**	**241**
Administrative expenses	−55	−60	−65	−70	−76	−90	−102	−121	−121
Goodwill amortization and other	0	0	0	0	0	0	0	0	−11
Operating Profit before Tax	**65**	**76**	**89**	**106**	**124**	**108**	**119**	**120**	**109**
Tax	−15	−17	−19	−14	−17	2	−3	−4	−3
Profit after Tax[d]	**51**	**59**	**70**	**91**	**107**	**110**	**115**	**116**	**106**
Net unrealized value movement in the year	394	113	389	211	417	−90	1,167	−676	−890
Net realized profit over opening valuation	56	77	78	113	136	180	350	453	−39
Capital Profits before Tax[e]	**450**	**190**	**467**	**324**	**553**	**90**	**1,517**	**−223**	**−929**

Sources: Adapted from Bill Barnard et al., "3i: Signposts and Destinations," Dresdner, Kleinwort, Wasserstein Research, June 2002, pp. 22 and 25; and 3i Group, "Annual Report," March 31, 2002, passim.

Notes:

1. As of March 31, 2002, 3i's beta was 1.39, the ten-year UK benchmark bond (ten-year) was 4.0 percent, and the UK Treasury Bill (ninety day, middle rate) was 4.1 percent.

2. This table does not include results for the publicly traded funds.

   a. 3i's loan, fixed-income, and equity share investments along with interests in joint ventures are considered financial fixed assets, as they are held for long-term investment purposes and are included in this line. This line does not, however, include realized or unrealized capital gains.

   b. These are management fees from the unquoted funds.

   c. 3i's Articles of Association prohibit the distribution of its capital gains, which are included in the capital reserve. The capital gains of subsidiary undertakings (foreign subsidiaries, such as Technologieholding), which are distributable, are also excluded from consolidated revenue and included in the capital reserve.

   d. This corresponds to the Revenue number (return for period before currency adjustment) in Exhibit 29.1a.

   e. This corresponds to the Capital profits line in Exhibit 29.1a.

EXHIBIT 29.5b

3i GROUP'S ADMINISTRATIVE EXPENSE DETAIL

Year Ended March 31 (£ millions)	1996	1997	1998	1999	2000	2001	2002
Wages and salaries	42.1	38.1	46.1	54.4	68.6	84.0	74.0
Social security costs	3.2	3.8	5.8	6.4	11.3	8.0	8.0
Other pension costs	0.4	0.5	0.6	1.9	3.6	5.0	16.0
Other admin. expenses	24.6	34.3	34.9	42.9	45.2	65.0	65.0
Total Admin. Expenses	**70.3**	**76.7**	**87.4**	**105.6**	**128.7**	**162.0**	**163.0**
Admin. expenses less allocation to capital reserve°	65.0	70.0	76.3	90.1	102.0	121.0	121.0
Average monthly number of employees	621	652	709	774	838	971	1084
% increase	4.9%	5.0%	8.7%	9.2%	8.3%	15.9%	11.6%
Average staff cost per employee (£)	£62,641	£65,031	£74,048	£81,008	£99,642	£99,897	£90,406
Total avg. admin. costs per employee (£)	£97,585	£117,638	£123,272	£138,434	£153,580	£166,838	£150,369
Growth in staff costs (%)	9.6%	9.0%	23.8%	19.4%	33.2%	16.2%	1.0%
Growth in total admin. expenses (%)	12.8%	26.6%	14.0%	20.8%	21.9%	25.9%	0.6%

Sources: Adapted from Bill Barnard et al., "3i: Signposts and Destinations," Dresdner, Kleinwort, Wasserstein Research, June 2002; and 3i Group, "Annual report," March 31, 2002.

Note: ° A proportion of the administrative expenses are charged to the capital account to reflect the costs of administering the funds for which a management fee is received.

held skill. Operating among small to medium-sized businesses that were often family-owned and had little history of external funding, the new organization had to invent not just itself but also an entire skill set.

Under Lord William Piercy, its first chairman, ICFC became somewhat of a financial maverick and an innovator, working across much of the economy and injecting a new measure of competition into London's financial circles. In the early 1950s, ICFC significantly undercut the prevailing fees charged to underwrite stock issues for medium-sized companies. Despite the controversy this generated, the organization developed a substantial underwriting business during that decade, even as the common rate for such services dropped by half. By the mid-1990s, though, 3i had essentially ceased underwriting.

ICFC helped create a greater awareness of the power and usefulness of equity for small companies, especially those that were family-owned. By 1950, equity positions made up 20 percent of ICFC's portfolio value; the balance was debt. All transactions were done from its own balance sheet. Starting in 1950, ICFC saw the chance to drive growth by expanding into Britain's regions, moving first into Birmingham and then, by 1953, into Manchester and Edinburgh. The local offices were encouraged to make independent investment decisions but also bore responsibility for them. This expanding branch network (29 offices by 1972) and devolved decision making contrasted with the clearing banks' strategy of centralized decision making and reduced attention to small regional businesses.[4]

4. 3i, "Fifty Years of Growth: 1945–1995," a private document.

EXHIBIT 29.5c

CONSOLIDATED BALANCE SHEET, YEARS ENDING MARCH 31, 2002, AND MARCH 31, 2001

(in £ millions)	2002	2001
Assets		
Loans and advances to banks	563	890
Debt securities	1,924	2,158
Equity shares		
—Listed	413	971
—Unlisted	2,964	3,030
Total equity shares	3,377	4,001
Interests in Joint Ventures	**35**	**46**
Goodwill	—	74
Tangible fixed assets	50	60
Other assets	184	210
Total Assets	**6,133**	**7,439**
Liabilities		
Loans from banks	519	617
Issue of debt securities	1,339	1,503
Other liabilities	53	58
Accruals and deferred income	181	210
Provisions for liabilities and charges	12	8
Subordinated liabilities	84	70
Subtotal	**2,188**	**2,466**
Called-up share capital	305	304
Share premium account	342	333
Capital reserve	3,022	4,084
Revenue reserve	276	252
Equity Shareholders' Funds	3,945	4,973
Total Liabilities	**6,133**	**7,439**

Source: 3i Group, "Report and Accounts 2002" (March 31, 2002), p. 39.

Note: These data cover only the investments from 3i's own balance sheet, both through 3i's own investment activity and its unlisted funds. Results for the publicly traded funds are separately published.

By the late 1950s, ICFC had begun raising debt directly from the market.[5] Except for the £10 million with which it was capitalized and a further £10 million stock issue in 1973, ICFC (and later 3i) funded all of its activities from its own cash flow.

ICFC also expanded its product line. In addition to buyouts and recapitalizations, it became involved in early stage venture investing. In 2002, early stage investing comprised 10 percent of the £1 billion invested, or almost £100 million ($143 million) (see Exhibit 29.6 for the proportion of investments by stage).

5. *Ibid.*, p. 6.

EXHIBIT 29.6

INVESTMENTS BY PRODUCT, AS OF MARCH 31, 1998–2002

Product	2002 (£ MMs)	% of Total	2001 (£ MMs)	% of Total	2000 (£ MMs)	% of Total	1999 (£ MMs)	% of Total	1998 (£ MMs)	% of Total
Start-up	95	9%	278	14%	82	6%	57	5%	29	3%
Management Buyout	332	32	617	31	440	32	365	32	381	37
Management Buy-In	29	3	88	4	142	10	241	21	164	16
Growth Capital	511	49	852	43	545	40	330	29	298	29
Share Purchase°	16	2	90	5	132	10	121	11	142	14
Recoveries†	56	5	47	2	35	3	33	3	23	2
Total	**1,039**		**1,972**		**1,376**		**1,147**		**1,037**	

Source: 3i Group, "Report and Accounts 2002" (March 31, 2002), p. 66.

Notes:

° Share purchase is the purchase of shares of a publicly traded company.

† Recoveries are corporate restarts.

In 1975, ICFC merged with Finance Corporation for Industry (FCI, founded in 1945 to provide large sums to help key sectors of British industry rationalize) to become Finance for Industry (FFI), although the other names continued to be used for sector-specific activities. The firm's investment rate almost doubled in the latter half of the 1970s, with interests ranging from property and consulting firms to shipping, along with the core business of providing long-term investment capital for small businesses. The firm continued its tradition of investing in technology and backed a number of companies that became significant successes, including Bond Helicopters, Caledonian Airways (later British Caledonian), and Oxford Instruments, the pioneer of magnetic resonance imaging (MRI).

In 1981, the CEO, Jon Foulds, decided to remake the company's image and unify the disparate names and far-flung activities under a single brand. After much debate, FFI, ICFC, and FCI became 3i (Investors in Industry) in 1983 (see Exhibit 29.7 for logo). Foulds also expanded internationally. 3i established an office in Boston, Massachusetts, in 1982 to support the UK technology portfolio and expanded to Paris the next

EXHIBIT 29.7

3i'S LOGO

Source: 3i Group.

year and Frankfurt in 1986. It started a joint venture in India and entered Australia through a wholly owned subsidiary. The Boston office evolved into 3i Ventures, dedicated to American-style venture deals.

3i also developed the United Kingdom's buyout business. For a number of reasons—to avoid carrying the portfolio companies on its books, to extend its financing ability beyond its own balance sheet, and to leverage its staff, which felt that its skills lay in investing rather than managing companies—the firm aggressively syndicated its deals. "Basically," admitted Larcombe, "we developed the UK businesses of firms that are our competitors today." The strategy made sense at the time. To a certain degree, 3i operated like a bank—it would provide funding to an experienced management team that bought a spin-out or took a company private and relied on the team's management and operational expertise. One 3i executive might be responsible for thirty or forty companies, a ratio that precluded close involvement. Only when 3i and its funds began taking majority ownership positions in 1994 did the firm start playing a more active management role.

By the mid-1980s, 3i had become a financial conglomerate. It was active in shipping finance, plant leasing, property development, and corporate finance, in addition to consulting and venture operations. It had offices in the United States, France, Germany, Italy, Spain, India, Japan, and Australia and a network throughout the United Kingdom. It was also still 100 percent owned by the clearing banks and the Bank of England.

In 1985, the clearing banks and the Bank of England finally agreed that 3i should be floated on the public markets. Resolving issues around 3i's tax status and finding a time when the markets looked favorable delayed the floatation for nine years. By then, though, 3i's track record compared favorably with that of other alternatives: a 332 percent return between March 31, 1983, and September 30, 1993, versus 414 percent from the FTSE All-share Index (similar to the S&P 500) and 320 percent from investment trusts on average.

To prepare for the floatation, 3i undertook an intense analysis to determine the cost-effectiveness of its various divisions. It discovered that the core effort of making long-term capital investments in small to medium-sized companies had been carrying the rest of the firm, along with an oversized management staff. In response, 3i refocused on its core business, shed the others, and reduced headcount by 45 percent, to 570.[6] "We decided that our strengths were in private equity," said Larcombe, "not financial services in a wider sense." 3i continued its Japanese joint venture but closed the U.S. office.

3i was floated on July 18, 1994, with a market capitalization of £1.6 billion ($2.5 billion), a 13.5 percent discount to the net asset value as of March 31, 1994. At this time, the UK was just emerging from the recession of the early 1990s, so the offer was oversubscribed only 1.1 times and yielded 75,000 new shareholders.[7] By September of that year, 3i's market cap had risen enough that it was included in the FTSE 100.

Third-Party Funds

3i began managing its first third-party fund in 1994. This effort helped reduce the dependence on syndicate partners in the buyout business and also generated a respectable fee stream. The side-by-side fund raised third-party money from institutional investors, such as pension funds, endowments, and insurance companies, to invest alongside 3i in defined sectors (see Exhibit 29.8 for funds). By 2002, 3i's six funds managed €7 billion ($7 billion), and it was raising the €3 billion ($3 million) Eurofund IV (half committed

6. Anonymous, "The Ayes Have It," *Investor's Chronicle* (May 20, 1994), p. 11.

7. Ewan Macpherson, postscript, in Coopey and Clarke, *3i: Fifty Years of Investing in Industry*, p. 394.

EXHIBIT 29.8

3i'S THIRD-PARTY FUNDS UNDER MANAGEMENT

Name	Year Raised	Total Commitment (€ MMs)	Third Party (€ MMs)	3i (€ MMs)	Focus
Eurofund 1	1994	442	306	136	Continental Europe
UK MBO 1°	1994	290	145	145	UK midmarket buyouts
UK MBO 2	1996	706	298	408	UK midmarket buyouts
UK Smaller MBO	1997	587	204	383	Smaller UK buyouts
Eurofund 2	1997	748	374	374	Continental Europe
UK Midmarket MBO	1997	2,142	1,071	1,071	UK midmarket buyouts
Eurofund 3	1999	2,244	1,122	1,122	Continental/Pan-Europe
Eurofund 4	first close 9/02	3,000	1,500	1,500	Continental Europe midmarket buyouts
Totals		**10,159**	**5,020**	**5,139**	

Source: 3i Group information and Sharon Corr and Rob Misselbrook, "3i," Lehman Brothers Equity Research, November 13, 2000, p. 7. £ converted to € using 1.7:1 ratio from November 2000.

Note: ° MBO stands for management buyout.

by 3i) to invest in midmarket buyouts. These funds had two advantages—they allowed 3i to take on larger deals than its balance sheet alone would support, and co-investing with them permitted 3i to take majority ownership positions without consolidating the subsidiaries' results for reporting purposes. There was no cherry-picking, as 3i invested in the exact same deals and the same people managed the money. In fact, the deal-doers were blind to the source of the funds they invested. For the fiscal year ended March 2002, such fund management had generated £35 million ($55.6 million) in fees.

3i also managed publicly traded funds that invested primarily in publicly traded companies. The first of these, 3i Small Quoted Companies, was founded in 1991 and managed by 3i Investments plc, a wholly owned subsidiary of 3i Group. In 1999, 3i Investments took over Biotechnology Investments Ltd., a publicly traded biotechnology investment group that had been established in 1981. This fund focused on both public and private bioscience companies. It participated up to 30 percent in 3i Group's private investments in the sector. 3i European Technology Fund, founded in 2000, concentrated on investments in public European high-tech companies. The same small-cap experts who managed 3i's publicly traded portfolio also managed 3i Investments. The money was pre-existing; 3i did not raise it. It did allow its name to be used for branding purposes and charged a fee between 1.5 percent and 2 percent of either committed funds or total fund value. Some £800 million ($1.14 billion) was invested in these vehicles, and management fees generated £6 million ($8.6 million) in the year ended March 2002.

The connection with 3i allowed the funds to share 3i Group's nonconfidential research on public companies and gave them the chance to buy shares when portfolio companies went public. The fund managers had the option of purchasing shares of these firms at the offer price and without the issue premium. 3i Group's shareholders would be indifferent to the identity of the purchasers as long as a market was created.

The Modern 3i

In 2002, 3i Group comprised 174 separate legal entities to comply with the regulations in all its countries of operation. Its market capitalization was £3.5 billion ($5 billion), down from a peak of £10.7 billion in September 2000.

3i Group included:

- The original organization, which made debt and equity investments from 3i's capital account. By law, the proceeds of these investments were to be reinvested in other transactions.

- A series of funds, raised from third parties, that were invested and distributed as traditional private equity funds.

- A number of foreign subsidiaries, which had been independent private organizations that 3i bought and subsequently integrated.

- A series of closed-end funds that held public securities.

It had 45,000 shareholders, including major pension funds (Scottish Widows Investment Partnership), insurance companies (Prudential), and investment firms (Fidelity), and also a large number of individual investors, including retirees, who had been attracted to the company's name and business when it floated.

3i since 1997: An International Strategy

In 1997, Brian Larcombe became chief executive of 3i Group. He had joined 3i as an investor-trainee in Manchester upon graduating from college in 1974. After eight years, as he said, "I got tired of doing deals and thought being involved in managing the business would be fun." He became a local and then a regional director, then finance director and a member of the executive committee in 1992.

3i in 1997 had twenty-four offices in the United Kingdom, four in Europe, and joint ventures in Japan and Australia. Its business ran the gamut from £500 million buyouts to £5 million early stage technology investments, and gross assets stood at £3.4 billion (£1.3 billion net).[8] Said Larcombe: "We had set up some international offices, but they operated in isolation. We weren't integrated. Our offices in Paris and Milan had the basic 3i operating approach, but there wasn't a strong sense of the synergistic benefits. You could say that we weren't a 'one-room' company."

By 1997, 3i had long held the dominant share of the fragmented UK private equity market. That year, it made 14.5 percent of all investments, measured by funds invested, almost twice the level of the runner-up. In 1994, the year it floated, 3i had accounted for 25 percent of all investments by funds invested and 48 percent of all deals. 3i's executives felt that the domestic private equity market, at 0.1 percent of gross domestic product (GDP), was fairly well developed. By comparison, the United States' private equity market was 0.4 percent of a GDP eight times larger, and the most active private equity firm in 1997 had a 2.7 percent share (see Exhibit 29.9 for market concentration figures). "It was obvious that if we were to continue to grow, we had to become international," said Larcombe. Added Patrick Dunne, director of marketing, "We set the goal that we would be number one or number two in every market of importance."

This decision coincided with the start of the technology and venture capital boom in the United States. U.S. venture and buyout companies began moving to the

8. 3i Group, 3i Group plc, Accounts and Reports, 1997, p. 7.

EXHIBIT 29.9a

UK AND U.S. PRIVATE EQUITY MARKET CONCENTRATION, 1997

	UK ($ MM)	U.S. ($ MM)
Total PE investment	$1,360	$30,793
Nominal GDP	1,287,000	8,159,000
PE as % of GDP	0.1%	0.4%

UK Top Ten VC Firms	Invested Capital 1997 ($ MM)	% of Country Total	U.S. Top Ten VC Firms	Invested Capital 1997 ($ MM)	% of Country Total
3i Group plc	196.97	14.48	DLJ Merchant Banking Partners	815.80	2.65
Cinven Ltd.	109.10	8.02	Kohlberg, Kravis, Roberts & Co.	640.15	2.08
Candover Investments plc	108.35	7.96	Schooner Capital	617.46	2.01
Permira Advisers Limited (FKA: Schroder Ventures Europe)	105.65	7.77	Warburg Pincus, LLC (FKA: E.M. Warburg, Pincus & Co.)	601.10	1.96
Bridgeport Capital Ltd.	98.69	7.25	J.P. Morgan Partners (FKA: Chase Capital Partners)	597.64	1.94
UBS Capital	94.61	6.95			
UBS Capital	94.61	6.95	Texas Pacific Group	475.8	1.55
CVC Capital Partners	93.10	6.84	WH Advisors, Inc.	420.20	1.36
Royal Bank Private Equity (RBPE)	84.04	6.18	Cypress Advisors L.P. (AKA: The Cypress Group)	418.33	1.36
Electra Partners Europe	77.53	5.70	Advent International Corporation	402.6	1.31
Phoenix Equity (FKA: DLJ European Private Equity)	58.30	4.29	Individuals	397.26	1.29
Total Share of Top 10	**$1,026.00**	**75.40%**		**$5,386.00**	**17.50%**

Source: Compiled by casewriter from Economist Information Unit Country Profiles and Venture Economics.

comparatively underdeveloped, less-crowded, and less-price-competitive European and UK markets. Said Paul Waller, director of fund operations at 3i, "In a way, this was a benefit as it drove us to increase the level of our game."

In 1999, 3i re-entered the United States with offices in Menlo Park, California, and Waltham, Massachusetts. The following year, it purchased established firms in Finland and Germany and the Bank of Austria's investment division, and in 2001 it added a Swedish operation. It also had operations in Singapore, Japan, and Hong Kong. The way in which 3i entered each country and the suite of services it chose to offer differed. Dunne explained, "We don't have a cookie cutter that we use everywhere. We vary our approach to match the local conditions, our own strengths and needs at the time, and the maturity of the market."

EXHIBIT 29.9b

UK AND U.S. PRIVATE EQUITY MARKET CONCENTRATION, 2001

	UK ($ MM)	U.S. ($ MM)
Total PE investment	$7,727	$70,552
Nominal GDP	$1,530,000	$10,082,000
PE as % of GDP	0.5%	0.7%

UK Top Ten VC Firms	Invested Capital 2001 ($ mil.)	% of Country Total	U.S. Top Ten VC Firms	Invested Capital 2001 ($ mil.)	% of Country Total
3i Group PLC	796	10.3%	Warburg Pincus, LLC	2,162	3.1%
Apax Partners & Co. Ventures Ltd. (AKA: Apax UK)	579	7.5	Hicks, Muse, Tate & Furst, Inc.	1,458	2.1
Cinven Ltd.	449	5.8	J.P. Morgan Partners (FKA: Chase Capital Partners)	1,105	1.6
BC Partners	408	5.3	Forstmann Little & Company	926	1.3
CVC Capital Partners	352	4.5	Goldman, Sachs & Co.	716	1.0
Royal Bank Private Equity (RBPE)	331	4.3	New Enterprise Associates	614	0.9
Terra Firma Capital Partners Ltd.	322	4.2	The Carlyle Group	562	0.8
UBS Capital	278	3.6	CSFB Private Equity (AKA: Credit Suisse First Boston)	559	0.8
Candover Investments plc	221	2.9	Heartland Industrial Partners	548	0.8
Alchemy Partners	190	2.5	DLJ Merchant Banking Partners	507	0.7
Total Share of Top 10	**$3,926**	**50.8%**		**$9,157**	**13.0%**

Source: Compiled by casewriter from Economist Information Unit Country Profiles and Venture Economics.

Buy or Build

In deciding how to enter a country, 3i looked at a number of factors, including the maturity of the market, the most appropriate products to offer (early stage or buyouts), and the most effective type of distribution channel. It had purchased firms in Germany, Finland, Austria, and Sweden, and established a joint venture in Japan. In the rest of the world, including the United States, 3i built its operations from the ground up (see Exhibit 29.10 for acquisitions). By 2006, 3i planned to have 10 percent of its portfolio in the United States and 5 percent in Asia (see Exhibit 29.11 for 3i's office network).

3i had made its first European acquisition in February 2000, when it purchased Technologieholding, the leading German early stage technology investor. 3i already was the market leader in German private equity, with offices in seven cities. Technologieholding was number two and growing quickly. Its early stage technology focus complemented 3i's emphasis on buyouts, later-stage technology, and expansion capital. In

EXHIBIT 29.10

3i'S ACQUISITIONS SINCE 2000

Date	Country	Name of Firm	Purchase Price ($ MM)
Feb '00	Germany	Technologieholding GmbH	$148
May '00	Finland	SFK Finance Oy	$10
Dec '00	Austria	Bank Austria TFV High Tech–Unternehmens Beteiligung GmbH (80%; 20% already held by 3i Technologieholding)	$65
Feb '01	Sweden	Atle (60% of Atle purchased through a joint venture and spun off; purchase price reflects the cost of the entire operation)	$521

Sources: 3i Group information from press releases and http://www.3i.com/3i_interim_report_2002, accessed May 2, 2003.

EXHIBIT 29.11a

3i OFFICE NETWORK, AS OF JANUARY 2003 AND AT FLOATATION (1994)

Region	2003				1994			
	Offices	% of Total Offices	£ Millions Invested (Incl. Funds)	% of Total Funds	Offices	% of Total Offices	£ Millions Invested (Incl. Funds)	% of Total Funds
United Kingdom	9	28.0%	3,390	63%	18	75%	3,248	88%
Continental Europe	19	59.0	1,683	31	6	25	292	11
Rest of the World	**4**	**13.0**	**280**	**6**	**0**	**0°**	**102**	**1**
United States	2	6.5	200	4	0	0	NA	NA
Asia-Pacific	2	6.5	80	2	0	0	NA	NA
Total	**32**	**100.0%**	**5,353**	**100%**	**24**	**100%**	**3,642**	**100%**

Sources: 3i Group, "Report and Accounts 2002," March 31, 2002; 3i Group, "Reports and Accounts for the Period Ending March 31, 1995"; Barnard et al., "3i: Signposts and Destinations," Dresdner, Kleinwort, Wasserstein Research, June 2002, p. 60; and 3i Group, http://www.3i.com/pdfdir/3i_interims02_suppinfo.pdf, accessed May 2, 2003. Excludes publicly traded funds.

Note: ° 1994 Rest of the World investments reflect the remaining portfolio of U.S. investments and the 3iBJ joint venture with the Industrial Bank of Japan; thus they have no offices associated with them.

addition, 3i's established processes and systems helped the smaller firm manage its back office, which had been strained by unexpected growth. The combined firm became the largest German technology investor by a factor of six.

The integration process presented some challenges even though, as Dunne said, "One of the joys of having such a big portfolio is that you can learn from their experiences as well as our own. So we had seen almost every possible way to mess up an acquisition integration." A major challenge was location—Technologieholding had a close overlap with 3i Germany. Some offices had to be closed and, although no jobs were lost, some managing partners had to take less prestigious titles. According to Dunne, "We did the hardest first. All the rest have been much smoother because we learned so much in Germany."

EXHIBIT 29.11b

3i'S PORTFOLIO BY GEOGRAPHY (AS OF SEPTEMBER 30, 2002)

	Investments (including Co-investment Funds)	Portfolio Value Excluding Co-investment Funds (in £ millions)	Portfolio Value of Co-investment Funds (in £ millions)
United Kingdom	1,552	2,831	559
Continental Europe	723	1,152	531
United States	73	198	2
Asia	26	70	10
Total	**2,374**	**4,251**	**1,102**

Source: 3i Group, http://www.3i.com/pdfdir/3i_interims02_suppinfo.pdf, accessed May 2, 2003.

Note: All figures exclude investments in joint ventures.

EXHIBIT 29.11c

EXIT PROCEEDS BY GEOGRAPHY (PERIOD ENDING SEPTEMBER 30, 2002)

(in £ millions)	Proceeds
United Kingdom	535
Continental Europe	79
United States	5
Total	**619**

Source: 3i Group, http://www.3i.com/pdfdir/3i_interims02_suppinfo.pdf, accessed May 2, 2003.

Note: Excludes carry, partnership distributions, joint ventures, and co-investment funds.

3i acquired the Finnish firm SFK Finance Oy for £6.9 million ($10.8 million) in May 2000. Dunne explained:

> The market there was fairly small. SFK was an excellent firm with dominant market share, and we knew the staff well. It was run by a terrific guy who had great telecommunications and technology expertise. Buying it allowed us to fill several holes at once—we had a strong position in Finland, the cultural fit was good, and we added some specific technical expertise to the team worldwide.

Ere Kariola, managing director of 3i Finland and founder and former head of SFK Oy, explained his reasons for making the merger:

> Finland is a small country. You can only get so big, raise so much money, and invest in so many deals here. There were nine of us in the firm, of a range of ages, and the younger guys were ambitious; they wanted to earn more money and move up. You can't really move up in a nine-person firm. 3i offered a fair price but more than that, they opened the world to us.

3i's History • **527**

Suddenly we had options for people—one of our investors is now with 3i Boston. They brought the resources of a big company and a good balance of control and flexibility.

3i contributed its own expertise to the Finnish operation, as well. One of the Finns learned that his former employer, the recently privatized Finnish national telecom firm Sonera, was planning to spin out a division. SFK had never done a buyout. 3i, however, had extensive experience in the area. Kariola said, "3i brought in a couple of buyout experts and someone who had been in that business. The deal was uncontested and wrapped up very quickly. Now we have buyout expertise in-house and have done a few on our own." As the tech market had slowed, buyouts had become a larger part of the firm's business.

In addition, 3i made use of the talents of the Finns. Not only did one investor move to the Boston office, but Kariola became head of the telecom sector team.

In February 2001, 3i completed its entry into Scandinavia with the purchase of the Swedish firm Atle. Atle also operated an industrial holding company, which 3i did not want to purchase, so the deal involved a joint venture, an acquisition, and an immediate demerger of the two divisions. As with SFK, 3i had known the Atle staff for some time and felt that the cultural fit was good. Atle's portfolio, like 3i's, was fairly balanced between buyouts and early stage investments.

The Danish office, on the other hand, was established organically. The three Scandinavian offices were under the umbrella of 3i Nordic with a dedicated director, yet each still retained its own name (3i Finland, 3i Sweden, and 3i Denmark). Dunne commented, "The integration of the Nordic offices went very smoothly. For one thing, we had experience by now. But also, because there was no established 3i presence, we didn't have to combine forces on the ground."

In December 2000, 3i had filled in its German presence by acquiring TVK, the four-person investment division of Bank of Austria. The two groups had worked together previously, and the integration went smoothly. Said Dunne, "With a strong German team, this was basically in-fill. We had started a Swiss office organically; we felt it was helpful to have a presence in Austria."

In entering the U.S., 3i used a different strategy. Said Larcombe:

The U.S. is a big, fragmented market. We couldn't go in and buy a firm that would give us significant market share. But it's important to be on the ground there, because so much is happening in early stage investments. It made more sense for us to set up our own operations, establish deal flow, syndicate some deals, and slowly become a presence. As we did so, we kept asking ourselves, "Why buy 3i?" We had to be able to offer a compelling reason for firms to go with us rather than any of the myriad of U.S. venture capitalists.

3i had had offices in California and Massachusetts in the early 1980s, only to close them in 1991. Allan Ferguson, the current head of the Boston office, had run the earlier venture operation and explained:

In 1991, 3i was getting ready to float, and international conglomerates at that time traded at a discount to their net asset values. Additionally, the banks that owned 3i wanted dividends, and early stage tech investing didn't generate dividends. 3i itself needed an income stream, too—it invested off its own balance sheet. So there were a number of reasons for 3i to pull out.

Furthermore, 3i had become concerned that its structure left it vulnerable to litigation. Its partners played active roles in their companies and sat on the boards. Without the protection of a limited partnership structure, 3i feared it would be known as having "deep pockets" and become the target of lawsuits from disaffected investors.[9]

During its earlier tenure in the United States, though, 3i had assembled a portfolio, much of it in biotech. Rather than cut the companies loose, 3i's U.S. organization dissolved and then reformed as Aspen Ventures, with 3i as its sole limited partner. It was to liquidate the portfolio in an orderly way.

3i never entirely left the United States. In 1995, when Ferguson left Aspen to establish the healthcare practice at Atlas Ventures, 3i invested in that firm. 3i even continued to back some of its old portfolio companies—when one lost a major partner, 3i made an additional investment.

In 1999, Ferguson decided to leave Atlas as it shifted toward a more balanced investment strategy. He contemplated retirement until 3i asked him to start up its U.S. effort, saying, "You don't know how to retire." Ferguson agreed, but cautiously:

> I did a lot of due diligence before coming back. A number of things had changed—the shareholders were experienced institutional investors that understood venture investing, not a handful of banks focused on dividends. 3i needs an active international strategy to stay in the FTSE 100, and it's committed to early stage technology investment as shown by its dominant position in many European technology markets. And tech has been good to 3i—it received a 100-to-one return for backing Mobilcom, one of the first floatations on the Neuer Markt.

By July 2002, 3i U.S. had invested in fifty-two companies. Ferguson did not see the company expanding beyond its current locations: "With offices in Menlo Park and Boston, we're starting to see all the important deals. Right now, we don't see being anywhere else in the United States. We have fifteen investors in the two offices, and our Boston office is the most international of any—we have two Americans, two Canadians, a Finn, a German, and two Brits."

Joint ventures

In 1990, 3i had established 3iBJ, a joint venture with Industrial Bank of Japan, essentially to learn about the market. The business focused on growth capital deals and made roughly 100 investments over the next decade. In January 2001, 3i formed a new business focusing on Japanese buyouts. In the $128 million buyout of Vantec, Nissan's logistics division, 3iBJ did the first true management buyout of a Japanese firm. The market, however, was slow to open, and in December 2002, 3i pulled out. "We'd looked at 300 deals and done one," said Dunne. "Although our one deal turned out to be a very good one, it was likely to be another decade before the market really opened up. It was a tough decision—it will be difficult for us to re-enter the country—but it seemed to be the right thing to do."

Making It Work: Financially

3i employed the type of budgeting process typically found in corporations. Rather than raising funds from limited partners (aside from the side-by-side funds), it invested from its balance sheet, relying on the income stream from past investments and exits from its portfolio companies to fund continuing investments. Each fiscal year (April 1 to March 31) was a new vintage year, and each office would submit a budget to London. The budgets estimated the amount of money that the portfolio

---

9. Coopey and Clarke, *3i: Fifty Years of Investing in Industry*, p. 358.

would require, the available capacity of the investing team, and the size of investments that the team hoped to make in the coming year. The London office reconciled and challenged the data; Boston's Ferguson said, "We're always wrong, but at least it's a start."

The side-by-side funds raised money through road shows to potential investors, just as most limited partnerships did. Paul Waller, director of fund operations, handled this process, leaving the deal-makers to focus on investing. Said Dunne, "It means that the investors can do what they do best."

The fiscal-year vintaging created some unusual dynamics. For one, the firm could never plead poverty—if a 1999 vintage company needed money, the current budget year would supply it but account for it under the 1999 vintage. Dunne explained, "It means we can look at each case on its own merits and fund it if it deserves funding." As a result, 3i's term sheets included "pay or play" clauses lest other investors leave it holding the bag. 3i even reported its performance based on fiscal year. Some entrepreneurs found it incomprehensible that an investor would not think in terms of funds.

The recent market slump had affected 3i's returns just as it had those of all other PE firms, but through a different mechanism. 3i's buyout investments generated a significant dividend stream. Cash inflows were kept in fairly liquid short-term vehicles to allow their rapid deployment. When the investment rate slowed in 2001, these cash balances built up, reducing overall returns. Nonetheless, said Ferguson, "There's no pressure to do more deals. We're expected to invest responsibly, not to get the money out the door."

As part of its annual reporting process, 3i undertook an exhaustive portfolio valuation process. Given the variety of its investments, the methodology was explicitly set out and had not changed since the 1994 public offering (see Exhibit 29.12a for guidelines). Analysts considered the valuations conservative, especially as compared with those of competing technology venture funds.[10] Between 1999, when 3i began breaking out its technology portfolio by valuation method, and 2002, the amount valued at cost or below had doubled, to 48 percent, and that at imminent sale (that is, about to go public, or in the mezzanine stage) had fallen from a high of 7 percent to 1 percent (see Exhibit 29.12b for valuation methods).

Making It Work: Organizationally

A typical U.S. bicoastal venture partnership managed two offices in three time zones with concomitant logistical headaches. By July 2002, 3i operated thirty-six offices worldwide and had invested over £1 billion ($1.5 billion) in 550 companies during the previous year. Larcombe said, "Some people say that we're big, bureaucratic, and slow. But not where it counts." Waller added, "We're as slow as we can be and as fast as we need to be."

3i's organization attempted to make maximum use of its size. Marketing's Dunne observed, "What's the point of being big if you don't make more money at it? Scale in itself is a hindrance. The challenge is to make it work for you." Each country had its own team; the United States had two (one on each coast). Over the countries lay a matrix of products—such as buyouts and growth—or sectors—such as technology; health care; software; telecommunications; and electronics, semiconductors, and advanced technologies (ESAT). Thus, Kariola from Finland was both the managing director of 3i Finland and the leader of the telecommunications team.

Local staff sourced deals. Over one-third of 3i's 2001 deals came through proprietary sources. Of those remaining, half were awarded to 3i on nonprice factors, such

10. *Ibid.*, p. 10.

EXHIBIT 29.12a

3i'S PORTFOLIO VALUATION METHODOLOGY

Quoted [Publicly Traded] Investments

Quoted investments are valued at the closing midmarket price at the balance sheet date, except for investments quoted on secondary markets including AIM and the Neuer Markt, which are discounted by 25 percent. Where there are restrictions on dealing in quoted investments, an appropriate discount is applied to the restricted shares.

Unquoted [private] equity shares

A three-stage valuation process is used:

1. The first stage is to value all unquoted equity investments in the manner described below:

   a. New investments are generally valued at cost for the first twelve months or, if later, until the receipt of audited accounts covering a period of at least six months since the date of investment.

   b. Any investment in a company that has failed or is expected to fail within the next twelve months is valued at nil.

   c. The value of other investments (except technology investments) is arrived at by applying 3i's proportion of equity shares held to the valuation of the company calculated by multiplying the latest audited earnings by the average price earnings ratio of the relevant sector of the FTSE SmallCap Index (or international equivalent), adjusted downward by 3i to exclude loss-making companies. If the result of this calculation is less than half of 3i's share of net tangible assets, then the investment is valued at half of 3i's share of net tangible assets. The value of technology investments is arrived at as set out above except that where the investment is in a company which is performing to plan the valuation is not reduced below cost.

2. All investments valued at more than £4 million by the first stage of the process, together with any investments which the local office responsible for the investment considers to have a value in excess of £4 million, are individually reviewed in line with internal guidelines for factors that may affect the value and their valuations may, as a result, be adjusted. These factors include:

   • Reliable financial information more recent than the audited accounts;

   • Nonrecurring profits and losses and abnormal tax charges;

   • Imminent sale or IPO;

   • Significant third-party transactions, which includes further rounds of finance to technology companies where there are substantial new outside investors and significant milestones have been achieved;

   • Potential issues of shares dilutive to 3i or other shareholders;

   • Forecasts by the investee business of lower earnings;

   • An industry standard basis of valuation, for example property companies, which are valued by reference to their net assets;

   • Large cash holdings; and

   • Very high gearing.

   This process applies to approximately two-thirds of unquoted equity investments by value.

(Continues)

EXHIBIT 29.12a (CONTINUED)

3i'S PORTFOLIO VALUATION METHODOLOGY

3. The third stage is to apply the following discounts to reflect the illiquidity of unquoted investments:
   - Investments valued at cost or half net tangible assets: nil
   - Investments valued at expected disposal proceeds or IPO value: 10 percent
   - Other investments: 25 percent

Unquoted fixed income shares and loan investments

Unquoted fixed income shares and loan investments are generally valued at cost unless the company has failed or is expected to fail within the next twelve months when they are valued at the lower of cost and net recoverable amount.

Source: 3i Group, "Reports and Accounts 2002," p. 67.

EXHIBIT 29.12b

PORTFOLIO VALUE BY VALUATION METHOD OVER TIME

(£ millions)	2002	2001	2000	1999	1998
Imminent Sale or Floatation	51	106	241	88	59
Listed	413	818	1,103	742	687
Secondary Market Quoted	89	266	483	75	85
Earnings	1,210	1,033	1,226	1,192	1,509
Cost	1,077	1,078	626	404	276
Net Assets	132	147	144	113	102
Other	405	401	262	120	46
Loan & Preference Shares	1,732	1,956	1,885	1,823	1,713
Total	5,109	5,805	5,970	4,557	4,477

Source: 3i Group, "Reports and Accounts 2002," p. 67.

as its willingness to become operationally involved or the strength of its international contacts. Boston's Ferguson recalled a situation when a potential investee company had challenged him to find contacts at a major international telecommunications firm. When he disclosed 3i's close ties with five senior executives, 3i won the deal, despite offering a lower price.

The actual deal-approval process had some local variations but followed the same general pattern. It was a highly iterative process, rather than a yes/no response like a bank credit review. As Waller said:

It is more a case of the relevant deal team coming together regularly to agree on the key issues and determine the due diligence processes, assess the findings, and decide deal tactics. At all times we are trying to make comparisons across the network to make sure we have a best-of-breed approach

EXHIBIT 29.12c

TECHNOLOGY PORTFOLIO VALUE BY VALUATION METHOD OVER TIME (£ MILLIONS)

	2002 (£ MMs)	% of Total	2001 (£ MMs)	% of Total	2000 (£ MMs)	% of Total	1999 (£ MMs)	Total
Imminent Sale or Floatation	10	1	44	2	171	7	24	2
Listed	219	13	475	20	603	25	287	29
Secondary Market Quoted	71	4	248	11	471	20	42	4
Earnings	94	5	69	3	168	7	94	10
Cost	827	48	841	36	449	19	221	23
Further Advance	170	10	227	10	143	6	38	4
Net Assets	11	1	1	0	2	0	3	0
Other	48	3	79	3	28	1	7	1
Loan & Preference Shares	266	16	345	15	344	14	258	26
Total	1,716		2,329		2,379		974	

Source: 3i Group, "Reports and Accounts 2002," p. 68.

and are fielding the most appropriate internal and external team to work on any one opportunity.

Once a deal had been found, the local team would do quick due diligence, pulling in outside expertise where necessary. Waller commented, "It sounds like one of those jokes, 'An Englishman, an Irishman, and a German. . . .' Those are the sorts of teams we can put together really fast." If the initial findings were positive, the deal would go to a review group for a "hunting license," an approval of an investment up to a certain amount, usually predicated on the satisfaction of various conditions. Buyouts would go to the buyout panel, consisting of the most senior buyout directors in Europe; venture capital investments went to one of the four global sector teams. The investment committee, composed of the executive directors, would see the deal at some point—once for a straightforward investment, several times if the issues were complex or the financial commitment large.

Once the "hunting license" had been granted, the team would continue its due diligence. An important quality control component of the process was a due diligence mentor. This individual, an executive director, acted as a sanity test, someone who was not involved in the "scent of the chase."

For venture capital deals, the sums were smaller and approval took place at the global sector level, after a significant amount of input from team members. The U.S. process was a case in point. The U.S. investor would list the deal in a log and report any changes in weekly videoconferences between the East and West Coast offices. When the investor was ready for formal feedback, a deal summary would be written and presented in a "fast forward" session. This gave the team a chance to ask questions, suggest deal structures, and contribute to due diligence. Formal approval came from the

U.S. investment committee (Ferguson along with the managing directors in the California office). Because of the continuous communication, directors would have discouraged unattractive deals before they appeared at the investment committee; most investments that appeared at the committee would be approved.

Large deals (above £5 million, or $7.8 million) went to the executive committee's investment committee in London. The investment committee met twice weekly and could be convened on twenty-four hours' notice by any country director.

3i had significant resources in its due diligence. Through the Independent Directors' Program (IDP), it had a database of 600 current and former executives with whom it had worked. Along with answering questions during due diligence, these individuals also provided a pool of potential board members after a deal was completed. By 2002, recruits from the IDP filled more than 1,000 seats at 3i's 2,606 portfolio companies. They were paid by the company, not 3i. Another group of industry experts made up the Industry Group, a panel of twenty executives with extensive experience in any of 3i's target industry sectors. They acted as an advisory panel for 3i's investors, both during the assessment phase and later, when 3i was actively involved in the company.

A local investor could access this expertise through a proprietary intranet. A database held extensive information on each member of the IDP, down to previous positions, personality traits, and preferences for future assignments. A search for individuals with airline industry experience could turn up a dozen possibilities, each with a detailed resume and an account of the individual's track record with 3i.

The intranet had proved tremendously valuable. Larcombe recalled competing for a deal in California when the company challenged him to produce solid introductions to three members of the boards of FTSE 100 companies within forty-eight hours: "It really wasn't so hard. I just went to the database and made a few calls and there we were." A series of news groups allowed sector teams to share knowledge, ask questions, and air comments. One note asked for information on the U.S. Army's procurement processes. Within hours, responses included the contact information for a good friend of Colin Powell, the U.S. secretary of state and former Army chief of staff, and similar data for the leader of the integration of the East and West German armies after reunification. Observed Larcombe, "None of us is as smart as all of us." Commented Dunne, "I don't think this could have been done ten years ago. Winning in the knowledge management game is about attitude and plumbing. The intranet has been a great piece of plumbing."

Dunne's "Message of the Day" provided another way to spread knowledge and build pride and team spirit. Each morning, employees received a brief note highlighting a recent 3i event, whether an exit, a personnel change, or an investment (see Exhibit 29.13 for examples).

Dunne had recently led a major internal branding effort. "We want our customers to know that they're at 3i. Regardless of whether it's Singapore or Sweden, the offices should all have the same feel," he said. At the same time, he was wary of too much conformity. Each office tried to reflect the local environment to some extent—the Stockholm office had light wood, the Milan office had a stunning interior with a view of the Duomo, and the Menlo Park office was "sleek, very Californian." Dunne explained: "Much more important than what the offices look like is how our staff treat the people they contact. That's why in re-energizing the brand we put so much focus on the values. The industry had become arrogant in the bull market and less endearing as a result!"

A book that described the 3i brand highlighted five values: empathy, authority, rigor, commitment, and widening horizons. With everyone they encountered, staff members at 3i were urged to leave an impression that they were engaging, well informed, confident, straightforward, and unstuffy. "You have to remember," said Larcombe, "that we're

---

EXHIBIT 29.13

MESSAGE OF THE DAY SAMPLES

When they logged into the intranet in the morning, 3i employees received a Message of the Day, written by Patrick Dunne, director of marketing. A few examples:

Bonne Chance, Guy!

Guy Zarzavatdjian returns to Paris today to head up 3i in France. Guy worked for 3i in France for 10 years before moving to Amsterdam in 1998 to establish 3i Benelux.

Every success Guy!

PS: Pape Bouba Diop is looking like good value! [Note: This was a French soccer player during the 2002 World Cup.]

Ever had that 'Damn, I can't find my cow' feeling?

Well, worry no more because 3i Spain have just backed Gesimplex who have solved the problem. A microchip is placed within a ceramic ball that, once swallowed, is non-digestible and non-expellable. So cattle owners can now reliably trace their cattle. It is apparently moosic to the ears of Australian farmers.

Well-done to ranch hands Felipe Muntadas, Carlos Mallo, Keith Ellis, Isabel Stegemeijer, and Pilar Aran.

Money, Money, Money

Well-done to 3i Stockholm—we finally invested in a company called ABA. The MBO of this Swedish Kroner 600 million business is a coup for 3i. ABA was founded in 1896 and today is a world leader in hose and pipe sealing.

So thank you for the music to Lars Erik Blom, Gustav Bard, Charles Martin, Peter Morlidge, and Hans Werner.

PS: Let's hope the winner takes it all!

Source: 3i Group.

---

dealing with a wide diversity of people—the way you communicate with and motivate an investment banker is different from the scientist or the entrepreneur."

Larcombe agreed about the importance of the brand, saying, "It's the glue that holds us together." 3i's approach to training helped to reinforce this. Regardless of their home office, new employees at 3i went through a mix of on-the-job and formal training. They attended induction days in London and ongoing sessions that met in a number of countries. The mentoring program often provided a mentor from a different country—Finland's Ere Kariola, for instance, had a mentor in the Berlin office.

In addition, sector teams had "away days" when they gathered outside the office to exchange information and learn about the state of their industry and also spent some time getting acquainted. During the winter of 2001, Kariola's telecom team had gathered in Finland for meetings and a half-day of skiing and snowmobiling. Dunne said, "It's all about building a team spirit. Strong internal relationships spark more ideas, and when favors are asked across the world, they will be delivered quickly rather than negotiated!"

3i invested heavily in networking, with a gathering of some sort at least every month. One month would see the leveraged buyout group gathering its top thirty-five investors, another would see a meeting of the top 30 or 100 managers, in addition to product group and country team meetings. Dunne commented, "There's a purely commercial reason for it—if we don't have a good network internally, how can we convince people that we have a good one externally?"

Leveraging the Investment

Larcombe said, "My concern is whether we are adequately leveraging the investment in our network." This could occur, he felt, through two ways: internally and externally.

Internally

The internal leverage would occur through using the best people most efficiently. This would ensure that 3i invested in not just the best antigen-development company in Spain, but the best one in the world. Waller commented, "It's so ironic that venture capital, which preaches globalization to its companies, is the last bastion of regionalization." The intranet, the IDP, and the training program all were intended to break down the barriers between people separated by time and geography.

Externally

External benefits would accrue to the portfolio companies, and, in the end, to the stockholders. The Industry Group and the IDP increased the chances of finding exactly the right board member for a company, or the best way to approach an operational challenge. In addition, 3i's size provided economies of scale. Kariola had held a conference for all the telecommunications companies in the portfolio. During the first day, the ninety CEOs had talked about issues of common concern and made contacts, some of which had become joint ventures, partnerships, or merger talks. On the second day, Nokia, Ericsson, and other large telecom equipment makers attended the event. Kariola said:

> If I were a little company, it would be much more difficult to see Nokia. If I were a conventional venture capitalist, it would be much more difficult to get the head of Nokia R&D to visit my company. But now I'm adding value to his processes. I'm giving him economies of scale. He can take a day and see ninety companies. I'm not wasting his time. 3i gives us that kind of access.

Similar conferences for health-care companies had yielded similar results. At a U.S. conference for technology companies that 3i Boston's Ferguson had organized, IBM had met deNovis, a portfolio company that made software to automate health-insurance claims processing. After signing a partnership deal with the firm, IBM credited 3i for "providing the marketplace headlights" that brought the software maker to the computer giant's attention.[11]

People at 3i

Before it went public in 1994, 3i had been viewed as a training ground for venture capitalists because it could not offer carry and was not a public company. The original compensation scheme was described in the 1970s as "simple [and] across-the-board . . . based on a combination of skill, responsibility, and merit, which had kept the organization unified and loyal, with its ultimate promise of an attractive pension."[12] In the

11. "3i Leverages Global Network to Bring Added Value to Portfolio Companies," company press release, (July 10, 2002).

12. Coopey and Clarke, *3i: Fifty Years of Investing in Industry*, p. 367.

1990s, 3i had addressed that issue, offering a notional carry scheme tailored to local market conditions (but overall still on the low side of U.S. scales). Dunne said, "Stuttgart is not Silicon Valley. It sounds obvious, but we need to tailor incentives to reflect the local expectations." Liz Hewitt, director of corporate affairs and investor relations, added, "We aim to provide a total compensation package that will attract world-leading people. That has to vary for each country and taxation scheme."

Compensation started with a salary in the upper quartile of the industry. In addition, 3i offered a bonus scheme, which awarded between 0 percent and 100 percent of an individual's annual salary based on achieving defined performance goals at the individual, team/office, and 3i Group level. Carried interest varied between countries and sectors. In technology and buyouts, 3i had to offer it to be competitive. Each fund had a pool of "carry points," a portion of which would be awarded to an investor for a particular deal. A key point was that these were transportable—investors could carry the carry if they moved to another posting. The points would be converted to cash at distribution. Moving to different countries did entail some costs, however. If a Finn moved to the United States, salary and carry rose, but the employee lost the pension and vacation days that were standard in Finland.

3i also offered stock options throughout the organization, awarded as a percentage of salary. To minimize taxes in some nations, employees could take their bonuses in options. Dunne and Waller both agreed: "There's more to life than money. While 3i has people who are inspired by making money, they're bigger than that, they have fascinating lives outside work. At 3i, you have a wonderfully stimulating environment; you're doing great things with interesting people. If you want to move around, you can do so."

Larcombe saw advantages in internationalization for recruiting people to 3i. "Opening the offices has meant we could hire more good people, or move them around," he said. "It's nothing new to a corporation—take Jane Crawford, who opened up 3i in Asia Pacific. She's just moved to Frankfurt to run our businesses in the German-speaking region. She brings five years' experience in a start-up. She'll add a whole new outlook to the place."

Said Hewitt: "We bring people in and if they stay three years, they'll stay five. A lot leave at three or five. If they stay more than five, they'll stay for a long time. Here, we talk about careers. We develop people's strengths. It's very corporate, but then, we're corporate, not a boutique."

The executive team had, on average, twenty years with the company, and all had started out as investors. Two, including Chris Rowlands, who had recently been recruited to re-energize the growth capital business, had rejoined 3i after significant careers outside the firm. Sometimes the company was criticized for being inbred and moving some of its best investors into management roles. A number of the country-managing directors were hoping to develop a dual career track to encourage talented investment professionals to continue to do deals.

The UK Business

3i still operated eight regional offices in the United Kingdom with investments in 1,600 companies.[13] Some of the UK investments were relatively recent, but many were remnants of the old 3i and had been in the portfolio for a long time. They generated a healthy dividend stream but were not candidates for an attractive exit. To free up the invested capital, 3i had begun actively managing these with an eye toward exits. Dunne

13. This excludes the head office in London.

said, "We want a balanced portfolio. Having the three core product groups (buyouts, technology, and growth capital) gives us a blend of yield and capital growth as well as a diverse risk profile by company stage."

Speaking about the business of investing in small and medium-sized firms, Dunne said:

> These are companies that want minimum interference. They're owner-managed, and the owners want to keep their positions until retirement. 3i wants to manage these firms in a nonintrusive way and has a strong and experienced staff doing so. These people have strong ties to their communities, they're well respected, and they work well with a larger number of firms than someone with a strong private equity bent would.

Larcombe added, "These investments were supposed to exit based on natural market turbulence. They're good companies and low maintenance because they don't expect to see us very often."

3i IN THE NEW MILLENNIUM

Larcombe knew that he and his team could take pride in their company. Since 1994, the firm had generated $12 billion in exits, and 168 companies had gone public from its portfolio. He felt that the buyout business built real value in its companies, rather than relying upon financial engineering for returns. The venture capital operation was becoming known even in the United States—a recent newspaper article had called it "the biggest venture firm you've never heard of."[14]

Although 2001 and 2002 had been difficult, Larcombe felt investors and entrepreneurs were attracted by 3i's longevity. As Paul Waller said: "Investors are nervous these days. One of the things they really like is that 3i has been around for fifty years. We are a long-term business. They're locking up money for ten years, and they know that three years into that commitment, we won't have run off to the Bahamas or disbanded."

As he went into the meeting, Larcombe reflected on 3i's history with business cycles and thought: "During a downturn, the market leaders establish the framework to come out stronger. We have to prove that our international network will provide superior returns. If we can do that in this environment, we'll excel in the recovery."

---

14. Beth Healy, "3i Group: The Biggest Firm You've Never Heard Of But Will," *The Boston Globe* (May 6, 2002), p. C-3.

Appendix: A Note on Private Equity Information Sources

Finding information about private equity-backed firms and private equity organizations is often difficult. If the firm is privately held, it is likely to attract little outside scrutiny and to disclose scant public information. Even if the firm is publicly traded, its coverage by the press may be infrequent. These problems are even more severe for private equity organizations. Private equity organizations tend to be extremely reluctant to disclose information about their successes, much less their failures.

Despite these difficulties, there are numerous occasions when it is critical to obtain information. One may be assessing a private firm as a strategic partner or a potential investment, or a private equity organization as a potential employer. This note summarizes the most useful information sources about these organizations.

Before beginning, however, it should be admitted that the most important information source is not discussed here: word-of-mouth. There is no substitute for informal "due diligence." Private equity organizations will often make fifty or even seventy-five calls before deciding to invest in a firm. A similar level of scrutiny may be appropriate before one accepts a position or undertakes a strategic alliance with a private firm.

INFORMATION ABOUT PRIVATE FIRMS

Business directories are an important, but rather limited, source of information about private firms. Directories such as CorpTech's *Corporate Technology Directory*, available via the *OneSource Global Business Browser* database, Gale Group's *Ward's Directory of U.S. Public and Private Companies*, and various state and industry directories provide basic information on employment, sales, industry focus, and year of formation. (Since these are based on survey responses, they are not always accurate!) For more detailed information, one must turn to other sources.

A rich source of information is the press. Almost every firm, no matter how publicity shy, generates some press attention. The easiest approach is to search well-indexed databases such as ProQuest's *ABI/Inform*, which covers academic, general business and

Professor Josh Lerner prepared this note as the basis for class discussion. I thank Erika McCaffrey of Baker Library for assistance.

trade publications. The *Factiva* database, a joint venture between Dow Jones and Reuters, provides full text of the *Wall Street Journal* back to 1979, newswires, newspapers, and regional business publications, while *OneSource* covers many of the smaller trade journals and newswires. *LexisNexis* includes the *New York Times*, several newswire services, and many smaller papers. It also pays to check with industry contacts as to the key trade journals that they read. Asset Alternatives publishes industry specific newsletters (*Venture Capital Analyst: Health Care Edition* and *Venture Capital Analyst: Information Technology Edition*), which provide news about specific investments.

Three databases are the best sources for detailed financial information on private firms. First, Venture Economics, a unit of Thomson Financial, provides comprehensive information on venture industry through its *VentureXpert* database. The data compiled includes detailed profiles of venture capital and private equity-backed firms, as well as information on exits by IPO or trade sales and more general industry data. Typical *VentureXpert* profiles are reproduced in Exhibits A.1a through A.1c. *VentureXpert* is available via the Web and also a client–server version where other Thomson products are also available, such as the *Mergers & Acquisitions* database, which provides information on corporate transactions, including joint ventures.

A second company, VentureOne, provides more detailed profiles in the *VentureSource* database, including information on directors and detailed business profiles. While their coverage does not extend as far back in time as Venture Economics' and only includes venture-backed firms (rather than other private equity-financed firms), the accuracy and detail of their information is generally superior. A sample report is shown in Exhibit A.2. Like the *VentureXpert* database, *VentureSource* allows one to undertake extensive screening—e.g., it is possible to identify all Internet firms that received seed financing in 1997 and were based in Massachusetts. *VentureSource* is a professional database, with subscriptions restricted to limited partners in private equity funds and corporations making direct investments.

Finally, information on debt financing is available through a Dun & Bradstreet credit search. This includes information on both bank loans and trade credit. It is far better to discover that a firm has defaulted on previous contractual obligations before entering into a business relationship with them rather than afterwards!

Private firms sometimes make information available about themselves. It is certainly worth checking to see whether the firm has a site on the World Wide Web. This is easy to determine using the Yahoo index, the *OneSource* database, and the various search engines such as Google. It may also be worthwhile to contact the firm: frequently, one can get the standard kit of information sent out to the press and/or potential customers without being asked too many questions. While it may be easy to get this information, it may not always be accurate. In addition, a lot of helpful information may be available through a Web site specializing in that particular industry. For instance, Recombinant Capital—which markets a high-priced database on biotechnology-pharmaceutical and information technology alliances—has put much ancillary information about these firms on its Web site (www.recap.com).

A final source of information on private firms is the most specialized and expensive. On occasion, one may be interested in establishing a relationship with a firm that has previously engaged in litigation. For instance, one may wish to enter into a collaborative venture with a firm that has previously litigated a key patent. Obtaining an understanding of the dispute may be important in evaluating the firm. These court records are readily available through a company called Federal Document Retrieval, owned by Thomson Research, which will photocopy some or all of the records. Some court records are also available on *LexisNexis*.

EXHIBIT A.1a

SAMPLE VENTURE ECONOMICS REPORTS

Company Founding Date: 9/5/95
Status: Public
IPO Date: 6/12/98
Industry: Business and Office Software (VEIC 2731)
Date Last Updated: 10/7/00

NetGravity, Inc.
1700 S. Amphlette Blvd.
Suite 350
San Mateo, CA 94402
United States
Phone: 650-655-4777
Fax: 650-655-4776
www.netgravity.com

Business Description: Develops advertising management software for the Internet and online marketing communications. NetGravity's AdServer manages online advertising and solves needs for Web marketers. AdServer schedules ads with an online interactive ad calendar and optimizes the placement and scheduling of ads.

Product Names:

AdServer Enterprise
AdCenter
AdServer Network

Investors

Firm	Fund	Focus	Rounds of Participation
Hummer Winblad Venture Partners	Hummer Winblad Venture Partners II	Early Stage	1, 2, 3
Hummer Winblad Venture Partners	Hummer Winblad Technology Fund II	Early Stage	1, 2, 3
Hummer Winblad Venture Partners	Hummer Winblad Venture Partners—Unspecified Fund	Expansion	2, 3
London Pacific Life & Annuity Co.	London Pacific Life & Annuity Co.	Generalist	4
Redleaf Venture Management	Redleaf Venture I, L.P.	Early Stage	3
TTC Ventures	TTC Ventures	Early Stage	4
Vector Capital	Vector Capital I	Later Stage	1, 3, 4

Investment Rounds

Date	Stage	Number of Participating Investors	Round Amount ($Th)
1/12/1996	Early Stage	3	3,000.0
4/19/1996	Early Stage	3	105.0
3/13/1997	Expansion	6	4,300.0
1/1/1998	Expansion	3	8,682.9

Exits

IPO/Acquistion	Date	Offer Amount/Purchase Price ($M)
Went Public	6/12/98	$27.0

Executives (truncated list)

Name	Title	Phone
Rick Jackson	Vice President, Marketing	650-655-4777
John Hummer	Board Member	
Tom Shields	Vice President & CTO	650-655-4777
Larry Wear	Vice President, Service	650-655-4777

EXHIBIT A.1b

SAMPLE VENTURE ECONOMICS REPORTS

Private Equity Performance Report

Investment Horizon Performance as of 6/30/00
Calculation Type: Pooled IRR

Fund Type	3 Mo	6 Mo	9 Mo	1 Yr	3 Yr	5 Yr	10 Yr	20 Yr
SEED VC	−2.9	8.3	24.3	36.0	35.7	38.2	17.4	12.6
EARLY STAGE VC	5.4	35.8	138.9	198.2	90.2	70.9	34.9	25.3
BALANCED VC	2.1	27.1	135.3	159.4	58.9	46.4	23.9	17.2
LATER STAGE VC	3.8	21.2	60.1	69.7	38.2	36.5	24.5	18.9
ALL VENTURE	3.9	29.0	112.4	143.4	63.1	51.2	27.4	19.9
SMALL BUYOUTS	−2.7	3.2	11.8	14.0	13.4	18.4	16.7	25.6
MED BUYOUTS	−0.2	8.3	43.5	50.3	24.2	18.3	15.1	21.3
LARGE BUYOUTS	−1.2	10.0	27.4	35.3	26.0	25.0	22.8	21.9
MEGA BUYOUTS	−0.3	10.9	15.5	17.6	17.3	16.4	16.9	18.9
ALL BUYOUTS	−0.9	9.3	20.0	23.6	19.3	18.5	17.2	20.1
MEZZANINE	−3.8	−0.7	1.9	3.5	6.6	9.8	11.0	11.1
ALL PRIV EQUITY	1.0	16.7	48.2	58.9	34.4	29.9	21.6	19.9

Source: Venture Economics (TFSD)/NVCA   *Type:* Summary Performance Report

Industry Investment Report

Disbursements per Company Industry
1/1/00 to 9/30/00 Rounds 1 to 99

Company Industry	No. of Comp	No. of Firm	Avg Per Comp	Avg Per Firm	Sum Inv. ($M)	Pct of Inv
Internet Specific	2,124	1,255	18.72	31.67	39,751.52	49.72
Communications	465	572	25.50	20.73	11,856.98	14.83
Computer Software	784	822	14.01	13.36	10,985.27	13.74
Semiconductors/Other Elect.	193	334	25.61	14.80	4,943.00	6.18
Medical/Health	281	282	9.67	9.63	2,715.96	3.40
Biotechnology	143	215	13.69	9.11	1,958.08	2.45
Computer Hardware	113	250	15.90	7.18	1,796.22	2.25
Business Serv.	85	124	15.48	10.61	1,315.73	1.65
Industrial/Energy	52	80	22.87	14.87	1,189.45	1.49
Consumer Related	118	165	10.08	7.21	1,189.20	1.49
Fin/Insur/RealEst	71	102	13.86	9.65	984.32	1.23
Transportation	22	30	17.15	12.58	377.41	0.47
Manufact.	26	50	11.38	5.92	295.98	0.37
Utilities	4	12	44.72	14.91	178.88	0.22
Other	19	20	6.00	5.70	113.95	0.14
Construction	9	17	12.58	6.66	113.19	0.14
Computer Other	9	20	9.12	4.10	82.05	0.10
Unknown	4	11	15.40	5.60	61.60	0.08
Agr/Forestr/Fish	6	16	6.79	2.55	40.73	0.05
TOTAL	**4,528**	**4,377**	**17.66**	**18.27**	**79,949.50**	**100.00**

EXHIBIT A.1c

SAMPLE VENTURE ECONOMICS REPORTS

Firm Type: Private Firm Investing Own Capital
Firm Founding Date: 1989
Cap Under Management: $28.0 M
Membership Affiliations:
Date Last Updated: 10/31/00

Hummer Winblad Venture Partners
2 South Park
2nd Floor
San Francisco, CA 94107
United States
415-979-9600
415-979-9601
www.humwin.com

Investment Portfolio (truncated for display purposes)

Name	Status	Status Date
@Large Software, Inc. (FKA:Celerity, Inc.)	Privately held	
AdForce (FKA:IMGIS, Inc.)	Went Public	5/7/99
Arbor Software Corporation	Went Public	11/6/95
Berkeley Systems, Inc.	Acquired	4/1/97
BigOnline, Inc. (FKA: BigBook, Inc.)	Acquired	11/24/98
Books That Work	Acquired	4/4/97
Cenquest, Inc. (FKA:Amicus Interactive, Inc.)	Privately held	
CenterView Software, Inc.	In registration	2/27/97
Central Point Software, Inc.	Acquired	6/1/94
CoroNet Systems(FKA:Soleil Network Technology)	In registration	11/8/95
Dean & DeLuca Inc.	In registration	5/9/00
DevX.com, Inc.	Privately held	
eHow, Inc.	Privately held	
Viquity Corporation (FKA: ecom2ecom, Inc.)	Privately held	
Watermark Software, Inc.	In registration	8/18/95
Wayfarer Communications, Inc.	Acquired	6/30/98
Wind River Systems, Inc.	Went Public	4/15/93
Works.com	Privately held	
Zembu Labs	Privately held	
Zero Gravity	Privately held	

Funds Managed

Name	Size ($M)	Stage	Vintage
Hummer Winblad Venture Partners	72.0	Balanced Stage	1989
Hummer Winblad Technology Fund	0.7	Later Stage	1990
Hummer Winblad Technology Fund II	1.2	Early Stage	1993
Hummer Winblad Venture Partners II	60.6	Early Stage	1993
Hummer Winblad Venture Partners— Unspecified Fund	NA	Expansion	1996
Hummer Windblad Venture Partners III, L.P.	99.0	Expansion	1997
Hummer Winblad Venture Partners IV, L.P.	315.0	Early Stage	1999

(Continues)

EXHIBIT A.1c *(CONTINUED)*

SAMPLE VENTURE ECONOMICS REPORTS

Investment Profile

	Num of Comp	Avg per Comp	Sum Inv $Th	% of Inv
Investment Total	75	6,335.1	475,129.6	100.0
State Breakdown				
California	50	4,313.8	215,690.7	45.4
Massachusetts	6	24,207.3	145,243.7	30.6
Washington	4	9,107.8	36,431.3	7.7
New York	4	6,734.5	26,938.0	5.7
Georgia	2	11,336.4	22,672.8	4.8
Oregon	3	3,000.8	9,002.5	1.9
Texas	1	7,755.0	7,755.0	1.6
North Carolina	1	3,424.0	3,424.0	0.7
Illinois	1	2,389.3	2,389.3	0.5
Pennsylvania	1	2,282.3	2,282.3	0.5
Minnesota	1	2,035.0	2,035.0	0.4
Arizona	1	1,265.0	1,265.0	0.3
Nation Breakdown				
United States	75	6,335.1	475,129.6	100.0
Industry Breakdown				
Computer Software	32	7,058.8	225,882.4	47.5
Internet Specific	32	6,506.9	208,219.9	43.8
Computer Hardware	6	1,290.8	7,745.0	1.6
Consumer Related	2	11,141.2	22,282.3	4.7
Communications	1	11,000.0	11,000.0	2.3
Fin/Insur/RealEst	1	0.0	0.0	0.0
Business Serv.	1	0.0	0.0	0.0
Stage Breakdown				
Early Stage	55	2,153.7	118,455.1	24.9
Expansion	47	4,404.3	207,003.1	43.6
Later Stage	17	8,804.2	149,671.4	31.5
Buyout/Acquisit	1	0.0	0.0	0.0

Executives

Name	Title	Phone	E-mail
Mark Gorenberg	General Partner	415-979-9600	mgorenberg@humwin.com
John Hummer	General Partner	415-931-5579	jhummer@humwin.com
Chuck Robel	Chief Operating Officer	415-979-9600	crobel@humwin.com
Deborah Wright	Chief Financial Officer	415-979-9600	dwright@humwin.com
Hank Barry	General Partner	415-979-9600	hbarry@humwin.com
Dan Beldy	Associate	415-979-9600	dbeldy@humwin.com
Ann Winblad	General Partner	415-979-9600	awinblad@humwin.com

EXHIBIT A.2

SAMPLE VENTUREONE REPORT

Magnifi

www.magnifi.com

Last Update: 10/98
Last Update Type: General Update

CONTACT INFORMATION:

1601 South De Anza Boulevard
Suite 155
Cupertino, CA 95014
Financing Contact: Ranjan Sinha, President & CEO

Phone: 408-863-3800
Fax: 408-863-7210

COMPANY OVERVIEW:

Business Brief:	Developer of automated marketing, supply-chain management software
Financing Status:	As of 09/98 the company is seeking to raise a $10 million round of venture financing that will start on 11/1/98 and is anticipated to close in the later first quarter of 1999. This round is open to new investors.

Founded:	02/96	**Industry:**	Software Development Tools	
Employees:	45	**Status:**	Private and Independent	
		Stage:	Shipping Product	

INVESTORS:

Investment Firm	Participating Round #(s)
Gideon Hixon Fund	1, 2
Draper Fisher Jurvetson	1, 2
Convergence Partners	2°
IDG Ventures	1°, 2
Crystal Internet Venture Fund	1, 2

FINANCINGS TO DATE:

Round #	Round Type	Date	Amount Raised ($M)	Post $ Valuation ($M)	Company Stage
1	1st	06/97	3.0	6.0	Shipping Product
2	2nd	11/97	5.1	NA	Shipping Product

FINANCIALS:

(A = Actual   E = Estimated   P = Projected)

($MM)	1998A
Revenue	0.00
Net Income	0.00
Burnrate ($K/Month):	0.41

(Continues)

EXHIBIT A.2 (CONTINUED)

SAMPLE VENTUREONE REPORT

EXECUTIVES AND BOARD MEMBERS:

Name	Title	Background	Phone
Ranjan Sinha	President & CEO	Date joined: 2/96 Cofounder, WhoWhere	408-863-3807
Eric Hoffert	Chairman & CTO	Date joined: 2/96 Senior Technologist, Apple Computer	
Chris Crafford	VP, Engineering	VP, Rightworks	
Pat Greer	VP, Professional Services	VP, Wallop Software	
Phillip Ivanier	VP, Business Development	Executive, MIT Media Lab; Executive, Apple Computer	
Jim Ogara	VP, Sales & Support	VP, DEC	
David Dubbs	Director, Marketing	VP, Marketing, LookSmart; Principal, Consulting Firm, Intellectual Capital Partners; Executive, AT&T	
Stewart Alsop	Advisory Board	Partner, New Enterprise Associates	650-854-9499
Gordon Bell	Advisory Board	Executive, Microsoft	
Dave Davison	Advisory Board	Cofounder, New Media Magazine; Partner, Knowledge Venture Partners	
Shane Robinson	Advisory Board	VP, Engineering, Cadence	
Skip Stritter	Advisory Board	CTO, NeTpower	408-522-9999
Susan Cheng	Board Member, Venture Investor	Partner, IDG Ventures	415-439-4420
Eric DiBeneditto	Board Member, Venture Investor	Partner, Convergence Partners	650-854-3010
Dan Kellogg	Board Member, Venture Investor	Partner, Crystal Internet Venture Fund	440-349-6025
Randy Komisar	Former Officer	CEO, LucasArts; WebTV	650-233-9683
Robert Pariseau	Former Officer	Date joined: 11/97	

BUSINESS INFORMATION:

Overview: Developer of automated marketing, supply-chain management software. The company develops Web-based marketing solutions to automate the marketing supply chain and its core activities and workflow, including encyclopedias, channel management, customer acquisition/retention, business intelligence, and campaign management. The company's patent-pending core technology supports unstructured marketing files such as video images, PDFs, and business documents, and integrates with the RDBMS to allow ROI assessment on marketing investment and establish a marketing process history. The production solution, MarketBase, links the internal and external collaborators of product or campaign development into a common, Web-based platform for managing the marketing process.

Product: Marketing automation software for managing product and advertising development, establishing marketing encyclopedia, acquiring/retaining customers, and supporting channels and customers.

Customers: Customers include CNN, ABC, PBS, Boeing, Time, Citibank, the U.S. Navy, GM, and Microsoft.

Market: The company estimates a $2 billion market for its products by the year 2000.

OUTSIDE PROFESSIONALS:

General Business Banking: Cupertino National Bank
Auditor: Coopers & Lybrand
General Counsel: Venture Law Group

END OF REPORT—Magnifi

° *Lead Investor*

INFORMATION ABOUT PUBLIC FIRMS

Public firms must file extensive information with the U.S. Securities and Exchange Commission. This makes finding out about these firms much easier. To track a company, the basic information is in the firm's initial public offering prospectus (description of the business, five years of financial results, directors and officers, principal shareholders, and financing history), the annual 10-K filings (description of business and financial results), and proxy statements (officers and directors and principal shareholders). The most recent financial information is available in the quarterly 10-Q statements.

All these documents are available from Thomson Research in hard copy, microfiche, (for the past fifteen to twenty years) on CD-ROM, and via the Web on the *Thomson Research* database. Much of this information as well as news stories is also available in summary form on the Bloomberg machines. Since mid-1996, most companies have made filings in electronic form, which are available (text only; pictures are not included) on the Internet at the EDGAR site, www.sec.gov/edgar.shtml. The *Thomson Research* database contains images of U.S. SEC and International public company filings, including prospectuses, proxies, and registration statements since 1989 for most companies.

Firms must also file "material" documents. Firms differ in how they define what is material, but generally a firm going public will file copies of its financing agreements with private equity organizations and strategic alliances with larger firms. These will often have a wealth of information not disclosed elsewhere. In many cases, a press release will describe a strategic alliance in glowing terms, but the agreement itself will reveal the alliance is much more limited in scope. It is interesting to note how often Wall Street analysts repeat what is in the press release, without bothering to check the agreement! When a firm goes public, it will typically file all material documents in a registration statement that accompanies the IPO prospectus, more technically known as an S-1 or an S-18. The index of a typical registration statement is reproduced in Exhibit A.3. If the firm signs an important strategic document after it is already public, it will typically be filed in a statement known as an 8-K. These are also available from Thomson Research and (since mid-1996 for most firms) at the EDGAR Web site. Firms often will file repeated amendments to their registration statements, scattering key documents across their statements. This makes it very frustrating to find documents. Making life a little easier is the fact that subsequent 10-Ks often list earlier documents filed by the firm and indicate when they were filed. *LexisNexis's SEC Filings & Reports* databases provide a searchable directory of all such filings and any exhibits contained therein over the past five years. In general, firms make it difficult to find the most interesting items.

Analyst reports are a somewhat useful source of information. A number of analysts seem to do little more than rephrase corporate press releases, but others do careful and insightful studies. Analyst reports are one of the few public sources of financial projections for firms. Perhaps the easiest way to obtain analyst reports is contacting the head of investor relations at the firm or else the analysts directly. Analysts covering each firm are listed in Nelson's *Directory of Investment Research*; and the dates of recent analyst reports are indicated in the *Bloomberg* news file. Alternatively, many full text reports are available through Thomson Research's *Investext* database. Financial projections are available in Thomson Research's *FirstCall* database and *Bloomberg*.

Several databases provide information about the financing activities of public firms. The *Thomson Research* database, which provides reports on offerings during the past ten or more years and is screened by many criteria, is easier to use and can be downloaded to a spreadsheet. Much more comprehensive, is Security Data Company's (SDC) *Global New Issues* database. This contains more detailed information, and it can be downloaded onto a spreadsheet for easy analysis. *Hoover's Online* offers quick access to basic company facts and financials, as well as IPO information via IPO Central.

EXHIBIT A.3

SAMPLE REGISTRATION STATEMENT INDEX

INDEX TO EXHIBITS

Exhibit Number	Description	Page
1.	Form of Purchase Agreement	69
3.1	Articles of Incorporation of Registrant, as amended	88
3.2	Bylaws of Registrant, as amended	106
3.3	Form of Amended and Restated Articles of Incorporation of Registrant to be filed on the date of closing of the offering made under the Registration Statement	135
5.	Opinion of Wilson, Sonsini, Goodrich & Rosati P.C.°	
10.1	Registrant's 1981 Incentive Stock Option Plan and forms of Stock Option Agreement	139
10.2	Registrant's 1981 Stock Purchase Plan and form of Purchase Agreement	165
10.3	Registrant's 1987 Employee Stock Purchase Plan	180
10.4	Stock Purchase Agreement dated July 14, 1981, among the Registrant, certain management shareholders and purchasers of its Series A Preferred Stock	192
10.5	Agreement dated September 8, 198,2 among the Registrant, certain founding shareholders and purchasers of its Series B Preferred Stock	233
10.6	Agreement dated July 22. 1983, among the Registrant, certain founding share holders and purchasers of its Series C Preferred Stock	305
10.7	Amendment made as of June 21, 1984, to agreement dated July 22, 1983, among the Registrant, certain founding shareholders and purchasers of its Series C Preferred Stock	391
10.8	Agreement dated January 9, 1985, among the Registrant and purchasers of its Series C Preferred Stock	478
10.9	Note Purchase Agreement dated November 22, 1985, among the Registrant and certain of its shareholders	571
10.10	Note and Warrant Purchase Agreement dated May 23, 1986, among the Registrant and certain of its shareholders	605
10.11	Agreement dated June 30, 1986, among the Registrant and purchasers of its Series D Preferred Stock and warrants to purchase Series D Preferred Stock	642
10.12	Registration Rights, Right of First Refusal and Amendment Agreement dated November 11, 1986, among the Registrant, purchasers of its Series D Preferred Stock and warrants to purchase Series D Preferred Stock, Twyford Seeds Limited ("Twyford") and certain management shareholders	771
10.13	Second Registration Rights Agreement dated November 25, 1986, among the Registrant, purchasers of its Series D Preferred Stock and warrants to purchase Series D Preferred Stock, Twyford and ML Technology Ventures, L.P. ("MLTV")	815
10.14	Addendum Agreement dated November 11, 1986, between the Registrant and McCormick & Company, Inc. ("McCormick")	850
10.15	Note Purchase Agreement dated November 11, 1986, between the Registrant and Twyford	858
10.16	Joint Venture Agreement dated November 11, 1986, between the Registrant and Twyford	995
10.17	Research, Development and License Agreement dated November 11, 1986 between the Registrant and McCormick†	1,191
10.18	Master Agreement dated November 25, 1986, between the Registrant and MLTV	1,226
10.19	Technology Agreement dated November 25, 1986, between the Registrant and MLTV†	1,261
10.20	Development Agreement dated November 25, 1986, between the Registrant and MLTV†	1,281
10.21	Joint Venture and Purchase Option Agreement dated November 25, 1986, between the Registrant and MLTV	1,322

(Continues)

EXHIBIT A.3 (CONTINUED)

SAMPLE REGISTRATION STATEMENT INDEX

INDEX TO EXHIBITS

Notes

° To be supplied by amendment.

† Confidential treatment requested.

Many publications cover the public marketplace, and highlight financial innovations of all sorts. Among the best are *The Red Herring*, which focuses on high-tech firms, current issue online at www.redherring.com; *Investment Dealer's Digest*; and *CFO*. The periodicals are well worth scanning on a regular basis.

INFORMATION ABOUT PRIVATE EQUITY ORGANIZATIONS

Among the most difficult to track are the private equity organizations themselves. Most actively avoid the press. While they disclose considerable information to their limited partners in annual reports and offering memorandums, these documents are generally confidential.

To obtain information about private equity organizations, one must thus use other means. It is worth searching *Factiva, LexisNexis,* and other databases for the occasional mentions of these firms. Both *VentureSource* and *VentureXpert* databases can be used to construct detailed profiles of various funds.

Often one is forced to rely on industry directories. *Galante's Venture Capital and Private Equity Directory* (on CD-ROM) profiles venture capital and private equity organizations alike; venture capital organizations only are profiled in *Pratt's Guide to Venture Capital Sources*. The *Pratt's* guide is quite useful, as it has been published for several decades. This allows one to answer questions such as which partners have left the firm and how capital under management has changed. There are several other directories that list U.S. private equity firms, such as the National Venture Capital Association's *Membership Directory*, but these are substantially less informative. An online directory has been developed by Infon, from which data on 3,000 venture capital firms can be screened by industry, stage, round and geographic criteria. Similar to Infon is Capital IQ, www.capitaliq.com, which has a unique combination of market data on both the private and public capital markets, and software tools for research and analysis. A subscription is required.

Many venture capital organizations make some information available through the Internet. The easiest way to find these is through Yahoo: the list is located at Business and Economy/Finance and Investment/Corporate Financing/Venture Capital. The quality, informativeness, and accuracy of these Web pages vary widely. Most buyout organizations have been more cautious about embracing this technology. A few of the many more general sites about the venture capital industry overall are informative, though most are pretty dreary. Among the best are PriceWaterhouseCoopers' MoneyTree Survey, www.pwmoneytree.com, a quarterly study of venture capital investment in the U.S., and Accel Partners, www.accel.com. Additional sites are listed at my home page, www.people.hbs.edu/jlerner. Both the Venture Economics and VentureOne Web sites have frequently-updated venture fund profiles as well.

While the above sources include some buyout firms, many more are listed in Reed Elsevier's *America's Corporate Finance Directory*, McGraw-Hill's *Corporate Finance Sourcebook*, and SDC's *Directory of Buyout Financing Sources*.

The names and nature of a fund's investors is potentially very valuable information. Two directories provide this information and are also useful for fundraising. SDC's *Directory of Limited Partners* has better coverage; but considerably greater detail is available in Asset Alternatives' *Directory of Alternative Investment Programs* which is also available on CD-ROM.

Occasionally, information may be needed about the private equity industry in general. These sources fall into three broad classes: statistical analyses, legal guides, and general overviews. In addition to the publications cited below, especially the *Private Equity*

Analyst and the *Venture Capital Journal*, there are several sources of statistical data. Particularly useful is VentureOne's *Venture Capital Industry Report & Planning Guide*. The annual reviews of Venture Economics and the National Venture Capital Association are also helpful. VentureOne also does a variety of other special reports. They are summarized and may be order at www.ventureone.com. Venture Economics releases quarterly investment statistics and trends on fund raising, industry performance, investments and exits in a series of press releases which can be found in the press room section on the Venture Economics Web site at www.ventureeconomics.com. For data on LBOs, it is useful to check the November/December issue of *Mergers and Acquisitions* and the Security Industry Association's (less useful) *Securities Industry Fact Book*.

The primary sources for returns and performance data for the private equity industry are Venture Economics' *Investment Benchmarks Reports*, which are prepared in three separate volumes: venture capital, buyouts, and European private equity. This performance information is also available in more detail via the aforementioned *VentureXpert* database. It is important to note that these sources essentially give aggregate returns—compiled over many funds. Much fund-by-fund return data is now available on the Web sites of various institutional investors, particularly public pension funds. A visible example is the California Public Employees Retirement Fund at www.calpers.ca.gov.

A second source of information relates to the legal status of private equity activities. The most useful reference guides are Joseph Bartlett's *Equity Finance*, the Practicing Law Institute's annual volume *Venture Capital*, Michael Halloran's *Venture Capital and Public Offering Negotiation*, and Jack Levin's *Structuring Venture Capital, Private Equity and Entrepreneurial Transactions*. The first is the best general overview; the second the most useful in-depth analysis.

Finally, there are more general overviews. Many collections of "war stories" by venture capitalists exist, which may make for enjoyable reading. Less entertaining but probably more helpful are the academic overviews of the industry: especially Fenn, Liang and Prowse's *The Private Equity Market: An Overview* and Gompers and Lerner's *The Venture Capital Cycle*.

Information is available about European private equity firms in the European Venture Capital Association's *Yearbook*, which has extensive statistical information, and the *Investment Benchmarks Report* from Venture Economics. *European Private Equity* also from Venture Economics, the *Venture Capital Report Directory*, *Galante's Venture Capital and Private Equity Directory* and Initiative Europe's *Europe Buyout Review*, *European Fundraising Review*, and *Who's Who in Private Equity* all provide information on European venture capital firms. Many national venture capital associations in Europe publish detailed annual reviews and directories in their native languages. For instance, the British Venture Capital Association prepares a membership *Directory* and *Report on Investment Activity*. The European Venture Capital Association has done a series of monographs on legal aspects of private equity investing across Europe that are very helpful.

Information on Asian private equity organizations and general trends is available in the Asian Venture Capital Journal's *Guide to Venture Capital in Asia*. *Galante's Venture Capital and Private Equity Directory* has much useful information. Venture Economics publishes statistical overviews of the venture capital industries of a number of Asian nations.

The final source of information is publications devoted to the private equity industry. These include not only news stories, but also detailed profiles of organizations and the firms in which they invest. The most useful periodicals about the U.S. market are the *Venture Capital Journal*, *Buyouts*, and the *Private Equity Analyst*. Detailed accounts of transactions are contained in *Private Equity Week*; available in full text in *OneSource*. The specialized world of small business investment companies is covered in the *NASBIC News*. Asian private equity is covered in the *Asian Venture Capital Journal*. The European private equity scene is dealt with in the *European Venture Capital Journal* and Euromoney's *LatinFinance* handles Latin American funds.

WHERE TO FIND RESOURCES

Asian Venture Capital Journal
Three Lagoon Drive, Suite 220
Redwood City, CA 94065
650-591-9300 phone
650-591-5551 fax
www.asiaventure.com
Asian Venture Capital Journal
Guide to Venture Capital in Asia

Aspen Law and Business
A Division of Aspen Publishers Inc.
7201 McKinney Circle
Frederick, MD 21701
800-234-1660 phone
800-9019075 fax
www.aspenpublishers.com
Structuring Venture Capital, Private Equity and Entrepreneurial Transactions [Levin]
Venture Capital and Public Offering Negotiation [Halloran]

Asset Alternatives
170 Linden Street
Wellesley, MA 02482-7919
781-304-1400 phone
781-304-1440 fax
www.assetnews.com
Corporate Venturing Directory & Yearbook
Directory of Alternative Investment Programs
Galante's Venture Capital and Private Equity Directory
Latin American Private Equity Analyst
Private Equity Analyst
Venture Capital Analyst: Health Care Edition
Venture Capital Analyst: Technology Edition

Blackwell Publishing
350 Main Street
Malden, MA 02148
781-388-8200 phone
781-388-8210 fax
www.blackwellpublishing.com
"The Private Equity Industry: An Overview" [Fenn, Liang, and Prowse, *Financial Markets, Institutions and Instruments*, Vol. 6, No. 4]

Bloomberg, L.P.
499 Park Avenue
New York, NY 10022
212-318-2000 phone
917-369-5000 fax
www.bloomberg.com
Bloomberg Database

British Venture Capital Association
3 Clements Inn
London WC2A 2AZ
United Kingdom
020-7025-2950 phone
020-7025-2951 fax
www.bvca.co.uk
British Venture Capital Association *Report on Investment Activity*
Directory/British Venture Capital Association

CalPERS
400 P Street
Lincoln Plaza
Sacramento, CA 95814
888-CalPERS (225-7377) phone
www.calpers.ca.gov

Capital IQ, Inc.
22 Cortlandt Street, 9th Floor
New York, NY 10007
212-791-9505 phone
212-791-9509 fax
www.capitaliq.com
Capital IQ database

CFO Publishing
111 West 57th St., 12th Floor
New York, NY 10019
212-459-3004 phone
212-459-3007 fax
www.cfo.com
CFO

CorpTech
300 Baker Ave.
Concord, MA 01742

800-843-8036 phone
www.corptech.com
CorpTech Directory of Technology Companies

The D & B Corporation
103 JFK Parkway
Short Hills, NJ 07078
800-234-3867 phone
www.dnb.com
D&B Credit Search

European Venture Capital Association
Minervastraat 4
B-1930 Zaventem (Brussels)
Belgium
32-2-715-00-20 phone
32-2-725-07-04 fax
www.evca.com
EVCA Yearbook

Factiva, a Dow Jones & Reuters Company
200 Burnett Road
Chicopee, MA 01020
800-568-7625 phone
413-592-4782 fax
www.dowjones.com
Factiva

Federal Document Retrieval (Thomson Research
Services)
1455 Research Blvd., 3rd Floor
Rockville, MD 20850
800-874-4337 phone
800-403-9949 fax
Litigation file services

Gale Group
27500 Drake Road
Farmington Hills, MI 48331-3535
800-877-GALE phone
800-414-5043 fax
www.gale.com
*Ward's Business Directory of U.S. Private and
    Public Companies*

Hoover's, Inc.
5800 Airport Blvd.
Austin, TX 78752
512-374-4500 phone
512-374-4501 fax
Hoover's Online

Infon Corporation
Suite 347
555 Bryant Street
Palo Alto, CA 94301
800-654-6366 phone
650-649-2676 fax
www.infon.com
The Infon Venture Capital Database

Initiative Europe
Betchworth Huse
57-65 Station Road
Redhill RH1 1DL
United Kingdom
44-0-1737 784200 phone
44-0-1737 784201 fax
www.initiative-europe.com
Europe Buyout Review
Europe Mezzanine Review
European Fundraising Review
Venture Industry Review
Who's Who in Private Equity

John Wiley & Sons, Inc.
605 Third Avenue
New York, NY 10158
877-762-2974 phone
800-597-3299 fax
www.wiley.com
Equity Finance [Bartlett]

Latin Finance
2121 Ponce de Leon Blvd., Ste. 1020
Coral Gables, FL 33134
305-448-6593 phone
305-448-0718 fax
www.latinfinance.com
LatinFinance

LexisNexis Group
P.O. Box 933
Dayton, OH 45401-0933
800-277-9597 phone
www.lexisnexis.com
LexisNexis Academic

McGraw-Hill Companies (LexisNexis)
P.O. Box 182604
Columbus, OH 43272
877-833-5524 phone
614-759-3759 fax

www.mheducation.com
Corporate Finance Sourcebook

MIT Press
Five Cambridge Center
Cambridge, MA 02142-1493
617-253-5646 phone
6l7-258-6779 fax
www.mitpress.mit.edu
The Venture Capital Cycle [Gompers and Lerner]

National Association of Small Business
    Investment Companies
666 11th Street, N.W.
Suite 750
Washington, DC 20001
202-628-5055 phone
202-628-5080 fax
www.nasbic.org
NASBIC Membership Directory
NASBIC News

National Venture Capital Association
1655 North Fort Myer Drive, Ste. 850
Arlington, VA 22209
703-524-2549 phone
703-524-3940 fax
www.nvca.org
National Venture Capital Association Latest
    Industry Statistics
National Venture Capital Association
Membership Directory
National Venture Capital Association Yearbook

Nelson Marketplace (Thomson Financial)
195 Broadway
New York, NY 10007
888-280-4864 phone
www.nelsons.com
Directory of Investment Research

OneSource Information Services
300 Baker Avenue
Concord, MA 01742
978-318-4300 phone
978-318-4690 fax
www.onesource.com
OneSource Global Business Browser

ProQuest
300 North Zeeb Road
P.O. Box 1346
Ann Arbor, MI 48106-1347
800-521-0600 phone
www.umi.com
ABI/Inform Database

The Red Herring
1931 Old Middlefield Way, Suite F
Mountain View, CA 94043
650-428-2900 phone
www.herring.com
The Red Herring—suspended print publication
from 3/03–9/04, available online

Reed Elsevier (LexisNexis)
P.O. Box 933
Dayton, OH 45401-0933
800-340-3244
www.lexisnexis.com/corpfinancedir
America's Corporate Finance Directory

Securities Data Corp. (Thomson Financial)
195 Broadway
New York, NY 10007
646-822-2000
thomson.com/financial/fi_investbank.jsp
Buyouts
Directory of Buyout Financing Sources
Directory of Limited Partners
European Venture Capital Journal
Global New Issues Database *via* SDC Platinum
Investment Dealer's Digest
Mergers and Acquisitions
Mergers & Acquisitions Database via
    SDC Platinum
Pratt's Guide to Venture Capital Sources
Venture Capital Journal
Venture Capital Yearbook
VentureXpert Database

Securities Industry Association
120 Broadway, 35th Floor
New York, NY 10271-0080
212-608-1500 phone
212-968-0703 fax
www.sia.com
Securities Industry Fact Book

Thomson Financial/ Thomson Research
22 Thomson Place
Boston, MA 02210
800-321-3373 phone
617-330-1986 fax
research.thomsonib.com
Compact D Database
FirstCall Database
Investext Database
Laser D Database
Thomson Research Database

U.S. Securities and Exchange Commission Filings
Edgar Database
www.sec.gov/edgarhp.htm

Venture Capital Report
Foxglove House
166 Piccadilly
W1V9DE
United Kingdom
44-0-20-7907-2900 phone
44-0-20-7907-2930 fax
www.vcr1978.com
Venture Capital Report Directory (UK & Europe)

Venture Economics (Thomson Financial)
195 Broadway
New York, NY 10007
888-989-8373 customer service
646-822-3230 fax
www.ventureeconomics.com
Investment Benchmarks (separate series for venture capital, buyouts, and European private equity)
National Venture Capital Association Yearbook
Private Equity Week
VentureXpert Database via SDC Platinum
Yearbook Australian Venture Capital Association

VentureOne Corporation
201 Spear St., 4th Floor
San Francisco, California 94105
800-677-2082 phone
415-357-2101 fax
www.ventureone.com
IPO Reporter
Venture Capital Industry Report &
  Planning Guide
Venture Edge
Venture IndustryData: Quarterly Statistics
VentureSource Database

Glossary

Acceleration A provision in employment agreements that allow employees to exercise all or some of their stock options before the vesting schedule allows, typically in the event of the acquisition of the firm.

Accredited investor Under the '40 Act, an individual or institution who satisfies certain tests based on net worth or income.

Adjusted present value (APV) A variant of the net present value approach that is particularly appropriate when a company's level of indebtedness is changing or it has past operating losses that can be used to offset tax obligations.

Advisory board A set of limited partners or outsiders who advise a private equity organization. The board may, for instance, provide guidance on overall fund strategy or ways to value privately held firms at the end of each fiscal year.

Agency problem A conflict between managers and investors, or more generally, an instance where an agent does not intrinsically desire to follow the wishes of the principal that hired him.

Agreement of limited partnership *See* partnership agreement.

Angel A wealthy individual who invests in entrepreneurial firms. Although angels perform many of the same functions as venture capitalists, they invest their own capital rather than that of institutional and other individual investors.

Anti-dilution provision In a preferred stock agreement, a provision that adjusts upward the number of shares (or percentage of the company) held by the holders of the preferred shares if the firm subsequently undertakes a financing at a lower valuation than the one at which the preferred investors purchased the shares.

Asset allocation The process through which institutional or individual investors set targets for how their investment portfolios should be divided across the different asset classes.

Asset class One of a number of investment categories—such as bonds, real estate, and private equity—that institutional and individual investors consider when making asset allocations.

Associate A professional employee of a private equity firm who is not yet a partner.

Asymmetric information problem A problem that arises when, because of his day-to-day involvement with the firm, an entrepreneur knows more about his company's prospects than investors, suppliers, or strategic partners.

Best efforts An underwriting which is not a firm commitment one.

Beta A measure of the extent to which a firm's market value varies with that of an index of overall market value. For instance, a stock with a beta of zero displays no correlation with the market, that with a beta of one generally mirrors the market's movements, and that with a beta greater than one experiences more dramatic shifts when the index moves.

Bogey *See* hurdle rate.

Book-to-market ratio The ratio of a firm's accounting (book) value of its equity to the value of the equity assigned by the market (*i.e.*, the product of the number of shares outstanding and the share price).

Bulge bracket A term frequently used to refer to the top tier of most reputable and established investment banks.

Call option The right, but not the obligation, to buy a security at a set price (or range of prices) in a given period.

Callable A security on which the security issuer has an option to repurchase from the security holder.

Capital structure The mixture of equity and debt that a firm has raised.

Capital under management *See* committed capital.

Carried interest The substantial share, often around 20 percent, of profits that are allocated to the general partners of a private equity partnership.

Catch up A provision in limited partnership agreements often used in conjunction with a preferred return. The provision allows the general partners to receive all or most of the distributions after the limited partners receive their capital back and the preferred return. Such a catch up typically remains in force until the general partners have received their contractually specified share of the distributions (e.g., 20 percent).

Certification The "stamp of approval" that a reputable private equity investor or other financial intermediary can provide to a company or individual.

Claw back A provision in limited partnership agreement that requires general partners to return funds to the limited partners at the end of the fund's life, if they have received more than their contractually specified share.

Closed-end fund   A publicly traded mutual fund whose shares must be sold to other investors (rather than redeemed from the issuing firm, as is the case with open-end mutual funds). Many early venture capital funds were structured in this manner.

Closing   The signing of the contract by an investor or group of investors that binds them to supply a set amount of capital to a private equity fund. Often a fraction of that capital is provided at the time of the closing. A single fund may have multiple closings.

Co-investment   Either *(a)* the syndication of a private equity financing round (*see* syndication), or *(b)* an investment by an individual general or limited partner alongside a private equity fund in a financing round.

Collar   A combination of an equal number of call and put options at slightly different exercise prices.

Committed capital   Pledges of capital to a private equity fund. This money is typically not received at once, but rather taken down over three to five years starting in the year the fund is formed.

Common stock   The equity typically held by management and founders. Typically, at the time of an initial public offering, all equity is converted into common stock.

Community development venture capital   Venture capital funds organized by non-profit bodies, often with the twin goals of encouraging economic development and generating financial returns.

Companion fund   A fund, often raised at the same time as a traditional private equity fund, that is restricted to close associates of a private equity group. These funds often have more favorable terms (e.g., reduced fees and no carried interest) than traditional funds.

Consolidation   A private equity investment strategy that involves merging several small firms together and exploiting economies of scale or scope.

Conversion ratio   The number of shares for which a convertible debt or equity issue can be exchanged.

Convertible equity or debt   A security that under certain conditions can be converted into another security (often into common stock). The convertible shares often have special rights that the common stock does not have.

Cooperative Research and Development Agreement (CRADA)   A collaborative arrangement between a federally owned research facility and a private company. These were first authorized by Congress in the early 1980s.

Corporate venture capital   An initiative by a corporation to invest either in young firms outside the corporation or in business concepts originating within the corporation. These are often organized as corporate subsidiaries, not as limited partnerships.

Credit crunch   A period when, due to regulatory actions or shifts in the economic conditions, a sharp reduction occurs in the availability of bank loans or other debt financing, particularly for small businesses. The early 1990s were one such period in the United States.

Cumulative redeemable preferred stock   *See* redeemable preferred stock.

Deposit-oriented lease   In venture leasing, a lease that requires the lessee to put up a cash deposit, usually ranging from 30–50 percent of the total lease line.

Dilution   The reduction in the fraction of a firm's equity owned by the founders and existing shareholders associated with a new financing round.

Direct investment   An investment by a limited partner or a fund of funds into an entrepreneurial or restructuring firm.

Disbursement   An investment by a private equity fund into a company.

Distressed debt   A private equity investment strategy that involves purchasing discounted bonds of a financially distressed firm. Distressed debt investors frequent convert their holdings into equity and become actively involved with the management of the distressed firm.

Distribution   The transfer of shares in a (typically publicly traded) portfolio firm or cash from a private equity fund to each limited partner and (frequently) each general partner.

Down round   A financing round where the valuation of the firm is lower than that in the previous round.

Draw down   *See* take down.

Due diligence   The review of a business plan and assessment of a management team prior to a private equity investment.

Earnings before interest and taxes (EBIT)   A measure of the firm's profitability before any adjustment for interest expenses or tax obligations. This measure is often used to compare firms with different levels of indebtedness.

Employee Retirement Income Security Act (ERISA)   The 1974 legislation that codified the regulation of corporate pension plans. *See* prudent man rule.

Endowment   The long-term pool of financial assets held by many universities, hospitals, foundations, and other nonprofit institutions.

Equipment takedown schedule   In a venture leasing contract, the time when the lessee can draw down funds to purchase preapproved equipment.

Equity kicker   A transaction in which a small number of shares or warrants are added to what is primarily a debt financing.

Exercise price   The price at which an option or a warrant can be exercised.

External corporate venture capital   A corporate venture capital program that invests in entrepreneurial firms outside the corporation. These investments are often made alongside other venture capitalists.

Financing round   The provision of capital by a private equity group to a firm. Since venture capital organizations generally provide capital in stages, a typical venture-backed firm will receive several financing rounds over a series of years.

Firm commitment An underwriting where the underwriter guarantees the firm a certain purchase price, by buying the securities from the firm and then reselling them. In actuality, the transaction is not finalized until the night before the transaction, so the risk the underwriter runs is usually very low.

First closing The initial closing of a fund.

First dollar carry A provision in limited partnerships that allow general partners to receive carried interest once the capital actually invested has been returned to the limited partners. The more traditional alternative is that both the invested capital and the management fees must be returned to the limited partners before the general partners receive carried interest.

First fund An initial fund raised by a private equity organization; also known as a first-time fund.

Float In a public market context, the percentage of the company's shares that is in the hands of outside investors, as opposed to being held by corporate insiders.

Follow-on fund A fund that is subsequent to a private equity organization's first fund.

Follow-on offering *See* seasoned equity offering.

Form 10-K An annual filing required by the U.S. Securities and Exchange Commission of each publicly traded firm, as well as certain private firms. The statement provides a wide variety of summary data about the firm.

'40 Act *See* Investment Company Act of 1940.

Free cash flow problem The temptation to undertake wasteful expenditures which cash not needed for operations or investments often poses.

"Friends and family" fund *See* companion fund.

Fund A pool of capital raised periodically by a private equity organization. Usually in the form of limited partnerships, private equity funds typically have a ten-year life, though extensions of several years are often possible.

Fund of funds A fund that invests primarily in other private equity funds rather than operating firms, often organized by an investment adviser or investment bank.

Gatekeeper *See* investment advisor.

General partner A partner in a limited partnership who is responsible for the day-to-day operations of the fund. In the case of a private equity fund, the venture capitalists either are general partners or own the corporation that serves as the general partner. The general partners assume all liability for the fund's debts.

Glass-Steagall Act The 1933 legislation that limited the equity holdings and underwriting activities of commercial banks in the United States.

Grandstanding problem The strategy, sometimes employed by young private equity organizations, of rushing young firms to the public marketplace in order to demonstrate a successful track record, even if the companies are not ready to go public.

Green Shoe option A provision in an underwriting agreement that allows the underwriter to sell an additional amount (typically 15 percent) of shares at the time of the offering.

Hedging A securities transaction that allows an investor to limit the losses that may result from the shifts in value of an existing asset or financial obligation. For instance, a farmer may hedge his exposure to fluctuating crop prices by agreeing before the harvest on a sale price for part of his crop.

Herding problem A situation in which investors, particularly institutions, make investments that are more similar to one another than is desirable.

Hot issue market A market with high demand for new securities offerings, particularly for initial public offerings.

Hurdle rate Either *(i)* the set rate of return that the limited partners must receive before the general partners can begin sharing in any distributions, or *(ii)* the level that the fund's net asset value must reach before the general partners can begin sharing in any distributions.

Implicit rate Also known as the implicit yield, the implicit rate in venture leasing is the annual percentage rate of return before considering the impact of the warrants included as part of the transaction.

In the money An option or a warrant that would have a positive value if it was immediately exercised.

Inadvertent investment company An operating company that falls by accident under the '40 Act's definition of an investment company.

Initial public offering (IPO) The sale of shares to public investors of a firm that has not hitherto been traded on a public stock exchange. An investment bank typically underwrites these offerings.

Insider A director, an officer, or a shareholder with at least a certain percentage (often 10 percent) of a company's equity.

Intangible asset A patent, trade secret, informal know-how, brand capital, or other nonphysical asset.

Internal corporate venture capital program A corporate venture capital program that invests in business concepts originating inside the corporation.

Intrapreneuring A corporate venture capital program that invests in business concepts originating inside the corporation. The term often is applied specifically to efforts in which the corporation intends to reacquire its new ventures.

Investment adviser A financial intermediary who assists investors, particularly institutions, with investments in private equity and other financial assets. Advisers assess potential new venture funds for their clients and monitor the progress of existing investments. In some cases, they pool their investors' capital in funds of funds.

Investment bank A financial intermediatory that, among other services, may underwrite securities offerings, facilitate mergers and acquisitions, and trade for its own account.

Investment committee A group, typically consisting of general partners of a private equity fund, that reviews potential and/or existing investments.

Investment Company Act of 1940 Legislation that imposed extensive disclosure requirements and operating restrictions on mutual funds. A major concern of publicly traded venture funds has been avoiding being designated an investment company as defined by the provisions of this act.

Investment trust *See* closed-end fund. This term is commonly used in Great Britain.

Investor buyout (IBO) *See* management buy-in.

Lease line Similar to a bank line of credit, a credit that allows a venture lessee a certain amount of money to add equipment as needed, according to a preapproved takedown schedule.

Lemons problem *See* asymmetric information problem.

Lessee The party to a lease agreement who is obligated to make monthly rental payments and can use the equipment during the lease term.

Lessor The party to a lease agreement who has legal title to the equipment, grants the lessee the right to use the equipment for the lease term, and is entitled to the rental payments.

Leveraged buyout (LBO) The acquisition of a firm or business unit, typically in a mature industry, with a considerable amount of debt. The debt is then repaid according to a strict schedule that absorbs most of the firm's cash flow.

Leveraged buyout fund A fund, typically organized in a similar manner to a venture capital fund, specializing in leveraged buyout investments. Some of these funds also make venture capital investments.

Leveraged recapitalization A transaction in which the management team (rather than new investors as in the case of an LBO) borrows money to buy out the interests of other investors. As in an LBO, the debt is then repaid.

Licensee In a licensing agreement, the party who receives the right to use a technology, product, or brand name in exchange for payments.

Licensor In a licensing agreement, the party who receives payments in exchange for providing the right to use a technology, product, or brand name that it owns.

Limit order In an underwritten IPO, the price-dependent orders made by individual or institutional investors: for example, the agreement by an investor to purchase 10,000 shares, conditional on the price of the offering being under $12 per share.

Limited partner An investor in a limited partnership. Limited partners can monitor the partnership's progress but cannot become involved in its day-to-day management if they are to retain limited liability.

Limited partnership An organizational form that entails a finitely lived contractual arrangement between limited and general partners, governed by a partnership agreement.

Liquidation preference provision In a preferred stock agreement, a provision that insures preference over common stock with respect to any dividends or payments in association with the liquidation of the firm.

Lock up A provision in the underwriting agreement between an investment bank and existing shareholders that prohibits corporate insiders and private equity investors from selling at the time of the offering.

Look back *See* claw back.

Management buy-in (MBI) A European term for an LBO initiated by a private equity group with no previous connection to the firm.

Management buyout (MBO) A European term for an LBO initiated by an existing management team, which then solicits the involvement of a private equity group.

Management fee The fee, typically a percentage of committed capital or net asset value, that is paid by a private equity fund to the general partners to cover salaries and expenses.

Managing general partner The general partner (or partners) who is ultimately responsible for the management of the fund.

Mandatory conversion provision In a preferred stock agreement, a provision that requires the preferred stock holders to convert their shares into common stock. Typically, holders are required to make such exchanges in the event of an initial public offering of at least a certain size and at least a certain valuation.

Mandatory redemption provision In a preferred stock agreement, a provision that requires the firm to purchase the shares from the private equity investors according to a set schedule. Typically used in the case of redeemable preferred stock investments.

Market maker The service provided by an investment bank or broker in insuring the liquidity of trading in a given security. As a part of its duties, the market maker may accumulate a substantial inventory of shares in the company.

Market-to-book ratio The inverse of the book-to-market ratio.

Mega-fund One of the largest venture capital or private equity funds, measured by the amount of committed capital.

Mezzanine Either *(a)* a private equity financing round shortly before an initial public offering, or *(b)* an investment that employs subordinated debt that has fewer privileges than bank debt but more than equity and often has attached warrants.

Milestone payments In a licensing agreement, the payments made by the licensee to the licensor at specified times in the future or else when certain technological or business objectives have been achieved.

Naked short In the context of a security underwriting, a case where the underwriter sells more shares than agreed upon (and those allowed under the Green Shoe option). In this case, the underwriter must buy back shares in the open market after the offering is completed to close out the short position.

NASDAQ The U.S. stock exchange where most IPOs are listed and most firms that were formerly backed by private equity investors trade.

Net asset value (NAV) The value of a fund's holdings, which may be calculated using a variety of valuation rules. The value does not include funds that have been committed but not drawn down.

Net income A firm's profits after taxes.

Net operating losses (NOLs) Tax credits that are compiled by firms that have financial losses. These credits generally cannot be used until the firm becomes profitable (or returns to profitability).

Net present value (NPV) A valuation method that computes the expected value of one or more future cash flows and discounts them at a rate that reflects the cost of capital (which will vary with the cash flows' riskiness).

Operating lease In venture leasing, a short-term lease in which the customer uses equipment for a fraction of its useful life. Obligations of ownership may remain with the lessor, including maintenance, insurance, and taxes.

Option The right, but not the obligation, to buy or sell a security at a set price (or range of prices) in a given period.

Out of the money An option or a warrant that would have a negative value if it was immediately exercised.

Participating convertible preferred stock *See* participating preferred stock.

Participating preferred stock Convertible stock where, under certain conditions, the holder receives both the return of his original investment and a share of the company's equity.

Partnership agreement The contract that explicitly specifies the compensation and conditions that govern the relationship between the investors (limited partners) and the venture capitalists (general partners) during a private equity fund's life. Occasionally used to refer to the separate agreement between the general partners regarding the internal operations of the fund (e.g., the division of the carried interest).

Patent A government grant of rights to one or more discoveries for a set period, based on a set of criteria.

Phantom stock A form of compensation, sometimes used in internal corporate venture capital programs, where employees receive payments that imitate those received from holding stock options, but where they do not actually hold equity. These compensation plans often have negative tax and accounting consequences.

Placement agent A financial intermediary hired by private equity organizations to facilitate the raising of new funds.

Point One percent of a private equity fund's profits. The general partners of a private equity fund are often allocated 20 points, or 20 percent of the capital gains, which are divided among the individual partners.

Post-money valuation The product of the price paid per share in a financing round and the shares outstanding after the financing round.

Preferred return A provision in limited partnership agreements that ensures that the limited partners receive not only their capital back, but also a contractually stipulated rate of return on their funds before the general partners receive any carried interest.

Preferred stock Stock that has preference over common stock with respect to any dividends or payments in association with the liquidation of the firm. Preferred stockholders may also have additional rights, such as the ability to block mergers or displace management.

Pre-money valuation The product of the price paid per share in a financing round and the shares outstanding before the financing round.

Price-earnings ratio (P/E ratio) The ratio of the firm's share price to the firm's earnings per share (net income divided by shares outstanding).

Primary investment An investment by a limited partner or a fund of funds into a private equity partnership which is raising capital from investors.

Private equity Organizations devoted to venture capital, leveraged buyout, consolidation, mezzanine, and distressed debt investments, as well as a variety of hybrids such as venture leasing and venture factoring.

Private placement The sale of securities not registered with the U.S. Securities and Exchange Commission to institutional investors or wealthy individuals. These transactions are frequently facilitated by an investment bank.

Pro forma Financial statements that project future changes in a firm's income statement or balance sheet. These often form the basis for valuation analyses of various types.

Prospectus A condensed, widely disseminated version of the registration statement that is also filed with the U.S. Securities and Exchange Commission. The prospectus provides a wide variety of summary data about the firm.

Proxy statement A filing with the U.S. Securities and Exchange Commission that, among other information, provides information on the holdings and names of corporate insiders.

Prudent man rule Prior to 1979, a provision in the Employee Retirement Income Security Act (ERISA) that essentially prohibited pension funds from investing substantial amounts of money in private equity or other high-risk asset classes. The Department of Labor's clarification of the rule in that year allowed pension managers to invest in high-risk assets, including private equity.

Public venture capital Venture capital funds organized by government bodies, or else programs to make venture-like financings with public funds. Examples include the

Small Business Investment Company and Small Business Innovation Research programs.

Put option   The right, but not the obligation, to sell a security at a set price (or range of prices) in a given period.

Putable   A security which the security holder has an option to sell back to the issuer.

Qualified investor   Under the 1996 amendments to the '40 Act, an individual or institution who satisfies certain tests based on net worth or income. The minimum amounts for attaining such a status are higher than those for accredited investors.

Red herring   A preliminary version of the prospectus that is distributed to potential investors before a security offering. The name derives from the disclaimers typically printed in red on the front cover.

Redeemable preferred stock   Preferred stock where the holders have no right to convert the security into common equity. The return to the investor, like that of a bond, consists of a series of dividend payments and the return of the face value of the share, which is paid out at the contractually specified time when the company must redeem the shares.

Registration right provision   In a preferred stock agreement, provisions that allow the private equity investors to force the company to go public, or to sell their shares as part of a public offering that the firm is undertaking.

Registration statement   A filing with the U.S. Securities and Exchange Commission (e.g., an S-1 or S-18 form) that must be reviewed by the Commission before a firm can sell shares to the public. The statement provides a wide variety of summary data about the firm, as well as copies of key legal documents.

Residual value   In venture leasing, the fair-market value of the leased equipment at the end of the lease term.

Restricted stock   Shares that cannot be sold under U.S. Securities and Exchange Commission regulations or that can only be sold in limited amounts.

Reverse claw back   In a limited partnership agreement, a provision that requires limited partners to return funds to the general partners at the end of the fund's life, if they have received more than their contractually specified share.

Right of first refusal   A contractual provision that gives a corporation or private equity fund the right to purchase, license, or invest in all opportunities associated with another organization before other companies or funds can do so. A weaker form of this provision is termed the right of first look.

Road show   The marketing of a private equity fund or public offering to potential investors.

Roll-up   *See* consolidation.

Round   *See* financing round.

Royalties   In a licensing agreement, the percentage of sales or profits that the licensee pays to the licensor.

Rule of 99   A provision in the '40 Act that exempted funds with less than 99 accredited investors from being designated investment companies. This rule was relaxed in a 1996 amendment to the '40 Act.

Rule 10(b)-5   The U.S. Securities and Exchange Commission regulation that most generally prohibits fraudulent activity in the purchase or sale of any security.

Rule 16(a)   The U.S. Securities and Exchange Commission regulation that requires insiders to disclose any transactions in the firm's stock on a monthly basis.

Rule 144   The U.S. Securities and Exchange Commission regulation that prohibits sales for one year (originally, two years) after the purchase of restricted stock and limits the pace of sales between the first and second (originally, second and third) year after the purchase.

Running rate   *See* implicit rate.

Seasoned equity offering   An offering by a firm that has already completed an initial public offering and whose shares are already publicly traded.

Secondary investment   The purchase by a limited partner or a fund of funds of an existing limited partnership holding from another limited partner.

Secondary offering   An offering of shares that are not being issued by the firm, but rather are sold by existing shareholders. Consequently, the firm does not receive the proceeds from the sales of these shares.

Shares outstanding   The number of shares that the company has issued.

Small Business Innovation Research (SBIR) program   A federal program, established in 1982, that provides a set percentage of the federal R&D budget to small, high-technology companies.

Small Business Investment Company (SBIC) program   A federally guaranteed risk capital pool. These funds were first authorized by the U.S. Congress in 1958, proliferated during the 1960s, and then dwindled after many organizations encountered management and incentive problems.

Social venture capital   Either community development venture capital or public venture capital (see definitions).

Special limited partner   A limited partner who receives part of the carried interest from the fund. In many cases, the first investors in a new fund are given special limited partner status.

Staging   The provision of capital to entrepreneurs in multiple installments, with each financing conditional on meeting particular business targets. This provision helps ensure that the money is not squandered on unprofitable prospects.

Stapled fund   A fund raised at the same time as another private equity fund, which invests on a *pro rata* in a subset (defined in advance) of the fund's transactions. Sometimes the term is used to refer to funds which invest in all transactions by the fund, but which is raised from a different class of investors (e.g., international limited partners).

Stock appreciation rights   One type of phantom stock compensation scheme.

Straight preferred stock   *See* redeemable preferred stock.

Super majority voting provision   In a preferred stock agreement, a provision that requires that more than a majority of the preferred stock holders approve a given decision.

Syndication   The joint purchase of shares by two or more private equity organizations or the joint underwriting of an offering by two or more investment banks.

Take down   The transfer of some or all of the committed capital from the limited partners to a private equity fund.

Takedown schedule   The contractual language that describes how and when a private equity fund can (or must) receive the committed capital from its limited partners. In venture leasing, the period after the lease begins when the lessee can draw down funds for the preapproved equipment to be purchased.

Tangible asset   A machine, building, land, inventory, or another physical asset.

Term of lease   In venture leasing, the duration of the lease, usually in months, which is fixed at its inception.

Term sheet   A preliminary outline of the structure of a private equity partnership or stock purchase agreement, frequently agreed to by the key parties before the formal contractual language is negotiated.

Tombstone   An advertisement, typically in a major business publication, by an underwriter to publicize an offering that it has underwritten.

Trade sale   A European term for the exiting of an investment by a private equity group by selling it to a corporation.

Triple-net full-payout lease   In venture leasing, a long-term lease in which the lessee's lease payments cover the entire cost of the leased equipment and the lessee assumes all responsibilities of ownership, including maintenance, insurance, and taxes.

Uncertainty problem   The array of potential outcomes for a company or project. The wider the dispersion of potential outcomes, the greater the uncertainty.

Underpricing   The discount to the projected trading price at which the investment banker sells shares in an initial public offering. A substantial positive return on the first trading day is often interpreted by financial economists as evidence of underpricing.

Underwriter   The investment bank who underwrites an offering.

Underwriting   The purchase of a securities issue from a company by an investment bank and its (typically almost immediate) resale to investors.

Unrelated business taxable income (UBTI)   The gross income from any unrelated business that a tax-exempt institution regularly carries out. If a private equity partnership is generating significant income from debt-financed property, tax-exempt limited partners may face tax liabilities due to UBTI provisions.

Unseasoned equity offering   *See* initial public offering.

Up-front fees   In a licensing agreement, nonrefundable payments made by the licensee to the licensor at the time that agreement is signed.

Valuation rule   The algorithm by which a private equity fund assigns values to the public and private firms in its portfolio.

Venture capital   Independently managed, dedicated pools of capital that focus on equity or equity-linked investments in privately held, high growth companies. Many venture capital funds, however, occasionally make other types of private equity investments. Outside of the United States, this phrase is often used as a synonym for private equity.

Venture capital method   A valuation approach that values the company at some point in the future, assuming that the firm has been successful, and then discounts this projected value at some high discount rate.

Venture capitalist   A general partner or associate at a private equity organization.

Venture factoring   A private equity investment strategy that involves purchasing the receivables of high-risk young firms. As part of the transaction, the venture factoring fund typically also receives warrants in the young firm.

Venture leasing   A private equity investment strategy that involves leasing equipment or other assets to high-risk young firms. As part of the transaction, the venture leasing fund typically also receives warrants in the young firm.

Vesting   A provision in employment agreements that restricts employees from exercising all or some of their stock options immediately. These agreements typically specify a schedule of the percent of shares that the employee is allowed to exercise over time, known as a vesting schedule.

Vintage year   The group of funds whose first closing was in a certain year.

Warrant-based lease   In venture leasing, a lease that requires the lessee to grant equity participation to the lessor, usually in the form of warrants.

Warrants   An option to buy shares of stock issued directly by a company.

Window dressing problem   The behavior of money managers of adjusting their portfolios at the end of the quarter by buying firms whose shares have appreciated and selling "mistakes." This is driven by the fact that institutional investors may examine not only quarterly returns, but also end-of-period holdings.

Withdrawn offering   A transaction in which a registration statement is made with the U.S. Securities and Exchange Commission but either the firm writes to the Commission withdrawing the proposed offering before it is effective or the offering is not completed within nine months.

Index